The
Butterfly
as
Companion

The Butterfly

MEDITATIONS

A volume in the SUNY series in Religion and Philosophy
Robert Cummings Neville, Editor

as Companion

ON THE FIRST THREE CHAPTERS OF THE *Chuang Tzu*

Kuang-ming Wu

STATE UNIVERSITY OF NEW YORK PRESS

Published by
State University of New York Press, Albany

For information, address State University of New York
Press, State University Plaza, Albany, N.Y., 12246

Library of Congress Cataloging-in-Publication Data

Wu, Kuang-ming
    The butterfly as companion.

    (SUNY series in religion and philosophy)
    Includes bibliographies and indexes.
    1. Chuang-tzu. Nan-hua ching. I. Chuang-tzu.
Nan-hua ching. English. Selection. II. Title.
III. Series
BL1900.C756W793   1990   299'.51482   87-17986
ISBN 0-88706-685-2
ISBN 0-88706-686-0 (pbk.)

12 11 10 9 8 7 6 5 4

To Wen-yen
My Companion

Contents

Acknowledgements

My intercultural, interdisciplinary meditations put me under immense and various debts of gratitude in many fields, imaginable and unimaginable, a small portion of which will be apparent from the American, Chinese, European, and Japanese works listed in References. I must, then, confine myself to a handful of persons who have rendered immediate and indispensable aid.

Messrs. (the late) John Wild, John Smith, William Christian, and George Schrader of Yale University were maieutically responsible for what is coherent in my thinking; they remain my Confucian fathers and Taoist mothers.

Robert Neville is my neo-Confucius, after whose discerning systematic dust I stare in awe, vainly hoping that some of this dust may rub off on me. His (by me) undeserved enthusiasm and (from him) unreserved encouragement introduced me to the press and the world. Beth Neville's skillful collages show me how to unify ideas without unifying them; her jacket design enhances the pages it embraces.

Then James Parsons came to devote "ten thousand" hours to Englishing, criticizing, and collating every word on the page. He persuaded me to the present title, rearranged the structure of the book, designed the title page and part-title pages, compiled the Indexes and Conversion Table, and finally proofed with me through galleys and pages.

David Hall continues to shelter me under the aura of his absence, the wings of his Uncertain Phoenix that ferry me from one provocative idea to another. Roger Ames, with his winsome smile, arranged for purchases of some essential Chinese books.

My wife Wen-yen has been my companion through the ups and downs of those five odd years of un-Taoistic struggles devoted to the creation of this book, gently capping them with tedious labors, straightening out my inconsistent romanzations, preparing the references to Chinese and Japanese works, indexing Chinese and Japanese names, and advising me on many other editorial matters. These pages are dedicated to her.

Were I to continue like this, my lifetime would not be enough to finish it. Suffice it to say that without these my respected companions, this *Companion* would not have come about—the defects of which indicate that I myself must continue to learn from them.

Foreword

Robert Cummings Neville
Boston University

Chuang Tzu is among the very few philosophers to admit the world to be as weird as it really is. His book begins by remarking a fish that becomes a bird, both a skillion miles long in size; the size and flight of the bird are so incomprehensible to a cicada as to be humorously absurd. The famous image of the butterfly dreaming to be Chuang Tzu, or maybe Chuang Tzu dreaming to be a butterfly, makes the weird point: reality is always for-a-perspective; and *that* point is for-a-perspective; the perspectives perceive one another as incommensurate; and the perspectives subtly and often without notice are transformed into one another so as to manifest the truly catholic nature of perspectives, which is not a perspective at all. The transformation is the thing, like the butterfly whose being is transformation.

One of the faster transformations of the current intellectual scene is the fad for deconstructionism. A text does not fix a state of affairs, deconstructionism points out, but is a processive interpretation of it, in turn requiring interpretation so that nothing is fixed and every interpretive "take" transforms the experiential perspective. Though deconstructionism as a fashion might have the pace and scale of the cicada's life, the point about transformation is an ancient, slowly evolving truth. Its flight from Chuang Tzu to Wu Kuang-ming has the scale and dignity of the epic recurring journey of the great bird (formerly fish). The wisdom, erudition, and humble self-understanding of Wu's Taoist deconstructionism is to the fuss of contemporary literary theory as Peng's flight is to the hop of the cicada.

As in his earlier *Chuang Tzu: World Philosopher at Play*, so in this book Wu Kuang-ming takes his philosopher to present not only a contemporary option but the best expression of that option. Here Wu's method is not primarily comparative and dialectical, as was his earlier book, but that of scholarly exhibition. *The Butterfly as Companion* is a word-for-word translation, an image-by-image exposition, an idea-by-idea analysis, and a whole-in-every-part interpretation. Chuang Tzu's three chapters are but a few pages, and Wu's very long commentary reflects the scale celebrated in the opening image of the fish-bird. There is a formidable scholarly apparatus here, something of which only a thinker of Wu's profound background in the languages and cultures of China and the West could create. I know of no other book that is as detailed and sensitive as this one about any text whatsoever (and I bear in mind the traditions of commentary about Jewish and Christian scriptures). Nor do I know of any scholar other than Wu who could have mobilized such a formidable apparatus with the love and attention necessary to produce this masterpiece of philosophical scholarship.

The story is told of H. J. Paton that after completing his massive two-volume study of the first half of Kant's *Critique of Pure Reason*, he couldn't entertain the thought that Kant might not have the whole truth. There is nothing like that sense about Wu's book. Formidable though it is, the effect of Wu's study is to lighten one about the text, to lift one from the words of Chuang Tzu to the play of one's own ideas. Finishing this book, one not only knows more but lives better. Partly this is the intrinsic effect of Chuang Tzu's own writing. But largely it is because Wu knows how to continue Peng's flight over our territory, circling through our own lives.

Preface

There was in ancient China a Taoist called Chuang Tzu who dreamed of being a butterfly. He suddenly awoke and realized that he was not a butterfly; but then, upon reflection, he was not sure. Was he he who had dreamed of being a butterfly? Or was he a butterfly now dreaming of being he? Thus it was that the butterfly became his companion, in dreaming and in waking, to his life reflections, to his zestful, jestful living.

This book is a companion, fluttering like a butterfly, to the first three chapters of the ancient book of Chuang Tzu, which consists of the seven chapters Chuang Tzu was believed to have written, followed by their companion chapters (twenty-six remaining today).

Why have I chosen to write only on the three beginning chapters of the *Chuang Tzu*? For the following spontaneous reasons: First, anything more than three chapters would have become unwieldy: "A big book is a big evil."

Secondly, the *Chuang Tzu* has only beginnings and no end. Even they are so many that one can begin and end anywhere in the *Chuang Tzu*; they are really "no beginning."[1] The *Chuang Tzu* is unfinished and unfinishable. By concentrating on the first three chapters, this Companion underscores this.

Thirdly, this implies that any portion of the *Chuang Tzu* is coherent in itself. Three rounds of different coherent descriptions are enough to excite the reader to go out and continue on his own. For, Chuang Tzu says in many ways in the Seven Inner Chapters: "Let the reader carry on." And there came the Outer Chapters, and Miscellaneous Chapters, then the *Lieh Tzu* and the *Huai Nan Tzu*, and so on.

Fourthly, in my opinion, the beginning three chapters sum up the entire *Chuang Tzu* in the fashion of a Chinese box. Chapter One is a cosmic and historical version of Chapter Two, which is an existential-thoughtful version of Chapter One; both chapters describe the whole *Chuang Tzu*. Chapter Three sums up the Seven Inner Chapters, which in turn are the essence of the *Chuang Tzu*. To deal with the first three chapters, then, is to deal with the entire *Chuang Tzu*.

Let me explain the structure of my contributions to this book.

First of all, a companion to this *Companion* seems to be called for, and this I offer in the Prologue. After Chuang Tzu's butterfly's invitation to the reader come explanations, first of what "companion" is, then of how poetic the *Chuang Tzu* is. Thus, the Prologue prepares the reader for entry into Chapters One, Two, and Three. Following the Chinese text, each chapter begins with an almost literal translation, poetically arranged (as that text is here, but without disturbing the original word order) to bring out the rhythm and cadence of Chuang Tzu's thought. Coupled with each translation are textual glosses, weaving a tapestry of the meanings of the *Chuang Tzu* in both Chinese and English. Then my meditations, which closely follow the Chinese text and its translation, stanza by stanza, sentence by sentence, sometimes word for word, pondering on the force, coherence, and meaning of the thought. The Epilogue meditates on the resonances among meaning, irony, and play, manifesting the significance of the *Chuang Tzu* as a whole.

Standing alongside and pervading everything else in this *Companion* is the Chinese text of the first three chapters of the *Chuang Tzu*. The text reproduced here is taken from the earliest extant version of the Chuang Tzu, that edited by Kuo Hsiang (died A.D. 312).[2] Keeping the original word order, I have arranged it in free verse and given numbers to the lines. In order to read this text in the usual way of reading Chinese writings (that is, from the top down and from right to left), it will be necessary to begin on the page opposite the first page of the Translation of each chapters, where the Chinese text begins.

Thus, it may be said that, at the heart of this book, the text of the *Chuang Tzu* and my *Companion* to it stand together, face to face.

PROLOGUE

Companion to the Butterfly

PRELIMINARY MEDITATIONS

A. Invitation by a Butterfly

1. You have at hand, my dear reader, Chuang Tzu's first three chapters, undisturbed—their poetic texts, their literal translations, their glosses, and meditations thereon. All this is self-reflexive, yet it opens out to the reader. This is, I dare say, a poetic invitation by a butterfly, in the form of its journal. We remember that butterfly. It is the one dreamed by Chuang Tzu, that Taoist bum in China during the fourth century before Jesus Christ was born.[1]

From such simple information we can gather several things. First, Chuang Tzu dreamed of being the butterfly, and so it belongs to him. Yet it has some advantages over him. It can flutter freely among the flowers; he cannot. It is innocent; he is not. It may be currently dreaming of being him; he, now that he is awake, cannot. His name, "Chuang Chou" was given by his parents and is not himself; the butterfly has no such problem, because it has no name. Its essence is fluttering—from one idea to another, one event to another, one life to another, fluttering from a dream to its awakening to another dream. It does not deny the distinction between awakening and dreaming, reality and illusion, knowledge and ignorance, Chuang Chou and butterfly, or even the reality of uncertainty. It just affirms its situation as it "flutters" from one thing to another. Its "name" is fluttering.

We must be warned, however, against "investigating" the dream as some of the wise philosophers do, asking whether dream is an "experience," whether it is "verifiable," whether in a dream "error" is possible.[2] Asking such questions is like asking what shape the wind and clouds have. The wind is neither square nor round, any more than dreaming is waking. Error, experience, and verification are notions of the waking world; they have as much to do with dream as the wind and clouds have with shape. Such investigation entangles us in much gobbledygook. We might as well try to catch and store the wind in a box.

In any case, dear reader, count yourself fortunate. You can enjoy and follow a butterfly fluttering back and forth between dream and reality without denying either. You will flutter with it between ancient China and the modern West. You will live vigorously and zestfully.

Thus this journal is an invitation. You are invited to join in our common joy of meditative fluttering, continuing the journal. *This* journal is thus incomplete. You are now one of the butterflies that play life—have you seen any butterfly that does not enjoy fluttering? Whether or not you are the butterfly or Chuang Tzu may be an interesting question, but it does not detract from your enjoying yourself.

    2.   But how about death—can we enjoy that? If the birth of a baby is joy to everyone, why is not death as joyous? After all, both are events that bring to pass something new—one to come into life, the other to complete it, and that with an added lived experience of going out of life. If it is fun to come in and begin life, it must be fun also to finish it and get out. If change is the spice (if not the essence) of life, I cannot see why changing-out-of a particular life cannot be as much fun as changing-into it.

    Of course change is accompanied by a little dizziness. An airplane takes off. It rocks and soars; we feel dizzy. Soon it stabilizes itself and we enjoy the scenery. Then it comes down. Again, we are rocked and dizzy at things getting bigger. Then the landing, and people on the plane look relieved. Death is a landing. We should be "relieved."

    Or perhaps it is rather like this. After landing we deplane to go to our new schedule of living. "Deplaning" is another departure, another beginning, for something new. Our "deplaning" from life may well be another beginning of something new. Chuang Tzu imagined so in his Chapter Two, lines 245–49. The disappearance of the plane, that ordinary daily living of ours, should be an exciting thing.

    Does this require reincarnation? Not necessarily, for even if there is no reincarnation, a disappearance is as much fun as reincarnation; we remember Buddha wanted Nirvana, a "blow off." And Chuang Tzu gleefully learned from talking with a (his own?) skull.[3]

    There are at least four possibilities after death—simple disappearance of this earthly body, its glorification, its continuation as before, or else things getting more miserable. And any of these possibilities can give us joy.

    If death is our simple disappearance, it would also be a disappearance of sorrows and worries, and we won't be worrying about our disappearance. If death is our glorification, nothing can be better; it should be a celebration.[4] In either case we cannot understand why we are sad at the deathbed.

    If death is a continuation of the life we have lived, we should also rejoice in death because we have a second chance. Even if we are caught in the predetermined wheel of eternal returns to the same life, Nietzsche and Camus are at our side to give us the courage of Zarathustra and Sisyphus.[5]

And, to think of it, words of comparison such as "same" and "different" make no sense in this context. They can be said of my life only by one who is (1) both in and out of myself and (2) remembers my past life. But there is none such except, perhaps, God. Even if a god existed he is not myself; *I* cannot feel pain because of his knowledge of my life eternally recurring. Besides, as a butterfly I can always find some new meanings in the "same" life, whether the last life or the next. All in all, there exists no eternal recurrence for the butterfly whose "name" is fluttering.

What if death leads us to a *worse* situation than now? We must remember that misery comes from a misfit between our life-of-desire and the environment. "Misfit" is a correlative term like "quarrel"; two parties have to agree to disagree, to quarrel. When we forget our desires (and ourselves) their "quarrel" with the environment simply cannot happen. More on this theme later.[6]

Death is as much of a change as birth is. Birth is a joy; death should also be. Whatever "goods" my birth (I use "good" as a verb) also "goods" my death.[7] The fact that we love life shows that every day is good; since death is an everyday occurrence, every death is also good. Not to think so is itself a misery. (Now do not tell me to look at miseries and frustrations around us. They are late comers on the heel of our decision not to think every day a good.)

"Oh, no; you are wrong," a sophist-logician like Hui Shih (a good friend of Chuang Tzu) would say. Birth is a positive (gain); death is a negative (loss). If the first change is joy, the second change should be sorrow. Our butterfly answers, "This is valid only if you think of 'positive' and 'negative,' not of 'change.'" Both are changes—change in one direction is as much of a change as change in an opposite direction. "Gain" and "loss" are terms of desire, not of change.[8] Or rather, gain and loss are cages of obsession, not of desire. It is one thing to desire something, it is another to be obsessed with it, such as with gain. Once we let go of that obsession, we see that loss is fun, too. For what are sports and sportsmanship for?

No player wants to lose the game, of course. Yet the unbeatable team spoils the game; eliminating all defeats eliminates the game itself. The defeat teaches us not just how to win next time but, more importantly, how to take it like a man. The point of the game is not (just) to win but to cultivate sportsmanship through defeats, as well as victories.

One plays a game in order to enjoy it; to enjoy the game is to experience the excitements of its ups and downs, to "enjoy" its "changing" tides. So in life, the point of which is to *enjoy* the excitements of the *changes*, its wins and losses, even death—for only life experiences its death. No defeat, no game; no death, no game of life.

3. Conversation with Hui Shih the sophist reminds us that Chuang Tzu has a position of no position. This strange description can be clarified by comparing Chuang Tzu with Confucius and Hui Shih.

Compared with Confucius, Chuang Tzu's position is that of *no position*, opposing the orthodoxy which destroys humanness by artificially promoting a definite position. Here Chuang Tzu has a position whose content is *no* position in contrast to that of Confucius.

Nonetheless, it remains that Chuang Tzu does have a *position* of no position, opposing Hui Shih the sophist who has no position at all. Hui Shih's is a sophism, pure negation wallowing in logical nonsense and dazzling platitudes.

Having no position of his own, Hui Shih is intent only on attacking others. He ends up in a dead end. As a thinker, he naturally wants to spread his view universally. Yet since all he does is pure negation, his universalized negation must also apply to himself. Thus he has to negate himself, and becomes unable to negate any more. In the end, Hui Shih has nowhere to pillow his head.

In contrast, by opposing Hui Shih's opposition, Chuang Tzu does affirm (by way of opposition) every view, including his own way of "no-position" and opposition, without being stuck in it. Life is larger than logic; in life p is not exactly not-not-p. Insistence on p indicates an "orthodox" dogmatic affirmation; insistence on not-p is a sophistic iconoclasm. Assuming not-not-p indicates an affirmation without affirmation, an affirmation that accommodates opposition, a position of no position, an affirmative non-position.

By opposing opposition, Chuang Tzu has two non-positions. First, Chuang Tzu can tarry like a butterfly wherever he happens to be and then flutter away, leaving no trace behind. Chuang Tzu enjoys roaming nonchalance, at home everywhere without claiming anywhere his home.

Secondly, Chuang Tzu's non-position enables him to *use* Confucius and Hui Shih for Chuang Tzu's own self-expression. In his polemic with Hui Shih, Chuang Tzu does not just debate but enjoys Hui Shih's eristics, inviting Hui Shih also to enjoy it together. How much Chuang Tzu treasured such dialogical enjoyment is shown at Hui Shih's grave where Chuang Tzu sorely missed him as Chuang Tzu's "partner" or "material."[9] This is not a selfish use of Hui Shih but a cooperation between an artist and his partner-material, an exquisite sharing of creative enjoyment in mutual echoing and responding. Chuang Tzu also responded to Confucius both negatively and positively, now criticizing Confucius, now affectionately calling him "Chung Ni," now putting Lao Tzu's thoughts in Confucius' mouth, honorifically calling Confucius "K'ung Tzu," perhaps hinting that Confucius was after all promoting being himself and natural, as Chuang Tzu has been arousing us to be all along.[10]

Thus Chuang Tzu's is a position of no position, soaring beyond others' positions by sauntering among them.

4. The book of *Chuang Tzu* consists of stories and sayings. Sayings can be arguments and their poetic parodies, rhymed or not. Stories are not epic, ornate, or eerie, but spicy and memorable.

Confucius said that to ponder poetry is to "know what is to come when told what has happened." This is in fact what "learning" is, repeatedly to "warm up the old and know the new," to "revert [extrapolate] to the three [corners of the square] when one is lifted."[11] Similarly, Chu Hsi said of Confucius' *Analects* that we must spend time repeatedly meditating on the implications hidden in the passage, whether outwardly simple or abstruse.[12] Such is the peculiarly Chinese way of *reading* worthy writings.

We must likewise tarry and dwell on the *Chuang Tzu*; its passages echo our life situations. To chew on them, to draw implications from them, is to meditate on the meaning of life. To enjoy them is to enjoy life.

But why not enjoy life itself; why bother with the *Chuang Tzu*? Chuang Tzu himself says something similar, that we must forget words once we get their intention, as we forget the net once we get the fish. Yet he continues, "Where can I get a man who forgets words so I can have a word with him?"[13] Why?

To make sense of life we can do nothing better than tell stories about it. Jean-Paul Sartre said,

> ...a man is always a teller of stories, ...he sees everything which happens to him through these stories; and he tries to live his life as if it were a story he was telling. ...While you live, nothing happens. The scenery changes, people come in and go out, that's all. There are no beginnings ...an interminable and monotonous addition. ...But when you tell about a life, everything changes; ...events take place in one direction, and we tell about them in the opposite direction. ...I wanted the moments of my life to follow each other and order themselves like those of a life remembered. I might as well try to catch time by the tail.[14]

Thus, to live humanly is to tell, to tell is to produce coherence, and to have coherence is to live humanly. Such coherence is elusive as a living fish, and the net of story-telling and mock-arguing is always needed to "catch time by the tail."

The beauty of Chuang Tzu's fishing net is that it resembles the fish, for here both the net and the fish need to be pursued. Chuang Tzu's sayings are too elusive for us comfortably to sit back and receive; to read them is to be aroused to ponder. And such is the way of netting a fish, catching our "time by its tail," its significance—and such is a human way of living.

We get the coherence of life through Chuang Tzu's fishing net. Lived coherence is neither a metaphysical system nor a rambling, neither analytically logical nor simply illogical, neither absurd nor calculable. Lived coherence is vast and vibrant, flexing itself like a fishing net to whatever comes.

Our human obligation is to discern and to live such "coherence." We cannot live without meaning; we live coherently and meaningfully or we die (as human). As we ponder on the *Chuang Tzu* we are in touch with lived meaning and coherence. We come to enjoy ourselves in it, come what may. And in doing so we add meaning of our own, proving ourselves to be life's creative participants. We discern and live, thereby enhance life. We change life by making life coherent, and *we* are in the meantime changed by living the coherence we continually create. Such is sensible living, our life imperative. To read the *Chuang Tzu* is to live it, thereby rightly living and enriching our lives.

5.   I have so far invited you to join Chuang Tzu's butterfly, or a butterfly's "Chuang Chou"—to enjoy fluttering about between knowledge and uncertainty, dreaming and waking, life and death. Such fluttering is in a position of no position, as opposed to Confucius (with a specific position) and Hui Shih (with no position whatever).

But who am *I* who thus invite you? What does this "invitation" amount to? "I" am one of your friends, sharing with you what I have found and how much I enjoyed fluttering with Chuang Tzu, the friend to us all. And so the invitation and the pages that follow expresses such companionship. This is a *Companion*, not commentary, to Chuang Tzu's writing. The next Meditation elaborates on this.

B.   Why Companion, Not Commentary

1.   The excitement, and so the problem, of studying the *Chuang Tzu* is twofold: (*a*) We must be "contemporaneous" (to borrow from Kierkegaard) with Chuang Tzu, that is, living the same time, life, and experience in the cultural and historical world of Chuang Tzu. This is a general problem in studying any historical document. (*b*) Besides, we must be evoked to live our lives as we never have lived. There is in Chuang Tzu an undiminished novelty that is *ours* to live. This is the peculiar challenge of studying Chuang Tzu. To consult textual criticism, the traditional commentary, helps solve the first

problem; to have a "Companion" should help meet the second challenge. We must now see how this is so.

The book of *Chuang Tzu* has many memorable vibrant phrases. To codify them—that is, authoritatively to parse and interpret them, to revere and follow them into indisputable standards for all truths and things—quickly turns Chuang Tzu into an orthodoxy. Nothing is deadlier to Chuang Tzu than a Chuang Tzu scholasticism which enbalms him in the temple of scholarship; he would rather be a turtle dragging its tail in the mud of real obscure living.

Søren Kierkegaard said that one can truly follow one's master only after the master's death.[15] Confucius would have agreed, but in a way perhaps surprising to Kierkegaard. Confucius said, "I transmit, I do not create";[16] he *thereby* revolutionized the tradition, radically democratizing the notion of "gentleman," universalizing the "heavenly decree," and insisting that becoming an upright individual is the first and the last requirement of a good ruler. That is what "transmitting the ancients" means. H. J. Paton, hardly a radical thinker, said of "traditions" and "the wisdom of our fathers":

> If we are to take the past as our guide, it is hard to see why we should follow the past ages in everything except in the one thing which makes them great, that is to say, in attempting like them to add something to human knowledge and … achievement. Mere imitation will contribute nothing to the sum of human values. … Even where we accept and seek to follow an authority, we cannot avoid the necessity of independent thought. The mere commentator may help others to understand, but he does not understand himself. To understand a past thinker we must think again as he thought, and to do so is not a matter of analyzing arguments and comparing texts, but of having the same experience and wrestling with the same problems. Without memory we cannot think, but we cannot make memory a substitute for thought.[17]

All this is profound and true. A phrase, however, gives us pause, "having the same experience." It is true that we must have the same experience of "adding something to human achievement." Yet "adding something" is to add something *new*, which cannot be the "same" with the past. When something is as new (different) as the other is, it is as unique and unrepeatable as the other. Both are the "same" in being different from each other.

Forest fires come; trees turn into ashes. Saplings then shoot up to the skies, as if none had done so before, just as the parent trees did before—thanks to the parents, thanks to *their* ashes, thanks to *their* clearings.

Such understanding of "following the tradition" revolutionizes the hermeneutics of classical texts. For example, a typical textual investigation of Chuang Tzu goes as follows: A word or phrase was used "thus and thus" by writers of Chuang Tzu's period, or by Chuang Tzu himself somewhere else; therefore, Chuang Tzu *must* also mean "thus and thus" in this particular place.

This assumes that Chuang Tzu never meant otherwise than he or other writers had meant before. But he did not promise us so; no writer does. One of the excitements of a good writer lies precisely in the subtle shift of meaning he commands as he writes.

Excitement differs from haphazardness, however. For the author *has* been influenced by other writers and has used that word "thus and thus" before. He may now want to use the word differently, as required by the new subject matter on hand; but his use is "different" only in terms of his and others' previous usage. The shift of usage is the shift of the past usage. Thus the excitement of the shift is recognizable in terms of (*i*) the past usage and (*ii*) the subject matter on hand, Textual investigation helps us on (*i*), but not much on (*ii*), which is yet the reason we read a writer.

Akatzuka Tadashi noted that Chuang Tzu has bits of contemporary myths and legends in the first chapter;[18] Akatzuka failed to see what such adoption of myth bits *means*. In his second chapter Chuang Tzu used notions current among commoners and philosophers; A. C. Graham pointed out some philosophical notions, yet missed common ones.[19] Both Akatzuka and Graham missed the fact that Chuang Tzu did not quote current notions and stories but *used* them as he liked. Furthermore, many commentators (such as Akatzuka, Han Shan, Fukunaga Mitsuji) pay exclusive attention to such notions as "one," "nothing," negations of the "many" and of wordly wranglings, and interpret all passages in this light.[20] They also tend to look to other writings and other occurrences in the *Chuang Tzu*, instead of *staying* with a specific passage, wrestling with it. This results in a version of Chuang Tzu that is vaguely nihilistic and otherwordly. The version no longer has Chuang Tzu's original vigor, intimate discernment, tantalizing obscurity, surprising freshness.

Thus, textual criticism has a negative function. It establishes *rough parameters* of meaning we can attribute to Chuang Tzu's phrases. We must respect such *parameters*; we cannot attribute to Chuang Tzu a meaning completely foreign to the usage in the ancient world, however prevalently meanings of this sort are adopted today. And yet any parameter of meaning is only a rough outline. As mentioned above, we cannot claim that since the writers of Chuang Tzu's times did not use the phrase in this sense, Chuang Tzu could never have meant this sense by the phrase. After all, we share a common humanness with people in Chuang Tzu's period, and the very purpose of Chuang Tzu's writing is to shock us out of common sense—and he was especially concerned with the common sense of his own period.

Thus we must appeal to our common humanity while dwelling in Chuang Tzu's writings, until we can intuitively move in his overall sentiment and thrust. At the same time, such perception itself must not be unrelated to the rough parameters of meaning established by painstaking research on textual-critical matters. In short, our understanding of the text is a subtle embodiment of the literary thrust and objective textual research.

2. Ch'en Ch'i-t'ien said that there are three difficulties in studying the *Chuang Tzu*—difficulties of deciphering the ancient text of Chuang Tzu, of interpreting his strange stories, and of discerning their philosophical import. To resolve these difficulties we must naturally start with textual exegesis. This is why so many commentaries keep appearing. Then he advised that among many commentaries those by Kuo Hsiang, Chiao Hung, Kuo Ch'ing-fan, and Ch'ien Mu are most comprehensive.[21]

It must be agreed that the difficulty of reading the *Chuang Tzu* is at least threefold, and that the textual-exegetical labors are an indispensable start toward understanding the text. We cannot, however, understand the *Chuang Tzu* by textual labor alone. We must further go on to ponder the implications of the text. Few have tackled the latter task.[22]

We think that the original text from Chuang Tzu's hand was intended to challenge our usual sense of rationality, but came unfortunately to be mingled with later emendations by the admirers, syncretists, textual copyists. It is now difficult if not impossible to disentangle the "wheat" of the original text from the "chaff" of extraneous additions and changes.

To make the matter worse, the *Chuang Tzu* challenges our common sense, which is our final arbiter in textual critical investigations. And so our textual hermeneutics has three pitfalls:

(*i*) Our usual critical rationality could be trusted to delete "unintelligible" passages and relocate "irrelevant" ones. An emaciated text, to our taste, emerges.

(*ii*) The text as a whole could be worshipped and swallowed, and we merely recite the text in irresponsible irrationality.

(*iii*) We could, by "weaving sense and nonsense," produce a "seamless whole" text. It now "cracks under the multiple strains of [our] craft," which in translation turns the *Chuang Tzu* into a "bland evasive English."[23]

If most translators (Giles, Legge, Watson) bordered on danger *iii*, then Graham is unique in leaning toward danger *i*, while many Chinese commentators tend to danger *ii*. These dangers are theoretically not unavoidable. We could heed the warning of textual critical scholarship against danger *ii*, while exercising our discernment and judgment against danger *i*; then danger *iii* will take care of itself.

Sadly, this is easier said than done. Trying to avoid dangers *ii* and *iii*, Graham not only falls into danger *i* but also clutters the text with unwieldy jargon. *Shih* (just to take Chapter Two) is rendered "'That's it' which goes by circumstance"; *wei shih* is "'That's it' which deems." Both are, however, words of daily usage picked up by logicians and thinkers, and can simply be rendered as "yes, this" and "for this reason."

All the preceding three dangers came from regarding the *Chuang Tzu* as a definitive, serious, scholarly disputation. The commentators and translators have completely disregarded the textual principle repeatedly put forth in the *Chuang Tzu* itself, which said, for example,

> He [Chuang Tzu] expounded them [his views] in odd and outlandish terms, in brash and bombastic language, in unbound and unbordered phrases, … not looking at things from one angle only. He believed that the world was drowned in turbidness and that it was impossible to address it in sober language. So he used 'goblet words' to pour out endless changes, 'double-rayed words' to give a ring of truth, and 'lodged words' to impart greater breadth. … Though his writings are a string of queer beads and baubles, … they are crammed with truths that never come to an end.[24]

In short, the book was meant to be a satirical stab in the back of our convention and common sense. We need, not just rational scholarship (textual-philological, socio-historical, cultural-philosophical), but a liberal dose of *sensitivity*—literary and rational. Graham's textual sensitivity is most helpful. We must go further. But how?

At least five questions can be asked about the *Chuang Tzu*:

(1) What does the tradition (the ancients) say about the book?
(2) What does Chuang Tzu say in the book?
(3) How does he say it?
(4) What does he mean?
(5) Why does he say so?

A vast number of exegetes wrote on the traditions of interpretation (question 1).[25] A few wrote on the contents and the style of the *Chuang Tzu* (questions 2 and 3).[26] Very few wrote on what Chuang Tzu meant (question 4), which is usually taken to be identical with an interpretive tradition (question 1). None wrote on why Chuang Tzu says what he says and in such a manner (question 5), which is usually buried under their busy concerns with historical circumstances.

Many thinkers (Confucius, Chu Hsi) can be understood by identifying what is said (question 2) with what is meant, thus making moot the questions about what is meant and why it is said (questions 4 and 5). This is how we handle disputation that is literal and serious. In contrast, Chuang Tzu evokes our reflection by ambiguities and elusive metaphors. He does not say what he means; he does not even point to what he means, which is less important than what is aroused. The difficulty, and so the fascination, of Chuang Tzu is that he peculiarly requires *our* involvement. Such involvement gives rise to the preceding five questions, each distinct from the other.

This does not mean that nothing definite is in Chuang Tzu or that what he says is not important. What he says directs what he evokes, which has a relatively definite range. But what will be evoked in the reader is not completely known. The *Chuang Tzu* is alive, with a character.

We do have the so-called Chuang Tzu scholarship, but it does not help us understand Chuang Tzu in the manner in which the comparable Chu Hsi scholarship helps us understand Chu Hsi. Scholarship usually means a concern with the tradition of interpretation (question 1); reading Chuang Tzu only in such traditional light leads us *away* from Chuang Tzu. That familiar Japanese adage, "He who reads 'Confucius' misses Confucius,"[27] (echoed by Mencius' warning—"Better be without the book than giving it full credence!"),[28] applies here with a fatal vengeance. To be trapped in the Chuang Tzu tradition (question 1) is to be embalmed in historical irrelevance.

3.   Commentary as such follows the hermeneutical tradition, authorizes definitive readings, and establishes the text in the shrine of the Classics. No literary activity is more lethal to Chuang Tzu's spirit. An "authoritative commentary to the *Chuang Tzu*" is as hazardously irrelevant as an "authoritative commentary" to Nietzsche, Kierkegaard, or Gabriel Marcel.[29]

In contrast, the "companion" answers and continues Chuang Tzu's call, "Where can I get a man who forgets words so I can have a word with him?"[30] The companion attempts with critical sensibility to transmit the seismic impacts of Chuang Tzu's sayings on our taken-for-granted life, preserving all his tantalizing ambiguities.

The authoritative bookishness of a commentary enshrines the turtle shell, killing the vigor of a living turtle wagging its tail (implications) in the mud of textual and lived ambiguities. The free individuality of a companion highlights and savors the intention of the *Chuang Tzu*—free individual concord.

The condescendingly called Outer and Miscellaneous Chapters in the *Chuang Tzu* are actually an early collection of such "companion" essays evoked by the Inner Chapters. They belong to the big circle of "friends"[31] called "the *Chuang Tzu*." This *Companion* (with all its defects) aspires to continue and expand that critical circle of friends.

Accompanying the reader, the "companion" enables him to read the text on his own and "reach his own interpretation" of it, as Max Black puts it in the Preface to his *Companion to Wittgenstein's "Tractatus"*. Then Black says that there "can be no question ...of any 'definitive' reading" of the *Tractatus* because his own views "have oscillated" while he was writing.[32] He does not aim at the authoritative interpretation, but perhaps at helping the reader savor the excitements of the *Tractatus*, as this *Companion* to the *Chuang Tzu* does.

Interestingly one can, while writing a companion, change one's mind. One cannot, while writing an authoritative commentary; "authoritative" means *definitive*, that is, unchanging. In contrast, changing one's mind while writing shows how the text excites the reader; the excitement qualifies him to write a companion effectively to transmit the text's power of excitement to other readers.

4.   I am not a professional historian or literary critic, and so am qualified to try such a companion. Not being a historian, I need not wear the mask of analytical objectivity; not being a literary critic, I need not complicate explanation by excessive rigor. I eagerly absorb advice from historians and literary critics, then throw away half of it. My criterion is my discernment gained by personal dwelling, with their help, in the *Chuang Tzu*.

The purpose here is to call attention and to invite you, the reader, to plunge into the *Chuang Tzu* without prejudice. You would soon realize, as I repeatedly have, that to plunge into the *Chuang Tzu* is to plunge into yourself and into your world. A concrete example of such hermeneutical transmission is given in Meditation C.

C.   Conversation With A Roadside Skull

Let us take a delightful story in one of the so-called Outer Chapters, Chapter Eighteen, where Chuang Tzu supposedly had a dream conversation with a skull at the roadside. Not believing in the skull's confession about its self-enjoyment, Chuang Tzu asked if it wanted him to ask the Arbiter of Fate to restore its former life with its body, family, and friends.

The skull frowned severely, wrinkling up its brow. "Why would I throw away more happiness than that of a king on a throne and take on the troubles of a human being again?" It said.[33]

1. I have eight points about the story:

(1) A scholarly consideration may go like this. The story is definitely from the hand of a late Taoist friend of Chuang Tzu's, for at least two reasons:

First, the story is pervaded with too much otherworldliness, not like Chuang Tzu's usual mood, as Kuo Hsiang, as well as Tsuda Saukichi,[34] would have said.

Second, the final scene, as quoted above, gave away the clumsiness of a later writer who inadvertently forgot that a skull has no brow to knit, much less a tongue to speak with, or brain cells to think and enjoy life with. (I omit all other considerations about literary style and phraseology.)

(2) However, if we forget such debate based on common sense (which Chuang Tzu wanted to challenge anyway) and simply read the story, then we will feel a breeze going through *our* skulls. We feel liberated; we realize that we have been carrying our skulls as we live on. We can knit our brows and still live on as if we had only skulls and nothing else.

And then we realize that this story is for us who are alive and yet carry death as we live on. This is a profoundly *this*-worldly story then. The very fact that the author lets the skull knit its brow connects it with the living, who have both skull and brow. Thus we have by-passed all the scholarly debate.

(3) Yet literary criticism in the preceding fashion does have its function; by adhering to common sense the criticism calls our attention to the story's departures from common sense. Such departures alert us to the author's intention and deepen our appreciation of the story in our own way.

(4) In any case, that the above description of point 2 agrees with Chuang Tzu's overall sentiment can be seen by checking 6/45ff, 18/15ff, 22/9, 77ff.

(5) Let us continue our thoughts on point 2. Enjoy our living death—this is the story's message. This contrasts with the prevalent mood in some existential literature, such as Kierkegaard's "sickness unto death" (despair) or Camus' defiance against the "absurdity of life" (disintegration of our life-accomplishments in death). Chuang Tzu's *living* in death makes life enjoyable; we live as if we were already dead.

Such living differs also from the Buddhist way of life which counsels us to *die* during our daily living. Since everything is vacant, to the point that even the notion of vacancy is vacant of meaning, there is no point in committing suicide. The base line is death, in which life matters little; we die while living. In contrast, the brow-knitting of the skull has its eyes (?) on enjoyment. It *lives* with the heaven and earth, with which it makes seasons, as if it were the king on the throne. The skull lives on, and it is such skull-living that Chuang Tzu proposed. When Chuang Tzu tapped the skull and slept on it as pillow, the skull's vibration of joy resonated into Chuang Tzu. Such resonance is called "conversation in a dream."

(6) But who wrote this story? To say it is a later disciple or friend of Chuang Tzu does not help answer the question. For the skull-to-skull resonance is so personal a matter that no one other than Chuang Tzu himself would have known it. Perhaps "Chuang Tzu" here functions as "Chuang Chou" does at the end of the second chapter. "Chuang Tzu" is a *wo*—the identifiable, objectifiable self, to be looked at and talked with. Who then is conversing with the skull? It must be the authentic transcendental *cogito*, the *wu* which begins the second chapter.

That is to say, the conversation with the skull must have been that between the *wo*-skull and the *wu-cogito*-self of Chuang Tzu. Such conversation later "leaked out" into the conversation among friends in whom "there was no disagreement in their hearts," saying,

> Who can look upon nonbeing as his head, on life as his back, and on death as his rump? ...Who knows that life and death, existence and annihilation, are all a single body? I will be his friend![35]

The "conversation" here is the resonance of the self with the self, and the resonance of the self with other selves.

Everyone alive literally sleeps every night, pillowed on his skull. This conversation is then a universal one, a continuation of the meditative joy of that butterfly dream that concludes the second chapter, and of that nourishing dance through suffering that pervades the third chapter.

(7) The dry empty skull has three reasons for its joy that can never be taken away: It is a skull, it is dry, and it is empty.

> (*a*) There may be a roadside skull, but there cannot be a roadside skull-in-general. The *skull* is unmistakably that of a particular individual; it is "mine."
>
> (b) Not even the devil (if any), much less vultures, wolves, and earthworms, would take a second look at it. For it is a *dry* skull; no one would care to touch it, much less harm it.
>
> (c) This dry skull is dry because it is empty; I cannot get any *emptier*. Yet it is still myself and no one else. Being the lowliest bottom to which I can go, the I/it is invincible.

Thus the dry skull is my identity which no one dreams of taking away. This is my ultimate emptiness, my ultimate self and safety, therefore my ultimate joy, me and my dry skull.

What joy? Well, now that its skin and flesh are shed, its blood dried, it ages no longer, but makes its happy rounds of seasons with the heaven and earth.

"With the heaven and earth [it] makes [rounds of] spring and autumn" (18/27) is the neat phrase casually tossed out by the dry roadside skull to describe its ineffable joy. "The heaven and earth" is nature; "spring and autumn" is the round of seasons. "With nature to make seasons" is to let nature roll in season after season, to let all spaces be at all times, to roll space and time into one—in short, to let things be as they are. This is joy unperturbed through ups and downs, season after season. The entire universe contributes to the skull's making of happy seasons.

"With the skies and the earth to make the spring and the autumn," said the roadside skull, the death at any roadside on life's way. Death is as close to me as the skies that cover me and the earth in which I live, every day of the season. Every day, in its turn, is as vast and eternal as the skies above and the earth around. I *am* my skull, as much at home in death as I am in the skies and the earth, in my everyday life. Death is as close as my life, and my life as close as my death; and so if I desire my life I should desire my death, and live on with my skull at any roadside of my life. And then my life will be as happy as that joy of the dry skull on the roadside, "making the spring and the autumn with the heaven and earth."

This phrase describes or, rather, presents the essence of the roadside skull's joy. How? In two ways.

First, the moment of experience is the event in the spatio-temporal atmosphere (*ch'i*), as expressed in the usual poetic phrase, "pine wind." It is space (pine) and it is time (wind), co-happening, co-steeping, con-fused—an experiential Hun Tun. We isolate the words and arrange them into an orderly logical explication—"winds in the pines," "winds through the pines"—and then the primal integrity of the initial concreteness is lost. The original impact is "pine wind," not to be tampered with, but to be felt with our senses, our spine, our life.

When, secondly, such experiential integrity goes as vast as the skies and the fields, and as endless as the springs through the autumns, the experience *makes* the universe in all its spatio-temporal richness. And such is the joy of the roadside skull whose subjecthood (he is *someone's* skull) is intact and whose subjectiveness is empty (he is dead). There exists "pure experience," devoid of all distortions and encumbrances of the flesh and blood—fatigue, boredom, selfishness.

Crickets must have played hide and seek in the skull both among themselves and with their predators. Insects must have come in for cover during the summer heat and rain, and during the winter cold and wind, if they were still around. Field mice may have nibbled at it for calcium, and found it less palatable than horns shed by deer. And it outlived all of them. Night hootings of the owl filled it with echoes of the sleepy moon, barely seen in the cracks of the clouds. Half hidden in the blowing dust, the skull blended in with the scene of the wild.

Thus the skull forever gazes at the skies and the fields, happily making its seasons with them. "No one bothers it, as it bothers no one." "Joy unspeakable which is yet no joy," joy vainly sought by emperors and tycoons, moralists and mystics, just comes and stays when the spring comes, and comes again and stays again when the autumn comes. "All changes are gone through into one," as "the under-heaven is safely tucked away in the under-heaven." All this is mine as long as I live with my own skull. To live with my own skull amounts to living with the heaven and the earth, season after season.

And so, my dear reader, when you are sad or hurt, frown with your own skull, on which you pillow your sleep every night. You will end up finding no frowning. Live as your skull does—with the heaven and earth, season after season.

This is Buddhism in reverse. Buddhism says that every *thing* is merely an aggregate of thing-elements, which in turn are puffs of imagination, unreal. Chuang Tzu says things are like music ("piping"?). Music is made of rubbings-together of things and their elements—metal, hollows, vibrations. Music is beautiful, and beautiful things are made of their skulls, their inanimate thing-elements. This is the musical joy of skulls. And so all these pairs are real and beautiful—skull and joy, the inanimate and the animate, things and heaven-and-earth. They interchange and integrate. Beautiful! Where is your hurt now?

(8) But does this description of "*i* (heaven-earth) *wei* (spring-autumn)" exhaust its meaning? Not quite. This description tends to confuse "instrumental *with*" *(i)* with "together *with*" *(yu)* and to confuse *treating-regarding wei* with *making-doing wei*. And such confusion brings out Chuang Tzu's style of writing. Let me elaborate.

Usually "*i (a) wei (b)*" means at least two things: (1) "With *a* as material to make *(wei) b*"—in this case, with the heaven and earth as material to make the rounds of seasons. This differs from "our springs and autumns are as endless as heaven and earth" (Watson, 193), much less "participating in the making of seasons with heaven and earth." (2) Another connotation in common usage is that *a* is not *b*, but it is now made as *b*, as in "*i* (you) *wei* (father)" or "*i* (enemy) *wei* (friend)." Properly speaking, *a* is not *b* ("you" are not "father," "enemy" is not "friend"), but now is made as, that is, recognized and treated as, *b*.

With this linguistic convention, the paradox of Chuang Tzu's phrase is manifest. Three points can be raised:

(*i*) (*a*) Given the linguistic convention, the phrase means that heaven-earth is not properly to be treated as spring-autumn, which the skull now does. (*b*) Yet what else can be more proper than somehow to connect heaven-earth with seasons? Watson's rendering (cited above) is quite understandable. (*c*) Yet, again, heaven-earth is spatial; spring-autumn is temporal. To treat something spatial as something temporal is as inappropriate as treating color as weight, though they are connected. Thus something proper is treated as something improper—(*a*), (*b*)—and something improper is treated as something—(*c*).

"*I* (heaven-earth) *wei* (spring-autumn)"—this phrase has two possible meanings: to treat (regard) heaven-earth as spring-autumn, and to make spring-autumn with (by using) heaven-earth. And these two meanings coalesce. Heaven-earth is unthinkable without spring-autumn. Spring's soft dreams, autumn's dry colors, summery steely vigor, and wintery ravaging white are the atmosphere of heaven-earth, which make up the seasons—without mentioning either heaven or earth.

Thus we make spring-autumn with heaven-earth, resulting in treating heaven-earth as spring-autumn; we make spring-autumn with heaven-earth because we always treat heaven-earth as spring-autumn. Here space (heaven-earth) and time (spring-autumn) are an Einsteinian continuum, the "one world" in which things move and have their being, and are themselves complexes of time-space. Things are seasonal; palpable things. The world is seasonal or nothing, in which seasons are, making the world of heaven-earth-spring-autumn.

(*ii*) But what does "making" seasons with heaven-earth mean? Does Chuang Tzu mean to say: (*a*) The skull is that nodal point where cosmic space (heaven-earth) intersects with, weaves itself into cosmic time (spring-autumn)? Or (*b*) the skull rejoices itself in rhythmization (if you will) of cosmic space? Or (*c*) the skull participates in the making of cosmic seasons without having its hands in it, doing nothing and nothing is left undone, having to do with it without having to do with it?

(*iii*) In sum, the phrase, "*i* (heaven-earth) *wei* (spring-autumn,)" is at once obvious and obscure, personal and cosmic, joyous and natural.

2. To all the preceding speculations someone might say, "Humbug!" He would say that the phrase must be defective, having originally been: "*i* (heaven-earth) *wei (x); i (y) wei* (spring-autumn)"—where *x* and *y* are now lost.

On the whole, he would continue: (1) the entire *Chuang Tzu* is too corrupt to be treated today; we no longer know how one thought is connected to another, and in such an argumentative book the defect is fatal. (2) Without knowing what words and phrases are authentic we cannot even begin to know what is going on. (3) What is left for us is to compare the similar texts in the *Huai Nan Tzu* which is closer to Chuang Tzu's period than Kuo Hsiang (whose text of the *Chuang Tzu* is the earliest one we have), and amend the *Chuang Tzu* with the *Huai Nan Tzu*. For instance, if the latter has *a-b-c* and the former has *a-c*, then one can amend *b* into the former.

My responses are as follows: To (3): The *b* may also be a later addition, whether Huai Nan Tzu's or someone else's; and no amount of formal or textual critical effort can banish this doubt. To (2): The corrupted text is not totally unintelligible. It conveys rather well the flavor and thrust of Chuang Tzu's style as different from that of Confucius and Mencius.

To (1): Behind the quest for textual purity and authenticity is an assumption that the difference between the presumed genuine text and the false one is crucial for understanding Chuang Tzu. But one of the peculiarities of the *Chuang Tzu*—judging from my response to 2—is that in Chuang Tzu this is not so; for Chuang Tzu *promoted* differences. Textual differences may enhance, rather than diminish the provocative character of Chuang Tzu's intentions and utterances.

There is, however, a right mode of provocation and a wrong one. My standard is that wrong provocation is one that is less flexible and less profound in implication. The Outer and Miscellaneous Chapters (especially Chapters Twenty-Eight through Thirty-One) produce Chuang Tzu, but mixed with an inflexible life-denying vituperation, especially against Confucius and against orthodoxies. There is a lack of double-edged subtlety, a lack of free montage-like shimmering of implications.

Our critic's other assumption is his belief in textual-critical methods. But the rambling unintelligibility of A. C. Graham's "restored" text (especially that of the third chapter, as we shall see) amply testifies to the limits of textual criticism. The criticism is effective only for the removal of spurious portions of text, not for positive reconstruction of the lost text. Its proper function is to remove, not to add.

And perhaps even removal should not be done without caution. Difference in diction and style may not be a sign of later addition, for the author does not promise us the same diction and style throughout. Textual criticism may cut too much. The paradoxical character of the text may not be a sign of textual corruption but an intended shocker to our common sense. Remove all ambiguity and paradox, and we remove the author with his text.

3. The question—"Is there any philosophical relevance to dipping into Chuang Tzu's *text*?"—raises the fundamental issue of hermeneutics in Chinese philosophy. The imagery of our conversation with *Chuang Tzu's* empty skull helps us understand the intricacies of the whole issue.

The fact is that we can do neither with nor without textual scholarship in our studies of the philosophy of the Chinese ancients, especially of Chuang Tzu. For, on the one hand, we must understand the ancient greats by studying the texts they left with us. Here, to neglect history is to be condemned *not* to repeat it in ourselves; we are babblingly lost in the barrenness of contemporary ignorance. We simply have to carefully study their texts to discern what they meant, or at least what they may well have meant. Understanding the philosophy of the Chinese ancients is first of all a textual exercise in the history of ideas.

On the other hand, however, in the field of Chinese philosophy (especially in Taoism and in Chuang Tzu) to know history *is* to repeat it on our own today—fully alive, always different from yesterday. To stay in Chuang Tzu scholarship alone is to be embalmed in Chuang Tzu scholasticism; it is to miss him, and thereby miss ourselves.

The authentic Chuang Tzu scholarship is then an art of handling Chuang Tzu's dry skull, fully alive. The text is "dry" and ancient, requiring the historical scholarship of textual hermeneutics. The text is "alive," calling us constantly as we handle it, telling us that *we* are dead, not it.

Chuang Tzu's text is his three kinds of words—"goblet words," "doublet words," "lodging words" (27/1-9). First, to quote Ezekiel backward, Chuang Tzu's dry bones and empty skull always come up to call *us* to stand alive. Such a call is Chuang Tzu's "goblet words" which tip *toward* us to alert us back to ourselves. His words call us to come alive, not just to them but to ourselves and to the world. Strangely, one way to come alive is to become as dry as the skull ["dry wood"], which will be meditated on when we come to Chapter Two, line 6.

Secondly, as we study Chuang Tzu's skull-text, we realize that it is radioactive with the double rays, as "doublet words," of both ancient wisdom and contemporary judgment. His empty skull becomes ours; we have to fill it with our brain, flesh, and blood, much as our bones are clothed in the flesh and blood of daily ongoings.

And then, thirdly, we realize that we have never been more alive to the text, to ourselves, and to the world. The dry empty skull talks to us *in* us now; the talk is his "lodging words," true Chuang Tzu scholarship. Such scholarship is a subtle art of weaving textual scholarship *under* our contemporary understanding. The etymology of "subtle" and "understanding" suggests nothing less than that our understanding should come from standing-under, under-going the text—so underwoven with the textual scholarship that we do not know whether our understanding (of the text, ourselves, the world) is ours or its, a seamless subtle whole in which the conversation with his/our skull is constantly carried on.

We thus come alive, with and within Chuang Tzu's skull-text. First, we come alive and respond, with the help of traditional hermeneutics of the text, to Chuang Tzu's call; so as, secondly, to come alive to ourselves and to the world; thereby, thirdly, to come back to the text for more serene evocation.

Here "objectivity" is as foreign as staying out of Chuang Tzu. For our first reading in the hermeneutic tradition arouses our curiosity. We are intrigued by ambiguous phrases, vibrant with alternative readings, some more plausible than others, some mutually contradictory. But the text is alive and calling; we cannot turn away. We probe deeper to find more alternative implications and coherence; our minds "fly off in a new direction at every re-reading" (Graham). We meditate on the text as we live on, come back to it, and find more implications. We thus move back and forth between the text and our daily living, and in the meantime we mature in our understanding of the text and of ourselves in the world. Such a round of existential conversations with Chuang Tzu's empty skull which becomes ours *is* "Chuang Tzu scholarship" truly so called.

One such round of conversations is reported in this *Companion*; it cannot by its nature be a commentary. "And such conversation is an indescribable joy co-rhythmic with the coming and going of the seasons," so adds Chuang Tzu's empty skull in us.[36]

D.   The Poetic *Chuang Tzu*

1.   "Just as the cosmic hymn was a perfect expression of the philosophy of Prajapati, and the memorial dialogue was a perfect expression of the philosophy of Plato, so the poetic vignette was a perfect expression of the philosophy of Chuang Tzu." In these terms, James D. Parsons has on occasion

related the highlights of his studies in the literary genres of philosophy—most recently in a personal communication to me. I take Chuang Tzu here to be the concentrated symbol of Chinese philosophy. Every book on Chinese poetry that I have encountered treats Chinese metaphysics. Conversely, there is hardly a book on Chinese philosophy which does not cite and explain at least one Chinese poem. Poetry and philosophy come together so naturally in China that people seldom even bother to notice their symbiosis or, rather, their being two aspects of a unity in nature, whether nature in us or outside.

Therefore, it is of significance to look into what it means to be *poetic*. To be poetic is to be self-involved. A piece of writing is poetic when:

(1) its content (what it says) involves its form (how it says it);

(2) one place in the writing explains and illuminates other places;

(3) its thought progresses self-reflexively; its beginning, middle, and concluding thoughts mutually enhance, entwine, and entertain; with the consequence that

(4) it involves the reader in an open-ended quest for more implications, sometimes mutually reinforcing, sometimes mutually contrasting.

Thus, to be poetic is to be open-ended, unfinished, ever ready for future involvement, devolvement, development. These various involvements render the reader one with the poetic writing, involving the poetic writing with the reader. This is self-ing involvement, self-involvement, creating a new self; it is "poetic."

Rhythm (metre) and versification (parallelism, alliteration, and the like) are literary devices for structural involvement. Writing in verse is called "poetry," which may or may not be poetic writing; verse is neither needed nor enough to make a writing poetic. Some verses are not poetic; some poetic writings are not in verse.

Many say that the *Chuang Tzu* is poetic;[37] few look into its meaning. The *Chuang Tzu* is poetic in that its thoughts cluster in a web—one thought points to another which explains it, then the pair point to another, and the movement goes on—and back. Clusters of thought co-mirror, co-imply into layer after layer of meaning. A spiral of thought loops in loops, twisting back to itself only to start over again in a new direction, from a fresh perspective. "Loop" sounds linear.[38] It is rather a co-deepening co-resonance; to enter its pulsing rhythm is to enjoy life.[39]

In such co-echoing, thoughts themselves have poetic cadence which renders them intelligible. Usually stories are told, for story is coherent in its layers of recursive meaning. Besides, stories are freely cut into bits, mixed into a montage, co-implicating, co-explicating. All this describes "poetic writing," with or without the traditional literary patterns of poetry.

2. *Can* such writing be called "poetic"? Well, what is the so-called "poetry" like? Besides (*a*) co-responding rhythm, it (*b*)conforms to the established rule of versification—metre, rhyme, and cadence. And Chinese poetry (*c*) opens out to the Beyond, "the Landscape beyond landscape" with "radiant transparency," "touching many things with few words."[40] Thus poetry is poeticity, *a* and *c*; *b* reinforces them.

Every expression has its rhythm; "[a]ll literatures are, in their infancy, metrical, ... based on ... regularly recurring rhythm."[41] Later, our literary style was codified into "rules of versification"; they fixed, standardized, and stranded our expressive rhythm.[42]

Now Owen Barfield must say that "prosaic" and "poetic" are irrelevant to literature. "On the roof/ Of an itinerant vehicle I sat / With vulgar men about me ..." is *verse*, and *prosaic.* " Behold now this vast city, a city of refuge ..." is *prose*, and *poetic*.[43] Chuang Tzu writes in poetic prose.

3. All this agrees with the "poetic" in China. *Shih* has two meanings. In a narrow sense, *shih* is poetry rigidly rhymed and metred, as distinguished from non-metred writing (*wen*). In a wide sense, *shih* is literature that expresses intention (*chih*)—that is, inner thoughts and feelings that chant, as distinguished from the descriptive report of external affairs (*shu*). Poeticity is used here in the latter, wide sense,[44] which has its own inevitable natural cadence, rhyme and metre, as the wind of our feeling brings up patterns of ripples in the waters of literary expression. But the wind has little to do with human convention; such natural ripples may or may not conform to the traditional canon of metre.[45]

Such *shih* in the wide sense naturally came to include the best of literature, even the description of facts, external or internal. If the Grand Historian Ssu-ma Ch'ien wrote poetic descriptive literature of the external fact, then the grand man Chuang Tzu wrote poetic literature of the internal fact.

4. The *Chuang Tzu* is poetic; its thoughts resonate. It is like a historical novel; it describes life imaginatively. It is like an incomplete historical novel of a poetic sort; it imaginatively reconstructs (poetry) human actuality (historical novel). A historical novel such as the *Shui Hu Chuan*[46] imaginatively reconstructs a likely story out of spotty historical information. Since the evidence is spotty, imagination is required; since it is historical, imagination cannot fly wild.

The "actuality" that Chuang Tzu describes, however, is an imagined one. He does not describe what has happened but what had *better* happen, had better be lived. The reader must himself reconstruct it as he lives it. Again, the *Chuang Tzu* is thus incomplete. To adapt Lin Yün-ming, the *Chuang Tzu* is the "dragonfly" which "dots" the reader's "waters" of life and imagination, "touching without touching them."[47] The poetic resonance in the reader evokes him into becoming the historical novelist of his own life.[48] Chuang Tzu would have smiled at Oscar Wilde's saying,

> To give an accurate description of what has never occurred is not merely the proper occupation of the historian, but the inalienable privilege of any man of parts and culture.[49]

Chuang Tzu's writing embodies rhythm in his self-expression of ideal actuality, manifesting its inner affinity with our life rhythm; yet it is too "bombastic" and "goblet-like" to become codified. His writing is poetic, not poetry in a narrow canonical sense, bits of which it also includes. Owen Barfield's words recur:

> ... [T]he earliest verse-rhythms were 'given' by Nature in the same way as the earliest 'meaning.' ... Nature herself is perpetually rhythmic. ... We can only understand the origin of metre by going back to the ages when men were conscious, not merely in their heads, but in the beating of their hearts and the pulsing of their blood—when thinking was not merely of Nature, but was Nature herself.[50]

Chuang Tzu echoed those primal ages of life expressiveness where meaning, rhythm, and being alive were one, as will be envisaged in our Epilogue. No wonder Chuang Tzu has so influenced Chinese poetry that we cannot understand Chinese poetry without him.

5. But what about metre? *Chinese* poetry is for Wen I-to something worth remembering, recording, and cherishing.[51] Here words are used in such a way as to "arouse aesthetic imagination," that is, "felt change of con- sciousness,"[52] the "way" of wedding rhythm and music to sense. One such wedding is by metre, the rhythmic recurrence of words and notions. The usual metric rules are only one variant among many such rhythmic patterns.

Prose describes meaning; poetry sings it. The poetic meaning happens when the reader co-resonates rhythmically; the strict convention of metre is such spontaneous co-resonance in the folk songs and folklore adopted and codified by recognized poets and institutional ritualists.

We cannot, then, judge non-metric poetic sentences as "not poetic." Chuang Tzu's sentences, whose sentiment pervades almost all subsequent

Chinese poetic diction, cannot be branded "not poetic" just because they do not conform to the rules of versification. Not to see poeticity in Chuang Tzu's writing because of its overall lack of metre makes as much sense as not to see rationality in Socrates's speech because of its overall lack of syllogistic jargon.

    6. In short, the entire *Chuang Tzu* is poetic,[53] not because its wording conforms to the canons of poetic style, but because its thought has poetic thrust; and the poetic thrust is part and parcel of his thought. We cannot understand Chuang Tzu until we appreciate his thought arranging itself poetically. His thought is a "poetic philosophy." It has two characteristics: it is poetic and it is a philosophy.

    To begin with, Chuang Tzu's poetic thought is a delight; it is both frivolously profound and wholesome. First, frivolity is here united to profundity; "[h]e is frivolous when he is profound and profound when he is frivolous" (Lin Yutang.[54] Second, not infrequently Chuang Tzu laughs at shallow worldliness—its assumptions, ideals, desires, and fears. Both these elements combine to jolt us into laughing at ourselves without bad aftertaste, cleansing us into a fresh start. Chuang Tzu's poetic philosophy is a wholesome delight.

    Moreover, Chuang Tzu's writing gives us a philosophy. It is as comprehensive as Lucretius's *On Nature*, for instance, which is in verse and has been compared to Chuang Tzu. They are both similar and different. They are similar in that they treat concrete matters philosophically and deliver their thinking poetically. They help us gain enlightenment without resorting to conventional religion.

    They are different on two counts. First, Lucretius's wording conforms to the current standard of poetry, while Chuang Tzu's does not. Yet Chuang Tzu's poeticity is so much a part of his philosophy that missing his poeticity amounts to missing his thought. In contrast, our comprehension of Lucretius does not require attending to his poetic style. Russel M. Geer's excellent translation of Lucretius is in prose.[55]

    Secondly, while Lucretius tends to detailed argumentation, Chuang Tzu argues, or rather mock-argues, to lead us somewhere. His argumentation is playfully poetic, and his "somewhere" is hilarity that is affirmative, wholesome, and contagious. Lucretius has the world of silent atoms with rational-indifference (*ataraxia*); Chuang Tzu's world is a lively interchange among concrete integrities of things (*wu hua*).

    7. In other words, Chuang Tzu's thought is a peculiar unity of poetizing, parodying, and philosophizing. His thinking is a poetizing because it has

cadence and swing. Although perhaps lacking in traditional metre, his thinking follows the "cadence, metre, and rhyme" of life, that is, that living inevitability which is free, rhythmic, and co-creative with us who are, in turn,
changed subtly by such life vicissitudes.

Chuang Tzu used traditional categories without being bound by them. That
is, he parodied the then-current philosophies; his writing is an "ode beside and
under" (*para-oide*) traditional philosophies, miming them so as to point at life.
In his hands, notions and phrases hover and romp in actualities.

All this sounds academic until we see what is actually involved. In life
things do not always go as expected. We expect poverty to deprive; it usually
does. But poverty also civilizes, and that on a historical world-wide scale; it
almost single-handedly, as it were, produced the ancient vibrant Oriental
civilizations. Chinese philosophy does have a Yin-Yang theory to describe this
real oxymoron, "civilizing poverty"; the Yin-Yang interdependence in their
mutual denial somehow differs from the antagonistic Hegelian dialectic. Yet
even the Yin-Yang theory is more of a description than an explanation of the
coherence of mutual denials. Chuang Tzu's way is to see this truth of actuality
as "poetic," that is, poetically coherent, the one involving the other as its self-
reflecting content. To express such poetic coherence is to mime the one so as
to point at the other—to parody it, using the one to express the other.

This amounts to saying that Chuang Tzu engaged in a sort of philosophizing. We have two ways of philosophizing—we can watch for systematic
logical consistency; we can also discern the shifting implications of actuality
and express them intelligently. Chuang Tzu philosophized in the latter way,
letting the former way take care of itself. He lets the systematic character of
our thinking grow into an atmosphere in which our discernment breathes its
life. It is a spontaneous philosophizing of the concrete, a subtle weaving of
philosophical montage under (*sub-tilis*) life's bewildering implications.

Thus for Chuang Tzu poetizing, parodying, and philosophizing become
practically synonymous. His poetico-philosophical parodies unite the self, its
discernings, and its living, by letting them be themselves—as Chapter Two
eloquently shows. That is why his writing is elusive as the fish, the bird, the
mole, and the rabbit, alerting us to become alive with them.

8. We see then a need for grouping Chuang Tzu's text in its poetic
atmosphere, a need for arranging his writing in free verse without disturbing
its original word-order (even reading from top down, from right to left).[56] This
poetic arrangement illuminates obscure passages, reveals how Chuang Tzu's
notions cohere into clusters of thought, how the clusters relate one to another,

how such relations compose a fascinating rhythm of progression. The poetic arrangement brings home to us the risible rigor that stomps and echoes. If the arrangement will not solve all textual and philosophical puzzlements, it will give us a convincing frame in which to solve many of them. The delight is that both the textual and philosophical problems can be solved in the same frame.

To repeat: The poetic arrangement of the first three chapters of the *Chuang Tzu* text does not imply that Chuang Tzu wrote standard poetry; his sentences are on the whole not in traditional verse form.[57] Instead, such an arrangement aims at bringing out poetic reverberations among Chuang Tzu's thought clusters and their spiral progression.

An almost literal translation is attempted, trying to convey to the English reader the poetic vigor of the original. If the reader feels difficulty in reading it, he must be reminded that, even discounting my clumsy rendering, he would have to wade (with his fellow Chinese reader) through poetic turgidity in the archaic original too, in order to savor its vigorous resonance that nourishes.

9. My original plan was to put pronunciation and translation along with *each* Chinese character, as in the intriguing arrangement in the translation of passages from the *Mencius* toward the end of I. A. Richards's *Mencius on the Mind*. But the plan proved to be unwieldy.

I have tried instead to use (*a*) the same number of English words in the same positions in sentences as in the Chinese original, and (*b*) the same English words for the same Chinese characters throughout.

I have failed, of course, on several occasions in both of my own restrictions, notably in *b*. I used the same "with" for *i* (instrumental "with") and *yü* (together "with"). I used different English words for the same Chinese characters—"of," "in," and "to" for *yü*; "fief" (verb) and "border" (noun, adjective) for *feng*; "what" and "why" for *ho*; "fall in with" and "middle" for *chung*. Just by looking at the English "no" or "not" the reader cannot tell whether it is for *pu* or for *wu*. Although *i* has two meanings, of emphasis ("rather") and duplication ("also"), Chapter One leans on "rather" ("also" occurs only on lines 13, 53, 103), while Chapter Two leans on "also" ("rather" occurs only on lines 9, 56, 71—*i* did not occur in Chapter Three. And the like.

But on the whole I believe I have kept the promise to be consistent about my own restrictions. In this way, I have tried to convey the vigor of Chuang Tzu's original sentences and the allusive power of an identical character in different contexts.

My translation is no more "precise" than others; "precise translation" is an impossible and dangerous notion. This translation is simply another trial at understanding the Chinese *Chuang Tzu* in English, to be read alongside others.

Chinese (especially Chuang Tzu's Chinese) is so different from our contemporary English that in its English translation obscurities and ambiguities are bound to occur. They are explained in the ensuing Glosses and Meditations, to which the translation serves as the reference point (as well as the start of our journey into Chuang Tzu and into ourselves).

10.   Five specifics on the Translation and the Glosses remain to be mentioned:

(*a*) Attempts at literal and consistent translation may have resulted in barbarism, which it is to be hoped, however, will enable the reader to feel the rhymed vigorous flow of Chuang Tzu's thought and words.

Such vigorous beauty puts to rest many guesses on how one cluster of stories and thinking is connected to another, especially in Chapter One; brings out Chuang Tzu more coherently, simply, rhythmically, meaningfully, and convincingly than any translation in any language; and exposes puns, cross references of key terms, and thereby the coherence of Chapter Three without resorting to the mutilation hypothesis. Explanatory glosses at the end of the translation of each chapter indicate many such gains in our understanding and appreciation of the *Chuang Tzu*.

(*b*) Word-for-word translation is in **boldface**, while additional English words required for understanding the text are in lightface. When the morphological distinction made in English indicates a change of meaning that is customary in Chinese, then I do not make the boldface-lightface distinction in translation. For instance, to take from Chapter One, "**bluish**"(line 12), "**piling**" (line 14), and "**governed**" (line 78) are totally boldfaced, although equivalents of the morphemes "-ish," "-ing," and "-ed" do not formally exist in Chinese. But when the morphological distinction made in English indicates a change of meaning that is uncommon in Chinese, then I do make the distinction between boldface and lightface within words. For instance, to take from Chapter One again, "**record**ing" (line 6), "**hair**y" (line 36), "**govern**ing" (line 78), and "**actual**ized" (line 122) are partly boldface and partly lightface, indicating a notable semantic change in Chinese. In this area, however, personal taste obviously comes in, and there would be room for dispute. I choose to err boldly in details, if need be, in order to call attention to the distinction.

Usually a Chinese character is rendered into an English word, but when a Chinese character requires several English words, they are hyphenated: *yu* is "there-exists," *wu* is "there-exists-no(thing)," *lei* is "is-of-a-kind," and so on. When several Chinese characters coalesce to form a notion, hyphens are put inside parentheses between the translated English words or within a word; *fei chih* becomes "no(-)pointer," *pu yen* becomes "un(-)said," and so on.

(*c*) Five characters of negation may be mentioned—*wu^a*, *wu^b*, *pu*, *fei*, and *wei*. The following comments are mainly based on my internal glance at Chuang Tzu's usage and on Ting Fu-pao's "*Encyclopedic Commentaries on Shuo Wen Chieh Tzu* " (*Ku Lin* for short).

Although both *wu*'s are pronounced the same, meaning almost the same, and the latter *wu^b* is preferred by contemporary Chinese, Chuang Tzu prefers the former. The former ancient *wu^a* means "empty," "hidden-invisible," as if behind a curtain warding off arrows of our vision, or as if a fugitive eluding the world's eyes. It is connected in meaning and in shape with "origin." I translate it as "there-exists-no" or its synonyms.

The latter, contemporary *wu^b* is cognate with *wu^c*, "weed-filled wilderness," "neglected wasteland," "decayed or humanly useless vegetation." K'ang Yin says that *wu^b* is a pictogram of the shaman magically restraining wild animals for hunting purposes—possibly by dancing (*wu^d*) with his hand on the ox's tail. *Wu^b* perhaps means "denial" (*wang, wu^e*) in general. It occurs only six times[58] in the original text of both Chapter One and Chapter Two; it does not occur in Chapter Three. I translate it as "no" or "not." With such understanding we can savor the differences between Lines 12 and 88, and Lines 83 and 125, in Chapter One.[59]

Pu,[60] "not," an active denial, is originally our inability to reach the bird in the sky; *fei*, "not-that," a logical denial of what is said, is originally the bird's two wings in opposite direction. *Wei*, "yet-to," occurs only three times each in Chapter One and Three, but quite often in Chapter Two. It implies the budding originative power of being (as in *wei yu*, "yet to-be," *wei shih*, "yet to-begin.")

(*d*) I have adopted the long-accustomed Wade-Giles system of romanization, still widely used, and in which portions of Chinese text in many books in English have been published. A Conversion Table for the Wade-Giles and the new Pinyin systems appears at the end of the book.

I make one personal departure from the Wade-Giles system. Instead of *p'eng* as given in Wade-Giles, I use *p'ung*, both because it rhymes with *k'un* and because it is closer to the Chinese pronunciation. The same applies to *fung* (not *feng*). I do not insist on my idiosyncrasy all the way however.

(*e*) A Chinese term often hovers among several English meanings, one of which must be chosen in translation; any translation is thus "dogmatic" and "inaccurate." Explanatory glosses, keyed to the words and phrases to which they refer, caution the reader to tread lightly in various places and give the original allusions, cross references, implicit rhymings, untranslatable particles, alternative readings, historical backdrops, traditional debates over the correct meaning, and the like.

Translated words and phrases frequently occur in English alone in the Meditations, unaccompanied by the Chinese, and are for the most part put inside quotation marks. These quote marks not only indicate that there is a Chinese source for such words and phrases; they also signal that by consulting the Index, the reader will be able to find most of these words with their characters, along with references to their most significant occurrences throughout the book. Chinese words are given in the Index in the alphabetical order of their transliteration, so that when the transliterated form is known it will also be easy to find the ideogram.

Each of the central chapters of this book has two parts. First we have the Chinese text, followed by an almost literal Translation with its explanatory glosses; then come Meditations that attempt to evoke coherent understanding of the *Chuang Tzu*. This format, initiated in Chapter One, is repeated two times, for Chapters Two and Three. Thus, the following pages trace the poetic contours of the *Chuang Tzu*, so that you, the reader, may continue your "butterfly-flutterings" in meaning, in irony, in play—in life.

Chapter One

HSIAO
YAO
YU

逍
遥
遊

Soaring
—And Roaming

THE KUO HSIANG TEXT

The text of the first three chapters of the *Chuang Tzu* reproduced in this book is that of the earliest extant version of the this classic work, from the hand of Kuo Hsiang (died A.D. 312). Kuo's manuscript was copied during the Sung dynasty (960–1279) and printed in the 1922–23 edition of *Ssü Ku-i Ts'ang-shu,* compiled by Sun Yü-hsiu. I have arranged the text in verse lines, while leaving the word order intact. The individual characters are, of course, as Kuo Hsiang wrote them.

The original text is presented here following the printing conventions of the Chinese tradition. This means that the front and the back of each page are exactly the reverse of what they are in the Western tradition: one reads from the top down and from right to left and turns to the next page by going to the other side of the page on the left. Thus, the first printed page of the Chinese text following the part-title pages of Chapters One, Two, and Three is not the beginning of the text for that chapter but the end. The Kuo Hsiang text for each chapter begins on the left-hand page opposite the beginning of the Translation for that chapter and continues toward the front of the book.

For further remarks on the text and its translation, see the Preface, note 56 to the Prologue, and the note at the beginning of the Translation of Chapter One.

南華眞經卷第一　郭象　子玄　註　陸　德明　音義

今夫犛牛
其大若垂天之雲
此能爲大矣而不能執鼠

160

今子有大樹患其無用
何不樹之於無何有之鄉廣莫之野
彷徨乎無爲其側
逍遙乎寢臥其下
不夭斤斧物無害者
無所可用安所困苦哉

165

今子有五石之瓠

何不慮以為大樽而浮乎江湖

而憂其瓠落無所容

則夫子猶有蓬之心也夫

VII

惠子謂莊子曰

吾有大樹人謂之樗

其大本擁腫而不中繩墨

其小枝卷曲而不中規矩

立之塗匠者不顧

145

今子之言

大而無用眾所同去也

150

莊子曰

子獨不見狸狌乎

卑身而伏以候敖者

東西跳梁不避高下

中於機辟死於罔罟

155

120

惠子謂莊子曰
魏王貽我大瓠之種
我樹之成而實五石
以盛水漿其堅不能自舉也

125

剖之以爲瓢則瓠落無所容
非不呺然大也 吾爲其無用而掊之

130

莊子曰夫子固拙於用大矣
宋人有善爲不龜手之藥者
世世以洴澼絖爲事
客聞之請買其方百金
聚族而謀曰
我世世爲洴澼絖不過數金
今一朝而鬻技百金
請與之

135

客得之以說吳王
越有難吳王使之將
冬與越人水戰
大敗越人裂地而封之

140

能不龜手一也
或以封或不免於洴澼絖
則所用之異也

110　　　　105

之人也之德也
將旁礴萬物以為一
世蘄乎亂孰弊弊焉以天下為事

之人也
物莫之傷
大浸稽天而不溺
大旱金石流土山焦而不熱
是其塵垢秕穅
將猶陶鑄堯舜者也
孰肯以物為事

115

VI

宋人資章甫而適諸越
越人斷髮文身無所用之

堯治天下之民平海內之政
往見四子藐姑射之山
汾水之陽窅然喪其天下焉

85

肩吾問於連叔曰
吾聞言於接輿
大而無當往而不反
吾驚怖其言猶河漢而無極也
大有逕庭不近人情焉

90

連叔曰其言謂何哉
曰藐姑射之山有神人居焉
肌膚若冰雪淖約若處子
不食五穀吸風飲露
乘雲氣御飛龍
而遊乎四海之外
其神凝

95

使物不疵癘而年穀熟
吾以是狂而不信也

100

連叔曰然
瞽者無以與乎文章之觀
聾者無以與乎鍾鼓之聲
豈唯形骸有聾盲哉
夫知亦有之
是其言也猶時女也

若夫乘天地之正
而御六氣之辯
以遊無窮者
彼且惡乎待哉

故曰至人無己
神人無功
聖人無名

堯讓天下於許由曰
日月出矣而爝火不息
其於光也不亦難乎
時雨降矣而猶浸灌
其於澤也不亦勞乎
夫子立而天下治而我猶尸之
吾自視缺然請致天下

許由曰
子治天下天下既已治也
而我猶代子吾將為名乎
名者實之賓也吾將為實乎
鷦鷯巢於深林不過一枝
偃鼠飲河不過滿腹
歸休乎君子無所用天下為
庖人雖不治庖尸祝不越樽俎而代之矣

故夫知效一官行比一鄉

德合一君而徵一國者

其自視也亦若此矣

而宋榮子猶然笑之

且舉世而譽之而不加勸

舉世而非之而不加沮

定乎內外之分辯乎榮辱之竟

斯已矣

彼其於世未數數然也

雖然猶有未樹也

夫列子御風而行泠然善也

旬有五日而後反彼於致福者未數數然也

此雖免乎行猶有所待者也

III

湯之問棘也是已

窮髮之北有冥海者天池也有魚焉

其廣數千里未有知其脩者

其名為鯤

有鳥焉其名為鵬

背若泰山翼若垂天之雲

摶扶搖羊角而上者九萬里

絕雲氣負青天然後圖南

且適南冥也

斥鴳笑之曰

彼且奚適也

我騰躍而上不過數仞而下

翱翔蓬蒿之間此亦飛之至也

而彼且奚適也

此小大之辯也

適莽蒼者三湌而反腹猶果然

適百里者宿舂糧

適千里者三月聚糧

之二蟲又何知

小知不及大知小年不及大年

奚以知其然也

朝菌不知晦朔蟪蛄不知春秋

此小年也

楚之南有冥靈者以五百歲爲春五百歲爲秋

上古有大椿者以八千歲爲春八千歲爲秋

而彭祖乃今以久特聞眾人匹之

不亦悲乎

野馬也塵埃也生物之以息相吹也

天之蒼蒼其正色邪其遠而無所至極邪

其視下也亦若是則已矣

且夫水之積也不厚則負大舟也無力

覆杯水於坳堂之上則芥為之舟置杯焉則膠水淺而舟大也

風之積也不厚則其負大翼也無力

故九萬里則風斯在下矣

而後乃今培風背負青天而莫之夭閼者

而後乃今將圖南

II

蜩與學鳩笑之曰

我決起而飛搶榆枋時則不至而控於地而已矣

奚以之九萬里而南為

南華眞經卷第一

北冥有魚其名爲鯤鯤之大不知其幾千里也
化而爲鳥其名爲鵬鵬之背不知其幾千里也
怒而飛其翼若垂天之雲
是鳥也海運則將徙於南冥
南冥者天池也
齊諧者志怪者也
諧之言曰
鵬之徙於南冥也
水擊三千里摶扶搖而上者九萬里
去以六月息者也

TRANSLATION WITH GLOSSES

I. The Big

1   In the **Northern Darkness there-exists** a **fish; its name** is
     called K'un the roe. The size of **K'un** being so **huge,**
     we do **not know its** measure, **how-many thousand li** it is.*
     It **changes and makes** himself into a **bird; its name** is
     called P'ung the roc. **P'ung's back** being so huge,
     we do **not know its** measure, **how many thousand li** it is.*
     It **rages-up and flies** off; **its wings** are **like clouds**
     of the size huge enough to **hang over the heavens.**
     This bird—once the **sea moves, then** it will **set-off** for
     the **Southern Darkness.**
5   **That-which** is **Southern Darkness**—it **is the Heavenly Pond.***

     That-which is *Tall-Tales of Universal-Harmony**—it **is**
     that which is (known for) **recording marvels;**
     The **words of** *Tales* **say,**
     "The **set-off of P'ung for** the **Southern Darkness is**
     The **waters** having been **roiled*** **three thousand li** high,
     the **one-which beats** the **whirlwind and**
     rises **up ninety thousand li,**
10   The **one-which leaves** (for the South)
     with the sixth month blowings.*

     Does it see (from up there) **heat-hazes?*** **Bits** of **dust?**
     Living things mutually blowing-about? Especially
     The **bluish blue of heaven**—is **it** its **correct color?** Or is
     it due to **its distance and there-being-no** way **to arrive-at**
     its **limits?**

---

*Starred items are treated, by line numbers, in Glosses following the Translation. The
Chinese text of each chapter of the *Chuang Tzu,* arranged in verse style, precedes my
own contributions to the chapter: Translation, Glosses, Meditations. This translation
is designed to match that text line for line and, in the words that appear in **boldface**
type, as much as possible word for word. Words and parts of words in lightface type
are required either to complete the meaning or to make the translation grammatical in
English. See the Prologue, Meditation D.10.

Its looking down is also like this only."*
Besides, mind-you,* if water's piling is not deep enough,
    then for its bearing a big boat, no power.
15   Overturn a cup of water up-on a hollow in the hall,
    then bits of trash will make* boats.
    Place the cup on-it, then it will stick;
    the water is too shallow and the boat too huge.
When* the piling of the wind is not deep,
    then for its bearing of huge wings, no power.

And so only* with ninety thousand li can the wind,
    then, stay down under.
And only after-that can it now* mount on the wind-back,
    shoulder the blue heaven, and
    things never hinder, block it.
And only after-that will it now head-for the south.*

II. The Small

20   The cicada with the little-dove* laugh at this, saying
"We leap, rise,* and fly, dashing between elm and
    sapanwood; then sometimes we do not arrive
    there and fall* to the ground only.*
What's-all-this fuss about ninety thousand li up
    and going south?*

He-who goes to the nearby woods takes three meals and
    come-back; his stomach is still so full.
He who goes a hundred li spends the night-before
    grinding the grain;*
25   He who goes a thousand li spends three months
    gathering food-supplies. As for
Them,* those two "worms"*—again,* what should they know?*

Small understanding does not reach huge understanding;
    small years of life does not reach huge years of life.
How do we understand its being so?

The morning mushroom does not understand twilight or dawn;
    the summer cicada does not understand
    spring or autumn.

30   Such are the **small years.**
      In **south of Ch'u there-exists** a creature called **"ming ling"**;*
              with **five hundred years-of life** it **makes** one **spring,**
              with **five hundred years-of life** it **makes** one **autumn.**
      Once **up**on an **old** time, **there-existed that-which** (was called)
              a **huge Ch'un**-tree;
              with **eight thousand years-of-life** it **made** one **spring,**
              with **eight thousand years-of-life** it **made** one **autumn.**

      And yet **Forefather P'ung*** is **now** for longevity **specially**
              widely **heard; multitudes** of **men** try to **match him.***
      Is it **not rather pitiful!**

III. The Big and the Small

35   Even **T'ang's questioning of Chi was** about **this only**:
              ("Do up, down, and the four directions have a
              limit?" Chi replied, "Beyond their limitlessness
              there exists another limitlessness.)*
      To the **north of** territories so barren as to **end**
              our search for small **hairy** grass there,
              there-exists that-which is a **dark sea**; it **is**
              the Heavenly Pond. **There-exists a fish in-it.**
      Its width stretches **several thousand li; yet**
              there-exists not **one-who understands its length.**
      Its name is K'un.

      There-exists a bird in-it; its name is P'ung.
40   With a **back like Mount T'ai, wings like clouds of**
              the size huge enough to **hang** over the **heavens,**
      It is **that-which beats** the **whirlwind**
              in a **ram's horn** spiral **and** rises **up ninety thousand li.**
      He flies **over the cloud breath** energies,*
              shoulders the **blue heaven;**
              after thus, he **heads-for** the **south,**
      Journeying, besides, to the **Southern Darkness.**

      The **marsh sparrow laughs at it, saying,**
45   **Besides, where** is **that** bird **going?***
      I bounce and spring up, not going-beyond several yards,
              and dropping **down,**

Flapping, flopping among weeds, brambles—such is rather
>the ultimate anyone can arrive-at of flying [that is,
>down to the ground]!
And, besides, where is that bird going?"*
Such is the distinction between the huge and the small.

IV. The Commen Men and the True Men

50   And-so, he-whose understanding effectively-fills
>one office, whose walking benefits* one village,
Whose virtue matches one ruler and qualifies to
>serve one state—
His look-at himself is also like such
>little creatures' self-estimation.

And Mrs. Sung Jung so grinning laughs at him;
Besides, all the generation praises him,
>and would not add more diligence;*
55   All the generation says that he is-not good,
>and would not add disillusionment.
Settling in the divisions of inside-outside, distinguishing
>the boundaries of honor, disgrace—
He lives thus only.*
That man, with his attitude toward this generation,
>is yet to be found so fidgety, fidgety.*
Although thus, still there-exists something
>yet to be planted firm.

60   Now, Lieh Tzu drives the wind and walks—
>he is so airy; he is good.
Fifteen days—and afterwards he returns.
>That man among those-who convey happiness,
>is yet to be found so fidgety, fidgety.
In such act, though relieved of walking, still there-exists
>that-on-which to depend.

Now, if there be someone like him-who, by charioting-on
>the correct nature of heaven, earth
And, driving distinctions-changes* of
>the Six heavenly Breath Energies,

65 With such energies **roams** where **there-exists-no end—**
    How besides, would **that** man have to **depend-on** anything?

    And-so they **say:** "In the **ultimate**ly-arrived **man**
            there-is no (need for) **self**-asserting
    In the **spirit**-filled **man**
            there-is-no (need for) **merit**-striving;
    In the **holy**-hearkening **man**
            there-is-no (need for) **name**-labeling."

V

70 **Yao, ceding** things **under-heaven to Hsü Yu,* says,**
    "The **sun, moon have come-out, and** the **torch fire** is
            not blown off;
    Its act **toward light, is** it **not rather trouble** in vain?
    Timely **rains have-come-down, and flooding irrigation still**
            continues;
    Its act **toward marsh**lands, **is** it **not rather labor** in vain?
75 Now, **you-sir, stand** at the throne **and** things under heaven
            are **well-governed, and I still** vainly **officiate** it.
    I look-at myself as **so lacking** in qualification,
            and **request-to convey** things **under heaven** to you."

    Hsü Yu said,
    "**You, sir,** are **governing** things **under heaven.**
            Now that things **under heaven** are **already governed;**
    And I am to **still replace you; will I make** a mere **name?**
80 **That-which** is **name—it is a guest of actuality;**
            will I make a mere **guest?**
    The **tailorbird nests in deep woods,** yet does **not go-beyond**
            one-branch;
    The **mole drinks-at rivers,** yet does **not go-beyond**
            filling a **belly.**
    Go-home, rest,* Ruler; for **me there-exists-no**thing
            for **which** to **make use** of things **under heaven.***
    After all, **although** the **kitchen man**
            does **not govern** the **kitchen,**
            the **ceremony-official** does **not step-over**
                wine-casket and **sacrificial-stand** and **replace him.**"

85   Chien Wu put a **question to Lien Shu, saying,**
      "**I heard words from Chieh Yu;*****
      They are **big and there-exists-no**thing **proper,***
          going-on and not returning .
      For **me his words** are **frightening,**
          as-if the **Milky Way and there-exists-no limits.**
      There-exists in-them huge extravagance,*
          not near human reality."

90   **Lien Shu said, "What** did **his words call?"**
      He **said, '"The Mount of Miao Ku Sheh, there-was** a
          spirit-filled man residing in-it;
      With **skin like icy snow, gentle-shy* like** a **young girl;**
      Not eating five grains, sucking winds, drinking dews;
      Charioting cloud breath energies,* **driving flying dragons;**
95   **And roaming* out of** the **Four Seas;**
      His spirit,* concentrated,*
      Lets things not be **plagued, and yearly grains ripen.'**
      I took these words to be **insanities and do not believe** them."

      Lien Shu said, "So it is!
100   '**In the blind man there-exists-no**thing **with** which to share in
          the **spectacle of emblems, ornaments;**
      In the **deaf man there-exists-no**thing **with** which to share in
          the musical **sounds of drums, bells.'**
      How-could there-exists blindness, deafness,
          solely in **figure and skeleton?**

      In-fact, it exists also in understanding.
      These words are they which **are as-if you** at this **time.***

105   **This man, this virtue-power,**
      Will widely pervade* myriads of **things,** which **with** this power
          he **makes into one.**
      Although the **generations long for peace,**
          who (among such men) would **fretting, fretting-ly**
          make business with things **under heaven?**

      This man*—
      None of anything **harms him.**

110 Huge flood stretches to heaven and does not drown him;
Huge drought—metal, stones melt, soil, hills scorch; and
it does not sear him.
This man is the one whose very dust, siftings*
Will still smelt, mold Yao, Shun. Among such men,
Who would consent to make business with things?"

VI

115 Sung men were selling ceremonial hats,
and they went to Yueh.
Yueh men cut-short their hair, tatooed their bodies;
they have no use to make of them.
Yao governed-well people under heaven; pacified political
businesses of all territories within the seas.
He went-on to see the Four Masters
in the Mount of Yao Ku Sheh.
Returning, on the sunny* bank of the Fen Waters he,
so dazed, lost on-it his businesses under heaven.

120 Hui Tzu called Chuang Tzu, saying,
"The king of Wei gave me seeds of huge gourd.
I planted them, and they actualized a filler of five bushels.
With it I filled water and soup; it
was so heavy, I-alone was not able-to lift.
I split it to make a ladle;
then it was unwieldy as a gourd,
no where-to accommodate*.
125 Not that it is not so horrendously huge,
but I called* it 'no use' and smashed it* to pieces.
(Isn't your theory like the gourd?)"*

Chuang Tzu said, "Now, you-sir, are certainly clumsy at
using something huge.
Among Sung men there-existed one-who was good at making
salve against hand chapping.
Generation after generation, with silk bleaching
they made business.
A traveller-lobbyist heard it,
and requested to buy its secret formula
for a hundred pieces of gold.

130 He **gathered** a **band** of his clan **and consulted, saying,**
'We, **generation** after **generation,**
    have been **making** the business of **silk bleaching,**
    not going-beyond several pieces of **gold.**
Now, in **one morning,** and we **sell** the **skill**
    for a **hundred** pieces of **gold.**
I **request** that we share it **with him.'**

The **traveller got it—with** it he **lobbied the king of Wu.**
135 **There-was trouble** with Yueh. The **king** of **Wu let him**
    serve as **general.**
That **winter, with Yueh men** they had a **naval battle.**
He inflicted a **huge defeat** on **Yueh men.** The conquered
    territory was **split and fiefed to him.**

Now being **able not** to **chap hand is one** and the same.
If **some** was **fiefed with it,** while **some** others were
    not relieved of silk bleaching,
140 **Then** this **is** due to the **difference of what use**
    people put to things.

Now there-is for **you-sir** a **gourd of five bushels** capacity.
Why not be **anxious** about **making with it**
    put a huge tub and floating-around in rivers, lakes?*
And you, instead,**worry-about its**
    being so **'unwieldy as a gourd, no where-to accommodate.'**
Then obviously **there-exists, still, in-you-sir,** a **mind** full
    of underbrush!"

VII

145 **Hui Tzu called Chuang Tzu, saying,**
"There-exists with me a **huge plant; men call it Shu.***
Its huge trunk* is **knobbly, bumpy, and does not fall-in-with**
    measuring **inked line;**
Its small branches are **curled, crooked, and does not fall-in-with**
    compass, square.
Stand it on the **road**side, and a **carpenter** would **not**
    look-around at it.

150   Now these **words of yours-sir, are**
      Huge and there-exists-no use, what the multitudes
          leave alone in the **same** way."

      Chuang Tzu said,
      "Have **you-sir alone not seen wild-cats, weasels?**
      They **crouch** their **bodies and hide;**
          with this pose they **wait** for **those-who stray.**
155   **East, west, they jump, race, not avoiding high, low,**
      And fall **in the middle of spring traps, dying in nets.**
      Now, in contrast, the **yak ox—**
      Its size **huge like clouds of** the size,
          huge enough to **hang** over the **heavens;***
      Such a one is, indeed, **able-to be-called huge,**
          and not-able even to **catch mice.**

160   Now, for **you-sir, there-exists** a **huge plant**; you are
          distressed that **there-is-no use** for **it.**
      Why not plant it in the '**village of there-exists-no**thing,
          not even with **what** reason that **there-exists** anything at all,'
          the '**field of vast none**';
      Rambling-ly, there-exists-no making beside it,
      Roaming-ly, you lie asleep beneath it.
      You would **not die-young** by **axes;**
          among **things there-does-not-exist that-which harms** you.
165   You say,'**There-exists-no use to-which** it **can** be put';
          then **how-could-there-be what** makes you **suffer hardships?**"

Glosses

Title: "'Mid pleasures and palaces though we may roam,/ Be it ever so humble, there's no place like home," say those famous lines of J. H. Payne. Chuang Tzu would smile and reply: Yes, but for the ultimate man his pleasures and palaces *are* his homes, and any humble place *is* pleasure and palace.

"Like us, the Libyan wind delights to roam at large," says Arnold. Chuang Tzu would smile and say: It is what this and the next chapters say.

"Let the winged Fantasy roam," says Keats. Chuang Tzu smiles, we can see, and replies: My P'ung Bird *is* just that.

"Type of the wise who soar, but never roam," says Wordsworth. Ah, Chuang Tzu would say, again with smiles: But the wise do both, as this chapter shows.

And so, the chapter is titled "Soaring and Roaming," to fit **Hsiao Yao Yu** of the original title.

On Lines 1–19: *To begin with, at the risk of repeating what is said in the Meditations, especially in B.1, the following glosses outline briefly the unity of lines 1–19. Then we will go into details.*

Line 1:

Pei ming, ("northern darkness"): *North* symbolizes the northern and Yin pole of the universe. This is where the *ch'i* ("breath energies") of things originate and change into Yang.

Darkness reminds us of that *hsuan ming* (6/45, 17/78) where things originate. This is the yet-to-begin-to-exist (Ch. Two, lines 131, 155, etc.), "the Tao of not-Tao" (Ch. Two, line 186).

In view of such implication, "northern darkness" is perhaps not originally *explicitly* meant to be "ocean." I therefore take line 5 (and perhaps lines 35–39, the entire section III) as gloss, as A. C. Graham has it (*Chuang-tzŭ*, pp. 43–44).

I wonder why Graham still translates *ming* as "ocean" throughout.

Interestingly, in Genesis 1:2 "darkness," the "abyss," and the "waters" describe the primordial state of the universe. The Bible has the Supernatural Power that tears apart darkness from light, which came from the Light out of his Fiat—what violence! Chuang Tzu in contrast sees things naturally moving from Yin-darkness to Yang-darkness.

Yu ("there is"): To have something softly, spontaneously, equivalent to a noncommittal "there exists."

Yü ("fish"): This is the Yin power (natural and ordinary) to beget and begin. This is the Tao that *can* be tao-ed, the second thought in Lao Tzu's beginning line of the *Tao Te Ching*.

In China, fish is strong, rich, joyous, reproductive, and awesomely supernatural (since few animals can live in water), yet everywhere in water, so common (Williams, *Outlines of Chinese Symbolism*, pp. 183–86). Chinese sentiment toward fish shares something in common with world mythologies about fish.

The Hindus saw the first Avatar of Vishnu as Pisces-Aquarius, half-fish, half-man, and viewed Christ as Piscean Avatar. The Talmud called the Messiah *Dag*, the fish. The Phoenician and Philistian *Dagon*, the Chaldean *Dannes*, and the Greek *Phoibos* were all fish men. Jesus, like Jonah, is a fish man, symbol of the Life Principle within the primordial ocean (Matthew 12:40). The fisherman's Ring is worn by the pope.

K'un: This fish has two characteristics. First, it has a name K'un, at once the smallest ("fish roe"; Chu Kui-yao has a long section on it) and the greatest (as described in the next sentence, perhaps parodying on *K'un*, "elder brother").

The power to begin is always unobtrusive. The mustard seed is one small dot, yet grows into the greatest of shrubs. This small-great power to begin (*shih*) is enfolded (*yu*) in the Northern Darkness (yet-to-begin-to-be, *wei shih yu*).

Line 2:

Hua ("change"): Besides, this natural beginning is an initiation of change (*hua*), first changing itself (into a bird), then changing its location (flying and migrating, *fei* and *hsi*—almost rhyming), to the Southern Darkness. To begin is to change; this is creation.

Niao ("bird"): At once its name is given, P'ung (rhyming with K'un), meaning a bird (*niao*, alone) with friends (*p'ung*). It is alone but not lonely, the Yang-correlate of the Yin-fish. (On what it means to be lonely, see Meditations to Ch. Two, C.2.2.3.)

Lines 3, 4: And then we have movement after movement ("rages-up," "flies," "sets off")—very noticeable, in contrast to the invisible mysterious existence of K'un in water.

Lines 4, 8, 10: Yet, mind you, these movements are never violent and destructive, but always wrapped within nature—"when the sea moves (*yün*)," "going on the sixth-month gale (blowings, breathings [*hsi*], of nature)." The Bird's movement (*hsi*, "setting off") always goes with Nature's movement (*hsi*, "blowing"). Even the Bird's angry arising (*nu*) has to do with the oceanic movement (*yün*)—*nu* is reverse pronunciation of *yün* (Akatzuka).

Thus the magnificent descriptions of the Fish and the Bird—stressing the big and the far—are yet about something natural, spontaneous, non-miraculous. The extraordinary is the ordinary. It is the glories of living Nature that are extolled here. Chuang Tzu would have chimed in with Carlyle who mumbled, "natural supernaturalism."

Thus is Chuang Tzu's "creation story" that differs from usual supernaturalism, such as the great Unusual Power (creator God) struggling to kill monstrous Darkness, or issuing a piercing Fiat from which came the Light to pierce and separate the world in two—night and day. Instead of such a violent dichotomy, Chuang Tzu has a story of natural movement *of* the dark nature itself, mysteriously moving from darkness to darkness, from north to south, year to year, awe-inspiring, yet a perfectly normal natural movement.

Line 6:

Ch'i Hsieh ("Tall Tales of Universal Harmony"): Nature is for Chuang Tzu a *ch'i hsieh*, letting us record wonders everywhere, a universal harmony of marvels. This is the *Tiao Kuei* ("Ultimate Ruse," Ch. Two, line 262) of nature that harmonizes all things (*ch'i wu*, cf. Ch. Two, lines 116–17). Perhaps (the book of) Ch'i Hsieh is the Ch'i Wu Lun, of Tiao Kuei. Chapter Two of the *Chuang Tzu* is just a brief summary of it.

Line 10:

Liu yueh hsi ("six-month blowings"): This is the *ch'i* of nature that changes every six months. *Hsi* is "breathing" (Akatzuka Tadashi) or "rest" (Kuo Hsiang)—a restful rhythm of breathing of nature. And it can mean the six-month gale, a seasonal wind (Hsuan Ying), perhaps the "earthly piping" in Ch. Two, lines 11, 12 29.

Line 11:

Yeh ma ("heat hazes"): Such natural breathing is the same breathing as that by *yeh ma* ("wild horse" or "waving heat-hazes") and by *ch'en ai* ("dust storms" or "turbid *ch'i* of life").

All these movements—the Bird rising up and flying, beating the whirlwind and rising ninety thousand li, setting off on the sixth-month gale, things blowing at each other—all these *express* the "heavenly piping" in Ch. Two, lines 12, 31.

Lines 12–19: In this atmosphere of the heaven, everything below is as blue and marvelous as everything (the sky) above. Nature is at once *natura naturans* and *natura naturata*, nature nascent and nature nurtured.

Now, we can go into detailed comments on the whole chapter.

Line 1:

Yeh ("is"): This character serves as the ending of a sentence, a copula, an emphasis, or a rhyming device (with emphasis). *Yeh* on line 11 must be a question-particle; see gloss there.

K'un: As both Chu Kuei-yao and Burton Watson noted, many commentators thought that Chuang Tzu started with K'un that means the tiniest fish imaginable and the biggest fish imaginable—the "roe" and the "whale."

Chu (pp. 2–4) strongly argued that *K'un* means both "roe" and "whale" in common parlance (though on different occasions); therefore there is nothing peculiar in using *K'un* here to mean "roe" or even both "roe" and "whale."

I do not see how this argument disproves Chuang Tzu's peculiar humorous use of *K'un*, meaning *both* "roe" and "whale" at the same time; no common parlance allows that. Much less does the argument prove that Chuang Tzu did *not* use *K'un* for his special purpose beginning the entire book with something that is yet to begin, to let something begin to be many big and small creatures imaginable (cf. Ch. Two, lines 155–59).

In fact Chu gives us not a rebuttal but a backdrop, if not a back-up, for this interpretation. For by giving us the common usage of *k'un,* Chu gives us the background against which Chuang Tzu launched out his creative imagination, the material out of which Chuang Tzu molded an expression of his creativity. (On the general principles of the creative use of [textual] tradition, see the Prologue, B. 1 and 2.)

But if *K'un* can mean both "roe" and "whale," can *ming* mean "darkness," "ocean", and "misty (drizzle?)" all at once? (Cf. *hsuan ming* ["mysterious darkness"], *ming hai* ["dark ocean"], *ming mung* ["dark mist"].)

For another hermeneutical probe critically benefiting from textual-literary scholarship, see preceding Prologue C.

Line 2:

Wei ("make") means, says Wang Shu-min (1:21) (on line 15), *wei* ("call," "mean," as in Ch. Two, line 161). So, I suspect, does the word on lines 1 and 2. Cf. line 125.

P'ung could mean *fung*, "wind" (Kuo Mo-jo). This interpretation makes the Bird correspond with the various pipings (and the belching of the Great Clod) in Ch. Two, lines 11–15, etc.

Furthermore, K'un and P'ung may symbolize the spirits of the heaven and earth, as in *Shih Ching* ("Classic of Poetry"; Akatzuka). See my Meditation, A.2.

Line 4:

Yeh (marker at the end of sentence): Emphasis (Ma Chien-chung, p. 339). Cf. line 128.

Line 5:

Che means "he who," "that which," "one which," "what is called," and may also have a rhyming function throughout.

Line 6:

Ch'i hsieh: "Tall Tales of Ch'i," "Universal Harmony," or "All Jokes," supposedly the title of a book. Or else "Mr. Ch'i Hsieh," the recorder of marvels and wonders. There may be an implicit and humorous reference to the "tall tales" of universal harmonies of all things in Chapter Two, titled *Ch'i Wu Lun.* If so, Mr. Ch'i Hsieh may well be Chuang Tzu himself, and the book called *Ch'i Hsieh* would be the *Chuang Tzu.* Chuang Tzu quotes from himself as an authoritative source of what he says.

Line 8:

Chih ("of"): "When" (Wang Li, *The Ancient Chinese*, p. 459); cf. Ch. Three, line 13.

Line 9:

T'uan ("beat"): "Circling up as whirlwind" or "gathering up the whirlwind" (Kuo Ch'ing-fan). Ch'en Ku-ying has *po*, "to capture" or "to hit, beat." All these are graphic and dramatic expressions.

Fu yao ("whirlwind"): This is a gradual pronunciation (*huan yen*) of *piao* or *p'iao* (both meaning "whirlwind"; Akatzuka). Cf. lines 41, 91.

Line 10:

Liu yueh hsi ("six-month blowing"): *Hsi* can mean: (1) "breath," and the sentence reads, "is gone six months before it takes a breath" (Graham); (2) "the breath of nature, the wind," and the sentence reads, "is gone with the six-month gale" (Watson); or (3) "rest," and the sentence reads, "it goes for six months before it takes its rest" (Kuo Hsiang, Ch'eng Hsüan-ying). I side with (2), which is consistent with line 11.

Che yeh ("that which is") begins and ends this "paragraph."

Line 11:

Yeh (marker for sentence ending), Wang Shu-min (1:3-4) says, means *che* ("that which"), but here, I suspect, it is a rhymer meaning *yeh*, a rhetorical question particle expressing excitement, together with line 12. Wang Yin-chih (pp. 99–100) cites 27/20–21 (Watson, p. 306) for the latter use of *yeh*.

Yeh ma: "Wild horses" can here mean "dust flying" or "heat hazes" (Chu Kuei-yao, p.7).

These three noun phrases may be repetitions of the same thing—heat-hazed dusts flying (as wild horses do), as if blowing breaths about. The repetition indicates P'ung's excitement from above at seeing things so small down below.

Or else, the three noun phrases may each indicate a distinct thing, expressing P'ung's wonder at whether what it sees is wild horses or dust flying or things blowing at each other. This also expresses P'ung's excitement.

Line 13:

Tse i i ("this only"): Graham takes this phrase as "then ceases (rises no higher)," claiming that Chuang Tzu never used it in the sense of "only" (*erh i i*); he cites 19/59 and 23/66 as evidence (Graham, *Chuang-tzŭ: Textual Notes to a Partial Translation*, p. 42).

But Ch'en Ku-ying cites Wang Yin-chih and Ch'en Pi-hsü to insist that the phrase does mean "only" (*erh i i*). Line 13 then describes how similar P'ung viewing of the below from up there is to our viewing of the far (line 11) and the sky (line 12) from down here (Kuo Ch'ing-fan). "And that is all."

Lines 13, 14, 16:

Yeh ("is") Although Ma Chien-chung (pp. 336, 338) plausibly says it means "when," I stick to "is," as a copula, which is closer to the original meaning.

Line 14:

Ch'ieh fu ("besides," "mind you") means, says Ma Chien-chung (p. 281), *ch'ieh* ("besides") with emphasis (*fu*). *Ch'ieh* means "besides" throughout in this chapter, but it is mostly just a particle of emphasis in Chapter Two. (See gloss to line 78, Ch. Two.)

Line 15:

Wei ("make") means "make ... as" (Wang Li, *Ancient* p. 378).

Chih ("it") either refers to "trash," or is a mere emphasis (Wang Yin-chih p. 201), as in line 22. Cf. Ch. Three, line 27 and gloss there.

Yeh ("is"): Although Wang Li (*Ancient*, p. 246) says it means "for" (judgment of reason), I stick to "is," as a copula.

Line 17:

Ssu: "And then" (emphasis, Akatzuka, 1:29), "only ... then."

Tse ssu: "Then" (Dobson, *A Dictionary of the Chinese Particles*, p. 691).

Line 18:

Erh-hou nai-chin: "Afterwards only now," same as *nai-chin erh-hou*, that is, "from now on" (Ch'en Ku-ying). In any case, the phrase is emphatic, "and then, and only then, can ..." See Graham, *Textual Notes,* p. 43.

Line 19:

T'u nan ("head for [the] south"): "Plans for [the] south, " that is, sets eyes to the south" (Watson) or "sets its course for the South" (Graham).

Line 20:

T'iao ("Cicada") symbolizes regeneration, happiness, and prudence (Williams, *Outlines of Chinese Symbolism*, pp.70–71).

Hsüeh chiu ("little doves," literally "learned birds") know what is to come. See Meditation A.3. They happily think they know everything and ceaselessly chatter, as they flutter about, about P'ung.

Line 21:

Chueh ch'i ("leap," "rise") means "sudden swift rise," corresponding to Pung's magnificent *nu erh fei* ("raging up and flying"; line 3). It took five long lines to describe P'ung's flight up (lines 3, 4, 7, 8, 9); it takes a mere short line for small creatures to flutter about (line 21). P'ung was silent; small ones chatter as they flutteringly cast a know-it-all glance at the P'ung. These contrasts show this portion to be the start of a new section.

K'ung is "hit" (Ts'ui Chuan) or "throw" (Ssu-ma Piao).

Erh i i ("only") rhymes with *tse i i* ("only") on line 13.

Line 22:

Hsi i ... wei ? ("what's all this ... about"): *Hsi* is *ho* (what?). I ... *wei* is used as a rhetorical question, implying a negation of what is said. Akatzuka cited *ho i ... wei* ("What does he need [refinement] for?" *Analects* 12/8). Cf. Wang Yin-chih on *wei,* p. 62. Also see line 83 for a similar rhetorical use of *wei.*

Line 24: Or "take ground rice enough for an overnight's stay" (Lin Yutang, *The Wisdom of China and India*, p. 630).

Line 26:

Chih ("they") means "these" (*tz'u*) or "those" (*pi*), according to Wang Li (*Ancient*, pp. 317, 359, 379).

Ch'ung ("worms") describes little creatures.

Yu ("again") is an emphatic negation—"How would they know?" Cf. Dobson. *A Dictionary of the Chinese Particles*, pp. 954–57.

Line 31:

Ming ling: Watson has "caterpillar"; Graham, Lin Yutang, and Y. P. Mei follow Kuo Ch'ing-fan and Chu Kuei-yao, taking it to be a tree, "ming-ling tree"; Ch'en Ku-ying took it to be "divine turtle." For Y. P. Mei's translation, see Wm. Theodore de Bary, Wing-tsit Chan, Burton Watson (eds.), *Sources of Chinese Tradition*, p. 66.

Line 33:

P'ung tsu ("forefather P'ung"): A remote rhyming with P'ung, perhaps.

P'i ("match") is *pi* ("parallel," "comparison," "example")—"Whenever people talk about long life they compare it to P'ung Tsu as an example" (Wang Li, *Ancient*, p. 379).

Line 35: This line is difficult. I followed the consensus among the commentators in putting this line at the beginning of a new section. This arrangement requires an addition from *Pei Shan Lu*, as Kuan Fang, (p. 76), Ch'en Ku-ying, and Watson admit. But "whether this passage was in the original *Chuang Tzu*, or whether, if it was, it belongs at this point in the text, are questions that cannot be answered" (Watson, p. 31). The convenience of putting this line here at the start of a new section is that the seeming repetition here will be packed into Chi's answer.

An alternative possibility is to see this line as a conclusion of the previous section. The advantage of this arrangement is fourfold: (1) It seems to be a good conclusion on the discussion of the small and the big—*t'ang* symbolizes *ta* ("huge," "big"); *chi* rhymes with *chi* ("extreme," "ultimate"), implying *chi ta* ("extremely big"); (2) *yeh shih i* ("is this only") corresponds with *tse i i* ("then only") on line 13, making it a good conclusion; (3) the futility of scholarly discussion correlates with both the chitchatting small creatures and line 33, *pu i pei hu*("[is it] not rather sad!"), the phrase that ends many sections and chapters in the *Chuang Tzu*; (4) unless we add the conversation (as Ch'en Ku-ying did, as it is here), the word *wen* (question) does not make sense in the next section.

Prudence (to follow generations of commentators) dictates putting this line at the start of a new section, and insert a legendary conversation.

Line 42:

Ch'i ("breath energies") means, as in line 64, the "breaths" of clouds, that is, the energies and vapor of clouds. Lyall Watson has written a book titled, *Heaven's Breath: A Natural History of the Wind.*

Line 45:

Ch'ieh ("besides"): Here, as in lines 45, 48, 54, 66, etc., it is emphatic. Cf. gloss to line 14.

Line 47:

Ao hsiang ("flapping, flopping"): The phrase reminds us of *hsiao yao* ("roam"; see part of the chapter title and line 163). Also see 23/43—*hsü hsing hsiang-pan erh kuei* ("with leisurely steps and a free and easy manner, he returned home"; Watson, p. 215).

I ("rather") is emphatic; cf. lines 13, 33, 52, 72, 74, 103. Cf. Prologue D. 9.

Lines 48: Here ends Ch'en Ku-ying's quotation-range which begins on line 35.

Line 50:

Pi ("benefit") is *pi* ("protect"; Wu Ju-lun, Graham), or "equivalent" (Kuo Ch'ing-fan), "fit for" (Ch'en Ku-ying), "capable of uniting all the villagers" (Kuan Feng), "impress" (Fukunaga, Watson).

Ho ("match"): Or "fulfills the demands of an emperor and wins his confidence" (Kuan Feng, Ch'en Ku-ying, Akatzuka, etc.)

Line 52:

Yeh ("is") is, says Ma Chien-chung (p. 338), a particle which rounds up what has gone before, and connects it to the next clause beginning with *erh* (which is emphatic on line 53).

Line 57: Cf. *tse i i* ("only"; line 13), *yeh shih i* ("is this only"; line 35). Kuan Feng interprets it as "That is why he can be like this."

Line 58:

Ch'i ("his") introduces a phrase (Ma Chien-chung, p. 58–59), and also (perhaps) refers to his manner of behavior. Kuan Feng has "In the world, such a man is rare" (p. 76, Note 10).

Line 59:

Shu ("planted"): Literally means "to plant solidly," and rhymes with *shuo* on lines 58, 61. Cf. line 161.

Line 64:

Pien ("distinctions-changes"): Both Kuo Ch'ing-fan and Ch'en Ku-ying take it as "change" (*pien*). Huang Chin-hung says that *cheng* ("regularities," "correctness") contrasts with *pien* ("changes"; *Chuang Tzu chi Ch'i Wen-hsueh*, p. 52). See also Ch. Two, line 219 and my gloss there.

Although Wang Shu-min also decides on "changes," he has a section (pp. 10–11) identifying *pien* as *pien* ("discrimination"). If Wang is correct, it means that Chuang Tzu implies here that the correct (ex)changes-and-debates are based on "real discriminations" of Six Live-Energies (*ch'i* means "breath," "vapor," "energy," cf. gloss to line 42) of the universe. Kuo Ch'ing-fan has a long explanation (1:20–21) of what these Six Live-Energies are.

Line 70:

Hsü Yu: (1) Does this phrase pronounce "*hsü*" ("hill," "empty")? (2) Or else, can the phrase mean "allow therefrom," that is, "that from which permission comes," "what makes freedom possible," "the root of freedom," or even "true freedom"?

(3) A third possibility is proposed by several people. Yang K'uan forcefully argued that Hsü Yu is identical with both Kao Yao and Po I, the first Lawgiver(s), all of which are different names of the mountain-god(s). Yao is another mountain-god connected with it (them), the connection with whom is the basis of a good government (*Ku Shih Pien*, 7:1:345–52, 398–400, and 7:3:376–77). Agreeing with Yang, Ku Hsieh-kang added that Yao is a sun-god (*ibid.*, 7.3.85). Ch'en T'ing, Sung Hsiang-fung, and Chang T'ai-yen in their various books and essays agree with speculation of this sort.

If their consensus is to be accepted, then Hsü Yu is thoroughly imbued with nature—nature less personified (as if *we* knew better) than nature personal, in which (whom?) we live and have our beings.

Line 76:

Ch'üeh jan ("so lacking"): Literally, "defect-ly."

Line 83:

Kui hsiu hu ("go home," "rest"): "No more" (Chu Kuei-yao), "Let such your words of ceding rest" (Kuo Ch'ing-fan), "Go home and forget it" (Watson), "Go back to where you belong" (Graham), "Let the rulership go back to you" (Akatzuka).

Yü wu so yung t'ien-hsia wei ("for me there exists no use of things under heaven"): "I am useless to the world" or else "I have no use for the (rulership of the) world." For the rhetorical use of *wei,* see gloss to line 22.

Line 85: These names may be various names of mountainous places (mountain-gods?). See Note 83 to Meditations.

Line 87:

Wu tang ("there exists nothing proper"): "Without grounds," or "no limit" (Akatzuka), "not appropriate" (Ssu-ma Piao).

Line 89:

Ching t'ing ("extravagance"): "Too much"—see a detailed explanation in Chu Keui-Yao, pp. 19–20.

Line 92:

Ch'o yüeh ("gentle-shy") is gradual pronunciation (*huan yen*) of *jo* ("weak," "tender"); it perhaps matches the "skin" (Akatzuka). Cf. *fu-yao* is also a gradual pronunciation of *piao* or *p'iao* ("whirlwind") on lines 9, 41.

Line 94:

Yün-ch'i ("cloud-breath energies"): As in lines 42 and 64, this phrase signifies the vaporous live energies of the heavens.

Line 95:

Hu: Rhyming word, emphatic, as in lines 100, 101, 107.

Line 96:

Shen ("spirit"): As in lines 68 and 91. Graham has "the daemonic" to match the "daemonic man." On *shen*, see my Meditations to Ch. Three, B.4.5.1.

Ning ("concentrated"): See Meditation C.1.2.a on the relation between invulnerability and concentration of spirits.

Line 103:

Fu ("in fact"): Emphatic.

Line 104: The line is difficult. It can mean "As your words just now have shown" (Kuo Ch'ing-fan, Watson) or "When he spoke these words he was like a maiden ready for a suitor" (Ssu-ma Piao, Graham). Also cf. Ch. Two, lines 118, 134.

Line 106:

P'ang po ("widely pervade") may be a gradual pronunciation (*huan yen*) of *p'u* ("pervade") or *po* ("wide-spread") (Akatzuka). Ssu-ma Piao has *hun-t'ung* ("mixing together"), which Graham adopted. Watson has "embrace." Sung

Ching-ju and Chang Jung (in their commentary on *Tung Lai Po-i*, p. 111) have "to be filled up."

Line 108:

Yeh is an emphasis (Ma Chien-chung, p. 339); cf. line 4.

Line 112:

Shih ("this") perhaps means *chih* ("only"); emphatic, says Wang Yin-chih.

Line 113:

Chiang ("will") perhaps means *ch'i* ("he"); emphatic (Wang Yin-chih).

Line 119:

Yang ("sunny"): It is the southern foot of a mountain (Fung Yulan) or the northern bank of a river (Graham, Watson; see Akatzuka 1:53). Akatzuka and Watson add, "[and when he got home] north of the Fen River" (Watson, p. 34).

Line 123:

Chien ("heavy"): Or "Its [low] solidity is such that by itself it cannot be lifted up, when filled up inside" (Ch'eng Hsüan-ying), "not solid enough to stay upright" (Graham).

Line 124: This is adapted from Watson; I prefer it because of its vagueness. Other interpretations are: "too shallow to hold anything" (Kuo Ch'ing-fan, Fung Yulan), "sagged and spilled over" (Graham, taking *hu lo* literally), "too huge to hold anything" (Chien Wen-ti, Wang Shu-min, Akatzuka). The last interpretation takes *hu lo* to be synonymous with *hu lo* or *k'o lo*, or takes *hu lo* to be gradual pronunciation of *kuang*. All of these re-interpretations mean "huge".

Line 125:

Wei ("make", "call") is *wei* ("called") (Kuo Ch'ing-fan, Akatzuka); cf. line 1.

P'ou ("split") rhymes with *p'ou* ("smash to pieces").

Yeh is probably *che* ("it," "that-which"; Wang Yin-chih, p. 87).

Line 142:

Lü ("anxious"): Or "to wrap around with cords" (Kuo Ch'ing-fan, Ch'an Shou-ch'ang); or "to hollow out" (Ma Hsü-lun, Hung I-hsuan). Where and how they got these exotic meanings is beyond me.

Chiang hu ("rivers," "lakes"): Originally an abbreviation of three rivers and five lakes, the phrase later came to mean "the world," or "civilian" (private) as opposed to being employed by government.

Line 144:

Fu is emphatic and rhymes with *hu* ("lake") on line 142.

Line 146:

Shu ("tree") rhymes with *shu* ("name of tree"; line 146).

Line 147:

Ta pen ("huge trunk") is "trunk" (Huang Chin-hung), "big root" (Kuo Ch'ing-fan).

Line 149:

Ku (look around") rhymes with *shu*, *shu* (as stated on line 146), *mo* ("inked"; line 147), *ch'ü* ("crooked"; line 148), *chü* ("square"; line 148), *t'u* ("road"; line 149).

Line 156:

   Pi ("trap") appears both alone (*pi*, "to avoid or hesitate"; line 155) and as part of a compound phrase (*chi pi*, "*trap*," line 156).

   Wang ku ("net") rhymes with *fu* ("hide"; line 154).

Line 158: The same phrase about the huge clouds appeared in lines 3 and 40, where it described the tremendous activities of P'ung the roc flying far. Here the phrase describes the rock-like self-possessedness of the yak. Is the chapter itself meant to be as great (in these two senses)?

Lines 159, 160, 161:

   Shu ("rats") may rhyme with *shu* ("trees"; lines 59, 146). Cf. lines 36, 37.

Line 163: Line 162 and 163 are almost poetic ones. Fung has "By its side you may wander in nonaction, / Under it you may sleep in happiness," which well captures the poetic thrust.

Line 165: This is another pair (or two pairs) of poetic lines, which Graham renders thus: "Spared by the axe/ No thing will harm it. / If you're no use at all, / Who'll come to bother you?"

MEDITATIONS—THREE READINGS

A. The Stories

1. A story connects events in life in an open coherent manner; they come together in a story to make sense to us. "While you live," Jean-Paul Sartre told us, "days add on to days without ryhme or reason....But when you tell [a story] about life...the pomp...of a beginning" comes about, followed by a sequence, and then by the end. Moments are "caught up by the end of the story which draws them on."[1]

Science is a "story" in the language of a logico-mathematical system, as inductively and deductively tight as we can make it to apply to events. Unlike science, myths and stories are loose and open, for all their coherence. Story is a yarn that we we spin out of our strands of meaning and continually add to.[2]

Such open coherence is inevitable when we want the precise and comprehensive understanding of things. For the more precise our explanation becomes the more aware we become that we have only one among many possible perspectives from which to explain things. As we strive for comprehensiveness by incorporating more and more perspectives in our total vision, our systems becomes vaguer and more general, that is, looser and more open. And then such loose coherence itself can serve as a metaphor that leads us from one familiar region of meanings to a novel one. As the horizon of loose coherence expands, the yarned implications of each perspective grow richer. Myths and stories are an inevitable result of our attempts at precise *and* comprehensive understanding of the world.

We can either believe in stories and myths for their own sake, or live in them as we live in language, using them to express the web of things. Chuang Tzu *used* bits of myths, legends, and stories, freely quoting and misquoting from them, to reflect the "heaven's net" (Lao Tzu)[3] that is vast and loose yet losing nothing. Such free use of myths and legends is to show a continuation with the tradition and culture in which Chuang Tzu was brought up, on the one hand, and to make a creative use of cultural tradition to strike out in a new direction, on the other. Such a collage of bits of myths, legends, and stories formulates anecdotes that reflect a coherence in living, much like the notion of "honor" reverberates with allied cultural connotations in various human situations.

Such peculiar story-telling fascinates us, luring us into living out our life in the new significance evoked in our appreciation of Chuang Tzu. And we are made healthy. For story is our twilight talk that unites the night of the unconscious with the daylight of cognition. As we live in our stories we are made whole in the total coherence of our cognitive consciousness with unconscious psychic pulls.

Sartre warned us that we tell lies when we tell a story about life.[4] Things are not neat as in an epic story—a hero meeting problems of life, challenging various breakdowns of expectations to reach problem resolution. Our life is not like that, but merely piecemeal.

But there is a difference. Telling a lie lies to the listener, telling a story belies the story(-teller). Both tellings lie, but they differ—one deceives people intentionally, the other interprets the world inevitably, despite oneself; one knows the truth and hides it, the other seeks to spread it; one impoverishes life, the other gives life coherence.

In fact, telling a story enriches life, showing us how paradoxical the actual world is. The world is understood only coherently, by interpretations that differ. The world then accommodates different understandings—often mutually exclusive, as quantum mechanics and Zeno's paradox vividly illustrate. Any interpretation is partial to a specific standpoint, and is less than the entire world; interpretation is mis-interpretation, a lie despite itself. The truth of the world accommodates many lies is order to be understood.

This is enrichment of life, that truth requires lies. For many lies of this sort help minimize lying to the world. Stories are told with a wink, inviting the listener to interpret and enjoy, that is, to live in them for a while—as if tarrying in motels, one at a time, to savor different scenes and feels of the world. Stories enrich the listener in various (vicarious?) life experiences. The listener sheds dogmatism and grows open-minded, empathic, worldly.

Chuang Tzu's montage of story-bits tells least lies to life, being unorganized as life is, giving us not the meaning of life but tantalizing glimpses; they invite us to make sense out of our life with their suggestions. The looseness of his story-telling has its justification. The montage of story-bits intimates the moving coherence of the heavenly web that is loose but leaks nothing. Since the Great Tao does not declare itself as such, it is now declared as not-such.[5] Since the constant Tao cannot be tao-ed (identified and expressed clearly) as constant,[6] it is now tao-ed as not-constant. And the book of *Chuang Tzu* is born—irrelevant, inconstant, allusive.

Life coherence is as elusive as a living rabbit, and so a lively snare of story-telling is needed. As mentioned earlier,[7] Chuang Tzu's snare aptly resembles the animal—both need to be pursued. Chuang Tzu's sayings are so "out of line" with our usual understanding of the world that we cannot help but be provoked to ponder. And participatory pondering in bits of stories is itself a healthy exercise in living.[8]

So far, four images have been used to describe myths, stories, and legends: yarn, heaven's net, twilight talk, and montage. They point to a salient feature of life—concrete open coherence. "Yarn" is an intertwining of cultural meaning-fibres into an open coherence. "Heaven's net" intimates a montaged system in which things move, flexibly and meaningfully. "Twilight talk" points us to the unity of day talk of reason with night talk of our innermost imagination. And Chuang Tzu's writing is such a healthy cosmic montage of story-bits.

Such montaged story-argument-bits are justly called "goblet sayings."[9] A goblet tips to pour in things as they come, and tips to pour out things as they flow over. These tippings-in and tippings-out present what is inexpressible— the Way things and ourselves go. To illustrate these goblet stories and their bits we now turn to the first chapter of the *Chuang Tzu*, titled "Hsiao Yao Yu," hesitantly translated as "Soaring—and Roaming."

2. "The Northern Darkness has a fish; its name is K'un."[10] So begins the entire book of *Chuang Tzu*. In the ancient Chinese mind the world is the central region of China surrounded by a barbarous wilderness which opens out to the horizon of waters. The dark waters are the utmost limit of our world and our wildest imagination.

Chuang Tzu starts with the very ultimate of the distant horizon—to the north. "North" is a region of the Yin, that is, the shaded, the hidden, the pit (*k'an*, perhaps rhyming with *k'un*), the water, and the winter. It is where the breaths (*ch'i*) of weather and things rise and gradually shift to the Yang. It is the beginning of the Five Elementary Ways of things that change and inter-change in the yin-yang cycle.[11]

This ultimate North is pervaded with oceanic darkness. The "dark" (*mimg*) is also mysterious waters, deep, far, hidden, silent, and confused, as expressed in a later phrase *ming ming*, variously translated as "mystery, mystery," "darkly shrouded," the "darkest dark" that originates things.[12] This may well be the region of con-fusion, the Hun Tun that ends the Inner Chapters. In fact, this Northern Darkness may well be another expression of the mystery of the Hun Tun.[13]

This horizontal region is far from barren; there lives a big fish.[14] The region is impregnated with life that is invisible.

"Fish" in China is life that is extra-ordinary, for it lives where no one or-dinarily can. It is incarnation of freedom from restraints, power of regenera-tion, perseverence, strength to avert evil (almost martially), harmony, abun-dance and wealth, and literary eminence.[15]

This Fish is said to be so "big that no one knows how many thousand li it is." To talk about its hugeness this way amounts to engaging in an understand-ing that does not understand (one of the main themes in Chuang Tzu's thought).

This enormous Fish must possess all qualities imaginable to a superlative degree. Yet Chuang Tzu described the Fish with only one characteristic, its stupendous size, as if nothing else need be mentioned.[16] After all, nothing needs to be said about something as common as a fish. Thus the Fish sums up the common at one with the uncommon. "They move without leaving any trail behind, act without leaving any memory of their deeds."[17] These words of a later chapter in the *Chuang Tzu* describe the fish perfectly, though they were meant to refer to people in the Region of Perfect Virtue. Fish live in the realm of Perfect Virtue.

And then Chuang Tzu alluded to what it means to be truly big. He named the big Fish *K'un*, which is also "fish roe," the smallest of the fish.[18] The name of the Fish is "the Biggest-Smallest"—as if to tell us that the truly big is what is also small, or at least what includes the small.

Secondly, part of the character, *k'un*, also pronounced *k'un*, implies "elderly," "multitudes," "together," and so on. This Fish may be alone, but he is not lonely; he is impregnated with noble sociality or solidarity.

Finally, *k'un* reminds us of *hun*, con-fusion, abundance-together. The story may hint at the truth that in the far horizon of our world and our imagi-nation, to the far North, a hidden life of con-fusion is living in the realm of Primal Con-fusion, the Perfect Hun Tun, that passes all our understanding.[19]

And then—in due course? suddenly? (Chuang Tzu does not tell us)—the Fish is "changed" into a bird, and the story begins to move along. In ancient China the bird and the fish are interchangeable, for both share the ability to live in places where no other animals can survive—in the sky above, in the water below.

What does "change" mean for Chuang Tzu? The *Chuang Tzu* tells us that *change* is a ceaseless general characteristic of all things.[20] A thing's change involves both growth into itself[21] and death[22] into species-transformation.[23] Human activities of teaching and government should promote and partake of such cosmic transformation.[24] Death and life are two aspects in the rounds of species-changes among things. Many chapters in the *Chuang Tzu* end climactically with such cosmic changes.[25] We should participate fully in the ontological transmutation of things (*wu hua*), so much so that we forget ourselves-changing in it.[26]

No wonder the important verbs with which Chuang Tzu begins his book are to "have-exist" and to "change," no less than a species-change from an extraordinary creature in the sea to another extraordinary creature in the sky. Yet such spectacular change may be just a simple event of the bird eating up the fish,[27] a daily happening, part of the routine "soaring and roaming" with the trend of things.

Being alone, the Bird has the name *P'ung* which implies big and social—as can be seen by its synonym, *fung*, regal phoenix, and by part of the character, *p'ung*, also pronounced *p'ung*, "friend."

The Fish and the Bird are somehow related and even interchangeable; or so it seems to be suggested in the parallelism of description—"The *K'un's* size being so huge we don't know he measures how many thousand li" (line 1), "*P'ung's* back being so huge we don't know he measures how many thousand li" (line 2).

It is time we look at the situation as a whole. In the depths of the horizon far north, the Yin Pole, lives the Fish, the spirit of Yin life. The breaths arise to originate weather and animals, only to shift to the Yang, the south, incarnated in the Bird. The roaming Fish may have embodied the moving spirit of the earth, and the soaring Bird the spirit of the spacious sky, when the one is changed into the other dynamically.[28] This species-change is natural and agonal—for the Fish may have been eaten by the Bird.

Furthermore, if *K'un* is taken in the plural (of *ch'i;* Chapter Three, line 48), then *hua* can mean a change of identity, a (re)birth of *K'un* into *P'ung*. This is perfectly in line with *hua* meaning sometimes death, sometimes birth (re-production) (22/40). Thus the change (*hua*) is not just change in time and in individualities (birth eating fish) but also evolution in species—from the fish to the bird. It means also the change in realm, from the Yin of amorphous nondescriptive vastness to the Yang of scheming striving vastness; vastness remains vastness, but what a difference it makes! The nestled and nestling Yin is now turned into the restive Yang, treking toward the Yin-waters yonder, that new Darkness in the south, perhaps in the restful Marsh (Chapter Three, line 35). Such is the vast rationale of the common actuality behind the bold imagination, fresh, innocent, and surprising.

The natural impelling shift of things is further brought out by a "vigorous flying up" of P'ung heading for the Southern Darkness. The majestic trek, with his wings outstretched like clouds over the sky, is in fact changes. For the oceanic movement is a seasonal shift, part of the wheel-like turning of the universe, and the Bird merely responds to its call. And so P'ung's trek is part of the shift of cosmic breaths from the northern Yin of autumn and winter to the southern Yang of spring and summer. -

P'ung goes from the Yin-depths to the Yang-depths which are the natural ("heavenly") Lakes. Or else, since the Yin is the South bank of a river, perhaps the species-trek can be called that from one Yin-Yang unity (the Yin-fish in the Yang-waters) to another (the Yang-bird toward the Yin-waters). Thus the vast movement of the vast cosmos is captured by Chuang Tzu's imaginative writing that first roams in the depths of the ocean and then soars up to the heights of the sky.[29] It is "too big for word" and logic; it can be done poetic justice only by myths and stories, these "tall tales" (ch'i hsieh), to which we will come back. At present our eyes are still fixed on the Bird.

The Fish turned Bird turns his eyes to the South. The *South* is the bright sunny Yang, where all things are heading, where clear recognition resides. Yet it is *dark*; there the waters of deep mystery are shrouded in ignorance. The trek is also that of intellection, from ignorance to *its* understanding. Mr. Knowledge in Chapter Twenty-Two roams north to the Black (deep-mysterious) Waters, then wanders back south to the White (bright-sunny) Waters, and gains understanding. Yet he goes from waters to waters—mysteries pervade throughout. Such roaming lets Mr. Knowledge grow into the understanding of no-understanding, for the mystery of actuality unveils itself as mysterious.[30]

Things go from darkness to darkness, Chuang Tzu says. Can we pursue darkness? No, because darkness is a deep lack, and no one can pursue a lack. "Going to darkness" must mean not its pursuit but a happening to ourselves, as our own births from the wombs in which we were unawares. We can only prepare for such happening by being ourselves. At home in the region of nothing we can grow unhampered into ourselves and into the world; we can freely soar and roam there.

After the Fish in the unknown darkness is changed into the Bird, the Bird sets his eyes to the darkness *yonder* (in the sense described above, perhaps), the Lake of Heaven, the "reservoir of naturalness," in which he can be as he is, without struggle. After all Darkness is the space that allows and nestles, if we but take it as our comfort and our poetry. It is where we become privy to profound secrets of the world; and it is as personal a place as daylight is public. Darkness is forever fresh, the realm where we forever *first* trespass. We do well to cultivate our sense for darkness, our repose in the deep Lake, the Hun Tun, the we-know-not-what. We were conceived and born there; our life is nourished in it.

Sadly we do not know the night; we do not even like it. We despise its depths and mysteries. We do not feel our way in the night any more, but rob and probe it with flashlights of reason, senses, and tools,[31] and laugh at those night-fumblers. We are cicadas and small doves, having lost a perspective of the starry night. We do not let the luring silence of darkness envelop us, as the Fish and the Bird did. We see darkness only as a metaphor for the absence of life, and forget that fish live there. We lose ourselves in the luminous shallows of clarity. We laugh nervously; we critize endlessly. We *think* we know, and lose our refuge from the machinery of clarity. We think we can afford to lose the poetry of the fish,[32] now that we take darkness to be a mere nuisance.

We cannot fight for the magic of darkness, however. We can just "smile" at the laughters of cicadas and doves. We smile in silence and in the ambiguities of Northern Darkness. And then we "prepare" for "foods" for our long silent trek—alone—to the luminous depths of the Southern Darkness (what gibberish to the ears of "clear-headed" cicadas). We go with the seasonal wind, the invisible force of a nothing that pushes and supports. We call the journey a Soaring and a Roaming (*hsiao yao yu*).[33]

To accommodate the "scholarly requirement" for critical literary support of the above stories, Chuang Tzu then quotes from "*Ch'i Hsieh*"—which could be the name of a book or a person, or of a book from the state of Ch'i, or mean "total harmony," or "all jokes," tall tales.

We see a bitter irony here. Chuang Tzu follows the customs of scholarship; and in his following he exposes its preposterous character. For as the Wheelwright told his Duke Huan, the knack and the logic of actuality cannot be recorded in dead letters. Scholarship is mere chaff and dregs of the old. The knack of turning the wheel cannot be handed down in writing; we must learn it at each fresh moment when we concretely respond to the turning. The turning of the Wheel of the Cosmos is like the movement of the ocean that churns up the "sixth-month breath," the seasonal whirlwind, the "wheezing of the Huge Clod." Our understanding must soar up with it to roam into the clarity of the Southern Deep ignorance.[34]

The breath-taking height of the epic flight is expressed in a reversal of perspectives. How high the Bird flies is measured not by how high it looks to us down here but by how small *we* look from up there. The "high up" is measured by the perspective looking down. The Bird flies up by the breaths of nature; looking down, it sees heat-hazes and dust winds rising like many short-lived breaths of earthlings. Everything is pervaded with the blue sky, and blue horizon, and the blue below.

The big bird requires a big environment and big imagination, not "a cup of" water or of wind, a cupful of predictable commonsense. We must go beyond the clutter and chatter of daily ongoing to hear the fluttering of silent wings in the waves of wind, freely soaring up ninety thousand li beyond small creatures of the earth, to head for the horizon yonder, the Southern Darkness, the Yang Pole.

Mind you, however, the horizon and the pole are those of *this* world. Flying far and forward the Bird looks down. To soar over the world is not to fly away from it but to accept it from the perspective of the sky.[35] The "perspective of the sky" is to be had in the environment yonder, the realm of freedom, in which we can accept our world in a new spacious way. We now see the "sky" of the Bird. We will soon hear about longevity, how eight thousand years to a huge Ch'un Tree is a mere spring. The Bird and the Tree describe the big frame in space and time in which we arrange things of our world in a fresh manner. To fly beyond the earth with the wild Bird of our imagination is to receive our world back in the perspective of the big sky and the patience of long years of the Tree.

In Paul Tillich's impressionistic book, *The Courage To Be,* nonbeing is taken to be the threat of being, what prevents the self from affirming itself. Following nonbeing we will despair in death, meaninglessness, and guilt. We must counter it by the courage of self-affirmation in transcendence and in acceptance. The God who is transcendence, "the God above God," is the power of acceptance. We revolt against nonbeing by accepting such Power of acceptance, and we can accept everything in spite of the threat of nonbeing.[36]

Chuang Tzu would have smiled in silence to Tillich. For Chuang Tzu nonbeing is a vast sky in which we can receive everything in perspective. Soaring up there, we can now afford a disarming smile and roam in this world, in the perspective of the sky, the nonbeing.[37]

Laughter is first expressed among the small creatures of the earth (cicadas and doves) against the soaring irrelevance of the big Bird. The petty chitchatting laughter implies both its self-condemnation and a legitimate warning to the Bird.

On the one hand, in laughing at the big Bird, the small twittering creatures expose their neighborhood-boundedness, and thereby affirms the greatness of the P'ung Bird. On the other hand, their laughter points to a danger in P'ung's epic flight, for it can fly *away*, and die in the poverty of transcendence pure and simple.

To transcend all things is to accept them from the sky; soaring above things must enable us to roam among them. Such a dialectic of transcendence among the big Bird and the small ones, such strange truth of going-beyond as coming-back with spacious acceptance, is the topic of the rest of the chapter, culminating in the memorable dialogues on the true meaning of "usefulness" as the use of the useless.[38]

The common sense of small cicadas and doves chitchattingly rejects the wild flight, the vast ocean and sky, of the big Bird. "We have exhausted ourselves fluttering from one small twig to another. What's all this about going ninety thousand miles to the south?" Such is also a natural reaction of petty scholars.[39] "We have got enough immediate problems to worry about; why irresponsibly fly that far?"

In reply Chuang Tzu first appealed to contrasts in time—morning mushrooms can never understand the Ch'un Tree which counts eight thousand years as a mere spring, for instance. Then he ironically appealed to the Record of Legendary Conversation between the wise Emperor T'ang and a wise man Chi.

This is Chuang Tzu's second appeal to the record, a standard scholarly procedure of authenticating one's claim. Yet extravagance by definition "breaks the record," going beyond any approval of communal commonsense.

What is poignantly ironic in Chuang Tzu here (as before) is that he drives home to the reader the record-breaking perspective from the sky by mock-appealing to the authority of legendary conversation.

Such masterful irony is accomplished by two ploys. First, T'ang could mean "vast" and Chi could mean either "small" (as needle) or "ultimate" (homonym with *chi*, the cosmic pole).[40] Thus either Emperor T'ang asked Mr. Ultimate, or Mr. Vast asked Mr. Extremely Small, about the extremely small or big. The conversation itself is extraordinary.

And to make the matter poignantly hilarious (the second ploy), the reply repeats the previous story of the big Fish and the big Bird *plus* the laughters of small birds as they hop among the twigs![41] In any case, this serves to highlight the debate-on-the-difference (*pien* can be "debate" or "difference") between the big and the small.

Difference is more than that in size, however. Sung Jung Tzu is supposedly big enough to quietly laugh at the "small" officials who fulfill their duties dutifully, winning fame in their neighborhood, even throughout the empire. Yet not even Mr. Sung is "big enough." Chuang Tzu from now on builds up a crescendo of what truly "big" means. To see the crescendo we must look again at the whole sweep of the story.

3.   "The Northern Darkness has a fish ... [which] changes itself into a bird ..." This is a story about something (*yu*), not nothing. But the story is about something (fish, bird) in the deep-and-dark (*ming*), in the far-away and

fan-tastic (wind, sky, darkness), in the we-know-not-what. Of course the earthly and luminously logical cicadas and doves will laughingly chitchat about the story. Their "scholarly" day-talks pride themselves on moving ceaselessly[42] from one logical twig to another and back to the same twig—often even failing to reach back. They never go far but live only in the daylight of logicality, forever criticizing each other. For them fantasy is too dark, too big, and too far to comprehend, and so deserves to be laughed at.

And the *Chuang Tzu* collects fantasies. After describing the "big and far," then the "small and near," Chuang Tzu now builds his story from the small-near up to the big-far, and shows how surprisingly indispensable the big-far is for our living, in fact so close to life that it is what life truly is.

Chuang Tzu adds one higher ideal onto another. A conscientious official is admired all over the district and the empire. He is small, however, being trapped in the values of his community, and is justly laughed at by Sung Jung Tzu, a man above worldly fame. Yet Lieh Tzu is on a higher level than Sung; Lieh Tzu soars with the seasonal wind, perhaps with our big Bird (or is *he* the Bird?). But we have someone going farther yet; he freely rides the normalcies of the heaven and earth, a man of all seasons (six breaths).

This man roams boundlessly within the universe. He is beyond us, not because he is above us but because he is at home everywhere among us, unhampered even by his self-concern (he has no self), his evaluation (no merit), his fame (no name). He roams (*yu*) in darkness and among the twigs, in government offices and in the field, in the wind and in calm lakes. He tarries wherever he happens to be, and the place is no longer big or small, far or near—it just *is*. Nothing is either dark or in daylight, fantastic or trivial—it is just home. This is true transcendence, going beyond both the ordinary and the extraordinary.

The two short stories on politics that follow address such extraordinary (second story) ordinariness (first story). The first story tops and criticizes the very best of Chinese political ideals—a solicitous ceding of the throne to the sagely-wise. The sage rejects the offer, for the sage is the tailorbird that uses one branch as its home, living as it does among cicadas and doves, yet is as much aware of its vast surroundings as the big Bird. The sage is the mole that drinks only a bellyful in the river, yet is as much at home in the vast ocean as the big Fish. Who among us is not like a mole and a tailorbird? Yet how many of us are like the sage?

The "big" then is less a description of the merely big than of the élan of transcending the self, re-situating the self, moving. To be big is to be bigger than the "big" self here and now, changing the habitat (the ocean, the sky), changing the perspective (from below, from above), letting the "small" be small (smiling at the laughing chitchats of cicadas and doves, mole-drinking a bellyful from the river, tailorbird-nestling on a branch in the woods).

The second story (lines 90–98) says that the spirit of the sage is "concentrated," indivisible, and so he is as indestructibly healthy as a maiden. His healthy spirit miraculously renders his surroundings healthy, himself freely living in the fire and in the water. He lives as if as far away (in the Ku She Mount) as the Milky Way, yet those sagely emperors are as close to him as his "dust and siftings." He lives amidst life's turmoil, natural or political. Yet the worst cannot touch him; he is beyond it. In the final analysis he lives (as the end of the chapter has it) in the Village of Not-Any-Existence (*wu ho yu*), that is, the realm of something (*yu*) that is a nothing. He roams in the Field of Vast Nothing (*kuang mo*), moving without moving, freely sleeping and nondoing, reminiscent of the Darkness and the Fish which started the chapter.

This fantastic Sage is beyond the notion of utility—he is profoundly useful (for life) in all his uselessness (for living), as described in the final six short stories.

4. Clinching the whole chapter of fantasies with a dialogue on "usefulness" (*yung*) distinguishes Chuang Tzu from all irrelevant mysticism and nihilism. Chuang Tzu's is a philosophy of an enlightenment of worldliness from the sky.

But this worldliness was produced by one seemingly useless story after another. The first story (lines 115–16) about the ceremonial caps summarily stresses the uselessness of a venerable tradition of *other* times. Sagely emperors much admired by the Confucians are so many ceremonial caps. No wonder the sagely emperor Yao was dumbfounded into a daze after having visited the Four Masters in the faraway mountain.[43]

Sadly we have ancient caps *inside* our heads. We ceremoniously revere and cling to what should count as useful and lose sight of the really useful in the "useless." We are cluttered (*p'ung*) and blinded by the very notion of "use."[44] Labelled "too big" (the gourd) and "too trite" (hand-salve), those things have "no room" (*wu so jung*) in our scheme of things. Fixation on preconceived "uses" freezes our discernment of use. Not fixation but flexibility, not changing things but changing our attitude, freely uses things.

The supreme test came when Chuang Tzu was confronted with Hui Shih the flexible sophist, who judged that Chuang Tzu's words were as useless as the dumb tree. Chuang Tzu then compared Hui Shih to the resourceful wildcat and weasel,[45] whose own resourcefulness kills them in a trap. Use cannot be contrived, but comes only naturally from the situation.

We have neither a preordained system (the caps) to use nor inner resources (the weasel) to wrest usefulness out of things.[46] On the contrary, we do well to cleanse ourselves from "usefulness" and "resources." Becoming uncluttered and forgetful, we leisurely roam in the world, and a flexible fit with the situation will come unawares. "Forgetting the waist is the fit of the belt," says Chuang Tzu later.[47] We know that the "belt" of our situation fits us when we forget ourselves in it. This is being use-less (wu yung), beyond the notion of "use," a life without "distress and suffering."[48] This is to "roam around and lie asleep below" a big useless tree, doing nothing. Or rather, we do do something—we plant that big and useless tree, but this is a doing that is a useless not-doing (wu wei).

Thus we go from the uselessness of the "useful" (caps) to the use of the "useless" (gourd, salve); and again from the "useless" to the real uselessness of the "useful" (weasel), and then back to use of the "useless" (big tree). The chapter that begins with the big Fish and the big Bird ends with the big Tree— the chapter swings from the useless to the useless. Such going back and forth is the roaming that soars high beyond the ordinary world, and thereby roams within it. The chapter roams in the use of the useless.

The "use of the useless" is significant for the pragmatic frame of the Chinese mind and the technological West. The phrase could mean somewhat as follows:

(1) Usefulness is relative to a specific perspective and demand of the situation, and something useful in one context becomes useless ("waste," "pollution") later in another context.
(2) For things to be continually useful, the *user* must change his perspective as the situation changes. He must not be stuck in one perspective.
(3) Freedom from a tradition-bound perspective requires that the user live in a situation-of-no-situation, the Village of Not-Any-Existence, and in an uncluttered inner landscape, the Field of Vast Nothing. Then he can afford to distance himself from the usual (notion of) utility and appreciate the "useless" things (tree, yak).
(4) All this amounts to a unity of things common and uncommon (ch'i wu lun), a soaring to the beyond that goes a-roaming in the ordinary (hsiao yao yu)

Two dynamic notions conclude this chapter—non-doing (wu wei) and the use of the useless.[49] Such notions abound in the Chuang Tzu —"the great Jen is not-jen," "the Tao of not-Tao," "doing with others without doing with them," and the like.[50] They all share one characteristic—"a of not-a ," as if to say, "Go beyond (negate) the usual *a*, then you will find the true *a*. Soar beyond *a*, and you will roam in *a*." Reverse your perspective; see the other side. Negate what you negated. Then you will see that *a* negated twice becomes *a* rendered flexible, cautious, and alive. In this manner, the very meaning structure of a notion comes alive, soaring and roaming. (Doing of) not-doing and (use of) the use-less are two such dynamic notions that conclude this chapter.

And the whole Chuang Tzu presents this dynamism. A soaring movement out of the Northern Darkness in quest for the Southern Darkness of the Heavenly Lake turns out to nestle a roaming stillness beside a useless Tree. All activities of the seven Inner Chapters conclude with Mr. Hun Tun at the center of the universe, meeting with the North Ocean and the South Ocean. The first chapter starts with a soaring animal for a definite goal, and ends in a human quietude that roams; the second chapter starts with human quietude that participates in the pipings of heaven, earth, and men, and ends with the hustle and bustle of animals (snake, cicada, butterfly), which interchange and interdepend to produce the identity of a "self." And Chapter Three applies this dialectical unity of quietude and dynamism to human suffering—we can be "at home" (*an*) in the "undoing" (*chieh*) of an ox, a leg, our life, and cosmic fire. And in this manner the chapter unwittingly sums up the *Chuang Tzu*.

5. "But seriously," someone retorts, "one does not need to be Hui Shih the sophist to wonder how much 'cash value' such incoherent tall tales have. What do all these mental acrobatics amount to, anyway? Any use?" And Chuang Tzu would say, "There we go again." Such serious query for "cash value" and "use" shows a one-track mind, a tunnel vision. To this frame of mind any mythical deviation from our devoted routine (cultural, logical) is a disturbance in the practical order of things.

Actually we are deprived of relaxed self-distancing in this pragmatic world. We are unable to entertain, much less enjoy, unusual alternatives which push our life forward. Our urgent solemnity nips flexibility-to-shifts of perspectives, rendering us humorless and anxious. We wear ourselves out in routines; when routines break down, we break down.

Pragmatism is glued to facts. The *fact* of the matter is, however, we are larger than facts, than our practical concerns. "What if we were a big Fish, a big Bird?"—such imaginative flight widens our repertoire of alternatives. We realize that we come from such a humus of potentials, the dark Northern Ocean. We must change into a big Bird and fly far to the Southern Ocean, to the mysterious depths of fresh imagination. We go from ocean to ocean with waves of mysteries, and become familiar with their uncanny novelty. We are prepared for their refusal to be classified into varied uses according to records and traditions. For we cannot leave the Dark and the Oceanic, in which we soak ourselves as we soar and roam from the northern unawareness to the southern awareness. We are nourished in the mysterious Deep, the Humus of existence. We realize that life is greater than whatever we accomplish and whatever happens to us (*factum*). We are the creator, not the slave, of facts.

Such a realization keeps us going, rendering us at home in this world full of surprises, "roaming around and lying asleep below" the "useless" Tree of life, refreshed. The chapter itself is a flight of the Bird, our soul soaring and roaming from the Dark to the Deep, the mysterious Lake of naturalness. If our practicalities make us "distress and suffer," this irrelevant exercise in pretending (= stretching ourselves forward) to be other than what we actually are[51] fulfills us. This exercise is not brainstorming; we do not storm but romp, roam, and stretch our wings of imagination in the storms of life. It is the uselessness of cosmic frolic that is most useful to life.

This roaming frolic (*yu*) reminds us of repetition (Kierkegaard), recurrence (Nietzsche), and the cyclic view of history (Greeks and Buddhists). But *yu* differs from repetition. Repetition assumes a re-cognition (remembrance) of how things transpire. We do not see a "recurrence" of events unless we remember how things have been, compare them with the present state of affairs, *and then* judge that these two series of events, the past and the present, are the same. And we conclude that we are trapped in the cyclical recurrences of dreary identicalness. Thus, repetition is a loaded notion, whereas frolicking, roaming *yu* is not, because *yu* does not remember, compare, and judge, but merely lives the now to the full, before going to the next "now." In the world of the butterfly and the fish changing into the bird, there is no "recurrence."

Repetition is almost synonymous with meaninglessness, as the Greeks and the Buddhists discerned.[52] In contrast, *yu* is significantly enjoyable, and forward-looking within the frame of present enjoyment. After all, the "same" route makes for different ways of life when walked in different stances and perspectives and to "walk (and roam) in a different perspective" is what *yu* is.

6. But what about suffering? Unless Chuang Tzu's magnificently useless soaring and roaming succeeds in dealing with suffering, all this proposal of cosmic frolic amounts to irresponsible nonsense.

Did Chuang Tzu deal with suffering? He did and he did not. On the one hand, he dealt with suffering in almost every chapter, including the first chapter which we just considered. Sages are great in their healing power— they heal us from plagues (line 97), flood (line 110) and drought (line 111).

They can heal us because, as Hsü Yu said, they know their "place" like the tailorbird occupying only one branch in the forest and the mole drinking only one bellyful out of the river (lines 81, 82). They know how to fit into nature, and so they are fit and do not suffer, and can help others without helping them. They practice their own non-doing—that irrelevant serenity in their activity as the Fish, the Bird, the Yak, the Tree. Nothing harms their concentrated spirits; nothing makes them distressed or causes them to suffer. The final phrase of the first chapter is "distress and suffer"; sages are out of distress and suffering and can make us so.

On the other hand, Chuang Tzu did not treat suffering as the major issue of life; the above passages had to be culled from the text centering on his main concern of nonchalant soaring and roaming. Although a burning issue, suffering was not for him the central concern, as it was for Buddha; nor was suffering an important issue for Chuang Tzu, as it was for Jesus. Buddha came to solve *the* problem of suffering, of which Jesus came to make a redemptive use. For Chuang Tzu suffering is a mishandling of life; the *problem* of suffering is itself a mistake. Suffering is not to be solved but to be let be, to dissolve of itself, as snow in the spring sun of our right living. To live rightly is neither living redemptively (Jesus) nor living enlightenedly (Buddha), but living appropriately, that is, fittingly to the changing climate of things, now soaring, now roaming—and *that* is Chuang Tzu's central concern. Myths in most civilizations usually have heroes undergoing suffering so as to solve it and live "happily ever *after*," not before or during the story. Myths (and their bits) in Chuang Tzu's writing are themselves moving images of happiness *amidst* suffering, happiness that is as nonchalant as animals and trees.[53]

The essence of suffering is violence, which includes (for Chuang Tzu) violence against oneself, such as "morality."[54] Chuang Tzu would say that vio-lence originates in opposition, including opposition to one's natural tendencies, one's spontaneity. The way to oppose suffering and violence, then, is to "oppose opposition," that is, to *stop* opposition, to go the opposite way of violence, to *be* non-violent, even to ourselves.

And so, to stop violence we do not violate violence but stop opposing opposition, and go along with whatever comes. In fact, whatever comes is recognized as "violence" only when we oppose it. To deal with it we go along with it—this is the weapon that deals a death blow to violence. This is why the Chinese martial arts (the arts of death) are at the same time arts of health and vigor. Chuang Tzu's non-violence does not provoke opposition (as Gandhi's did), but flies and flows (soars and roams) *with* the seasonal winds of this world.

When virtually all sages tell us that being a child is the height of sage-liness, such praise falls on the deaf ears of a child. He is unimpressed, even slightly annoyed, when lovingly told that he is a "perfect boy." The reason is simple; the child needs no such sayings. He *is* that boy, and there is nothing spectacular about being himself. Fish do not feel wet in water, and no amount of eulogy on the virtues of life in water touches them. Children do not treasure childhood.

We see that these sayings, and in fact all "sayings," are made by, for, and to the outsider of a situation. A saying is redundant to the insider to the point of irritation, for he does not feel or need that *about* which all sayings say. Thus we would not feel pain when *in* pain; we would not feel irritated when we yield to an injustice. Such yielding can of course be an abject defeat. "Defeat," however, is an evaluation word from outside, a label put on our outside. To those living in injustice there is no injustice, no defeat, irritation, or pain. We may know it, we may take it, absorb it, and sooner or later it dissolves itself.[55]

Now, to know it and to take it anyway is sageliness. We have here a sagely discernment that would deign to utter such useless pronouncement as "We are at home in suffering and injustice." This saying is analogous to "Children are sagely": the saying is both inside childhood and outside it. The saying is out-side enough to judge the value of childhood and to use labels; the saying is inside enough to feel the value of childhood, or rather, to live it. Those who knowingly yield to "injustice" (a label and a disvalue) is as sagely as the sagely pronouncement about the sageliness of a child.[56]

Similarly, when we are in pain, we just take it as it is. "Pain" is a label from outside; by dwelling in the situation we take off the label ("pain") from our consciousness. "Happiness" is also a label. To a boy born deaf, a lack of enjoyment of sound does not bother him. Christopher Nolan is a boy born with many handicaps. Happily his mind opens out to the world. He is in and out of himself at once. It is natural, then, that he was irritated at outsiders peeping into him. He said,

> Feeling beastly-nasty,
> Many discuss me so—
> Can he hear? Can he see?
> Can fools fly? Evidently no![57]

These are words that come from inside, angry. Christopher Nolan's anger gives us two important points.

First, there comes a time when oppression does hurt us. We cannot and should not suppress our anger at being massacred like dodo birds.

But this is the "anger out of not-anger," an important phrase with which Chuang Tzu ended his twenty-third chapter. The anger of no anger differs from both Hitler's obsessive hatred of the Jews and Gandhi's many colleagues's ingrained animosity against the British. Justified or not, both are turbulent vengeful angers out of anger, having nothing to do with the anger out of no anger of Bonhoeffer, Gandhi, and Christopher Nolan. The anger of no anger is quiet, restful, at bottom.

Secondly, the anger of no anger does not exclude cautious intelligent actions, any more than innocence excludes anger. Besides, innocence does not imply inability, nor does spontaneity stupidity. The whole of Chuang Tzu's fourth chapter is devoted to this subtle, essential, yet difficult point. A quiet appropriate act born of an inner understanding of the tyrant, as the act of a tiger tamer, is in the end one that is more effective than any other; the tyrant-tamer's acts stamp out tyranny as no other act does, and that at a minimum cost, injuries or otherwise, both to the tyrant and to the victims.

For the words of Christopher Nolan are those from inside, and born of the situation. Words can be born of and dwell in the situation; if we let them speak out from the bottom of our hearts, they will echo the situation. And we follow their lead to go with the winds of this world. To go with the winds of this world is to be at home in the inevitables (what cannot be helped).[58] To follow oneself is to be spontaneous (what one cannot help but be).[59] Both followings[60] lead to our health and nonchalant happiness in life.[61] Such is Chuang Tzu's *dissolution* of suffering, ranging from poverty to tyranny, amputation, and terminal illness.[62]

To soar and to roam is an enjoyment of life that is not, mind you, a violent excitement but a daily routine, the constant Tao of things. To soar is to live in the perspective of the sky. To roam is to rise and fly *with* things. Not to soar and roam is to suffer in life. To soar and to roam (*hsiao yao*) is to leisurely frolic (*yu*) as a mole who knows his river and his place in it. Such a place is forever shifting, sometimes into sunny comfort, sometimes into dark hazards.

Thus, all these implications of *hsiao yao yu* yarn themselves into a chapter title that aptly sums up the moving coherence of a Chuang Tzu's story-telling, those twilight tall tales, those montages of bits of myths and legends that reflect life as it should be lived.[63]

B.   Roaming, Laughing

In his *Fear and Trembling* Søren Kierkegaard admiringly gave us four readings of "how God tempted Abraham and how he endured temptation, kept the faith, and a second time received again a son contrary to expectation"; the legend is as terrifying as it is beautiful.[64]

Chuang Tzu and the legend of Abraham have one thing in common—they need to be read and reread. I would also admiringly give three readings of the first chapter, four of the second chapter, and three again of the third chapter. The *Chuang Tzu* is not terrifying, but as fascinating and beautiful as the legend of Abraham, and more enjoyable by far.

In miming Kierkegaard, then, I think I put Kierkegaard's story of Abraham upside down—into Chuang Tzu's jestful "fish stories." Here Abrahamic terror is replaced by Chuang Tzu's levity of a profound sort. I have given one reading (A); I will here give another (B) and then another (C). He who has an ear, hear.

1. The *title* of this chapter strikes us as full of lively movement yet never violent—an unhurried *hsiao yao yu*. Of all the chapter titles in the *Chuang Tzu*, perhaps only this one has a single unequivocal meaning, for *hsiao* is *yao*, and *yao* is *yu*. With slight variations of implication, they share one core meaning— playful soaring and roaming. Nothing seems more definite than this, yet this definite core meaning is also indefinite—soaring roaming freedom is as playful and unpredictable as a gust of wind.

This unequivocal unpredictability of free roaming is rightly placed at the beginning of the entire *Chuang Tzu*. Such free roaming is the "hub," to adapt Lao Tzu,[65] that is empty and alive at the center of "thirty spokes" in the wheel of the universe.

Hsiao Yao Yu is a threefold verb; the title unmistakably speaks of movement. The movement is between two extremes—the big and the small, the far and the near, the common and the uncommon, the useful and the useless, and the Northern Darkness and the Southern, that is, according to Wang Fu-chih's *Chuang Tzu Chieh*, between the primordial chaos, or rather, con-fusion, Hun Tun, and "separation-and-clarity" of things. At the same time the very reading of the title—*Hsiao-Yao-Yu*—exudes peace and roaming at ease.

To look more closely at the three characters:

Hsiao is interchangeable with *hsiao*, "to dissolve" (as in water), though both *hsiao*'s mean "roaming." Wang Fu-chih read in *hsiao* (keeping the two meanings in mind) a traversing far in time, passing through series of events as one forgets them one by one (as the flight of a bird which leaves no trace behind).

Yao is synonymous with both "far" (*yao yüan*) and "waving" (*yao*). It is to travel far in space, traversing many horizons that keep changing. Such travel is with ease and leisure, "as an old man having an after-the-meal stroll, moving himself about for digestion."[66]

Yu originally meant both the unrestrained flow of a banner in the wind and a fish swimming in water in playfulness.[67] It is a self-satisfying movement that fulfills itself.[68] And this meaning is also at the basis of both *hsiao* and *yao*. It is the movement of self-variation, as in casual play or a game, most congenial to imagination, because it is the nature of imagination to vary itself, in which a given variation suggests a novel one, which in turn stimulates more novel ones. Thus imaginative freedom is often regarded as synonymous with playful creativity. Even the physical body, as Charles Darwin suggested, continually diversifies itself in contents in historical situations, and Darwin's suggestion is itself the feat of his imaginative creativity in historical situations. To go (*yu*) far (*yiao*) and wide (*hsiao*) creatively is life's joy—of growing into oneself in the world.

2.   The *beginning* of the *Chuang Tzu* is vast, vigorous, vibrant, risible, natural, and supernatural. This is in contrast to three other representative books in Taoism—the *Tao Te Ching*, the *Lieh Tzu*, and the *Huai Nan Tzu*.

The *Tao Te Ching* begins with a solemn paradox, "The Tao tao-able is not the constant Tao,"[69] a laconic metaphysical meditation. The *Lieh Tzu* begins with an ordinary teacher about to take off from the political chaos of his country. He was asked by his students to leave some precious words before leaving them. Thus the *Lieh Tzu* has an academic and political beginning. The *Huai Nan Tzu* begins with the Tao and the Beginning in a poetico-speculative essay laced with affected cadence. To read it is to savor an overripe fruit, sickeningly thick with aroma of *that* species of fruit. None of them is as crisp and alive, spontaneous and jovial, as the *Chuang Tzu* .

Beginnings reveal what is to follow. The *Tao Te Ching* is mystical, its metaphysico-meditative eye glued to the Cosmos; all human conduct should be patterned after the Way of Nature through personal cultivation and even political manipulation. The *Lieh Tzu*'s concern is with man, even to the point of toying with the futility of man against the background of unknowable nature. The *Huai Nan Tzu* borders on alchemic religiosity tinged with an encyclopedic ambition toward the entire current scholarship, embracing politics, science, and instructions on how to survive in difficult times. In contrast, the *Chuang Tzu* is forever roaming in life in all its variations and its naturalness that goes beyond itself.

This is of course not to say that each of these writings is *confined* to those themes, but to say that they treated various themes, each of them from the perspective of sentiments peculiar to themselves. Such peculiarity is a cue, a root basic metaphor, in which each writing treated various themes and problems.

3. It is interesting to compare the beginning of the first of the seven Inner Chapters[70] with the last story of the Hun Tun that ends those chapters.

The Northern Darkness is the primordial Deep, the primeval Hun Tun or Non-Separation. The Southern Darkness is the mystery of Separation-and-Clarity, represented by emperors *Shu* (the formed or speedy) and *Hu* (the no-form or knowledge) that together killed the Hun Tun. Such change (*hua*) is a common occurrence in the universe. Seen this way, the great Fish-Bird Story that begins the *Chuang Tzu* must be a parody of standard cosmogony with which a respectable treatise begins. Let us see how it goes.

In the beginning was pre-cosmogonic Non-Separation. In that primeval situation existed a mysterious Fish-force, alive and pregnant with all potentials of life. This Fish-force changed itself into the big Phoenix, a mysterious force of Nature that natures. This Fish-Bird soared up from the dark Realm of Non-Separation, traversed thousands of li toward the rich world of Separation-and-Clarity, the world as we have it.

This is a cosmogonic journey, timeless yet in time. Whenever we see things we feel the thrust of this great journey. Whenever we have the arrival of a baby or the sprouting of a blade of grass, we see the arrival of that Fish-Bird, that Marsh Pheasant trotting by the Heavenly Lake of the Southern Deep (cf. Chapter Three, lines 35–37).

The all too mundane character of this "cosmogony" can be seen when compared with the solemn Biblical cosmogony. There the Spirit of God was hovering over the face of the waters. The earth was without form and void; darkness was on the face of the deep. Then God's awesome Fiat echoed over the dark deep stretch of silence—"Let there be light!" And there *was* light.

In Chuang Tzu's natural landscape, the Fish and the rising Tide coupled with the Bird and the primeval Gust, are enough to stir our imagination back to where things began and are in fact still beginning. These natural yet supernatural beings take the place of austere and decisive Biblical creation. Such natural innocence also differs from the bloody cosmogonies of Hesiod and of Babylonian antiquities.

4. Chuang Tzu is not only natural but jocular, and that in ways which make us think. Two examples are in order, the presumed literary "source" to his stories, and the naive laughter which proves to be anything but naive.

To quote from reputed "weighty words"[71] is a Chinese custom, thereby lending credence to one's saying. Chuang Tzu followed the custom, yet his "literary source"—the *Ch'i Hsieh*—is an ironic one. For *ch'i* can mean either "all (without exception)" or "the state of Ch'i," *hsieh* can mean either "harmony" or "jokes," and *ch' i hsieh* could be the name of a man or of a book, such as "collection of tales from the state of Ch'i."

Combined, the phrase offers three levels of meaning. On a serious level, the phrase can mean "the book of universal harmony" or "collection of sayings from Ch'i (region, dynasty, man, or people)." On a half-serious level, *ch' i hsieh* can mean "collection of jokes from Ch'i (or by Mr. Ch'i)." On a hilarious level, *ch' i hsieh* can mean "book of all jokes."

When any meaning is chosen, the reader's mind is obliquely referred to other meanings. Thus any combination of these implications evokes a smile; to meet the phrase is to be tickled. All harmony is in all jokes; an arrangement of universal harmony is the arrangement of many jokes. To cite from authority is to cite from the devil-may-care.

Chuang Tzu's second jocular twist is the laughter of petty creatures (cicadas and small doves) who heard about the fantastic journey of a fantastic Bird. To them it is an enormous waste of time and energy to wait for the June gust and tide, while preparing a six long months' supply of food to take off for the uncertain and therefore uninteresting territory.

We see here the first irony—the big is laughed at by the small, the fantastic ridiculed by the trivial, the profound by the prosaic, and the poetic by the pragmatic.

The initial reaction of the Phoenix is to smile back at the petty doves; the daily humdrum accomodates no primeval cosmogony, small understanding and years do not reach huge understanding and years. The great Lieh Tzu traversing on the wind is beyond the imagination of proud officials of petty loyalty. Of course "low-grade people laugh greatly on hearing the Tao, which is no Tao unless laughed at."[72] We are reminded here of Xavier Rubert de Ventós who said,

> For Søren Kierkegaard, the ethical 'stage' is conventional ... the stage of the small virtues ... of decorum and good reputation, of respectability, and the prompt performance of 'civic duties,'... a world from which we must break loose in order to reach the absolute, unique, ... and absurd experience ... the radical experience of existence itself.[73]

On second thought, however, the laughs of the small are justified after all. "What's so big about being big?"—a little boy quipped at the big bully. Hegel may not have observed his own irony when he said that the master depends on his slave to be master, for although the slave also depends on his master to be slave, *his* dependence on the master is less than the master's on him. The greatness of dependence is directly proportional to the greatness of a person, as Chuang Tzu twice reminded us, "only then can he ... " (lines 18, 19). The big Bird had to wait for the wind, the tide, and the sky; he had to collect food for a six-months' journey. The small birds need none of that.

To be truly "big" then does not belong to the big Bird, but includes being *both* big and small. It is to change, not only from the big Fish to the big Bird, but from the big to the small and back to the big, as the sage Hsü Yu was great by virtue of knowing his place with a tailorbird and a mole. The distinction between the big and the small still stands, yet the distinction is a map for journeying back and forth, not for setting up exclusive bigotry in mutual ridicule.

5. Having traveled from the primal Fish and Bird through the worlds of small creatures, civic community, sages, we come to a self-critique of all these descriptions.

We have traversed from the big to the small, from twigs to the end of the world, from the ephemeral to the long-lived, from the serious to the ridiculous, from Lieh Tzu who depends to the ultimate man who rides, from politics to sages.

Now, Chuang Tzu turns to the self-critical meta-talk about "use" and how useful all the above are. As the ceremonial miters are useless for the the tatooed Yüeh people (supposedly fools) who cut their hair short, so the reputed "useful" things can become useless. As the huge gourd can be a great float and the chap hand-salve can be an aid to a great campaign victory, so the reputed "useless" things can be useful. And if there is a tree of which absolutely nothing useful can be said, we do well to think of "useful" inner resources which can prove to be a death trap. Uselessness itself can be useful for survival. Thus the chapter ends with self-referential consistency that sounds inconsistent—great utility is useless.

In such a manner the chapter casually tosses off new themes to build a new way of life—use of the useless, non-doing, non-existence. The rest of the book is devoted to clarifying those enigmatic and enticing notions—playfully.

Why do we need a playful setting for basic themes? Simply because delightful fantasy is the force of creation. Frisky roaming *is* creation, romping through various realms, unifying all into a deep sense of delight. Chuang Tzu imperceptibly moves from the grandiose "Fish story" of cosmic creation to refreshing individual creativity, which is yet laughed at by small doves. Creation now turns out to be everywhere in fresh "useless" creativity, for which the jocular style is an appropriate atmosphere. Read Chuang Tzu and smile; levity is the spring of light-and-lissome life against dead-ends and problems. To look into the pattern of creativity is to peep into the mysterious workings of levity. Chuang Tzu presented creation by way of recreation, roaming playfully through the first chapter. To follow him is to become creative in one's own recreation.

C. A Close Look

The first chapter of the *Chuang Tzu* sums up the whole book. The chapter is concerned with a "cosmology of freedom" (to borrow Robert Neville's felicitous phrase). the universe pulsates with freedom, therefore one can rest in the restless universe, being at home in action. One can romp through the universe, one's native habitat. One is always free in it, roaming, and to it, soaring. But one is not at liberty to be free *from* it—either thrown out of it, estranged senselessly, or to wrest oneself in revolt from being trapped (choked) in its futility.

Chuang Tzu's is the cosmos of freedom on which one can ride and ponder in magnificent frolic; otherwise one shall unwittingly drift into miseries of egotism, nihilism, moralism. This universe of freedom is that of creativity in polarity of tarrying and soaring, as illustrated by the big Fish and the big Bird. Their relation is as follows:

(1) Only the bird can see things from above; it rises and surveys from the sky. And only such a rising bird can be described. No wonder the fish is dropped after a few lines. The fish tarries and roams *in* water, and only lives its life. No rising, no survey, no description.

And yet the bird can fly up and *away*, disappearing in abstraction. The revolt of existentialism and phenomenology is needed only in the bird world.[74] Perhaps the bird's flight needs the fish's tarrying and roaming, being itself.

(2) The bird is predominantly striving; only fish can mutually forget each other in rivers and lakes, darting and roaming around in self-enjoyment. Yet to be *intelligently* enjoyed, such "fish"-enjoyment needs a bird's eye view of things. We have a "fish-story" before a "bird-story" here; a bird-story is followed by a fish-story which ends the seventeenth chapter. It takes both the soaring bird and the roaming fish to be free and creative in the limitless universe.

(3) The fish-bird relation is like that between being awake and being in a dream. To *know* that one may never know whether one is awake or dreaming, is both to be and not to be in both states, as Chuang Tzu discovered in the famous butterfly story that ends the second chapter. Such interweaving of both states is expressed when he said, "I call you a 'dream'—I am also a dream."[75]

(4) To see such sub-weaving of meanings in life is a happy living. It is a discernment, bird-like, of meanings roaming in rivers and lakes of life, fish-like. In contrast to the platonic gazing at eternal forms separate from this world, this is the fun of soaring and roaming, changing with and within things. "You and I came to watch change, and now change has caught up with me."[76]

Change (*hua*) is what connects the Fish and the Bird, and weaves the entire *Chuang Tzu* from underneath to describe the cosmology of freedom. The message is this: The self and the universe go hand in hand together when we *let* fun, freedom, and creativity join themselves. This theme will be elaborated by examining three points: (1) the "loop" structure of the chapter, (2) creation without creation, and (3) self-critique.

1. *A "loop"*: **1.1.** The first chapter can be divided into three parts. In *A Concordance to the Chuang Tzu*[77] what I call Parts A and C occupy exactly 13 lines each, and Part B has 21 lines. Within the Translation, Part A comprises segments I and II; Part C, segments VI and VII; and Part B, everything in between.

First, let us look at Parts A and C; they are parallel in a reverse manner.[78]

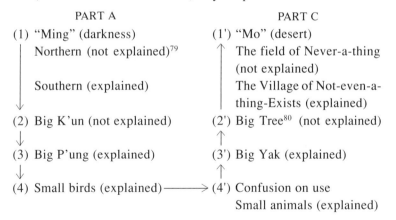

PART A	PART C
(1) "Ming" (darkness)	(1') "Mo" (desert)
Northern (not explained)[79]	The field of Never-a-thing (not explained)
Southern (explained)	The Village of Not-even-a-thing-Exists (explained)
(2) Big K'un (not explained)	(2') Big Tree[80] (not explained)
(3) Big P'ung (explained)	(3') Big Yak (explained)
(4) Small birds (explained) ⟶	(4') Confusion on use Small animals (explained)

We see that as Part A moves from 1 through 2 and 3 to 4, Part C moves from 4' through 3' and 2' to 1'. Parts A and C form a cosmic-comic roaming, a delightful "loop." Part A is about what is the case—a playful naturalness. Part C is about what should be the case—a playful naturalness.

Substantially, however, what is and should be the case is treated in Part B; Part A prepares for it, Part C examines and deepens it.

Part A prepares for Part B by describing creation in change. The big creature pities the small with smiles; the small laugh at the big. In mutual laughter the smallness of the small is *manifested*, together with the bigness of the big. Such manifestation is a creation.

Part B is a reversal of Part A. Here the story of the big Fish and Bird is repeated; but only their bigness is stressed without mentioning their change. And then the reversal comes; to grow "big" is to decrease daily until there is not even oneself, much less merit (work) or name (influence). Growth is a non-doing ("no merit") and non-doing-with ("no name") in a "no self."

The culmination of such growth is effected by the irony of laughter, of which two hilarious stories are told. The first story tells how Mr. Hsü Yu rejected the model emperor Yao's offer of the throne. We see a twofold irony here. On the one hand, only the good ruler who need not step down knows how to cede his throne, analogous to the religious paradox that only a good man who needs no repentance knows how truly to repent before infinite holiness (which only the good can recognize). It takes a good emperor to realize the futility of the candlelight of his goodness as he recognizes the sun of sageliness, as well as the fatuity of his political irrigation while under the seasonal rain of sainthood. This is one irony. On the other hand, a good emperor need not step down—the world is so well governed, why step down? He is "stuck in his position," condemned, if you will, by his goodness. For when we have the reality of good government, changing the ruler is merely to decorate with a name. This is that with which the sage Hsü Yu chided Yao. Hsü Yu is no decoration to the throne; he is beyond the political good. This is one more irony.

The second story describes a Divine Man, who is so mysterious as to sound silly to the ordinary people in quest of an ordinary goo. Mr. Chien Wu (Mr. Self?) the ordinary man, admits to thinking of the story as silly—first laugh. To such thinking Mr. Lien Shu (Mr. Linkage?)[81] gave a chuckle as he describes the Divine Man. For the deaf-and-blind are not confined to the physical realm. The spiritual deaf-blind are impervious to the Divine man from whose dust and siftings alone sagely emperors can be produced—second laugh.

The height of being is, then, reduction of being, until one goes to the Darkness in which big beings reside. Only laughter intimates this mysterious Realm, the laughter of both the small and the great. Reduction and laughter, then, are the two ingredients in the high Realm, where the non-self of the Ultimate Divine Sage resides.

We have three stories about such a Sage. The *first* story is about Mr. Hsü Yu, or perhaps Mr. Allowing.[82] Although he is at the bottom of the series of teachers, he is most perceptive, even openly critical of his teacher.[83]

The story exhibits an essential traits of the True Man, never meddlesome but allowing everyone to be himself. He refuses Yao's ceding of the throne, advising that each animal, including himself, is satisfied with where he is. The Sage is without name (distinction), as he is in himself, like a fish, a bird, a tailorbird, a mole.

The *second* story tells about a Divine Man roaming in the mountain mists, gathering dews as he gathers himself and rides on the vitality (breaths) of the universe. As he becomes pure, concentrated in spirit, the crops naturally grow. He is a man without merit.

In the *third* story the emperor Yao went up to the mountain and saw four such masters. Yao was so moved that he forgot all about his kingdom. He became with them a man without self.[84]

All this sounds like useless idle talk. Chuang Tzu agrees that such talk is "useless" but not "idle." These stories are like a big useless Tree, planted in the never-never land of the Vast and Nothing, where even the glorious Mr. Sung[85] failed to plant himself.

Nothingness is regarded in the West as an enemy, to cope with which is nihilism's problem. But one can cope only with something, not nothing. Nihilism is, then, itself a problem. And yet nothingness does "seep in," as it were, and corrode oneself in the same manner as one's skin deteriorates in weightlessness. Nihilism does have a problem after all.

Chuang Tzu, in contrast, applauded becoming nothing, that is, nameless, merit-less, and self-less. How can one become so? Since one is not a nothing, one can only become one *with* a nothing, somewhat like music dipped in silence. In Yehudi Menuhin's performance, for instance, the sound stands out in silence and the silence stands out in the music. Or rather, the sound hugs silence and becomes one with it, presenting it; sound and silence become background to each other. The louder the music, the deeper the silence, each interfusing with the other.

I can only be sound, not silence. For a sound to be a silence, I must become an echo of silence, a silhouette of silence and its shadowing-forth. As a shadow gives depth to a thing, so an echo shadows forth silence, a nothing. This is perhaps the silence of an I-Thou world which Martin Buber glimpsed.[86]

1.2. "But all this sounds entirely incredible and unintelligible," someone may protest. Two notions may aid our understanding, though neither was used by Chuang Tzu. One is Lucretius' "atoms"; another is the Biblical notion of "womb."

1.2.a. In the tradition of Leucippus, Democritus and Epicurus, Lucretius said that atoms are indestructible because, by definition, they are uncuttable, indivisible, therefore void cannot penetrate them. They are individuals, solid, incorruptible, hence imperishable by void.[87]

Henry G. Bugbee meditatively joined the "purity" of living with the "truth" of our *act* of consideration.[88] We can say that Chuang Tzu joined Bugbee's purity of the self with Lucretius' voiding of the void in atoms in the Ultimate Divine Sage—he is immune from life's harm because his spirit is "concentrated" (line 96).

It is, in the final analysis, only half true to say that there are forces that destroy and forces that delight and purify. We can be attentive ("pure"), and the force of the universe (*liu ch'i*) blows through us and stays in us; we will be delighted and purified. We can *cope* with it, tame it, manipulate it; *we* then divide it into two, the force with us and the force against us. And we shall be in for trouble. This is why Chuang Tzu condemned *chi-hsin* and extolled *chi*, both difficult to translate into English. *Chi* is that mysterious spring and vector of things; *chi-hsin* is that frame of mind which machinates on this *chi*, the machine-mind that distances itself from *chi* to plot on it.[89]

1.2.b.   Chuang Tzu's Ultimate Divine Sage is pure not because he voids the void in him but because he *is* void, not because he accomplishes something but because he is nameless, merit-less, and self-less. How does such void-Sage help us to indomitable health? The answer perhaps lies in the sagely void wombing us into sagely void.

Phyllis Trible in her moving description of King Solomon's judgment between two women's quarrel over a baby (with passages from Job, Jeremiah, and Psalms), called attention to the linkage of *rahamim* (compassion; plural) to *rahem* (womb; singular), the power to bring forth life. Noticing further that this womb-like compassion is also attributed to biblical men, Trible was unable to explain the trans-sexual character of "compassion" and "womb."[90]

Solomon, Hosea, Jesus, and others are men with the womb-power. Of course men impregnate wombs; men enable womb's enablement. And behind all this is God's "formative power in the uterus," closing and opening wombs in judgment and blessing.[91] God is the uterus for all uteruses.

Thus *rahamim* is metaphor to God. *Pace* Trible who did not know what to do with the male metaphor of God, we can see how malehood serves as the womb-power that opens the womb; we see woman, man, and God coming together at wombhood. If malehood is womb to the womb, then God is behind them enabling their mutual wombing functions. God is the Womb of all wombs.

Trible correctly said that "womb" is an all pervasive metaphor for the formative power of being. Womanhood should justly be celebrated as the physical bearer of this metaphor. But womanhood is not without its own dialectic. Women are *both* men's model and dependent on men for their wombhood. Women are the model for men; the essence of humanhood lies in the womb—enablement and letting-become, in short, creativity (cf. Genesis 1:28). At the same time women are dependent on men, because women sometimes depart (as do men) from their wombhood. Solomon had to womb out women's wombhood (1 Kings 3:25); not until 3:26 (after Solomon's inducement) was one of the two women described as *mother*, "the woman whose son was alive." In their fight for possession of the baby, two women wandered out of motherhood, or rather, their very wombhood went awry in their eagerness to nurture the baby. They needed the wombing wisdom of the male Solomon to bring them back to themselves. Solomon occasioned their self-revealments and allowed them to decide their own case.[92] Male Solomon wombed forth their own wombhood, and God enabled Solomon to do so.[93]

We must remember that womb is an empty chamber, and as such, as the void, it enables life to come forth. Void should be both voided and retained. It should be voided because it separates and destroys, as Lucretius noted. Yet separation is the only way for things to become individuals, as Hesiod, Anaximander, Heraclitus and other pre-Socratics noted.[94] Void is that in and through which creation takes place. As an arena and an agent (separator), void performs the function of Plato's Demiurge, though Plato himself may not have realized it.

Perhaps Chuang Tzu's self-less Sage likewise enables the creation of wholeness. His sagehood has two components—a womb-like emptiness and an atom-like purity. Emptiness enables others; purity establishes himself. Both combined describe his creativity. As Socrates' emptiness enabled his midwifery, so Chuang Tzu's sage merit-lessly draws forth others. Perhaps purity *is* the womb. Perhaps reduction through laughter attains creative purity. Laughter is a womb-like activity; for laughter is usually evoked, an active passivity. The sage is laughed at ("How useless!"), in which he wombs forth the smallness of the laughter, as Solomon, being a man, let the woman manifest her womanhood.

Such creation without active creation is what Chuang Tzu called a mirroring and an echoing,[95] the solid atomic purity against which things bounce into being, and the empty womb-chamber in which things echo forth themselves. Indestructible atomic purity redounds into womb-like creativity, in which things self-create.

2. *Creation without creation*: Chuang Tzu's sage is pure as atom and empty as womb, in which he creates by not creating. How does he do it? To answer the question, we must go out of Part B (in which we have tarried) to look at Parts A and C, and the climax turns into an anticlimax. The sage is pure emptiness; the more we watch him the less we see in him. He is revealed only by the way he lives as nameless, merit-less, and self-less. Such revelation comes about not by watching him but by laughing at him in small cleverness.

We must see Part B at work in Parts A and C, looking again at Parts A and C in the perspective of B. We remember Plato's Sun of Goodness, itself too bright to be visible; Chuang Tzu's realm of Darkness is invisible because it is far and dark. Yet both Plato's Sun and Chuang Tzu's Darkness can be felt in their effects. Parts A and C are Part B's orbit and its self-revealment.

One soars from the faraway Darkness where one simply is to another faraway Darkness of clarity. Since it is dark all the way one feels that one is going from nowhere to nowhere. One simply goes, which means that one "changes" one self and one's habitation.

The Dark is the deep and far, the primordial unorganized state; in such a Dark Ocean there is (simply "is," timelessly *yu*) a fish named K'un. We remember that K'un has three implications: fish roe, the small not-yet-beginning to be; the fantastic big whale, the universal being; and perhaps *hun*,[96] aperion (boundless indefinite), a con-fusion, an ambi-guous ambience for roaming in the subliminal, about to issue in beings.

The roaming takes three stages: the change, the flying, and the laughter. First the subliminal K'un is changed into the liminal P'ung Bird, pushing itself to the threshold of life, the heavenly Pond. The change (birth? *hua*)[97] here is a transport, being carried away out of oneself, analogous to the Socratic mania.

The K'un fish is indescribable, mysteriously roaming in the Northern Darkness, hidden. Such hiddenness is broken into by big Bird P'ung's soaring in the whirlwind toward the Southern Darkness. The relatively smooth first round of change from the hidden to the manifest is then confronted with the small birds' noisy laughter, whose petty dynamism (shared by loyal officials) is answered with the quiet smile of Sung Jung Tzu.

This second round of contrast between the manifest and the hidden is repeated in the contrast between the humane government of Yao, his proposal to cede his throne (first surprise) to Hsü Yu, Hsü Yu's refusal (second surprise), and the quiet Divine Man in the mountain mist (third surprise). The chapter ends with three rounds of argument (in three stories) on use, culminating in quiet fulfilment in uselessness.

The small birds' ridicule of the big Bird is like Hsü Yu's rejection of the "great" emperor Yao's ceding. The small birds' laughter, "We strive, rise, and fly, dashing between elm and sapanwood ... such is a rather ultimate of flying.

Yet where does he think *he's* going?" (lines 21, 47–48), echoes Hsü Yu's impatience, "Tailorbirds nest in deep woods, yet occupy no more than one branch; moles drink at the river, yet drink no more than to fill the belly ... I have no use for the empire" (lines 81–83). The small doves are like Hsü Yu and his tailorbirds. Nature accepts them as Chuang Tzu accepts the charge that all these are "useless." The "great" busying for living must be cut down—the cosmic journey, the model government, useful gadgets (ceremonial hats). Small is beautiful.

Uselessness releases us from constant worries about use. In uselessness we are released into a vast field of relaxation; the field is for nothing in particular, fit for wandering and sleeping around; we just go on living like a fish, a yak, a tree. In this field of Not-Even-Existence, *Erehwon*,[98] we are refreshed into ourselves, becoming mighty and "huge as clouds hanging over the sky" (line 158). Uselessness is profoundly useful for life.

For all this is what makes everything happen by itself. This is what the Divine Man is—be at one with the mountains, flowing with the cosmic breaths, and things great and small will obtain as they are. To be useful, one must be useless; to be involved, one must be frolicsome. Freedom is achievement; to laugh is to fulfill.

This is the freedom of roaming around, covering the big and the small, the quiet and the moving, the natural and the human, the useful and the useless. Roaming is a stop(*chih*)-and-start(*ch'ih*) that make up the ideogram *ko*,[99] shared by all three characters, *hsiao*, *yao*, *yu*, of the title of Chapter One. Roaming is an integration of motion and quietude, a walk without walk without walkin, a stop without stopping, forever resting in the restless universe.

Such roaming covers three realms, one calling forth another. The first realm is that of the big mysterious, described at the beginning and the end of the chapter. The chapter begins with a big and useless statement, "In the Northern Darkness there is a fish whose name is K'un." Each phrase in it is answered by another phrase at the end of the chapter. The Northern Darkness is echoed by the Field of Never-a-Thing, and the Southern Darkness by the Village of Not-Even-Existence. The there-is is answered by advice to "go rambling away and doing nothing," "roaming around and lying asleep," under a motionless tree. The big Bird is answered by the Yak, "huge as clouds hanging over the sky," and the name K'un is answered by the "Shu" tree—both indescribably big and useless.

Interspersed between the beginning and the end of the chapter, aroused by the first "fish-story" (the first realm) into existence, are myriads of things, the second realm. These things are small creatures and little dutiful officials.

Finally, there is an "Individual" in the midst of those worlds of things, the realm of the true self. The simple existence (*yu*) of K'un is changed (*hua*) into selfless, meritless, and nameless disutility of doing-nothing, simply being-oneself. This self roams beyond the dust and dirt, wandering freely in the service of inaction.[100]

Such is the "creation story" of Chuang Tzu.[101] It is a creation that is not at all creation. For small creatures came into being by their laughing at the big ones, who in turn were manifested thereby as "big"; against the background of deep Darkness myriads of things thus arise to feel that they are "OK" and "can" (*k'o*) do things themselves,[102] as they compare themselves with such useless and intangible beings as big Bird, big Fish, big Yak, big Tree, Hsü Yu, Divine Man, and Chuang Tzu himself. This is creation by not-creating, "creation" by laughter; small birds' ridiculing *hsiao* (laughter) brings out their small existence, and Sung Jung Tzu's unperturbed *hsiao* (smile) brings out his big-ness. In the beginning was the Tao, and the Tao was with *hsiao*, and the Tao was *hsiao*, through which everything came to be.

"But this is to put the cart before the horse," someone may say. "It is not laughter that creates; it is the existing things which are ridiculous that occasion laughter. We exist first, and then we laugh." This objection assumes existence-as-such without properties—emptily existing prior to those properties. But there is no bare existence as such; it is a phantom concoction of philosophers. "Existence" is always existence-with-properties in a specific concrete mode. Existence is always existence-as-*a*, for instance, existence as a plebean or in a magnificent nonchalance. Such concrete existence comes to be, among others, in laughter. Petty laughter brings out the small birds' tiresomely petty existence; an understanding smile brings out Sung Jung Tzu's magnanimous existence.

It is thus correct to say that laughter creates out of nothing. Ordinary existence does not first exist, then become ordinary; it comes into existence-as-ordinary by its laughing at the extraordinary. And such creation by laughter is made possible in the Darkness, the Field of Vast Nothing, the Tao. When lowly people hear the Tao, they laugh boisterously at it—if they did not laugh the Tao would not be Tao.[103] They are caused to exist by their laughter evoked by Tao, and then they say they did it all by themselves. That is the power of non-being, too deep for words and for laughter. To roam in it is to be refreshed, where we daily create in laughter.

The creation of the big is also by the laughter of the small. The big Bird P'ung is a magnificent charismatic bird, a target of many desires—P'ung is a literally a "bird" accompanied by a community of "friends." Yet his supposedly epochal flight is turned into an unexpected target of ridicule; the hero is turned an anti-hero. The flight is to all appearance useless, for use assumes a feasible purpose and a definite destination; but "where does he think *he's* going?" Thus such a big flight is manifested in the laughter of the ordinary. This is the story of "roaming" creation and laughing transmutations in many a sense, the story of the "arts of Mr. Hun Tun."[104]

As with all ancient writings in China, the *Chuang Tzu* begins with the origin of things. Yet it alone builds up a series of self-negations with laughter, irony, frolic, as if to insist that the freedom of playfulness and roaming *is* the beginning of all things.

But it is "as if to insist." Chuang Tzu did not explicitly say so; he exhibited and expressed it. He who has ears beware. To an ordinary reader this roaming chapter is just that, frivolous and unworthy of attention. The reader is all too eager to go on to the second chapter, not realizing that the second chapter is an elaboration on the first. In fact the entire *Chuang Tzu* is the fish K'un, the yet-to-begin-to-begin-to-be, and the Ming, the dark jumble of things not yet definite, arousing the reader to convert himself into a P'ung bird of free flight to the Southern Deep.

After all, freedom is a transport. One is free in himself when free *to* himself, self-possessed when de-centered, self-transporting and self-transforming. The self is such a unity of opposites, a perpetual source of unrest, an arousing to the P'ung's flight. To be transported is to travel far from one's old habitat (old self), and so to be self-transported this way is to be authentically oneself in freedom. Thus to be authentically oneself is to be a pilgrim in and beyond the old world, free in and with regard to one's environment. To be oneself is to arise and fly and to transform; to be autonomous is to shatter "autonomy." To be self-possessed is to be dispossessed in a spontaneous self-transformation. True possession (*yu*) of life is ecstatic, a self-translation (*hsi*).

In sum, Chuang Tzu's sentiment can be described as follows:

(1) Cosmic creation for Chuang Tzu is connected with individual creativity; the "all"-creation has a lot to with "every"-creativity.
(2) Creativity means going into something other than before, something novel. To go in such a way in life is "roaming."
(3) Something novel here is something delightful, laughable, unexpected, a psychic as well as physical "soaring."

Therefore cosmic creation has a lot to do with laughter that is connected with individual soaring and roaming.

3. *Self-critique:* It is time to take stock, time for self-critique. This came in the form of an attack by a sophistic dialectician Hui Shih and Chuang Tzu's answers. The conversation further reveals the self-involving development of Chuang Tzu's "system."

We can start by asking ourselves whether Chuang Tzu is another irresponsible sophist, that is, how useful what Chuang Tzu says is for living. Answers to this question naturally divide into three: (1) The comparison of Chuang Tzu with Hui Shih, in which Chuang Tzu's relation with Socrates is touched on, and (2) the "logic" of Chuang Tzu that is alive, his "system" that is on the move with life itself. The result is (3) life lived in "fun."

3.1 *Chuang Tzu and Socrates:* Although the relation between Socrates and the sophists is "subtle,"[105] their relation is easier to see than that between Chuang Tzu's use of evocation and a charlatan's use of logic.

Good things are "useful," and for sophists useful things can be indefinitely arranged according to whatever desires we have in the changing situations. The sophists then merely indulged themselves in whatever is useful. In contrast, Socrates asked *what* a thing is useful for, and *what* the aim of human existence is. It is "that quality, characteristic mark, or formal structure that all good things, no matter how relative, ... must share if they are to be good at all."[106] From this Guthrie draws a general conclusion: "... the Socratic search for definitions and [his method] ... rather include and transcend than undo the work of Sophists ..."[107]

Guthrie's insight that Socrates includes and transcends more than it undoes the sophists is instructive. Sadly, however, our quest for the means of distinguishing Chuang Tzu from a sophist cannot benefit from the Socratic search for definition. For Chuang Tzu has no such fixed point on which he stands opposed to the sophists. Yet Chuang Tzu's method of evocation is not for aimless sophistic dispersion but for fruitful life peregrination.

Both Chuang Tzu and the then-current sophists (Hui Shih, Kung Sun Lung) played with arguments. Yet Chuang Tzu played with arguments so as to result in peace and insouciance, while Hui Shih produced petty wrangling without end. Hui Shih's words dazzle the hearer with their paradoxes, juggling definitions. Hui Shih's talk is a word trickery that makes no dent on actuality.

Chuang Tzu's words are *patently* and hilariously false. Their falsity arouses the reader into seeing things in a fresh light, and the fresh outlook reveals new aspects of actuality. Sophists juggle words to jag the audience; Chuang Tzu jigs with oddities to jab at the falsity in life. Both are lampoonists, but the sophists merely confuse and entertain us, while Chuang Tzu emancipates us with entertainments. And Chuang Tzu even jigs with Hui Shih's own arguments, hoping to jab Hui Shih free from his own cleverness. Instead of Socratically examining him, Chuang Tzu lets Hui Shih develop himself, sometimes by playing his own game with him, humorously following along Hui Shih's way and landing the "arguments" on a nonsense and quibble, sometimes by telling tall tales to tease him out into his own senses. Futhermore, Chuang Tzu enjoyed talking with him so much that later Chuang Tzu had to stop at Hui Shih's grave; there he sighed his own loneliness with a story of how much a carpenter misses his "material" and "partner."[108]

In short, Socrates argued for the sake of finding truths—Socratic arguments had a "great use" for truth. Hui Shih argued for the sake of argument—his arguments were "useful" for winning the argument. Chuang Tzu argued for the sake of—nothing. For Chuang Tzu, "for the sake of" makes no sense—Chuang Tzu's arguments were "useless."

Hui Shih manipulated not the argument but truth to win the argument. Socrates manipulated not truth but arguments to discover truth. Chuang Tzu enjoyed himself manipulating arguments and roaming in the realm of truth. Truth is not so much something to be found as an ever-present horizon and ambience *in* which to dwell and ambulate, as the fish in the water roaming in self-forgetfulness and a mutual forgetting.

Socrates was serious about truth. Hui Shih was serious about the arguments. Chuang Tzu was neither serious nor not-serious—he was non-serious with both the argument and truth. For Chuang Tzu played with arguments in truth, as an adult plays "da, da" with babbling babies. An adult neither despises the baby and stops talking with him, nor engages in a conversation as seriously as the babies do among themselves. The adult *enjoys* talking with the baby.

An important question remains. If the sophists were "villains" in philosophy, why did both Socrates and Chuang Tzu spend so much time with them? Because within the so-called "heresies" of sophists there is a grain of truth; they are profoundly alive, flexible, and amidst the confusion of the day, dared to traverse various schools of thought.

It is well-known that sophism is a latter-day phenomenon of an intellectual era. By the time the Greek sophists came on the scene, there were roughly three kinds of philosophers vying for reputation. There were nature-philosophers such as Thales, Anaximander, Anaximenes, Anaxagorus, who sought for the original matter as material principle that makes the world as it is. Then there were dynamic philosophers who saw the world-principle either in the fire and change (Heraclitus) or in whirling atoms (Democritus). And finally, opposing both are the static ontologists such as Parmenides, Zeno, and Melissus, who claimed that the universe is One, unchanging, full, and so on. Surveying all these, the sophists decided that man is the measure of all things; they engaged in a sophistic manipulation of propositions and views expressed so far by others, in order not to find what there really is but to win the argument.

A somewhat similar situation obtained in ancient China. There were schools of cosmology, such as the I-Ching and the Yin-Yang. There was Confucianism on human decency, and Legalism on the strategy of coercion. Between the Confucian and the Legalist schools there appeared Hsün Tzu for self-discipline, and so on. Taking advantage of the confusion, there arose the school of sophists, such as Kung Sun Lung and Hui Shih, who dazzled the audience with a fascinating survey of various views in a "hop, skip, and jump" fashion, combining them in a surprising sophistic display.

Neither Socrates nor Chung Tzu could ignore such a critical juncture in intellectual history. Plato's Socrates proceeded to *use* the sophistical technique of dialectics to oppose the sophists and to meticulously search for the universal definitions of notions and things, thereby to reach the Form that is eternally valid. Socrates' model was geometry; his Sun of Goodness (the Form) was the object of our vision, or rather, the Ideal through which vision (intellectual or otherwise) was made possible. It was the Idea, a vision, that was important.

In contrast, Chuang Tzu *trailed* the sophists like a detective. Chuang Tzu followed their technique of sophistry and extracted an important truth. The Chinese sophists inadvertently exhibited a philosophy, a "system" and "logic" that is as alive as life itself. For they followed their instincts and roamed in the realm of logic. Their very logical irresponsibility fascinated Chuang Tzu, for their behavior served as the symbol of a "live" logic. As a result, Chuang Tzu produced a "system" that is alive. To this we now turn.

3.2. *Life-"logic":* The first chapter, *Hsiao Yao Yu,* can be regarded as an allegory on the liveliness of the "system" of thinking in life. This thinking reflects the living organism; this thinking is, as the word "organism" suggests, not without its structure, pattern, and coherence. Such thinking reflects a living system. Life is like the fish K'un, silently alive and immersed in the vast dark depths of the universe. And such an immersed system of silent life will inevitably change into another system like the bird P'ung, then come to be in a "laughing" relation with others (such as small animals).

Whether such systematic thinking is like the fish immmersed deeply in the dark waters of life, or like the bird rising high into the sky of abstraction, it must have its autonomy, its self-sameness. Yet it must not be too self-conscious. For part of the trouble with a visible, self-consciously spun-out system is that it tends to be ossified into irrelevance or trivialities. It ends up forcing the protean actualities of life into its procrustean bed, no matter how much and how often it revises itself. The systematic character of thought should be as oblivious to itself as the tree is to itself—which is perhaps a visible replica of the invisible big Fish in water.

Is there a meta-rule, meta-system, as it were, to all such organic systems of thought? Yes, Chuang Tzu would have replied. It is the "system" of Hsiao Yao Yu, of leisurely romaning *(p'ang huang)*, [109] which is a system for no system. For such a system has no rule except following itself drifting *out* of its routines. It "spills over" outside itself. And an overflowing system is not a system, which is a self-contained logical network with which we explain things. A system should be self-contained in the sense that it must have a set coherence which explains things (including itself) without exception—at least so we think. However, a system's job is to explain, that is, to refer to life, which is beyond any *set* explanation. As a result, a system that refers to life overflows beyond itself, defying what we take a system to be—hence, it is a system of no system. Such a spill-over[110] can be explained as follows: (*a*) No book can contain in it *all* that it says; (*b*) no system can be completed. And so (*c*) the best way to produce a logical system that is alive (comprehensive and referring to life) is not to stick to the traditional way of continual revision but to go two ways: a way of story-telling and a way of self-involvement.

3.2.a. *Books:* Chuang Tzu told us a story about a wheelwright who dared to say that his lord's book-reading is a dealing with chaff and dregs. When it was demanded (on pain of death) that he produce an explanation, he answered that the feel at hand when chiseling a wheel cannot be verbally passed on even to his own son, who has to learn it afresh in *his* raw concrete contact with the wheel and the tools.[111]

Another story concerns Lin Hui who strapped his baby on his back, threw away his precious jade disc, and fled from China. The baby is bothersomely less valuable than the jade—his deed does not make sense. Asked, he replied that the profit relation between him and the jade breaks away in disaster, which seals tight the heavenly relation of mutual belonging between him and his baby. And yet this is not an explanation, but a mere description of something concrete that is beyond explanation.[112]

Both stories show that books and words tell about life, which is beyond words. Factual information can, we think, be conveyed in writing. But the information worth writing down is worth more than bare facts, and value-laden facts are difficult to transmit with literal accuracy.

> To transmit words that are either pleasing to both parties or infuriating
> to both parties is one of the most difficult things in the world. Where both

> parties are pleased, there must be some exaggeration of the good points; and
> where both parties are angered, there must be some exaggeration of the bad
> points. Anything that smacks of exaggeration is irresponsible. Where there
> is irresponsibility, no one will trust what is said, and when that happens, the
> man is transmitting the words will be in danger.[113]

Similarly, almost all of the major historical incidents have been the targets of
intense debates among historians. No wonder Chuang Tzu described the ideal
Utopia as a place where there are no historical records.[114]

But how about technical instruction, from which valuational overtones
should be absent? Yet it is precisely here that the wheelwright (in the story just
cited) despaired of any possibility of writing down (or verbally transmitting)
what should be done to make good wheels. He can only confess, "I caught it
in hand and feel in mind-and-heart. Yet I cannot teach *it* to my son."

Books refer beyond themselves to life; "themselves" here means the written meaning, what makes sense. Books are concerned only with what makes
sense, for only what makes sense can be written down. Yet all words make
sense only generally. General truths can be written down, such a "Men are
mortal," and they are tiresomely trivial. We usually use words to convey
(describe) life, which is incorrigibly concrete; there is no life happening in
general any more than there is human face in general. This means that words
are powerless to convey exactly what is worth conveying—concrete life hap-
penings.

If the intention of the book is beyond the book, then the intention is
beyond what can be told, what makes sense. That is why Socrates was against
books. Written words produce only a "semblance" of truth. Socrates sighed,

> You might think they spoke as though they made sense, but if you ask
> them anything about what they are saying, if you wish an explanation, they
> go on telling you the same thing, over and over forever.[115]

The words must tell what makes sense to express what is beyond sense;
they must say what they cannot, and so do not, say.

Socrates discounted only *written* words; Chuang Tzu distrusted all words,
spoken or written. Yet Chuang Tzu admitted that conveyance must go on, for
without saying something, what is beyond expression can never be conveyed.
In this manner silence and speech mingle, and in their mutual weaving appears
the sub-texture (subtlety) that is beyond and within both words and silence, the
living truth of things. The situation of "neither silence nor speech" is what
exhausts (*chi*) expressive effectiveness for the highest realm (*chi*) of Tao and
things.[116] Concretely speaking, one mode of such saying without saying is to
tell stories.

3.2.b. *Story-telling*: Daily living can be told imperfectly in a story. A story can imperfectly be translated into a logical system, which can be matched, Kurt Gödel claimed, by a number system. But Gödel then added that such a mathematical system is not provable in *that* system; no sound and complete deductive system of mathematics can be attained.[117]

In other words, any system is incomplete—be it mathematical, logical, narrative, or organic, and so it inevitably refers outside itself into another system and in the end into life. A most flexible system of statements is a *story* which is both open and coherent, a yarn of meanings that intertwine and can be added to or abridged at will.[118] Furthermore, the story refers back to the *way* in which it is told, since the style of story-telling is part of the life that lurks behind the story.

Such consideration warns us against taking a description (story) *literally*, for it says more than it actually says. This supports a hermeneutics of evocation, metaphor, irony, and situational implication (such as "It is raining" implies "I believe that 'it is raining' is true"). An interpretation is an over-interpretation beyond what is explicitly said. A right interpretation differs from a wrong one in that, as Rudolf Bultmann more than once said, the former illuminates the life situation of the reader who participates in interpretation, while the latter hinders such illumination.[119] As Michael Polanyi said, myths "are clearly works of imagination; and their truth, like the truth of works of art, can consist only in their power to evoke in us an experience which we hold to be genuine."[120] A legitimate over-interpretation enhances life-discernment; an illegitimate one only complicates the text.

3.2.c.i. *Self-involvement:* There are two characteristics of the logic that is alive: self-involvement and story-telling. The first is the predominant method used in the second chapter of the *Chuang Tzu*, the Ch'i Wu Lun, and the second, the method in the first chapter with which we have been concerned, although both chapters used both methods. We will consider self-involvement first, then return to story-telling.

One of the characteristics of the logic that is alive is self-involvement, a feedback mechanism, a self-involved consistency *and* inconsistency. Both consistency and inconsistency are integrated into the organic system of self-involvement. This is intimated in the first chapter in the build-up of Part A to Part B, then it's deepening through the self-critique of Part C.

Suppose logic can be dynamic; logic changes, even its rule (and rate) of change changes. Then what is it that is reasonable and not random in all this? This is the question Chuang Tzu must answer; even Heraclitus must lay down an unchanging rule, "Strife is father of all."

Chuang Tzu would have followed Heraclitus' manner of saying and answered the above question with the rhythm of self-consistent (self-involved) inconsistency. This "rule" differs from that of Heraclitus in that this is both unchanging (since it is a rule that applies universally, even to itself) and changing (since inconsistency is built into itself). This is what generates the mutual *internal* involvement of dreaming and awakening, life and death, production and destruction, one and many, big and small, knowledge and ignorance, moving and at rest. Self-involvement does not merely mean that the pairs are often those of contraries, and are correlative, in the sense that without the one in the pair the other does not make sense. These three points constitute that famous Yin-Yang Theory. It means further that the one exists *within* the other. This is what makes Chuang Tzu's description so much alive, for he is merely following the rule of life, what Nietzsche called the biological principle that begets the famous will to power—though Nietzsche did not elaborate on what the biological principle is.

Life has a rhythm of systole and dyastole, inhaling and exhaling, nocturnal coming-back and daytime going-out—and, similarly, self-referential consistency and inconsistency. Self-referential consistency is analogous to the organic coherence of life's feedback system; it gives integrity to life, and gives coherence to the system of the "life" of a view, preserving it from random dissipation and death. Self-referential inconsistency is analogous to growth, transformation, and even adventurous transmigration. This is what prevents a system (be it life or narrative) from becoming autophagous, chewing itself up in a convolution of logical spirals, spinning out tiresome tautologies or falsehoods. In contrast, paradoxes and false statements, knowingly entertained, can serve as antinomies to goad our dogmatism and make us think. They tender a theme incomplete, inviting the reader to participate in it, involving the reader in exploring further implications.

Self-referential consistency is self-involvement. Self-involved inconsistency is other-involvement. Both belong to a "live" system of ideas. Both conspire to make up an irony which is both focussed and dehiscent, self-responsible and evocative of novel horizons. This is the world of transforming-and-transmigrating, a happy roaming in fresh territories from the Northermost Darkness to the Southernmost Mystery, from everywhere to nowhere, in a great uselessness that nonchalantly turns out various uses.

And such is the rule of nature, its biological principle, alive and reasonable internally (no fixated self, no merit) as well as externally (changing, migrating). This is what Paul Ricoeur dryly called "the logic of immanent development."[121]

What is important to note is that life has no distinction between self-involved consistency and inconsistency. Both are mixed in the great stories of life. The chapter on happy Soaring and Roaming is just such a collage of stories of life.

A story is an elaboration of a specific idea, a logical system applied to life, moving about in it. A dialogue is two stories in one, one complementing and enriching the other. The *Chuang Tzu* has many stories and dialogues. They differ from ordinary essays and treatises, which merely display their contents. In contrast, the surface meaning of stories and dialogues are so self-evident that often its very obviousness constitutes its oddity, forcing the reader to step aside and loop the writing back to the *modus operandi* either of the stories, or of their characters, or the reader's own life. The obviousness is the oddity which involves the reader in the stories' and dialogues' unexpressed self-movement of referring back to themselves and to life.

In the *Chuang Tzu*, stories seem to have been randomly collected.[122] However, this collage of stories soon attracts the reader's attention to the manner in which the stories refer one to another, either by the one "laughing" at the other, or by the one elaborating on the other from a slyly (and slightly) different angle, or exploiting some key notions in a new direction, or simply explaining some key notions by the manner in which the stories are arranged. Part C demonstrated such self-involved explanation on Divine Man (the Sage). Thus these stories mutually develop the implications they produce. And the total meaning of the collage of stories emerges in the meantime.

The characters of the dialogues do not merely discuss the topics of their conversation. They are themselves involved in the contents. The way in which the talk is carried on—whether in jest or in seriousness, or Mr. Jestful confronting Mr. Serious—reflects forth the deeper meaning of the theme discussed.

For instance, the last dialogue in the chapter warns that Hui Shih's weasel-like rhetorical talents shall trap him and threaten his survival, and Chuang Tzu's seemingly useless idle talks establish ("plant") life in the security of a leisurely roaming, while so much laughed at and puzzled about in the chapter. Thus the point loops back on to the entire chapter and clinches its importance.

Furthermore, by jumping out of themselves these stories and dialogues leap out of the book into the reader's life. It has been the reader who was intrigued into these extra-literary moves. As he involves himself in such meta-moves, he finds his life involved in the truths those stories adumbrate (but do not state). And he soon realizes that *that* involvement is part of what is conveyed; life-truths cannot be had without getting involved, any more than he can begin to swim by paying for a swimming lesson without getting wet. Truths of life involve the reader's own self-examination which leads him beyond daily chores and profits. The truths these stories present loop onto real life by looping the stories back onto themselves via the reader's involvement. Self-involvement is such going out of the stories, going back on themselves, and in the meantime hitching onto the reader. Such is an evocation of life.

Storied self-involvement has the character of self-referential consistency and inconsistency, and the tension of both constitutes the challenge to the reader to get involved in digging out the implications for life.

But, of course, to state so boldly the logical and biological principle of life is true neither to life nor to the *Chuang Tzu*; neither *explicitly* says such things. The "principle"[123] that has been described so far is really a mere cipher pointing to the flexible rationality of actuality as alive as life itself. Or, rather, perhaps the so-called "principle" is invisible, like life itself. The principle is only intimated in its living activities, as a flexible bone-structure barely discernible in the flesh-and-blood movements of the body. Chuang Tzu used the phrase, "goblet words" to describe it, tipping to let things in and righting itself to let things out, ever adapting to the fluctuating world.[124] No wonder only such maneuvers are described in the chapter of Soaring and Roaming; to go beyond them is to go against life. What has been done so far is to "peek" ultrasonically at the inner structure of life, and let it go. Peeking too long stops life too long for unnatural probing. Fortunately we have a way of peeking at life-on-the-move, and that is to tell a story.

3.2.c.ii. *The flow of life in stories*: One of the characteristics of the logic of life is its flow. This is amply adumbrated by the telling of a story, which *moves* with the events it describes.

Chuang Tzu told us a story of the big Bird which soars to clean our hearts. And then he told one story after another. He skillfully wove them into a collage or montage; as we move in it we get resonance of meanings.

First, the small cannot comprehend the big; a big Sung Jung Tzu can smile back at them. But then, secondly, the laughter of the small needs to be taken seriously by the big after all, for neither the big Bird nor the big Sung Jung Tzu has planted himself in the Village of Not-even-existence in the Field of Vast Nothing (lines 59, 161).

And all these stories so far are a mere way-station to the realm of the ultimate divine Sage. Another series of stories are told to elucidate this ultimate realm—Mr. Hsü Yu's refusal of Yao's throne, the Divine Man's habitat in the faraway mountain, and Yao's forgetting of the throne when he met those four Masters. Then come another series of stories about use, ending with the "use" of the useless things, as do all the stories told in this chapter.

Telling stories like these composes and executes a "living order." Such stories can deeply move us—from our accustomed territory to a new one. Stories are metaphor in the original sense, what carries us over to new place—new ideas, new activities, new cultures, new perspectives—and we live there by that metaphor. Metaphor has this power because it is a mini-story powerful enough to pervade our life. Stories of war are so captivating as to dominate the world of argument; we argue as if we engaged ourselves in warfare. Money stories are powerful enough to dominate our thinking about time; mathematics and vision are metaphors that dominate science. We live and move in metaphors; we call them root metaphors, paradigms, assumptions, postulates, even prejudices, but call them what we will, we cannot live without them. We live by the mini-stories of metaphors. For metaphors shape our views and pattern our lives. Unfortunately no metaphor by itself covers all aspects of life; every metaphor hides some aspect of life as it stresses others.[125]

We need to move freely in and out of metaphor, always trying out new ones, using old ones in a new light, living in one metaphor in one situation, living in another metaphor in another situation. For such moves in and out of our particular life orientation, we need to be evoked by a new metaphor into shifting out of our old one. The *Chuang Tzu* is one such meta-metaphor. For the *Chuang Tzu* does not present us with a specific metaphor but, with an evocative collage of metaphors, helps us *move* among metaphors.

Or perhaps Chuang Tzu may well have his own metaphor, for no one can live without metaphor. His freedom of Hsiao Yao Yu implies that for him, the world is bigger and freer than our own metaphors. This is a metaphor of no metaphor. It is a metaphor because it is a view opposed to some others, such as a mechanistic metaphor of the world. It is not a metaphor because it has no definite system and contents to orient us. It wants *us* to invent our own metaphors and freely live by them, modify them, and discard them for new ones. Chuang Tzu's free "system" of metaphors is exhibited by a collage of stories, one referring to another, which reflects back with deeper implications. Such a mutual involvement is the frame in which we freely roam.

Lucretius' purpose is similar to Chuang Tzu's—to provide a clear "understanding" of the world to liberate us from metaphors that scare and stifle us.[126] However, Lucretius took *his* metaphor of nature, atomism, to be *the* correct one, and thus trapped himself in the metaphor he produced.

The world of computers is in a similar predicament; a computer does not change its metaphor. Human life is not lived in computer-computation, but shifts its metaphors.[127]

The big Bird was laughed at by doves and cicadas, perhaps not because the

Bird was big, but because it was clumsy—waiting and preparing for so long for the take-off, as if to show that his only goal of life is to soar. It lacks the nimble practicality of small birds and officials.

Yet the soaring can mean soaring beyond our accustomed world of old metaphor. Soaring is a self-transmigration from one metaphor to another, hence self-transformation; our life-metaphors change, therefore our selves and our world change. Short-term practicability stays in the same world; it drains the self, which is helpless when confronted with a huge gourd.

Similarly the big Yak and the big Tree seem clumsy and useless, yet they are at home in the environment of no environment—the Field of Vast Nothing, the Village of Not-even-existence; they are not stuck in any single metaphor.

And all these echo the two Deep Darknesses which started the chapter. In these vast Nothings-and-Depths these useless big creatures roam; they change themselves in their change of life-metaphors. Since they inhabit nowhere (in particular), their peculiar habitation facilitates their freedom. Such is bigness of the self- and world-metamorphoses. Such is the vastness of free and easy soaring. Such is the lesson of those fantastic stories which delight young and old without benefiting our busy-ness, because they make us pause, put us at ease, and set us in our happy self-transmutation and cosmic transmigration.

As mentioned above, to change one's metaphors freely is to undergo self- and world-metamorphoses. It is to change from the world of big Fish to that of big Bird. It is to soar with Nietzsche's Eagle without Nietzsche's ridicule.

Thus to go through world-metamorphosis is to be inwardly pure and peaceful. It is to plant that big useless Tree in the Village of Boundlessly Not-even-existence, roam and drowse under the Shu tree. To outwardly change is to be inwardly at peace—and one is happy, for one is now free from hurt and anxiety.

For to be inwardly at peace is to be pure, to become as integral an individual as the Lucretian indestructible atoms. To be at home in oneself is to be at one with oneself, to be one single whole, unmixed throughout, and indestructible. As Lucretius' atoms are outwardly invisible, so Chuang Tzu's individualism is objectively indescribable. As Lucretius' atoms are freely in motion and indestructible, so Chuang Tzu's pure individuals roam and soar, free from hurt and anxiety. Yet such purity is unteachable, because each individual is as he is, and *he* has to find his own purity. Chuang Tzu gave us an advice of no advice: "Be pure."

3.3.   *Fun*: But of course such immortal happiness raises new questions. How do we avoid frivolity when we pursue creative laughter? Why not-doing and drowsing? To go into them is part of what it means to roam in the realm of no realm. Such roaming cleanses and lightens life—and strengthens it. This is "fun."

As surely as there is a subtle distinction between genius and insanity, so surely are creativity and frivolity indistinguishable in actuality. A professor in French literature[128] objected to my using the peculiarly American word, "fun"; it is too frivolous to describe the solemn objective of life. He insisted on "happiness" as the true end of life.

He is *of course* correct, for frivolity cannot be a life objective to aim at but a life slippage to be avoided; and it is the "of course" that is the crux of the matter. For Chuang Tzu says that life objective *is* life slippage. To strive to attain something is a sure way to miss it; conversely, to *let* life "slip" is to "attain" the goal of life. From this perspective, "fun" is a fitting description of Chuang Tzu. There is a distinction between fun and happiness, yet in the final analysis we are not sure (with Chuang Tzu) as to whether such a distinction, with our moral tinge of preferring happiness over fun, is justified.

The point is admirably (and playfully) made in Chuang Tzu's description of being awake and being in a dream. It is *after* having been awakened that Chuang Tzu realized that the distinction exists, and *then* wondered whether he was really awake or now in a dream, and *then* pronounced that it does not matter–as long as we know the distinction, and know that we cannot know which situation we are in. That is, as long as we are *awakened* to our being *not* sure whether we are awakened or not, we are all right.

Fun-and-happiness parallels dreaming-and-awakened. They are distinct and inseparable; they are different and they interpenetrate. The ideal state of life is not "ideal" but ordinary—a subtle mixture of fun and happiness, frivolity and profundity, silly senseless banter and free creative laughter, the lazy snooze of a bum and that of a sagely bum, a "bumming around" and a roaming in which creativity soars. In the end, what counts is to discern that they are inseparable. Such discernment is evoked by laughter at the delightful story of fantastic senselessness, told with gusto and sparkling insouciance. This is its danger and its glory, and both for the same reason—it is so incredibly easy, easy to slip, and easy to soar!

Such "fun" is synonymous with *yu*, playing around, roaming around. The notion of *yu* may well have three ingredients—to wander, to frolic, to play a game. To wander throughout the heaven and earth is an explicit meaning in the *Chuang Tzu*. Watson is to be commended for his consistent rendering of *yu* as "to wander" whenever the word occurs.

To frolic (*hsi*) is a standard meaning mentioned in the *Kuang Ya*. Although *yu* as "to frolic" explicitly occurs only three times,[129] all these occurrences are important. In 9/9 all three meanings are combined.

Also, usually "to frolic" and "to play a game" go together; to play a game is of course to enjoy oneself in it. Playing a game is mentioned often, and that in unexpected places. Chapter Three is totally devoted to the theme of "dancing one's occupation" in life, including that of lowly butcher. Much emphasis was similarly put on the lowly wheelwright, the ferryman, the bell-stand maker, and the buckle maker.[130]

Chuang Tzu's attitude to games is instructive. On the one hand, he took war to be a mere game.[131] On the other hand, he took quite seriously such pastime avocations as catching cicadas, fishing, archery, hunting, horse racing, music, watching fish play, and bird watching.[132] They all reveal what life is and how to live it. Serious occupations are treated playfully, and playing games is treated seriously. Life is "fun" in a serious sense.

And we must remember that the three implications of *yu* referred to above are all present in all its occurrences, though emphases may differ from one case to another. To wander and roam is to playfully roam with frolic. To frolic is to wander around playing. To play is to enjoy oneself letting the mind roam wherever it takes fancy. Thus to be oneself is to have fun roaming in the cosmos—and such fun is creation (Chapters One and Two). It is to enjoy oneself—and such enjoyment becomes dance (Chapter Three). It is to have fun in the world, and it is a roaming fun (Chapters Four and Five). Have fun among friends—and they come with no strings attached (Chapter Six). Roaming in fun throughout the future, one is on top of the world (Chapter Seven).

It is only fair to note that seriousness is not opposed to frolic, for both are two ways of being enthralled. Seriousness keeps frolic from going flippant, and frolic keeps seriousness ever free and unstuck. All in all, to freely roam in frolic and in playfulness is what things originally are and what we ought to be—that is, to be ourselves, in the fun of soaring and roaming.

4.   Need we repeat? The leisurely roaming under the useless Shu Tree is characterized by an innocent delight in the sunshine, a feeling of destiny that allows oneself to roam in adventure, the freedom of the big Bird and his altitude of exuberance. A free spirit warms the self in its cool flight, living no longer in the fetters of yes and no, love and hate, fluttering off aloft and seeing things beneath him, having nothing to do with those chatters of small birds who know nothing about themselves, and so can only be concerned superficially with things which have nothing to do with them. This big Bird has

renounced everything customarily revered, and renounced reverence itself. Indeed the roaming under the useless Tree *is* the soaring up in the forbidding heights. And how peacefully all things lie in the light of deep darkness, as seen from the robust air of vast chill and heights of deep valleys. There the big Bird joins the little ones. To such joining we shall now turn.

Chapter Two

CH'I
WU
LUN

*Things, Theories
—Sorting Themselves Out*

305 300 295

吾待蛇蚹蜩翼邪
惡識所以然惡識所以不然

昔者
莊周夢為胡蝶
栩栩然胡蝶也
自喻適志與
不知周也
俄然覺
則蘧蘧然周也
不知周之夢為胡蝶與
胡蝶之夢為周與
周與胡蝶則必有分矣
此之謂物化

290　　　　285　　　　280

化聲之相待若其不相待
和之以天倪因之以曼衍
所以窮年也
何謂和之以天倪
曰是不是然不然
是若果是也則是之異乎不是也亦無辯
然若果然也則然之異乎不然也亦無辯
忘年忘義
振於無竟
故寓諸無竟

VII

罔兩問景曰曩子行今子止曩子坐今子起
何其無特操與
景曰吾有待而然者邪吾所待又有待而然者邪

既使我與若辯矣

若勝我我不若勝邪

若果是也我果非也邪

我勝若若不吾勝

我果是也而果非也

其或是也其或非也邪

其俱是也其俱非也邪

我與若不能相知也則人固受其黮闇

吾誰使正之

使同乎若者正之既與若同矣惡能正之

使同乎我者正之既同乎我矣惡能正之

使異乎我與若者正之既異乎我與若矣惡能正之

使同乎我與若者正之既同乎我與若矣惡能正之

然則我與若與人俱不能相知也

而待彼也邪

255   250

夢飲酒者旦而哭泣
夢哭泣者旦而田獵
方其夢也不知其夢也
夢之中又占其夢焉
覺而後知其夢也
且有大覺而後知此其大夢也

VI

而愚者自以爲覺
竊竊然知之
君子牧乎
固哉

260

丘也與女皆夢也
予謂女夢亦夢也
是其言也其名爲弔詭
萬世之後而一遇大聖知其解者
是旦暮遇之也

245 240

長梧子曰

是黃帝之所聽熒也而丘也何足以知之

且女亦大早計

見卵而求時夜見彈而求鴞炙

子嘗為女妄言女以妄聽之奚

旁日月挾宇宙為其脗合置其滑涽

以隸相尊眾人役役聖人愚芚

參萬歲而一成純萬物盡然而以是相蘊

予惡乎知說生之非惑邪

予惡乎知惡死之非弱喪而不知歸者邪

麗之姬艾封人之子也晉國之始得之也涕泣沾襟

及其至於王所與王同筐牀食芻豢而後悔其泣也

予惡乎知夫死者不悔其始之蘄生乎

235   230   225

死生无變於己而況利害之端乎

乘雲氣騎日月而遊乎四海之外

若然者

疾雷破山風振海而不能驚

河漢沍而不能寒

大澤焚而不能熱

至人神矣

王倪曰

V

瞿鵲子問乎長梧子曰

吾聞諸夫子

聖人不從事於務

不就利不違害不喜求不緣道

无謂有謂有謂无謂而遊乎塵垢之外

夫子以爲孟浪之言而我以爲妙道之行也

吾子以爲奚若

且吾嘗試問乎女

民溼寢則腰疾偏死鰌然乎哉

木處則惴慄恂懼猨猴然乎哉

三者孰知正處

民食芻豢麋鹿食薦

蝍且甘帶鴟鴉耆鼠

四者孰知正味

猨猵狙以為雌麋與鹿交鰌與魚游

毛嬙麗姬人之所美也

魚見之深入鳥見之高飛麋鹿見之決驟

四者孰知天下之正色哉

自我觀之

仁義之端是非之塗

樊然殽亂

吾惡能知其辯

齧缺曰

子不知利害則至人固不知利害乎

若有能知此之謂天府

注焉而不滿酌焉而不竭而不知其所由來

此之謂葆光

故昔者堯問於舜曰

我欲伐宗膾胥敖南面而不釋然其故何也

舜曰

夫三子者猶存乎蓬艾之間若不釋然何哉

昔者十日並出萬物皆照而況德之進乎日者乎

齧缺問乎王倪曰

子知物之所同是乎

曰吾惡乎知之

子知子之所不知邪

曰吾惡乎知之

然則物無知邪

曰吾惡乎知之

雖然嘗試言之

庸詎知吾所謂知之非不知邪

庸詎知吾所謂不知之非知邪

有左有右有倫有義有分有辯 有競有爭

此之謂八德

六合之外聖人存而不論

六合之內聖人論而不議

春秋經世先王之志聖人議而不辯

故分也者有不分也辯也者有不辯也

曰何也

聖人懷之

衆人辯之以相示也

故曰辯也者有不見也

夫大道不稱 大辯不言 大仁不仁 大廉不嗛 大勇不忮

道昭而不道言辯而不及仁常而不成廉清而不信勇忮而不成

五者園而幾向方矣

故知止其所不知至矣

孰知不言之辯不道之道

160

165

170

有未始有無也者有未始有夫未始有無也者

俄而有無矣而未知有無之果孰有孰無也

今我則已有謂矣

而未知吾所謂之其果有謂乎其果無謂乎

天下莫大於秋豪之末而大山為小

莫壽乎殤子而彭祖為夭

天地與我並生而萬物與我為一

既已為一矣且得有言乎

既已謂之一矣且得無言乎

一與言為二二與一為三

自此以往巧歷不能得而況其凡乎

故自無適有以至於三而況自有適有乎

無適焉因是已

夫道未始有封言未始有常為是而有畛也

請言其畛

故以堅白之昧終而其子又以文之綸終

終身無成

若是而可謂成乎雖我亦成也

若是而不可謂成乎物與我無成也

是故滑疑之耀聖人之所圖也

為是不用而寓諸庸此之謂以明

IV

今且有言於此

不知其與是類乎其與是不類乎

類與不類相與為類則與彼無以異矣

雖然請嘗言之

有始也者

有未始有始也者有未始有夫未始有始也者有有也者

有無也者

140　　　　　　　135　　　　　　　130

彼非所明而明之

其好之也欲以明之

唯其好之也以異於彼

三子之知幾乎皆其盛者也故載之末年

昭文之鼓琴也師曠之枝策也惠子之據梧也

無成與虧故昭氏之不鼓琴也

有成與虧故昭氏之鼓琴也

果且有成與虧乎哉果且無成與虧乎哉

道之所以虧愛之所以成

是非之彰也道之所以虧也

其次以為有封焉而未始有是非也

其次以為有物矣而未始有封也

有以為未始有物者至矣盡矣不可以加矣

古之人其知有所至矣惡乎至

III

125 120

其分也成也其成也毀也
凡物無成與毀復通為一

唯達者知通為一

為是不用而寓諸庸
庸也者用也用也者通也通也者得也

適得而幾矣因是已
已而不知其然謂之道

勞神明為一而不知其同也謂之朝三

何謂朝三

曰狙公賦芧曰朝三而暮四衆狙皆怒曰然則朝四而暮三衆狙皆悅
名實未虧而喜怒為用亦因是也

是以聖人和之以是非而休乎天鈞 是之謂兩行

115 110 105

樞始得其環中以應無窮
是亦一無窮非亦一無窮也
故曰莫若以明
天地一指也萬物一馬也
以馬喻馬之非馬不若以非馬喻馬之非馬也
以指喻指之非指不若以非指喻指之非指也
可乎可不可乎不可
道行之而成物謂之而然
惡乎然然於然惡乎不然不然於不然
物固有所然物固有所可
無物不然無物不可
故為是舉莛與楹厲與西施恢恑憰怪
道通為一

100　　　　　　　95

道隱於小成言隱於榮華

故有儒墨之是非以是其所非而非其所是

欲是其所非而非其所是則莫若以明

物無非彼物無非是自彼則不見自知則知之

故曰彼出於是是亦因彼彼是方生之說也

雖然方生方死方死方生

方可方不可方不可方可

因是因非因非因是

是以聖人不由而照之于天亦因是也

是亦彼也彼亦是也

彼亦一是非此亦一是非

果且有彼是乎哉果且無彼是乎哉

彼是莫得其偶謂之道區

80

夫隨其成心而師之誰獨且無師乎

奚必知代而心自取者有之

愚者與有焉

未成乎心而有是非

是今日適越而昔至也是以無有為有

無有為有雖有神禹且不能知

吾獨且奈何哉

85

II

夫言非吹也言者有言

其所言者特未定也

果有言邪其未嘗有言邪

其以為異於鷇音

亦有辯乎其無辯乎

90

道惡乎隱而有真偽言惡乎隱而有是非

道惡乎往而不存言惡乎存而不可

65   60   55

已乎已乎

旦暮得此其所由以生乎

非彼無我非我無所取

是亦近矣而不知其所為使

若有真宰而特不得其朕

可行己信而不見其形

有情而無形

百骸九竅六藏賅而存焉

吾誰與為親

汝皆說之乎其有私焉

如是皆有為臣妾乎

其臣妾不足以相治乎

其遞相為君臣乎

其有真君存焉

如求得其情與不得

無益損乎其真

75   70

一受其成形不亡以待盡

與物相刃相靡

其行盡如馳而莫之能止不亦悲乎

終身役役而不見其成功

苶然疲役而不知其所歸可不哀邪

人謂之不死奚益

其形化其心與之然可不謂大哀乎

人之生也固若是芒乎

其我獨芒而人亦有不芒者乎

子綦曰
夫吹萬不同而使其自已也
咸其自取怒者其誰邪

大知閒閒小知間間
大言炎炎小言詹詹

其寐也魂交其覺也形開
與接為搆日以心鬪
縵者窖者密者

小恐惴惴大恐縵縵

其發若機栝其司是非之謂也
其留如詛盟其守勝之謂也
其殺如秋冬以言其日消也
其溺之所為之不可使復之也
其厭也如緘以言其老洫也
近死之心莫使復陽也

喜怒哀樂
慮嘆變慹
姚佚啟態
樂出虛
蒸成菌
日夜相代乎前而莫知其所萌

25 20 15

子游曰敢問其方
子綦曰
夫大塊噫氣其名為風
是唯无作作則萬竅怒呺
而獨不聞之翏翏乎

山林之畏佳大木百圍之竅穴
似鼻似口似耳
似枅似圈似臼
似洼者似污者

激者謞者叱者吸者
叫者譹者宎者咬者
前者唱于而隨者唱喁
泠風則小和飄風則大和

30

厲風濟則眾竅為虛
而獨不見之調調之刁刁乎
子游曰
地籟則眾竅是已
人籟則比竹是已
敢問天籟

莊子內篇齊物論第二

I

南郭子綦
隱几而坐仰天而嘘
嗒焉似喪其耦

顏成子游立侍乎前曰
何居乎
形固可使如槁木而心固可使如死灰乎
今之隱几者非昔之隱几者也

子綦曰
偃不亦善乎而問之也
今者吾喪我汝知之乎
女聞人籟而未聞地籟
女聞地籟而未聞天籟夫

TRANSLATION WITH GLOSSES

I

1 **Tzu Ch'i** of **South Wall***
Reclined* on his **armrest and sat;** he **looked-up-to heaven and**
    sighed-deeply,*
So **loosened-up, seeming** to have **lost his counterpart.***

Yen Ch'eng Tzu Yu, standing in-attendance before him, **said,**
5 **"Why is-this?***
One **can** indeed **let the figure** become **inherently as dry wood;**
    and yet **can** one **let the heart-mind** become
    inherently as dead ashes?*
He of now who reclines on his **armrest is-not**
    he of earlier who reclined on his **armrest."***

Tzu Ch'i said,
"Yen, is it **not rather* good that***
    even **you*** asked about **it!**
10 **For-the-moment now I*** have **lost me-myself,***
    do you understand it?
Do **you hear men's piping, and** are **yet** to **hear earth's**
    piping;
Do **you hear earth's piping, and** are **yet** to **hear heaven's**
    piping?"

Tzu Yu said, "I venture-to ask-about their secret ways."
Tzu Ch'i said,
15 **"Well,** the **Huge Clod*** belches out **breath;**
    its **name** is **called wind.**
This is well if **only there-is-no starting-up;** once it **starts-up,**
    then **myriads** of **hollows rage-up*** howling.
Do **you alone not hear them roaring, roaring?***

The **winding recesses of mountains, forests; hundreds** of
    spans of **huge trees, their hollows** and **openings**—they
Seem noses, seem mouths, seem ears;
20   **Seem sockets, seem bowls, seem mortars;**
There are **those-which seem pools, those-which seem puddles;**
Those-which shout-like-waves, those-which whistle-like-
    arrows, those-which screech, those-which suck;
Those-which yell, those-which wail, those-which moan,
    those-which scream.*
Those-which are **before sing 'yu——,'** and **those-which**
    follow sing 'yung——.'*
25   **Breezy wind, then a small harmony** of chorus; **whirling wind,**
    then a **huge harmony** of chorus.

Fierce wind relieved, then multitudes of hollows are **made**
    empty.
Do **you alone not see them waver, wavering, quiver,**
    quavering?"*
Tzu Yu said,
"Earth pipings—these, then, are **multitudes of hollows only.**
30   **Men's pipings—these, then,** are **rows of bamboo** tubes **only.**
I **venture-to ask-about heavenly pipings."**

Tzu Ch'i said,
"Well, he-who* blows-on myriads not in the **same*** way,
    and lets them be **themselves,*** that is, letting
    all of **them pick** themselves—
He-who rages-up, who is he?"

35   **Huge understanding widens, wide**ns;
    small understanding is **picky, picky.**
Huge words burn,* burn; small words chat, chat.

Those-who* sleep—their **souls crisscross;**
    those-who* are **awake**—their **figures open,**
With outside **contacts** to **make alliance;**
    daily, with mind-heart to **fight.**

Those-which-are vast, those-which-are sly, those-which-are
        subtle*—
40   Now they are in **small fears—jumpy, jumpy**; now they are in
        huge fears—devastating, devastating.*

They* **"issue like springed arrows"**—this is what people **call**
        "arbitrating between *this-yes* and *no"*;
They **"stay as** if they were under **sworn oaths"**—this is what
        people **call defending** what they **win;**
They **"fade like autumn** and **winter,"**
        with these **words** they say, **they** now **daily dwindle;**
They **drown in what** they **make;** they **can not let** themselves
        restore themselves;
45   **"Those-which*** are **clogged** are **as if sealed,"***
        with these **words** they say, **they are old, stagnant;**
Their **hearts-minds of** being **near death—none** can
        let them **restore** their **daylight** vigor.

Now **delighted**, now **angry;** now **lamenting,** now **glad;**
Now **anxious,** now **sighing;** now **fickle,** now **obstinate;**
Now **modest,** now **willful;** now **insolent,** now **fawning*** —
50   As if **music coming-out-of empty** holes;
Vapor forming mushrooms.
Day and **night** they **mutually alternate with** what goes
        before and none understands where he sprouts from.

Can we know **only** these? **Only** these?
Can we, **dawn** or **dusk,*** but for a moment **obtain this,**
        that with which, all these were **born from?**
55   "If there **is-no 'that, 'there-is-no** identifiable **I-myself;**
        if there **is no I-myself, there-is-nothing whereby** to
        pick."
This is rather* near the matter, **and** yet we do
        not understand that whereby they are **made, let be.***
It seems **like there-is** a true **commander, and** yet we
        especially do **not obtain its clues.**
We can walk it, **trusting ourselves,*** and yet
        we do **not see its figure.**
There-is manifest **reality and** yet **there-is-no figure.**

60   (Let us quest for the Commander in my self. Let me ask you:)
         A **hundred bones, nine hollows, six organs—**
         all are **complete and present* in-me.**
      With whom do **I** the subject **make family** ties?
      Are **you pleased** with **them all? Then*** your liking them
         implies that **you may*** have **favorites among-them.**
      In such a situation **as this,** do **all** that **there-are**
         make your favorite **servants, maids?**
      Then perhaps they have **nothing adequate with** which
         mutually to **govern**; or
65   **Then** perhaps **they take-turns mutually making rulers,**
         servants; but
      Then, there-is, perhaps the **presence** of a **true**
         ruler among-them.
      As it is, **seeking** and **obtaining its rea**lity
         with not obtaining it, give
      No benefit or **loss to its truth.**

      Once men **receive their formed figures,** they would **not**
         forget them, **with*** which to **await** their **exhaustion.**
70   **With things** they now **mutually fight,**
         now **mutually follow-along;***
      Their walks exhaust as gallops, and none is **able-to**
         stop them—is it **not rather sad?**
      To the **finish** of their **bodily-lives*** they **slave, slave,***
         and do **not see their formed merits,**
      They **so extremely tire, slave** themselves,
         and do **not understand where they** should **go-home—**
         can we **not lament** them?
      Even if **men call** them **"not dead,"** why does it **benefit***
         anything?
75   **Their figures change; their hearts-minds with them** do **so—**
         can we **not call** them **hugely lamentable?**

      Lives of men—are they **inherently muddled like this?**
      How-could* I-myself (being one among men) be **alone muddled**
         and among **men there-exist also those-who** are **not**
         muddled?

Well,* if men were to **follow their** pre-**formed minds-hearts***
    and take **them** as their **teachers,**
      then for **whom alone, indeed, there-exist-no teachers?**
Why must there-be they [teachers] only for **those-who**
    understand the world's **alternations and** let their
      hearts-minds pick (of) them **selves?**
80   Even **those-who** are **foolish—there-exist**
      such teachers (**with** ours) **among them.**

(On the other hand,) if being not-**yet formed in heart-mind**
    and already **there-is** *this*-yes against *no**—
This is to **go-to Yueh today and arrive-there earlier,**
    yesterday. **This is** to **take no existence as* existence.**
If you **take no existence** as **existence, although**
    a **spirit**-filled **Yü*** were to **exist** here and now,
      he would **not, indeed,** be **able-to understand** you,
Let **alone*** I myself; **what, indeed,** can I do?!

II

85   Well, they say, "**Words are-not that-which* blows** wind;
    in the **one-who** has **words, there-exists** something
      expressed in the **words.**" But
What he used **words** for **is especially** not **yet determined.***
Is-there in-fact anything expressed in **words?**
    Or is-there anything **yet** to **try** being put in **words?**
Or shall we **take** it **as "different from twittering sounds**
    of baby birds"—then
Is-there also a **distinction? Or is-there-no distinction?**

90   (The Confucians and Mohists may say,) "**How-could Tao** be **hid,**
    and then **there-exist** *true-false* distinctions;
      how-could words be **hid, and** then **there-exist**
      (these-)yes-no distinctions?*
How-could Tao go-on to any place **and not be-present?***
    How-could words be-present and can not be acceptable?"

Tao is **hid by small formings;**
    words are **hid by glory** and **splendor.**

And-so* there-exist *(these-)yes-no* distinctions
   of the **Confucians** and the **Mohists.**
   With these distinctions
   they **"yes"** their "others" 's* *no*
   and **"no" their** "others" 's *yes.*
If we **desire** to **"yes"** *their** no's and **"no"** *their* yes's,
   then there is **none like** judging things **with** the
   standard of the illumination of **clarity.**

95   (For as Hui Shih the sophist would say:) "**There-exist-no
   things** which are-**not** the *that*; **there-exist-no
   things** which are-**not** the *this(-yes).*"
   Yet seen **from** *that*, even *this* is **not seen** (as *yes*);
   if we **understand** a thing in terms of **itself,*** **then** we
   understand it (as *yes*).
And so (Hui Shih) **says,** *"That* **comes-out of** *this*(-yes);
   this(-*yes*) **also follows-on*** *that.*" This
   that-this relation is treated by the **theory of
   co*-birthings.**

Although this is **so,** it is true that **as births,
   so deaths, as deaths, so births;**
   As *can*,* **so** *can not*, as *can not*, **so** *can*; and
   As following-on *(this-)yes*, **so following-on** *no*;
      as following-on *no*, **so following-on** (this-)*yes.*
   (But all this is so confusingly indeterminate.)
100   **With this** reason, the **holy man** goes **not by** this route of
   co-birthings, **and illuminates them all from
   heaven.** This is **also*** "**following-on** the grand *(this-)
   yes* of all."

(And then we can see that) *this*(-*yes*) **is also** *that, that*
      is **also** *this*(-*yes*);
That is **also** one *yes*-and-*no*, *this*(-*yes*) **is also**
      one *yes*-and-*no.*
Indeed, are-there in-fact *that* and *this*? **Indeed, are-there not
   in-fact** *that* and *this*?
Where **none of** *that* or *this* **obtains its
   counterpart***—people **call** it the **Tao Pivot.***

105   Then the **Pivot begins** to **obtain its middle** point
        of the **circle**, and*-**with** it, it **responds**
        till **there-is-no end.***
This(-*yes*) is **also one** "**there-is-no end**";
    no is **also one** "**there-is-no end.**'
And-so I **said,** "There is **none like** judging things
    with the standard of the illumination of **clarity.**"*

(As for Kung Sun Lung, another sophist, let me say this:)
    With a **pointer** to **show** a **pointer's not-being** a **pointer,**
    is not like* **with** the **no-pointer** to **show** a
    pointer's not-being a **pointer;** similarly,
With a **horse** to **show** a **horse's not-being** a **horse,**
    is not like with a **no-horse** to **show** a **horse's**
    not-being a **horse.***
110   (Stretched far enough, such thinking would show that after
        all the) "**Heaven** and **earth are one pointer;**
        myriads of **things are one horse.**"

Things **can** be acceptable **by** our saying that
    they " **can**" be acceptable;
    they **can not** be acceptable **by** our saying that
    they " **can not**" be acceptable.
The **tao** of things, we **walk it** and it is **formed; things** we
    call them so **and** they are **so.**
Why are they **so?** They are **so by** being called "so";
    why are they **not so?** They are **not so by** being called
    "not so."
But **there-exists** in everything **what** is **inherently*** **so;**
    there-exists in everything **what can inherently** be
    acceptable.
115   **There-are-no things** that are **not so; there-are-no things**
        that **can not** be acceptable.

And-so, for this reason,* **take-for-example, stalks with**
    pillars, lepers with Hsi Shih (the famed beauty), the
    grotesque, the strange*—
Tao goes-through them all, **making*** them **one.**
Their division is* really their **formation;**
    their formation is really their **breakdown.**

Commonly, in **things there-exists-no formation with**[=or]
breakdown; they are **again gone-through, made one.**

120   **Only he-who** has **attained understands** going-through
and **making** them **one.**
For this reason he does **not use** things (according to his
pre-formed opinion) **and lodges them-in*** the **ordinary.**
What is ordinary is after all what is truly **used;**
     what is used is what is **gone-through;**
     what is gone-through is what is truly **obtained.**
Going everywhere, **obtaining, and being completely** in Tao
     —this is **only** to "**follow-on** the *this-yes* of all";
This **only and not understanding its** being so—
     we **call it Tao.**

125   In contrast, **laboring** the **clarifying spirits** to **make** them
     one, and not understanding their already being the
     same—we **call** it "**morning, three.**"
What is called "morning, three"?
Mr. Monkey-Keeper, **giving-out** chestnuts, said, "**Morning,
three and evening, four**, all right?" The **multitudes**
of **monkeys** were **all angry.** He said, "**If so, then,
morning, four and evening, three.**" The **multitudes** of
monkeys were **all pleased.**
In either situation, whether in **name** or in **actuality,**
     there is **yet** to be any **waning, and anger, delight**
     were **made use** of (to accomplish the keeper's intention).
This **is also** an example of "**following-on**
     the *yes-this* of things."
With this* reason, the **holy man harmonizes them with**
     (*this-*)*yes* and *no* of things,
     and rests in the **heavenly balance.***
     This it is which is **called*** "**double walk.**"*

III

130   **Men of old—there-existed-in their understanding what**
has **arrived** at the ultimate. **How-could** they have
arrived there?

There-existed those-who took things as
    yet to **begin** to **exist.**
Such **ultimate!** Such **exhaustive** understanding!
It **can not** have anything **with** which to **add** to!
Next understanding to **theirs took** things as **exist**ing;
    and borders are yet to begin existing among them.
Next to **theirs took borders among-them** as **exist**ing;
    and the (*this-*)*yes-no* distinction
    is yet to **begin existing.**

That-which is a **manifestation of**
    (*this-*)*yes-no* distinction, **is**
    that **with** which **waning of** the **Tao is** produced;
135   **That with** which **waning of** the **Tao** occurs, **is**
    that **with** which **forming of love** happens.
Yet **indeed, is-there in-fact forming with waning?**
    In-fact, indeed, is-there-no forming with waning?

There-exists forming with waning,
    hence* the **lute-playing of Mr. Chao** the musician;
There exists **no forming with** [=or] **waning,**
    hence* the **lute-not-playing of Mr. Chao.**
The **lute-playing of Chao Wen,** the **rhythm-hitting of**
    Teacher K'ung (another musician), the **dryandra*-leaning**
    and arguing **of Hui Shih** the sophist—
140   Are these **three masters' understandings complete?*** **All of**
    them **are those whose** careers **prospered.**
    And-so they were **recorded** for **later years.**
Only with what they were-given-to
    they **distinguished** themselves **from others.**
With what they were-given-to they **desired** to **clarify them**
    (what they were given to, their professional expertise).
These **were-not what others** needed to be **clarified and**
    they still insisted on **clarifying them.**
And-so (Hui Shih) **finished** his life
    with the **obscurities of "hardness, whiteness,"**
    and his [Wen's] **children again finished** their lives
    with the **lute-strings of Wen** their father.

145   They **finished** their **bodily-lives;**
             there-were-no accomplishments **formed.**
             Are men **like these** famous, **and can** be **called**
                "well-**formed"?** Then, **although** commoners,
                we are also well-**formed.**
             Are men **like these** famous, **and can** not be **called**
                "well-**formed"?** Then **things** together **with us**
                are not well-formed.
             For **this reason the brilliance of dim submergence is**
                what the **holy man heads-for.***
             For this reason he does **not use** things (according to his
                pre-formed opinion) **and lodges them-in** the **ordinary.**
                This it is which is **called** judging things
                "**With** the illumination of **clarity.**"

IV

150   **Now there-are indeed words about**
                something like **this** preceding.
             I do **not understand**—are **they of-a-kind**
                with the "**this-yes"?** Or
                are **they not of-a-kind with** the "**this-yes"?**
             But once "**of-a-kind" with "not of-a-kind" mutually**
                make a new "**kind" with** each other, **then**
                there-is-nothing with which to **differ with "that."**

             Although it is **so,** I **request** to **try** to have a **word**
                about **it.**
             There-exists what begins. (This requires that)
155   **There-exists what** is **yet** to **begin*** "**there-existing** what
                begins." (This in turn requires that) **there-exists**
                what is **yet** to **begin** "**there-existing** what is **yet**
                to **begin** 'there-existing what **begins'.**" (In short,)
                there-exists what exists, (which implies that)
             There-exists what exists-not. (This again requires that)
             There-exists what is **yet** to **begin** "**there-existing what**
                exists-not." (This in turn requires that) **there-exists**
                what is **yet** to **begin** "**there-existing** what is **yet**
                to **begin** 'there-existing what **exists-not.**"

All of a **sudden, and**—there-**exists** what **exists-not.** *

    And I do not **yet understand**—

    which is in-fact what "**exists**,"

    which is what "**exists-not**,"

    or "**there-exists** what **exists-not.**"

Now, then, there-exist already* in **me-myself** words

    with which I **call** something,

160   **And** I am **yet** to **understand what I call**—is

    it in-fact a **calling** of what **exists?** Is

    it in-fact a **calling** of what **exists-not?***

(The sophist says,) "**None under heaven** is more **huge**

    than the **tip of autumn feather**," and "The **huge mountain**

    is **called*** 'small'";

"**None** is more **long-lived than** the **child died-young**,"

    and "Our **Forefather P'ung** (the longest lived of

    men) is **called** he-who has '**died** too **young**'";

"**Heaven, earth, with I-myself** are born **at-the-same-time**,"

    and "**Myriads of things with I-myself make one.**"

Now-that they have **already*** been "**made one**,"

    does the **word** still, **indeed, obtain** its **existence?**

165   **Now-that** I have **already called it "one"**, does the **word**

    still, **indeed, obtain** its **no-existence?**

The **one** with the **word make two;**

    two with the "**one**" **make three.**

Starting **from this, with** which to **go-on,** even a **skillful**

    calculator is **not able-to obtain** the answer—**and how-much**

    less can **those common** people!

And-so, with going from no-existence to **existence**

    we **arrived-at three; and how-much** more would we arrive

    at if we were to **go from existence** to **existence!**

There-should-exist-no going among-them.

    Only* follow-on the "**this-yes**" of all.

170   Well, in **Tao** (mounds taken as) **borders** are **yet** to

    begin to **exist**; in **words, normal**cy is **yet** to

    begin to **exist. For this** reason, we say things

    and boundaries come to **exist** (like raised paths

    between fields).*

I **request** to have a **word** about **their boundaries.**
Lowly "**left**" exists; honorable "**right**" exists.
   Social **classes** exist; **right** manners exist.
   Divisions exist; distinctions-disputations exist.
   Wranglings exist; contentions exist.
These it is which men **call** the "**Eight Virtues.**"
What is **outside of** the **Six Cosmic Correlates,*** the
   holy man lets be **present and** does **not sort.**
175   What is **inside of** the **Six Cosmic Correlates,** the
   holy man sorts and does **not argue** about what is right.
As for the **records of managing** the **generations** of people of
   the **former emperors** during many **springs and autumns,***
   the **holy man argues** about what is right
   and does **not distinguish-dispute.***

And-so, among **those-who divide,**
   there-exist (as their basis) things **not divided.**
   Among **those-who distinguish-dispute,**
   there-exist (as their basis) things
   not distinguished-disputed.
You **say, "What** does it mean?" I say,
"The **holy man embraces them** all without discrimination.
180   But **multitudes of men distinguish-dispute** them; **with** their
   distinguishing-disputes they **mutually display** themselves.
And-so I said, 'For those-who distinguish-dispute
   there-exists something they do **not see.'**

Well, Huge Tao does **not declare** itself as such;
   Huge Dispute does **not say a word;**
   Huge Benevolence is **not benevolent;**
   Huge Courage does **not hurt.**
Tao shown-forth, and it is **not Tao.**
   Words disputed, and they do **not reach.**
   Benevolence made a **norm, and** it is **not comprehensive.***
   Modesty made **fastidious, and** it is **not trustworthy.**
   Courage employed to **hurt, and** it is **not well-formed.**
The **Five Items** are **round but almost tend** toward developing
   sharp-edges.*

185   And-so, understanding stops at what it does not
        understand—this is to **arrive**-at-the-ultimate.
What is it that **understands disputes of not** having a **word?**
        Tao of not Taoing?
If **there-exists** something **like an ability**
        to **understand** these—
        this it is which men **call** the **Heavenly Treasury.**
Pour into-it and it is **not full; bale out-of-it**
        and it is **not drained**—
        and we do **not know that-by which it comes.**
This it is which men **call** the **Shaded Light.***

190   And-so, in **what** were **earlier** times,
        Emperor **Yao asked of** his subject **Shun, saying,**
        "**I-myself desire** to **attack** tiny tribes, **Tsung, K'uai, Hsü-ao.**
        Yet, **facing South** on the throne, I am **so** uneasy
        that I can **not** let-myself-go; **what is its why-so?**''
Shun said,
"**Well, those** so-called '**Three Masters**' are **as-if** maintaining
        their **presences** in the **midst of mugwort underbrush.**
Yet **you-sir** can **not so let**-yourself-go;
        what is the reason?
        In **what** were **earlier** times,
        ten suns came-out at-the-same-time
        and **myriads** of **things** were **all shone-bright.**
        And how-much more so with
        him-whose virtue is-beyond suns!''*

195   Mr. **Chew Chipped*** asked of Mr. **Royal Horizon, saying,**
        "Do **you-sir understand** that **of which things** have the **same**
        positive approval of '**yes**'?"
He **said, "How** would **I*** understand it?"
"Do **you-sir understand what you-sir** do **not understand?**"
He **said, "How** would **I understand it?**"
200   "If **so, then,** in **things is-there-no understanding?**"
He **said, "How** would **I understand it?**

    Although it is **so,** let me **try experimenting**
        on having a **word** about **it.**

How-can I understand that what I call understanding is-not
    not-understanding?
How-can I understand that what I call not-understanding is
    understanding?

205   Besides, I will try experimenting on asking of you.
If people sleep in moist places, then they will develop
    loin pain, die paralyzed. Are the eels so?
If people dwell in trees then they will be trembling,
    goose-fleshed, pulling-back, frightened.
    Are the monkeys so?
But then, of these three parties, who is it that understands
    the correct dwelling place?
People eat vegetables, meat*; deer eat tender-grass;
210   Centipedes relish snakes; owls, crows, savor mice.
Of these four parties, who is it that understands
    the correct taste?
Gibbons are taken by baboons as mates;
    bucks with does accompany; eels with fish roam.
Mao Ch'iang, Lady Li, were what people admire as beauties.
Fish, seeing them, plunged deep; birds, seeing them, flew
    high; bucks with does, seeing them, leapt, ran.
215   Of these four parties, who is it that understands
    the correct beauty under heaven?

From my point of view about them,
The buddings* of benevolence, rightness; the paths of
    'this-yes,' 'no'—they are all
So tangled-up, confused.
How am I able-to understand their distinctions-disputes on
    what counts as correct?"*
220   Mr. Chew Chipped said,
"If you-sir do not understand benefit, harm,
    then does the ultimately-arrived man
    inherently not understand benefit, harm?"
Mr. Royal Horizon said,
"The ultimately-arrived man is spirit-filled.
The huge marshland brush blazes,
    and is not able-to sear him;

225　The Yellow **River** and the **Han** River **freeze,**
　　　　and are **not able-to chill** him;
　　The **swift thunder**bolt **splits mountains,** the **wind shakes**
　　　　the **seas, and** are **not able-to startle** him.
　　He-who is **like so**
　　Chariots-on cloud breath energies, **rides the sun** and **moon,**
　　　　and roams out of the **Four Seas.***
　　Death or **life, there-exists-no difference to** himself;
　　　　how-much less with the **buds of benefit, harm?"**

V

230　**Mr. Jittery Magpie asked of Mr. Tall* Dryandra-Tree,**
　　　　saying,
　　"I heard this-from the Master*—
　　'The **holy man** does **not pursue the business of**
　　　　worldly **duties—**
　　He does **not go-to benefit,** does **not defy harm,** does **not**
　　　　delight in seeking, does **not go-along-with Tao;**
　　When **there-is-no calling** of something, **there-is calling;**
　　　　when **there-is calling** of something, **there-is-no**
　　　　calling*— and he **roams out of** the **dust, grime.'**
235　The **master took** it **to be words of vague romanticism,***
　　　　and I* took* it **to be the walking of mysterious Tao.**
　　How-about my dear **sir, what** do you **take** it to be **like?"**

　　Mr. Tall Dryandra Tree said,
　　"This is **what** even the **Yellow Emperor,**
　　　　on **listening** to it, would have been **puzzled** about;
　　　　and with what would **Ch'iu*** be **adequate**
　　　　to understand it?
　　Besides, you also calculate with **huge dispatch—**
240　You **see** an **egg, and** at once **seek** a rooster announcing
　　　　the **endtime of the night;** you **see** a crossbow
　　　　pellet, and at once **seek** a **dove roasted.**

　　I-for-one will **try to make you** some **abandoned words** about it;
　　　　how-about you with abandon* listen to it?

Now, these are the words: Standing **beside** the **sun, moon;**
> **clasping-under-arms space, time;**
> **making them fit, unite** together;
> **putting their dim confusion** in place;
> **with** the title of **serfs, mutually honoring*** —although
Multitudes of **men slave, slave,***
> the **holy man, a stupid sluggard, participates** in
> **myriads of ages and forms one lump*** —
He lets **myriads** of **things** become **so,**
> as they are, **exhaust**ingly,
> **and with this** growth lets them **mutually enfold.***

245 How-could I-for-one understand being pleased-with
> death's not-being a delusion?
How-could I-for-one understand hating-death's
> being-not like him-who is young, exiled,
> and does not understand going-home?
Li her Ladyship was child of the border-man of Ai.*
> In the beginning when the state of Chin obtained her,
> she wept, her tears drenching the collar of her robe,
Until reaching the time when
> she arrived at the king's place, with the king
> she had the same square bed, ate hay-grain-fed cattle—
> and afterwards regretted her weeping.
How-could I-for-one understand those-who are dead not
> regretting their longings-for life of their beginning few
> days?

VI

250 Those-who dream of drinking wine—come* morning, and
> they wail, weep;
Those-who dream of wailing, weeping—come morning, and
> they field hunt.*
While* in their dreams, they do not understand
> their being in a dream;
In the middle of their dreams they again interpret
> their dreams in-them.
Awakened—and only afterwards to they understand their
> having been in a dream.

255   **There-is*** indeed a **Huge Awaken**ing—and **afterwards**
         they would **understand** all **this** to be **their huge dreams.**

     And yet **those-who** are **fools take** themselves to be **awake.**
     So saucy, saucy,* thinking that they **understand them**selves—
     Now, presuming to be '**ruler,' now,** '**herdsman.'**
     How inherently **incorrigible!**

260   **Ch'iu with you—both are dreams.**
     I-for-one call you 'dream'—I am also dream.
     This is its saying—its name men **call 'Ultimate Ruse.'***
     After myriads of generations, and then for **once** we may
         meet him-who is a **Great Holy** man and **understands**
         the **undoing of its** mysteries—yet
     This is paradoxically to **meet him** at any **dawn,**
         any **dusk.***

265   (In the meantime) **now-that let* me-myself**
         with you dispute-distinguish.
     If **you win** over **me-myself,**
         then **I-myself** do **not win** over **you**(—they say).
     But **are you in-fact** on the '**yes'-side?**
         Am I-myself in-fact on the '**no'-side?**
     If **I-myself win** over **you,**
         then **you** do **not win** over **me-myself**(—they say).
     But **am I-myself in-fact on the 'yes'**-side?
         Are you in-fact on the '**no'-side?**
270   **Or* is one-of-us** on the '**yes'-side?**
         Or is one-of-us on the '**no'-side?**
     Or are both of us on the '**yes'-side?**
         Or are both of us on the '**no'-side?**
     If even **I-myself with you** are **not able-to mutually**
         understand, then other **people** will of course
         inherently receive our darkness.

     Whom should **we let correct them** (our disputes)?
     '**Let him-who** shares the **same** opinion with **you correct**
         them'—but **now-that** he already shares **with you** the
         same opinion, **how** would he be **able-to correct them?**

275   'Let him-who shares the **same** opinion with **me-myself correct
               them**'—but **now-that** he is already the **same as I-myself,
               how** would he be **able-to correct them?**
       'Let him-who differs from me-myself with you correct
               them**'—but **now-that** he already **differs from me-myself
               with you, how** would he be **able-to correct them?**
       'Let him-who is the same as I-myself with you
               correct them**'—but **now-that** he is already the **same
               as I-myself with you, how** would he be **able-to correct
               them?**
       If **so, then, I-myself with you with** other **man—
               all*** of us are **not able-to mutually understand.**
       And yet do we still **depend**-on '**that** man' who '**understands**'?

VII

280   (Thus) the **mutual depending of** those **changing 'sounds'*** is
               like their not mutual depending at all; (rather,)
       Harmonizing them with heavenly equality,* following-on them
               with** their own **flows** which **spread-far-and-wide—
       This **is that with** which to live to the **end** of our **years** of
               life.
       What is **called 'harmonizing them with heavenly equality'?
       We say:** (Affirm as) '**yes**' the '**not yes**';
               (allow as) '**so**' the '**not so.**'
285   **If*** the '**yes**' is **in-fact** the **yes, then there-is-no
               distinction-dispute, also, over** the **difference of
               the'yes'** from the '**not yes**';
       If* the '**so**' is **in-fact** the **so, then there-is-no
               distinction-dispute, also, over** the **difference of
               the** '**so**' **from** the '**not so.**' (In short,)
       Forget years; forget the '**right**' (and the '**wrong**');
       Roam-and-stop* at where **there-is-no boundary.
       And-so lodge them-in** the '**there-is-no boundary.**'

290   Mr. **Double Nothing*** asks Mr. Shadow, saying,
               '**A-while-ago you-sir** walked; now **you-sir stop.
               A-while-ago you-sir** sat; now **you-sir rise.
       Why is-there-nothing** specially **you** to **behave*** as yourself?'

Mr. **Shadow** says, 'Am **I*** he-for-**whom there-is** something to
    depend on **and** then become **so** (as I am)?
    Is **what I depend-on, again, that-for-which there-is**
    something to **depend** on, **and** then becomes **so** (as it is)?
Do **I depend** on something as the **snake** does on his **skin,**
    as the **cicada** does on his **wings?**
How-would I **know that with** which it is **so?**
    How-would I **know that with** which it is **not so?**'

295   In **what** were **earlier*** times,
    Chuang Chou* **dreamed, making** a **butterfly.**
    So flitted, flitted, he **was** a **butterfly.**
    Indeed, he **showed*** what he him**self** was, **going** as he
        pleasantly **intended!**
    He did **not understand Chou.**
300   **So sudden**ly, he **awoke.**
    Then—so **thorough**ly, **thorough**ly, it **was Chou.**

    (But then he did) **not understand**—
    did the **dream of Chou make** the **butterfly?**
    Did the **dream of** the **butterfly make Chou?**

    Chou with the butterfly—
    there **must-be, then,** a **division.***
305   **This it** is which men **call 'things changing'.**"*

Glosses

Title: **_Ch'i Wu Lun_:** Two points of contention have traditionally been tossed about on this title, which is proverbially difficult to interpret: (*a*) whether this chapter is a *lun* ("theory," "discourse," "discussion") about *ch'i wu* ("unity," "equality," "parity," "arrangement," among things), or a *ch'i-ing* of *wu-lun* ("theories of things"), or a *ch'i-ing* of things (*wu*) and theories (*lun*), and (*b*) what *ch'i* means, whether "arguing for the natural parities of things," or "letting (recognizing) things sort themselves out into their natural parities."

As is noted in my Meditations, to argue for any *one* of these positions is not to let things sort themselves out into their natural parities. As Graham noted, this chapter proposes a "synthesising vision," and that, I may add, with touch light as a dragonfly's tail occasionally kissing the water as it flies over a pond. Such playful soaring and roaming among theories and things welcomes every position without committing to any.

Line 1: Since the center of the city is occupied by upper class people, the South Wall is a plebeian district, if not a ghetto.

Ch'i is *chi*, "the base." Therefore the name may imply Mr. Basis among the commons.

Line 2:

Yin ("reclined"): Every commentator I know of says that *yin* is "to lean on" something. I would not be surprised, however, if Chuang Tzu has another common meaning in mind, "to hide," as in lines 90, 93 (though even there some commentators [Chang Ping-lin, Fukunaga] might prefer "lean on.")

If the meaning "to hide" is adopted, Mr. Tzu-ch'i would be hiding in the armrest as he leans on it, becoming well-nigh indistinguishable from it. This interpretation will not only fit with the close interrelationships among three pipings that immediately follow this episode; it will also fit with the end of the chapter, where there is the close interrelationship between a snake and its skin, between a cicada and its wings, and between Chuang Chou and his dreamed butterfly. All of these without exception point to an integration among things and theories, sorting themselves out into mutual parities, that is, a *Ch'i Wu Lun*.

Hsü ("sigh deeply") is gentle breathing that contributes to becoming empty (*hsü*) to hear and overhear three pipings. Mr. Tzu-ch'i breathes out his objectifiable self (*wo*) so as to emptily accommodate all things alike. *He* becomes here a pipe, emptily chorusing with other sounds. Cf. "empty chamber" in 4/28–32.

Line 3:

Ou ("counterpart"): Although Yü Yüeh said it sounds and means *yü* ("lodge"), and Wang Shu-min still insists on *ou* ("ploughing"), most commentators prefer *ou*, meaning "associates," "wife," or "body" (as in line 6), as Watson said.

I would prefer to take *ou* as the self's counterpart that is recognizable, identifiable, and objectifiable as "self" (in one's self-consciousness), or recognizable (by others) as an identity or even an object (a name for instance, such as Chuang Chou, line 296). On this interpretation *ou* (as *ou*) is a *wo*-self distinct from the *wu*-self. This interpretation fits line 10; see gloss there. Cf. also line 104.

Or else, *ou* can mean *yü* ("lodge," "habitat") or *chi* ("temporary lodge"; Yü Yüeh). Then, again, it signifies interdependent interchange and flipflopping of subjects, such as in the dream story which ends this chapter.

The first interpretation perhaps explains *yu fen* ("distinction"), and the second, *wu hua* ("interchange") in lines 304–305.

Lines 5:

Ho chü hu ("why is this?"): *Chü* could mean (1) *ku* ("reason"; Ssu-ma Piao)—"Why is this?" or (2) *ho* ("what," emphatic; most commentators)—"What is this?" or "What is the matter?" (Wang Yin-chih says [p. 121] that *chü* is just a marker for emphasis.)

Line 6: Wing-tsit Chang and Akatzuka see a special emphasis in *erh,* assigning different meanings to two occurrences of *ku*; "The body *may* be allowed to be like dry wood *but* should the mind be allowed to be like dead ashes?"

Line 9:

Erh is "you" (Huang Chin-hung, Akatzuka).

Pu i: is "not rather", emphatic; as in line 71, and Ch. One, lines 34, 71, 74.

Yeh may well be *che* ("that," "that-which," "one-who"; Wang Yin-chih, p. 97) as in line 101.

Line 10:

Chin che ("for the moment now") is literally "these-(moments)-which are now." I suspect this phrase also echoes *chin ... che* on the previous line.

Wo ("I") quite consistently means objectifiable self—except for line 268, where Kuan Feng, Lu Shu-chih, and Lin Yün-ming have *wo* as it should read, but Kuo Hsiang has *wu*, which is (unfortunately) followed by Hsüan Ying, Ch'en Shou-ch'ang, Wang Hsien-ch'ien, Wang Fu-chih, ts'ao Ch'u-chi, and Lu T'ieh-ch'eng. Happily, Nishida Chozaemon and Sakai Kanzo have *wo*; Sakai claims to have it from *Su-pu Ch'ung-k'an*. See Notes to the Meditations, Ch. Two, note 28.

Line 15:

Ta k'uai ("huge clod") is either the earth (Yü Yüeh) or between heaven and earth (Lin Hsi-i, Ch'u Po-hsiu, Chu Kuei-yao).

Line 16:

Nu ("rages [up]") is the same as P'ung's mode of flight (Ch. One, line 3). This may explain and reconcile the preceding interpretations of *ta k'uai*, which may well be either a demythologized P'ung or the Northern Darkness that bred and facilitated the change of K'un into P'ung. Silence is followed by noises.

Line 17: The sentence parallels line 27, where vision is stressed (in silence).

Line 23: Two points may be noted: (1) Rapid parallelisms convey busy commotions. Ch'en Shou-ch'ang (among Chiao Hung, Hsüan Ying, Wang An-shih) was quite excited about it. (2) Ch'en pointed out rhymed sentences in lines 21 through 27. According to Ch'en, line 19 patterns after men, line 20 patterns after things, and line 21 patterns after earth.

Line 24: Notice how *yü* rhymes with *yung*, and the character for *yung* is shaped like that of *ou*. Counterpuntal responses here correspond with *ou* ("counterpart of the self") on line 3. Line 25 explicitly mentions this fact, before things calm down into emptiness.

Line 26:

Hsü ("empty") corresponds, of course, with *hsü* on line 2. This is where it all starts (*tsuo*), and he who occupies this situation is a happy man, as Mr. Tzu-ch'i is.

Line 27 corresponds not only with line 17, but also with lines 9 through 12. This concludes the explanation of the situation of Mr. Tzu-ch'i.

T'iao t'iao, *tiao tiao* ("wavering," "quivering"): Before going into explanations, we must note that they rhyme, and that the first pair is heavy aspirated *tieh yin* ("duplicates") and the second pair is light and unaspirated *tieh yin*.

Because branches cannot move without the wind which has ceased by now, Chu Kuei-yao (p. 44) guessed that the characters may be synonymous (because of similarity in character-shape) with *chün* ("balanced") later (line 129, and 23/45; cf. 27/10), which is in turn synonymous with *t'iao* ("Harmonious"), to signify the first character in the title, *ch'i*. One wonders whether such a maneuver is needed.

Line 33: Or "blows in myriad different ways" (Wing-tsit Chan), "lets them self-cease" (Graham).

Yeh is *che* (Wang Yin-chih, p. 97), and is in the middle of the sentence as *che* is in the next sentence (line 34). "Park themselves" explains "lets them be themselves."

Line 36:

Yen ("burns"): If "big words" are taken favorably *yen* can mean *tan* ("clear and limpid"; Li I, Chu Kuei-yao). *Tan* also rhymes with *chan* ("chatty").

The trouble with this amendment is that (1) we have no textual support for it, (2) it is a radical change of meaning. Besides, *yen* is not terribly out of rhyme with *chan*.

After all, it is also possible, and more natural, to take both "big wit" and "big words (or debates)" unfavorably, lumping them with "small wit" and "small words." This is what I did. Akatzuka also took an unfavorable view on all knowledge and words in this part.

Line 37:

Yeh is *che* (Wang Yin-chih, p. 97).

Line 39:

Che ("that one") is usually taken to refer to our heart-mind. But the word could refer to fights (line 38) or even wit and words (lines 35, 36).

Line 40: Or "All these activities end up, one way or another, in small jumpy fears or big overwhelming fears" (Akatzuka).

Line 41:

Ch'i ("that") is usually taken to refer to our heart-mind (line 46). But the word could more plausibly refer to wit and words (lines 35, 36), both of which eventually come out of heart-mind.

Lines 41, 42, 43, 45: Graham plausibly surmised that here Chuang Tzu "might be either the author or the commentator of these verses about" our uneasy "heart, the organ of thought" (*Chuang-tzŭ*, pp. 50–51).

Line 45:

Yeh is *che* ("that-which"; Wang Yin-chih, p. 97).

Line 54:

Tan mu ("dawn," "dusk") is "for a moment" (as in the short moment of dawn or dusk). This line echoes line 264.

Line 55: Graham plausibly surmised that Chuang Tzu is here discussing "a quotation or a provisional formulation of his own."

Line 56: Or "... by whose order do they come into play" (Lin Yutang, *The Wisdom of Laotse*, p. 235).

I is "rather," emphatic.

Line 58:

Chi ("oneself") could have been *i* ("very much," "enough"; Lin Hsi-i). *i hsin* is then identical with *hsin i* ("certain enough," as in *shih i* ["yes, indeed"] of lines 29, 30, [53], 123), and the sentence reads, "we can act on it—that is certain enough" (Watson).

Line 60:

Ts'un ("present") has, according to Graham, the connotation of "belong in, be where it belongs, keep where it belongs, etc." (*Later Mohist Logic*, p. 206). He translated this line as "The hundred members, nine apertures and six organs are in him as his constituents without anything missing" (*Chuang-tzŭ*, p. 51).

This interpretation makes line 91 read "How could Tao go anywhere without being present as belonging to something? How could saying be present as belonging to someone and yet cannot exist as such?"

Unfortunately Graham did not bring out this point in his actual translations of lines 60 (quoted above) and 91 ("By what is the way hidden, that there should be a genuine or a false? By what is saying darkened, that sometimes 'that's it' and sometimes 'That's not'?"—*Chuang-tzŭ*, p. 51).

Line 62: Or "Or have you preference?" (Wang Hsien-ch'ien, Lin Yutang).

Lines 62–68:

Ch'i ("that") is probably *nai* ("then"; Chu Kuei-yao, quoting Wang Yin-chih).

Yu ("there exists") is probably *huo* ("may," "might"; Chu Kuei-yao, quoting Wang Yin-chih).

In this paragraph these two particles play a significant logical-rhetorical role in arguing for the existence of the inscrutable True Lord.

Line 67:

Ju means "as" (cf. lines 6, 42, 45, 63, 71) and the sentence can also read, "Situations such-*as* we succeed or do not succeed in seeking out his true identity do not benefit or discount from his authenticity."

Line 69:

Wang ("forget"). There are three interpretations: (1) Many common editions (*ssu pen*) have *wang* ("perish"), which makes the sentence read "They do not lose it till it exhausts its life" (Watson), or "Though it won't die right away, eventually it will" (cf. Akatzuka). (2) Other commentators prefer *wang* corrected into *hua* ("change") in light of 21/20 (Liu Shih-p'ei, Ch'en Ku-ying, Kanaya Osamu); and the sentence reads "Let us not change it till it naturally exhausts itself."

The second interpretation (2) should be discarded. (*a*) There is no reason why we must correct the Inner Chapters themselves. (*b*) Besides, such a favorable interpretation is out of line with the accusatory tone of this paragraph. (*c*) Finally, line 75 also has *hua* ("change"), and it is very difficult to square the meaning on that line with the meaning on this line.

Although the first interpretation (1) (*wang*, "to lose or die") may be acceptable, I prefer (3) the way it stands in the present text (*wang*, "to forget") because the paragraph (*a*) treats psychological matters and (*b*) corresponds with *wang* ("forget") on line 287, where to forget our years is urged. The latter *wang* begins the chapter, deploring the sorry state of our not-forgetting; the former *wang* ends the chapter, extolling the happy state of our worry-less forgetting.

I ("with") means *erh* ("and," "in the end"; Akatzuka).

Line 70: Akatzuka said that this line corresponds with line 44.

Jen ("blade fight"): Or *jen* ("made pliable" [through pounding]).

Mi ("follow along"): Or *mo* ("pulverized" [by grinding]).

Line 72:

Shen ("body") is a singularly appropriate word for a life that includes bodily life, an actual going through of life, and corresponds with *hsing* ("bodily figure"; line 69); cf. line 60.

I i ("labor, labor") means "driven (like a slave) by their fighting or following with things" (line 70); cf. line 243.

Line 74: That is, no matter how men call them not dead, they are as good as dead.

Line 77:

Ch'i ... i ("that ... also") is emphatic.

Ch'i ("that") here is descriptive (*chuang shih*, Wang Yin-chih, p. 114), and almost equivalent to *ch'i* ("how could"; cf. Watson). Or else, *ch'i* ("that") can be taken as "or" (*keng tuan*, Wang Yin-chih, p. 119), which makes the sentence read "Or am I the only stupid one, and there are still others not stupid?"

In any case, self-involvement in the accusation against all men is a significant part of this chapter's argument. (See line 261.)

It is obvious that *ch'i* ("that") has been used throughout (till line 78) to carry
rhetorical (and logical) resonance.

Line 78:

Fu (marker for sentence beginning) and *tu ch'ieh* ("alone indeed") are emphatic.
Ch'ieh as "indeed" (Wang Yin-chih, p. 180) is controverted by P'ie Hsueh-hai,
who takes it to be "will" (pp. 609, 655; cf. *Ma Shih Wen-t'ung*, p. 234; quoting Ch.
One, line 19). I side with Wang, however, because "indeed" is smoother,
"will" does not change the meaning much, and most commentators do not even
bother to translate *ch'ieh*, showing that they agree with Wang.

Ch'eng ("to form") has the connotation of "set up, already completed, finished," etc.
Cf. lines 118, 119; and gloss to line 92.

Ch'eng hsin ("formed minds") corresponds with *ch'eng hsing* ("formed figure";
line 69).

Line 79:

Tai ("alternate"): Cf. line 52. This is perhaps a synonym of *hua* ("change"; lines 75,
280, 305) and *man yen* (line 281), to be explained later (logically in lines 96–107,
existentially in lines (295–305).

Lines 82:

Shih fei ("this-yes, no"): This important distinction occurs for the first time here.
It could mean: (1) "yes and no" (*shih* also means "is," *fei* also means "is not"); (2)
"(what) [we] affirm as true and (what) [they] negate as false" (*shih* also means
"this"); (3) "right and wrong," "appropriate and inappropriate" (and its discernment); (4) "truth and falsehood" (and its discernment). The first logical
sense is perhaps uppermost in the discussion, but the other three are not too far
behind. Lin Yutang summed up well when he said, "*Shih* and *fei* mean general
moral judgments and mental distinctions: 'right' and 'wrong,' 'true' and 'false,'
'is' and 'is not,' 'affirmative' and 'negative,' and 'to justify' and 'condemn,' to
'affirm' and 'deny'" (*The Wisdom of China and India*, p. 636, note 10).

I translate *shih* as *(this)-yes* or *this-(yes)* to allow for emphasis sometimes
on the former, sometimes on the latter. For consistency, I would translate:

    shih as "yes-this";

    fei as "no";

    wu as "there-exists-no," "there-is-no," "no existence";

    pu as "not"; and

    pi as "that."

I "a" wei "b" is literally "with *a* to make *b* (in our mind)," and so "take *a* as *b*." Cf.
lines 88, 131, 132, 133, 212, 235, 236, 256; Ch. Three, line 48 (possibly line 3);
as well as my Prologue, C.I.7(c) and 1.8.

Line 83:

Yü is a sagely legendary emperor wise enough to dam the flood for his people. The
pronunciation mildy rhymes with *Yueh*.

Line 84:

Tu ch'ieh ("alone . . . indeed") is emphatic; cf. line 78.

Line 85:

Yeh (marker for sentence ending) is *che* ("that which"; Wang Yin-chin, p. 97).

Line 86: Or "If he-who says is himself not determinate" (Akatzuka)—as shown in *yen cheh* ("one who has words") on line 85.

Line 89:

Pien ("distinction") can also mean "debate," which makes the sentence read "Yet is there really good argument for it at all?" (Cf. Graham.)

Line 90: Cf. lines 181–83, 185–86. Cf. also *Tao Te Ching*, Chapters 1, 18, 78, 81.

Yin ("hide"): Cf. gloss to line 2.

Line 91:

Ts'un ("present"): see gloss to line 60.

Lines 91, 98:

K'o ("can"): Or "How can words exist and not be *acceptable* (as words)?" (Watson). The only drawback to this rendering is that it is too long and clumsy. *K'o* means "can"—logical, physical possibility and moral acceptability.

Line 92:

Hsiao ch'eng literally means "small accomplishment," perhaps implying small shrewdness or hack-work, used here obviously in a derogatory sense. I translate it as "formation" to correspond with lines 69, 78, 118, 119, etc., to mean "to establish, put things together, bring into being," and even "to pretend, scheme, fraud." Cf. gloss to line 78.

Lines 93, 94:

Ch'i ("that") is rendered "other" (line 93) and "their" (line 94), and that by *all* commentators I have consulted. I am uneasy about this but I have no better alternative.

Lines 93, 96:

Ku ("and so") means *tse* ("then") according to Wang Yin-chih, p. 124. Cf. glosses to lines 137, 138, 140.

Line 95:

Tzu means "from" in the third sentence, and "self" in the fourth, as I would also take it generally to mean later.

Chih ("it"; the first occurence) is corrected by Yen Ling-feng and Ch'en Ch'i-t'ien into *shih* ("this"), to parallel *pi* ("that") of the third sentence. The whole line then becomes "By *that* it (*this*) is not seen (as *this*); by *this* it is understood (as *this*)." The result may be the same, but *tzu* can now be consistently translated as "by" (or "from the perspective of"). Unfortunately I have yet to see any ancient text having *shih*, although Lin Yün-ming has a gloss saying that "*chih* (knowledge), I suspect, may be *shih* (this)."

Line 96:

Fang ("as . . . so"): All of the sources I checked agree that it etymologically means two boats lashed together side by side (cf. 20/22). Graham said that from it comes (1) the dynamic meaning of "to compare"—develop characteristics side by side. (2) Also "proceed, rise up, side by side," as here, and "while" (line 252) proceeding with an event or time side by side. (3) Nominalized, "method," "formula," or "recipe" (line 13; Ch. One, line 129—that from which one takes one's direction (*Later Mohist Logic*, pp. 186-87. Also see Dr. L. Wieger, *Chinese Characters*, p. 217; K'ang Yin, *Wen-tzu Yuan-liu Ch'ien-Shuo*, p. 140; as well as *Shou Wen Chieh Tzu*, Chapter 8B, pp. 6–7.)

Yin ("follow on"): K'ang Yin (p. 521) said that it originally meant a man lying in bed from which it follows that something follows (*chiu*) something else, which is what *Shuo Wen* (6B, 12) has. Graham has "depend on, have as grounds, by this criterion, criterion" (*Mohist Logic*, pp. 214–15).

Wang Yin-chih (pp. 29–30) cited many examples to show that *yin shih* ("follow on this") means *yu shih* ("likewise," as has been explained).

Line 100:

Sheng Jen is "holy man," one who is discerning-hearkening (Ch. One, line 69; Ch. Two, lines 129, 148, 174–79, 196–219).

I ("also") rhymes with and responds to Hui Shih on line 96."

Line 104 is where Mr. Tzu-ch'i of South Wall resides (line 3).

Tao shu ("Tao pivot"): Is it *axis mundi*?

Line 105:

I ("with") is *erh* ("then"; Wang Yin-chih, p. 22). Or "responds endlessly."

Line 107: Cf. line 94. The words are the same, but the meaning slightly differs.

Line 108 discusses the "can" (*k'o*).

Pu jo is "not (as good) as."

Line 109 discusses the "so" (*jan*). In sum, difference *can* be used to show the sameness, the self-so-ness. On Kung-sun Lung, see Graham's *Mohist Logic*, pp. 457–68, as well as P'ang P'u, *Kung-sun Lung i-chu* (in mainland China) and Hsu Fu-koan *Kung-sun Lung-tzu Chiang-shu* (in Taiwan).

Line 114:

Ku ("inherent") implies something inherent.

Line 116:

Ku wei shih: "Because of this reason (*wei shih i ku*)" (Kuo Ch'ing-fan); "then, in order to clarify this point" (Kanaya Osami); "because of this, therefore (*wei shih, ku*)" (Wang Hsien-ch'ien). In any case, it is wrong to take the phrase as a technical term, as Graham did; there is no textual evidence for such as interpretation.

T'ing is "stalk" (common view) or "beam" (Ssu-ma Piao).

Hui kuei chüeh kuai ("grotesque," "strange") has many interpretations: (1) as translated (Chu Kuei-yao, Wang Pi. Chiang Hsi-ch'ang); (2) "things, generous, strange, deceptive, abnormal" (Ch'eng Hsüan-ying); (3) same as *tiao kuei* ("supreme swindle," "ultimate ruse") on line 262 (*Ching-tien Shih-wen*).

Line 117:

Wei i is "make them into one," or "call them one" (cf. line 161; Ch. One, line 2).

Line 118: Or "What is separation to some is production to others, etc."

Yeh (marker for sentence ending) is *che* (Wang Yin-chih, p. 97); cf. lines 134, (140), 141, 142; and Ch. One, lines 104, 114.

Line 121: Or "Lodge himself-in"; cf. line 289. This line contrasts with "slaving (oneself) for others" (i i) on lines 72, 243.

Line 122: Chang Ping-lin said that *yung*[a], *yung*[b], t'ung, and what is today pronounced as *te* all mutually rhyme, because *te* is a borrowing of what is today pronounced as *chung* which was pronounced *tung* (as quoted by Ma Hsü-lun in *Chuang Tzu i-cheng*, p. 73).

Line 123:

Te ("obtain"): (1) "Let things obtain and develop themselves as they are" (common view); (2) "being self-possessed" (Lin Yutang, Wing-tsit Chan).

Shih: (1) "Go," "arrive"; (2) "fit," "comfortable."

Chi: (1) "Complete," "ultimate"; (2) "almost," "near." Wing-tsit Chan has "When one is at ease with himself, one is near Tao."

I (marker for sentence ending; "already," "only") and *i* ("only," "already") are rhymed. There is an untranslatable play on words and phrases between *yin shih i* ("following on this-yes only") here and *shih i* ("this-yes only") on lines 29, 30, where *shih ... i* is translated "these ... only."

Line 124:

I erh ("only-already," "and") is either *i jan erh* ("having been ended, then"; Akatzuka) or *tz'u* ("this"), a repeat of the above situation, *yin shih erh i* ("following on the yes of things only," Wang Yin-chih, p. 23). Cf. Ch. Three, line 2.

Incidentally, Yen Ling-feng said that line 122 plus the first sentence on line 123 may be an ancient gloss mistakenly copied into the main text. If we cut them, we get a sentence structure here similar to that in lines 100 and 149. Ch'en Kuying (p. 70) agrees.

Line 129:

Shih ("this") is repeated three times, with some rhetorical effect. Cf. line 100 and Ch. Three, line 23.

Chün ("balance") is *chün* ("equality") or *t'ao chun*, "the potter's wheel" to mold pottery. Pottery here refers to either things or man's character (Ts'ui Chuan). Fung Yulan, said that *t'ien chün* is synonymous with *t'ien ni* on line 281. See his *Chung-kuo Che-hsüeh Shih*, p. 291. Derk Bodde's translation fails to bring out this point, in *A History of Chinese Philosophy*, I, 233.

Shih chih wei liang hsing ("This it is which men call 'double walk'"): Or "arriving at this is called walking double courses." For *liang hsing*, see lines 58, 71, 290.

Line 134:

Yeh (marker for sentence ending): See gloss to line 118.

Lines 137–49: This section is extremely obscure in details, though the main idea is fairly clear. Being almost at the middle point of the entire chapter, this section is an important transition from the first half to the second. It (1) sums up the previous discussion (cf. Akatzuka, 1.96–97):

line 130 refers back	to lines 35,–120;
line 134	to lines 93–107;
lines 135–38	to lines 118–19;
lines 139–47	to lines 11, 36; and
line 148	to line 57;

and at the same time (2) lays down what is to come:

line 131 refers forward	to lines 150–69;
line 132	to lines 170–94; and
line 133	to lines 195–219.

All of these will be developed into the very self-involvement of the subject-ego in the cosmic process of co-happening.

Line 137, 138, 140:

Ku ("and so") is *fu* (marker for beginning a new topic; "well," "now"; Akatzuka); *ku* ("ancient"; Hsüan Ying); *tz'u* ("this"; Chang Ping-lin); or *tse* ("then"; Wang Yin-chih, Ch'en Ku-ying). See also Fung Yulan's translation of Kuo Hsiang's explanation, with which Fung apparently agrees, in *Chuang Tzu: A New Selected Translation with an Exposition of the Philosophy of Kuo Hsiang*, p. 54.

Line 139: Or "tune the zither" (Ma Hsü-lun), "beat time" (Ts'ui Chuan), "lean on the dryandra desk" (Ch'eng Hsüan-ying). The last phrase is ironic. Hui Shih was leaning on dryandra (tree? desk?) as a *dispensable* backdrop against which to advance his argumentation. Little did he know that true knowledge (of no-knowledge) is in the silent tree. See line 230.

Line 140:

The first sentence: Or "The knowledge of these three was near perfection" (Wu Yen-hsü, Shih Te-ch'iang, Lin Yün-ming).

The last sentence: Or (1) "practice their art to the end of their lives" (Lin Hsi-i); (2) "their names have been handed own to later ages" (Ts'ui Chuan); (3) "all are those whose careers are well-formed" (Li Mien).

Lines 141–43: Or "What they were given to was very (*i* ['with'] is *i* ['already'] and may in this context mean 'very') different from that (='cosmic knowledge' on line 130), which cannot be clarified by what they were given to yet they still insisted on clarifying what they were given to" (Akatzuka, cf. Graham).

Line 144: Ch'en Ku-ying has conveniently compiled a list of various interpretations of the second sentence, as follows:

Lun ("strings"): (1) "lute strings" (Ts'ui Chuan); (2) "business" (*hsü yeh*; Ch'eng Hsüan-ying).

Ch'i tzu ("his sons"): "sons of Chao Wen" (Kuo Hsiang); (2) "sons of Hui Tzu" (Lin Yün-ming); (3) sons of all three gentlemen (James Legge).

Line 148:

Hua ("dim") is either *hu* ("dim"; cf. *Tao Te Ching*, Ch. 21; Shih Te-ch'ing) or *luan* ("confuse"; Ssu-ma Piao, Wang Hsien-ch'ien).

I ("submergence") is "doubtful" (as it means), "indistinct" (Fukunaga); *ning* ("not radiant," "submerged," "concentrated"), or *t'ao* ("contained," "hidden"; Ch'eng Hsüan-ying). Cf. line 189.

T'u is "set one's eyes on" (as in Ch. One, lines 19, 42); *pi* ("despise"; Huang Chin-hung), or *sheng se* ("dispense with"; Kuo Hsiang).

Clearly, then, we have two opposing interpretations on this sentence, a favorable one and an unfavorable one. I chose the former both because it involves less exegetical acrobatics, and because it goes smoothly with what follows. The unfavorable interpretation reads, "The glitter of glib implausibility is despised by the sage" (Chiang Hsi-ch'ang, Ma Hsü-lun, Graham).

Line 149: Cf. lines 121, 289; and also 94, 107.

Lines 154–60: Cf. an interesting gloss by Graham in *Chuang-tzŭ*, pp. 55–56. My reaction to it is twofold. First, no-existence (*wu*) has three meanings: (1) something other (than what is designated as existing), (2) nothing, and (3) non-being. Cf. my *Chuang Tzu: a World Philosopher at Play*, Aria I. Graham vacillated unawares between (1) and (2); he was not even aware of (3). Secondly, Graham sees only Chuang Tzu's refutation of the then-current logic. Such a refutation is undoubtedly an important intention of Chuang Tzu. Yet we cannot neglect Chuang Tzu's ultimate intention to lead the reader further on into non-being and interchanges among beings. This section has laid down a thread for this.

Line 155;

Wei shih ("yet to begin"): I suspect that Chuang Tzu uses this phrase as a technical term. In fact, *wei* ("yet," "not yet") alone could be a technical term. The possible meaning of *wei* as "never" (as Watson rendered it) makes the entire section cumbersome and meaningless.

Line 158:

Yu wu: (1) "There exists no-existence."

(2) "Existence and no-existence."

Lines 159–60: Or "Now I have just said something. But I don't know whether what I have said has really said something or whether it hasn't said something." (Watson)

I: "only," "already" (cf. lines 123, 169).

Lines 161, 162:

Wei ("make") is *wei* ("call"). Cf. Ch. One, line 2.

Lines 164, 165: Cf. Ch. One, line 78.

Lines 163–69: Graham said that Plato said something similar in the *Sophist*, and "that Chuang-tzŭ never does say that everything is one (except as one side of a paradox [5/7–8]), always speaks subjectively of the sage [as] treating [everything] as one." (*Chuang-tzŭ*), p. 56) I wish to add that the reason why Chuang Tzu never says that things are one is presented here—we can go from one to three (and many), as well as from many to one.

I ("only," "already"): Cf. line 123.

Line 163: I tried to make contemporary philosophical sense out of this in my *Chuang Tzu*, p. 51.

Line 170:

Fung is "mound," "heap," "border."

Chen is "raised passage between fields," and may mean "barriers" or "boundaries." Another reading is: "It is because of this that there is distinction (or division)" (*wei shih erh yu chen yeh*).

Line 172: Chiang Hsi-ch'ang claimed that the former four describe Confucianism, and the latter four describe Mohism. Watson glossed that "Chuang Tzu is deliberately parodying" the "virtues" of Confucians and Mohists.

Line 173: Or (perhaps) "They go to what we call Eight Virtues."

Line 174:

Liu ho ("six correlates"): *Ho* means "pair" or "correlate." Six Correlates signify the universe. Cf. *liu ch'i* ("six breath energies") in Ch. One, line 64.

Hsü Shen's gloss on the *Huai Nan Tzu* (I.2.b) says that *liu ho* is made up of:

(1) early spring correlated   with early autumn,
     mid-spring   with mid-autumn,
     late spring   with late autumn,
     early summer   with early winter,
     mid-summer   with mid-winter,
     late summer   with late winter; or

(2) four directions and up and down (heaven and earth).

Lines 173–76: There may be some contrasts implied:

line 174 (*lun*[a]) contrasts with   virtues 3 (*lun*[d]);
line 175 (*i*)   with virtue 4 (*i*);
line 176 (*pien*)   with virtue 6 (*pien*);

and this contrast may include virtue 5 (cf. line 177; also see lines 118, 285–86, 290–94, 304; and Ch. One, line 56.) Virtues 7 and 8 are deemed unworthy of the holy man, and are discussed in lines 180–81, 265–79.

Also, it is possible that:

line 174 corresponds   with Heavenly Piping,
line 175   with Earthly Piping, and
line 176   with Human Piping (cf. lines 11–12).

Line 176: This is Wang Hsien-ch'ien's view. Akatzuka thinks that these refer to *The Annals of Spring and Autumn* and *The Classics of History*, two favorites of the Confucians.

Line 183:

Ch'eng (literally, "to form") is *chou* ("comprehensive") according to *Chuang Tzu Ch'ueh Wu* and Kuo Hsiang.

The line can also be interpreted in a favorable light: "Tao manifested yet does not lead (but lets each lead itself), sayings disputed yet does not reach (but lets the hearer reach the conclusions for themselves), benevolence made constant yet does not complete (the beloved), modesty is clean yet is not always faithful, courage may hurt yet does not give mortal hurts (or 'does not overwhelm,' taking *ch'eng* ('to form') as *wei* ('awesome'), in accordance with Akatzuka)."

Line 184:

These Five Things perhaps parodies the Confucian "Five Ethical Principles" (*wu lun*).

Yüan, fang are "circle, square," but Akatzuka cited *Lü-shih Ch'un Ch'iu, Huai Nan Tzu*, and *Ta Tai Li* to say that the contrast may correspond with heaven (circle) and earth (square). The whole sentence then reads, "are circles without obstruction (line 105), being close to the Method of Nature." But Akatzuka himself treats *fang* as "rule."

Another interpretation (Kuang Feng, Fukunaga) takes *fang* to mean "squared," with "edges and angles," that is, "become flawed." I follow this interpretation because of its simplicity and naturalness.

Line 186: Since *pu* ("not") goes with verbs and adjectives, *yen* ("word") and *tao* ("way") are both verbs or adjectives.

Line 189:

Pao kuang can be: (1) "hidden light" (Feng and English); "Shaded Light" (Watson); "Store of Light" (Legge). They followed Lin Hsi-i.

(2) Graham has "Benetnash Star," adding that "as a metaphor for the prime mover of things Chuang-tzǔ chooses not the stationary North Star but the circumpolar star which initiates the cyclic motions" (*Chuang-tzǔ*, p. 57). He followed both Chu Kuei-yao and Wang Shu-min who quoted from *Huai Nan Tzu*, 8.5.a, which has *yao kuang* that supplies foods to myriads of things, resides at the center of the Dipper Constellation, controls twelve time-divisions, raises Yin and Yang, and arranges for the births and deaths of things.

(3) Another interpretation says *yao Kuang* is an appearance of the vapor (breath)-energy of harmony (*ho ch'i*). (4) Ts'ui Chuan has "the light that now appears, now disappears."

Lines 190–93:

Yao had been honored by the Confucians as *fang hsün* whose august brilliance (*ch'in kuang*) was supposed to have spread all over the world. Chuang Tzu matched it with the inherent virtue of things, represented by Yao's *subject*, Shun, who described natural virtue as compatible if not superior to ten suns, which may represent human virtue since they are not natural, making all natural living beings unlivable, and have a lot to do with the human virtue of the Archer *I* who shot down nine of them, as recorded in the *Huai Nan Tzu*, 8.5ab). This is of course another gloss on the Hidden Light, and an irony (cf. Akatzuka).

Line 195:

Nieh ch'üeh ("chew chipped"): See my Meditations, B.11.2.

Line 197–244:

Wu ("the I") is an authentic subject. Cf. line 10.

Line 199: This line goes beyond the Socratic level; Socrates died because he said "yes" to the question in line 198.

Line 209: Or hay-fed and grain-fed beasts (Graham, cf. Watson).

Line 217:

Tuan ("buddings") is "bud," "beginning," or "principle."

Line 219:

Pien ("distinctions-disputes"): Cf. lines 176, 273–77. It can mean "discrimination" (Graham, Watson); "difference" (Wing-tsit Chan), or perhaps "disputes on the difference between what is proper and what is not." This paragraph (lines 195–219) alludes, of course, to the contrast between *cheng* (the proper, real, correct, normal") and *pien* ("the debatable, changeable"). See Ch. One, lines 63–65.

Lines 223:

Shen ("spirit-filled") is "daemonically marvelous, skillful, versatile." See Ch. Three, Meditations, B.4.5.1.

Line 228, with Ch. One, lines 42, 64–65, may be another description of divine freedom in Lines 67–68 and 108–14.

Line 230:

Ch'ang ("long," "tall") can mean *chang* ("elderly," "venerable"); cf. archaic *yü* ("I for one") on lines 241, 245, 246, 261. See also line 139.

Line 234: Or "In saying nothing he says something, and in saying something, he says nothing." (Cf. Graham, Fung, Lin Yutang; cf. lines 159, 160).

Line 235:

Meng lang ("vague romanticism"): Chu Kuei-yao took it as *lan man* ("scattered"); Akatzuka thinks that the phrase is a rhymed gradual pronunciation of *wang, mang mo, mang yang, man lan* (cf. line 241; Ch. One, line 119).

Wo is identifiable objectifiable self (cf. line 159), not *wu*.

Line 238:

Ch'iu: Akatzuka took it as Mr. Tall Dryandra Tree, making the sentence read "How much less would I be able to know it?" (lines 84, 167). But as a given name most commentators have taken it to refer to Confucius. I leave it vague as Ch'iu.

Can a tree talk? "Yes, in its silence," Chuang Tzu says here. Its silence teaches us the secrets of the Tao of things. Sciences are one mode in which we are taught by nature; stories are another one. The silence of nature is absolutely eloquent about the ultimate (the ultimately ordinary) of things.

That the tree's replies begin here is clear enough. But where do they end? See gloss to the last line, line 305, which I take to be the end of the tree's replies.

Line 241:

Wang is "abandoned" (Graham); "reckless" (Watson); "at random" (Fung, Lin). Cf. line 153.

Line 243:

I li hsiang tsun ("with/as slaves, mutually honor") opposes the usual courtesy of *i kui hsiang tsun* ("as nobles mutually honor"). Cf. line 72.

Line 244;

> *Ch'un* (literally, "pure") is taken by Akatzuka (I followed him) as *t'un* ("lump," "collection," "gathering"). Akatzuka also said that *hun, tsun, t'un,* and *yün* rhyme, and Ch'en Shou-ch'ang confirms it.

Line 247:

> *Li* is literally "beautiful." Is there a pun here?
>
> *Ai* is not clear on where it is, but from its being homonymous with *ai* ("love"), there may be a pun here too.
>
> *Shih* is literally "beginning, at first." Cf. lines 131–33, 154–58.
>
> Kuo Ch'ing-fan, Wang Shu-min, and Lin Hsi-i, among others, claimed that this lady is that notorious Li Chi offered by the state of Li Jung to Duke Hsien of Chin. *Tso Chuan* devoted several sections to her, who later caused great commotions in Chin. See James Legge, *The Chinese Classics*, 5:113–46. Would this historical background indicate the dangerous futility of human attachment (or loyalty) of whatever kind?

Line 250:

> *Erh* is "and then." See Ma Chien-chung, p. 297.

Line 251:

> *T'ien* ("field") is *t'ien* ("hunting").

Line 252:

> *Fang* (literally, "as ... so"; here, "while"): See lines 96–98, and note gloss on *fang* from line 96.

Line 255:

> *Ch'ieh* ("besides") is "by and by," according to Lin, and Feng and English.

Line 257:

> *Ch'ieh ch'ieh jan* ("so saucy, saucy"): Watson has "busily and brightly."

Line 262:

> *Ti kuei* ("ultimate ruse"): *Ti* means either *chih* ("attain," "arrive," "ultimate"), *chüeh* ("swindle": Ma Hsü-lun), or *shu* ("beginning": Chu Kuei-yao).
>
> *Kuei* means "far away from common sense, extraordinary, grotesque" (cf. line 117). The two characters together may correspond to *ch'i hsieh* ("Tall Tales of the Universal Harmony") in Ch. One, line 6.

Line 264:

> *Shih* ("this") is *tse* ("then"; Wang Yin-chih, p. 203). Cf. "Tomorrow a Sage may arise to explain it; but that tomorrow will not be until ten thousand generations have gone by. Yet you may meet him around the corner" (Lin Yutang).

Line 265:

> *Chi shih* ("now that let") may be *jo huo* ("if") according to P'ei Hsüeh-hai, p. 335. But I stuck to the original meanings of the terms.

Line 271:

> *Ch'i* ("that") is *ni i chih tz'u* (word supposing a hypothetical situation) for Wang Yin-chih, p. 114.
>
> *Huo* is "any one of us."

Line 272: Or "Everyone has his own inherent darkness (prejudices)" (Ch'en Ku-ying). Interpreted thus, this line belongs with line 273, which starts a new paragraph. But then *tse* ("then") is left untouched.

Line 278:

Chü ("both," "all") can be two ("both"; as in line 271) or more than two ("all"; as here)—as Wang Li, pp. 601–2, said.

Line 280:

Hua sheng is "changing voices," perhaps referring to earthly and human pipings in lines 11, 12.

Lines 280–82: Some texts (Kuo Hsiang, Chiao Hung) put this portion after line 286. Chiang Hsi-ch'ang and Wang Hsu-min said that this portion should be in the present order, which is also the order of the texts of Hsüan Ying, Wang Hsien-ch'ien, Lin Yün-ming, and Ch'en Shou-ch'ang.

Ni ("equality") is "division" (*fen*; Wang Hsien-ch'ien); "equality" (*chün*; Chu Kueiyao); "beginning" (*tuan*: Hsüan Ying); "limit" (*ya*, Akatzuka; *chi*, Ts'ui Chuan); "whetstone" (*yen: Ching-tien Shih-wen*).

Line 285, 286:

Jo is "if"; "like" (as in lines 41, 43, 57, 76, 146, and 147) also has this connotation.

Line 288:

Chen ("roam and stop") is to (1) "stop, end" (*chung, chih*; Chu Kuei-yao, Ts'ui Chuan); (2) "go through without obstruction" (*t'ung ch'ang*; Kuo Ch'ing-fan); or (3) "soaring and roaming" (*hsiao yao yu*: Lin Hsi-i).

Line 289:

Ku ("and so") is "then" *(tse)*. See line 93.

Yü chu wu ching ("lodge them in the No-boundary"): Cf. lines, 121, 149.

Line 290:

Wang liang ("double nothing") is a gradual pronunciation of *mang* in *mang mei* ("vague"; Akatzuka). It means "penumbra," the outer shading of a shadow. On this story and the ones that follow see my Meditations, B.13.1, B.13.5, C.2.2.1.

Wang ("nothing") could be a remote reference to *wu* ("no-existence"); cf. lines 157–59).

On *liang* ("double"), cf. *liang hsing* ("double walk") in line 129.

Chu Kuei-yao has many other interpretations of *wang liang*, all of which seem in this context irrelevant conjectures. My interpretations, "Double Nothing" and "Neither (shadow) Nor (substance)" in B.13.1–7, are relevant conjectures, fitting with line 129.

Line 291:

T'e ts'ao ("characteristic behavior") is independence that is peculiar and constitutive of one's constant characteristics.

T'e ("special") is *te* ("virtue"; Akatzuka) or *ch'i* ("to keep," "hold"; *Ching-tien Shih-wen*; cf. "habit" in Aristotle).

Ts'ao ("behavior") is constant pattern of one's behavior (*chieh tu*), or "independent will and behavior" (*tu li chih ts'ao*; Ch'eng Hsüan-ying).

Lines 292-93:
Wu is "the true I"; cf. line 10.

Line 295:
Hsi ("earlier," "originally yesterday") is logical, ontological, and chronological "before"—cf. line 7, 82.

Line 296:
Chuang Chou is a personal proper name perhaps signifying the identifiable *wo*, especially in conscious logicizing (cf. lines 79, 146-47, 159, 163, 216, 265-79, and perhaps 191 also). See note 10 to my Meditations that follow. Also, there is an easier hypothesis for the appearance here of a proper noun; see gloss to line 305 below.

Line 298:
Yü ("showing," as in argumentation): Cf. lines 108, 109. I follow Graham here, though *yü* could mean *yü* ("happy"; Li I).

Line 304:
Fen ("division") is a distinction recognized by the human mind and can be argued about, as in lines 172, 177.

Line 305:
Hua ("change"): Cf. line 280; Ch. One, line 2.

The overhasty happiness of the dreaming (dreamed?) butterfly in lines 295–99 may be compared to the overhasty excitement of Mr. Jittery Magpie (in line 239), to be sobered into the deep nonchalance of Mr. Tall Dryandra Tree. The silence of the Tree is of course a personification of the unity of "division" and "change," in lines 304–305.

An interesting question is whether or not the tree's replies (beginning at line 238) end here. The ending is usually taken to be at line 264, or at most up to line 289 (Huang Chin-hung, Fukunaga)—without explanation. I see no reason why the end cannot extend to the very end of the chapter, line 305, as I have assumed in this Translation.

If this hypothesis is accepted, then we can naturally believe the tree bluntly to be telling about that "Chuang Chou" who dreamed about being the butterfly, perhaps while he was drowsing under the tree—as suggested at the end of Ch. One, (line 163).

Another interpretation of the proper name, "Chuang Chou," is suggested in note 10 to my Meditations that follow.

MEDITATIONS—FOUR READINGS

After an almost literal translation of poetically arranged text of the second chapter (word order undisturbed), we have here four meditations: (A) An integrated survey of the chapter as a whole, (B) a section-by-section (sometimes word-by-word) look at the text, (C) a speculative flight into what all this might mean, and (D) a discussion of what it can mean for our living.

A. Survey

Every reasonable man can be said to make his world. He connects ideas in a certain way, and his system is born. Then things (*wu*) begin to appear as "ox" (*niu*) and such, "cut" (*wu*) out of non-separated Darkness (*ming*); they appear as connected in the way his ideas are connected, and his world is born. And so, to think is to connect ideas systematically, and to make a system of ideas is to make a world of things (*wu*).

It is natural, then, that how the world of things appears depends on how one thinks and makes a system of idea, *lun^a* in Chinese. *Lun^a* is words (*yen*) of *lun^b*. *Lun^b* has at least two meanings. On the subjective side, *lun^b* originally meant "to collect and arrange (bamboo) tablet-pages" by seeking and following their natural order, that is, arranging pages and books according to their contents; hence, it now means "sorting things" according to the natural grain of the jade-of-things (*wen li*), or "thinking rationally" according to the thread and way of things. In this subjective sense, *lun^a* is words arranged in the natural order of things.

Objectively, the arrangement of ideas (*lun^a*) is a wheel (*lun^c*), that is, a *lu lu* ("crank pulley") at work, a dynamic wheeling of things. In short, our thinking-and-reasoning (*lun^a*) is for the Chinese a natural reasonableness; to be rational is to be natural and to see naturally.

Chuang Tzu came in at this point and said that to think things rationally is to see things in a heavenly (natural) wheeling of things (*t'ien ni*). To describe such natural wheelings Chuang Tzu used the character *ch'i*, things arranging themselves democratically, a spontaneous system of ontological reciprocity. "Equality" is a natural description here, an absolute parity of interaction and interdependence among things, even among wings and cicada, dreaming and being awake, and so on. It takes a Great Awakening to notice this natural self-arranged equality among things.

Ch'i originally means ears of grain in the field waving in the sun. They look roughly identical in size, shape, and color—hence the translations, "arrangement in order," "equalization," and the like. But each ear is different from others, each alive and unique in itself, responding one to another freely. The world is a field, a configuration, of such living, responsive, and democratic self-arrangement among things.[1] The title of the second chapter, *Ch'i Wu Lun*, is thus not accidental; it says that the natural order must be recognized (*lun*[a]) as self-arrangements (*ch'i*) among things (*wu*). For if the arrangements were imposed on them,[2] the world would go to pieces. Since dynamic self-arrangements among things make up the world, their *being*-arranged unmakes the world in confusion (*luan*). And so the chapter title, *Ch'i Wu Lun*, is tentatively translated as "Things, Theories—Sorting Themselves Out" or, as it might be, "On the Equal Self-Arrangement Among Things."

The living self-arrangement among things is structured in a twofold manner: On the one hand, their *self*-arrangement bespeaks distinct non-collapsible identities of things. On the other hand, the fact that it is self-arrangement *among* things indicates that such arrangement obtains in their mutual interaction, to the extent of interdependence and interchanging of identities. These two qualities—distinct identities (*yu fen*) obtained in their interchanges (*wu hua*)—make up the world.[3]

How thoroughgoing such dynamic reciprocity is is brought out in the story of Penumbra and Shadow toward the end of this Chapter. The story goes as follows:

> Mr. Double Shading (Penumbra) asked Mr. Shadow, saying, "A while ago, sir, you walked; now you stop. A while ago you sat; now you rise. Why, in you, is there no consistent independence?"
>
> Mr. Shadow said, "Am I like this because I have something to depend on? Is what I depend on like it is because it in turn has something to depend on? Do I depend on something as a snake depends on his skin and a cicada on his wings?" (Chapter Two, lines 290–293).

Two points can be noted. First, we see how inappropriate, if not self-defeating, it is for Penumbra to ask Shadow in this way, seeing that Penumbra itself has to depend on Shadow for all the activities of standing, sitting, and walking. The question, *if* valid, answers itself; as the questioner (Penumbra) depends on something external to it, so the respondent (Shadow) depends on something external to *it*.

And yet, secondly, the validity of the question can after all be seen, because the relation of dependence can be reversed; Shadow's existence depends on its profile, which is Penumbra. It is then as true to say Shadow depends on Penumbra as it is to say Penumbra depends on Shadow. Similarly, the relation between Shadow and the thing of which it is Shadow is also a reciprocal dependence. As Penumbra defines Shadow, so Shadow shadows forth the thing, which is given depth and concreteness by its shadow. As Samuel Todes said,

> ... the quality of viewing is normally marked by the quality of shadow, and without shadow we see nothing. ... We see things best when we see them ... together with their shadows. ... [The shadows] help us to *see things* ... by clearly outlining for us what remains to be better seen than is optically possible in the given visual context ...[4]

And then, we remember Shadow cited two examples to show the mutual dependence among things—snake's skin and cicada's wings. As the skin and the wings depend on the snake at the cicada to exist, so the snake and the cicada depend on their skin and wings to survive. Things mutually wait on one another, and are waited on by one another (*hsiang tai*), to exist. All this illustrates a radical *interdependence* among things, even in cases such as those above where we usually expect unilateral dependence. Chuang Tzu further elaborated this ontological interdependence by the following three points:

(1) Each thing is judged to be "so" in its being so, and "not so" in its being not so, as logicians such as Mo Tzu claimed.[5] If so, then a thing exists not only because of its being identical with itself (self-identify), but also because of its being fit to be judged as such (value judgement). Such a judgement is not just a subjective one, for sophists (Hui Shih, Kung Sun Lung) claimed that the this is involved in the that, both casually and logically. Chuang Tzu freely used the sophists' notion, "*fang*," to assert four co-responses among things:

(*a*) Where there is a this, right, there is a that, wrong.
(*b*) Because there is a this, right, there is a that, wrong.
(*c*) As soon as there is a this, right, there is a that, wrong.
(*d*) Whenever there is a this, right, it is followed by a that, wrong.

In this manner things are inextricably interrelated for their unique identities (lines 95–99).

(2) Their interdependence extends to the reversibility of argumentation about them. For instance, if Hui Tzu (and possibly Mencius) said that "Heaven, earth, and I were born at the same time," and "myriads of things and I make one" (line 163),[6] then Chuang Tzu can produce a counter-argument *in*

their manner, this way. Claiming *oneness* of all things amounts to producing *two*, namely, (1) the claim, and (2) the claiming act. Add "oneness," the referent of the claim, and Chuang Tzu now has *three* (the claim, the claiming, and its referent) from the claim of "oneness" of all. This shows us that if the sophists can go argumentatively from many to one, then Chuang Tzu can likewise go from one to many (lines 163–69).

(3) The validity of judgement depends on the perspective from which it is made, and the perspective depends in turn on the subject and his situation. A man will get backache and paralysis by sleeping in a damp place, but not a roach. The prospect of living in a tree terrifies a man, but not a monkey. "Now, of all three parties, who understands the correct places to be?" Asks Chuang Tzu (lines 205–15).

What is more, the subject itself is not unchanging. Lady Beautiful (*li chi*) wailed pathetically when captured by the enemy. But as she was treated with sumptuous meals and royal beds, she came to relent her initial tears (lines 245–49).

Thus Chuang Tzu has produced three points. First, things are as they are, each in its own way responding to others. Secondly, things are so interdependent that universally valid judgement is impossible. When we say or argue one thing about a particular case, we must at the same time say or argue something else about it. Thirdly, the validity of judgement depends on the perspective from which it is made. And the perspective depends on the subject, which is not unchanging.

These three points are interwined in a significant manner. If the specificity of things entails their specific *relations* with others (point 1), then such interdependence prevents a particular proposition and argument from being *unqualifiedly* valid (point 2). The validity of judgment and argumentation now depends on the life-*situation* of the subject (point 3). Validity is perspectival and existential.

To such interrelatedness of things and thinking, we can respond with three attitudes.[8] We can either neglect it and become *dogmatic* or be obsessed with it and become *relativistic* (namely, indifferent and withdrawn), or we can *participate* in it and allow ourselves to freely respond to it. Only the last is the correct way.

To neglect the interdependence among things and thoughts produces *dogmatism* like that of those monkeys in Chuang Tzu's sardonic story. They angrily insisted on "morning, four [nuts] and evening, three" when the monkey keeper offered "morning, three and evening, four." Such dogmatism locks us in our own illusion and prejudice (lines 125–29). Then our psychic wranglings drown and haunt us day and night (line 70–80). After all, winning an argument over our opponent warrants no validity to our position. Both or either of us may be either right or wrong. And no third party—whether he agrees with one or both of us—can decide for us, precisely because he agrees with one or both of us (line 265–79).

If neglecting things' interdependence leads to monkey-like bigotry, then being obsessed with the interdependence induces *relativism*. Relativism can take two forms: Indifference, saying, "It does not matter which view is taken," and withdrawal, saying, "None is valid or important." Chuang Tzu did not advocate such indifferent withdrawal from this world. The subject should not be an impotent observer detached from things' endless *fang*'s.

If dogmatism throws a monkey wrench of staticity into the dynamic reciprocity of things, then indifference withdraws the subject from such reciprocity. Dogmatism, indifference, and withdrawal amount to pulling the subject out of this world. And since living participation in the ontological mutualities is crucial for making up the world, allowing dogmatism, indifference, and withdrawal to prevail unmakes the world.

Therefore, Chuang Tzu proposes that the subject embody the Pivot of the Way (*tao shu*) of things' mutualities. The subject must fit himself in the Pivot, fit the Pivot "in the center of the Circle" (*huan chung*) of the world, and thereby respond endlessly and freely to things by "following along" (*yin shih*) (line 123) and "walking both" (*liang hsing;* line 129) ways—the way of things and the way of the subject. The subject should be as active and responsive a participant as the monkey keeper is.[9]

Such free response is not a matter of technique but our very mode of living and acting, so much so that our own identities are interchanged as a result. But what is the status of the subject who proposes all this? Chuang Tzu would respond with another story.

Near the end of the chapter, Mr. Tall-Dryanda-Tree (*ch'ang-wu tzu)* quietly told chatty Mr. Jittery-Magpie (*chü ch'üeh tzu*), "Ch'iu [Confucius?] and you—both are dreams. I call you 'a dream'—I am also a dream" (line 260–61). To call someone a dream is to deny him a real status. At the same time, a valid claim requires the real status of the subject making it, which in turn requires that the subject be awake and alert. For one might claim to be in a dream while dreaming, and such a claim is unreliably dreamy.

But can the subject who is awake claim that he himself is now dreaming? That a wakeful claim to be dreaming is perfectly legitimate (though unexpected) is shown in Chuang Tzu's delightful story of his butterfly dream that concludes the chapter:

> Before, Chuang Chou dreamed being a butterfly. Flitting-and-flitter-
> ingly, he was a butterfly. Is it that in showing what he himself was, he did as
> he pleased? He did not understand that he was Chou.
> Suddenly he awoke. Then—it was solidly and surprisingly Chou.
> But, then, he did not understand—had Chou dreamed being a butterfly,
> or was a butterfly now dreaming of being Chou?
> Here we have Chou with a butterfly—there, then, must "exist a division."
> Just this is what is called "things changing" (lines 295-305).[10]

In this story we see not one but two dreams, which are produced by reflecting on one dream after having been awakened from it. These two dreams
are Chuang Tzu dreaming and the butterfly dreaming, and they are found to
be interconnected though mutually exclusive.

We usually suppose dream to be something unreal, but we seldom note
that dream is also a distinct world in itself made by the dreaming subject. And
the verdict on this constructed world to be "dream" is made not from inside
that world (while we are dreaming) but from *outside* of it, realizing that we
have now been "awakened" from that particular dream. And then we find that
each dream is a world in itself, each different from all others. The world of the
butterfly differs from that of Chuang Tzu, each with its own integrity, and
he/it cannot have both at once.

Chuang Tzu said in the story, however, that our awakening does not settle
the issue but raises it. For we have an additional problem. Now that we are
awakened enough to reflect on our "awakened" situation, we do not know
whether or not we are currently dreaming a different dream (cf. Meditation B.
13.2). Is Chuang Tzu really himself or a mere butterfly currently dreaming of
being Chuang Tzu? If each dream has its integrity (because they cannot be
mixed together), it also has its own uncertainty (because each trails on the
other).

The dream story can now be applied to world-making. Since each world
is as it is in itself the subject cannot recognize it, much less assess it, without
going outside of it ("awakened" *from* it); for how could Chuang Tzu have
knows he was not a butterfly unless awake from *its* world? Yet once outside,
that world is so different from the other that the subject is disqualified from
judging it adequately; for how could Chuang Tzu the man assess the world of
a butterfly? Each world is at once as it is in itself, differing from the other, *and*
connected with the other. "I call you 'a dream'—I am also a dream."

The dream story shows that it takes an awakening in order to be able to
reflect on the dream status of the present self. In fact, the self *must* be awake
before it is in a position to realize that it is eternally flip-flopping between its
having dreamed and its currently dreaming. And the self can respond to the

realization by freely changing from the subjecthood of a Chuang Chou (having dreamed) to that of a butterfly (currently dreaming), and back to Chuang Chou again, endlessly.

Here the distinct identities of the butterfly and the Chuang Chou have to hold. These two dreams are distinct; one cannot dream both at once. Besides, dreaming implies a dreamer, and two non-consecutive dreams imply two dreamers. They are real and distinct, and cannot be a matter of relativistic indifference. At the same time, there is an endless change-over of the status and identify of the dreamer, having nothing to do with Stoic quietude. And finally there is an inevitable involvement of the dreamer, the subject, who is anything but an ideal observer severed from the world.

"But to say, 'I am also a dream,' amounts to relativism caught in its own tail, defeating itself," so an objection may run: "For the truth of the statement requires that the subject be awake, and yet the statement claims that the subject is dreaming. Thus if the statement is true, it is false; the statement rests on its own denial."

Chuang Tzu might answer as follows: Even if I am not dreaming, now that I am "awake," I am not sure which subject I am—Chuang Chou, which I think I am, or someone else (butterfly?), dreaming to be Chuang Chou. And no matter which I am, now that I am "awake" and so "not sure," I cannot shake myself from my *dream* status—either as currently dreaming or as having dreamed. And this dream status stuck to myself is expressed by "I am also a dream."

And so this is how the situation stands. I am aware of being in a dream, or unable to get out of dream status, whether having dreamed or currently dreaming. And this dream-awareness is due to my being *awake*—now that I am awake, I am not sure. The situation, then, not only satisfies the logical requirement of a wakeful claimant for his claim to be true; for he must be awake to make his claim of *being* a dream, as we saw in Chuang Tzu's dream story. It also indicates the radical interrelation among the identities and the statuses—being awake, being in a dream, Chuang Chou, butterfly—which are at once distinctly and respectively real, *and* mutually dependent and trailing. This is what Mr. Tall Dryandra Tree means when he says, "I call you 'a dream'—I am also a dream."

Let us go a step further. If we compare a dreaming self to a nothing and a wakeful self to a something, then we see how even a nothing and a something are mutually dependent. Such dynamically interwined complex of being and nothing is expressed in the notion of "piping" (*lai*). The sound of a pipe obtains when the hollow of the pipe meets the belching of nature (the huge Clod, *ta k'uai*)—the invisible wind. The sound of a pipe obtains when the hollow of the pipe meets the belching, which is also a nothing. A hollow responds to the wind by sounding itself forth. Likewise, as a nothing, as dreaming, the subject sounds forth a something, a statement, "I am also a dream" (cf. lines 11—27).

This world is made up of the human pipings of the selves freely taking part in the real endless interchange of identities and responding to clamors of "monkeys" of things. Such human piping spontaneously responds to the pipings of the earth and of the Heaven—now a monkey keeper, now a buttterfly, now a Chuang Chou, "now a dragon, now a snake, shifting with the times, never holding to one course only. Now up, now down, measuring things with harmony, drifting and wandering with the beginning of things, thus thing-ing things (*wu wu*) without being thing-ed by things (*wu yü wu*)."[11]

To put it differently, there *exist* (*yu*) in this world several worlds of things, each distinct (*fen*) from the other. Things-and-worlds (*wu*) are yet interdependent-and-interchanging (*hua*), such that to say *p* on something assumes a non-*p* or even an anti-*p*, which yet gives rise to *p*. To roam in and out (*yu*) of these things in these worlds is to let things (*wu*) self-arrange and equalize (*ch'i*) themselves, to respond endlessly, to walk two ways, and thereby to overhear the heavenly piping (line 12).

B.   A Detailed Look

Here are some notions in the second chapter to which I found myself drawn. They are roughly in the order in which they appear in the chapter. Tarrying there, I found new landscapes and atmosphere. My world was renewed, opened, far and deep. I can assure you, my dear reader, that inexhaustibly more of such scenes as the following are hidden in this chapter. What follows is a mere handful of samples, hopefully to stimulate your own look into the chapter for your inspirations.[12]

1.   *Ch'i Wu Lun*: Each of the Seven Inner Chapters is titled with three pregnant characters. Of these titles, that of Chapter Two seems clearest yet most obscure. On the one hand, the chapter is clearly a treatise of a somewhat theoretical sort, and *Ch'i Wu Lun* reflects this sentiment. On the other hand, we can only vaguely promise what this title could mean. To trace its meaning is to come to understand this chapter, yet the meaning seems to move on as we look again and again.

Ch'i has at least three possible meanings: sorting-and-arranging, equal, and perhaps (mind-)fasting. *Lun* has at least four possible meanings: logicizing-arguing, arranging in order, wheeling, and threading-reeling. Obviously *ch'i* and lun overlap in "arranging." *Wu* can be seen as things (*niu*) cut out (*wu*) by *lun*; things are seen as *ch'i* if our *lun* is things self-*lun*-ing.[13]

Such are our etymological and textual clues. What follows are meditations on what all this could *mean*.

1.1. Such men as Nietzsche, Kierkegaard, and Kafka were convinced that they were unique Individuals, self-obsessed, excluded, and set apart from the crowd. In writing so, they hit *our* inner sympathetic cords—*everyone* is unique. Everyone thinks troubles are unique. Even after being assured that everyone has similar pain and troubles, his sense of *unique* pain remains. It is not that he disagree with that assurance; he is convinced that perhaps everyone does have a more or less similar if not the same kind of problems. But such knowledge does not diminish his sense of being uniquely-in-pain. The general knowledge of pain and the sense of unique pain go together. We are, then, equal in our uniqueness; we are *all* unique; this is one possible understanding (*lun*) about the equality (*ch'i*) of things (*wu*).

1.2. Many uses of logic conform to basic logical rules, which are thus universally applicable. We understand things because they fit structures of reasonableness. We understand many different metaphysical systems and rational arguments for the same reason—they all conform to logicality, meaningfulness, and reasonableness. Thus we can say logic (*lun*) trivially unifies (*ch'i*) all things, including systems and arguments (*wu*).

Yet things (thoughts, arguments, and metaphysical systems) differ one from another. People oppose one another by relying on the same logical rules. There is no single set of logical rules for using logical rules, nor is there a single metaphysical principle for constructing metaphysical systems. This argues against the possibility of one grand system (of whatever sort) that covers all things, arguments, and metaphysical systems.

But then, what about this argument-against-the-possibility? Does this argument (*lun*) cover (*ch'i*) myriads of things (*wu*)?

1.3. Another meaning of *lun^a* could be the way of *lun^c* ("wheels") of things. Ch'i Wu Lun then becomes "all (*ch'i*) things (*wu*) mutually involving and arranging (*ch'i*) themselves in wheels and wheels (*lun^c*)," the way of "things changing". To see the way things go in this manner we become involved likewise (*yin shih, man yen*). Things are thus in a merry-go-round that is really merry.[14] To participate in it is to change (*hua*), the verb that began Chapter One and ends Chapter Two: *hua* is *lun^c*, *lun^b*, or *lun^a*.

Such a wheeling of things is inexpressible (remember the story of the wheelwright)[15] because expression opposes its denial and wheeling does not.

Such a wheeling is always beginning (always "yet to begin to begin to ...),[16] and so without definite beginning or end. Probing into the origin of things, we find that existence and non-existence, one and three, involve each other; arguing parties involve each other; shadow and penumbra involve each other; dream and awakening involve each other.

This chapter describes such mutual involvement, in which we walk, taking two roads, affirming together pairs of opposites (death and life, yes and no, can and cannot). All are various earthenware freely turned forth from the potter's wheel (*t'ien chün, lu lu*), the heavenly wheel, the Pivot of the Way of things (*tao shu*).

Such a turning is neither moving nor stopping, but both. As Al Chung-liang Huang said,

> The minute you use two words, there seem to be two different things. He is moving; he is quiet. T'ai Chi integrates these two extremes. When you meditate, you realize you are moving and being quiet at the same time; your energy is furiously moving, extending, feeling, while your physical self is settling down quietly. Watch a potter centering the clay on the potter's wheel. You see that furious motion of the turning—yet the clay seems not to move; it does not budge because it is centered. It is right there, as if it is standing still.[17]

Ch'i Wu Lun seems to be concerned with *wu*, "things," the many-ness of something other than the self. The chapter is advertized as *ch'i*, a "sorting out" (Graham) and an "equalizing" (Watson) of the other-than-self.

But the chapter starts with the self lost (in) itself, and ends with the self as the other, the butterfly. Perhaps, then, another interpretation of *ch'i* could be *chai*, fasting. Here it means either self-fasting or thing-fasting. If self-fasting, Ch'i Wu Lun says, "By self-fasting, that is, losing subjective discrimination, we can see things wheelingly arrange and interchange among themselves." If taken to be thing-fasting, Ch'i Wu Lun amounts to a disputation on fasting things away, so as to attain unpurturbed clarity of unity with the "Heavenly Reservoir or Treasury," the "Heavenly Balance," the "Shaded Light." Both views are acceptable; they complement each other.

1.4.   Rhythm, such as that of music, is something peculiar. It exists only to a person who thinks it exists; or rather, it exists to a person to whom it exists. This subject-related existence has a twofold significance. Rhythm exists only when it is *recognized* and responded to as rhythm, and rhythm exists only as resonance that *spreads*. Both to resonate and to spread as resonance, that is what the existence of rhythm means. Rhythm means co-responding, co-resonance, in which individual resonance represents individual identity.

But then such symphonic resonating rhythm is both a single rhythm and many individual tunes. This is the meaning of "oneness in nature," that *ch'i* which is glibly translated as "equality." It is both one and many, total and individual, one living solidarity that is individually autochthonous. Subatomic particles (as a system) are such, human body is such, friendship is such; family, society, history, culture, the eco-system of nature, are such; in fact, anything that is *actual* at all is such. This sort of *ch'i*-rhythm is natural, moving, and composed; *Ch'i Wu Lun* says that in nature things sort and even themselves out.[18] Modern physics and ancient intuition in the *I Ching* tell us that things (*wu*) are such a rhythmic system (*lunª, lunᵇ*) of resonating togetherness (*ch'i*).

To hear their piping (*wen ... lai*) and to see their silence (*chien chih t'iao-t'iao, chih tiao-tiao*) is to hear and see the cosmic rhythm (lines 11–12, 27). To thus enter into the rhythm of things we must lose our selves in it, that is, become absolutely quiet inside ("dead ashes") and out ("dry wood"; line 6). Then we see that we usually call such "tunes of things" life and death, good and evil, right and wrong, beauty and ugliness, fortune and misfortune, formation and breakdown. This is the story of life we are going to hear and see, the story of the logic of the life of things.

2.   If the first chapter starts with Northern Darkness, then the second chapter quietly begins with Mr. Southern Limit (horizon?) of the City (*nan kuo*). There in the Northern Darkness was a fish changing into a bird to fly to the Southern Darkness; here in the Southern City-Limit is Mr. Dark-Basis losing himself to hear pipings, especially the Heavenly piping. There in the first chapter two animals were in silent actions changing, rising, flying. Here two people are talking serenely, one in self-less hearing, another in awed asking. Could it be that the epochal journey from Northern to Southern Darkness is from animality to humanity (from fish to bird to self-less man), from nameless darkness so as to prepare for the takeoff, to a serene city dwelling so as to overhear the heavenly piping in self taking off (from) the self? Is the first chapter that of activities in the world and the second chapter that of meditative overhearing of the world? Is the first chapter the takeoff and the second chapter the arrival?

In any case, the name Nan-Kuo Tzu-Ch'i starts the second chapter, and this name is perhaps not without significance. Usually the name is taken to refer to some historical personage whom Chuang Tzu admired. But we would not be surprised if the name *also* alluded to something symbolic.

The ancient Chinese city was surrounded by a city wall against bandits.

Nan kuo literally means "the southern city wall" or "to the south of the city wall" where the commoners gather.[19] *Tzu* is "man" or "Mr." *Ch'i* is either "very, variegated, or dark grey (or red)"[20] or "basis, root.[21] Thus *Nan-Kuo Tzu-Ch'i* can mean Mr. Basics at the common throng of the plebeians, amidst their hustle and bustle. He is the "man living at the unrecognized southern city wall and embodying the basic Tao."[22] This contrasts with Fukunaga Mitsuji, who said that the man lived in the quiet outskirts away from city congestion, forgetting worldliness and even himself, enjoying the life of composure reminiscent of the great flight of the P'ung Bird.[23] On the contrary, I think Akatzuka is right in placing Mr. Nan Kuo in the midst of city life; he still kept himself untainted, given to soaring and roaming in the sky. The famous poem of T'ao Ch'ien's comes to mind:

> Building a hut amidst common men,
> Without hearing clamors of horse or coach—
> May I ask you how it is possible?
> When the heart is distant, the place itself becomes
> > out of the way ...
> . . . .
> Birds flying, two by two return.
> In all this there is true meaning;
> Wanting to explain it, words are already forgotten.

How about that awed Mr. Yen-Ch'eng Tzu-Yu? Akatzuka took *yen ch'eng* to mean "elegant city" (*yen ch'eng*), and took *tzu yu* to mean a person (*tzu*) like pennant (*liu*) or scallops along the lower edge of a flag (*yu*); that is, he is a city dweller and minor follower of Tao, yet without deep understanding.

I hesitate. After all, Mr. South-Wall Basis praised him; he cannot be a shallow person. *Yen Ch'eng* may mean someone as accomplished (*ch'eng*) as Yen Hui, the best disciple of Confucius; *Tzu Yu* may refer to another disciple of Confucius; he was a man of literary sensitivity, and forty-five years younger than Confucius.[25] He must be an inquisitive young man with fine Confucian sentivity. His inquiry may signal Chuang Tzu's intention that Chuang Tzu's ideal man is beyond the Confucian ideal, recognizable as a strange ideal, yet unintelligible in Confucian terms.

3.1. What strange thing did this sensitive young Confucian see in Mr. Basis of the Common? Chuang Tzu took care to describe the strange Mr. Basis three times.

First, Mr. Basis was presented descriptively; " ... reclined on his armrest and sat; looked up to heaven and sighed deeply, vacant, seemed to have lost his counterpart" (lines 2–3). He was not watching anything, but looked up to the sky, barely breathing ("sighed deeply"), as if having lost his reciprocal, which could be either himself or things in general.[26]

Secondly, Mr. Yen-Ch'eng Tzu-Yu reported objectively what he observed. From outside, an observer senses the change —"Can the figure really be 'allowed' to become 'as' dry wood, and can the heart-mind really be allowed to become as dead ashes?" (line 6). There is a change (shih ju) into unresponsiveness. We usually take it to mean self-preoccupation. In this case, unresponsiveness goes to the extent of not responding to oneself. One has died to oneself, without even self-awareness.

Finally, we see Chuang Tzu's subjective presentation of Mr. South-Wall Basis. For the above objective impression is mistaken. Mr. Basis does respond to Mr. Yen-Ch'eng's query. What is lost is his "counterpart," that is, his self-as-looked-at-from-outside, from the standpoint of others. The newborn baby is glum and self-composed, yet not without awareness.[27] It is the self-made-conscious-of-itself that he lacks.

Walt Whitman's *Song of Myself* can be instructively compared with Chuang Tzu's passage here. Both are nature lovers; both take care of themselves. Yet somehow they are different. "Song of Myself" can mean either "song about myself" or "I myself singing myself;" in either case, it means "I love myself," and "the I always goes with things, with many worlds of things." Chuang Tzu, in contrast, saw the I (wu^f) forgetting the I (wo), the I awakening to the possibility of being in a dream, as a dreamed entity. This is the "loss" of the wo-self to the wu-self. There is a radical oneness of being and nothingness, or rather, a radical oneness with oneself that ultimately means oneness with things without losing distinction. Whitman has "song to myself"; Chuang Tzu has a self-less overhearing of pipings of men, earth, and heaven.

What does the self losing the self mean? What does overhearing nature's piping mean? The first question will be taken up immediately, in 3.2.; the second question comes later, in 3.4.

3.2.   *The self losing the self*: Reading the second chapter, we are struck by Chuang Tzu's consistent use of the wu-self that differs from the wo-self.[28]

The authentic wu-self[29] appears in its un-selfing, that is, mind-fasting (hsin-chai) or wu-chai-ing, wo-chai-ed. It is the self that lets go (shih ju) of its obtrusive self (wo), that is fasting away the objectifiable, identifiable companion-self (yü; cf. ou, line 104). The true wu-self is, in turn, authenticated in its activity of self-fasting and self-losing (wu sang wo).

The object-self (*wo*) is "obtrusive" in that, as Kant said, it has its "experience" only by *imposing* its synthetic-apriori forms on reality, on thing-in-itself. To know is to dictate, to legislate-question-and-demand-answers-in-terms-of-the-question-and-get-them.[30] It is to stir up human piping, and hear earthly piping *in terms of* human piping.

If this obtrusive self is let go of, then the authentic self, the self that has been doing the losing, the self-shed self will appear as the self-that-has-lost-itself, as empty as dry wood and dead ashes (*kau-mu ssu-hui*; cf. *hsü*). Such *wu*-self is a catharted self, whose authenticity is certified precisely in its activity of self-catharsis (*sang wo, sang ou*).

Two corollaries follow. The first is about the "reality" thus seen. The second is the self-activity that obtains in this manner. Let us start with the second implication.

Wu shows itself as a negative force that *loses* the objective phenomenal *wo*-self. *Wu* shows itself in the disappearing of *wo*. *Wu* selfs itself in its un-selfing.

Wu-wei can be understood in this context, and our understanding of *wu-wei* sheds light on the un-*wo*-ing of *wu*. Chuang Tzu did not adopt Lao Tzu's phrase, *wei wu-wei*.[31] For the phrase is not only redundant but has two dangers. It tends to make *wu-wei* into some*thing* to be contrived; in *wei*-ing such *wu-wei*, the *wei* is re-introduced. In actuality, however, the activity of *wu-wei* obtains of itself *in* the *wu*-ing of *wei*. *Wu-wei* appears *in* its own act of self-disappearance; it is authenticated by its self-catharsis.

Similarly, *tzu wei* or *tzu-jan* is not an innocent notion. It is not whatever that exists as it is, but an activity that self-authenticates in and through its negative movement of self-loss. It is not a random reckless whatever-goes. As the self-act goes through its own fasting away, *it* appears of itself as natural, free, and spontaneous. For to do something requires an agent. When the agent does its own cleansing away of its self, it appears of itself as authentic-*wu*. Such spontaneity is a catharted one, a home-coming to the self.

To such a sobered *wu*-self and its activity of *wu-wei* and *tzu-wei*, reality appears as it is (*ku jan, t'ien lai*). To put it in Kantian language, the thing-in-itself appears in a Kantian not-knowing; we know actuality in our not-knowing (*wu chih*, even *pu chih*). Such knowledge of not-knowing reminds us of Socratic knowledge through ignorance. Reality is affirmed and known beyond words and knowledge. It is in this Realm of no-realm that we come to "know" that things are "equal," in an active sense of reciprocal interchange and dependence (*wu hua, fang-sheng fang-ssu, yin-shih yin-fei, fang-k'o fang-pu-k'o*). *Ch'i wu* is a situation of participatory democracy of beings that appear to the self in its self-fasting.

The firemen at the fire station play cards and even break their bones drilling fire drills, but so far they do *nothing* "real." Their drills and their playing prepare them for real fire. When the real fire breaks out, they "do nothing." They just hop on to the fire engine and do what they have been drilling. They practice as if what they do is real, and they do real things as if, in practice, *unreal*. Thus they do unreal things in reality; they "do nothing" real to do real things. They do real things as-if not real, both while they are drilling (in which they are serious in a make-believe world) and while putting out real fire (as if playing a game in a make-believe world).

"Chuang Chou" (the knowing, indentifiable, nameable, phenomenal self) dreamed, then awoke, then wondered. *In* such dreaming, awakening, wondering, there is the real subject-self (*wu*) that *understands* the mutual interchanges and distinctions of things. It is when I participate in these experiences that I come to understand: this is participatory knowledge. It is here that the things-in-themselves appear together (*ch'i wu*) and are known through being unknown.

3.3. *Reciprocal change*: Mr. Yen-Ch'eng Tzu-Yu, the observant Confucian disciple, exclaimed at Mr. South-Wall Basis, change: "The man ... now is not the one ... before," (line 7). Mr. Basis admitted the change (*hua*?): "I (*wu*) have lost myself (*wo*)" (line 10).

The *wo* that is shed off and lost is the self identifiable as a particular something, an entity persisting with oneself as its "counterpart" (*yü*), as "the self." Here it is the so-called "Mr. South-Wall-Basis" judging, clinging to himself, the subject that is full of himself (self-consciousness). Thus the *wo*-self is the this-yes (*shih*), the completion-formation (*ch'eng*), as opposed to the that-no (*fei*) and the breakdown (*huei*). The *wo*-self is umbra against the penumbra, the Chuang Chou against the dreamed butterfly. The *wo*-self originates division (*fen*), a subjective regarding of the objects as different from the self, a mound (*feng*) turned into a boundary (*chen*), a division between fields.

It is all right, however, to regard things as different one from another; "make insistence on 'this-yes,' and boundaries come to exist like raised paths between fields" (line 170). It is all right to do so as long as we acknowledge (*i ming*) ourselves regarding them as such, and stop making anything out of it, but let ourselves be and let things be (*yin shih, ying*).

In order to let things be as they are and let our *wo*-self continue regarding things, we must lose (or loosen)[32] our *wo*-self, or rather, lose our love of identifiable self; we do well to stop taking our self as *this wo*-self, as a Chuang Chou, as correct ("this-yes"), and so on.

Once we have lost our identifiable *wo*-self, we can accommodate and participate in the differences and divisions (*fen*) of things. Our participation is equivalent to knowing that everything "can" (*k'o*) be as it is, that things have their own "so," their own "can" (line 114). We can participate in each thing, each *yes*, each *this*, each *can*. Such participation is called things-(inter)change (*wu hua*; line 305)—fish changing into bird, Mr. South Wall Basis letting himself become like dry wood and dead ashes, Chuang Chou dreaming himself a butterfly. Things-interchanging is also myself-changing. It is because of this that there is distinction (another interpretation of line 170).

3.4.   And having lost oneself, one immediately *asks*, "Do you hear ... piping?" (lines 11, 12). Such is our way of participating in things.

To listen (*t'ing*) is to attend and gather. To hear (*wen*) is to empty-mindedly let in. To listen is to collect; to hear is to accept. To listen is to collect things; to hear is to let things collect of themselves. As the subject makes room inside (as a chamber), the ways of things will come in and collect themselves there. What we see is no longer the subject listening and collecting, but the waves of things gathering themselves, flocking themselves *there* in a room, an emptiness, an environment in which things become themselves.

To let things in is to see that things become of themselves and we do not know how this happens, or what lets things be (*shih tzu-chi*)[33] is. We only hear ways of things as waves of things, their rhythm, their flow in their beautiful pattern, vibrating in ourselves.

The subject *wu*-self loses itself (*wo*), and then it can hear emptily the heavenly piping, the wind blowing. To hear is to listen with the breaths of things; one becomes an empty room to accommodate things, for the ways of things gather themselves in emptiness. All this describes mind-fasting (4/24–34).

I used to think that I listen to music in order to live (well), but now I suspect that perhaps we all live in order to listen, not with ears (only) but with our spine of souls. And the growth of a person is measured not by years but by growth in *this* direction, to be able more and more to "hear" things and "overhear" the silence of things, that is, their actuality and what makes them as they are. Such hearing and overhearing are equivalent to letting things in, and letting oneself disappear in things, and letting oneself *be* in them, as adumbrated in the story of Chuang Chou dreaming to be a butterfly at the end of the chapter. There is disappearance without disappearing, unity in difference and transformation.

> The Great Man ... is like the shadow that follows a form, the echo that follows a sound ... making himself the companion *(p'ei)* of the world ... He dwells in the echoless, moves in the directionless ... and proceeds to wander *(yu)* in the beginningless ... His face and form blend with the Great Unity ...

which is selfless. ... He who fixes his eyes on nothingness—he is the true
friend of Heaven and earth.[34]

But what sort of "piping" is it that we hear and overhear when we lose our
wo-self and blend with things? We know holes make sounds. Why? Wind
arises and blows; that's why. The wind arises; why? Who made it so? The
answer to the latter two questions is "somewhat like the relation between holes
and the wind." Holes are something negative, a lack; the wind is something
invisible, the power of a no-thing. And our questions are also a lack, asking
to be filled, and to be filled with something like the wind. That *something* must
be as powerful as the wind, as no-thing, as invisible, blowing the wind to blow
forth sounds out of a lack, a hole.

Yet this "something" is not identical with the wind or holes; it is less than
that no-thing, the wind, and more lacking than the "lack" of holes. It is that
mysterious Darkness to the North. It is an inexpressible No-thing, to which we
can allude only by questions, as in the beginning of the chapter,[35] or by admis-
sions of ignorance ("How would I understand it?"), attempts at saying something ("Although thus, let me try to say something about it"), or saying things
"with abandon" ("I will try for you to say some abandoned words; you with
the same abandon listen").[36] All these are modes of saying without saying,
adopted toward the end of the chapter.

Now, if holes and cavities make the earthly piping, and our questions and
trials make the human piping, what is unique about the heavenly piping of
which both these pipings are an expression?

To begin with, we realize that heavenly piping is not a piping as other
pipings are, but a piping-enabling power, much as medicine is not healthy as
our body is, but as an health-producing agent. That is why silence is also part
of heavenly piping; "Are you alone not seeing them wavering, quivering?"
(line 27). We are reminded of such expressions as "God is light" and "God is
good." God is light in the sense that God produces light while surrounding
himself with darkness;[37] God is good in the sense that God produces good,
and rains on both the good and the bad people.[38] Heavenly piping is similar
in this respect to God.

Heavenly piping differs, however, from God and medicine in one respect—it is a power that is yet to begin to let there-exist something that is yet
to begin to exist (lines 154–160). In other words, heavenly piping is the spring-
power (*chi*) and seed-power (*chung*) of all pipings, not separate from them as
God and medicine are from their productions. To borrow Aristotle's language
of four causes, heavenly piping is not merely the efficient cause but also the
formal cause and perhaps the material cause of all pipings—though perhaps

it is not their final cause. For everything is self-caused, having its own integrity; it is innocently and naturally its own self-sovereign.[39]

And perhaps this is why the image of "piping" is used by Chuang Tzu. Piping is wonderfully vague about self-creation. On the one hand, it is as it is, a unique piping all to itself. On the other hand, it is produced by, and produces, a nothing—it produces sound, as invisible as a nothing, and it is produced by a nothing, a hollow or cavity blown through by a breath of air that is invisible and bland. And the same wind produces so many pipings. Furthermore, piping can mean echo and resonance, sounding back and forth that is as individual as it is mutual, as considered a while ago.[40] All of these are symbolic of heavenly piping, that mysterious dark power of enablement that is itself a non-being.

3.5.   It is interesting to see references to vision and light in this chapter. They are as follows, groupable in two clusters:

GROUP A

Fierce winds pass on, then all hollows become empty;
Are you alone not seeing them wavering, quivering?   (*lines 26–27*)

Tao is hidden by small formations; words are hidden by vain show.
And then there exists this-yes and that-no ...
If we desire to "yes" their no's and "no" their yes's, then there is nothing like
   by the light of clarity.   (*lines 92–94*)
For this reason he does not use things according to his judgment but lodges
   them in the ordinary. It is this which we call "by the illumination of clarity
   and nature."   (*line 149*)
Pour into it and it does not fill, bale out of it and it is not drained—and we do
   not know where it comes from.
It is this which we call the Shaded Light.   (*lines 188–89*)
How much more so with him whose virtue brightens more than the
   sun's!   (*line 194*)

GROUP B

For the appearance of this-yes and that-no is what makes for Tao's
   deformation.   (*line 134*)
Others were not clarified yet they insisted on clarifying it to them.
Therefore Hui Tzu ended his life with the obscurities of "hardness and
   whiteness ... "   (*lines 143–44*)
Tao manifest, and it is not Tao.   (*line 183*)

These are all the references I know of to sight and light in this chapter. Group B refer to philosophical debates, whose abstruse topics are illustrated in Group A. Therefore Group A deserves attention.

In Group A, to see is to see emptiness, to see silence (lines 26–27), to see "withered wood and dead ashes" (6), to see the very loss of the self (10). Vision is for detection of a lack, emptiness, ignorance of the origin of things (54, 188).

Thus such vision is an audient one, what is commonly called contemplative or meditative vision. This is where we hear the invisible wind starting up and things raise their howlings, thereby realizing that everything is equal (*ch'i*) — by seeing things of quiet (*chi*) and empty-hollow (*ch'iao, hsü*). Such seeing of equality in the emptiness of things is in turn due to the emptying of the self (*hsin chai, sang wo)* where the ways of things collect (*tao chi yü hsü).* A self-emptying leads to a hearing of the winds arousing things. Such hearing in turn leads to an audient seeing of vacuous quietude. And in such pervasive quietude we realize (are awakened to) the equality of all things.

Silence after music—what is it? What does it mean? Three things can be said.

(1) Silence after music is a rest from music in order to digest music, to feed on it and grow silently in it—thereby to become part of it. Such music-digestion, as any digestion, is inaudible, silent, even to our consciousness. Growth takes place unawares.

(2) Silence after music is a background against which the music just heard stands out as music. It is soil to music, an environment in which music grows.

(3) Silence after music is neither music nor unrelated to music. It is something, or rather, a no-thing, that goes with music to make a musical whole. It is something visible to accompany something audible—to make that piping of heaven.

4. As to allusions to Something that lets things sprout as they are, three descriptive modes stand out: to blow and arouse (*ch'ui, nu*), to let-be oneself and self-adopt (*shih tzu-chi, tzu-ch'ü*),[41] and the question form in which such meditative phrases are cast.

Three points can be made about those three descriptive modes. But before going into these points some words on "principle" are in order. We can say there exists something as a ruling principle that is active constantly in things. Principle is etymologically connected to principality and prince, as both David Hall and Robert Neville noticed. Neither liked the rigidity and tyranny that such rulership entails. Hall "solved" the problem by putting principle in things—he goes for "autonomy." Neville "solved" it by going to the "vague" metalevel principle of abstraction and generality.[42]

They are to be commended for sensing the problem of principle in Western philosophizing. Unfortunately neither offered totally satisfactory solutions. Hall still needs an overruling principle for those individual principles, something like the principle of preestablished harmony. Neville must pay the price of abstraction and imposition. His new language and new grammar aspire to *take over* all our expressive modes. His system threatens to be another principle. Now we can consider Chuang Tzu's three points.

(1) Chuang Tzu dissolved the problem by two steps: (*a*) He admitted the necessity of principle that overarches all things, and yet (*b*) insisted that we do not-know it.

The unity of these two points—our intimation of the necessity of principle plus our ignorance of it—entails three points mentioned at the beginning: (*i*) There is at least the activity of blowing and arousing; (*ii*) such activity is actually a letting-be oneself and a self-adopting. Actually we see just *things* themselves becoming as they are, things adopting themselves, in commotion of existing, analogous to various howlings and hissings when it blows, although the "it" remains unnoticed; (*iii*) but what is this "it" that blows? We must let it stand as our *question*. It is a Kafka-esque "lord," an unknown true lord (*chen chai*). Our nickname "wind" is just that, a sobriquet. We can say the wind comes by difference in atmospheric pressure, which in turn is produced by the tilt and rotation of the earth. All this is what we *say*, another howling, another nicknaming. For we can always ask for the origin, the principle, the lord, of all such "difference" "tilt," and "rotation."

(2) And so this is how we stand —"there must be" and "we do not know." This is a steadfast refusal to go into a comprehensive-systematic metaphysics on the one hand, or into a comprehensive and systematic scepticism on the other. We embody in ourselves such a principle, such an acknowledgement, and such ignorance.

Such i-gnorance is so important that Chuang Tzu expressed it in more than one way:

(a) He used rhetorical questions: "... he who arouses them, who is he?" (line 36). "How can I understand ... " (195–201, 203–204, 245–249). "How can I know that with which this is so?"(294).

(b) Chuang Tzu denied explicit knowledge: "It seems like there exists something genuinely in command, yet only we do not get its clues" (57). "He did not understand—had Chou dreamed being a butterfly, or was a butterfly dreaming of being Chou?" (302–303).

(c) Chuang Tzu used *wuᵃ* (a negation of existence) as a summary of our intuition-and-ignorance of the principle: "no figure" (*wu hsing*; 59), "not-said anything" (*wu wei*; 160, 234), "going should not exist" (*wu shih*; 169), "in life or death there exists no change to the self" (*wu pien*; 229), "no dispute as to the difference" (*wu pien*; 285), "no limit" (*wu ching*; 288–89), "no constant independence" (*wu t'e ts'ao*; 291).

(d) Chuang Tzu appealed to the revered "knowledge of the ancients"— about there not yet to begin to be things (130).

(e) Chuang Tzu kept saying, "I propose to try to say something" (153), "I try for you to say some abandoned words" (130–31), "suppose there exists a saying" (150), "I try to say" (202), where "try" means "experiment in ..."

(f) The most startling announcement is undoubtedly Chuang Tzu's saying connected with dream, "I call you 'a dream'—I am also a dream" (261), where "call" (*wei*) is the same as "what people call" in "Things we call them so and they are so" (112), and is as hesitantly experimental as those sayings in (e) above.

In any case, a dream realized as dream indicates an awakening, a not-dream; thus, "dream" is a self-negating notion, a notion that includes its own negation to obtain. In addition, it belongs to the dream that we can never be sure whether we are awakened or in a dream; again, here, we have a combination of certainty with its own negation—we are certain that we are not certain. In some such manner Chuang Tzu assures us that we are very certain about our being uncertain about the principle of things.

(3) What does such insistence (certainty) about our uncertainty of principle indicate? At least two facts: (*a*) The principle of things is also *within* us, so much so that it *is* our subject-ive undergoing of the experience of existence as existence. We embody (*wu hua, hua sheng*) the principle of existence, though we are not identical with it (*yu fen*). (*b*) We have no-knowledge of it. Knowledge requires distance. To know is to see, and without distance we neither know nor see. When we *undergo* the experience, we have an intimate taste of such experience of being ourselves. But we do not-know it. We are uncertain as to *what* it is, and are sure of our uncertainty.

Incidentally, *fen* is a subjective intuition of objective distinction, which Chuang Tzu used *feng* ("mound") and *chen* ("raised paths in the field") to express. Similarly, *wo*-self is owned by *wu*, the subject-existing-in-itself. Such distinction in the usage of words is maintained in this chapter.

5. Now we are in a position to move on to the negative aspect of what has been considered so far. To blow forth sayings (theories, distinctions) and things (subjects, events) with the wind, the *ch'i* ("equality"?) has negative as well as positive significance. Negatively obsessed with sayings and things, we become "big" and "small wits," expanding and picking holes (35–36), shouting "morning, three" (126), shedding tears of Lady Beautiful (247–49), all of them tragicomedies. But to *know* that obsession brings tragicomedy leads us to wandering delightfully between dreaming and being awake, flipflopping our identities—and these are the positive consequences. Let us go into the negative aspect first.

Not to lose the *wo*-self in our participatory interchange among things is to "enslave ourselves for life" (72), damaging all our thinking, our notions, and our regards. The most obvious roads to damage are objectivation and clarification. For the Tao made manifest is not the Tao, discrimination put in words does not reach far, benevolence made constant is not universal, fastidious modesty cannot be trusted, and daring attack never wins (183). Thus we have a pair of contrasts—losing the *wo*-self and participating in the interchange of things, on the one hand, clinging to the *wo*-self and becoming enslaved and obsessed with the bewildering interchanges among things, on the other.

This chapter has another pair of thoughts—"not-yet-beginning-to-be," and the "one" (see B.9.2). Somehow these two notions are related, and serve to *anchor* the above pair of notions (the interchange and the self-loss) firmly down to actuality, preventing them from flying into abstraction and/or mystical irrelevance. After all, our world is the rich Heavenly Treasury (187) that is real enough to make us relent our tears (245–49). To a world that includes dreams and deaths we do well to be awakened (255, 300).

In order to be awakened *out* of self-obsession, we must consider what such obsession includes—it includes human piping that is full of "formed mind" (78, 81). What is such mind?

We are surrounded (if not overwhelmed) with human piping. In this all too human world we rush and gallop to and fro, fight or follow things, and fight within ourselves (71). All such self-destruction comes from our set ideas about what is to be affirmed and what is to be denied (*shih fei*), what is to be approved of and what is to be disapproved of (*k'o pu k'o*; 93–99). This in turn comes from our "(pre-)formed mind-and-heart," our pre-suppositions, presumptions, prejudices.

To stop our painfully meaningless hustle and bustle, we must see *how* and *wherefrom* our preformed mind arises in the first place (52, 54, 56).

Lines 35 through 84 constitute a warning against failing to lose-oneself to overhear the heavenly piping. Following our preformed mind as our teachers, we come to be obsessed and possessed with diverse confusions, all sound and fury. But this section may also be taken as a continuation of the question, "... but he who arouses them, who is he?" (34).

And both interpretations cohere—a warning and a pressing forward. If we do not vacate ourselves from ourselves, we shall be slaves to our set minds. We will then have approvals and disapprovals, then daily struggles within ourselves and with things—we will be constantly rushed and harried. We then must see how set-minds arise, hence the original question, "... but he who arouses them, who is he?"

This question is to be considered and answered in lines 85–107. But, now, note that the piping is echoed by a blowing. "Great understanding ..." (35) is a transition from and an emphasis on "who does the arousing?" Unless the question is answered we will be in eternal miseries.

In order even to *ask* this question, however, we must first lose ourselves and our set-minds. For to ask intelligently such a question is to identify it as a problem, and identification requires distancing from it, that is, to lose the *wo*-self and go outside of the problem.

But then to go out of the problem to identify and look at the problem is to have started solving it. For once we lose the *wo*-self, we can empty-mindedly listen to the heavenly piping, the echoes of nature, *within* the sound and fury, the hustle and bustle of things which change, co-arise, and complement one another. As we see them, we ourselves come to take part in them, ourselves interchanging with them (*wu hua*). Again, we come to that dream story that enjoys the interchange of the *wo*-self (Chuang Chou) with others (butterfly), as in a dream.

6.   Let us now go to lines 85 through 107. Saying something is not a prejudiced blowing (as Confucians and Mohists have it, leading to the kind of "suffering" we have been discussing), but a being-blown by that something which affirms both the this (*shih*) and the that (*pi*). And we respond to them as true human piping sounding forth what it overhears empty-self-ly. This is a true human piping, not a blowing but a being-blown. Human piping is true and meaningful if it is blown through by earthly piping of the this and the that.

And these *this*'s and *that*'s are in fact also being-blowns themselves. The "wind" of things blows where it wills, and things now appear, now disappear (*fang sheng fang ssu*), and a *yes*, an affirmation, causes and is caused by a *no*, a negation (*yin shih yin fei*), appearing now as "right," now as "wrong" (*fang K'o fang pu k'o*).[43] This is why the sage does not take sides but looks at them from the perspective of heavenly piping, "illuminates them all from heaven" (line 100), that is, goes according to the (self-)affirmation of all things (*yin*

shih). He sees that "that" is also a "yes," and the "yes" belongs also to "that."
"That" is also a one yes-and-no, "this" is also a one yes-and-no—it does not
make sense to claim opposition.

This condition is called the "pivot of the way" of things; when the pivot
is fitted into the "ring" of the ceaseless "yes" and ceaseless "no," we can then
respond to them ceaselessly. The Greek gate-god Janus faced both ways, in
opposite directions. Chuang Tzu wants us to be a Janus of the universe, or
perhaps the pivots at the center of the circles of things co-arising. Soon he
would propose to walk both ways, formation and breakdown, as the ways of
nature swing to and fro.

Let us put all this from the perspective of a judging subject. As we are til-
ted (*p'ien*)[44] toward the side on which we stand, then *this* appears. If *this* is
taken as *that* (from the standpoint of *that*), then *this* becomes incomprehensible even by *this*. *This* is said to be known only when *this* is known-as-right-
and-acceptable. And, paradoxical as it may sound, to be in such a state of self-
knowledge, self-affirmation, and self-justification gives rise to the *that* and
the *no*, because self-affirmation means other-negation, and negation implies
acknowledgement of the *existence* of the other to be negated. *That* and *no*
emerge out of *this* and *yes*.

Chuang Tzu says this is the origin of Hui Shih's sophistry. Chuang Tzu
agrees with him, saying that as soon as a birth takes place, death begins to
emerge, and as soon as death happens, birth is not far away. Because of *this*
(right) *that* arises (as a wrong), and because of *that*, *this* arises in contrast to
it.[45]

Such reciprocity and co-incidence in time, space, and causal relation
(*fang*) is the network of things that explains their existence and justification.
This is not to dazzle us (as Hui Shih dazzles) or to deny the existence and
relation of things (as Buddhism does), but to affirm them all—logic, relativity,
and existence. Thus Chuang Tzu explains the origin of all things, space, time,
and reasoning.

The pivotal notion here is *fang*,[46] which means "for a while, about to,
because of," and the like—a fit term to express causal, processive, and often
instantaneous co-arisings among things. Standing in this *fang*, we see things
and judgments as inter-dependent, from which "differences" ("division" or
"discrimination") arise. Differences can mean those in things and in subjects
(*shih-fei, pi-shih*). Differences can also mean those in time, in the process of
formation and breakdown of things, life and death.

Now, if differences of things and judgments appear because of interdependent co-happening, then they stop bothering us when we stop being

obsessed with them (*pu yu*) and stop exercising such judgment (*pu yung*). Or, positively speaking, we can stay at the pivots of the swinging door called *fang*, and fit the pivots and doors in the "center of the circle" of co-incidence in the world (104–105), somewhat as follows:

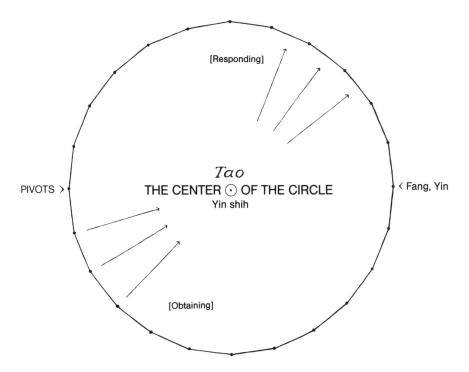

Whether the door opens or closes, the movements of the door are the *same* to its pivot-hinge. The pivot and hinge can be taken as having limitless *yes*'s and *no*'s. Whether swinging in one direction ("yes") or in another ("no"), the swinging remains the same movement to the door.[47]

This sameness is characterized as *yin-shih* (100; cf. 123, 128). For we can now afford to recognize- the-"yes" (*shih*) to (*yin*) any situation, right or wrong, life or death.

7.1. *Lines 108–129*: This is a "double walk," affirming both sides like the monkey-keeper who goes along with monkeys' adamant insistence on "morning, four" without abandoning his original intention of seven total (125–29).[48]

Then we shall see that things have their own-*so* (*ku jan*), and their "ways" of being are formed by being "walked" (112). We "can" (*k'o*) now afford to explain an affirmation with its negation (using a no-pointer to show that a pointer is no-pointer), accepting every judgment. Similarly we can afford to affirm things in their differences (using a no-horse to show that a horse is no-horse), accepting every thing as "such" (*jan*; 108–109, 113–14).[49]

This is to see how Tao "goes through them into one," from *this* to *that*, and back; this is to double-walk, both in *this* and in *that*. Such is how we dwell in many ordinaries, ever starting with what-is-as-it-is and affirm things-as-they-are. Such resting in the natural balance is what harmonizes things with their *yes*'s and *no*'s. We can now call things "so" and they are "so."

7.2. "By a pointer showing its not being pointer; by no-pointer showing a pointer's not being pointer (cf. horse)" (118, 119): It is not important as to *what* each of these assertions means or logically amounts to, as all commentators I know of labored on. It is important instead to show *that* either logical route works, and each route has its own chain of reasoning. It is profoundly important to stand at the fork of these two logical roads, appreciate both, then walk both, going freely in and out of both. This is to tarry at the pivot and to respond endlessly and freely.

After struggling, seeing, and walking the two routes, we come to realize that "heaven and earth are one pointer, and myriads of things are one horse" (110). Here again Chuang Tzu did not intend to be impaled on a logical contradiction. Instead he meant to point to the "live" oneness, the dynamic at-one-ness with various things, the endless variety of things, in which we can be at home. Such one-among-many can be seen in the way that parent are related to their children. On the one hand, parents love their children without discrimination, relating themselves to them in the same parental manner. On the other hand, their relation to each child is unique, each different from the other.

7.3. We can sum up what is said above in four points:

(1) Why are things so?—as they are. They are so in their being so. Why are they not-so? They are not-so in their being not-so. Things have their inherent "so" and "all right"-ness. Nothing is not "so," nothing is not "right." Thus things are affirmed in *their* own right; they are at *one* in their uniquenesses. Such is the way things go; their Way goes-through them into oneness.

(2) This affirmation of oneness-in-uniqueness is a dynamic one, a *fang*. (a) It is processive: Things are now arising, now perishing, now O.K., now not-O.K. Where there is birth, there is death; where there is right, there is wrong. (b) It is causative: The right causes and depends on the wrong, death is caused by and causes life.

(3) We must illuminate all in the life of Heaven, that is, in naturalness, as-they-are-ness. We must explain (fingers as) non-fingers with non-fingers. This is a judgmental consistency of rightness. We must also explain (horses as) non-horses with non-horses. This is an ontological consistency of self-so-ness. This is in opposition to Kung Sun Lung the logician-sophist who explained fingers with non-fingers and horses with non-horses.

(4) In such consistent application of the law of consistency both to things (horses) and to judgments (fingers), in such unity and consistency lies the parity (*ch'i*) of things and theories; "heaven and earth are one finger; myriads of things are one horse."

7.4   We can see Chuang Tzu's unique liveliness in his discovery of the oneness of things. For the extent of being human and alive is gauged by the extent to which one can draw implications (unexpected as well as expected) out of an incident—be it literary, psychic, or historical. Such peculiar drawing of implications would have been impossible without that particular person; it is he who draws those implications out of this incident. In this sense he is a creator, a poet. The extent of being alive is proportional to the extent to which one is a poet. It is the power with which one branches *out* of the given situation (literary, psychic, historical) of one's ordinary life.

We have two examples in this section alone showing how alive Chuang Tzu is. Chuang Tzu quoted approvingly from the current sophists' phrases and jargon, such as *fang* and *yin* and *shih fei*; he agrees to the usage of those famous logical terms. And then, he develops them in a surprising and fresh direction; he connects them with the interconnections and interdependence among things. He even sees deep meaning behind common terms such as to "let" (*shih*), not "yet to begin" (*wei shih*), and connects them to the above sophistic terms, *fang, yin,* and the like.

Another example is Chuang Tzu's statement, "Myriads of things are one horse." This is an oblique quotation from the current sophist Kung Sun Lung, because it is close enough in sentiment to Kung's "None of the things is not finger" and "White horse is not a horse" to be recognizable as from Kung, yet Kung nowhere made this statement. It is a creative adaptation from Kung Sun Lung. Chuang Tzu seems to say by such parody of Kung Sun Lung that: "Suppose we accept Kung Sun Lung's thesis. Then it would be more consistent of him to apply 'non-horse' to non-horses. But then, if we stretch him far enough, everything is 'horse'—as long as 'non' is built into the notion of 'horse'. But then, the original intention of Kung Sun Lung—that is, to hair-split, divide, and confuse,—is challenged. But all this has been in the mode of

Kung's argumentation. We did not invent anything new, logically or example-wise. And so by following Kung Sun Lung we go beyond him and perhaps negate him." It is abrogation by fulfillment. Such is how alive Chuang Tzu is.

7.5. *Lines 120—29* have a strange string of notions, such as use (*yung*), ordinary (*yung*), going-through (*t'ung*), and obtaining (*te* or *tung*; see gloss to line 122). What is the relation among them?

As Fukunaga noted,[50] Chinese thought has a peculiar semantic principle, to wit, "Words of a sound flock together in sense; like sound, like sense." This principle is often exploited to explain a notion or to prove a point—such as saying that "*Li^a* is *li^b*" (the essence of proper-ritual for conduct is in its practice), "*Li^a* is *li^c*" (such essence is in discrimination), *Li^a* is *t'i* (li is the substance of all conduct). Likewise, *chih* (finger) is *chih* (signifier-pointer); *ma* ("horse") is *ma* (marker) (lines 108–10; 7.1). Similarly here. Fukunaga cited similarities in sound among the four words: *yung^a-yung^b-t'ung*, and *te*, which he took to rhyme as *yo, yo, yo*, and *tok*. But I suspect that we have here four groups of words: *yung^a-yung^b-t'ung, te(tek)-tao, shih^a-shih^b*, and *chi(ki)-i-chih*. The first group is basic to all the rest, and deserves explanation.

The group *yung-yung-t'ung* is somewhat like "used" and "being used to," or "adapted" and "being adept at." In any case, philosophers have long toyed with two "baskets" (categories) of necessity ("needed") and sufficiency ("enough"); things can be thrown into either, neither, or both baskets.

Things throwable into the "needed"-basket are the so-called four necessities, clothes-food-houses-transportation. They are the necessary conditions of life. Things throwable into the "enough"-basket are objects of fine arts, tenderness, the sunrise, and the like. They are the sufficient conditions of life.

That is, things "needed" for our living are just that and no more. Adequate supplies of life necessities alone do not quite make us happy; those who are quite happy with money *alone* are often regarded as not up to the human level. Life necessities are not the sufficient conditions of life. They are only *useful*, extrinsic values of life.

Things "enough" to make us enjoy ourselves, such as proper attire and conviviality, give us a lift. But they are, so we say, incapable of filling our stomach. They are sufficient but not necessary conditions of life. They are intrinsic values but useless for living. Such is our common-sense distinction between the enough and the needed, the sufficient and the necessary.

Five points can be noted about the above distinction. First, there are things which do not fit into either basket. An electric pencil sharpener is neither needed nor enough to give us zeal or joy.

Second, things needed can be and often are greeted with enjoyment. One can enjoy making money, plumbing, cooking, and so on. Things needed for survival can produce artistic satisfaction (such as architecture). These things can become necessary and sufficient conditions for life, as long as we take a properly artistic and childlike attitude to them.

Third, Chuang Tzu's point is that such a "bleed out" (*t'ung*) of use into enjoyment can be reversed. That is, things enjoyable but useless can be and are often in fact more useful than ordinary useful things, as the latter part of the first chapter stresses. All work and no play not only makes Jack a dull boy; Jack may go depressed and die. Besides, since "use" changes as time and subjects change, and since things enjoyable are rich in diversity of kinds and ranges, those who are attentive to things enjoyable are more resourceful (*t'ung*), more well-balanced, and happier (*te, shih*). What is useless can, should, and often does bleed out into something profoundly useful. This is his phrase, "use (out) of the useless."[51]

Fourth, the "ordinary" daily life (*yung*[b]) *requires* such blend and traffic (*t'ung*) between the useful and the useless, the needed and the enough. This is what Chuang Tzu means by *yung*[b], which has *yung*[a] ("use") as its part. Those who are capable of such traffic are those who are "worldly wise" (*t'ung*, as in *t'ung ta*); the word *t'ung* again has *yung*[a] ("use") as its integral part (line 122). Such people "go both" ways (*liang hsing*),[52] having mastered the ways ("Five Elementary Ways"?) of things.[53] They are at home ("dwell") in the ordinary (*yü chu yung*[b]), the truly rich ones who tap the heavenly resources in life (*t'ien fu*).

Fifth, in order to attain such a level of enjoyable freedom we must first discard our obsession with "use" and simply inhabit (dwell in) the ordinary (*pu yung erh yü chu yung*). Then, without our knowing it our life will be full of things both useful and enjoyable, while we follow along (*yin shih*). This is the Way of life (*tao*).

"But all this is common sense; what else is new?" Someone may ask. "And that's precisely my point," Chuang Tzu may reply. For his point was: Be common-sensical. *Yung, yung, te, t'ung*, as well as *shih, shih*, are all common words. That common way of life is *the* Way things go.

8.1. *Lines 130–49*: Finally we arrive at the bottom ("ultimate") of things. This segment shares with the segment considered in Section 6 (lines 85–94) the same conclusion, "by illumination" (*i ming*); in fact, this segment explains that segment, and exhibits a faint parallelism:

(90) Tao is "hidden" ... and
then there exist "yes and no."

(92–93) Tao is hidden by "small
formation" ... then there exist
yes and no of Confucians and
Mohists.

(95) Seen from "that," even this is
"not seen" as yes.

(100) Holy man does "not (go this)
route" ...

(134) The "appearance" of "this-yes
and no" is what makes for Tao's
"deformation."

(134-35) This appearance of "this-
yes and no" is ... what makes for
love's "formation."

(141) Only by what they like did
they feel "distinguished" among
"others."

(148–49) Holy man ... does "not
use" (things according to his
judgments) ...

But this segment clarifies *ming* as opposed to *mei*. By *mei* ("darkness," "foolishness") Chuang Tzu means that foolhardiness of those (three) "gen-iuses" who made clear (*ming*) what they liked; in their cleverness they insisted on clarifying (and illuminating; *ming*) to others what they were not clear about.[54] Because they were "close" to perfection, because they were "mas-ters," they were dark-and-foolhardy; their folly was most apparent in the "chop logic" (Graham) of "hardness" and "whiteness," two of their pet notions with which they confound the world. Their clever clarity *is* their dark folly.

This segment is thus centered on the "ultimate" of ancient knowledge and on the true meaning of *ming* ("illumined," "clarified," "enlightened"). Both knowledge and illumination culminate in the single notion of yet-to-begin-to-be (*wei shih yu*). We on our part must dwell in the realm of "yet-to-begin-to-have-yes-and-no," where there is no "formation" or "deformation" (lines 136–38), where we discard the "false brilliance" (of geniuses; line 148).[55] To be enlightened about this, we must "dwell in diverse ordinaries" where there are no experts, whether they are musicians or logicians. This is to go "by clarity-illumination."

Now that yet-to-begin-to-have-yes-and-no is explained, we can go to yet-to-begin-to-have-things; this is Section 9, which discusses lines 150–69. Then, equipped with that insight, we can begin to live rightly amidst "yet-to-begin-to-have-boundaries"; this is in Section 10, on lines 170–94. The pre-liminary explanation of yet-to-begin-yes-and-no is expanded in Section 11, on lines 195-229. Lines 130–33 can thus be regarded as a sketch of what is to come:

Level 1 (130–31): " ... there existed in their understanding something ultimate, [to wit,] there existed some who thought there had not yet begun to exist things." This is to be treated in lines 150–69, and discussed in Section 9.

Level 2 (132): "Their next thought ... there had not yet begun to exist borders." This is to be treated in lines 170–94, and discussed in Section 10.

Level 3 (133): "Their next thought ... there had not yet begun to exist *this-yes* and *no*." This is to be treated in lines 195–229, and discussed in Section 11.

And so we have three levels of yet-to-begin-to. Level 3 is the start and the closest to us; it is about our "judgment." The next, level 2, is about the natural borders (*feng*) of "things" (as opposed to our "subjective discrimination" and judgment). The highest, level 1 is about the "primal beginning of all things," in which our words fail.

Chuang Tzu courageously plunges into level 1 first, in lines 150–69. Then he explicates level 2 of how things are as they are, *naturally* distinct and divided by natural borders, in lines 170–194. And then in lines 195–229 he shows us how to live in this world of natural distinction with *our* natural "discriminatory" faculty. We shall see that this order is that of seeing things as they are, then realizing that *we* ourselves are part and parcel of those "things," mutually distinct and interchanging.[56] This will be the theme of what is left of the second chapter. Our living among things is then in the mode of yet-to-begin-to-be with them, at the primal basis of all.

We can see that the "argument" of this chapter is poetically tight. It is not just something that is "pervaded by the sensation, rare in ancient literature, of a man jotting down the living thoughts at the moment of inception," as Graham saw it.[57] Graham happily discerned the fresh poetic power of Chuang Tzu's thoughts at their "inception." He missed Chuang Tzu's poetic *connection*, the poetic system that forms the tissue of those living thoughts. The system is as alive as the living thoughts themselves.

8.2. What does "*yet-to-begin-to-be*" mean? Why is it so attractive, so important to us today?

If the child is father to the man because the child is not-yet-a-man, then the not-(yet)-a-child must be greater than the child and the man put together. Not-(yet)-things then must be greater than things, for no-thing "things things," enabling them to be as they are. And this is what we usually mean by "God."

But "no-thing" is greater than God because God is still something, and yet at the same time God *is* that no-thing himself (in the above sense). God then is better and greater than himself; we are reminded here of Tillich's "God above God," which clinched his *Courage To Be*. God is Self-Transcendence.

Translated into a "situation," no-thing is a con-fusion, a Mr. Hun Tun, comparable to Greek and biblical chaos. Translated into "action," no-thing is

a "no-phenomenon," a no-finding, an in-nocence (non-harming, non-disturb-
ing) that finds the great "Dark Pearl," nobody could find, a failure that
succeeds.[58] Translated into "man," no-thing is those social outcasts ("bums"
we call them) who show forth virtue even through their bodily handicaps.[59]
They "talley with virtue."

9.1. *Lines 150–69*: Suppose I give an utterance here (*tz'u*), that is, utter
something from "here," out of myself, the subject. Then I do not know whether
or not this utterance-here (*yen yü tz'u*) is "grouped with" the *this-yes* (*shih*).
But then, both being-grouped and being out-of-group can again be grouped
as one group, as belonging to the same category of "grouping." And so the
here and the there (*pi*) will have no difference.

Even so, let us try and say something anyway. When we say "something,"
it is the beginning of "something" existent. We see then immediately that there
is behind it a "yet-to-begin to begin an existence" of "it," and the prospect becomes dizzying—we will then go behind that yet-to-beginning and discern a
yet-to-begin to begin yet-to-begin an existence, and so on. We have now a
series of yet-to-begin to yet-to-begin to ...to begin an existence, ad infinitum.

And of course we also see that "existence" implies its contrast, its "non-
existence" (from which it stands out as existing). Suddenly non-existence
pops into existence, and we have the same series of not-yet-to-begin not-yet-
to-begin ... not to exist, ad infinitum. And we do not know whether the existence of non-existence is to be counted as existence or non-existence.

Similarly, I have just said something (as above). Is this something-said
(*wei*) really something, or is it really nothing? I have to agree, then, with
sophists (such as Hui Shih)[60] who said that the entire world is no greater than
the tip of the fine autumn hair, and that the great mountain is really small, or
that none is longer-lived than a dead child, and that Methuselah died young.
I can even push Hui Shih and say, "Heaven, earth, and I were born at the same
time," and, with a side glance to Mencius,[61] say that "myriads of things and
I make one." In short, if thing can be lumped with no-thing everything is one
with everything else.

But then, now that we have uttered and got "one," do we have no more to
say? We do, indeed. For surely in uttering "one," we get *two*—the word "one"
and what is meant by that word. But then these two and the original "one"
(what there is) make *three*. If we go on this way, not even the great calculator-
mathematician can get the entire series, much less (ourselves who are) ordinaries. Moreover, if we go from non-existence to existence and get to three,
how many more (complex things) would we get if we go from existence to

existence! We had better not "go" then, but follow whatever there is as it is (*yin shih*).

The word *shih* is interesting. We see how Chuang Tzu coaxed from such a common word further surprising implications, although those implications are not contrary to the common meanings of the word. *Shih* is a yes and an is and a this, a here, a me. We affirm and approve of whatever is closest to ourselves, in fact, ourselves. We almost hear Chuang Tzu chuckling here. Furthermore, *shih* is contrasted with *pi* and *fei*. *Pi* is the thing out there, a reality or an utterance by someone out there, and by implication something not-me, therefore, not-yes, a no. Here Chuang Tzu comes in and says that you (*pi*) have your set of yes-and-no, *shih-fei*. And I have mine here (*tz'u*), too. And so, to affirm-and-follow-along-with (*yin shih*) such universal having of sets of yes-and-no, this affirmation is the Great Shih; hence, the *Yin-shih*, that is, an affirmation of the as-is in *each* case, from *its* perspective.

9.2.   We see two root-notions at work here—"one" and "yet-to-begin-to-be". First, the oneness of all things is preceded by "where there is birth, there is death; where there is *can*, there is *cannot*" (lines 96–97), "where there is a following on *yes*, there is a following on *no*" (line 99). And the oneness of all precedes "what is really so" and "what can really be accepted" (line 114), as well as "double walk" (line 129). In other words, "one" is another expression of the parity (*ch'i*) of all things in interdependence, ever co-arising to say, "Heaven, earth, and I were born at the same time" (163).

Secondly, the yet-to-begin-to-be ties together things, boundaries, and yes-and-no. The yet-to-begin-to-be is at once an ontological justification, an anchoring, of actualities, *and* also a tracing to their origin—in the yet-to-begin.

But then, is there any relation between the one and the yet-to-begin? Chuang Tzu was silent here. Perhaps that famous word, "going-through" (*t'ung*; line 120), can serve as the pivot of the workings of both the one and the yet-to-begin; and the final portion of the chapter (lines 220–305) can be regarded as an explanation of this going-through in freedom. What does this going-through mean?

The yet-to-begin-to-be describes, among other things, childhood. Let us look at a child. We can look at children with the child's eye, and we can look at them with the adult's eye. Children are invincibly innocent. They can do anything, even sex and violence, with absolute composure. "Child molester," "child pornography" are horrors only to adults; they are adult categories.

The same can be said of children starting early on "adult stuff," such

as music, sports, three R's, and the like. They are in fact not trained to be
"whiz kids"; they just imitate adults. When they "count," they merely memo-
rize; they do not always understand its meaning. When they "read," they
pronounce sounds of letters; they do not always understand what they read.
When they undergo a certain motion, they do not always appreciate the
beauty of music or gymnastics; they just do it. They are invincibly children,
innocent of adult things, whether they be "crimes" or "achievements."

To come around back to such childhood and see children with the child's
eye, and then to see things in the child's perspective, is to become a child,
and to become invincibly innocent. He shall be pure (line 244) of everything,
of success as well as of crime. Such composure is instinctively admired.

Let a child be a child; and let ourselves be as innocent as a child. Then
we will shed our adulthood (line 10), immune to being perturbed by successes,
failures, and worries (lines 35–84). We shall be incorruptible, invincible
(lines 233–44), innocent (lines 3–6, 23/41). Successes and failures are "one"
to us, for we are invincibly "one" with ourselves. This is what it is "to go-
through" all with perfect composure, a roaming in the world without hurt.

10.   *Lines 170–94:* When we make natural territories (*feng*) into set
standards (*ch'ang*), then all sorts of restrictive boundaries come to be. Someone produces (*wei, yu*) "left," and "right" comes about; fixing distinctions
among people, and what is right appears. When distinctions (*fen*) and discriminations (and debates) (*pien*) arise, then competition and strife follow.
Such is what is called "Eight Virtues"; Chuang Tzu's wry smile peeps through
the phrase.

In contrast, living in the original world of yet-to-begin-to-be, out of
Six Realms, the holy man exists *(ts'un)* without distinctions *(lun).* Living in
the Six Realms, the holy man distinguishes without debating (*i*) about *yes*
and *no.* If there is any writing warning about ancient worthies, then perhaps
the holy man will debate without discrimination (*pien*).

Since all these distinctions are conventional, where there is "distinction,"
there is no-distinction, and where there is "discrimination," there is also no-
discrimination. Tao does not profess itself (182), knowledge professes ignorance (185); "natural riches" are hidden (187), and "natural lights" are shaded
(189). This is the power of the yet-to-begin-to-be, enriching all things at
their primal root, "without their knowing it."

This is not to say that there are no regulations. The circle and the square
are what people use as standards, yet they are not what people "invent" and
"approve of,"[62] but are the actuality of things as they are. Those "Five Things"

(184) can, if taken not accusingly[63] but approvingly, be said to be *true* to "what is so" in things without external imposition. Tao is then displayed as not-Tao, in which we can debate and discriminate with words and allow their meanings to remain unattainable. We can be constant in humanness without accomplishing anything, be clean in conduct without letting people trust us, and be courageous without being overwhelming (183).

In other words, by rendering our standards sinuous, those Five Things will go flexing with things as things come and go. *We* shall be true to the situation.

This brings us to the conversation between two sagely emperors, Yao and Shun. The image of the sun, the laudatory image of Confucianism for Yao, is here disparaged, being compared to the nuisance of "Ten Suns" in ancient myths.[64] "Underbrush of mugwort" ordinarily a disparaging image of uncouth barbarity, is treated as uncarved naturalness, through which Yao's virtue does well to shine forth, as Shaded Light,[65] perhaps. Yao should not conquer the three stiff-necked barbarous tribes with his solar might. Instead, he should let his own human naturalness (*te*) shine unobtrusively through their brushy hearts. Finally, the story skillfully lets the junior Shun gently instruct and persuade his senior Yao, a beautiful illustration of how the mighty Yao should proceed.[66] Later, in Chapter Three, we shall see the lowly butcher Ting instruct his Lord Wen Hui on living well.

11.1. *Lines 195–229*: The original authentic self (*wu*) and knowledge or understanding (*chih*) appear here. This is the new segment that lasts to the end of the chapter, although for convenience it will be further divided, adding two more segments.

So far in this chapter words and statements (*yen*) have been treated, together with what the statements refer to, such as existence (*yu*), knowledge (*chih*), things (*wu*), virtue (*te*), and the like. Statements and their referents are now combined in one notion of *knowledge* (*chih*). This segment explains the allegedly obvious (though highly treasured) statement in the previous segment, "Understanding stops at what it does not understand— this is ultimate" (185). The explanation culminates in the notion of awakening *(chüeh).*

All this investigation leads us back to what the chapter started with— the original authentic *self* (*wu*). This return unifies the self and knowledge, whose mutual relation is explained here.

The relation turns out to be a radically dynamic interchange. The authentic self is by no means a static "something" to be taken for granted.

Descartes said "I" exists as long as I think. Chuang Tzu would say "I" exists as long as I change with my knowledge of wonderment ("How can I understand?")[67] and my playful attempts at expressing such a situation ("Although it is so, let me try to say something," "I will try for your sake to say abandoned words; you with abandon listen.")[68]

The self changes in wonderment over three changes, in which it obtains itself. First, there is change in knowledge, as described above. And then such uncertainty of knowledge empties *right* and *wrong* (*yes* and *no*) of content, because the criteria of *yes* and *no* change, and we do not have the unchanging universal right. Thirdly, this shift of perspectives culminates in an *awakening*. It is not an awakening that settles in true knowledge and certainty, but an awakening that wonders, an awakening to uncertainty. It is an awakening to the interchanges of things, including my identifiable self (*wo*).

And it is precisely *within* this puzzlement over radical "interchanges" (of identities) "among things" (including my self), this awakening and recognition of the vicissitudes of actuality, that the continuity of the authentic self is obtained. The I continues as such precisely in its recognition of its own discontinuities as it participates in the interchanges among things. The original authentic self (*wu*) is the yet-to-begin-to-be my identifiable phenomenal self (*wo*),[69] the primal subject that stops and stays at its not-knowing, and knows such not-knowing.

11.2. To begin with, we have a dialogue between Mr. Nieh-ch'üeh and Mr. Wang Ni. Both are supposed to be holy men,[70] the height of human excellence. Their conversation covers all three levels of the roots of things ("yet-to-begin") as outlined in 8.1.

Nieh-ch'üeh, literally "chew chipped." Mr Chew Chipped is Mr. Muncher, munching on things until his teeth chipped, a Mr. Gaptooth.[71] Interestingly it happens to coincide with the name of the famous sword whose blade is chipped, and whose fame came from a swindler making a fortune out of advertizing it to be the sword worn by the renowned swordsman-emperor Ch'ing Hsiang of Ch'u in the Warring Period.[72] We sense sarcasm in the name Mr. Chew Chipped, a man of intellectual acumen whose false fame consists in his chipped intellect!

Wang Ni is literally "royal horizon or boundary," with a side glance at *T'ien Ni*, "natural boundaries" or "heavenly equalities" (2810). *Wang* in the *Chuang Tzu* usually means human royalty, and so "royal horizon" must signify something of human excellence; he is both the teacher of Mr. Nieh-chüeh and a student of Mr. Wearing-Cloak.[73] He is between the human and the divine. True to his name, as "royal horizon," he stops at his legitimate limit, gaining a link to *T'ien Ni*, the heavenly horizon or equality. This agrees with another interpretation, saying that Wang Ni may have affinity with *Wang Ya*, "deep and vast horizon of the waters."[74] Or else Wang Ni may have connection with *T'ien Ni* ("heavenly-natural boundary"), analogous to *t'ien yen* ("heavenly-natural whetstone").[75] Such ambivalence is used as a linkage of human spontaneity with naturalness in the world. This linkage is repeated in the name of Mr. Chü-ch'ieh in the next segment (see Section 12.1).

The topic of their conversation is whether there is knowledge of "that of which things have the same approvals of 'yes'," that is, what things commonly affirm. This common affirmation can mean either (1) what is the same among things, or what makes things the same, or (2) what they all affirm and approve of as "yes," as correct, that is, the universal criterion of "right" and "desirable." This is an important question if one is to follow the yes of things (*yin shih*).

Mr. "Royal Horizon" (Wang Ni) answered, "How would I understand it?" And he repeated it three times. The answer is a confident ignorance, an uncertainty that knows its own reason why it is not certain, a knowledge of ignorance, an understanding that stops at what it does not understand, a knowledge culminating in its limit. (Similarities to the philosophy of *docta ignorantia* of Nicholas of Cusa will be evident throughout this discussion.)

Such knowledge of uncertainty is then elaborated with many concrete examples in actuality, such as different "correct" lodgings, foods, and beauties for different species of living beings. We must note here that uncertainty of this kind differs from confident agnosticism or the anything-goes sort of arbitrary indefiniteness, for we do know that different species do have their respective "correct-proper" lodgings, foods, and beauties. Our ignorance is not here, but in what it is that they all agree on as *the* proper lodging, food, beauty. In any case, such considerations show both an ex-pansion of our perspective in nature and a shift of the very judging subject that goes with the shift of propriety.

Then comes the question, "But what about the knowledge of 'benefit from harm,' the knowledge of survival? Isn't survival commonly affirmed as a most important 'object of universal approval'? Though professing ignorance on matters of universal concern, is the ultimate man so ignorant as not to know of such an object of universal acknowledgement as this?" A keen question indeed.

Wang Ni's answer seems high-pitched and far-fetched. The "ultimate man" is "divine"; he is never hurt amidst natural catastrophes, but rides on the normalcies of clouds, the sun and the moon, and roams beyond the

Four Seas. The problem of benefit and harm is a "small issue"[76] for him indeed.

The reason is that "death and life makes no difference" in him or to him. The phrase is ambiguous. It can mean: (1) "making no difference *in* him"—the ultimate man is not touched by death and life, but is unborn and undying, perhaps by virtue of being in the realm of yet-to-begin-to-be, beyond the Four Seas; (2) "death and life are not different (but are the same) *to* him"—although the ultimate man can be born and can die, he is indifferent to them, perhaps by virtue of the change of identities that death represents.[77]

Both Mr. Royal Horizon and Mr. Chew Chipped seem to take the phrase in the first sense. Mr. "Jittery Magpie" in the next story (beginning with line 230) takes the first sense; Mr. Tall Phoenix Tree takes the second sense.

All in all, after a long discussion (if not digression) on relativity and co-arising of yes and no, approval and disapproval, we finally come back to the problem (with a new depth) of what-things-commonly-"yes." We began by trying to find a commonality among things, the universals in things. We now find that the judging *subject* has a lot to do with the answer. Each species has its own universal, and those universals clash. We have no common universal. What does it mean?

11.3.   So-called abstract paintings and absolute music can mean many things, even conflicting things, to many people, and to the same person on many occasions. We usually say that it is the audience who read into the painting and the music whatever *they* fancy, with which the art object has nothing to do. Hence the description "abstract" and/or "absolute," that is, loose, independent, unrelated. But this is misleading, for the painting and the music are what trigger in the audience those meanings and emotions, which would not have happened without the art objects. Those objects do influence subject-responses in some way. And yet it is difficult to understand how the same art objects can trigger off many unrelated and conflicting reactions.

Another example is the notion of nature. On the one hand, "nature red in tooth and claw" seems true. Animals survive in a chain of depredations—the lion eats the lamb, the lamb eats the grass. On the other hand, nature is an arena of mutual support—the lion weeds out the weaker lamb and strengthens the species. Nature is then both a hierarchical eating society and a world of partnership.

Dangers are everywhere in nature. Even in mutual benefit there still exists devouring, and inter-specific cooperation does not always guarantee *individual* survival. Species survival often requires the self-sacrifice of individuals, as in deaths of the male insects as they mate or the worker bees dying in stinging their enemies.

Nature is thus both a motherly cradle and a monstrous cruelty. Living beings must practice both violence and cooperation to survive, a coincidence of opposites in actuality. Here our logical standard of consistency is challenged. The ultimate man is he who discerns this *fact* and rides *on* it.[78]

12.1. *Lines 230–89*: Mr. Jittery Magpie and Mr. Tall Phoenix Tree are living things in nature, unlike the two conversants in the previous section. First we go to their names, then to their talks.

Chü ch'üeh is jittery magpie chattering, almost reminding us of jitters in fear, *chü ch'ieh*. *chü* describes small birds (such as sparrows) looking around in caution as they peck on food. Magpie's chirpings are supposed to harbinger some auspicious news, bringing in joyous events. Chuang Tzu may have felt sympathy for the little intellect's noisy nosings-around, and took them to be like the natural chirpings of a jittery magpie. Their noisy inquiries must, however, be addressed to silent nature, in which they dwell and alight as a magpie on a phoenix tree.[79]

The "phoenix tree," *sterculia platanifolia*, is perhaps the commonest tree in China. It is commonly called Chinese parasol tree, and is said to be the national tree of China. It is reputed to be the only tree on which "the phoenix" would rest—that big P'ung bird, an auspicious sign of peace and concord. It is ironic that instead of the phoenix, a magpie is on the tree to ask questions. Although also auspicious, the magpie is much smaller and less awesome than the phoenix. The Chinese pronunciation of the tree, *wu*, reminds us of both *wu* the original self and *wu* an awakened understanding. In any case, the tree neither moves nor talks, and it stays tall and long. Mr. Tall Phoenix Tree is long in silent implications.

This segment treats natural chitchats and natural silence. Nothing is more common than jittery little birds chattingly perching on a common tree; the conversation is yet more profound than those chitchats among the little doves and cicadas about an unusual phoenix in the first chapter (lines 20–22, 44–48).

The scene also reminds us of the conversation that ended the first chapter under and about a big tree *shu*, smelly, unsightly, useless. Having persuaded the logician Hui Tzu about the use of the useless, Chuang Tzu may have actually dozed off under the tree (whatever it is), dreaming this conversation between the magpies and the tree, and also dreaming that butterfly which ends this chapter. This fulfills the description, "roaming around and lying asleep under the tree" that ends the first chapter (163).

12.2. But what is the magpie-tree conversation about? To answer, we must go back to the previous segment.

There, the question "Do you know what things commonly affirm?" picks up the thread that began with "*that* comes from *this*; *this* also depends on *that*"(96), and left off with "Now, are there actually *that* and *this*? Are there actually no *that* and *this*?" (103). The previous segment considers the relativity of perspectives in concrete details, concluding with a confident freedom of sagely ignorance. This segment also sums up what has gone before, and prepares for a new height of meditation—the interchanges of things reaching the self.

We remember Mr. Royal Horizon answered, "How would I understand what things have in common?" (196–97). Then he gave his reason for his ignorance. It is because each species has its own criterion and perspective for "what things commonly affirm," he would not know how to tell among those criteria and perspectives.

But does such ignorance entail the absurdity of not knowing what all living things universally affirm, the value of knowing benefit from harm, the value of survival? Mr. Royal Horizon's answer was an abrupt one—the ultimate man could not care less about any such notion, but merely rides on things, roams beyond the Four Seas. Death and life makes no difference in/to him.

The conversation between two human excellences—a chewing chipped one and an unmoving horizon—abruptly ends. The dialogue is now picked up by another pair, two naturals, moving birds and unmoving tree. They appropriately start where the last talk ended, with the ultimate man, but attend this time to his personal behavior and his dealing with the world. Mr. Magpie noisily (and rightly) poses a dilemma: "Do you think such description of the ultimate man is fantastic *or* profound?"

The answer is, after cautioning against shallow excitement at exotics, again enlightening, pushing the dialogue beyond the horns of the dilemma. "I will try for you to say some abandoned words; you with the same abandon listen" (241).[80] The sentiment repeats the previous "But let me try to say ..." (202), and describes the self-abandoned overhearing of the heavenly piping (12). The sentiment is that of the natural silence of a tree, analogous to an answer from someone observed as "dry wood ... dead ashes" (6).

Then Mr. Tall Phoenix Tree bursts forth into poetry, half-describing the ultimate man, half-exhorting Mr. Magpie:

Standing beside the sun and moon,
Holding the rounds of space and time,
Fitting himself with them all,
Putting their confusing muddle in their places,
As serfs mutually honor.
While multitudes of people slave and slave,
The holy man is a stupid sluggard—
Thus he participates in myriads of ages and forms one lump;
Myriads of things fulfill their being so,
And by this mutually enfold (242–44).

And then, perhaps after a pause, Mr. Tree goes on, "As for the supposedly important question of death and life, I am not sure whether delight in life
is not a delusion, nor am I sure whether hating death is not like an orphaned
youth not knowing to come home. That Beauty (*li chi*) of Ai[81] came to wonder
whether being happily married (even by force) is not after all a good thing.
Death may well be a happy marriage (by force)—unless, of course, *you* yourself see to it that violence be eased off by a new awakening, as if from a dream."

Such an awakening is a going-beyond of a special kind. We remember
that initially Mr. Tree looked up in his ignorance to the holy man going beyond the Four Seas. The authentic self (*wu*; 219) differs from the ultimate
man (223). Then the beyondness is denied, and the holy man is put (back?)
in his (proper) ignorance (243). Now the beyondness is that of awakening
from a dream, which will turn out to be an Awakening *into* the dream, the
Great Awakening (255). This is a reconciliation of beyondness with a
mixing-with-all-things. The divinity of the ultimate man is here his holy
stupidity. The holy man now becomes one with the universal as-is (*jan*) and
the universal *yes (shih)* (244).

12.3. "Do you know what things commonly affirm" Yes, if we are
willing to go back to our primal ignorance, mixing, melange, and dream-
like con-fusion, *to* which we are awakened, a Great Awakening to a dream.
In other words, the answer to the question depends on the metamorphosis
of the self, and that a change into uncertainty. We remember that the Cartesian *cogito* hangs on its concern for the ego, its *egology*; Chuang Tzu's know-
ledge-of-all hangs on a non-egology. This answer brings us back to the beginning of this chapter: "I have lost myself, do you understand that? I now overhear the heavenly piping" (1–12).

The irony remains here. This knowledge obtains by continually asking
rhetorically. "How would I know that?" Such quasi-Socratic ignorance is
ignorance in a special condition of the knower, as in a dream.

Thus we come to an intimate connection between knowledge and dream. To know truly is to know as in a dream. This is a surprising declaration. How could it be so?

First, we know that, ultimately speaking, it is the constant shift of the knower's perspective that produces all sorts of "knowledge"—now weeping to the knowledge of misery, now relenting having wept,[82] because of the knowledge that it has been all to the good; now drinking in the knowledge of life's comforts, now wailing in the knowledge of life's miseries; now crying, now hunting; now a lord, now a herdsman.[83] Now we know that all these varieties of knowledge are presumptuous and incorrigible, cocksure and obstinate.

But, secondly, to know all *that* is to be awakened from it all, a dream. For all such constant shifts can only be characterized as "dream." And only by being awakened can we know that all this has been a dream; only by a Great Awakening can we know that all this varied knowledge has been a great dream.

Strangely, in the third place, although an awakening dispels a dream, the Great Awakening does not, but instead acknowledges that (1) "both the wise Confucius and you are dreams," and (2) "I call you 'a dream'—*I* am also a dream" (260–61).[84] Such a saying is so strange that it can only be dubbed "ultimate grotesques" or "Great Swindle," and if any great holy man comes to solve such a riddle it will be the rarest moment indeed (262–64).

For, fourthly, you and I can never solve a problem such as this by discussion. Neither winning an argument nor relying on a third party's judgment can decide who is in the right. To rely on such hollow voices of changing opinions (*hua sheng*) amounts to relying on nothing (280).

Instead, we had better harmonize all with the "heavenly horizon" and "balance," or rather, the "natural grindstone" that churns out things incessantly,[85] to which we trust ourselves and our judgments (or knowledge?) in the "ceaseless flow of things far and wide."

What does it mean to harmonize with the heavenly horizon? Things are yes or no, so or not-so. If it "*yes*'es the *no*" and "*so*'es the not-*so*," its being different from *no* or *not-so* requires no debates. We do well "to forget (the distinction between) years and right," and move around in the Limitless Realm (*wu ching*), live there till we complete our natural span of life.[86]

Thus, we are led by our quest for a fixed "what things commonly affirm" to that ever-swinging Swindle, hanging in midair—"Ch'iu with you—both are dreams. I call you 'a dream'—I am also a dream." We must ever swing in the Limitless, even lodge ourselves and lodge things in it. There we go along with the limitless grinding of nature on all sides, forgetting distinctions of years and yeses.

12.4. Let us translate *lines 265–89* into our contemporary scene, or at least transpose them to the level of our understanding.

There were two men arguing. A Zen master said to one of them, "You are right." Then he turned to the other and said, "You are right." A third man could not take this and said, "But, Master, they are fighting and opposed. How can both of them be right?" The master thought for a while, turned to him, and said, "You are right, too."[87]

We see four points. First, when one takes up one position, takes a specific standpoint of a judging subject, there arises "right positions" and "wrong positions," where "right" means anything that agrees with him, and "wrong" is anything that disagrees with him.

Secondly, when the master takes the perspective of Mr. A (the *yes*), he can say that A is right ("*yes*-ing the *yes*"). Then, taking the perspective of Mr. Anti-A (the "not-*yes*"), he can say that Anti-A is right ("*yes*-ing the not-*yes*"; 284). Then, again, taking the perspective of Mr. Anti-Master, he can also say that anti-Master is right.

No matter where he turns (this is the third point), he can use the *same* statement, "You are right." In other words, "*this* (and *yes*) is also *that*; *that* is also *yes* (and *this*)" (101). And "if everything as 'this' (and so 'yes') is actually affirmed as 'yes,' then there is no dispute as to the difference between 'yes' and 'not yes'" (285). It is *thus* that he "harmonizes them all with heavenly equality" (281).

But, fourthly, what is this "thus" that harmonizes everything and every view? It must be equivalent to "following them with their own flow spreading far and wide" (281), following along with the changes of things. "Thus" is following-the-change. Such a following involves *changes* of the subject itself, which *lodges* itself and them all in where there is *no limit* (288–89).

12.5. We have in the previous sentence emphasized three notions that are hard to understand: change, lodging, no limit.

The original word for "change" is *chen* (288). I translated it "roam and stop" to accommodate three widely divergent opinions—stop and end, go through without obstruction, and soar and roam, as my gloss to line 288 indicates. Such is the change, which is neither to stay in it forever nor to fly away somewhere else. It is to lodge without lodging, to move without moving away, to be active in a situation. To be active in a situation is not to be wrapped and engulfed in it but to lead it by following it. *Chen* is thus difficult both to understand and to practice; only being naturally flexible can accomplish it.

The original word for "lodging" is *yü* (289). It is to tarry and be at home somewhere. But to tarry somewhere is to tarry somewhere definite; one cannot lodge where there is no limit (289). To be-*in* (*yü*) already implies being in a particular realm, calling forth a realm-with-a-limit (*ching*); and yet Chuang Tzu specifies that the realm is without limit (*wu ching*). Perhaps Chuang Tzu wants us to be somewhere without being somewhere, that is, being in it as if not being in it; that is, "roam and stop at where there is no limit." We have here a grand summary of Chapters One and Two of the *Chuang Tzu*.

12.6. But what does roaming and tarrying in the realm of no limit mean? Perhaps being with children comes closest to such a situation.

Children may be called the realm of no realm, realm without limit. They have no maturity, no knowledge, need caring, and constantly ask questions.

I once dreamed that I was with a tiny baby, helpless in my arms. He could speak, however, and constantly and innocently asked me questions. "Why? What do you do that for?"—the baby kept asking me; and I kept my silence, ashamed. I was awed by his innocent probing that was all too natural, to which I was speechless. For all those things that I do, I do not know why I do them. He kept nudging me to come out of myself, to reflect on whatever I was doing, and kept me *out* of my routine ruts. I had to be on the go.

And yet, for all his probing and throwing me off my balance, he was supremely at home in my arms. He seemed to be at home in his ongoing quest; there was nothing uneasy about him. He was confident, not in himself but in his questioning, and in my arms which he questioned. He was at home in me whom he questioned; he was at home without being at home anywhere. He lodged himself in the realm of no limit.

How about ourselves? We can watch children's thoughts, draw some lessons, then take off from them into our own business. Or we can watch children, tarry with them, draw one set of implications today, then another set tomorrow, and so on, and dwell in them forever.

The former route is usual to philosophers and psychologists. The latter route is the mother's (cf. Luke 2:51) and Chuang Tzu's. The former takes children to be a starting-point, to be left behind. The latter takes children to be a home, to be nestled in. The former grows out of childhood; the latter grows into Primal Childhood. The former becomes an adult; the latter becomes a child, always proving. We do well to dwell in such latter realm of no limit, says Chuang Tzu.

Dwelling without dwelling—this could be another meaning of realm without limit. There are times when we wish we were different—we wish we were not as sad, depressed, overwhelmed, or obnoxious, angry, haughty.

To get out of such a situation, it is no use trying to shake it off as if we were shaking dust from our shoes, however. For our situation is not a thing but that in which we were situated, very much a part of us. We cannot *take* ourselves off ourselves.

Instead, we must undergo our situation to get over it. Undergoing the situation, we will go through it; we will have dwelt in the realm of no realm. Or, we can choose a different set of situational conditions to help us out of our untoward situation. A smoker may not be able to refrain from smoking. But he can put himself in a situation where smoking is embarrassing or painful. He is dwelling in a realm of no limit. We ourselves change in the meantime.

12.7. Our uneasiness stays, however. We are not sure whether such a change of ourselves, such variation in many perspectives and knowledge, does not imply that we are "but a dream," an unreliable illusion. We are annoyed, in addition, at such indecisiveness of our knowledge and our situation—are we dead leaves in the wind?

To put this uneasiness to rest we must turn to the close interdependence and interchange among things and knowledge. We will go into Chuang Tzu's two further stories—the story of the Shadow and the shadow of the Shadow (penumbra), and the story of Chuang Tzu ("Chuang Chou") and the butterfly mutually dreaming one to be the other. We will realize that to characterize life and knowledge as dream is not to denigrate its reality but to be realistic and flexible about it. "Dream" here does not imply delusion; it implies radical interchanges among separate identities. And such interchange of the subjects is the radical itinerary, the roaming and soaring of the very subject which makes possible the radical equalizing of things and their views. To matters such as these, which clinch the entire chapter, we now turn.

13.1. *Lines 290–305*: This entire Meditation has one characteristic—swindling indecisiveness, swinging to and from between this and that, yes and no, me and you. Why this indecisiveness? Even Mr. Neither-(shadow-) Nor (substance)—that is, Mr. Penumbra—gets impatient and asks.[88]

What is taken, or mis-taken, to be "indecisiveness" here, answers Mr. Shadow the respondent, is really the "heart" of all things, that everything depends one on the other in a radically reciprocal manner. Penumbra depends on Shadow, whose fringe Penumbra is; yet Shadow also depends on its Penumbra, which is shadow's contour, that is, Shadow itself. And the same sort of reciprocity exists between shadow and a thing of which Shadow is a shadow, for the visual appearance of a thing depends on the visual depth given by its shadow.

"To think of it," continues Mr. Shadow, "all things are in such mutual dependence. Snake skin depends on a snake as cicada wings do on a cicada, yet without its skin and wings neither a snake nor a cicada could survive for long."

But now, what is happening here? What depends on what, really? One thing is certain: The very foundation of knowledge, the Cartesian certainty of the knowing self, is shaken. How so?

Listen. Last night Chuang Chou, that identifiable self (*wo*) of Chuang Tzu, dreamed that he was a butterfly swinging and sauntering as his fancy took him, *not knowing* that he was Chuang Chou. Suddenly he awoke, and he had to look around, curious that he was Chou himself after all. But now, now that he was awake, he did *not know* whether he was really Chou having dreamed of being a butterfly or really a butterfly currently dreaming of being Chou. Between Chou and butterfly there must be some distinction (*fen*, a subjective awareness of natural borders, *feng*). This reminds us of what Chuang Tzu told us before, "Seen from *that*, even *this* is not seen as *yes*; once understood in terms of itself, then it is understood as *yes*" (95). The standpoint of *this* (*Chou*) is distinct from *that* (butterfly). This sort of swinging back and forth between two distinct identities is what is called the constant change-over among things (*wu hua*).

The story ends here. We are led this far, to this Great Awakening, to the uncertainty of dream-like mutual interchange of the very subjects on which our judgments of actualities are based.

The heavenly piping is now seen to be the echoes of changes (*hua sheng*) in which we dwell and are. To be awakened to this fact is self-lessly to overhear the heavenly piping. Such is the oneness (*ch'i*) of things (*wu*), all moving back and forth, interchanging. For the self (*wo*) is now one (myself) and two (Chou and butterfly), two (Chou dreamt? butterfly dreaming?) in one; after all, it is I (*wu*) who have been puzzling over all this throughout.

Let us look closely at this "self" of Chuang Tzu. To be puzzled at myself, as to whether I am Chou or a butterfly, shows that I am the same I who have undergone different (identifiable) selves, Chou and butterfly. "I have been puzzled throughout" implies that there has been the same I who have undergone experience of being differing selves. For otherwise how would I know enough to be *puzzled* at myself in the first place? And yet how strange such puzzlement is—for how can I be different selves and yet remain the same self, same enough to be puzzled? To be puzzled at such matters is itself very puzzling indeed. But such is the concrete situation of myself—I am the same-different self. I am myself in a dynamic change of my very subjecthood and identity.

13.2.1. All this goes to show that "myriads of shapes and things are one change," as Ch'u Po-hsiu put it.[89] Things are really differences in unity and unity in differences; seeing that dream and awakening can never be the same, this is a coincidence of opposites. Such unity of unity (being one) with differences can only be had in the state of Great Awakening, that is, awakening from an awakening. It is an "awakening" when Chou thought he was not a butterfly; it is an "Awakening" from *that* awakening when Chou was not sure whether he was he or a butterfly.

Furthermore, as soon as he thinks he is Chou, he begins to wonder if he is Chou. As soon as he thinks he is a butterfly, the awakened "he" would label *that* state of mind as being in a dream. When he is a "Chou," he is no longer a "butterfly"; as soon as he wonders about *that*, he may well be a butterfly dreaming. There is a butterfly-like flittering from "Chou" to "butterfly" and back to "Chou."

Put differently, it goes like this. First, one can say, with Descartes, that the butterfly does not exist. For Chuang Chou *exists* to the extent that he awoke and wondered (doubted) whether he was really he having dreamed or really the butterfly currently dreaming. The butterfly does not wonder about its own existence as Chuang Chou does; therefore its existence is dubitable. Yet, secondly, to the extent that he doubts his existence, his *doubts* may be justified; he may really be not he but perhaps something else, such as a butterfly. In fact, he may be really a butterfly currently dreaming of being him. Besides, if "thinking" is all-inclusive, then a butterfly dreaming may be part of a butterfly thinking, which includes Chuang Chou wondering; perhaps the butterfly's dream includes Chuang Chou's Cartesian *cogito*. Therefore, by the fact that "Chuang Chou" wonders and exists, the butterfly exists. The worst of all this is that no one knows how to put to rest such flipflops of doubts and identities.

Such a ceaseless interchange of identities implies that (1) the death and life of identities has no effect on the original self (*wu, chi*), (2) the opposition of this and that, yes and no, knowing and no-knowing, has no final say, although they ceaselessly exist in turn and together, and (3) to live in this realization (Great Awakening) is to live in the "Pivot of the Way," and "to go-double," (and "go-neither"?), that is, to freely saunter and swing in the swing of things. All this amounts to a shaking of the foundation of our judgments, our *self*, our subjecthood.

13.2.2. We have three situational stages: dreaming, awakening, Great

Awakening; or not awakening, awakening from not awakening, awakening from awakening (awakening without awakening); or not knowing, knowing, knowing that we are not sure. Such is a logical description of our experiential odyssey on life's way. It can be said that *after* having gone through these stages we can experience them all at once, that is, be awakened from awakening while sleeping, and have the great awakening in a dream. Logically speaking, being in the uncertainty of the Great Awakening is being awake while sleeping. Experientially speaking, however, we must go through the Great Awakening before we can be awake and asleep at the same time (cf. 13.2.1).

On second thought, however, we ask: Is the preceding description classifiable as "logical." and an actual going through the stages, "experiential"? Can we even make a proviso of "after having gone through these stages"? As long as "we are not sure," as long as we can be awakened "without awakening," can we not have the Great Awakening while dreaming without having to go through the stages beforehand? All these questions collapse the distinction between experiential stages and logical ones.

Doesn't the three-stage distinction itself then fall apart? No. For not-knowing differs from *knowing* that we do not know, simple ignorance from knowledge of ignorance. Similarly, not-awakening differs from awakening, as much as awakening differs from awakening-from-awakening.

But how do they differ? This is where words and knowledge fail. As *knowledge* of being spontaneous destroys spontaneity, so knowledge of the *Great* Awakening is a situational oddity, if not an impossibility. The Great Awakening is as elusive as spontaneity, for both describe what it means to be truly alive. The great Tao is un-tao-able; the great Name (of life) is un-nameable. The most we can experience is, as Miss Kimberly DeMunn insisted (as she pushed me relentlessly into this "mess" in our honors class on Chuang Tzu), "it would not be until after we awoke that we would realize we had a Great Awakening."

13.2.3. Western philosophy has been preoccupied with problems of universals, metaphysics, and the like. Behind Platonic form, Aristotelian organism, Kantian transcendentalism, and so on, is an assumption that all these systems are produced by an unchanging (though mysterious) Subject. Western philosophy is egological; this explains the importance of Descartes' quest for the indubitable Ego and Kant's postulate of the transcendental Ego.

In contrast, Chuang Tzu tackled metaphysics by dissolving the standpoint of the subject. To lose oneself does not mean abolishing the self (for it is "the I which does the losing"), but the "abolition of a fixed subjective standpoint." We can then selflessly "follow the respective *yeses*" of things, "tarry in many ordinaries," and thereby dwell in the pivot of the Tao and respond endlessly.

Dissolution of fixation in the subject is called the Great Awakening. Such an Awakening does not leave dreams—to think that one can leave dreams would amount to another dogmatism. To greatly be awakened is to be awakened from both uncritical dreaming and uncritical awakening. For we may be still dreaming, and we are incapable of checking on it.

Such uncertainty, however, is not a dissolution of distinction but its confirmation; because being awakened differs from dreaming, we can be awakened to being uncertain about what we are.

Thus, if "theory" means definite cognition of an assured subject, as in Western philosophy, then Chuang Tzu's is a non-theory, a non-egological noncognition (uncertainty), a self-less not-knowing.

13.2.4. The butterfly flutters between sleep and not-sleep, between dream and not-dream, between the fish in darkness (not-dream, sleep—*ming* can mean sleep or ocean) and the bird toward darkness (dream, not-sleep-nor-awakening, something describable, moving). This "sleep" (with or without dream) is appropriately produced toward the end of the first chapter (line 163: "roamingly lying asleep") and the beginning of the second chapter (lines 3, 10: "vacant, seemed having lost his counterpart," "at present, I have lost myself").

Thus the beginning of the first chapter is recapitulated and elucidated at the end of the second, in the butterfly. The question remains: *What* is this butterfly? It is obviously not Chuang Chou; when he came in, it disappeared. Nor is it the Bird or the Fish; none of their descriptions fits the butterfly's light fluttering. Perhaps the butterfly *is* the "flutteringly" (297) and things "changing" (305), that is, the adverb and the verb, the activity of changes hoveringly in line with nature. And *that* is the self truly so called.

But, what have we done so far? We have gone around in a circle of mutual involvement, a *poetic* movement, explained in the Prologue as "The Poetic *Chuang Tzu*."

Stories proceed in a dream, neither awakening nor in deep sleep. The butterfly story asks us, "Are they really just a dream? Are we sure the 'Chuang Chou' is not dreamed by the butterfly?" Telling stories is as much a circular self-involved activity as our dream-awakening cycle is.

Chapter Two ends with an implicit summary of Chapter One (full of stories). Chapter Two says, "birth arises side by side with death; death arises side by side with birth," and this is a "circle" (97, 105). The sentence is applicable to "consciousness arises side by side with unconsciousness, and so on," that is, "awakening, knowing, or a Chuang Chou arises side by side with a dream, not knowing, or a butterfly, and so on," and this is a "circle." Chapter Two explains the logic of the stories in Chapter One, and of the entire *Chuang Tzu*. It is a movement from the Northern Darkness to the Southern, that is, from darkness to darkness, and that perhaps *in* darkness, as the end of the first chapter says, "roamingly lying down and sleeping" in the "village of there exists not, not even why there exists anything" at all.

If the logic of lucid consciousness is in a straight line, at which Western philosophy is adept, then Chuang Tzu's is the logic of dream, sleep, non-consciousness. The logic of Chuang Tzu is the way of movement of our deep non-consciousness, of our deepest total being. This is the circular logic that does not beg the question, but is a way of roaming, back and forth, in "that dark, impenetrable night that the mind calls up in order to plunge into it," as Albert Camus said toward the end of "An Absurd Reasoning" in *The Myth of Sisyphus*.

Only the mind's plunge is not "that of despair," as Camus continued, but of nonchalant roaming, as in a dream that nourishes. If there is a Sisyphus rolling the stone up to the hill only to let it roll down, and if there is a Camus who "must imagine Sisyphus happy," then Sisyphus is happy, less because "the struggle itself toward the heights is enough to fill a man's heart," as Camus mused, than because the stone *is* rolling and Sisyphus is roaming, uselessly, circularly.

13.3.   The second chapter ends with four stories. Let us look into them afresh.

The first three stories—penumbra and umbra, a snake and its skin, a cicada and its wings—have one thing in common, the reversibility of the relation of dependence. It reminds us of Hegel's surly story of the master-slave relation that can be reversed (in his *Phenomenology of Spirit*), of which Karl Marx took advantage. Chuang Tzu points us to a radical yet natural and serene reciprocity of dependence among things, a symmetrical interdependence.

In the last story of Chou and butterfly, the mutuality of interdependence becomes that of the change-over of subjecthood itself, an interchange of identities as disparate as a human being and a butterfly. The human being symbolizes a discoursing mind; the butterfly, a flittering flip-flop of life-and-death, ever regenerating into something else out of a previous life. It is parity in disparities.[90]

Thus these two points, interdependence (relativity) and interchange (non-egology), sum up the chapter. The result is a proposal to go along dynamically in the world, to follow along with the affirmation (*shih*) of each situation, each judgment, each entity, *as* each one changes into the other (*yin chih man yen*).

This argues for (*lun*) a dynamic parity (*ch'i*) among disparate things (*wu*); everything is alive, dynamic—argument, parity, things. "Argument" here is itself a journey *from* the self ("self-emptying") to its knowing (that is, "knowing of not-knowing" and "not-yet-existing") and its saying (that is, "saying without saying"), then to the interdependence and interchange among things and subjects-who-judge, always flip-flopping. This chapter argues our life's way; and such argument is itself part of life's way, and going on life's way is itself an argument.

What is *lun*, an argument? Graham translated it as "sorting."[91] Such sorting is like an actively turning whetstone *(ni)*[92] and balance *(chün).*[93] The life of things moves in a wheeling (*lun*) of parities (*ch'i*).

The *parity* (*ch'i*) we see is a dynamic one, the parity of interdependence (umbra and its penumbra, snake and its skin, cicada and its wings) and the parity of interchange (dream and awakening, Chou and butterfly, knowing and not-knowing). It is the parity of interpenetration both of functions and of indentities.

Things (*wu*) are thus ever swindling (*kuei*) our knowledge by ever swinging (*chen, tiao*) and changing (*hua*) themselves into something else. Such ontological dynamism assumes subjective awareness (*fen, pien*) of objective disparities among things (*chen, fung*).[94] For without distinction moving is impossible, as Parmenides rightly said.

In short, things have two aspects—disparity and change. The changeability of things depends on their having distinction. The objective manyness of things depends on the subjective dynamism of distinguishing (in saying, in knowing), and the subjective dynamism of existing opens out to (and dwells in) the pervading influence and confluence of the objective as-is. Here again, subjectivity and objectivity are in parity (*ch'i*), the dynamic parity of *fang* and *yin*, in which things occur.

In such a world we ourselves must enjoy ourselves swinging, sorting, and soaring within the realm of no-realm, that is, no definitive distinctions. We dwell in the realm as if dwelling out of it, and dwell out of if as if being in it. Such a dynamic unity of the parity of things (*ch'i*) is thus as synonymous with *yu* as *lun* is with *hsiao yao*. And we *are* things (*wu*).

13.4.   What are things? We must raise this question again with Aristotle and Heidegger. Things *have* their peculiar "wild meanings";[95] things have their own birth of meanings, "wild" when found. Such meanings are found to be singing their own ontological vibrations. Things have their waves of voices, their "hollows" that sing. As we "hollow ourselves" we can "overhear" and then become part of their voices; we call it language (*yen*). Our utterances can "sing the world"[96] with trees, hollows, birds, insects, subatomic systems of energy. Vibrations of our souls resonate with those of monkeys, cicadas, snakes, and butterflies. We become them as they become us, and we are one, one in all our differences. For without distinction there would have been no resonance which sings the world. World songs of the whales (*k'un*?) from the belly of the ocean (*ming*?) would never have arisen without cicadas and small doves *differing* from whales, snakes, butterflies, Chuang Chou. We are one natural song (piping of heaven?) in our differences. Such is the meaning of *ch'i*, the democracy of life.

We have thought about *ch'i* and *wu* repeatedly. Where is *lun*? That is what our talk is. It reflects that natural *lun* ("wheel") in the hands of the old wheelwright, who wheeled-as-he-talked with his Duke Huan about the skill of chiselling out a wheel; such activity is as different from dead bookreading and argument as living moments are from chaff and dregs of the old.[97]

In contrast to dead argument, the heavenly piping is simply the world singing itself out.[98] Since we are part of the world, if we let ourselves "self-empty" into "dead wood and ashes," we can listen in and join in with this singing. We can sing the world with whales and cicadas, even resonate with shadows, snakes, and butterflies. We will be *one* in the chorus of differences and interchanges. Do we hear the singing rhythm?

> 'Suppose a thing loses its shadow,
> Then it will become invisible,
> It will lose itself.
> A shadow gives a thing its depth, and
> Shadows it forth as its umbra, and
> Sounds it around as its aura,
> And gives it its "thing."

> 'Similarly,
> A penumbra surrounds an umbra
> To make an umbra an umbra.
> So does the skin to its snake, and
> The wings to its cicada—'
> So says Chuang Tzu.

> 'My shadow is my skin and my wings—
> My aura, my glory, giving me my self.
> Everything in the end interdepends with everything else.'

'There is a butterfly,' continues Chuang Tzu,
'Flittering to and fro
Between dream and real, between death and life,
Telling "Chuang Chou" that "he" that identifiable self,
Or that "me,"
May well be someone else
On whose dreaming he depends,
With whom he interchanges
In *his* dreams, and
On the difference from whom he interdepends to
Exist as himself.

I depend on you,
My shadow and my butterfly, to
Exist.

Thank you. ..."'

13.5. "Shadow" is an interesting notion. Besides Chuang Tzu, Carl G. Jung, and a Jungian writer, John A. Sanford, paid close attention to it.

A man without his shadow is a shadowy existence, a man in sheol. Why? Because shadow gives a man depth, which makes a man exist, a recognizable existence, perhaps even to himself.

What is depth? Carl G. Jung said it is the portion of our existence which escapes our conscious gaze, from which in fact we shy away our gaze. Our shadow is our dark forgotten corner, deep in us and quite powerful, our other self. Jung poured into this corner things of psychological significance, such as conscience, shame, undealt-with awkward experiences, secrets to oneself. This is nonetheless an essential part of the self, the other self that overshadows the conscious self from behind. Jung confessed:

> About this time [student years] I had a dream which both *frightened* and encouraged me. It was night in some unknown place, and I was making slow and *painful* headway *against* a mighty wind. *Dense* fog was flying along everywhere. I had my hands cupped around a tiny light which *threatened* to go out at any moment. Everything depended on my keeping this little light alive. Suddenly I had the feeling that something was coming up *behind* me. I looked back, and saw a gigantic black figure following me. But at the same moment I was conscious, in spite of my *terror*, that I must keep my little light going through night and wind, regardless of all *dangers*.[99]

The implications are clear. The little light was "my consciousness"; "the figure was a 'specter of the Brocken,' my own shadow on the swirling mists, brought into being by the little light."[100] And my little light, though "infinitely small and fragile in comparison with the powers of darkness, … is still a light, my only light."[101]

The same notions as Chuang Tzu used recur—wind, shadow, following, even unconsciousness. Yet what a different context from Chuang Tzu's in which Jung placed them! The italicized words in Jung's sentences clearly indicate the following: First, for Jung, the relation between the conscious self and its shadow of the (collective) unconscious other self is one of "terror" and antagonism. But, second, knowing this relation is an "encouragement" because such knowledge starts our efforts at making peace between the two selves. This is what psychiatry tries to accomplish.

This whole atmosphere, despite Jung's sympathy with Oriental insights, contrasts sharply with Chuang Tzu's. For Chuang Tzu, it is first of all important to have a Great Awakening to the uncertainty, not between consciousness and unconsciousness, but between the shadow and its penumbra, between the original ego (*wu*) and the flip-flopping of the empirical namable ego ("Chuang Chou") with other subjects, such (even) as a butterfly (not a shadow). Secondly, reconciliation is foreign to Chuang Tzu, for there is no antagonism and struggling terror. Instead there is an awakening, and then the Great Awakening, not to a resolution of problems but to a realization of and participation in uncertainty and the interchange of beings, of subjects, of names. Such is the root distinction between the Western and the Chinese ways of envisaging things.

A Jungian writer John A. Sanford wrote a novel, *The Man Who Lost His Shadow*,[102] which described a man who, having sold his shadow for money, was tormented by a lack of his essential self. He was neglected by others who could not see, hear, or touch him; he was buffeted about in human traffic, yet unable to make any difference in the world.

Only love, Sanford proposed, can *hear* (overhear?) that tormented shadowy man, and only love can redeem the shadow back to him. This is a Christian layer put on this richly imaginative and suggestive story. Perhaps care, attentiveness, and discernment could be more fitting than love, which includes them.

Again, the comparison with Chuang Tzu is instructive. Both Sanford and Chuang Tzu emphasized the importance of a poetic form of expression. Sanford used riddle poems as keys to solving the problems, and Chuang Tzu's story of the dialogue between the umbra and the penumbra is both unconventional and poetic.

Yet Chuang Tzu's story is stranger than Sanford's; Chuang Tzu's is more natural and more penetrating. Sanford had to appeal to morals (the man's loose and exploitative living, his shadow's accusations), to love (the little woman, Carolyn his girl friend), to mysterious plot, devil's Law, and magic. Sanford's story is a cleverly dressed Jungian morality play.

Chuang Tzu's story in contrast is made up of nothing but natural things—a man's shadow and his shadow of shadow, or rather, anything's shadow and its shadow of shadow. And the story grows stranger and deeper than Sanford's because the shadow was asked by and answered his penumbra, without showing the thing (or man) that is nonetheless present for their existences and conversation to take place. And the entire story is natural; it needs no artificial plot or morality to cohere it into a story.

Again, Sanford's story is in line with the typical Western mode of myth: An ideal smooth situation turns into disaster. Then comes a dramatic turning or a series of turnings, and the problem of the situation is solved. There is conflict and then its resolution—shadow versus self, past versus present, hate versus love.

Chuang Tzu's story is always natural—penumbra asking its own shadow, not shadow split from a person. It is natural yet unexpected, for whoever heard of a conversation between the umbra and the penumbra, and the penumbra asking a question about the umbra?

There is indeed a faint intimation of a problem. Penumbra asks if Shadow has been indecisive. Shadow answers with interdependence among all things. And such interdependence evaporates "problems," even without Shadow's knowledge. Everything is as natural as before, and that without knowing why for sure. The problem, if any, is not solved but resolved and evaporated. So much for "shadow."

13.6. Related to shadow is the notion of *dream*. Dream is the activity that most powerfully convinces us that we ourselves are part and parcel of the process of interchange among things. That is, we are one among things that mutually change, influence, co-arise, and co-cause one another. The subject who judges is *one* of the things judged. The very perspectives of judgement interchange, slide one into and from another.

"... Acting 'ruler,' 'herdsman,' and the like. / Incorrigible!" (258–59). The story of a ruler and a herdsman intertwined and exchanged in dreams is instructively elaborated by Lieh Tzu,[103] in many ways a synthesis of this sentiment. But the *Chuang Tzu* has no such long and well-developed stories, but only bits of mini-stories, often fleeting images here and there in phrases, notions, and words. Why? Perhaps this is to evoke many a Lieh Tzu in actual life. The reader must work himself into a particular coherent story. Perhaps the shortness and variety of mini-stories show the variety and interchange of situations and judgments in life.

This does not entail a denigration of individual integrity, distinctions among things, and subjective judgments. On the contrary, distinction is what enables interchange to happen. The subject who is strong enough to accommodate the change of the very subjecthood is a happy invincible sage.

And we ourselves agree to such change in our daily activities. Every night we sleep, dream, and wake up refreshed; the doctor is relieved if the patient can sleep well. We go on vacation, for a change of attitude and perspective. We change our attire for different occasions, change our automobiles, houses, decorations, positions of furniture, and the like. We have holidays and celebrations. Merchants seasonally change their merchandise and fashion. All these activities are meaningless unless they are good for us. They refresh, heal, and nourish life.

13.7.   Seeing implications in situations and statements is what is peculiarly human. Ordinary people are aroused to thinking and finding implications when confronted with unusual crises and aphorisms. Saints, poets, and those who are insane find unusual implications in the ordinaries. The degree of being human and alive is gauged by the degree to which one can find noteworthy implications in both the ordinaries and the extraordinaries alike.

Chuang Tzu has a knack for implications. He takes off into imaginative heights from ordinaries such as dead wood and ashes, wind and hollows, hearing, one, *fang*, *yin*, yes, beginning, monkeys, fingers, horses, fish and birds, uglies and beauties, wars, dreams, success and failure, and the like.

But then, how can we tell sages from the insane? Did Chuang Tzu distinguish wise and considered opinion from arbitrary irresponsible banter?

The final segment of the chapter (lines, 195–305) considers this problem. Chuang Tzu in the person of "Royal Distinction" (*wang ni*) says that the sage knows that he cannot distinguish and is *aware* of the problem, such mixing of the two, whereas the insane (Mr. Chew Chipped?) does not know and is not aware. The distinction lies in the *knowledge* of the impossibility of knowing the distinction.

Then Chuang Tzu goes on, saying that therefore we had better take his (or anyone's) words with a grain of salt; he has been talking "recklessly" and he is to be listened to "recklessly" (241). No one knows who is right or wrong, even after the debate and with a judge presiding—the Socratic knowledge with a vengeance. Socrates says he is called the wisest because he knows that he does not know much at all; Chuang Tzu says, "I call you 'a dream'—I am also a dream" (261). We may all be dreaming, and true knowledge consists in awakening to such a pervasive dream.

Then he goes on saying that he knows that he does not know what depends on what—shadow can be said to depend on its penumbra as well as the other way around, cicada can be said to depend on its wings as much as the other way around. Then he combines "dream" with "dependence." Such combination shakes the very basis for judgment, the absoluteness of a judging subject, an "ideal observer."

So, what is the distinction between the sage and the insane? Chuang Tzu would smile and say that you can say both that there is a distinction and that there is no distinction. There is a distinction in that the sage *knows* he is unable to see the distinction, whereas the insane does not know. There is no distinction because there is a parity in status between the two. This may be another way of asserting the parity of things.

13.8.   How does Chuang Tzu's attitude toward the relativity of things compare with the Buddhist's? Although both agree that things are correlative and we are somehow involved in them, the implications they draw from these "facts" differ. Their differences can be seen under two headings—things and ourselves.

For the Buddhist, things are moving in many circles of causes, co- causing and co-arising to annoy us, making us suffer. For Chuang Tzu things are not moving but alive, co-arising and co-dying, back and forth, and are equally important. *Ch'i Wu Lun* can mean a "description of how equally important things are."

For the Buddhist, all such annoyance (even joy annoys us) is caused by (rooted in) our desire and ignorance. If we cut our desire-clinging and ignorance, we will arrive at Enlightenment, that is, an awakening to a realization, and go beyond the circles of annoyance. For Chuang Tzu, we are part of such live interdependence among things. We must let go of ourselves so as to overhear, accommodate, and truly participate in the delight of such life flip-floppings. We are awakened to an onerous participation in the vicissitudes of things-transforming.

Both say ignorance is the cause of annoyance. The Buddhist awakening to knowledge dissolves our ignorance. Chuang Tzu's awakening to uncertainty (are we dreaming or awakened?) amounts to our knowledge *of* ignorance, affirmation of uncertainty. Buddhists awaken *out* of dreaming; Chuang Tzu wakes up *to* dreaming.

Both treasure unclinging. The Buddhist unclings himself to go beyond existence, even that of himself. Chuang Tzu unclutters and empties his self to tune in and partake of the pipings of all (men, things, heaven), to treasure and follow things, to walk both ways with monkeys-and-heaven, butterfly-and-Chuang-Chou, umbra-and-penumbra, skin-and-snake, wings-and-cicada, dream-and-awakening. Such is the joy of life-meandering so nonchalantly described in the first chapter.

All in all, Liu Hsien-hsin was closer to the truth when he said that "the Buddhists stressed the emptiness of all, discarding all; Taoists stressed the greatness of all, wanting all," than was Kuan Feng who identified Buddhism and Taoism.[104]

13.9. It is time to take stock. The first three chapters of the *Chuang Tzu* can be said to center on *hua*, "change."

Chapter One starts with the story of a big Fish changing (*hua*) into a big Bird, and Chapter Two ends with *wu hua*—things changing. Chapter One is titled *Hsiao Yao Yu*, a delightful change in steps and strides, perspectives, and activities. Chapter Two starts with Mr. South-Wall-Base "before," concluding with the story of Chuang Chou-dreamed versus a butterfly dreaming, in short, *things* interchanging.

The structure of *hua* is explained in Chapter Two. First one must be aware of such ontological interchange. Awareness requires becoming "dead wood and ashes" in regard both to the object-self (*yü, wo*) and to the entanglements with thoughts and worries, knowledge and schemes. Such awareness does not relieve one from change but enables one to come back home in change. One roams in change as one soars high in enjoyment of one's bird's eye view of the world. Soaring and roaming, one becomes one with all things. To paraphrase St. Paul, if for Onesimus to leave Philemon for a while is to receive him back forever (*Philemon* 15), and such is the decree of divine love, then for one to leave one's self for a while is to receive it back forever, and such is the Way of distinction and change among things.

To lose (*sang*) to be one (*i*) seems analogous to a Hegelian dialectical synthesis. For Hegel, synthetic oneness is a tension-filled unity such as that between the master and his slave or, as Marx applied it, the economic tug of war between the proletariat and the capitalist. Chuang Tzu's synthesis is a grandiose one—"All things are one horse," "All things are one with me." This is not Hegelian unity of enmity, much less a Buddhistic dissolution of identities. It is instead a synthesis (*i*) in change (*hua*), a dynamic interchange of perspectives and identities based on their distinctions.

Clearly there is an order—*hua* obtains only *in fen*; distinction has to be there before interchange happens.

All arguments, all pushes and pulls, are *fen*-activities. To realize this is to realize that we have been dreaming. All distinctions of me and you and our argumentative distinctions (*pien*) having been through, we come to realize that nothing is better than harmony (*ho*) with the heavenly whetstone of equality-in-distinction (*t'ien ni*).

In the meantime we experience all the wherefroms and wherefores (*yin*), and we now can use our experience as that-whereby (*yin*) we follow endless changes (*man yen*). We live out each year to the full (*ch'üng nien*), and we realize that we have been freely moving-about (*chen*) in the limitless realms, dwelling in the no-realm (*wu ching*). We have the distinctions of umbras and penumbras, goings and stops, sittings and risings, snakes and their skins, cicadas and their wings, Chuang Chou's and butterflies, ignorance and awakening. Then there are distinctions between now and then, something depended on and something else that *that* something depends on, a recognition of why it is so and a not-recognizing why, the so and the not-so, Chou dreaming and butterfly dreaming. *In* surveying all these distinctions (*fen*), we suddenly realize that we have already been engaging ourselves in changes (*hua*).

14.   The third chapter follows this pattern. Completion of our years (*chin nien*) is completion of our distinctness (*fen*), of our life's confines (*ya*), of the total self, body and all (*pao shen*). And such an act of completing is a carving-loosening (*chieh*), bringing out the distinctness (*fen*) of things. After all, things (*wu*) come into existence as if an ox (*niu*) were carved (*chieh*) with a knife (*wu; tao* with blood stains)[105] out of darkness (*ming*) of rich confusion (*hun tun*). By this cutting and carving, the Duke of Wen-hui is duke and the Cook Ting is cook, mutually distinguished.

Such is the secret of the completion of our years and completion of our self, that is, nourishment of our life. Cutting, in other words, is nourishment! From this angle, we can see that mutilation[106] of the Commander of the Right is "due to heaven"; completion of our years includes letting oneself be rendered unique-and-one-footed (*shih tu*). To be mutilated is to let-be unique as this specific Commander, completing one's years *as* this Commander. And of course to complete (*chin*; line 4) is to exhaust (*chin*; line 61), as that immortal Lao Tan did, completing himself by exhausting his years and dying. He completed himself because he loosened himself from the bond (*hsüan chieh*, "bond-loosened"). Thus to complete and exhaust oneself (*chin*) is not to know that one is exhausted but to pass on as the fire goes on, changing things in the process.

Thus distinction leads to change and change obtains in distinction. In carving-loosening an ox, one dances to the rhythm, that is, resting in the times and situating oneself on the course of things—to distinguish is already to change.

We are reminded here of some popular Buddhistic interpretations, almost irresistibly. A. C. Graham is an example, despite himself. Graham takes *chieh* to mean "liberation from selfhood," "(loosing or) losing selfhood," so that one comes back home to what has always been, "identical with everything conscious or unconscious in the universe." "I am everything." All this comes dangerously close to the Buddhistic obliteration of the specific identities of things.

This is because Graham takes the identities of things on a scale of space, not in terms of process and history. And he produces a complex, largely unintelligible justification for exalting the acceptance of mutilation and catastrophe as one's destiny.[107] He is ignorant of a much simpler Chuang Tzu—*fen* and *hua*, that is, *chieh* and *shun*, *shih* and *yang*.[108] Similar to frames in a movie film, *each* time slot (*fen*), each actual occasion, each *kairos* (*shih*), is eternity. Dwell in it (*an*) and things shall go (*hua*) smoothly forever. We can settle (*ch'u*) in this smooth (*shun*) cosmic process of changes (*hua*).[109]

And through such indwelling of interchanges my identity comes into existence, whether it be a Chou or a butterfly, a commander or a criminal (mutilated), a duke or a cook. My identity comes out intact, if only I allow it to (inter-) change (with things). This is a new theory of the immortality of souls (Chapter Three, line 61).

In short, all things are at one in such *fen* in *hua* and *hua* in *fen*; hence *ch'i wu lun*. To enjoy such dynamics of the universe is to *hsiao yao yu*. We "nourish ourselves" by "dwelling in" the cosmic dances that carve and undo these oxen of things.

C. What All This Means

1. *The chapter and its title:* The chapter titled *Ch'i Wu Lun* combines a theme of *ch'i*, the order and unity of things, with a theme of *wu*, many lively things. The view is thus a calmer and more complex one than Parmenidean monism alone or Heraclitean dynamism alone.

Objectively the bond that binds these two themes is the mysterious "heavenly Treasury" that is dark (*ming*) at both ends, the one at the North and the many at the South. Subjectively the bond is perceptive self-involved ignorance, awakening to uncertainty in the transformation of things.

The chapter is precariously similar to the sophistic dialectics of Hui Shih who juggled systems of logic, *lun*. But Chuang Tzu was rigorously responsible to meaning coherence that is self-involved. He differs from Hui Shih in maintaining a steady gaze at things, for the sake of which he clowned with logic coherently; but he never dazzled the reader with logical trickery as Hui Shih did.

For all his philosophical profundity, Chuang Tzu was always smiling in his sentences. If this chapter is a philosophical one, it is a magnificent philosophical parody on philosophy. It is a slippery chapter. In what follows three main subjects are presented: the title (Section 1), the contents (Section 2), and some interesting themes (Section 3).

1.1.   Marie C. Swabey began her book on *Comic Laughter* with a warning:

It is a misplaced hope to expect to fined here a comic treatment of the comic. ... What is important ... is that in the laughter of the comic insight we achieve a logical moment of truth; ... metaphysically, through some darting thought, we detect an incongruence as cancelled by an underlying congruence. We gain an inkling ... of the hang of things ... feel more at home in the universe by aiding in the discernment of values ... a revelation of the ideal ... [110]

I could not agree with her more, about the important function of the comic. I wonder, however, why in achieving discernment in the comic one is not comical. If the comic is an important avenue to discernment, a no-nonsense philosophical analysis of it smacks contextually odd.

It is undeniable that explication of the comic may somehow diminish its romping frolic, yet there is no reason why such explication itself cannot be enjoyable, if not comic. If the comic is an important avenue to truth, as Swabey correctly insisted, and if the exposition of it is to show us how this is the case, then the exposition is best when it exhibits the original comical flavor, showing how *that* flavor presents truth to us by presenting that flavor. Kierkegaard's treatment of Socrates' irony may be less ironic than Socrates' speeches, but Kierkegaard does display Socrates' subtlety, and in such display the ironic comes through to the reader.[111]

After all, an exposition of the comic and ironic should convey both clarity of contents and truthfulness to the writer's style, sacrificing neither for the other, so as to present the comico-ironic as an inevitable ploy in the provocation of truth in the reader. This is of course due to the fact that living truth must be experienced alive. One cannot investigate the wind by trapping it in a box. The wind of life is discerned by standing in the midst of its impact, not by analyzing it in a logical sieve. An exposition of the truth that comes via the comic and ironic cannot succeed by analyzing the comico-ironic, but by rearranging the reader's posture so that he can best be struck by the unexpected blow of the ironic. Such a blow, such evocation, can not be forced, much less analyzed; we must let it come, by facilitating its coming. All exposition is a removing of the blockage, a rearrangement of the environment, to let the subject-matter come.

The reason for having comical and ironic in philosophy is twofold. First, as Swabey pointed out, the hang of things and the discernment of values come to us alive and most effectively through laughter and smile. Second, *such* a seeing of truth is salutary. In playing off one point lightly and laughingly against another, the self is neither trapped nor unconcerned, but rendered free to see and savor the truth of the matter. It is a wholesome affair.

The second chapter of the *Chuang Tzu*, titled *Ch'i Wu Lun*, is a magnificent philosophical parody on philosophy. Very seldom is this fact noticed. Usually the chapter is taken to be a *serious* philosophical exposition of ontology or cosmology and a serious refutation of then-current schools of thought. Commentators usually take pains to explicate what they think to be Chuang Tzu's contorted train of arguments. For that purpose, they kindly give us background information on Chuang Tzu's allusions to then-current philosophical thought and hazard their ingenious explanations of Chuang Tzu's cryptic aphorisms. They miss the woods for the trees.

The chapter taken as a serious philosophical treatise is the chapter rendered unintelligible. We are hard put to find a consistent flow of argument in an arbitrary collection of random philosophical bits. We tour philosophical volcanic eruptions bombarding us with apothegms. And we blame this sorry state of affairs on generations of inept copiers bungling through the long chapter with one mis-copying after another.

One of the chapter's most sympathetic interpreters, A. C. Graham, takes the chapter to be a serious philosophical treatise and comes up with an ingenious view:

> Chuang-tzǔ was thinking aloud, jotting the living thought at the moment of its inception, of thought which is not yet systematic but 'existential' ...struggling with his own developing thoughts formulating an idea and then revising or attacking it. Sometimes perhaps he is criticizing a provisional formulation of his own; often certainly he is attacking an idea already current.[112]

Chuang Tzu is here described as an inceptive thinker struggling to attain "mature systematization," which finally came in his disciple's chapter on the Autumn Flood (Chapter Seventeen). This interpretation assumes that Chuang Tzu shares our ideal of thinking, to attain a coherent comprehensive metaphysical system. On this assumption the *Chuang Tzu* is a series of stuttering trials at the ideal, scattering the pages with bits of insights and half-baked stories. Such a sorry picture reflects more on *our* approach than on Chuang Tzu.

Suppose, therefore, we abandon the picture of Chuang Tzu struggling for serious systematic thinking, and take him as he is, living in his thinking, citing "famous" thoughts, some well-known, some concocted, quoting and misquoting, only to modify them or point to their alternatives. And suppose Chuang Tzu is doing all this quite intentionally, using, as he told us, his goblet words to pour out endless changes, marshalling odd and outlandish terms, brash and bombastic phrases, to arouse the world out of its turbidness.[113]

In other words, suppose we see this impish and provocative Chuang Tzu romping through the universe with his cosmic laughter, *parodying* a regular sober philosophizing process. Then we shall be impressed while reading the *Chuang Tzu* that such parodying is itself a sort of philosophizing, provoking us into thinking more effectively than any other mode, evocative of living "truths that never come to an end."[114]

Then the piecemeal character of the chapter suddenly takes on new significance. Half-baked bits of thought are tossed out only to be recanted, the established sayings of the famed are mentioned only to be refuted—all these seeming futilities fall into place. We see that Chuang Tzu is *playing* with arguments and thinking, poking fun at them. Chuang Tzu is here showing the reader how ridiculous it is to engage in serious arguments and disputes, for they are to be played with and played in. *What* the disputes are about is not to be disputed but to be lived.

Such parodying goes beyond Nietzsche's, who also wanted to express in as few words as possible the entire universe of truth, and arouse the world with his expressions. Sadly Nietzsche's ironies were abrasive, contemptuous of the "vulgar." He was proud of his pride in the great glorious Self. Chuang Tzu in contrast hid himself in smiles and similes. He lampoons without demolishing, letting his opponents demolish themselves. He attacked without messy formal attacks.

Graham was correct in noticing that the technical terms Chuang Tzu used came from the accepted document of Chinese dialectics, the *Mohist Canon*, such as *pien, liang, ch'u, sheng, ming-shih, chü, lei, chien-po, k'o, shih-fei, jan*.[115] It is well known that Chuang Tzu cited two celebrated sophists, Hui Shih and Kung Sun Lung, without mentioning their names. It is seldom noted that Chuang Tzu perhaps frivolously misquoted Mencius, "All things are complete in me," by saying "The myriads of things are one with me,"[116] and obliquely matched Mencius' serious pronouncement, "Heaven produces creatures, providing them with one root," with "The Way makes them all into me."[117] The very title of the chapter, *Ch'i Wu Lun*, perhaps carped Mencius' "It is the nature of things (*wu*) to be unequal (*pu ch'i*)."[118] Far from being immature, Chuang Tzu's knowing brush parodied recognized thinkers.

But he reserved his most scathing satire for the sophists, who were irresponsible in their verbal tricks. Chuang Tzu turned their frivolity back on them, and in so doing came up with novel metaphysical insights that revolutionized our way of life.

Graham said that the second chapter is widely regarded as "the most important chapter" in the *Chuang Tzu*, "the most important document of early Taoism outside *Tao Te Ching*."[119] One wonders whether he fully appreciated the far-reaching implications of his correct assessment.

1.2.   All expositors agree with Graham that the second chapter is a masterpiece. Few realize that it is a magnificent parody on philosophy. The perceptive reader immediately feels its punch when he confronts the title, *Ch'i Wu Lun*.

Lun means saying, dialogue, debates, thinking, judging, arguing, criticizing, or some or all of these, a treatise.[120]

Wu means not only ordinary visible things, but anything that exists, visible and invisible, the quick and the dead, and the beyond, the situational matters, events, species and varieties, and the like.[121] It can be used as the phrase, *wu wu*, "thinging things."[122] *Wu Lun* can mean the noisy clamor of public opinion.

Ch'i is an interesting notion. Among fifteen or so meanings, three stand out for attention: (a) Originally it was an ideogram depicting ears of wheat or corn arranging themselves in rows (similar heights, colors, shapes, and the like), waving in the sunny breeze. (b) Then it came to mean arranging or mixing things in a meaningful pattern—such as in the preparation of drugs or cuisine. A pharmacist and a chef are professionals who *ch'i* (verb) things for medical and culinary purposes. (c) Then came *ch'i* as adjective "equal" or noun "equality."[123]

The three preceding paragraphs can be summed up thus: *Ch'i* is not uniformity that abolishes uniqueness and variety of individuals, whose togetherness and parity it avidly describes. This sentiment was well expressed when Chuang Tzu said,

> The myriads of things live species by species, one group settled close to another. Birds and beasts form their flocks and herds, grass and trees grow to fullest height. ... men live with birds and beasts, group themselves side by side with the ten thousand things. Who then knows anything about 'gentlemen' or 'petty rascals'?[124]

Such is the *ch'i* of happy togetherness.

And *wu* includes human beings and human affairs; they are some of the "matters" of fact that comprise our world. Since we humans are *wu* among other *wu*'s, we ought to be able to "walk among the animals without alarming their herds, walk among the birds without alarming their flocks."[125] If they do not resent us, "how much less would men!"

Finally, *lun* is not logical syllogism or metaphysical system; this chapter has no definitive doctrines. For great discriminations are not spoken, and so "the sage debates but does not discriminate"(176). The purpose of this *Ch'i Wu Lun* is obviously to warn against misguided systematization, advising us to "forget the years; forget distinctions" (287), giving reasons why there should be no system. This is a chapter of "subtle, elliptical reasoning" (Graham).[126]

1.3. The three characters combined, *Ch'i Wu Lun*, have a variety of implications for the meaning of the chapter. I can see at least five, each related to the others. To save space, let C, W, and L stand for the three characters in the title, *Ch'i Wu Lun*. Let an arrow "→" stand for what is going on in the relations among these terms. Then the following summary interpretations of the chapter might result:

(1) *C→(WL)*: This chapter *ch'i*s (harmonizes, arranges, equalizes, mixes approximately) theories (L) of things (W).

(2) *(CW)←L*. This chapter is a theory (L) of (or theorizes about, or discusses) the *ch'i*-ing (C) of things (W), or how things (W) are *ch'i*-ed (C).

These two interpretations have been traditionally entertained. Huang Chin-hung said that the second interpretation was prevalent before the T'ang dynasty (618–907 A.D.), and that since the Sung dynasty (960–1279 A.D.) both interpretations have been held by various thinkers.[127]

Reasons advanced for the first interpretation are: Originally things have no yes or no (distinctions), said Lu Shu-chih, but distinctions among them arise in our set-mind, producing theories; and according to Wang Fu-chih, our troubles begin with fights over our views on things. In fact, our views on things *are* our troubles, as described in lines 35–84.

Reasons for the second interpretation are: "Theories about things," said Kuan Feng, are themselves "things" in the universe; once things are equalized words will automatically be equalized also. When the distinction between the self and the other is abolished, said Huang Chin-hung, all theories and controversies are automatically stopped. And so the second interpretation includes the first, which cannot include the second. Wu I added that the *Chuang Tzu* has phrases of WC (17/44) or CW (33/43), but no WL.

Besides these interpretations, three others may be considered:

(3) $(C{\rightarrow}W)+(C{\rightarrow}L)$: This chapter is on *ch'i*-ing (C) things (W) and *ch'i*-ing (C) theories (L).

(4) $C{\rightarrow}(W+L)$: This chapter *ch'i*s " things (W) and theories (L)," taken together.

(5) $(CW+W) {\leftarrow}L$. This chapter theorizes about (L) the relation between our *ch'i*-ing of things (CW) and things themselves, as they are (W).

More interpretations of the title may well be possible. But *which* interpretation is the right one? Traditionally, all commentators naively took this question to be a legitimate one, answering it in one way or the other. This question itself, however, must be questioned. For these interpretations overlap.

There is, then, a sixth:

(6) Chuang Tzu smilingly saying, "Take your pick." For any interpretation we choose will lead to others, and we may end up embracing all interpretations.

Such fluid goblet rationality[128] is typical of Chuang Tzu. And that for good reason, he would add, for it is a fitting way to reflect (on) the flow of reasonableness in actuality.

2. *Contents*: 2.1. *Outlines*: We see Chuang Tzu's live rationality again when we consider how *best* to outline the chapter. There are various possibilities, each of which shades into others. First, we will see three outlines typically given by commentators. Then, we will see my own four possible outlines.

2.1.1. Chang Ch'eng-ch'iu says there are eleven sections to the chapter:

(1) Three Pipings (lines 1-34)
(2) Mental wranglings and muddles (35-84)
(3) Words (85-107)
(4) Things (108-24)
(5) Formation and Deformation (125-49)
(6) Debates (150-89)
(7) Futility of political attacks (190-94)
(8) Virtue as beyond the distinction of life and death, profit and loss (195-229)
(9) Life and death are as sleeping and waking (230-64)
(10) No use debating (265-89)
(11) Self-forgetting lets all theories self-extinguish (290-305)

Kuan Feng comes up with five sections:

(1) Pipings (1–34)
(2) Muddles (35–77)
(3) Things (78–149)
(4) Knowledge and debates, all useless (150–289)
(5) Shadow and dream (290–305)

Chen Ku-ying has seven sections:

(1) Three pipings and loss of self-centeredness (1–34)

(2) Debates among different schools of thought, resulting in loss of true self (35–77)

(3) All these wranglings originate in prejudices, subjective obstinacy. Clarity of knowledge is needed to see impermancence and relativity of judgments and things (78–107)

(4) Tao brings everything into one (108–49)

(5) Oneness of self and universe (150–89)

(6) Three stories: Yao—inclusive in spirit; Nieh Ch'üeh—relativity of values; Chu Ch'üeh Tzu—life and death as one (190–289)

(7) Two stories: "shadow"—non-dependence; and "dream"—mutual transformation (290–305)

More examples of a similar sort could be given. Enough is shown, however, about what commentators usually give us. They are helpful in identifying topics treated in the chapter and showing us how they are arranged. The trouble with them is that they all look like dictionaries or indices, devoid of exciting coherence.

2.1.2 I see four new ways, philosophically more interesting, of outlining Chapter Two. They elucidate the meaning and coherence of the chapter.

(1) We can see three elements in the chapter: (*i*) The world of *things*, mutually transforming (*wu hua*) and arranging (*ch'i*). (*ii*) The *logic* of debate and dialogue—manifesting the mutuality of contraries. (*iii*) The *self* as the knowing subject, shedding its fixated self-assertiveness.

Here, (*i*) is about *ch'i wu*; (*ii*) and (*iii*) are about the objective and the subjective poles of *lun*. The chapter begins and ends with (*iii*); both (*ii*) and (*iii*) surround (*i*).

Furthermore, (*i*) is about non-being, (*ii*) is about non-saying, and (*iii*) is about non-knowing, and so:

(2) The chapter can be seen to have three interfused sections. It starts with non-being of the self, shading into a non-saying about things (*wu*) and

arguments (*lun*), leading to a discerned non-knowing of things, including the self—all of which amounts to a *ch'i*-ing of things and theories. To say (non-saying) so (non-knowing) about things interchanging (non-being) sums up the chapter, toward the end of the chapter.

(3) The chapter can be outlined in terms of three pipings, an important musical metaphor with which the chapter begins:

    (i)   Introduction: on three pipings (1–34)
   (ii) Piping of men: muddles (35–59)
  (iii) Piping of earth: double walk (60–129)
  (iv) Piping of heaven: shaded light (130–89)
   (v) Piping of men: Yao story (190–94)
  (vi) Piping of earth: *Nieh-Ch'ueh Tzu* story (195–229)
 (vii) Piping of heaven: *Chu-Ch'ieh Tzu* story (230–89)
(viii) Conclusion: shadow and dream (290–305)

(4) Dissatisfied with three pipings repeated twice, we may arrange the chapter in a loop, in five levels:

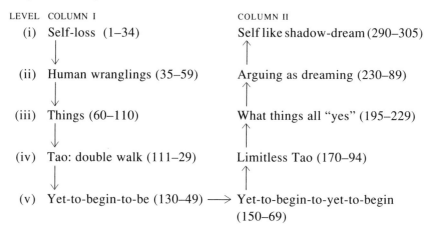

LEVEL COLUMN I   COLUMN II

   (i)   Self-loss (1–34)   Self like shadow-dream (290–305)

  (ii) Human wranglings (35–59)   Arguing as dreaming (230–89)

 (iii) Things (60–110)   What things all "yes" (195–229)

 (iv) Tao: double walk (111–29)   Limitless Tao (170–94)

  (v) Yet-to-begin-to-be (130–49) ——→ Yet-to-begin-to-yet-to-begin (150–69)

We see that column I is progressive from the self to the origin of things, from self-assertiveness to being aware of the suffering of futile wranglings (level ii), then from there to realizing the relativities of things (level iii). This realization leads us to see how formation and deformation, differences of policies, rights and wrongs, are all roads walked out by men and things (level iv). That gives us insight into the origin of things, the very Pivot of the Way of things (level v). So far the road has been negativities gradually improved on.

Such improvement allows us to go into the very beginning of things (level v in column II) and realize that Tao (the Way of things) is limitless (level iv).

Our non-knowledge is really our freedom to roam (level iii). We can now enjoy arguing with one another, knowing that all this may well be dreaming (level ii). Yet dreaming is not negative, since to realize our uncertainty about whether or not we are in a dream shows that we are "greatly awake" (level i). And so the initial "loss" of the self proves to be something very positive, giving us our true identity in non-knowledge and freedom in interchange with things. Such is column II, a reversal of column I.

Thus it all depends on the initial loss of our self-assertiveness. Without that loss, we are forever tossed in the agonies of daily problems with ourselves and with others, forever in the dark (*mang*) about the Pivot of the Way of things. With the loss of self-assetiveness level i becomes the piping of men (level ii), which spreads to the piping of earth (level iii), through which we discern the piping of heaven in the ongoings of things (level iv) and in their very Center-Pivot, the yet-to-begin to yet-to-begin things (level v). Thus we see mutual echoing of three pipings in five levels, not only in interaction with our surroundings (level iii) but in a comprehensive interfusion with all things (levels iv, v). With our self-loss column I is turned into column II.

Such an ideal world of mutual resonance (level v) is yet seen to consist in the ordinary (*yung, fan*). Level iv is the summarizing link typified by heavenly Equalizer, Shaded Light, heavenly Treasury, and the like. Level iii is consummated in a rhetorical question, "How do I know?" Level ii is an enjoyment in interaction with others, fully realizing that all this may be a dream. Level i is the scene of mutual transformation (*hua*), first into dry wood and dead ashes, then into a butterfly, forever ontologically involved one with another. Once we discard our set minds on things, our bigoted selves, we are able to watch the process of change, which gradually comes to ourselves.

2.1.3 These many possible ways of outlining the chapter can be taken in two ways. On the one hand, such multiple possibilities can show Chuang Tzu's failure to think things through. He may have busied himself catching inchoate thoughts, and no more. That we can interpret the chapter in so many ways may mean that it has no definitive meaning; the chapter might mean nothing significant, then.

On the other hand, seeing that the *contents* of the chapter are anything but insignificant, it could have been constructed multi-faceted. It could be a brilliant art work, designed to reflect life. Multi-dimensionality of meaning is not necessarily meaninglessness; life is a complex of meanings. The "ambiguity of life"[129] does not mean that life is meaningless, but a *tangle* of significant interrelations. And the chapter's ambiguous phrases may have been designed to faithfully reflect the ambiguities of life. If this is the case, then probing into the nuances of the chapter can give us nuances of life.

2.2. *Ontological interpretation*: I offer two interpretations of the chapter—ontological and methodological—according to two sides of the chapter. When we want to know *what* things truly are, we read the chapter ontologically. When we are excited and want to know *how* we can participate in them, we read the chapter methodologically. And it will be seen that these two interpretations dovetail. Then we shall see what they manifest—the logic that is alive with life, the goblet rationality.

2.2.1. *Contents and implications*: The chapter begins with Mr. South Wall Base sitting—neither lying (quiescence of energy) nor standing or running (agitation of energy), but in the natural state of sitting, as he was exhaling toward heaven. He was observed to become like "dry wood and dead ashes."

This famous phrase does not describe death but self-forgetfulness, the purest intensity of openness to things.[130] This state enables one to catch cicadas as easily as "grabbing them with his hand," to carve a bell-stand out of wood as if from a divine hand;[131] being *the* sagely stage[132] that takes part "in the beginning of things."[133] It *is* in fact the state of a newborn baby and calf, the beginning of life.[134]

Deathly alive as baby and dry log, Mr. Base described himself as having lost his self. Both T'ang Chün-i and Wu I pointed out[135] that since the lost self (*wo*) differs from the losing self (*wu*), who describes the situation, to lose one's self is not to die but die only to the assertive self, the formed and set mind (78). Self-loss is self-shedding as snakes and butterflies (293).

Then "three pipings" follows. Note how the pipings are introduced. They are not noticed until one is calm as dead silent ashes. One has to have become silent before one can come alive to cosmic musicality; "I lose myself in/to music," a musician said. Losing one's ego enables one to overhear the interactive involvements among three pipings.[136]

Piping comes when two non-beings meet, hollows in things and the blowing wind. "Gentle wind, then a small chorus; whirling wind, then a huge chorus" (25). Selflessly listening, we discern three pipings—the piping of men, of earth, and of heaven. And later, as the ashes blow up into hollows of the dry wood, *we* take part in the cosmic fugues, in the mutual shadowings-forth and transformations.[137]

Three pipings are both distinct and interactive. The piping of men is inspired by, as it interacts with, the piping of their surroundings, the piping of earth. And both pipings reveal their root, the piping of heaven, which manifests itself only in them. The Muses stir up nature into "being" of musical resonance, to which human beings respond by singing with it in their daily ongoings, and by sometimes composing music out of its inspiration.[138] How does all this come about?

The huge Clod belches out the wind, the breath of nature that blows forth lives; "the male [insect] cries on the wind above, the female cries on the wind below, and there is wind-change," that is, fertilization.[139] Blowing over the hollows, the wind calls forth the music of life.[140]

Many commentators follow Kuo Hsiang, saying that there is in fact no heavenly piping, which is a literary expression of a collective mutuality of earthly and human pipings. I disagree. Chuang Tzu has many "heavenly" phrases ("heavenly balance," "heavenly treasury," "heavenly horizon") indicating the existence of heaven. More importantly, without heavenly piping things are devoid of their cohering and originating principles; Chuang Tzu repeatedly meditated on Tao, shaded Light, and the Yet-to-begin-to-yet-to begin things.

Yet it is as illogical to deny the existence of the first principle (the beginning power, *t'ien chi*) as it is impossible to claim its knowledge and possession. To *know* something is (a) to take a definite position to the exclusion of others, and (b) to stand detached from it, objectifying, classifying, and manipulating it at will. And neither is possible in our relation to the first pervasive principle, that *in* which we know.[141]

We ourselves are human piping resonating with earthly piping. We are a "network of relations";[142] we can know things *in* such a web but not the web itself, much less what makes possible things, ourselves, and our relations. Aristotle "proved" the first principle, "A is A and not non-A" by a *reductio* argument.[143] We can only watch how our argument breaks down when we do not assume (start with and follow) "A is A." Plato compared the Form of forms to the "Sun" of ontological goodness. The sun cannot be looked *at*, but can only be felt *in* the visibility of things.[144] Similarly, only by watching the interactive relations between human and earthly pipings can we discern heavenly piping. All we know is our relations with things, not the first principle.

To know the unknowability of the first principle (*in* which we are) requires philosophical conversion, as Plato intimated in his allegory of the Cave. Chuang Tzu would say that such knowing of unknowing is an ontological revolution, no less than being cleansed from the objective, objectifiable, and objectifying ego (*wo*). The heavenly *chi* (natural power to spring forth life) can only be felt; it can not be known as we know an object. An old farmer scolded such a machinating mind (*chi hsin*),[145] which amounts to a detachment of oneself from the interconnection among things, an activity of the objectifying ego (*wo*).[146] The *wo*-self embraces the machine mind, forms a definitive opinion of things, and our suffering begins.

The first principle is real and unknowable (*chen chai, chen chün*; 55–59, 66–68; cf. 33–34). To embrace both its reality and unknowability is to be at home in the Pivot of the active Way of things (*tao shu*; 104).

This is to arrange things equally and in order, to talk so as to end talks, or rather, to talk as if there were no talk, and to act in the dark without fear. We are in the dark because we know that we cannot know the first principle. We are not afraid because we can discern its Light Shaded (*pao kuang*) through our enmeshed interaction with things.

This leads us to look into reciprocity among things, the cosmic fugal chorus of earthly and human pipings, which Chuang Tzu described alternatively.

But first as to our messy troubled inner life, a topsy-turvy world of intellectual push and emotional pull. Lines 35–84 describe the *necessity* of our self-losing.

This is the world of negative human piping, the psychic resonance of hatred and joy, exaltation and fear, and the cognitive resonance of slander and knowledge. People assert themselves, now in despair, now in pride, now against one another, now for themselves, not realizing that all this is mere hollow echoes of earthly and heavenly pipings, but ever staking their lives on such futilities (*mang*).

Painful "sound and fury" turns significant (echo) only when it alerts us to the intricacies of sympathetic resonance. Human piping should promote cosmic chorus, not pulverizing us in self-assertion and petty achievements. For assertive achievements hinder universal reciprocal thriving. Its Way is a Wheel (*huan*) that churns forth eddies of mutual transformations, endless this's and that's, approvals and disapprovals, all interdependent. Self-assertiveness blinds us to the Wheel, and we take up our position against out opponents. We do not (want to) realize that our (opposition) makes sense only in terms of our opponents, on whom we interdepend. In our blindness we turn our mutuality into mutual destruction.

How can this be? Look again at Mr. South Wall Base sitting, leaning on (or hiding behind) his armrest, his possession and his support, where he loses his self without losing himself, neither abandoning himself (*ch'i chi*) nor asserting himself.

It is in such a state that we discern cosmic inter-piping. Only a dry log produces sound, sounding forth against the silence of dead ashes. Sound comes when all such emptiness is blown by the invisible-intangible wind. Thus sound goes with my self-loss without losing myself. Invisible, intangible, untouchable, sound yet vibrates the receptor. Does vibration exist by itself?

The wind is also a vibration out of the huge Clod. A boy once remarked, "I wish the tree won't shake that hard, 'cause then we won't have wind." It is a revealing remark; the wind *is* the tree shaking. Yet the wind is also (felt as) an existence all its own; it is also correct to say the wind shakes the tree and breaks it down. The wind is neither itself nor a nothing.

When a withered tree meets the wind, we hear sound. Withered tree, wind, sound, all these share one thing in common—neither themselves nor nothing.

Wind is vibration, which is nothing in itself, but a thing vibrating. Yet that thing is not in itself its vibration. But, again, is it really all right to say that something is not in itself vibration? Where else is that something that vibrates except in its peculiar vibration?

And yet, without the wind of vibration, can something vibrate as itself? It stays quiet and hidden as if it were a hollow, a nothing, until vibrated or, rather, until it resonates to the wind of sympathetic resonance. Thus something is as it is when it vibrates to the wind, vibrating itself forth; "every object is inhabited, and we cannot make contact with the object unless we listen to it. Everything has a vibration, ... Japanese wind chimes ... hanging in the doorway and they made a beautiful sound in the breeze."[147]

Likewise, wind is an initiator of vibrations in many things as they respectively are, and yet it is nothing but a sympathetic resonance *of* something. The wind is itself and not itself. Thus in the wind-situation, in sympathetic resonance, activity and passivity, subject and object, existence and nothing, make sense in terms of one another.

If the wind is a cosmic force of resonance, then each existential sound is a manifestation of the world in the manner of a particular thing, as much of that sounding thing as the world sounding forth in that thing.[148] Chuang Tzu asked: "Blowing on the myriads differently, and letting them be themselves; all of them self-choose, but he who arouses them, who is he?" (33–34) Then he answered later: "I played it with unwearying notes and tuned it to the command of spontaneity. Therefore there seemed to be a chaos where things grow in thickets together, a maturity where nothing takes form ... "[149]

It is not quite right just to say wind, resonance, and vibration, as if they are not related. For resonating vibration is sound with particular structural interrelations among the sound, the wind, and the peculiar characteristic of each thing. Chuang Tzu used "piping" (music) to characterize the situation.

Music or piping is an organized group of sounds, a structured non-being that is not nothing. And piping is of three levels, each closely interrelated to the other two; we see in one the other two. The world is a mutuality of pipings of cosmic-and-individual life. To discern and live it is joy; to violate it in self-assertion is confusion and suffering.

The violation happens in human piping; human beings can assert themselves and destroy the cosmic chorus, turning it into violent noise. Yet even in such painful "music" of human life we can see indications of the structure of music, for even the human cacophony of pain has its rhythm, as is suggested by Chuang Tzu's hushed cadence of description in lines 35–84. It is, however, nothing after all because we can find neither its cause nor goal. All our suffering is so futile (*mang*; 76–77).

All this is because we "make" up our "mind" (*ch'eng hsin*) about our fleeting daily dealings, regarding them as eternally ours, stubbornly disregarding actuality, to wit, the fact that human piping is neither itself nor nothing but belongs to the hierarchy of the three pipings. We disregard actuality and "set our minds" (*ch'eng hsin*) on illusion, and this is to "take no-existence as existence" (83).

No wonder we suffer in our prejudice and petty accomplishments which eclipse (*yin*) the universal music, or, rather, shade (*yin*) us from the natural Tao. Such pettiness is manifested in Confucian and Mohist chitchats (*yen*) on *yes* and *no*, right and wrong.

But as the sophists frivolously said, things simultaneously produce one another, yes and no, right and wrong. Their frivolity alerts us out of Confucian-Mohist mistaken seriousness.

Yet if the sophists goaded us out of moral seriousness, the sophists themselves were stuck in *their* frivolity. The holy man does not take the road either of seriousness or frivolity, but goes in the light of nature (*chao chih yü t'ien*) and follows whatever actually is (*yin shih*; 100), and this is to dwell in the Tao Pivot without contraries, responding to all endlessly. *Yes* and *no* forever produce each other, mutually forming a circle (*huan*) of reciprocity which rolls and rolls. Clarity of things resides at its center, and to stay here is to be free. If they say frivolously that they can prove with a referring finger that the finger is no finger, the holy man (who stays in the center and hence is free) can frolic and prove with a non-finger that the finger is no finger. And similarly with a horse and a non-horse. For, does it matter? All things under heaven are one finger and one horse. This is the clarity gained at the center of the universe.

The self hollows itself into dead wood and ashes, and discerns the futility of our fixed judgments and feelings, which echo one another in the wind. Such echoing and mirroring is of two kinds. On the one hand, *things* (*wu*) that are and are not, being one and many, mutually produce one another. On the other hand, *our* theorizing and debating (*lun*) about things affirms and denies, again mutually depending one on another.[150] To discern such echoing and to take part in it is to do justice both to things and to theorizings (*ch'i wu lun*). How so?

The first echoing concerns the Way things go; the second concerns our knowledge. Things which come and go in birth and death, accomplishment and destruction, one and many, originate in heavenly Treasury (*t'ien fu*) which has its Pivot and Hinge that opens both ways (*tao shu*). To follow this Hinge of the Way of things is to *walk both* the way of "morning, three" and that of "morning, four" (*liang hsing*). To dwell in the heavenly Treasury is to stay in the illimitable Horizon of nature (*t'ien ni*), the Realm of no realm (*wu ching*).

This realm is where things not yet begin to not yet begin to be. To dwell there is to trail along whatever comes (*yin shih*), the unceasing vicissitudes (*man yen*). Being clear about (*i ming*) the Light that preserves and shines dimly through all (*pao kuang*), we are set free to ride and romp about (*ch'eng, ch'i, yu*) among the clouds, the sun and the moon, and beyond the Four Seas.

All this amounts to arranging and equalizing things and theories, to see that everything is fine as it is (*ch'i wu lun*).

With such luminosity (*i ming*) we now know the following two uses to be equally good: (1) to use the *not-finger*, what is finger-ed (pointed out), to show that finger-ing is no finger, and (2) to use *fingers* to show that finger-ing is no finger. In the end, all things under heaven are just one pointer-pointed (*i chih*); likewise, all things are one horse (108–10).[151]

If you protest that this is no argument but wrangling, Chuang Tzu would smile and say he was only paying back to the sophists with their own coin of sophistry. The same holds for "'Heaven and earth with me were born at the same time,' and 'Myriads of things and I make one'" (163), which sums up the sentiments of Mencius and Hui Shih.[152] Chuang Tzu admired them for reducing all things to one universal. And then in the next breath, Chuang Tzu solemnly went on to twist the One into three—the thing said, its meaning, and the saying itself.[153] What joy of playing around with arguments and pseudo-arguments!

Chuang Tzu's bantering with sophists and theorists makes a novel ontological point no one has made so far. To argue that finger-ing is not finger is to show (*yü*) that Tao manifested as such is not Tao (183). If the great Tao does not declare itself (182), then the true self is not self-conscious. If Tao

tao-ed is not the Tao, then self self-ed is not the self. Metaphysical preoccupation with the self (such as self-critiques of reason, of saying) leads to
selfish idealism of the world. If the Tao exists as un-tao-ed Tao (186), then
the authentic self appears in self-losing, in which the world is finally
understood as it is.

So the self must become like the dead wood and ashes before it can discern the world, the interdependence of mutual pipings at the great Clod's
beck and call, when the Clod belches out its wind-breath of life.[154] As the self
that is selfed is no self, so things that are thinged, that is, taken as independent
things in themselves, "eternal factuality" rightly loathed by Nietzsche, become our source of pain. It is pain produced by the phantom of independence.
Things truly exist only in their mutuality and involvement.

Such Tao of things is not-taoed (*pu tao chih tao*); such discernment is
not worded (*pu yen chih pien*), for to know all this is not to know. How so?
Because to "know" such reflexive echoing of life vicissitudes is to participate
in it. This existential involvement and reciprocity (*wu hua*) is a bewildering
"mutual dependence that is no mutual dependence" (*hsiang tai juo ch'i pu
hsiang tai*). Chuang Tzu gives two short stories which explain such knowing
of not-knowing.

The final two mini-stories (shadow, dream) are perhaps the most pungent
and evocative of all his stories; Chuang Tzu is understandably called the
Butterfly Dreamer (*meng tieh chu jen*) in Chinese literature. But people forget
that the dream story is preceded by an equally brilliant shadow story; people
forget it perhaps because it is less easy to understand. We start with the
shadow, then go to the dream, and then connect the two.

Penumbra demanded of Shadow, "A while ago you walked; now you
stop. A while ago you sat; now you rise. Why in you there is no constant independence?" (290–91). This is closer to nonsense than small birds' laughter
at the big Bird in the first chapter. Penumbra depends for its existence on
Shadow; how dare Penumbra demand Shadow's independence?

Yet Shadow is defined by its profile, its Penumbra. As Penumbra defines
Shadow, Shadow shadows forth its thing, giving it its depth and concreteness.
Skin and wings depend on their snake and cicada, whose survivals depend on
them. Similarly birth and death, right and wrong, co-wait-on and co-arise.

And *thinking* about all this is like Penumbra, which defines and depends
on Shadow. Thinking is also a disutility that defines and lets things be as they
are, the conscious "nothing" of Sartre that carves out things from the "slime"
of the In-itself.[155]   Todes said, "The cast of mind is the 'shadowing-forth of
… truths'. … Our mind is the shade of the tree of experience … "[156]

Such reciprocity is radicalized in the dream story that ends the chapter. Four points stand out:

(*i*) We are asked to consider an ordinary experience of *dreaming*, for life trivialities harbor fresh truths of things.

(*ii*) On awakening, Chuang Tzu realized that he had been dreaming. He now *knew* that he was Chuang Chou, not butterfly.

Then, being awake and alert, he acquired uncertainty. *Now* he did *not know* whether he was Chuang Chou having dreamed or butterfly dreaming. And he knew no way to dissolve his uncertainty.

(*iii*) We see four pairs of distinct entities and situations: (*a*) dreaming versus awakening, (*b*) butterfly versus Chuang Chou, (*c*) butterfly dreaming versus Chuang Chou having dreamed, (*d*) knowledge versus ignorance.

(*iv*) These distinctions intermingle. First, there do exist (for certain) *differences*; awakening is not dreaming, butterfly is not Chuang Chou. This is true whether the butterfly or Chuang Chou is dreaming or awake.

Secondly, such distinctions *intertwine* as follows. While dreaming, Chuang Chou was innocently certain (knew) he was a butterfly. Now that he awoke (in the know), he was not certain (did not know) what he was. Thus it takes an awakening (knowing) to reach uncertainty (not-knowing) about all four pairs of contraries above (*a, b, c, d*), as to where and what one is. To know is to awaken to intermingling, to see things changing, an ontological interchange (*wu hua*).

Two distinctions are significant: (*a*) being in a dream versus being awake, and (*b*) being a butterfly versus being Chuang Chou. Distinction *b* starts mutualities; distinction *a* turns them into existential involvement. Far from lifting us out of uncertainty, awakening plunges us into it. An awakening is a knowing not-to-know, a nagging suspicion about our still dreaming. It takes a Great Awakening (*ta chüeh*) to say, "I call you 'a dream'—I am also a dream" (261).

The chapter has a twofold conclusion: "Here we have Chou with a butterfly—there, then, must exist a division. Just this is what is called things changing" (305). Two points—distinction and (inter)change—are both real and necessary for each other. *Pace* Legge, Chuang Tzu's ontological insight differs from "Buddhism that holds that all human experience is merely so much maya or illusion."[157]

The same holds for the dream story. An awakening is necessary to become aware of the uncertainty about what one *is* in interdependence and distinction among dream-awakening, Chou-butterfly. Being in a dream is to be innocently certain of oneself, to blur the distinction, and to destroy mutuality. Distinction and interchange—*they* are mutually distinct and therefore mutually interchanging!

2.2.2. *Further implications*: We can see three intriguing points:

(1) An echo is usually louder than both the silence of the valley and the original sound it echoes; yet an echo sounds hollower than the space and the sound. Penumbra is usually more conspicuous than shadow, whose presence it signals; yet penumbra remains more fleeting than shadow.

Being noticeable, echo and penumbra call our attention, but not to themselves—they call attention to something else they advertize.

Such is the structure of actuality; what is noticeable announces something other that is hidden. B. Gentry Lee is a manager of Mission Operations and Engineering for Project Galilee to investigate the planet Jupiter and beyond—what noise! He claims to manage about two hundred scientists. A born speaker, he can hold his audience breathless for two hours, but does not do investigation. He is a famous echo and penumbra for the shadow, the scientists of the star probes. The stars themselves, in turn, are more silent, hid in the heavenly horizon of the heavenly treasury, the silent spacious universe.

That is how things arrange themselves (*ch'i wu*), silently, by mutual shadowing forth. Our thinking and writing about all this (*lun*) is a mere shadows, echo of echoes, adumbration and evocation, of all this.

(2) Chuang Tzu dreamed that he was a butterfly; now that he was awake, he was not sure about his identity. This is like playing a role, a favorite theme of Shakespeare and Sartre. Both sensed duplicity in play-acting; Chuang Tzu welcomes it as part of the playful joy of transmuting life.

Sartre's sarcastic description of both the woman at the cafe with her love and the waiter there,[158] exposes our ontological duplicity, the rift in the self. We are the For-itself, never catching up with ourselves. Shakespeare's plays illustrate our life as a stage, on which tales are "told by an idiot, full of sound and fury, signifying nothing." How sad.

But why be sad? Chuang Tzu would ask. We know we have reality and illusion, or rather, two actualities. We are not sure where we belong, forever oscillating between them. Let us then enjoy ourselves in the oscillation, even in our being not sure of oscillating. This is (self-referential) inconsistency self-involved, playfulness played out.

Both Shakespeare and Sartre are sad because they are too serious. Their sorrow stems from their platonic nostalgia for an absolute immobile authenticity, *the* true self, an impossible union of the actual and the ideal, the In-and-

For-itself. The culprit is platonic immobility, the ghost which refuses to move. Once we leave it alone and go our way, we enjoy our uncertainty and oscillation, fully awakened to it.

(3) All "definitive" argumentation is nonsense. If the subject of argumentation is itself uncertain, where is the definitiveness of those things argued *about*?

Instead, Chuang Tzu plays with arguments. He describes the self's disturbances, talks about things talked about by theories, talks about those talks, then talks about things again. He *uses* the phrases of those theories, always giving them a little twist, even parading their unintelligible combinations to sound profound. He uses such profound unintelligibles to shock and show us how wrong those theories are and how complex things are. Such parodies of theories sound like buffoonery, which tickles us into taking a second look at things.

Chuang Tzu disputes dogmatic assertions and their underlying dogmas about the subject and the mode of judgment. Three stories attack the subjectivist dogma. The first story about losing oneself starts the chapter; the other two about shadow and dream end it. Dogmas about logic and theorizing are attacked throughout the chapter—by romping through theories and sayings, and by inventing logical nonsense that sounds profound. He examined dog-mas about the eternal identities of things, the absolute validity of "my" views, and static logic itself. This is a Chinese "critique" of pure reason (*lun*), with winks and frolics.

The impossibility of reaching truth by argumentation is explained toward the end of the chapter. Argumentation assumes two entrenched and opposed positions. Neither party can know whether he is right even after winning the argument. Nor can the third party help them. For the third party either agrees or disagree with one of them, and he is not better than one of them. Or he disagree with both of them, and he is an outsider unable to decide between them.

So far, Chuang Tzu is perilously similar to a sophist who loves to argue; perhaps Chuang Tzu was arguing with a sophist. Isn't Chuang Tzu himself advancing a position of his own after all? Worse, Chuang Tzu proposed a "position" that is no position, a "truth" saying that truth is impossible to reach. But such an impression is premature, for Chuang Tzu capped his argument against argument with "I call you 'a dream'—I am also a dream" (261).

To say "I am dreaming" is an existential contradiction—to "say something" requires not being in a dream. But perhaps Chuang Tzu is saying Socratically that he knows that he does not know. But there is a difference.

Socrates' pronouncement is a heuristic device to good one into attending to self-knowledge and what one means (defines) when one says something.[159] Chuang Tzu in contrast sticks to his knowledge of no-knowledge of self-dream, from which he draws two conclusions;

(a) The subject is involved in the interchange of things, and
(b) True existence dwells in such a realm of mutual distinction and dependence.

These truths lead to the joy of ontological roaming, which is innocently executed in the first chapter. The first chapter starts with the big Bird soaring from one heavenly Pond and Reservoir to another, and ends in the mighty Yak unhurriedly ruminating under the Useless Tree. The second chapter starts with a death-like vital quiescence in which to discern the kaleidoscopic-fugal mutuality of cosmic pipings, and ends with existential involvement in the unceasing reciprocity of transformation. The first chapter proclaimed such ontological romping with stories. The second chapter practiced playing with arguments in the endless interchanges of things. All this playing and roaming is made possible by a loss of the self.

2.2.3. *Dialogue with Lucretius*: Strangely, all this significant roaming, made possible by self-kenosis, fulfills oneself; one is rendered indestructible.

In order to see this, "concentration" of spirit (*ning shen*) in the first chapter (96) is joined with loss of the self (*sang wo*) in the second chapter (10). The joining is effected by transposing Chuang Tzu's conversations with his contemporaries to one with the Western Lucretius on the topic of their common interest—"touch." To my knowledge, Lucretius was the first philosopher *explicitly* to conceive the central importance of touch, around which he organized a systematic understanding of the universe, the philosophy of "atomism." Touch is a "colliding" which leads to composing, a hooking together of units of matter (atoms) into things.

Lucretius' atoms are indestructible because they are without void inside; void is that through which separation from the self (destruction) takes place. Being without void means internally coagulated, concentrated, so that one looks like dry log and ashes from outside, in touch with oneself.

A true individual is one who is in touch with oneself, all over and at every spot, inside out. Such a person is indestructible. That primal "baby" favored by Chuang Tzu is always full of himself; whenever he shouts, eats, or smiles, he does so "because I want to," as he says. This is what it means to be pure and unmixed, "clean as spring water," full, refreshed, and in touch with oneself, having one's "skin like ice, snow" (Chapter One, line 92).

In contrast, "I miss you" means "I miss myself in you," and so "I miss myself"; "you" (in whom I am) being absent from me, I am also absent from me. Attacked by Hansen's bacilli, parts of the leprous body become numb, skin lesions occur, and hair, fingers, and toes drop off. Missing someone is an ontological leprosy attacking me with its bacilli of my absence (in someone's absence); parts of my heart become numb, spiritual lesions occur, and my heart and my soul drop off.

Missing someone differs from loneliness, a suffering from being *just* oneself. One can be lonely, missing no one in particular. Here oneself is not missed; one is full of oneself who wants more, the lack of which cuts into oneself. Loneliness is a lack of sharing; missing someone is a self-lack. Loneliness is being alone turned diseased; missing someone is not being alone turned diseased.

Yet both diseases have one thing in common; when one is lonely as the baby who misses his mother, one is out of touch with oneself. "I miss my mom" means "I am lonely, and I miss myself drained out to my mom." The baby wants to be touched from inside by mom (his inner strength), who by touching him brings him back to himself. Such is motherly presence; all other intimate presence[160]—friendly, sexual—are extensions of motherly presence, an intimate touch from inside.

No wonder Lucretius made so much out of "touch," the origin of things. Lucretian "collision" (how sad a substitute) touches off series of combinations called "things." If fullness indicates atomic imperishability, and if fullness is being in full touch with oneself, then keeping in touch keeps atoms going, forever creating things.

Unfortunately Lucretius did not extend touch to personal purity, fullness, and concentration. Nor did he realize that atoms can and should be extended to individuals, collision to touch, creation to nourishing and being refreshed. To extend Lucretius' insight beyond Lucretius in order to connect with Chuang Tzu, let us consider "love."

Lucretius has a curious chapter on love,[161] which is treated lamentably without explicitly resorting to his atomism. Love is described as a threefold tragedy: (a) a violent stab, resulting in a spurting of blood (life essence, spermatozoa) toward the stabber, (b) a desire to become literally one with the beloved (as in sex), resulting in failure, and (c) an illusion, always seeing the beloved as better than oneself, who is always haunted by such phantoms. Love is then a never-ending anxiety.

This description results from mixing two views of love—love as touch and love as an urge to merge. Though understandable as explanations of love, these two themes do not reconcile, hence love is tragedy. Lucretius took touch externally to accompany the impenetrability of things, while merging does not. External touch assumes at least two impenetrable things, which merging dissolves. Thus external touch collides with the urge to merge—and this is love, hence tragedy. Lucretius came to this conclusion because he had only the philosophy of external touch, a colliding of atoms, but love is something internal.

And touch is not just external. Human touch is characterized by two features:

(*i*) To touch is to *be touched*; activity and passivity are at one in human touch. Even the mechanical collision of metal balls generates new velocity and direction to each ball, irrespective of which initiated the collision. But this feature is especially central among human beings where to influence someone is *eo ipso* to be influenced by that someone.

(*ii*) To be touched is to be *touched inside*. An intended external touch seeps inside. A baby's touch moves his mother to tears, and the mother's touch puts the baby at ease both with himself and with his habitat. We are moved, positively or negatively, by a personal touch.

Combining these two features of touch among human beings, love can be described as an internal touch which assuages Lucretius about love.

(*a*) If touch can be internal, then an external touch can go into oneself, and the *stab* is gone. Stab is a forceful external touch breaking through the wall that shields the inside. Stab expresses hunger for an internal touch.

(*b*) The internal human touch dissolves frustration at the *failure* to merge two loved ones into one. An external intentional touch invites an internal touch, which fulfills the desire for merging by merging two persons while preserving their individualities.

(*c*) *Phantoms* of fantasy disappear as internal touch merges persons in love, much as we forget our wishes while happily looking into the wishing well.

Internal touch is not simple reciprocity. Its complexity is exemplified in sexual mutuality. To adapt Lucretius, the male enters the female who draws out his essence; they enter and influence each other, touching each other inside. Then their union grows independently into a new person. This person is a concentrate symbol (a thrown-together) of the merging of the two. As they are one in two, so their child *both* is and is not his parents.

And they are in turn changed by their activity of procreative union; they remained themselves as they are changed from lovers to parents, fulfilled, smiling at their child and at each other. Such is the structure of touch among persons. It is a merging of separate individuals into one, who yet remain separate individuals. And as individuals, they are mutually changed. Something comes about, a new creation. All these transformation occur in the personal internal touch.

This model of touch holds true among persons everywhere. It holds true even among non-humans. Atoms collide and produce molecules; events collide and take a new turn. Colors, sounds, and tastes merge and come out with new configurations. Chains of new creations and changes in previous entities take place. It is a mutual echoing, a shadowing forth and shading into each other, even a dreaming of each other. Here phantoms may well be reality, and reality phantom, and even they form a mutuality that touches inside.

Even situations can touch each other. Patrick Romanell bemoaned the tragic situation where two equally valuable and equally pressing moral imperatives collide; and we are forever caught in the blind.[162] But we can extend the preceding considerations about touch, and regard this as a creative moment of *chi hui,* a meeting *(hui)* of many situational intentionalities *(chi),* a critical moment of emergence of a new situation with new duties, an "opportunity" for a new future. It is in such situations of conflict that two moral values touch from inside and create a new moral situation, without dissolving the conflicting moral values. Thus every situation can be an opportunity *(chi hue)* for joining (touching inside) many moral demands into a new imperative; such is our world of creative opportunities in their uncertainties.

Chuang Tzu describes this world, where things and events co-touch to co-arise out of their common heavenly originating power *(t'ien chi),* the heavenly piping. Things and events are "OK and correct" *(k'o)* in their various affirmations and negations; the heights of things are relative without being arbitrary or illusory. For they all begin in the yet-to-begin-to-yet-to-begin-to-exist, where many fingers are one finger that points without point-ing, and the world is one horse in harmony with non-horses. Arguments are correlative yet not futile, reflecting the ever-moving Tao Pivot and heavenly Balance. Following the heavenly Horizons, we go with vicissitudes that touch and change. This is the actual, changing world that lets each one be as it is, reflecting and co-creating this world. We are happy in it.

Such happy co-creative activities can be characterized as those of touch. Individuals touch others to touch themselves, and vice versa. Parental touch brings about the baby's self-touch, without which it does not grow into a person. Sex and friendship are touches from inside, creating partners and new beings.[163]

To live is both to self-touch and to other-touch. To be full is to fully self-touch, which is a self-referential consistency; to be fully in touch is to fully other-touch, which is self-referential inconsistency.[164] At night we become pure and full in the self-touch of sleep; in the day we make new touches and new enrichments. That is why Chuang Tzu has to be awakened before he can not-be-sure whether he is a person ("Chuang Chou") or a butterfly. During the hours of awakening we other-touch so much that we are not sure whether we are we or others. Paradise is not far off; we are whole together and happy.

Needless to say, to wonder whether one is a person or a butterfly is to wander between them, and to be internally in touch with them both. Needless to say, the wanderings of Chuang Tzu among contraries (in the second chapter) show that he is fully awake. Those paradoxical sayings are verbal oscillations expressing wanderings among things. Playful roamings touch things and situations from inside, all over, and all over the universe. This is an arrangement and treatment of things with an understanding awakening. This is a roaming of creative touch among things and thoughts.

2.3. *Methodological interpretations*: Now, after all this has been said, *what* did Chuang Tzu tell us? Nothing much that is newsworthy. Not what is, but *how* to become, ourselves, must be the second chapter's theme. With this new methodological clue, we start afresh.

The chapter is filled with simple themes, yet is itself ambiguous. Although unintelligible, it is yet fascinating and somehow nourishing to the reader. How can something unintelligible be simple, fascinating, and nourishing?

The chapter reminds us of Mama Cass's little musical line in 1969; "Make your own kind of music." This line is peculiar in three ways. First, it is so *simple* that four years olds can recite it. Second, it does tell us something—urging us to make our own music. It is itself a kind of *music*, dominated by the consonant sounds that begin and end the word "music," meant to be sung. But, thirdly, it is not exactly a music like "Twinkle, Twinkle Little Star," but an *invitation* to music-making, not yet music. It is a not-yet-music music.

Chuang Tzu's second chapter is, like Mama Cass's line, simple and says something, yet it says nothing. It is structured and rhymed slightly, yet it is unintelligible, to be worked out by the reader.

The chapter starts appropriately with three pipings. "Music" is piped forth from a hollow through a nothing-power, the wind. The "music" comes out of the meeting and resonance among things that are really nothings. Earthly piping is resonance among such things (*wu*); human piping is thinking and debating about such things, a resonance with such thing-resonance (*lun*). Heavenly piping is what begins and arranges all this (*ch'i*), the yet-to-begin to yet-to-begin all these. This is the cosmic music, three levels of polyphonic fugue, produced in the meeting of wind with hollows, resonance among nothings.

Resonance requires at least two things for it to came about. Things arise by reciprocal interaction. Being and nothing, birth and death, accomplishment (formation) and destruction (deformation), and the like, are correlative; they co-arise dependently. And human thinking and debating about them co-relate with them.

In human argument any position can be matched with its counter position. Wise sayings can be twisted and even anti-quoted. The long middle portion of the chapter is full of such points and counter-points, quotations and mis-quotations, and even pseudo-quotations, that is, mimicries. Chuang Tzu matched a counter-saying to a saying he quoted, arguing, mis-arguing, even pseudo-arguing, that is, mimicking some famous argument. In all this he poetized and pseudo-poetized, parodying wise sayings with ironies, paradoxes, and plain jokes.

He produced a positive thesis out of Hui Shih's sophistic wranglings such as finger-non-finger, horse-non-horse. The thesis says, "All things are one with me," which seems to be a mimicry of Mencius (line 163; *Mencius* 7A4). And then Chuang Tzu attacked it, saying that he can get three out of this cosmic One.

And there is no way of resolving this argumentative impasse. A third party cannot help. He agrees either with either of us or with neither of us. If he agrees with either of us, how can he judge between us? If he agrees with neither of us, how can he arbitrate?

For any point evokes its counterpoints; any event produces its counter-events. To understand this is to cease to try and judge because, far from being eternal and infallible, the judging subject may well be dreaming (and changing). "When I say you are dreaming, I am, too." This is of course not to say that life is *but* a dream; for wings may belong to their cicada, who yet must depend on them to fly and survive. You shadow me forth as I do you, and both of us shadow forth our origin—the Way we go, the Not-yet-begin to not-yet-begin to begin. *It* shadows us forth, yet remains in shade.

Nor can we say we are for sure dreaming; it will be a denial of our dream. What we say in a dream cannot be trusted; we may not be dreaming if we say we are dreaming. We have only one thing for sure—"When I say you are dreaming, I am, too." If you say all are one, I say from one comes three; if you say there are many views, I say they are all shadows and dreams. And what I just said belongs to a dream also.

To understand all this is to go along with all this, and to do so is to "arrange and equalize" (*ch'i*) things (*wu*) and thinking (*lun*), and in your (the reader's) own way. And a "position" such as this, which is really not any fixed position but "the Hinge of Tao," is Heaven—heavenly Equalizer, heavenly Horizon, heavenly Reservoir, heavenly Piping. Put yourself here, and you can walk two courses at once—the course of things and the course of thinking.

This brings us to the piping of heaven. Such piping cannot be directly heard but can only be indirectly felt in our daily ongoings with things and thinking. That is why the self is treated at the start of the chapter, letting our subjective prejudice die as dry wood and ashes. The disappearance of antagonism between the subject and the object enables the self to hear hollows in the universe piping out knowledge and talks. All of them are equal, arranging themselves into pipings of men, of earth, and of heaven.

Now we make "our own kind of music" together. The melody is made up of trivial wood, ashes, monkeys, shadow, dream. Such melody is ever in the making, ever a not-yet music, always beginning to not-yet-begin. And Chuang Tzu did make *his* own kind of music for us to make our own. Chuang Tzu said a lot of simple, atrocious, funny, and beautiful things. And what he said is—"Make your own kind of pipings." When each of us makes his own kind of piping, it is his own yet not his. It is our piping of men to blend in with the polyphonic pipings of earth. And all this is the piping of life, of heaven, to be lived. The point is to make our own music of life.

In all this Chuang Tzu differs from the serious moralism and logicism of Confucius and Mo Tzu, from the mechanistic atomism of the Stoics, from Buddhistic transcendence, and from sophistic Hui Shih and Kung Sun Lung. To identify Chuang Tzu with sophism is as tempting as to see Socrates as a sophist. And Chinese commentators have been as prone to a Buddhistic interpretation of Chuang Tzu[165] as Western scholars are to a Stoic one.

But Chuang Tzu did not propose any specific ism. He merely wanted to *alert* us toward living the polyphonic ambiguities in the polythetic self involved logicality of the universe. We do well to roam in it as its parts.

3. *The logic of life*: The *Ch'i Wu Lun* chapter is a philosophical parody on philosphizing. The chapter is logic turned back on itself, a critique of reasoning turned hilarious. Such parodying is meant to be itself philosophical. Thus *how* Chuang Tzu performed his parodying becomes an interesting topic to consider. The mode of *ch'i* -ing intimates a kind of *lun* peculiar to

Chuang Tzu, and such *lun* is nicknamed "goblet rationality" or "the logic of life." We will look at (1) the traditional logic, and then (2) Chuang Tzu's goblet logic of life.

    3.1 *Zeno and the static logic*: **3.1.1.** George Lakoff and Mark Johnson say that our conceptual system structures what we perceive, how we get around in the world, and how we relate to people. And then they thougthfully added, "Our ordinary conceptual system, in terms of which we both think and act, is fundamentally metaphorical in nature."[166] They describe "metaphors" as "understanding and experiencing one kind of thing in terms of another."[167] Such metaphors consists mainly of both orientational "up" and "down" and ontological concretizing of experience into discrete objects and substances; from these two we derive metaphors such as personification and metonymy.

    What is significant here is twofold: (*i*) All our thinking and acting is incorrigibly *experiential*; our previous experience serves as "metaphor" to pattern our thinking and acting now in the world. (*ii*) The spatial and ontological metaphors of the West are basically *visual*. For only vision can at a glance survey space (up and down) and concretize our experience into discrete entities. The first point shall be taken up in the next section about Chuang Tzu's goblet rationality. We are here concerned with the Western tendency to vision.

    Western metaphors that structure our daily experience are basically visual, surveying. Tactility also surveys in a series of motions. Yet the tactile series takes time to obtain, rendering the space and the objects less accessible to us. Hearing is even less capable of bringing space and the discreteness of objects to us. Things seem to suddenly appear to us as sounds, and we feel them as dispersed impacts. There are no distinct observable entities in hearing.

    Sight and touch are predominantly the senses of space. It is not an accident that for Lakoff and Johnson "understanding is seeing" is a major mataphor to orient our activities.[168] Sight is peculiarly spatial because, unlike touch, sight surveys *in an instant* the total map of the entire object or situation, albeit from a specific perspective.

    The advantage of visually surveying the total situation in an instant is purchased at the price of time and motion, however. Our eyes must fix either on the moving object (and feel the background slide by), or on the scene behind the moving object (and feel the moving object zip by). And feeling is not seeing. Vision is motionless because it is timeless. We *fix* our gaze, and only infer motion from the failure of vision clearly to catch both the moving object and its stationary background.

    Geometric logic, as Bergson and Ortega used to call it, is primarily a timeless visual logic, a favorite of Parmenides, Zeno, Plato, and Aristotle. Even Lucretius who promoted touch for his philosophy cannot help but rely on the logic of sight to connect items of knowledge and matters of proof in his *On Nature*. His logic is in the controlling metaphor of sight—detached, static, surveying, and structural.[169]

Such static topological logic is used by Zeno against motion; yet the very *move* of his mind and argument shows that motion is immediately present in our experience.

Two of Zeno's four extant paradoxes concern the infinitely divisible units of space to be traversed in motion within the finite span of time—the tortoise and the arrow. Here, in both cases, he forgot to notice the *progressively* small increments to the motion of the tortoise, and such series of decreasing increments *converge* to a definite number. The words, "progressively," "converge," are motion-words. Zeno put them out of consideration and fell into these paradoxes.

In the paradox of the stadium Zeno forgot that the speed of one moving body C is double that of another moving body B that goes in an opposite direction (body A is stationary outside the stadium). Finally, the paradox that says that the body in motion is neither in the place where it is nor in the place where it is not, hence motion is impossible, shows that the geometric logic can conceive only of these two alternatives. Yet motion is precisely such a peculiar combination of these two places on a time scale, a *process* of combining. Motion appears in Zeno's static schema to be something as contradictory as subatomic and extra-terrestrial realities appear to the contemporary mind.[170]

It is noteworthy that Alfred N. Whitehead who proposed the philosophy of organismic *process* as reality loved to expound his thoughts in pithy quotables which tend to border on paradoxes. Paradoxes are logic on the move through its breakage. When used in the context of process, logical breakage is no longer something to be avoided or solved, but a nimble expressive *tool* for process. Chuang Tzu loved to use paradoxes also, not because of any love for wallowing in obscurities, but as handy intimations of the dynamics of living actuality.

W. V. Quine writes about paradoxes as follows:

> A veridical paradox packs a surprise, but the surprise quickly dissipates itself as we ponder the proof. A falsidical paradox packs a surprise, but it is seen as a false alarm when we solve the underlying fallacy. An antinomy, however, packs a surprise that can be accommodated by nothing less than a repudiation of part of our conceptual heritage.[171]

This is almost an expression of Western common sense—an alternative interpretation of these paradoxes is possible. Once the nature of our visual logic is noted, shock waves of the *para*-situation of our *doxa* (our paradoxes) ceases to be a conceptual catastrophe, as Quine envisioned it, but is seen as one of the ways for flowing actuality to register on our "sense organ of mind" (*hsin*). As sound waves vibrate our eardrums, so *para*-waves vibrate our *doxa*, our logical system. To perceive the vibration (*para-doxa*) of our logical eardrums is what Chuang Tzu called overhearing the piping in a death-like quietude.

Sometimes we listen wrongly, and we get audial illusions—"it is a falsidical paradox to say that Achilles can never overtake the tortoise; it is a veridical paradox to say that the moving body is neither in the place where it is nor in the place where it is not."[172] As we accept optical illusion to be no "illusion," given the situation and our eye-structure, so we will accept Zeno's *para*-illusion as an intelligible phenomenon, given Zeno's ignorance about mathematical convergence (in Achilles and the tortoise) and his geometrical frame of mind (in the moving body). As optical illusion is a legitimate fact which reveals the different media, so Zeno's "audial illusion" (as I would call it) is an important datum which reveals the peculiarity of *our* logical eardrums primarily tuned for static entities.

Furthermore, as optical illusion is an integral part of our learning optical truths, so audial illusion (on *para*-waves in our *doxa*) is one of our ways of listening to the living vibration of the universe. Paradoxes are no longer disasters to be dissolved, but an expression of our experience. Chuang Tzu's *Ch'i Wu Lun* chapter is an understanding of living actuality in such language.

For the understanding of living actuality to take place we must lose our set-mind (*ch'eng hsin*) which dogmatically judges paradoxes to be rational aberrations, for we prejudge here that our logical apparatus should monitor reality without being rocked, much less jarred. We must instead quietly let in the vibration that shakes our mind-chamber (*hsin-shih*), and we are received into the recesses of actuality. The *Ch'i Wu Lun* chapter is one report on such cosmic waves, as it were, by the perceptive mind of Chuang Tzu.

Such reception is a dynamic one. As vibration moves in, we move with it into actuality with understanding. Paradox is a rocking of our entire doxa-chamber. Achilles cannot overtake the tortoise; but he does in fact. And so we rock between the no and the yes, and we are aroused to discernment. A moving body can be neither where it is nor where it is not, and so motion has no logical pillow on which to rest its head. But of course motion is change of place, and so motion is in-and-out of place at once. Again, such thought stirs us. Living actuality must be discerned "live." Vibration must be received with vibration;

our mind moves as we listen to movement, moving to match up with natural pipings. Our logical system is tuned in vibrantly to paradox.

Aristotle's criticism of Zeno is instructive.[173] He accused Zeno of mistaking motion to be already completed at each stage of infinitely divisible junctures in the process of motion. But completed motion is no longer motion; motion is by definition "incomplete," always moving toward its completion of no-motion. Aristotle's impressive battery of technical terms (*energeia, entelecheia*, and the like) is designed to explain this completing process of motion *to* its goal.

But of course the unmoved goal, *telos*, is important; static actuality, not moving potentiality, is what counts. Things as they are, already complete, manifesting their maturity *in* their motion, simply have no place in Aristotle's system. Motion is a subordinate notion in him, always derived from its goal, the immobile completedness. Acorn is for the sake of an oak tree, and has no value in itself. Aristotle has the visual logic of stationary perfection, not the logic of life, logic on the move. "All men ... desire to know. An indication of this is the delight we take in our senses ... above all ... the sense of sight"; so begins his *Metaphysics*.[174]

3.1.2.   Some people of reason believe in analytic clarity. Every sentence must be clear, every move from one sentence to the next must be analytically valid and obvious. Each sentence must be clearly understandable and lucidly explicable with reasons. Therefore, writings that are metaphysical, prophetic, or lyrical are mere inspired nonsense. For as Socrates said of prosphesying poets, they say many (seemingly?) fine things, but understand nothing of what they say.

By adapting Zeno, an objection to this clamor for clarity can be raised. Between every move from one thesis to the next, it is always possible to insert a further explanatory thesis between the two. From thesis *a* to *b*, one can insert a mid-thesis *c* to make the transition *clearer*. And of course another mid-thesis *d* can come in between *a* and *c* to facilitate their move, and so on ad infinitum. Having become analytically fastidious, one can never advance a single logical step; analyticity paralyzes logical *motion*. Blind belief in analytical clarity, as any superstition does, kills logic. For an argument to move on, the request for further explanation must sooner or later be suspended at some point, where a self-evident transition, a jump, must be made.[175] Three points can be raised here:

(1) The first point is that this situation has at least four consequences:

(*i*) Fastidiously speaking, one cannot get an argument started. We are in a logical quagmire.

(*ii*) There always exists the prospect of supplying a new logical step ("new evidence") that leads to a new direction and a different conclusion, even one contrary to what was originally intended.

(*iii*) As long as a logical move is always a jump, how much logical rigor is satisfactory ultimately depends as much on the proposer's logical "taste" as its convincingness depends on the reader's logical "taste." The *intrinsic* nature of logical necessity is an impossible ideal if not a myth. Persuasiveness and necessity become synonymous, existing in the eye of the logical beholder.

(*iv*) One can even claim that at any point in an argument, the less the number of logical steps to be made, the more nimble the jumps and the greater the logical sagacity required to understand the point. Therefore, a valid argument that contains less steps and a more surprising conclusion indicates a mind that is logically more mature.[177] Contrary to Socratic condemnation of inspired sayings, logic endorses Nietzschean aphorisms. Look at Zeno. His thesis begins and proceeds logically; it ends with demolishing the "movement" of logical steps!

(2) Yet, one can claim that Zeno's paradoxes still stand defensible. For our usual reply of "$1/2 + 1/4 + \ldots = 1$" does not quite meet Zeno's challenge. Zeno would say that all this is fine if we can get started not from the end of "$1/2$" but from the other end, " $\ldots$ " For Zeno's request was: *Before* traversing the first half, one must traverse $1/4$, before which one must traverse $1/8$, before which $\ldots$ And since the end of "$\ldots$" cannot be in sight (it is an infinite series) we cannot get the series of addition started. We cannot move. And this is understandable given Zeno's static logic that does not calculate motion.

(3) But to *say* something, as Aristotle pointed out, is to *fixate* something as such. Logic is a system of saying things; therefore, logic is an inherently fixating activity.

Two ways have been invented thus far to use logic to point at motion. One way is to juxtapose different propositions (or stories) from different contexts, and make a montage of sayings, so as to alert the listener to what they point at. Another way is to say something (say, a story) that is patently false, and manipulate (change purposely) the context of discourse to provoke laughter—"Of course this is nonsense. But what a nonsense!"

The first is the way of paradox; the second, that of irony. Chuang Tzu used both. Asked for a principle of montaging propositions and context manipulation, Chuang Tzu would smile and point at the on-going daily living. One must pattern one's sayings after the frets and fribbles of life so that what one says reflects its flow. But daily livings crisscross without apparent rhyme or reason, and so this "principle" amounts to a principle of no principle!

3.1.3. Nietzsche said, "In the mountains the shortest route is from peak to peak: but for that you must have long legs. Aphorisms should be peaks: and those to whom they are addressed should be big and tall of stature."[178] We need long legs to go from one peak to another, and long legs here are the "tall" logical knack to sense the profundity of the connection between peaks, and between the peaks and the valley.

Not all connections, of course, are correct or profound. Some are arbitrary and meaningless. Some seem arbitrary and illogical, yet therapeutically effective. Some are inevitable. Distinguishing these connections one from another is part of the assigned walk for the long legs of the intrigued "select readers" (Nietzsche).

For this task regular logic will help as means, not as guide, for logical necessity leads to the dead end of Parmenides and Zeno. Logic then can only be used as a tool to arrange our findings into a coherent expression.

Someone might say that sometimes even such logical parsing must be kicked to make a trans-logical point. But even the kicking has a *reason* or two, which should be logically expressible. Admittedly the higher the insight, the greater the logical leap that is required for expressing and understanding it. Logicians may sometimes have to give up logical explanation and leap from one step to another. But even then we must use our long legs to explain how impossible it is to build a series of steps from the mundane here to the mystical there. Patient sympathetic understanding is indispensable; we should not condescendingly bulldoze mysterious peaks into a field of flat common sense.

Our eyes are not discarded when we "see motion"; we *use* our eyes with other senses synesthetically to feel or infer motion. Likewise, in understanding the dynamics of life, we do not discard visual static logic but use it to produce a rhythm of paradoxes, of montages of stories, of self-involving consistency and inconsistency.

Chuang Tzu said that we discard the sieve when we capture the fish.[179] For living truths we weave our logical sieve with the usual wire of visual logic; we discard the sieve after capturing the point—"Perfect saying discards saying."[180] That is why Chuang Tzu did not waste time talking about his talk.[181] The most his disciples did was to raise the question about how words and silence are related.[182] They also mentioned three kinds of sayings.[183]

3.2. *Three ways of saying:* 3.2.1. Sophists dallied with ordinary notions and cooked up outlandish sayings, which proved to be resolvable into plain falsehoods, mixtures of platitudes and falsehoods, or pure platitudes. In all these the reader is aroused without gaining insights into actuality. The sophists merely dazzled.

Both Socrates and Chuang Tzu used techniques of sophistic arousal to invite the audience into real probes. Chuang Tzu's words are "goblet saying" (*chih yen*), ever tipping *to* life—stories and sayings which are concrete and relevant. His words are "opportune-words." Such opportune words are "lodging words" (*yü yen)*, loaded with important situational implications. These loaded words are also "heavy" and authoritative (*chung yen*) with a double-layered (*ch'ung yen*; cf. shaded light) paradoxical ring.[184]

These three descriptive "words" indicate Chuang Tzu's way of using sophistic tactics—to approach the reader in his own situation (goblet words), calling his attention by authority and antinomy (double-layered words), pointing the way for him to explore the further implications lodged there (lodging words).

These implications turn out to be too deep for straightforward stationary logic. They are at the deep recesses of actuality and can only be captured with faltering speech (with a paradoxical ring) or simple silence (of which these words are echoes). What words say echoes what they do not say, that to which they call our attention, their "intention" (*i*), what is by nature unsayably actual. Then the listener realizes that this echo is itself part of the actual, which envelops the effort at reaching it; otherwise actuality is not real. The *Chuang Tzu* is actuality expressing itself through the reader's effort to capture it, or rather, to be captured by it and become it.

Three kinds of "words" can be used to illustrate the pattern of the operation of Chuang Tzu's vital logic:

(*a*) Self-involved consistency: existential implication and situation involvement (as in the purity of the true man in his self-forgetfulness);

(*b*) Self-involved inconsistency: irony, antinomy (as in dream, non-doing, no-knowledge, interdependence). Both these features describe lodging words (*yü yen*).

(*c*) Collation, collage and montage (*ch'ung yen*) of arguments, stories, anecdotes; loosely connected meanings which can be variously interpreted.

The kaleidoscopic effects of all these features together give the reader many meanings, according to how he *tips* the words as he does his goblet (*chih yen*).

Chuang Tzu's way is the logic, the vehicle, the *lun,* and the metaphor that carries us over to real life by evoking our participation in our own echoing, stammering expression of things; often we are a part of things (*wu hua*). To think about such a way, such logic, such *lun*s and words, is to think about (*Lun*) the arrangement (*Ch'i*) of things (*Wu*).

3.2.2.   The comical lies in a juxtaposition of incongruous elements, such as big nose and small hat, small pants and big shoes, and the like. Since life seems to us a juxtaposition of the incongruous, an appropriate mode by which to approach life may well be the comical.

If the tragic elements in life are characterized by being caught *in* their irreconcilable values that are equally pressing, then the comical attitude is what takes us beyond the tragic. And it may well be that the logic of the comical is that of life, the logic of the paradoxical (broken logic whose breakage measures the impact of the actual, as in double-layered words), of the ironic (the juxtaposition of two incompatibles, illuminating one with the other, as in lodged words), and of the mutual involvement in life (symbiosis of opportune relevants, as in goblet words). The *Chuang Tzu* is just such a comical book of the metaphorical logic of collages (and montages) of notions (and arguments).

Metaphor is category confusion, mixing of types, crossing of sorts. Such mixing is dangerous because it is a category mistake. Yet when such mistakes are used skillfully, they facilitate a shock to free us from tradition and fixation into seeing things in a fresh manner. Such freeing from the bonds of custom can be accomplished, not painfully as happened to the prisoners in Plato's Myth of the Cave, but with hilarity as in the *Chuang Tzu*. Thus the comical, the metaphorical, and the living are mutually related in the roaming, soaring freedom of life.

Life is movement or it is no longer life. Life moves out of the old and the fixed. Unless logic moves, we will forever make tautological statements, empty repetitions. Significant tautology is a contradiction unless we confer *metaphorical* meaning on it, as in "Boys will be boys."

Metaphor is one way in which logic moves, by hooking one meaning from one realm of discourse to another meaning from a different realm. The legitimacy of such hooking is discerned extra-logically, by how much significance it carries, or rather, evokes, in life, especially in the life of the audience. A meaningful metaphor is alive with life significance; a meaningless metaphor is a dead one.

3.2.3.   Suppose we decide to prove that progress in philosophy consists in an accumulation of many significant notions, similar to what has been done in the second chapter of the *Chuang Tzu*. Progress is good because the more and more meaningful notions we have the better we will understand the world and the more flexible we become.

But are we not going to be lost in so many notions? How do we choose from many notions the right ones for the right occasion? Is there a rule to guide a right use of notions? If coherent simplicity (such as oneness) is a sign of understanding, how can many notions be a sign of progress?

We may answer as follows. Since notions are human tools, no single set of notions is adequate for *all* situations. Sticking slavishly to our pet notions, we will end up being irrelevant, trapped, and conceptually collapsed. We must therefore be free to use several sets of notions as the situation changes. Such resourcefulness comes from having many notions. To grow in this way is progress.

And we won't be lost in many notions as long as we are in touch with the situation, which will dictate which notions we should choose and use. Drugs and equipment proliferate in the medical world; they are confusing when there is no patient. The patient's illness dictates when and how to use what drug and what instrument. The patient is the cohering point for all drugs and tools; the more tools and drugs we have the more resourceful we become in dealing with his illness.

This is to say that many tools have nothing to do with simple coherence. Each new situation imposes its own unity on our many concepts. Each situation uniquely regulates our many notions into a unity. Each situation differs from others, and can be construed from many perspectives (of many notions); our many notions grow into many *kinds* of them.

Thus the word "unique" is a plural; the one is many. The "one" is not idealistic, nor is the "many" simply conceptual; they are concrete situational "one" and "many." The more our notions are the richer will be our perception of many unique situations, whose unity life is, a concrete pluralistic monism. This is what *ch'i* means also, an arranging of the many in the one, which is in turn enriched by the many, and that in a concrete situation. This is a concrete *lun* which *ch'i*s things (*wu*).

But, someone may ask, are we sure such a pluralistic monism is totally free from *our* prejudice? What if our mind can only operate in these terms? What if all that we have indicated is a mere mirroring of ourselves in reality? Here to reply "It works" won't help, for we legislate what is means for something to "work."

Yet our inability to answer these questions does not mean we are trapped in ourselves. It only means we do not know. And so this concrete pluralistic monism is a *chastened* one.

Such considerations link us to the dreaming of the butterfly again. Since we know we do not know, it means we may well be having an interesting interchange between knowledge and ignorance, idealistic subjectivism and concrete situationism; our knowledge of such agnosticism is alive. Our knowledge of uncertainty is the only thing that saves us from the trap of circularity. We are in such a position of chastened freedom as to arrange (*ch'i*) things (*wu*) and our notions about them (*lun*) into one.

D.   Philosophy and "Things Even-ing Themselves Out"

1. This second chapter of the *Chuang Tzu* is enticingly enignmatic. On the one hand, the text is in Chinese characters, not in the undecipherable symbols of an unknown culture. As a language Chinese has been remarkably constant; classical Chinese is almost[185] as intelligible today as it was in the fourth century before Christ, when Chuang Tzu was reputed to have written his sentences in it.

This is remarkable if we consider the Indo-European languages. They evolved from Latin, Greek, and Sanskrit to different languages so distinct from one another that we must specifically study them in order to read them, even though we may know Latin, Greek, and Sanskrit. And knowing these modern languages does not enable us to read the classical languages, which we have to learn independently. In contrast, an average literate Chinese can read Chuang Tzu with a little help from a commentary. We can read his stories, all simple and straightforward.

On the other hand, however, we do not understand the chapter at all. Chinese characters are there staring at us with flickering conflicting meanings. We do not know what to make of those stories we thought we understood, much less their mutual connections. We guess that perhaps the original text had been dislocated, mutilated, miscopied. We do our best to collate, emend, relocate the text.[186] The text now makes a tottering sense.

Unfortunately, such "sense" as we make out of the obscure text is itself treacherous. It reflects *our* common sense, insipid and trite. Or else, it is full of semantic contortions. We wonder if we have not done damage to this phrase or that word before we came out with such "smooth" reading. Or else, the sense we make seems an insignificant part of the vast concatenation of conflicting profundities, a little surface scratch of the deep Something in the text.[187]

All this while we *feel* that this Something is alive, a chameleon that changes at will. Or rather, it is not even a particular Something but merely an echo of actualities that shift, and the shift is such that the *word* "change" does not apply here. For "change" is opposed to stability, something like a quagmire. But this Something that is not quite something, this shift that is not quite a change, *includes* stability. This shifting Something is not there objectively for us to pursue, but includes our pursuit, and puts us at ease. The Something that shifts is not a Heraclitean commotion, intangible and burningly unapproachable. It is rather like the continental shift or the shift of a seasonal wind, on which we depend like the "sixth month gale" ridden by the Bird and Lieh Tzu. This is the cosmic wind belched out of the "huge Clod" to originate pipings of things.[188] It is a shift we come from, depend on, tarry in. And yet we cannot ridicule it or look for its immutable law without courting our own disaster.

Thus the second chapter is puzzling because it is a heap of sorites in stories, a baffling collage of platitudes, an intelligible unknown. Or rather, let us change the imagery. This chapter is a bottomless lake whose bottom we can see. This is a lake whose bottom *we* think is clearly visible, till we delve into it. And then we find that the bottom is visible as bottomless! This lake is the *Chuang Tzu*, especially this chapter, which reflects the "heavenly lake" of life. For this is what life is. We can see the bottom of things; life is made up of familiar events like political upheavals and scientific breakthroughs. As soon as we look into any of them, however, it recedes into an unfathomable depth of concrete implications, one layer after another.

Chuang Tzu's second chapter is like that. Every word is plain and sparkling; we think we understand it, them. But when we try to explain what these sentences mean we are at a loss. Even after we find what we think to be an explanation, we find that Chuang Tzu has more to say.

Our commentator comes along and makes sense out of the sentences. And then we become unconvinced. *That* may be what Chuang Tzu meant, we say, but cannot be *all* of what he meant. And we make our own plunge into the text. We have actually attempted three readings so far, Meditations A, B, and C. But the reader may well feel that this is one plausible interpretation, but cannot be all of what Chuang Tzu meant. And the plunge continues. An indefinite variety of riches awaits us there, that "heavenly treasury" (*t'ien fu*).

Chuang Tzu's words are "shaded light" (*pao kuang*). They reflect and allude to actuality. Actuality also makes sense tantalizingly, as those words do, into which someone plunges for what Chuang Tzu takes to be the meaning of life. Then we become dissatisfied with being told what that meaning is, we plunge into the text and observe life anew. Chuang Tzu's words arouse us into life itself.

2. Such considerations bring up, apropos of this chapter, the question of the relation of Chuang Tzu to philosophy.

I. M. Crombie ended his two-volume study of Plato by asking, "Why do we call Plato a philosopher?"[189]—an intriguing question on Plato. Yet Chuang Tzu is so odd that I doubt if we can with equal confidence ask the same question about him as Crombie did about Plato. And perhaps Chuang Tzu knowingly wrote in such a way as to *destroy* our confidence in asking, "Why do we call Chuang Tzu a philosopher?" Chuang Tzu purposely criticized the customary manner of philosophizing (serial, argumentative) so as to induce the kind of discernment properly called "philosophical." To question Chuang Tzu the philosopher is in itself to question *our* very notion of philosophy.[190]

Crombie laid out the "method" that is "philosophical," the "manner," not (primarily) the "subject-matter," that distinguishes philosophy from other pursuits—clearing up conceptual entanglements, criticizing theories about life and the world with scientific standards of clarity and reasonableness, using deductive reasoning, forging and refining notions employed in such discussions, and making diagnoses of the type of pit into which such discussions may fall.[191]

There are two kinds of philosophy. Positivism by conceptual clarification shows why questions like "Is the will free?" and "Are material objects independent of our experiencing of them?" do not really arise. Deductive metaphysics hunts for self-evidently true axioms that are fertile of practical consequences, and by such deducing settles the kinds of questions that are unanswerable in empirical investigation.

But what earned Plato the title of "philosopher" is his critical scrutiny of any ideas, opposing both propaganda and blind swallowing of ideas (even when these ideas happen to be true). Therefore Plato is neither a positivist nor a deductive metaphysician.

All this is about Plato the rationalist. Interestingly enough, in the last two pages of his book Crombie distinguished Plato the poet from Plato the rationalist, implying that the latter is Plato the philosopher. Crombie did not raise the question whether poetry has any philosophical significance, why there are two Platos, whether the one Plato hinders or helps the other, and if so how.

In any case, his description of Plato the poet has an uncanny resemblance to Chuang Tzu. The following statement about Plato might be used to describe Chuang Tzu:

> ... he [Plato] disdained lucidity as he also disdained logical rigour. He thought perhaps that an undue attention to ... an argument or to the precise

words ... would distract attention from the realities ... under discussion; ... that an eye fixed steadily on realities was the only sure defence against the deceptions of words. At any rate it is his habit ... to suggest his points rather than to state them; ... commonly ... he uses ... prose-poetry to set them in ... [an] emotional atmosphere. For this reason there is not one Plato but many; you find in him ... what you are looking for, and if the plain sense of the words does not support your interpretation, perhaps you will be able to base it on the general feeling of the passage, or vice versa.[192]

Now, Chuang Tzu may agree with Crombie's rejection of both positivism and metaphysics, and join with Plato the poet; Chuang Tzu would, however, depart from Plato the rationalist. While Plato practiced the antidote to propaganda with logical scrutiny, Chuang Tzu would caution that propaganda can take the form of fascination with logical scrutiny. Plato's myth of innate recollection may have mitigated this danger; Plato the poet may have come to the rescue of Plato the rationalist. But now Plato is caught in a bind—myth does not go too well with logical scrutiny.

Chuang Tzu, on his part, abandoned not logical scrutiny but *belief* in it. He used it with discretion, his "gut-level" reasonableness. Such basic reason is what Max Black called "primitive," "minimal," and "compressed" rationality which, *pace* Black, we share with animals. Such basic rationality is also like poetry, in that both are open-ended and discernful.

Max Black cited the following cases: On seeing a mountain boulder hurtling toward me, I jump aside into a stream; a cat moving to its saucer full of milk; a chess player mumbling as he moves his pawns, "That to there? Will be captured. Same if go there? No. OK." All these examples are activities of "basic reason using," compressed practical enthymemes, reason at work. They are indispensable for survival, and as a basis for the elaboration of human intelligence, hence "basic."

Although animal behaviors fit patterns of "basic reason using," they are only "quasi-rational" for Black, because animals have no concept of reason or of a sign, "let alone fragments of verbal telegraphese, that often mark informal human inference." Nor do they have the retrospective power of articulating non-verbal rational acts.[193]

Chuang Tzu would applaud Black for defending reason as basic and indispensable for survival. He would, however, hesitate to describe animal intelligence as only quasi-rational. For Black rationality should exhibit all of the following qualities:

(*a*) particular behavioral pattern that makes sense,
(*b*) facilitates survival,

(c) and is amenable to rational elaboration (for self-critical learning) into a full-blown logical inference,

(d) by retrospective reconstruction,

(e) through verbal manipulation.

But even Black admits that "a reasoner who is maladroit at retrospective reconstruction is not necessarily to be censored as an inept reason user."[194] I wonder if Black sensed that (d) and (e) conflict with (b); Chuang Tzu went so far as to say that human articulated intelligence (d and e) confounds the world,[195] and he recognized rational value in animal judgments.[196] Chuang Tzu would say that therefore we do share with animals not primitive-compressed rationality but primal ("basic") life rationality, what could be called "animal reason" latent in Santayanan "animal faith"; "animal" after all means "living being." Our articulated cognitive rationality is not a slow replay of basic reason (as Black would have it) but its reinterpretation and remodelling in a specifically cultural manner. If anything, it is human articulated logicality that should be called "derivative," if not "quasi-," reason.

This is so for two more reasons. First, the animal behaviors noted by Black are not sleep-acts but fully conscious, reasonable, and are translatable into philosophical arguments. Secondly, what Black takes to be rationality proper, philosophical logicizing, has all the explicit layout that exists *only* in retrospect. And if it had existed at the moment of action, the agent would have perished; such a slow tedious chain of reasoning would have choked up quick appropriate action. Yet survival is what Black takes to be one crucial value and hallmark of being rational.

This is not, of course, to say that animal life-reason is not rationality. Philosophical logicizing and animal reason are *mutually* translatable. Black, as is customary among philosophers, urges that animal reason be wholly translated into logical reason. The merit of such logical translation is that we gain clarity of understanding. But this does not mean that we can relegate animal reason to a quasi-rational status, much less dispense with it. If anything, we must learn how to translate the tedious bookishness of logical rationality *back* into animal reason. The former is a preparation for becoming adept at the latter: we must unlearn the former to survive in the latter, as we must grow *out* of the driver's manual in the fast traffic of life vicissitudes.

But we are not animals exclusively. Translation of our bookish rationality into animal reason means (for us) logical discernment. *Our* "animal reason" should become a poetic one, perhaps in the form of story-telling (as Black himself said). Chuang Tzu called such a becoming a forgetting of words, a no-knowledge that understands.

In a recent book, *Patterns, Thinking, and Cognition,* Howard Margolis argues that our belief depends not just on "logic + interest," but also on pattern recognition—or "P-cognition," as he calls it. He curiously argues for this "black Box" serially and logically. The ingenuity of the book lies in proving pattern thinking by serial (logical) thinking, thus effectively converting the former into the latter.

Is this manner of proof satisfactory? One is at a dead end here, for three reasons:

(1) When one says that our belief depends on three modes of thinking—logic, interest, and recognition—how is one to prove their existences and their mutualities? Either one must use any one of these modes to prove them; or one must use them alternately; or one must use all of them together. But which route is the best? Why? How does one go about making this choice?

(2) In his Preface, Margolis calls our pattern cognition a "black box," in addition to logic and interest. This is already to assume separation, as he did when he said, at the beginning of the Introduction, that he "will be working out an analysis of cognition in which everything is reduced to ... 'P-cognition' ..." This is to ignore organic interrelations among his three modes of thinking. How does one go about proving both distinction and interrelation among the three modes?

(3) In neither (1) nor (2) above can one either use or not use one or all of these three modes of thinking to prove them. One cannot use one of these three modes because that would be partisan. One cannot use all of these three because that would beg the question, using them to prove them.

And yet one cannot not use one or all of them either. For (a) *ex hypothesi,* one has only these three modes of thinking; (b) if one uses any other mode of thinking to prove these three modes, one denies what one wants to prove—namely, that one has only these three modes of thinking. Or (c) if one does not want to say that we have only these three modes then one needs to say that we have four (or five or ...) modes of thinking, and the same problems start all over again in the world of our having four (or five or ...) modes of thinking.

In sum, this sort of book is impossible to write—logically, persuasively, pattern-recognitionwise, or in accord with whatever other modes we may have of thinking.

We seem to have only one way left. We simply must play and juggle with modes of thinking, keeping them in the air or on the playing field together, so as to evoke an awareness that we do have these modes and that they generally find expression in many literary genres.

This brings us to the relation of philosophy to poetry and to story-telling.

Story-telling has been treated in the first chapter. Here, we treat the relation between poetry and philosophy.

3. William Blake said somewhere that philosophy begins with poetry and ends with poetry. Chuang Tzu would add that if Blake is correct then philosophy should *proceed* with the logic of poetry (as Plato practised masterfully though intuitively), not mathematics (as Plato aspired to and practised consciously).

The logic of mathematics is serial, external, mechanical, coherent. The logic of poetry is mutual, interpenetrating, recursive, co-responsive, co-reverberating, and organic (Chuang Tzu said "musical"). The logic of mathematics appeals primarily to sight; that of poetry appeals primarily to hearing. The logic of poetry is reasonable without being calculative, logically compelling without being closed off in itself. The manner of its universal applicability is not mechanical.

Literary people must be warned that beauty without logical discernment makes no sense. Philosophers must be warned that logic without poetic discernment is barren. The combination of logical and poetic discernments is the logic of poetry, at once inevitable and open-ended. We must challenge logicians with poetry and challenge poets with logic; we must combine beauty with philosophy.[197]

Chuang Tzu's chapter of *Ch'i Wu Lun* is one such combination, enjoyable, even risible to the core, bantering without being silly. Chuang Tzu's sentences loosen the reader's lips and tickle his mental palate toward the truths of life without collapsing into laughter.

Chuang Tzu says that he writes so because life is so, and we had better live likewise. Our lived reason must operate in the logic of poetry, logically compelling and open-ended. What does "logical and open" mean in a poetic context?

Universal truths, if there be such, are necessary and sufficiently universal; but we are finite and free. All that we can expressly say is necessary but not universally true, that is, our assertions can at best be convincing, not unconditionally true; in fact, they are often false.

This means that what we can know (and say) is inexhaustible. Chuang Tzu says so as he starts his third chapter, adding that to brave such an inexhaustible world with our limited life is dangerous. Both Kant and Michael Polanyi put this point in terms of man's self-understanding. A *comprehensive* knowledge for man is impossible because our very act of knowing must be included among the items of our knowledge.[198]

It follows that we cannot and should not attempt a consistent system of *universal* truths. Every such universal system of absolute truths has proven to be an overstatement of a partial truth. What it affirms can be true; what it denies can also be true.

That a final absolute and universal assertion is impossible can be shown thus. (*a*) If we say "All are true," then it implies that "It is true that 'all are true' is false," making "All are true" itself false. (*b*) If we say "All are true except for the statement, ' "All are true" is false,' " or "All are false except for the statement ' "All are false" is false,' " then we cannot complete our assertion, because before we say, "It is true that P (=whatever we say)," we must say "It is true that it is true that P," before which we must say, "It is true that it is true that ... it is true that P," and so on, in order to prevent the "except"-clause to enroach on the assertion. This is why Chuang Tzu said, "Do not say, but 'follow what-is.' "[199]

Concretely, all that this amounts to is this! Things we thought to be false often have a grain of truth in them, if not themselves true. Chuang Tzu said something similar and deeper.[200] We can attain only glimpses of truth from a particular perspective—cultural, cognitive, or psychic. Our so-called "truth" is autochthonous, that is, parochial, soiled (soil-ed), or else an abstract nothing. Even the claim or ideal of culture-free truth is culturally determined—it is typically Western.

This explains how much infused life is with inconsistencies, how much more excited we are at villains, falsehoods, inconsistencies, mistakes, than at orthodoxies and proprieties. This also explains our excitement at half-truths and vague truths enshrined in proverbs, metaphors, aphorisms, lampoons, and tongues-in-cheek. Wittgenstein reminds us that a concept is like (always "like") a string twisted out of many different fibres.[201] We add that the *way* those fibres are twisted together differs as one goes from one language and culture to another, from one way of life to another. To understand is to understand the variety of ways of life. "Life in general" or "notion in general" is vacuous and meaningless.

But beware. This point itself should not be taken as another attempt at universal and consistent truth—or rather, it should and it should not be taken so. It should be taken as true universally in the sense that *every time* we see a system of universal truths we must look at it with some caution. Yet what is said here should not be taken as itself a consistent truth because otherwise what is said ("No claim is consistently true") contradicts what is claimed ("The claim, 'No claim is consistently true' is consistently true.")

This amounts to saying that we should *sometimes* learn from system builders; we should not wallow in inconsistency for its own sake.[202] Our claim to value inconsistent and partial truth must be a responsible act, that is, an expression of our loyalty to actuality. Our inconsistencies must come from our discernment of, and dogged follow-up on, actualities at the price of *our* notional consistency. Such is the "scientific spirit," the spirit of relativity of our claim *to* truth. "I once thought I was wrong, but I was mistaken," as a little joke says, and I am often not even sure of the truth of *that* joke. Robert Cummings Neville, in the concluding statement of his momumental systematic work, *Reconstruction of Thinking*, says, "The attempt has been made ... to state positions in as vulnerable a way as possible. For vulnerability is of the essence of truth." Here "vulnerability" can be taken as "vulnerability of our claim to universal truth."[203]

Life is a series of exceptions. To let them shine forth in short universal statements is the task of aphorisms. They make us think and apply them in our own ways in our own circumstances. This is how exceptions come to intimate universals. The logic of poetry in Chuang Tzu's "metaphysics" works, among others, in such a way—specials and exceptions in aphorisms stirring us into exploration on our own. Those specials are packed with alluring but insufficiently universal truths, goading us on.[204]

An exciting illustration of such "metaphysics" is this second chapter of the *Chuang Tzu*.

4. *Ch'i Wu Lun* is a *Hsiao Yao Yu* in thinking and theorizing. But few are aware of how much such a colorless statement involves. Thinking and theorizing for Chuang Tzu involves no less than a radical probing into the self, resulting in a self-less self and an awakening to one's perhaps-dreaming. Such self-probe and self-awakening to a perhaps-dreaming involves a corresponding revolution in our way of thinking the world and living in it. Plato's stable world of ideal prototypes of reality is gone. Things are ever changing and ever one, dynamic and rhythmic, in which we move fugally.

Ch'i Wu Lun is thus *Hsiao Yao Yu* radicalized, applied to our existence and our world. This is a philosophizing that opposes both the customary disembodied (ideal) subject eternally contemplating the world of abstract Reality (as in the West), and the customary social conventions sacralized to a cosmic family metaphysics (as in China). It is rather moving in, with, and as the world. Such moving is a carefree roaming and soaring that is the theme of the first chapter.

We remember the first chapter structured thus:

(*a*) The chapter starts with movement without motion—a Fish in the Northern Ocean,

(*b*) continues with many stories and many activities, and

(*c*) ends in another movement without motion—

"roaming around and lying asleep below it [the useless Tree]." (163)

We see the second chapter structured likewise:

(*a*) The chapter starts with movement without motion—Mr. South Wall-Base reclining, looking up, overhearing,

(*b*) continues with many stories and activities, and

(*c*) ends in another movement without motion—dreaming-awakening.

What is such parallelism *about*? *Hsiao Yao Yu* is traditionally taken to signify two things:[205] (*i*) *Things* are equal and equal in their respective appropriate places; (*ii*) the heart-and-mind of the ultimate *man* is both the big Bird and the small ones, the far and the near, eternally thinking things and "thinging things". The first interpretation is about "things," about cosmology; the second is about "heart-mind," about egology.

The debate is carried into *Ch'i Wu Lun*. Traditionally this chapter has received two interpretations: Either as a concern for the *Ch'i*-ing of *Wu-Luns* (equalizing of theories of things) or as a concern for the *Lun* (theory) of *Ch'i*-ing *Wus* (equalizing things).[206]

Both parties in the debate about the interpretation of these chapters share a common assumption, to wit, things and thinking are different. They believe that *Wu-Luns* (theories of things) are our subjective thoughts about things,[207] whereas things (*Wu*) are something objective, out there. They believe that to equalize *things* (or to let them even out) is not to equalize *theories* about things which are, as Mencius said, by nature not equal (3A4).

Chuang Tzu would have smiled and said that we think in terms of this dichotomy because we think that there is such a thinking subject over against things thought. Western philosophy predominantly revolves around this "gap."[208] This is an obsession that must be dissolved by the "self losing its self." This is not to destroy the self (as Buddhism would) but to realize that the identity of the self is not a fixed one. That is, although the self is not non-self, the distinction (*fen*) is a dynamic one, always interchanging with others (*hua*). The concluding story of the butterfly dream delightfully clinches what has been repeatedly explained and exhibited in the chapter. The distinction exists subjectively (*fen*), but the territory (*chen, fung*) shifts (*hua*).[209]

The chapter professing to be about things and theories starts and ends with the self. This shows that our identity can be interchanged with others, even things, from whose standpoint our original identity as subject is an object of *their* "thinking."[210] It follows that "to even" our thinking about things is to even things, for theory and things are so much a reflection of each other that no one knows which is an always-this and which an always-that, which is real and which dreamed.[211]

Even the style of Chapter Two reflects such kaleidoscopic uncertainty that is typical of deep truths of actuality. We must be charmed into reading the chapter repeatedly and be awakened to new meanings.[212] We will realize that no matter how much we get out of our readings we can never exhaust its implications, simply because we can never be sure what is its true definitive meaning.

What it intimates is at least this. Chuang Tzu in this chapter meditates on the state of affairs of the self that is lost in the fugue of interchange of identities with things and wanders between dreaming and awakening, among uncertainty, ignorance, and knowledge. This is what can be dubbed as a non-egology.

5. Let us go further into Chuang Tzu's non-egology. After confessing that he has "lost" his self, Mr. South-Wall-Base explained the situation with an overhearing of various pipings. And then he went into further stories of reciprocity of a this with a that, birth with death, and relativity of standards of value and things. All these stories and metaphors make a point—that the judging subject changes, interchanges, into and with others; not just perspectives but the very subjecthood itself changes. Here we have a relativism *of* the subject, an existential relativism.

But what is *it* that considers all this? How do we characterize *it*? We can only call it non-subject, that is, no ordinary subject describable as a this and a have-been-born, a Chuang Chou and a butterfly. Non-subject is what (*wu*-subject) does the losing of its self (*wo*-self), the *wu*-subject which forgets its self and can claim "no-*wo*."[213] It is not even Kant's transcendental Ego because Kant's Ego is a stable Noumenon, an absolute postulate behind every thinking and experience. Kant's Ego does not lose its self.

This does not mean, of course, that the subject does not exist, for otherwise there would be no one to perform self-losing, or to consider all reciprocity of identities. Nor does it mean that the non-subject "exists" as a Chuang Chou or a butterfly exists. And yet all we have (as existing) are just Chuang Chou and butterflies. "All of them self-change, but he who arouses them, who is he?"[214] And so we say that this sort of "subject" exists-as-not-existing, a non-subject.

Nor is this non-subject God, either. It is neither all-mighty nor all-knowing. This non-subject exists but can be characterized as not-existing and in other negative terms. Or rather, it cannot be talked *about* at all, because it is what begins talks about everything, a radical subject that encompasses even its own non-existence, its own self-losing, as well as itself as an object of thought.

To realize such non-subject we must lose our regular thinkable subject; hence "I lose myself." To this primal non-subject (non-ego) the world of things is "one" in their self-sorting (*ch'i*) and co-thriving (*fang sheng; yin shih*).

This chapter is thus a chapter on the logic of self-metamorphosis, the logic of the (inter-)change of the non-subject, where the usual logic assumes an unchanging self. This chapter cannot, then, proceed in the manner of the usual logic—and yet the usual logic is all we have.

The only way out of the predicament is for Chuang Tzu to *use* the usual logic prevalent among the sophists, and spar with them playfully. In his very sparring and playing with their logicizing Chuang Tzu merely says what *can* be said; he stays silent beyond the sayables, and lets the sayables say all the silly things and platitudes that any sane man would be above saying, indicating that what cannot be said is what is meant. "All these parables really set out to say merely that the incomprehensible is incomprehensible, and we know that already," says Franz Kafka.[215] Similarly, Chuang Tzu would say that he made a parabolic use of logic, using logic as a parable for something unsayable, a thrown-beside-the-inexpressible. It is in this way that actualities that can only be experienced are presented.

If "What can be tao-ed [identified as Tao] is not the always-Tao," as Lao Tzu claimed,[216] then what can be tao-ed can be tao-ed and then presented as not-the-Tao. Whatever thus negated can be said-as-negated, which will be a parable and finger-pointing to the always-Tao. Such finger-as-no-finger is a metaphor, story, dream, performance, presentation, of the Constant Tao. For such performance is silence that speaks. This is pre-sentation, an itinerary of the not-taoed Tao. The Tao "comes about as we walk it," as Graham translated line 112. It is a "two-way walk" of saying without saying, of waking up knowing that one is perhaps dreaming.

And it is a unity of three pipings. The objectifying and overhearing non-subject is equivalent to the heavenly piping in the world. The identifiably objectifiable self is the earthly piping. And the human piping is this our saying so. Such human piping can be an echo of the other two pipings as natural and spontaneous as they; and then we are supremely integral and happy. Or else we strive ourselves and assert our set-minds (that *wo*-self) in this turbulent world, and we suffer. To this theme we now turn.

Chapter
Three

YANG
SHENG
CHU

養生主

Nourishing Life
—Its Inner Principle

然則弔焉若此可乎

曰然

始也吾以爲其人也而今非也

彼其所以會之必有不蘄言而言不蘄哭而哭者

是遁天倍情

忘其所受

少者哭之如哭其母

有老者哭之如哭其子

向吾入而弔焉

古者謂之遁天之刑

適來夫子時也

適去夫子順也

安時而處順哀樂不能入也

古者謂是帝之縣解

指窮於爲薪

火傳也不知其盡也

提刀而立爲之四顧爲之躊躇滿志善刀而藏之

文惠君曰善哉吾聞庖丁之言

得養生焉

百步一飲

不蘄畜乎樊

中神雖王不善也

III

公文軒見右師而驚曰

是何人也惡乎介也天與其人與

曰天也非人也

天之生是使獨也人之貌有與也

以是知其天也非人也

老聃死

秦失弔之

三號而出

弟子曰

非夫子之友邪

曰然

IV

澤雉

十步一啄

25　　　　　　　20　　　　　　　15

始臣之解牛之時所見无非牛者

三年之後未嘗見全牛也

方今之時臣以神遇而不以目視官知止而神欲行

因其固然技經肯綮之未嘗而況大軱乎

依乎天理批大郤導大窾

良庖歲更刀割也族庖月更刀折也

今臣之刀十九年矣

所解數千牛矣而刀刃若新發於硎

彼節者有間而刀刃者无厚

以无厚入有間恢恢乎其於遊刃必有餘地矣

是以十九年而刀刃若新發於硎

雖然每至於族吾見其難為

怵然為戒視為止行為遲

動刀甚微謋然已解如土委地

莊子內篇養生主第三

I

1 吾生也有涯而知也无涯以有涯隨无涯殆已
已而為知者殆而已矣
為善无近名為惡无近刑緣督以為經
可以保身可以全生可以養親可以盡年

II

5 庖丁為文惠君解牛
手之所觸肩之所倚
足之所履膝之所踦

10 砉然嚮然奏刀騞然莫不中音
合於桑林之舞乃中經首之會
文惠君曰譆善哉技蓋至此乎
庖丁釋刀對曰
臣之所好者道也進乎技矣

TRANSLATION WITH GLOSSES

I

1   In **my life there-exist shorelines, and in understanding***
there-exist-no shorelines. With the **existence** of
shorelines to **follow** after the **no-existence** of
shorelines is **dangerous** enough **already.**
He-who already* knows such danger, **and** still* **makes** after*
understanding, is dangerous indeed.*

In the **making** of **"good" there**-should-**be-no*** going **near name**
and fame; in the **making** of **"evil" there**-should-**be-no**
going **near cane*** and blade. Instead, we had better
go-along-with the **spinal-artery** of energy,
with which we **make** our constant **passage.***
With it we **can maintain** our **body**-and-life;
with it we **can** keep our **life whole;**
with it we **can nourish** those with **family** ties to us;
with it we **can exhaust** living our natural **years.***

II

5   **Kitchen fellow,*** for **ruler Wen Hui,*** is **undoing*** an **ox.**
At the **touch of** his **hand, at** the **leaning of** his **shoulder;**
At the **stepping-on of*** his **foot, at** the **pressing of**
his **knee.**
So swoosh! So swing! (—the meat is whisked off the bone).
So swish!—the
knife performs through the ox, and **none** of the moves does
not fall-in-with* the **tune,**
Matching with the **Dance of Mulberry Forest, even* falling-in-**
with* the **collective** symphonies* **of Ching Shou.***

10   **Ruler Wen Hui said, "Ah! Good! How*** could the **skill** arrive-at
such height!''
Kitchen fellow, letting-go-of* the **knife, responded, saying,**
"What your **servant is-given-to is** the **Tao, being-beyond**
skill.

In the **beginning,** during the **time of** the **undoing of oxen**
    of your **servant, in what** was **seen**
    there-were-no-things that **were-not oxen;**
During the period **of three years after**wards,
    I was **yet** to **try seeing** the **whole ox.**
15 **While* now,** at the **time of** ox-loosening,
    your **servant, with spirit meeting, and**
    not with eyes looking, have the **sense** and
    understanding stop and the **spirit desiring, walk—**

Cleaving to heaven-given **lines,* cleaving-along huge seams,***
    sliding-through* huge hollows.
Following-on their inherently-so,* the **skill**ed knife has
    not yet tried passing through a **ligament, tendon—**
    and how much less a **huge bone!**

Fine kitchen fellows **yearly replace** the knife; it has **been**
    chipped. A **band**-of-common **kitchen** fellows **monthly**
    replace the knives; they have **been broken.***
Now the **knife of** your **servant** is already
    nineteen years old.
20 **What** have been **loosened-up** already **number***
    thousands of oxen, and the **knife blade** is
    like newly issued from the **grindstone.**

In *those** **joints there-exist spaces,** and in *this**
    knife blade there-exists-no thickness.
With no-existence of thickness to enter the existence
    of spaces—then, **spacious, spacious**-ly,
    for its roaming-about* the **knife, there must,**
    of course,* **exist more-than-enough ground.***
This is how I have been **with** the knife for **nineteen years,**
    and the **knife blade** is still **like newly issued**
    from the grindstone.

Although it is **so, every** time I **arrive at** a **band** of
    complexities* I see their troubles in the **making.**
25 **So** very **warily,** I become **cautious for*** it, my **look**-around
    stops for it, my **walk slows** down **for** it.
Moving the knife very delicately until—**Ho!** the **ox so**
    undoes itself, as the **soil thrown-to** the **ground.**

I hold the **knife and stand** up, **looking-around for it***
    in **four** directions. **Lost, hesistant for it** for a while,
    then realizing that my **intention** is now **fulfilled,**
    I give my **knife** a **good*** wipe **and store it** away."
Ruler Wen Hui said, "Good! I have **heard**
    the **words of kitchen fellow.**
I have **obtained** the **nourishing** of **life*** **in-them."**

III

30 **Kung Wen Hsuan*** saw the **Commander** of the **Right**
        and was **startled, saying,**
    "What man is this? How-could he be **singular*** **-footed?**
        Was it **heaven? Or*** was **it man?"**

    Then **said, "Heaven** it **was; it was-not man.**
    Heaven's giving-birth-to this* **was** to **let** him **alone**
        become unique,* while in the **outlook*** of **man there-exists**
        a **pairing.***
    With this I understand it is heaven; it **is-not man."**

IV

35 The **marsh pheasant,** living on
    Ten steps for **one peck,**
    A **hundred steps** for **one drink,**
    Not wishing* to be **fed in** a **cage.**
    To be **hurt*** in **spirit,**
        though living like a **king, is not good.**

V

40 **Lao Tan*** **died.**
    Ch'in Shih* **mourned him—**
    Three wailings, and he **came-out.**

    Disciples said,
    "Are-you-not a **friend of** the **master**'s?"
45 He **said, "I am so."**
    "If **so, then can** you **mourn for-him like this?"**
    He **said, " I can do so.**
    In the **beginning I took** him **as*** **that man** I have been
        admiring; **and now** (I know) he **is-not.**

Until-now since when **I entered and mourned,**

50   **There-were those-who** are **old weeping for him as weeping** for
         their child,

Those-who are **young weeping for him as weeping** for
         their mother*

Seeing that there is **that with which that** party **gathered***
         like **this, he* must** have had it **exist** in him
         that-which he did **not wish worded** and was **worded,**
         that for which he did **not wish wept** and was **wept.**

This is **escaping heaven, opposing real**ity, and
Forgetting what they* received.*

55   In **those old** days they **called it** the **cane of
         dodging heaven.**

As time **goes,** so he **came—**
         the **master** was the **one-who*** was **timely.**

As time **goes,** so he **left—**
         the **master** was the **one-who*** was **compliant.**

Being **at-home** in the **times and dwell**ing oneself in
         compliance, he was the **one-whom*** sorrows and **joys**
         were **not able to enter*.**

In **those old** days they **called this 'bonds of root-
         entanglements* loosened-up.'"**

VI

60   **Finger-pointing* ends at making firewood.***
That-which* transmits fire does **not understand
         its* exhaustion.**

Glosses

Title: *Yang Sheng Chu*: As will be discussed in Meditations, the title can be divided into two in two ways: (*i*) The *chu* of *yang sheng* ("the ruling principle of nourishing life"), and (*ii*) cultivating (*yang*) the *sheng chu* ("the lord of life"; cf. Ch. Two, lines 57, 66).

Chang Ch'eng-ch'iu quotes various authors on this issue (in his *Chuang Tzu P'ien-mu K'au,* pp. 61–62), and decides on the latter interpretation because the most important thing in life is what makes life possible, the "lord" of life. He takes "lord" questionably to mean the spirit as distinct from the flesh. Sakai Kanzō takes the former interpretation, because line 29 supports him. I also follow the former, both because it is more descriptive and because it has less danger of mind-body dualism. In the end, however, both interpretations amount to the same thing.

Line 1 has *ya* as its rhyme.

Chih is (1) "knowledge," (2) "understanding," (3) "thoughts and anxieties" (Lin Shi-i). Meaning (3) makes this line a summary of the first description of psychic wranglings in Ch. Two, lines 35–52, 69–73. I follow (1) because (2) is laudatory and (3) is forced. But for consistency with previous passages of the translation, I have rendered *chih* as "understanding" throughout.

Sui ("follow"; line 1) is bad; *yüan* ("go along with"; line 3), *i* ("cleave to"; line 16) and *yin* ("follow on"; line 17) are good.

Line 2 and line 1 have *i* as their rhyme. *I* usually means (1) "already," (2) "only" or "stop,"or (3) "nothing but."

I here may be (1) abbreviation of *i chih* ("already knowing such danger"; cf. Ch. Two, line 123), or (2) *tz'u* ("this," "thus"; Wang Yin-chih, Yang Shu-ta, Ch'en Ku-ying; cf. line 10). Both amount to the same thing.

Wei ("make"): Watson has "striving"; cf. Graham, *Later Mohist Logic,* pp. 209–10. *Wei* rhymes with *sui* ("follow") in sound and in meaning.

Wei chih ("make-after knowledge") contrasts with *pu chih* ("not knowing") in the final line 61.

Wei ("make") is bad; *chieh* ("undo"; line 5) and *yu* ("roam"; line 22) are good.

Erh ("and") is emphatic.

Line 3:

Ming, literally "name" (cf. Ch. One, line 69), rhymes with *hsing* ("cane," as in "punishment" by caning) and *ching* ("passage").

Wu ("no existence") means *wu* ("must not") for Ch'en Ku-ying, but I think it merely connotes it.

Wu chih ("[do] not [go] near") describes *chi'eh* ("undoing"; line 5, etc.) and *yu* ("roaming"; lines 21–23).

Hsing ("cane") echoes *hsing* (grindstone") in lines 23 and 25.

Tu can be (1) "the back center meridian-vein through the body," (2) "the back center fold through a dress," or (3) "discernment" (*Ku Lin*, 4:82–83; Chu Kuei-yao, Kuo Ch'ing-fan, Sakai Kanzō). (1) is popular with commentators, who sometimes liken it to medical "nourishment," apropos of the chapter title. (2) is endorsed by Lin Yün-ming, linking it with line 22. I think (3) is noteworthy—true discernment is connected with the center of our back where we cannot see. Thus our discernment is without conscious observation; it is a reality-trailing.

Ching can mean: (1) "constancy," "standard," resulting in *yu* ("playful roaming"; line 22), which explains another interpretation, (2) "route" or "passage" (Ch'eng Shou-ch'ang, Ma Hsü-lun, etc.). Cf. line 17.

The first sentence of line 3 is difficult. Every commentator I consulted denies that Chuang Tzu encourages getting away with doing bad, but they do not agree on what he meant.

Wang Shu-min (*Chuang Hsüen Kuan-kui,* pp. 105–107) disagrees with all fifteen interpretations he cited, and comes up with his own (pp. 108–109): "In being good at nourishing life, do not come close to shallow glories; in not being good at nourishing life do not come close to what hurts and maims you, such as what labors the body and saps vitality." This interpretation seems forced.

Ch'en Shou-ch'ang has "Coming close to fame and punishment are traces of good or bad; the mind ceasing to arise, then traces are gone also" (p. 23). This is an over-spritualizing.

Ch'eng Hsüan-ying (followed by Chang Wen-hu, Huang Chin-hung, and Fukunaga) has "No good deed is not going near fame; no bad deed is not going near cane. These are ordinary doings that labor and endanger our mind and soul"—meaning we had better stay clear of both doing good and doing bad.

In other words, "Do no 'good' to go near fame, *as* we do no 'bad' to go near cane." The word "as" is approved of by Ho Ching-ch'ün (*Chuang Tzu I I*, p. 31). "Good" and "bad" are in quotation marks, meaning good and bad as recognized by people. (I omit Lin Hsi-i's peculiar view.)

Line 4: The sentential tempo exudes roaming freedom of Hsiao Yao Yu, soaring and roaming.

This line has *-i, -in,* and *-ing* as its rhymes, and echoes (rhymes with) line 3 on *-ing,* as was also noted by Ch'en Shou-ch'ang.

Lines 1 and 2 are negative; lines 3 and 4 are positive. All these lines are crisp and short, fit to be an introduction to what follows.

Sheng ("birth") could mean *hsing* ("nature"; Ma Ch'i-chang, Wu Ju-lun), making the sentence read "we can fulfill our nature."

Ch'in ("family") can mean (1) "parents" ("We can even fulfill our Confucian filial duties, if we wish"); (2) "someone or something closest to us, our self" ("We can nourish our life"; Kuan Fong; cf. Ch. Two, line 61); or (3) *hsin,* "daily renewals" ("We can nourish our daily renewals"; Wang Shu-min).

Chin ("exhaust"): Cf. the final line 61. This introduction as a whole is indeed as brief as the conclusion (lines 60–61), both of which conclude with a "good finish"!

Line 5:

P'ao ting ("kitchen fellow") can mean (1) "a cook named Ting," as a carpenter named Shih ("Mr. Carpenter"?; 4/64, 24/48), or a wheelwright named Pien ("Mr. Wheelwright"?; 13/68; Fukunaga 1:114); (2) "a cook" (Lin Shu, *Chuang Tzu Ch'ien Shuo*, 2:2; Matthews *Chinese-English Dictionary*, s.v. *ting*—Thomas Merton adopted this interpretation); or (3) *pao* ("brother"; *ting* is a mere fellow— Ma Hsü-lun, Chu Kuei-yao). The last meaning is interesting; a cook is "brother" to his ruler!—(fellow human being?)

It must be noted that in ancient China, a cook was also a butcher—the killer *is* the nourisher here.

Ruler Wen Hui: Tradition (reputedly starting with Chu Hsi) identifies him as King Liang Hui with whom Mencius began his dialogues in the *Mencius*. Although this is a mere conjecture, it is philosophically significant. Mencius' sentiment is that "The gentlemen keep their distance from the kitchen" (1A7), and although Mencius' statement was addressed to King Hsüan of Ch'i, Mencius' thrust is always to avoid bloodshed. This line is a satirical jab at Mencius; rather butchery than "goodness"!

Lines 4, 5:

Ch'in ("family"), *chün* ("ruler") may implicitly echo *ch'in* and *chün* in Ch. Two, lines 61–66.

An exaltation of the cook is peculiar to Chuang Tzu, not only in contrast with Mencius but also with Buddhism, where a butcher let go of his cleaver and instantly became a buddha. Here the cook practices Tao by cutting up an ox! This goes against the grain of even such an able commentator as Ch'en Shou-ch'ang!

Chieh ("undoing") means (1) literally, "cutting up an ox by undoing its horns," as here; (2) "loosening" (as it will frequently be rendered in the Meditations), "untying," "undoing" (line 5); (3) "relief from trouble" (lines 33, 59); (4) "elucidating and dissolving doubts" (cf. lines 28, 29), "explaining things clearly" (cf. *chih* in lines 1, 61); or (5) "disentangling" (lines 24–27). Chuang Tzu may have had in mind lines 26, 31 (*chieh*).

See Graham, *Mohist Logic*, pp. 217-18, for "ox" as stock example among Chinese logicians, especially of disjunction, "X or non-X."

Lines 6, 7:

Chih ("of," "this") may well mean "goes" ("The hand goes to where it touches," etc.) as well as being required by the sentential rhythm. Cf. line 17. (Both lines have *i* as their rhyme.)

Lines 6-9 are dancing, rhythmic.

Line 8

Hua jan ("so swoosh") is the sound of the meat leaving the bone.

Tsou (perform") has double meanings of performing the carving and performing music. The line has *an* (*in*) as its rhyme.

Huo jan ("so swish") is the sound of the knife going through, rhyming with *hua jan*—although the sounds are more like one of Wilfred Owen's "half-rhymes." Both describe *hsiang jan* ("so swing"), echoingly.

Lines 8–9: There is parallelism among *chung* ("middle"), *ho* ("harmony"), and *hui* ("gathering"); cf. line 52.

> *Chung* ("falling in with") originally means "middle" (as in Ch. Two, lines 105, 258, and possibly Ch. Three, lines 39). It is also often used as verb, "fall in the middle of" (Ch. One, line 155) or "fall in with" (Ch. One, lines 147, 148, and possibly here).

Line 9:

> The Mulberry Forest Dance is for rain (Chu Kuei-yao)—is this another reference to "nourishment"?

> *Ho* ("harmony") rhymes in meaning, if not in sound, with *hui* ("gathering", "to-getherness", of instruments; Chu Kuei-yao), hence "symphonic"—cf. "orches-tra" (Graham). This line contrasts with line 52.

> *Nai* ("then") is *ch'ieh* ("besides"—Wang Yin-chih, p. 129; Huang Chin-hung, Akatzuka).

> *Ching shou* perhaps alludes to *tu ... ching* on line 3 (the *tu*-meridian going through the neck).

Line 10:

> *Shan* ("good")—such "good" is certainly not the kind that goes near name! This true "good" parallels the one in lines 27, 28, 39.

> *Kai* ("how"): Chu Kuei-yao claims it to be *ho* ("how ...!").

Line 11:

> *Shih* ("let go of") is *shih* ("throw away"; Lin Hsi-i).

Line 12:

> *Hao* ("is given to") here contrasts with the same character, *hao,* in Ch. Two, lines 141, 142.

> *Chin* ("is beyond") refers either to the cook (as rendered here) or to the way (as Watson has it), or both. This is in contrast to Ch. Two, lines 141–43.

Line 13–15 has a three-step progression (cf. lines 18-19): (1) Lines 13–14 is progress on *chien,* "turning on ox." (2) Then on line 15 *chien* (explained as *shih* to rhyme with *shen*) is left for *shen,* for which see Fukunaga, 2:347–50.

> *Yü* ("meet") is good, but *hui* can be good (line 9) or bad (line 52).

Line 15:

> *Fang* here means "while." See gloss to Ch. Two, line 96; cf. Ch. Two, line 252.

Line 16 runs rhythmically. *I* rhymes with and echoes *p'i ,* and so I tried "cleave to" (*i*) and "cleave along" *(p'i).* The following pairs rhyme in sense—*hsi* ("seam") with *k'uan* ("hollow"); *t'ien li* ("heaven-given line") with *ku jan* ("inherent so"); *tao* ("slide through") and *yin* ("follow on") with *ching* ("pass through").

> Wang Shu-min mentioned a "mix up" of *k'uan* with *ch'iao* in the Ch'eng Hsüan-ying manuscript, and of *ch'iao* with *k'uan* in Ch. Two, line 18, in the Chiao Hung manuscript. If we take these two words to be interchangeable (since their

meanings are identical), not a mix up, then *hsi* rhymes with *ch'iao* (= *k'uan*) in sound as well.

Li ("line") is natural veins and lines in (the jade of) actualities. Graham takes it to be the natural patterns, organizations, and configurations of things (*Mohist Logic*, pp. 191–92).

   Ku Lin said that the inner grains of jade are most apparent to inspection from outside, and so *li* came to mean carving-refining (*chih*, "governing"; cf. Ch. One, lines 75, 78) of jade from a jade block.

   From this original meaning *li* came to mean managing (governing) a situation according to its inner tendency. *Li* is the way things are structured originally and naturally (2:33-37). Neo-Confucianism (among others) turned this common natural notion into a technical term. Another natural-technical term is *ch'i* ("breath energies," "vaporous thrust"—cf. Ch. One, lines 42, 64, 94; Ch. Two, line 15). This is peculiar to Chinese philosophy.

Hsi ("seams") is seams of things, their natural folds, as in the back central folds of a dress (*tu*). Cf. Chu Kuei-yao. As the back central folds of a dress cannot be seen (when the dress is worn), so the cook traces with his knife the natural seams (and folds) of an ox without seeing them.

Tao ("slide through"): I followed Ch'en Ku-ying and Fung Yulan's interpretation, but it can very well mean "led by ..."

Line 17 as a whole is dynamic, rhythmic, and rhymed. Every commentator I have read passes over *chih* (a connective, generally meaning "of"), perhaps tacitly agreeing that the word is required by the sentential rhythm, somewhat like *chih* on lines 6 and 7. Can this line mean "as the skill of the knife passes by minute connectives it never goes to them"?

   In any case, this line is difficult. I noticed four interpretations:

   (1) Kao Heng greatly flexed his textual ingenuity to prove that *chi ching* ("skill ... pass") means *ni ch'u* ("to touch contrary-wise"), and that *wei ch'ang* ("yet ... tried") should begin the sentence.

   (2) Kuo Ch'ing-fan and Ch'en Ku-ying cited many commentators to show that *chi* ("skill") means *chih mo* ("tributary veins"), that *ching* ("pass") means *ching mo* ("main veins"), and that *wei ai* ("slight obstruction") should be added.

   (3) Li Chen and Fung Yulan took *ch'ang* ("tried") literally to mean "to attempt."

   (4) Kuo Hsiang, Lin Shu, and Ho Ching-ch'un took *chi* ("skill") literally to mean "skill," and *ch'ing* ("pass") as a verb to mean "to pass through."

   The last interpretation seems least forced, requiring least emendation, and my translation went accordingly, combining Fung and Feng-English. It must be noted that these four interpretations amount to the same thing.

Ku jan ("inherently so"): Cf. Ch. Two, line 114. Cf. Graham, *Mohist Logic*, pp. 189–90.

Ching ("pass") perhaps refers to line 3.

Wei ch'ang ("yet tried") is placed at the end of the sentence, perhaps because *ch'ang* slightly rhymes with *jan*.

Lines 18–20 have rhymes and parallelisms of two kinds of butchers, showing that they are on an equal level of clumsiness (cf. Ch'en Shou-ch'ang). This is a threefold progress, rhymed, as in lines 13–14.

Lines 18: Or "cuts the meat, breaks the bones" (Wang Fu-chih, Yü Yüeh, Wang Hsien-ch'ien). I followed another interpretation (Kuo Hsiang, Kao Heng) that takes these verbs to refer to the knife, because the latter interpretation makes for a simpler sentence construction.

Lines 19, 20, 22:

I is a mark of stress and rhyme, connoting "already" (lines 19, 20) or "of course" (line 22).

Line 20:

Shu ("number") can be a verb (as here) or an adjective ("several")

Hsing ("grindstone") may remotely refer (in sense, in sound) to *hsing* ("cane", "punishment"; lines 3, 55)..

Line 21:

Che ("that which") is emphatic (as *yeh;* Wang Yin-chih). Cf. *yeh* on line 1.

Line 22:

Yu is "roaming leisurely," the theme of Chapter One.

Yu hsieh ("existence of spaces") parallels *wu hou* ("no existence of thickness").

... hu ch'i yü ... ("...-ly, that in ...") is emphatic (Wang Yin-chih, Chu Kuei-yao).

Lines 20, 23:

Hsin ("new") may echo *ch'in* ("family"; line 4). Cf. the third possible interpretation in the gloss to line 4.

Line 23:

Shih i ("this with") can be compared to *i shih* on line 34.

Lines 24-27 are taken by Chu Kuei-yao (followed by Arthur Waley in his *Three Ways of Thought in Ancient China,* p. 48) to refer to the common butcher's practice. Waley also cited Kao Heng, whose view on this I failed to find. Watson (p. 51, note 4) decided against Chu-Waley-Kao's interpretation and followed the traditional view because caution in difficulties is also a part of a divine cook. All other commentators that I know side with Watson, some with good interpretation (e.g. Lin Hsi-i).

Wei, wei chih, ("make," "for it"): (1) Much of the rhythmic movement of this paragraph is due to the emphatic *wei,* which I surmised to be an emphatic particle (*yü chu*) as in Ch. One, line 22 (cf. my gloss there). But I forfeited this speculative interpretation.

(2) Wang Li (*Ancient Chinese,* pp. 457, 483) takes *wei* as abbreviated *wei chih* ("because of this [difficulty]"). Many Japanese commentators follow this interpretation. although I followed them, too, we must note that in the end both interpretations amount to the same thing.

Line 24:

Tsu ("band") is a gathering (*chü;* Lin Hsi-i), opposite of *chieh* ("loosening") in line 5. Chu Kuei-Yao takes it to mean *tsu p'ao* ("common cooks") as in line 18.

Line 25:

Ch'u jan ("so warily") is *wei chieh* ("become cautious").

Line 26:

T'u wei ti ("soil thrown to the ground") may connote "as the soil submitting itself to the ground/earth." even "returning home to the earth."

I ("already") may mean *chi* ("itself")—"the ox loosens itself."

Line 27: I followed Akatzuka in separating *man chih* ("intention satisfied") as an independent sentence after *ch'ou ch'u* ("hesitant"). This arrangement makes the meanings straightforward and natural, the meaning transition smooth, and the whole sequence of events natural and breath-taking. Lin Yün-ming's text agrees with this.

Wei chih ("for it") on line 27 may refer to *t'i tao erh lih* ("hold the knife and stand up"). That is, "looking around" and "lost and hesitant" may well describe how he stood up with the knife on hand.

Shan ("good") is *shih* ("wipe"; Kuo Hsiang, Ma Hsü-lun), or "clean and ready the knife for future use" (Lin Hsi-i, Ch'ien Mu). Both are speculative interpretations.

Shan ("good") echoes, of course, line 3 (such a lowly occupation as butchery will *not* "go near fame"), line 28 (such a delighted praise without ulterior motive!), and line 39 (not caged "safety"). Cf. the poignant passage in 6/58.

Lines 28–29: Not only did the cook feed Ruler Wen Hui with the *result* of his act (food for physical life), but he also fed his Lord with the *words* of his act (food for life-nourishment.) And the act is that of the bloody undoing of an ox!

Not to listen (*t'ing*) attentively, but to "hear" (*wen*) pervasively, the good words, even from the mouth of a bloody cook (Mencius said, "Gentleman keeps his distance from the kitchen" 1A7), *is* life-nourishing. Such bloody dismembering, when executed according to its natural lines, nourishes life.

Line 29—"Lightly, briefly, without further ado, the entire episode is completed. It is worth a careful look" (Lin Hsi-i). ·

Lines 30–34 have *yeh* as their rhyme, signifying a fast pace of thinking. Does this story parallel the previous one? The ox is now oneself, going along with the heaven's knife!

Line 30:

Kung Wen Hsüan is Mr. "Cultured-Lofty Official." Akatzuka takes *wen hsüan* as an ornate carriage, on which this officer rides.

Yu shih ("commander of the right") is an ex-commander for Akatzuka and Watson. Lin Hsi-i takes him to be the commander who *had* been mutilated. These two men may be acquaintances (Akatzuka).

Lines 31–34:

Shih ("this-yes") is repeated. The repetition may imply an emphasis, with the force of an affirmation as opposed to *fei* ("is not") in lines 32, 34. Cf. Ch. Two, line 93; the *shih fei* opposition due to specific perspectives.

Chieh ("mutilate") may be rhymed (in sense, sound) with *chieh* ("undo"), and perhaps contrasts with *yü* ("paired") in lines 31, 33. In any case, it has the double meanings of "lone footed" (explicit) and "great and honorable" (implicit), perhaps echoing the status of being an officer, of either the inquirer or the respondent. *Ch'i* ("that") may be "or" (Wang Yin-chih). Cf. Ch. One, line 12.

Line 31:

Yü usually, in this sort of context, (1) means "with" or "and" in the sense of "or" (cf. Ch. Two, line 67), but (2) could less plausibly be taken to mean "give," which makes the sentence read "Did heaven give [this fate] to this man?"

Line 32: Who said these words? The inquirer who mumbled the answer himself, or the respondent who proudly answered and thereby instructed the inquirer? Both interpretations have supporters.

Line 33:

Tu ("alone") is (1) unique in, (2) only one-footed (Lin Hsi-i).

Yü ("pairing") may ridicule the questioning particle, *yü*, on line 31. In any case, the character here can mean (1) "pair" or "pairing" (Lin Hsi-i), (2) "to participate" (Graham), or (3) "given," "inherited" (Watson). It may have a little of all three.

Lines 35–37: On this sort of harsh life of the wild pheasant, see Lin Hsi-i.

Chih ("pheasant") rhymes with *chuo* ("peck").

Yin ("drink") may rhyme with *fan* ("cage").

Line 38:

Ch'i ("wishing") is *ch'i* ("to pray", "to request"), *ch'iu* ("to implore," "to beseech"; Ch'en Ku-ying), *yüan* ("to be willing and desirous of"; Lin Hsi-i).

Ch'u ("fed") is *yü* ("to raise"; Ma Hsü-lun), and is bad. Only *ts'ang* ("store"; line 27) and *yang* ("nourish"; line 29) are good (*shan*).

Line 39: Kuo Hsiang and Ch'en Shou-ch'ang put *chung* ("middle") in line 38, and take the line to refer to the pheasant in the wild.

Chung ("middle") is *shang* ("hurt"; Kao Heng).

Wang ("king") is *sheng wang* ("beautiful," "brilliant," "prosperous"; Ma Hsü-lun).

Pu shan ("not good"), if taken in a laudatory sense, may mean "feeling so vigorous (*wang*) and good that it actually does not feel good (*shan*)."

Lines 40–41:

Ssu ("die") and *ch'u* ("come out") are rhymed.

Shih ("lose") and *chih* ("of," "this") are rhymed.

Line 40: Lao Tan's death must have meant a lot to Chuang Tzu. In the *Chuang Tzu*, "Lao Tzu" refers to the teacher of Taoist doctrines, and "Lao Tan" refers perhaps to the historical personage as well.

Line 41:

Ch'in Shih: *Ch'in* may mean *Ch'in jen* ("man from Ch'in"), a stranger (Matthews, *Chinese-English Dictionary*, s.v. *ch'in*). *Shih* ("lose") may be *i* ("ease," "err," or "out of office"; Ma Hsü-lun). Thus *Ch'in Shih* may mean an easygoing stranger, or he who plays as such.

Akatzuka offers another guess. The name pronounces identically with *chin shih* ("advance to lose"), or is a slow pronunciation (*huan yen*) of *chi* ("swift").

The name then means he who knows life's fast pace of passing. The brisk style of lines 40–47, and his manners, can support either or both of these.

Line 48:

Ch'i jen ("that man," "those people") could be Lao Tan (line 52) or the mourners (lines 56–57).

Yeh (marker for sentence ending) is perhaps *che* ("that which"; Wang Yin-chih, p. 97), and that perhaps in lines 56, 57, 58, and 61 also. Cf. Ch. Two, lines 9, 118, 134.

I wei is "take as" here. See gloss to Ch. Two, line 82.

Lines 50–51 have a wailing rhythm.

Mu ("mother"; line 51) is Taoistic (Lao Tan was a man).

Line 52:

Pi can be "he" (Lao Tan; Lin Yün-ming) or "they" (mourners; Ch'en Shou-ch'ang).

Hui ("gather") is a gathering of symphonic wailings. Cf. line 9.

Yen ("word," "have a word") can be *yen* ("mourning with the living for their misfortunes"; Kao Heng), contrasted with *k'u* ("mourning the dead"). Cf. *The Analects* 19:25; the very Confucian ideal is condemned.

Lines 53–55 have a swift judgmental rhythm. Here *hsing* ("cane") (line 53) rhymes with *ch'ing* ("reality"; line 55), *tun* ("escape"; line 53) is *tun* ("escape"; line 55), and *pei* ("oppose") is *pei* ("turn one's back on").

Shou ("receive") is "received from heaven" (inherited) or "received from Lao Tan" (taught).

Lines 56–58 have *yeh* (cf. lines 30–34) and *sh-* as their rhymes, and that at a rolling serene pace.

Yeh: See gloss to line 48.

Line 57:

Shun ("compliance") originally means flowing with a river (Ma Hsü-lun).

Yeh: See gloss to line 48.

Line 58:

Ch'u ("dwell") is one's rightful dwelling place, as in Ch. Two, lines 207, 208.

Ju ("enter"): Does the line describe Lao Tan or mourners?

Yeh: See gloss to line 48.

Line 59:

Ti ("root entanglements") means (1) *ken ti* ("flower stem connected to the tree"; Ma Hsü-lun), (2) "the Ruler," "the controlling Heaven" (traditional interpretation). Cf. Lines 53, 55.

I do not share the latter interpretation because Chuang Tzu never shared the view of going against the Heavenly Ruler (if there be such), whether in revolt (as in the West) or by doubting its existence or by manuvering our way out of it (as this interpretation suggests, and as in Hsün Tzu, Han Fei Tzu, Wang Ch'ung, *et al*.) But this interpretation is too powerful to be avoided; I will deal with it in my Meditation, as I have done in my *Chuang Tzu: World Philosopher*, pp. 127–28.

Hsüan ("bond"): Cf. *Mencius,* "… as if they had been released from hanging by the heels" (2A1). It means *hsi* ("ties," "bonds"; Chu Kuei-yao, Liu Yen-lin, Ma Hsü-lun). Lin Hsi-i made it mean "psychic entanglements."

Line 60:

Chih ("finger-pointing") means (1) "meaning" (Graham, *Textual Notes,* p. 13); (2) "counting with fingers" (Chao Hung, Wang Fu-chih); (3) "pointed [at] by fingers" (Lin Yün-ming); (4) "pick [out] with fingers" (Yü Yüeh, Wang Hsien-ch'ien); (5) "animal fat" (*chih*; Wen I-to, Kuan Feng); or (6) "solid and alive" (Lin Yün-ming).

Hsin ("firewood"): Cf. *ch'in* ("family members"; line 4). It could be our bodily life (Lü Hui-ch'ing, Lin Yün-ming, *et al.*), or bodily form (Ch'en Shou-ch'ang).

Line 61 is rhymed on *yeh* (cf. gloss to line 48), subtly indicating the supremacy of matter-of-fact naturalness over logical-psychic wranglings.

Ch'i ("it," "they") may stand for either fuel-logs or the fire.

Line 60–61: There is a subtle play on the bad *ch'iung* ("ending"; cf. lines 1, 2) and the good *chin* ("exhausting"; cf. line 4).

Wei ("make"): Ma Hsü-lun has an unnecessary note of taking it as *hui,* "splitting trees into fuel logs."

There are many interpretations of this passage; cf. Akatzuka, 1:153–54. The danger these interpretations commonly share is that they tend to *dualism*—form against spirit, body against heart-soul—and open themselves to the Buddhist's favorite exposition of the unreality of the this-worldly, as was done by Han Shan.

Interestingly, Kao Heng takes this paragraph in a bad sense, to allude to a man's being worn down by the fire of psychic wranglings and worries about the external affairs, not realizing that his time of death is coming. This interpretation nicely echoes Lin Hsi-i's interpretation of *chih* ("knowledge"; line 1) as *hsin ssu* ("thoughts and anxieties") eternally endangering our life.

I did not follow Kao Heng's interpretation because (1) it strikes too tragic a note for a chapter ending, and (2) *chin* ("exhaustion"; lines 4, 61) and *ya* ("shoreline," "horizon," "limits"; line 1; Ch. Two, lines 280–82 and see the gloss there) have good connotations, which prevent *wu ya* ("no existence of horizons") and *pu chin* ("not exhausting") from having bad connotations.

I stick to a literal rendering, to preserve the original rich crisp ambiguities.

On the whole, collapsing different terms synonymously, we can see the picture more clearly. Suppose we take "firewood" to mean *fire,* "exhausting" to mean *finishing,* "finger-ing" to mean our resources and activities, that is, *knowing,* and "fire transmitting" to mean *changes.* Then lines 60–61 say, in effect, that "our life activities (of knowing) are limited, but our life's *changes* (involvements) are limitless."

What is dangerous is *knowing,* which consciously follows-after its objects. One must turn knowing (at the beginning of the chapter) into not-knowing (at the end). Then one can follow-along (*yüan*) the inner thrust of things, including oneself. The cook's story describes this, and the rest of the chapter elaborates on its applications.

Yüan means "cleaving to natural lines, which leads (*tao*) through seams and hollows" (line 16); a thickless nothing entering a spacious nothing (line 22); a dancing resonance with things in spontaneous un-self-conscious walkings of the spirit (lines 9, 15, 22, 25–26). And this is what knowing means (line 61), which lets us into the limitless changes of life, illustrated throughout the rest of the chapter. This is also what the latter half of Chapter Seven elaborates.

Where there is fire, there must be fuel to feed it, which (or whose ending), however, the fuel knows not. He who follows such naturalness lives and finishes out his life without knowing when, where, and how his fire/life finishes. It amounts almost to immortality—it is im-mortality.

MEDITATIONS—THREE READINGS

Again, after translation, meditative understanding. We have three readings: (A) An integrated look at the chapter, considering its internal coherence, its relation with the first two chapters, and with the rest of the Inner Chapters, (B) a close look at sections and words, and (C) *our* understanding of its message.

A. Coherence and Interrelations

1. Up to now, *what* is the Way things are (and so the way of life) has been explained. The explanation spans two chapters, a fantastic cosmological and ontological journey into the root of things, as fascinating as it is all-encompassing, including the natural interchange of identities[1] and our roaming freedom.

But *how* do we participate in such cosmological enjoyment and become ourselves? How does such roaming ontological freedom actually work in this all too painful world? To answer questions of "how" is the theme of this third chapter.

With such questions we see the Bird in a new light. That Big Bird in the first chapter changes out of the darkness of the Northern "one-knows-not-what," flies through the first and the second chapters, and reaches the "dark" suffering of the Southern "clarity-and-separateness"[2] of beings, to become separate and clear as the self is to suffer.

The theme of suffering did exist in the previous two chapters—in describing the ideal man and the ideal state in the first chapter,[3] and those mental wranglings at the beginning, and the ideal man again at the end, of the second chapter.[4] But suffering is treated in passing there; here it is faced squarely. And Chuang Tzu came up with a surprising theme: it is *in* the darkness of suffering that we nourish our life (*yang sheng*)—not just body or just spirit, but the bodily life (*shen*) and the actual years of life (*nien*). The word "in" in the preceding sentence is crucial—this is an active "in," an undoing (*chieh*), that is, a resolution, an unravelling, whose principle (and method) (*chu*) is explained in this chapter.

Thus two new themes came out and are unified here: nourishing life in suffering. The unity in this chapter is as surprising as it is vigorously mundane.

It is *soaringly* surprising; no one else has proposed the unity of life in nourishing and suffering with such pungency and such economy (without love or
redemptive god). It is *roamingly* mundane, no evading the issues of harsh
actualities, no transcedence to the beyond, no abolition of either the self or
suffering. It fulfills the vistas of the first chapter.

And the unity of nourishing and suffering in this chapter is absolutely comprehensive about the affairs of *life*—putting together in parity (*chi*) two things
(nourishing and suffering) which occupy our attention (*wu*), with allusively
beautiful rationale and order (*lun*). It fulfills in actual life what is presented in
the second chapter.

Thus, if the first two chapters are about things outside the self, this chapter
concerns the nothingness of the self. If the first two chapters treat the fantastic
infinities of things (the self is one of them), then this chapter stresses the joy
of self-limiting that trails the facts of life, in the spine of the back of the self.
If the first two chapters ride and romp, this chapter follows, meets, and becomes free and contented. Such following is really a training of oneself, which
amounts to freely trailing things. Such freedom can afford to become as
nothing, thereby to be fulfilled in life.

2.   In short, this chapter is, as its title indicates, about nourishment of life
and its principle. The title has three characters whose meanings are fairly
straightforward: *yang* is "nourishing"; *sheng* is "life"; *chu* is "lord," or
"funda-ment," "principle."

When these three characters are combined to become the title of this
chapter, we see two possible interpretations. *Yang Sheng Chu* could mean (*i*)
yang sheng-chu, nourishing the life-master, the "true Lord" (Chapter Two,
line 66) of life, what makes life what it is. Thus interpreted, this chapter is
about nourishing the essence of life. Furthermore, the title could mean (*ii*)
yang-sheng chu, the master-principle of nourishing life, the essence of caring
for life. Both interpretations have been defended by various commentators.[5]

The second interpretation seems the more plausible, for three reasons.
First: "There seems to be something genuinely in command," Chuang Tzu
confessed, "only we cannot get its clues. We can walk accordingly, trusting
ourselves to it, yet we do not see its manifest form. There is its reality, but no
figure can be seen."[6] In Chuang Tzu's opinion, we know that "something in
command" must exist, but not what it is. If this is the case, then we cannot talk
about how to nourish it, and this chapter would have been impossible.

Secondly, this chapter is concerned with protecting our body, keeping our
life whole, nourishing those closest to us, and finishing out our natural years.

Impressed with his cook, Lord Wen Hui exclaimed that he has obtained nourishment of life. We must be like Lao Tan, being at home in "time" and settling ourselves in "following along," for then sorrows or joys cannot enter us.[7] All these descriptions concern life and *its* nourishment, not nourishing its principle or its Lord.

Thirdly, nourishment of life *includes* nourishment of the lord of life, whoever he may be. There is no need to choose between the two interpretations if we choose *Yang Sheng Chu* to mean the principle (*chu*) of nourishing life (*yang sheng*).[8]

3. Immediately, however, we meet a kind of textual problem that the previous two chapters do not have. According to Watson, "The chapter is very brief and would appear to be mutilated."[9] Graham goes further and says, "The chapter is short and scrappy, surely because of textual mutilation; it is unlikely that the compilers were short of material on so basic a theme."[10] And then Graham goes on to lend his kind hand to "restoring" at least the first part of the chapter, by adding passages to it from later chapters on the basis of similarities of phrases.

Unfortunately, similarity of wording does not automatically indicate that Chuang Tzu's original sentences have been dispersed in those places. In fact, Graham's additions seem less an elucidation of Chuang Tzu's thoughts than a haphazard potpourri of diverse thoughts in Chuang Tzu's phraseology, if not tiresome alliterations of his words torn out of context. All of the passages Graham picked smack of later concoctions, as both Akatzuka and Fukunaga also noted.[11]

It seems more fitting, then, to take Graham's additions as just that, *additions,* the afterthoughts of later writers inspired by Chuang Tzu, than to take them as parts of Chuang Tzu's original words that somehow got scattered into later chapters. The latter impression is more difficult to entertain than the former. For these additions hinder the coherence of the third chapter more than they enhance it. They distract us from the main flow of the chapter.

Curiously no Chinese or Japanese commentator (that I know) has said that the chapter was truncated or dislocated, much less proposed any reason for such a hypothesis.[12] The mutilation hypothesis came about perhaps for four reasons (I am just guessing): (*i*) The text is unusually short—the shortest in the Inner Chapters, and only sixteen characters longer than the shortest chapter in the *Chuang Tzu*, Chapter Nine, titled, "Horses' Hoofs." (*ii*) Most of its phrases can have more than one meaning, due to the abrupt shortness of their meaning-context. (*iii*) While "Horses' Hoofs" is coherent, treating one theme, this chapter has no less than six themes, all seemingly unrelated.[13] (*iv*) Worse, these seemingly random themes seem to contradict the title that advertizes the main theme of the chapter. The title promises the principle of life nourishment; the stories are about violence, death, and suffering. Thus the shortness of the chapter, its ambiguous phrases, its random themes, which contradict the title—all seem to point to the hypothesis, "The text appears to be mutilated."

My reply is threefold: considering textual style, contextual significance, and coherence with the other Inner Chapters. First, as to the text. The shortness of Chapter Three is hardly reason for claiming that it is muti-lated; Chapter Nine is shorter. The words and phrases here are not any more or less ambiguous than those in other chapters; if anything, the words in this chapter are clearer. Besides, they are studded with resonance of rhymes and allusions. In my opinion, this is a rare masterpiece of philosophical poetry. There is a natural distinct style, unsuspected cadence, rhyme, and progression of thought. Frequent rhymes and echoes show how phrases mirror, refer, and resonate among themselves, via sounds to meanings then back to sounds. Allusions and parallelisms are everywhere, so much so that we are led to believe that this chapter is not a bungled text but an accomplished one.[14] Any addition (a la Graham) would destroy the literary and philosophical integrity of the chapter.[15] Here Chuang Tzu was not imposing rhythmic form on alien facts; the rhythmic form emerges out of and expresses the intelligible progression of the sense of facts.

Secondly, as will be shown in the next two sections (4 and 5) of this Meditation, it is possible to present a meaningful transition from one story to another, thereby exhibiting a sensible loop-coherence embracing the entire chapter, which in turn can be shown to present a revolutionary thesis.

Thirdly, the six themes in this chapter can be shown to correspond with the main theme of each of the six other Inner Chapters. Thus, the third chapter can be taken as the gist of the Inner Chapters, as will be shown in Section 6.

Of course my reply is not conclusive. In the world of ancient texts, especially in the *Chuang Tzu*, nothing is conclusive. As Hu Shih dramatically illustrated, even passages that have previously been taken to be obviously sentential can be shown to be personal names by a newly discovered "original text."[16] In such a world, prudence dictates my objection to the multilation hypothesis with regard to the third chapter. If that hypothesis were true, it would justify a counsel of moratorium on our exegetical efforts. For all our attempts at emendation are merely more or less probable, and the mutilation hypothesis does not help us understand this chapter at all. If the hypothesis proves to be false, however, it would have unjustifiably hindered our best exegetical efforts. Thus if true, the hypothesis does not help; and if false, it does us harm. The best course is, then to proceed as if the chapter were intact, as most commentators have done. Before that particular "original text" appears to us, our only sensible approach to the ancient text is to observe the text *as it is*. Our responsibility is to see if *it* possesses its own integrity and progression of thoughts.

4.   We see at least two points in relation to the third chapter as it is. First, it has the mutuality of nourishment and suffering. Second, such mutuality characterizes the entire Inner Chapters.

First, there is mutuality of nourishment and suffering. The title is concerned with nourishing our life, yet in five of its six parts the chapter tells us about cutting up an ox, amputation, harsh wildlife, death, and fire—all external and destructive. We can even see a progressive character in the arrangement of the stories. First, we undo an ox. Then, our leg is gone. Then, after the harsh life of a wild pheasant, our entire person is off—in the funeral of Lao Tan our teacher. Finally, we are continually burned till we are burned out, despite our ignorance.

On a closer look—and perhaps this is what the chapter is designed for, to make us look closer, for the nourishment of life consists partly in coming to be perceptive—undoing an ox is entering its inner spaces with the thickless knife—it is not cutting but fitting and dancing, cutting without cutting. Likewise with amputation, death, and fire. Amputation (suffered perhaps for political reason) is a natural (*t'ien*) catastrophe; it is not something *we* (*jen*) expect to see in life. Death without pathetic wailings is an ordinary death. The fire passes on without concern for the logs because the fire burns not the logs themselves (they do not know) but the fuel (*chih*) in them. Burning is without burning for them; but when the fuel is spent, the logs are reduced to ashes. They thus finish themselves up naturally, "finishing out our natural years" (4).

In short, in all this suffering we must live as if we were dancing, following the heavenly and the natural, climaxing in not knowing we are burned up.[17] This is to nourish our lives. Nourishment occurs not high in the misty mountains away from this world's suffering, but in the very midst of suffering.

The chapter says two things, then. First, life is as sharp as the butcher's cleaver that cuts into the ox, whatever it is—the self, life, the world, society, nature, problems. Various natural and political mishaps can amputate us, in whatever sense—psychically, physically, financially. Death can happen to our teacher, our ideal, our parents, our children, even ourselves. Fire can burn on us as the fire of psychic and social-occupational disasters.

Secondly, we cannot and should not evade them. We live in their midst, yet can be without cut or burn. We can go on living without dulling our knife and find life as satisfying as the marsh pheasant does. The secret is to stay on with (*yüan*) the throbbings of our spinal arteries of life energy, not to follow after (*sui*)[18] the limitless knowledge with the limited life. Neither the limited nor the limitless is wrong; following after either one is.

Thus the chapter begins with the dangerous (insisting on knowing the limitless) and ends with the blissful (going without knowing), that is, enjoying our allotted years as the beautiful marsh pheasant amidst natural risks.

How do we find self-nourishing in dangers? Remember Lord Wen Hui who praised the lowly butcher for teaching him how to nourish life. The butcher is an agent of death, in the lowly caste; the Lord is the helmsman of social happiness. We would have expected the Lord to teach the butcher how to nourish life; it was the reverse. We must learn from the lowly nittygritty of the infliction and reception of suffering, which teaches us how to live happily *there*.

5. Contrary to our first impression that this chapter is "scrappy" (Graham), it can be found to be internally coherent. Those seemingly stray fragments can be seen to refer one to another, mutually dovetailing into a surprising theme. Such mutual weaving can be shown in five ways:

(1) Six fragments reflect on each other to comprise a loop and allude to the three characters in the title, in a manner similar to that we found in the second chapter (C.2.1.2.), and in the first chapter as well (C.1.1.).

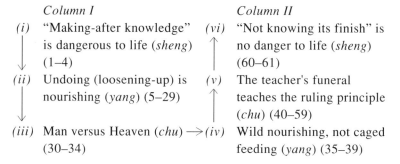

	Column I		Column II
(i)	"Making-after knowledge" is dangerous to life (*sheng*) (1–4)	*(vi)*	"Not knowing its finish" is no danger to life (*sheng*) (60–61)
(ii)	Undoing (loosening-up) is nourishing (*yang*) (5–29)	*(v)*	The teacher's funeral teaches the ruling principle (*chu*) (40–59)
(iii)	Man versus Heaven (*chu*) (30–34) →*(iv)*	Wild nourishing, not caged feeding (*yang*) (35–39)

If making after limitless knowledge exhausts and endangers our limited life (*i*), then to undo the oxen of things is life-nourishing (*ii*). Such undoing goes with a knife which can, by heavenly inevitability, make us singular-footed (*iii*). This process goes from *sheng* (*i*) to *yang* (*ii*) to *chu* (*iii*); this is column I of the loop.

But such heavenly (natural and wild) danger is worth risking, for no feeding in the cage can hide its being not-good; true nourishing (*yang*) comes in the wild (*iv*). Such wild-nourishing can end in the death even of our teacher; in his funeral, however, we discern the principle of life (*chu*) (*v*). If we follow along this principle, we can afford not to know our own finish; we can live (*sheng*) (*vi*). Thus we go from *yang* (*iv*) to *chu* (*v*) to *sheng* (*vi*). This is column II of the loop.

And so we start (*i*) and end (*vi*) with *sheng*, in which *yang* and *chu* alternately reflect and weave one on the other, first *yang* (*ii*) on *chu* (*v*), then *chu* (*iii*) on *yang* (*iv*). We have an interweaving of the title (*Yang Sheng Chu*) in the loop.

(2) We note that a line or a phrase can be found to be the main theme to each of the six segments of the text:

> *In segment I* (1–4) we stay on with the spine artery as our constant passage (3);
> *In segment II* (5–29) we let things inherently so lead us as (17) to enter the inner spaces of things with the thickless (22);
> *In segment III* (30–34) the reason for heaven's giving birth to such a singular-footed man is to let this man become unique (33);
> *In segment IV* (35–39) caged feeding is not good (39);
> *In segment V* (40–59) we can either go to the Cane of Escaping Heaven or be at home in "time" to loosen up the bonds of entanglements (59);
> *In segments VI* (60–61) fire transmits itself, not knowing its end (61).

We then realize that they form themselves into two columns of three points, as follows:

Segments	I	and	IV	explain the principle of nourishing life;
Segments	II	and	V	elaborate and apply it;
Segments	III	and	VI	show its results.

And so this chapter solidly delivers what its title promises.

(3) We see line 3 proclaiming the "fittingness" (*shih*; 56–58) of our staying on with the spine artery as life's constant passage, and see line 4 explaining its result, the freedom of "playing about" (*yu*; 22), in which we *can* protect our body, keep our life whole, nourish what is closest to us, and finish out our natural years.

These two main themes, fit and play, are explained in a reverse order:

THE PLAY	THE FIT
(*a*) Life dances with symphonic ↓ tunes of the ancients (8, 9)	(*d*) The bliss of life transmits in ↑ our ignorance (61)
(*b*) We delight in the Way things ↓ go (12)	(*b'*) We settle in "time" and ↑ "following along" (59)
(*c*) We cleave to inherent ──────> naturalness of things (16, 17)	(*c'*) Political inevitability is linked to natural inevitability (30–33)

This set is also a loop, going from (*a*) to (*b*) to (*c*) to (*c'*) to (*b'*) to (*a'*). This set also internally relfect one part on the other, (*a*) on (*a'*), (*b*) on (*b'*), (*c*) on (*c'*).

(4) When we look at the two longest stories in the chapter, the ox-undoing (5–29) and the funeral (40–59), we see correlations of a sort among their parts, indicated by line numbers:

5 and 40–41:	Introduction.
6–9 and 42:	Events.
13–15 and 48:	Contrasts between then and now.
15–17 and 49–51:	Description.
18–20 and 52–55:	Elucidation—*hsing* ("grindstone") echoes *hsing* ("cane").
21–23 and 56:	The cook's easy-going echoes the master's welcome coming.
24–27 and 57:	The cook's hard going echoes the master's sad going.
28–29 and 58–59:	Conclusion.

There is an interesting snag in the conclusion part. In the story of the cook, the undoing (28) is followed by the nourishing (29), whereas in the death story, the nourishing by settling ourselves in the times (58) is followed by the loosen-ing (59). The first story is focused on the undoing of an ox; in the second story the self is the ox, and attention is on letting undo.[19]

Why are these two notions (undoing, nourishing) reversed in the conclusions of the two long stories? Perhaps for two reasons: (*i*) the second story reversed its conclusion in order to link up to the first story, and (*ii*) to lead to the final conclusion in lines 60–61.

(5) The chapter's six sections can be seen to form themselves into two groups. In the *first group* key terms are arranged like this:

Staying-on-with (*yüan*) makes for the constant-passage (*ching*) in the first story;

Undoing (*chieh*) follows the natural Way of things (*tao*)
    in the second story;
Amputation (*chieh*) comes from natural Heaven (*t'ien*)
    in the third story.

This series is arranged in the order of ascending severity and mystery:
from staying-with to loosening-up to amputation in our life activities, and
from constant-passage to the Way to natural Heaven, in our life process.

In the *second group* key terms are arranged around the negative *pu*:

Not-good (*pu shan*) describes caged-feeding (*ch'u hu fan*)
    in the fourth story;
Cannot-enter (*pu neng ju*) describes bond-undoing (*hsüan chieh*)
    in the fifth story;
Not-knowing the finish (*pu chih chin*) describes the fire
    transmission (*huo ch'uan*) in the sixth story.

Thus the *pu*-phrases describe the situation (the how), and caged-feeding,
bond-loosening, fire-transmitting describe what is the case (the what). Again,
this series is arranged in ascending order of severity and ultimacy, from not-
good (external judgment) to cannot-enter (safety) to not-knowing (immortality) on our part, and from caged to loosened to goings-on in the situation.

The first group describes the principle of the life-nourishment; the second
group applies it. Both groups have the same structure: short introduction
(contrasts), long story (centered on *chieh*), and short conclusion (in ultimate
situation). Interestingly, the first group is full of activities dealing with things,
and the second group is pervaded with serenity in ourselves—both amidst the
pain of this world.

All in all, these five ways of looking at the story-fragments convince us
that the chapter is anything but fragmentary. They cohere and co-mirror into
a coherent whole, proposing the surprise principle of nourishing life in
suffering.

6. So much for the unity and coherence of the chapter. As to its
connection, or correspondence, with the rest of the Inner Chapters (the first
seven chapters in the *Chuang Tzu* reputed to have been authentically written
by Chuang Tzu himself), my bold assumption is that the third chapter can be
seen as a summary of the Inner Chapters, all concerned ultimately with happy
living-in-suffering.

Let us take another look at the arrangement of the third chapter:[20]

Story 1: Life is limited but knowledge is not. Life should not follow after knowledge but should instead stay on with lifes's own inner throbbings at its spine.

Story 2: The butcher cleaves to natural lines and undoes the ox.

These two stories concern the principle of nourishing life.

Story 3: The singularity of the one-footed Commander is due to natural Heaven.

Story 4: The marsh pheasant is happy strutting in the wild.

These two stories concern the foot, the walking, hence, the living.

Story 5: Lao Tan's death is an "undoing of the bond."

Story 6: The fire goes on, ignorant of its finish.

These two stories concern dealing with death.

Now, this arrangement can also be seen as the gist and structure of the entire Inner Chapters, if we realize how each story corresponds with one of the other Inner Chapters, in the following manner:

Story 1 corresponds with Chapter One, for its freedom and self-fulfilment;

Story 2 corresponds with Chapter Two, for its freedom within things;

Story 3 corresponds with Chapter Five, for its allusion to the sagely handicapped;

Story 4 corresponds with Chapter Four, for its allusion to freedom amidst risks in life;

Story 5 corresponds with Chapter Six, for its allusion to friendship and death; and

Story 6 corresponds with Chapter Seven, for its not-knowing and its freedom in the ultimate realm.

Such a scheme of correspondence has its strength in covering the entire seven chapters in the Inner Chapters. Its weakness lies in its necessity to reverse the correspondence at midpoint—Story 3 with Chapter Five, and Story 4 with Chapter Four.

An alternative scheme of correspondence is as follows:

Story 2 corresponds with Chapter Four, regarding "ox" as the world of men, where mind-fasted Yen Hui goes as freely in and out of risks as the thickless knife of the Cook;

Story 3 and 4 correspond with Chapter Five, seeing that

Story 4 is a positive explication of the free spirit in Story 3;

Story 5 corresponds with Chapter Six; and

Story 6 corresponds with Chapter Seven (both for reasons mentioned above).

This scheme has the advantage of not reversing the order of correspond-ence, but the disadvantage is that it leaves Chapters One and Two, and Story 1, unaccounted for. Perhaps we can say that Story 1 is not a story but a summary of the entire Chapter Three, and that since this chapter follows the first two chapters, this chapter does not need to treat them. But the explanation does not sound convincing.

In any case, if the experiment we have conducted seems at all plausible, the shortness of this chapter becomes understandable. The shortness demonstrates forcibly the coherence of this Chapter as a summary of the rest of the Inner Chapters (or at least all the chapters in the Inner Chapters that follow this one).[21] We can now go into the details of Chapter Three.

B.   Segments and Words

1.1.   *Line 1*: The first line is a model to the rest—tantalizingly unclear, although entirely (even trivially) clear on the surface.

On the surface it means what it says: Knowledge is limitless, life is limited; it is dangerous to follow after the limitless with the limited. This is clear enough and trivial enough. But what does it mean? Why so? How does this pronouncement illuminate or summarize the rest of the chapter?

Many commentators have had their hand in interpreting the line for us.[22] None has convinced us with the final explanation. This is worse than reading the *Tao Te Ching*, which at least intimates that we are confronted with some-thing deep. This line reads trite.

What anyone could hope for, then, is to be careful, try his best, and wait for something deeper and more convincing. Perhaps Chuang Tzu did mean the passage to be read this way, ever beckoning, ever challenging, ever alive. So obvious yet so obscure—this is what it means to be alive. Our life is mirrored in such passages as this.

1.2.   While the first chapter started with the surrounding world, the second chapter with our reaction to it, this chapter starts with "my life" (*wu sheng*); *wu* can be "my" or "our," the self that is true and truthful (as in Chapter Two).[23] The word "I" in this authentic sense appears at the crucial junctures in the chapter (and in life), where "I" see difficulties (24), hear the deep words of life nourishment from an unexpected place (28), consider someone to be the one (48), enter to mourn (49).

Furthermore, it is "my *life*" that is treated in this chapter, not death, which is never mentioned as such. Yet the chapter concerns all the mortal dangers of life. Perhaps Chuang Tzu tells us that despite our fear of various risks to life, its real danger is somewhere *else*.

The fact is that knowledge is beyond us, and the real danger lies in following after what is beyond us. He did not tell us what the danger is, because that is not the point of the chapter (although he repeated the warning—"Danger!" (*tai*)—twice). The point is a positive one, to come soon (3–4).

1.3. We must not overlook the connection between knowledge and danger. Lin Hsi-i in his usual surprising vein proposed that "knowledge" (*chih*) here means "thoughts" (*ssu*). With the limited actual (bodily) life we follow after limitless thoughts—such confusions, such vexations, no one knows when they cease, said Lin.

Now "thoughts" here are more psychic broodings than cognitive knowledge. Yet Lin may have a point. If ignorance is bliss, then knowledge must be (or at least lead to) misery. If knowledge is power, then power is also misery, or at least leads us to misery. If to brood over some unresolved thoughts is one sure way to hell, then to strain after knowledge is also hell, which is tension and imbalance.

Knowledge itself may not be dangerous; to follow after it is. For knowledge and brooding are cousins; to be capable of the one is to be capable of the other. And once one is in them, one tends to follow after them endlessly (*wu ya*); sadly, one's short life cannot afford it.

Two examples from this chapter may help. First, Lao Tan's disciples thought that he pursued (followed after) knowledge with his life, and so when his life ended they thought his teaching ended also. This amounts to thinking that Lao Tan devoted his life to the pursuit of his teaching, and to the captivation of his disciples lives, making them slaves following after his teaching. No wonder Lao Tan's death constituted such an immense misery to them (lines 40–59).

The second example is the final two lines (lines 60–61), saying that although our handling of firewood ends at making firewood, the fire goes on without *knowing* its finish. Knowledge is something conscious and explanatory, an explanation inserted between the knower and the known. Thus knowledge is knowledge with distance. And yet to know something is also to be familiar with it and to digest it cognitively. Thus we are tensed up between two pulls of knowing—to distance and to digest, to be apart and to be a part.[24] This is the eternally insoluble dilemma of knowledge, and to follow after such an eternal torment with our limited life is (to court) danger. Moreover, comprehensive knowledge is an impossibility, if not self-defeating. For to know all includes knowing our knowing, which is impossible; we can never catch ourselves knowing, with our knowing.[25]

All in all, to follow after knowledge with life is like pursuing the limitless with the limited, exhausting our life in the fire of frustration. "Fire" here is both suffering and life. The solution comes when we come to not-know. Not-knowing suffering is not knowing life's end, thereby being enabled to finish out our natural years. *How* we can do so is the main theme of this chapter.

2. *Lines 2–3: Wei* means "to do," "to contrive," "to make." Chuang Tzu understandably regards it as less than the ideal of life. Here *wei* is either contriving-making knowledge, as we make firewood (60), or contriving a "good" and a "bad" for oneself. Such *wei* implies conscious pursuit, a "following after knowledge." And this explains how risky indeed it is to "make (after)" knowledge (2)—not to mention the risks involved in the knowledge itself and in the mismatch of the bounded with the boundless.

And yet when we move and act we cannot help being conscious, if not also pursuant. The secret (guiding principle) of avoiding the risk of consciousness (if not contrivance) is to combine (not avoid) *wei* with *wu*, its negation. Hence line 3, "In 'making' 'good' we had better not (*wu*) go near fame (name), as in the 'making' of 'bad' we do not (*wu*) go near cane." We do the so-called "good" stealthily, not letting the left hand know what the right hand does; we are not self-conscious about it. It takes a thief to do good—to be safe from name (a social manifestation of self-consciousness, if not contrivance). We can then avoid being caught in disaster as bad as the "cane" for thievery. In short, never follow after the labels of "good" and "bad," even in our own consciousness, while we do something.

In an extra-ordinary situation of difficulty, we need a peculiar *combination* of *wei* and not-knowing (24–27). *Wei* is now almost an exclamatory particle that accompanies our care and concentration. Just think—a doing as an exclamation of selfless concentration!—as is well shown in the final description, "I hold the knife and stand up, looking around. At first lost and hesitant, I slowly find myself, satisfied. I 'good' my knife (lovingly wipe it) and store it away." (27).

But all this moves us more than it clarifies, and so Chuang Tzu gave us a hint with the phrase, *yüan tu* (3). *Tu* can mean something social or something medical. Socially it means "to investigate and ascertain," or "direct," or even "reprove"; or (as noun) "the spinal-fold of a dress." Medically *tu* means "the spinal meridian-channel for life-energy." *Yüan* can mean either "to decorate the hems of a dress," or "to stay along with something," "to follow along," "to move according to something;" or (as noun) as "cause," "destiny," a "connection," or a "hem."[26]

Putting these meanings together, *yüan tu* can mean: (a) decorating along the spinal fold-seam of a dress, (b) staying on with the spinal meridian-channel of life-energy, or (c) being pushed, and then responding—only when one cannot help it does one arise, only by following the push does one start (as in Lin Hsi-i.)[27] The first meaning is barely noted by commentators.[28] The second is most popular, even standard. The third is peculiar to Lin Yün-ming (to my knowledge).

We can see three implications for our ideal deeds running through these meanings. They are those which are: (*i*) non-conscious, not deliberate, (*ii*) a staying on with things, (*iii*) and crucial to life—in a word, we are at our best when we follow along with nature. We can then be non-deliberate; the spinal fold or artery cannot be seen, nor can a natural push be planned in advance. We can only stay *on* with them, with their natural way, being on it, being it.

One can either bike one's way *to* an intended destination, or simply bike as a born biker, and find one's destination. One can follow *after* something, or one can go along the river bank, without pushing the river. Such nondeliberative staying on with the spinal seam of a dress, the spinal artery of life energy of things, or an urge from beyond one's contrivance, is *crucial*. For it is spinal; one's life depends on it. If one stays on with the nondeliberative urge to stay on the spinal fold (or artery) of life energy, one can course through the folds and seams of the oxen of things; there will be no cutting or breaking. The course will be one's constant path of effortlessness.

Thus the phrase *yüan tu* has two possible meanings, both of which are jointly implied. First, we feel our way through the invisible vital spinal artery of the energy that pervades the inner self and the entire cosmos. Such energy (*shen*) passes through the tubes and spaces of a thing and makes it what it is. It is such vital paths of things that we go through. Second, we go through the spinal fold-seam of a dress that stitches pieces together into the dress we see, the dress, as it were, of things. To navigate through such seams is to track along the natural veins (inherent seams) of things (16–17, 22). Such tracking is invisible ("spinal") to our consciousness, and so is natural. We can then "cut through" things (such as oxen) without cutting them; we can merely loosen them up by unfolding their seams. Such riding on the spinal thrust of things contrasts with the tensed pursuit of the goal of knowledge in line 1. There is nothing wrong with the bounded or the boundless. The risk lies in the incongruity of the tensed matching of the two. The secret is to find the middle channel, the spinal seam, and stay on with it.

3. *Line 4*: To find the spinal route and stay with it is the guiding principle of nourishing life. The Cook told his Lord how he found this royal route of nourishment by being true to his lowly task of butchery, the task as much related to life as death is. His knife ceased to cut; it merely cleaved along the natural seams to loosen up an ox. And the Commander on the Right on his part realized the heavenly nature by staying with himself and becoming singularly himself, that is, singular-footed. He lived out his natural years with the wild pheasant in the ensuing story and the wise Lao Tan in the story after that of the pheasant.

All this is emphatically implied in line 4, where "can" (not *k'o* but *k'o i*) is repeated four times. The drawn-out pronunciation of *k'o i* and its repetitions give us the feeling of tarrying here and enjoying ourselves, then there, then there, in a free and unhurried roaming, as in the first chapter (Meditation A.6.). Line 22 describes a leisurely playing-about ("roaming," *yu*) of the Cook's knife as it enters the interstices in the ox. Lines 1 through 3 describe how to come to the freedom presented in line 4; in fact, lines 1 to 4 can be seen as a summary of Chapters One and Two.

We can protect and preserve our body (psychosomatic personhood), can fulfill (keep whole) our life, can nourish those close to us, thereby can finish out our natural years. These four freedoms can mean the same, a fourfold assertion of the freedom of living—if we take "to preserve," "to fulfill," "to nourish," and "to finish out" to be mutually synonymous, and also take "body," "life," "those close to us," and "our natural years" to be mutually synonymous.

Or else they can be taken as a summary of the third chapter:

The freedom of preserving our body describes that of nourishment
    that goes with the cook's knife;
The freedom of fulfilling our inner life urge describes the single-
    footed Commander and the marsh pheasant—both follow their
    own life urge without succumbing to foreign pressures;
The freedom of nourishing those close to us describes the true
    relation of Lao Tan to those around him;
The freedom of finishing out one's natural years describes how the
    fire (of life) goes on by not knowing its finish.

4.1. *Lines 5–29*: The cook's knife describes how to ramble away in life "without dying young by axes" (Chapter One, line 164; the conclusion of the first chapter) and all that implies.

The story begins with a name, *p'ao ting*. *P'ao* could either mean "kitchen" or serve as a homophone for "brother" (*pao*). *Ting* could be either a surname, Mr. Ting, or a "chap," "that fellow." Thus *p'ao ting* could be (1) Mr. Ting the cook, (2) that fellow in the kitchen, a cook, (3) brother Ting, or (4) fellow brother, a fellow human being.[29]

Chuang Tzu may have had all these meanings in mind when he produced "*p'ao ting*," which is significant. As Socrates' "slave boy" in the *Meno* taught us the universal truth of teaching-as-reminding, so this cook is a concrete particular that represents humanity. Every human being has a name, every particular human being is a proper noun, a concrete universal. I am humanity, and "all things and I make one" (Chapter Two, line 163).

Be that as it may, a cook is a cook is a cook. He is of the lowliest class in society, relieved of the danger of going "near fame." He nourishes his lord by undoing an ox. As long as his lord (though of the highest rank in society) is nourished and taught by the lowliest of his subjects, the lord is also relieved of the danger of fame. So, at a stroke the first line of the story (5) hit concretely at line 3—at least its first half. To be nameless is to be holy; and we have here, in the single lowly butcher knife, two nameless holy men, for "the holy man has no name" (Chapter One, line 69).[30]

Then we see the undoing of an ox, in order to feed. To feed is to "undo" in blood—pain can feed. And such bloody butchery can be a joy to behold (10), a dance in a prideful ancient rhythm, which echoes throughout the cosmos—after all, everyone must eat. The description (6–9) *shows* its rhyme and rhythm. Pain can be joy, pride, and rhythm. Such rhythm reminds us of the old ritual dance for rain. It is a cosmic dance tune that concretizes the history of the entire community (ritual dance) and echoes the cosmos (for rain):

> The hands touch,
> The shoulders lean,
> The feet plant,
> The knees press;
> Swoosh! Swish! The meat is whisked from the bones,
> The performing knife zings through the ox,
> Hitting the tune of the Dance of Mulberry Forest,
> The symphonic tune of the Neck and the Head (or
>   Passing through the Head).   *(Lines 6–9)*

All this is joy and expertise; and it is natural. To be an expert is to be experienced, trailing, tracking nature, becoming natural. Nature is rhythmical—in space and in season, at the right spot and time. To find and dwell in the spatio-temporal rightness is to be natural, to be an expert. No wonder the lord is delighted. It is the delightful expertise of undoing the ox of things.[31]

4.2. The beautiful movement of the cook's knife reminds the lord of two pieces of music, the dance of Mulberry Forest and the symphonic music of Ching Shou.

According to Chu Kuei-yao, the Mulberry Forest is a dance music named after a place called Mulberry Forest (in Sung territory), where the legendary Emperor T'ang cut his hair and fingernails short, presented himself as a sacrifice, and prayed for rain to relieve seven years of drought. The music is that with which to dance and pray for rain (for crops). "Mulberry" also symbolized home, peace, native soil, civilization.[32]

According to both Chu Kuei-yao and Wang Shu-min,[33] the Ching Shou is a symphonic music that is part of an orchestral suite called Hsien Ch'ih (the Universal Pond) that is also mentioned in 14/14. According to Akatzuka, Hsien Ch'ih is the mythologized Eastern Ocean where the sun rises, and the Hsien Ch'ih music is the music as vivacious and auspicious as the sunrise, to be played in the mid-spring month (February). Spring is the season of things sprouting in life, not at all the season of butchery.

There seems, then, to be bitter irony and profound truth here. Those musical pieces are unmistakably those of the spring, the rain, and the rising of life with the sun. The beautiful knife of the butcher is unmistakably that of autumnal slaughter, the opposite of the spring of life.[34] Here then life and death are joined in the dance—of life! The butcher's expertise is the skill that joins life and death, the spring and the autumn, in the dance that rises with the rain and the sun.

4.3. Such expertise is not mere skill, as the cook insisted, though it *is* skill. It is the skill of no skill, the experience in the Way of things, a following of the Way. The cook is given to it. How did he make it?

The cook must have paused here. He took a breath, then spread out a poetic architectonic, describing his favorite—the Tao of undoing an ox. It is a stun-ning triptych of moving pictures:

Lines 13–17: About himself and his three stages of progress from the past preoccupation with the ox ("saw nothing but oxen"), to his technical care on specifics ("never saw a whole ox"), to his yielding to the flow of spiritual (spinal?) vitality pervading his knife and his meeting with the ox ("the spirit walks as it desires"). It is a journey from the past to the present. The key terms are "cleaving-to" (*i*) and "spirit" (*shen*).

Lines 18–23: About the knife and its threefold contrast in the progress in the ox—his knife is not like the good cook's to be replaced yearly because it is chipped (because it chips into the ox), much less is it like the common cook's knife to be replaced monthly because it is broken (because it breaks into the ox). *His* knife is ever fresh off the grindstone, even after nineteen years of continual use. The knife "things things"—it enters into the ox and the ox loosens itself. The knife is not "thing-ed by things," because the cook does not use the ox to cut and chip the knife.[35] The key terms are "enter" (*ju*) and "nothing" (*wu*), not cutting; it is cutting without cutting.

Lines 24–27: About the unity of the cook and the knife in the difficult places, fully manifesting his expertise beyond expertise. It is a threefold unity of the self, the knife, and the difficulty. The key terms are "submitting" (*wei*) and "loosening" (*chieh*).

All this is a complex of implications in the simple phrase, a "loosening up of the ox" (5). The complex is a threefold description from three perspectives: the agents (the self, the knife, and their unity with the ox), the movement (the progress of the self to the spirit, the cutting without cutting, and the expertise in the difficult places), and the key terms (two terms in each section).

This structured complex, plus the beauty of the rhyme and rhythm of brief phrases[36] make this story a classic that delights every reader.[37]

Immediately we need to look into the number "three" and the number "nineteen" (line 19). Then we must discern what those key terms imply.

4.4. The number "three" (*san*) is one of the favorites of the Chinese. It has three implications:

(1) "Three" expresses the multiplicity of an object, and multiplicity in turn implies abundance and inexhaustibility.

(2) "Three" expresses an intensity of meaning: "three suns" means effulgence, "three tongues" means excessive talking, "three trees" means a forest, and so on.

(3) "Three" is the way of heaven, earth, and man.[38]

Although usually spatial, "three" is used processively by Taoism and in the *Book of Changes*, with all the preceding implications of abundance and intensity. Without explicitly treating "three," Chuang Tzu often resorts to "three" to express the processive dynamism of growth into sageliness,[39] as here in this chapter.

As for the number "nineteen" (*shih chiu*), I suspect that it may have come out of some combination of the following three motives:

(1) To purposely avoid any common symbolic meaning to number.

(2) To intimate profound intuitions such as these: Nineteen is one short of twice ten, and so "nineteen" has three components: ten, twice, and one short.

(a) "Ten" (*shih*) is written in Chinese as the crossing of a horizontal line and a vertical line, and is the most accomplished of numbers. The horizontal represents the east and the west, the vertical represents the south and north, and together they comprise the cardinal points and the center.[40]

(b) "Twice" is "two" (*erh*) and represents the heaven above and the earth below (or the power of the earth, "one" being the heaven), or the dual powers, Yin and Yang.[41] And so "twenty" must be a gathering of all the universe of things and their powers.

(c) "One short" then means "almost," just before reaching the fulness of perfection, and that is the best condition—being full yet having room yet to grow, for a complete fulness is a step before the decline.

Therefore "nineteen" signifies a dynamic fulness of movement, characteristic of the ever-fresh dancing of the ever-fresh knife of the cook.

(3) To compound the meanings of two numbers, "ten" and "nine." "Ten" has been described as the perfection of the universe. "Nine" (*chiu*) is (a) the ultimate of numbers or numerousness, (b) the ultimate Yang in the *Book of Changes*, (c) the south, as in the destination of the Big Bird (Chapter One, lines 4-5, 43), (d) a "long time," (*chiu*), "old," (*lau*), and (e) a "gathering" (*chu*), as of "pigeons" (*chiu*).[42]

Thus, no matter which meaning we choose, the "nineteen years" is a long and significant period of time.

4.5. As for the key terms in the cook's story, there are three sets—a verb and a noun, a verb and an adjective, and two verbs—all of them thoroughly dynamic and serene.

4.5.1. *Verb and noun: I*—to lean and "rely on," to be lovingly attached to.[43] The cook leans on the natural veins of the ox as he cleaves along its huge seams and slides through, as if the cook is lovingly attached to them. This is what the cook likes (*hao*, 12), and is also what the spirit desires (*yü*, 15); the intuitive thrust of the vital force leads the knife on through the ox smoothly. What is this vital thrust (*shen*)?

Shen has three meanings:

(i) That which draws out everything as it is, giving birth to things as they are, the élan vital of the universe, hinted at in Chapter One, and elaborated in Chapter Thirteen.

(*ii*) What *shen* does to man is his *shen*, the vitality and spiritousness of a man. Lack of human *shen* (one of the Three Treasures in human health) leads to unconsciousness or madness. Human *shen* is the alertness, the luster in the eye, the vitality behind *ching* the source of life and *ch'i* the ability to activate. Chapters 11, 14, and 15 are about the human *shen* and how to cultivate it.

(*iii*) The daemonic wonders one can perform when at one with *shen* is also *shen* (divine spiritedness), as in artwork.[44] This is almost like the Socratic *daemon*, though without its nagging foreboding, forbidding connotations. Chapter Nineteen is a collection of such marvels, various extensions of the cook's story here.

Now, the wonders that human beings can perform seem to arise (as Fukunaga said) out of the union of natural *shen* and human *shen*, but the union is less a Faustian selling off of one's identity than an invigoration of one's deepest vitality, the "force of human personality" (Kaptchuk), which somehow echoes in affinity with the cosmic élan vital. It is the Socratic daemon with a positive connotation, not dulling but sharpening one's awareness, sensitivity, and versatility with things, enabling one to be an expert as divine as the creator gods (*shen*). Heraclitus expressed this cosmic depths of the spirit of a person well when he said, "You could not discover the limits of the soul, even if you traveled every road to do so; such is the depth of its meaning (*logos*),"[45] although Heraclitus may not have meant what is meant here. Traveling every road is to travel the world (in all its divine meanings). Our inability to discover the limits of the soul signifies that the soul is coeval with the cosmos, in the midst of which it is. Hence our discovery of the world is through our probings into the depths of ourselves. To reveal or rather release such depths-of-ourselves which echo the world, is the Tao of the Cook who attained the divinity of his skill in the undoing (releasing?) of the ox.

What does such divine spiritousness have to do with the ordinary sensory faculties? Lines 13 and 14 treat this theme. Though both lines talk about seeing (*chien*), there is a difference. Sensory seeing (*kuan*) dominates line 13 where the cook sees nothing but oxen. Then cognitive-intent seeing (*chih*) dominates line 14, where he no longer sees the whole ox but merely specific places. And both seeings cease in line 15.

We are now as objectively serene as a skull.[46] The skull is unmistakably someone's, not an indistinct stone. But the skull does nothing to express its identity; it is as indistinctly quiet as any stone. And as such both the skull and the stone enjoy seasonal changes without those sufferings attendant on the self-assertiveness of the living (who usually are oblivious to carrying the skull within). Now we can be as indistinctly quiet as our skull and indistinctly quiet in our acts as the stony skull. Such skull-like serenity and vacancy lets the inner thrust of our vitality (*shen*) walk as it desires.

Shen is here joined with *yü* ("desire"), a peculiar combination.[47] The pull and urge of the spirit of man is so much at one with him that it can be called "desire"; it is the appetite of life itself that desires and pulls him as he goes *in* the ox. He is all knife in the ox; he, the knife, and the ox, all three, are at one in the desire of the spirit.

How about the sensory faculties, perceptual and cognitive? They have to stop. Their stoppage is also the stoppage of skill, which is exclusively of the sensory faculties. *They* have to stop before the divine inspiration takes over, for which the stoppage makes room. This situation echoes Chapter Two (lines 3–12) where the Master South-Wall overheard the pipings by becoming like dead wood and ashes, becoming one with the wind of the universe whistling and piping things, vitalizing things into themselves. The stoppage of faculties also echoes forward to Chapter Four (4/26–28) where Confucius teaches his best disciple Yen Hui how to empty himself to let the breath-energy (*ch'i*) listen of itself to itself. *Ch'i* is then functionally synonymous with *shen* here.

Both terms *i* and *shen*, describe how the *cook* performs.

4.5.2. *Verb and adjective*: As for how the *knife* goes about in the ox, the cook has two words for it: *ju* ("enter") and *wu* ("nothing").

Ju describes how the tree lets down its roots into the ground and spreads them as they grow.[48] K'ang Yin, said that *ju* delineated our house to go in and out of.[49] Chuang Tzu adds that our true ground and house is a nothing (*wu*), which originally must have had something to do with *yüan* ("source," "head," "chief").[50]

The knife goes into the ox as going home into its original ground, and *that* is a nothing, a space. Its going is a homecoming as smooth as a nothing (the thickless) entering a nothing (the interstices).

To enter is a serene verb, and one can hardly hear or see a nothing entering a nothing. Roomy and leisurely and unnoticed, there is a playful roaming, a natural happening. This perhaps expresses what Heidegger aimed at in his cryptic saying, "Nothing nothings." How much more concrete, how much more practical, Chuang Tzu is, when he said that the thickless enters the interstices, that is, a nothing entering a nothing.[51] Whenever we overhear the dance of nothing entering nothing, we hear echoes of Chapters One and Two.

4.5.3. *Two verbs*: Then comes the unity of all—the cook, the knife, and the ox—in a complex spot. *Tsu* is where arrowheads are collected,[52] where tissues and tendons twist and enfold each other, a complex (*com-plectere*) place too congested to pass through. At this point the doing-and-making (*wei*) is concentrated, the gaze stays, and the vigilance heightens, gathering themselves up in the single spirit. Here is an intensive inscrutable divine unity of the intuitive, the perceptive, and the conscious—"his spirit concentrated" (Chapter One, line 96). As this unity of the cook unites with his knife, the knife goes slowly in the ox; every move accomplishes a unity of the cook-knife with the ox. The knife nudges and enters; the ox slowly yields. There is no cutting, just continual inching, entering, as if there were no end to it. Then, all of a sudden, the flop comes. The flop is exclaimed, with two verbs, "to submit" (*wei*) and "to undo and release" (*chieh*).

Wei can mean "to entrust," "to submit," faintly connoting a homecoming, as "a lady following a man."[53] The ox-meat submits itself, as naturally as the soil comes home entrusting itself—to the ground.

Wei can also mean *wei*, the "crooked withered grass."[54] As the knife inches forward the ox undoes itself, releasing itself "sinuously" (as the withered grass) down to the ground. Withering symbolizes the autumn; its dance rhythm is that of the spring. Here in the unity of the cook, the knife, and the ox, is the unity of the autumn and the spring, death and life.

In the meantime, the cook has been in a trance, for his effort (*wei*) has been *part* of the rhythm of the spontaneous knife, which has, in turn, been a mere extension of the spirit sliding through the natural lines (*li*) in the ox. The rhythm has been soft and subtle, in which the knife and the ox quiver together—then the "problem" is suddenly solved. The ox is resolved and released (loosened), as the soil goes to the ground. Such is the dynamic serenity of the two verbs, *wei* and *chieh* . Such dynamism quietly "goods" (*shan*) the knife (27) as the invisible spirit (*shen*) dances to "good" our life (28–29) and our death (6/58).

Wei has been explained. What is *chieh* ("to undo," "to release")?

Chieh may be regarded as *the* central notion in this story of undoing the ox. The word has positive significance, and this story explains it. The story may be taken as an explication of a profoundly vague statement toward the end of the second chapter, "After myriads of generations and we meet one great holy man who understands the dissolution (*chieh*) of the mystery" (line 263).

The mystery can be understood from its "dissolution," *chieh*, which is an act of separating the ox horns (*niu chiao*) with a knife (*tao*).[55] Such separation lets things be as they are (*ch'eng*), as well as destroying (*hui*) them.[56] Things (*wu*) are oxen (*niu*) separated by knife (*tao* with bloodstains).[57] Separation (*fen*) is of course separation (pictured by *pa*) by a knife (*tao*).[58] In other words, things come about from separation between the self and the not-self. In the second chapter "things" are very much the target of attention.[59] What is added in the third chapter is the knack of separation, *in* which life (of the self and things) is cultivated. Free sauntering in the first chapter (*yu*) is the culmination of all this, the self, the separation, and the things.[60]

Let us go slower. Because of our subjective discrimination (*shih*), natural mounds (*feng*) become the raised paths between fields ("borders," *chen*),[61] and separation (*fen*) into things begins.[62] Separation (*fen*) is responsible for making borders (*chen*) out of the natural mounds (*feng*). Thus, *fen—chen—feng*; this is a description of human and natural differentiation (into various things) from the standpoint of beyond-the-self, that is objective perspective of things, as to *what* is the case. And this is what the second chapter described.

The third chapter treats various *things* from the standpoint of the self. The chapter tells us that because of the undoing (*chieh*) of the ox-no-longer-seen (15), the ox of things (*niu, wu*) comes out; and this is due to the spontaneous walking of the spirit-as-it-desires (15). Here to match the sequence of *fen-chen-feng*, the third chapter has *chieh-niu-shen*, a human-and-natural differentiation of things from the standpoint of the self, as to *how* the self goes about doing it, resulting in life-nourishment (*yang sheng*).

The self in the third chapter is the true one, the spirit-ed spontaneous one, unifying the subjective act with the objective responses from the beyond-act. The unity is the process of having-things (*yu*), which is a nothing entering a nothing, where nothing (*wu*) has a lot to do with the origin (*yüan*), the yet-to-begin-to-be (*wei shih yu*).[63]

To enter a nothing with a nothing is to nothing a nothing (*wu wu*, 22/67), *the* way to loosen up an ox in the third chapter, synonymous with "division" (*fen*) that produces distinct things (*wu*),[64] in the second chapter. Both chapters say, in effect, that to thing things (*wu wu*) is to nothing nothings (*wu wu*), as the later *Chuang Tzu* says.[65]

Such entering, thing-ing, nothing-ing activities are those of playing-about and roaming-around (*yu*), as described in the first chapter, with the knife-of-distinction (27).

Such loosening activities loosen *ourselves* from any tight spots in life (59), and we are born *with* things, as the second chapter proclaimed (Chapter Two, line 163). And we continue to go on, not knowing the finish (61). Going with the times and being at home in the situation (cf. 58), we neither die young nor live long (Chapter Two, line 162), neither mortal nor immortal, but simply immortal (61). Thus the third chapter understandably has no "death," only "finishing out our natural years" (4), "undoing" (5, 13, 20, 59), "going" (57), or at worst "danger" (1, 2) and "exhausting" (60). Everything, pain included, contributes to nourishing (*yang*) the im-mortality of our life (*sheng*).

4.6. *Lines 24–27, and 28–29*: Watson said[66] that this segment lends itself to two interpretations: (*i*) that of Arthur Waley (and Chu Kuei-yao) who said that this passage describes the mediocre (*tsu*, "rabble") cook; (*ii*) that of Watson and traditional commentators (Kuo Hsiang, and so on) who said this passage describes how the expert cook Ting handles the complex places (*tsu*, "meeting of a crowd").

It seems to me: (*i*) unthinkable for Cook Ting to devote more words than those on his own beautiful dance, to describing the inferior common cook, especially after having described his own dance; (*ii*) unthinkable for this concluding segment to describe what is inferior, ending the entire story with an anticlimax. I therefore side with the traditional view. This passage must describe the ideal cook's performance or, better, execution because, in Watson's words, "the extreme care and caution which the cook uses when he comes to a difficult place is also a part of Chuang Tzu's 'secret of caring for life.'"[67]

I would go further and regard this section as an implicit introduction to the rest of the chapter, in which three typical hardship in life are depicted—political mutilation (exemplified in the loss of a leg), precarious supplies of life necessities (in the pheasant's obtaining of food), and death (in Lao Tan's funeral). The conclusion (fire burning endlessly) is enigmatically significant.

Thus this section is both the climax of the story of Cook Ting and an introduction to the rest of the chapter. A skillful transition! Let us see how it goes.

The cook's expertise manifests itself when he grasps the nettle. Likewise, we can resolve (*chieh*) the complexities of life (*tsu*) when we ourselves are intimately involved with them, heart ("cautiously"), eyes ("look"), and hands ("walk") (25). And thus the beautiful execution is continued: going along with (*i*) the "grain" of things, being selflessly (*wu*) in (*ju*) unison with the rhythms of the wherefroms and wheretos of events, and those events and things loosening up (*chieh*) their difficulties, entrusting themselves (*wei*) to whatever will be.

Such is the principle (*chu*) of nourishing life (*yang sheng*) proclaimed (exclaimed!) by prince Wen Hui, who ironically is its recipient, not its author. The principle consists in the unity of loosening (*chieh*) and nourishing (*yang*), that the loosening is the way of nourishing.

If the Cook's story explains the principle of nourishing life, which was stated at the beginning of the chapter, then the rest of the chapter explains what it means to go slow with the knife of loosening and come out with "heart fully satisfied" (*man chih*; 27). Such unity of loosening with nourishing can be seen in all the stories in this chapter:

> In the story of loosening up the ox the stress is on nourishing (as Lord Wen Hui said), yet the story is surely about how delightful the loosening is;
> In the story of the Commander of the Right, the stress is on loosening (*chieh*, "amputation," 31, as homonym-almost-synonym of *chieh*, "undoing"), yet the story implies nourishing (*t'ien*, "heaven," 32-34);
> In the story of the marsh pheasant, the stress is on nourishing (pecking, drinking, 36–37), yet the story implies the dangers of being loosened in nature (38);
> In the story of Lao Tan's funeral, the stress is on loosening (the funeral) turned into a loosening of entanglements (59), and it implies the safety of being nourished in such a way of life (58);[68] and
> In the story of the firewood, the stress is on nourishing (unending transmission), yet the story is about the fire of loosening and dissolution.

All in all, an equation of life is established: To undo, in all its precarious connotations, *is* to nourish. Now we are in a position to go into other stories in this chapter.

5.1. *Lines 30–34*: Lin Yün-ming puzzled aloud at this most difficult passage. My interpretation is as follows:

While going through that mutilating experience in public employment, the excruciating pain is undeniable. Yet all that is, after all, included in the phrase, the heaven "lets (me) be my one-unique self" (33). It is the freedom of the "loosening" that pains me. Yet such pain can after all be affirmed as it is, when later I look back. "Without *that* experience I would not have been what I am now; it must have been from heaven, then," so I think (32).

This freedom of affirmation is neither an irrelevant optimism of romantic superstition, on the one hand, nor a calculated Spinozistic fatalism, on the other. It is not dreamy optimism because it includes the pain of the mutilating experience; it is not cold fatalism because we come to see the inherent reasons of things (*ku jan*) not in front of us (in anticipation and for the purposes of planning), but only at our back (now that we have passed through the experience), in our spine. We "see" the "inherent veins" of things without seeing them, as we trace the spine-meridian and the spinal seam of our life.

It is the live performance of that knife of nineteen bloody years of experience. It is an experiential freedom, drenched in the often mutilatingly painful, natural texture of things, an absolute realism.

5.2. Kung Wen Hsüan, Mr. Lofty Cultured Official, saw the Commander of the Right, and was startled (30). Why? There were so many people, some ex-officials, roaming the streets who have become footless. There was no reason to be startled.

Perhaps the footless man was still the Commander of the Right. If the man was recognized as an ex-Commander the rhetorical questions that followed would not have been asked—"What man is this? Why is he singularly one-footed? Was it heaven? Or was it man?" How can a footless man be a Commander of the Right? If by heaven (natural disaster or inborn), then he would not have been appointed as a Commander; if by man (punished by law), then he would have been removed from the position a long time ago. "What man is this?"

The answer, whether given by that Commander or mumbled through the mouth of Mr. Lofty Official, is profoundly ironic, if not enigmatic (33), for it can be taken in more than one meaning:

> "Heaven's giving birth to this" can also mean "heaven's letting him live as he does";
> "Letting be alone or unique" can also mean "letting be lone-footed";
> "Man's look" can also mean "man's outlook on life, his tendency to think in a certain way";
> "Pairing" can also mean "participating, this is, conforming to convention" or "given at birth, inborn."

Putting all these meanings together into a coherent sentence is not easy. But the general sentiment of the answer can be surmised as follows: "Heaven's letting him live as he does is to let him be uniquely himself (perhaps be lone-footed). This is what he was originally born with. Man's features may usually be paired—two legs, for instance. And so man's outlook on life may tend to conform to the usual convention, to see features in pairs as normal. But such a conventional outlook is also due to our inborn nature. Therefore, whether one-footed or two-footed, all our traits are due to heavenly nature."

But if, having been politically rendered lone-footed, the man still holds the post of the commander, is he not a fool who has failed to learn from his bitter lesson? But perhaps the situation is quite different. Judging from the next two chapters in the *Chuang Tzu*, the Commander may have become the Commander precisely *because* of his unique unusual lone-footedness, which took him out of usual competition for fame, and so made people feel that it was easy to get along with him. By and by, his gentle demeanor in his handicapped situation may even have won favor among the superiors, and he may have come to be looked upon as an incarnation of many virtues, as both the fourth and the fifth chapters show. But there may be another reason for regarding this lone-footed Commander as sagely. To this we now turn.

6. *Lines 35–39*: Although some commentators regard this segment as a separate story, distinct from the previous one,[69] many if not most others take this passage as part of the answer to the question put in the previous story. Both interpretations have their respective advantages. If taken as a separate story, this segment shows the prized freedom of roaming among risks of nature to nourish life, and such roaming is itself part of the nourishing which is elaborated in Chapter Four. If taken as a part of the answer to the question about the Commander on the Right, then this segment amounts to showing the reason why the Commander stays on as Commander. And here is why.

Even if the Commander lost his foot as punishment, and even if the answer to the question of how the misfortune happened was that it was due to "heaven," these two points can be both true if heaven means what has happened. That he is still Commander amounts then to his having gone along with what has happened, with what cannot be helped.

The answer gives us further point. If the reason for heaven's giving birth to this (man? event?) is to let him become unique (lone-footed), it was compared to being given his looks. Although political mutilation denies his having been born lone-footed, the heaven must have given *something* at birth which resulted in his losing a foot later in life. As Thomas Merton puts it, translating line 33, "When heaven gave this man life, it willed/ He should stand out from others."[70]

What this "something" is is explained in the pheasant story here. The pheasant does not wish to be fed *in* a cage, although life outside it is harsh and dangerous. A caged pheasant is not truly a pheasant; caging the pheasant is not "going along with" the ox-of-a-thing.

Similarly, heaven is what shaped the Commander's spirit to be commander, as it shaped his looks. For his spirit the natural place is the Commander of the Right. To hide from the position is to cage his spirit, that is, to kill it. Nourishing life requires the Commander to allow the spirit to be free, to accept risks as it goes along in the wilderness of politics. Nourishing his life-spirit involves exposing himself to bodily danger. His lone-footedness is the badge of this indomitable spirit, as the pheasant hopping ten hops for a peck, hopping one hundred hops for a drink.[71]

Thus linking the two stories throws light on both, enriching both. An interesting interpretation, incidentally, was offered by Wang Fu-chih who *contrasted* the Commander with the pheasant. He said that we should, when at the nitty-gritty, go near the cane of the Commander, rather than going near the name (fame) of the pheasant; for name (fame) is the punishment of heaven. But this interpretation seems forced and unintelligible.

Another interesting point before we go on. Line 39, "... though a king, it is not good," can be taken as a description of either life in a cage or life outside it. Graham and Watson take it to be the former—Graham saying, "One's daemon does not find it good even to be a king." Kuo Hsiang takes it to be the latter, saying, "its spirit is healthy, and consequently it forgets health."[72] Wang Shu-min's interpretation, which I followed in my translation, eliminates such ambiguity and sides with the former interpretation.

    7.1. *Lines 40–59*: This is another long story in the chapter, only slightly less in words than the Cook's story.

The passage may mean scolding Lao Tan, a mere historical personage, though a great teacher. He should not have spoken and acted in such a way as to leave his followers with lingering pangs of attachment when he left them.

The passage can also mean scolding the mourners (and so Confucian decency). They failed to understand their teacher's coming and going according to his time. When we follow him, dwell in our "time," and settle in our "going along," we can also be like him, being released from the tangles of sorrows and joys.

Although this story continues to treat the theme of the unity of loosening (59) and nourishing (58) that began with the Cook's story, this story brings the unity home to us by a reversal of several images.

To begin with, by shifting the main event from the Cook's preparation of steak to the legendary teacher Lao Tan's funeral, the stress is shifted from nourishment to the loosening in death. Then, the cook was the loosener; now, Lao Tan is the loosened. The cook handled the knife as a nothing; here the "knife" is an invisible inevitable death, and we are being handled by it. And yet the operation is the same. In both cases a loosening-release-resolution happens. In both, the smoothness of the loosening and the freedom from tangles are prominent. In both, the nourishing serenity is manifest; in both, we are nourished, though *this* time it takes enlightenment, and is more serious.

    7.2. Søren Kierkegaard said that one can truly follow one's master only after the master's death.[73] An illustration, if not proof, of this saying is here.

Lao Tan does a better job teaching us, now that he is dead, than while he was alive. For if we concentrate on his teaching, then his demeanor and his presence sadden us; our memories pierce us into weeping and wailing as if we had lost our mother or son. After all, he would have taught us more were he to be alive with us now. But if we concentrate on his entire life span, then we realize that "when he came, it was his time to come; when he went, he followed along" (56–57). If we stay on with the "itinerary" of his life, our entanglements with our own emotions, our emotional entanglements with him, are loosened away, and we are far away from the cane of escaping heaven.

It is in this manner that we truly follow our Master, embodying in our life his teaching and his ideal, when he is no longer with us. For he now teaches us with his life and death, not from his mouth alone.

Does this story have any relation with the previous ones in this chapter? It is not impossible to see that it has.

There is a contrast between the current ideal (Confucianism is perhaps its reflection and refinement) and Chuang Tzu's. To mourn for one's teacher as for one's family member is a high virtue in China. Ch'in Shih is (i) Mr. Great Loss, who has greatly lost the ideal of mourning for one's teacher, (ii) is now Mr. Great Easygoing, as nonchalant as a stranger to Lao Tan, and (iii) understands the fast-going vicissitudes of life, Mr. Fast Passing.[74] Thus in contrast to those mourners entangled in the gathering of sad-fond memories (50–52), Mr. Ch'in Shih intently watched and understood how the Master came and went—as smoothly as heaven wanted him to.

This is not only the true respect one pays the Master. It is also the attitude shared by Cook Ting who cleaves to natural lines, and slides along through seams and hollows (16), who enters the inner spaces with his thickless knife. This is also the manner of the singular-footed Commander, at home in his "misfortunes" as much as the easy strutting of the beautiful pheasant in the marshes. Risks are received into its life and was not even mentioned. It is not feeding in the cage but freely roaming in the wild (39), as free as the free roaming of the Cook's knife (10, 28), that is good.

The loosening-up, the undoing, starts with an ox and the lowly cook, Ting, who embodies the Way in his knife, and ends with the highest Master of the Way, Lao Tan, who embodies the Way in his life. He enacted in his life the very dance of the Cook, the knife, and the ox. Lao Tan is the drama itself.

It is the drama of life-nourishment. Nourishment is first mentioned in line 4, where its various implications are brought out—keeping the body (as the lowly cook did to his lord [29]), fulfilling the life urge (as the Commander of the Right did to his spirit [33], and as the pheasant rejected a wrong feeding [38]), nourishing those closest to us (as Lao Tan mothered his disciples [50]), and finishing out one's years (as the fire went on without knowing its finish [61]).[75]

It is also the drama of loosening up oneself and roaming around. First, the cook roamed around in his knife in the inner spaces of the cow to nourish and teach his lord. Such nourishing-teaching is itself a loosening up of the social convention—the lowly uneducated butcher is not supposed to teach or nourish the highest state authority whose legitimate role is to teach and nourish the people. Then we see the Commander loosening himself out of the confines of political etiquette and protocol, demonstrated in his singular-footedness. Such free independence is reflected in the unwillingness of the wild pheasant to be fed in the confines of the royal garden (38).[76] Then came the sauntering Ch'in Shih who ridiculed the mourning scene (loosening up the social convention and Confucianism) and the Master. For Chuang Tzu to mention the funeral of the supposedly immortal Master Lao Tzu is already to loosen up Chuang Tzu's own Taoist tradition. Finally, the fire should be roaming on beyond the fingering of the firewood, the base and tradition that supports the fire of life. This is another meaning of nourishing, to fulfil one's life in free roaming, loosening oneself out of any entanglements, natural, social, psychic.

7.3. The Chinese phrase *ch'i jen* on line 48 can be singular, "the man," that is, Lao Tan, or plural, "those people," that is, the mourners, or both. What does Chuang want to convey by such negative descriptive of line 48 and what follows in line 49–53?

Negatives always tantalize and challenge us. This passage must have inspired the later *Chuang Tzu* to come up with what Chuang Tzu must have meant. At least two passages can be cited, which are so important that they deserve quoting in full here:

> Thus it is said, To be filial out of respect is easy; to be filial out of love is hard. To be filial out of love is easy; to forget parents is hard. To forget parents is easy; to make parents forget you is hard. To make parents forget you is easy; to forget the whole world is hard. To forget the whole world is easy; to make the whole world forget you is hard.[77]

This passage may have in turn inspired the following also:

> Tzu-ch'i of Nan-po sat leaning on his armrest, staring up at the sky and breathing. Yen Ch'eng-tzu entered and said, 'Master, you surpass all other things! Can you really make the body like a withered tree and the mind like dead ashes?'
>
> 'Once I lived in a mountain cave. At that time, T'ien Ho came to pay me one visit and the people of the state of Ch'i congratulated him three times. I must have had hold of something in order for him to find out who I was; I must have been peddling something in order for him to come and buy.... Ah, how I pitied those men who destroy themselves! Then again, I pitied those who

pity others; and again, I pitied those who pity those who pity others. But that was long ago.[78]

We have been accustomed to admiring Confucius in the following quotation from the *Analects:*

> Tzu-kung said, Suppose one had a lovely jewel, should one wrap it up, put it in a box and keep it, or try to get the best price one can for it? The Master said, Sell it! Most certainly sell it! I myself am one who is waiting for an offer.[79]

We can see that Chuang Tzu's ideal goes farther than Confucius. These passages from the later *Chuang Tzu* go to the depths of humanness, deeper than the dazzling human achievements in history.

But what about the passage in the third chapter (40–59) which presumably inspired them? This passage is in itself insipid, serenely enigmatic. And no matter how many truths of the profoundest kind it inspires, it still remains remote, inexhaustible in its negative darkness. If those truths are like *yu wu* (the nothing that appears as nothing), then this passage is like *wu wu* (the nothing that hides itself, a nothing).[80] Such is one of the examples of the incomparable darkness (*ming*) with which the entire Inner Chapters started.

8.1. *Lines 60–61*: These two last lines of the chapter are profoundly vague, almost inexhaustible in their suggestiveness. Only three hints can be produced here: first, on an intuitive level, then a concentration on *ch'i* ("its," "their," 61), and finally on "fire."

Let us first see what intuition can reveal. What is pointed at (*chih^a*), what is intended (*chih^b*), what feeds the fire (*chih^c*), is what constitutes our "firewood" (*hsin*), the logs that live on as fire and make up our ups and downs of life. And they, the ups and downs of life, represent flames of the passions of life, we die in them, they die in us.

And yet, somehow such fire continues; it does not know its extinction. We carry on the fire; the fire carries us on. The fire has become part of our bone and blood, and we have become part of the fire. The self and the universe join and mingle, as the spinal artery becomes cosmic and our life-breaths become the vital energy (*shen*) of all things. We are the firewood, the fire, the cosmos; and the fire lives on in and through us. The Buddhists would presumably have been more than happy to see the fire blown off into nirvana.[81]

8.2. Let us now go slow and concentrate on the word, *ch'i* ("its," "their," 61). To what does this word refer? Three things are mentioned in this segment—the fingers (*chih^a*), the firewood (*hsin*), and the fire (*huo*). *Ch'i* can refer to any one or all of them.

If all of them are referred to by *ch'i*, the sense is clear. Everything is as happily intact as they are now, living on as if forever. This is to live in oneself, staying along with (*yüan*, 3) one's spinal artery of life energy.

If only one of them is referred to by *ch'i*, we must consider them one by one.

Chih^a: This word can mean at least three things—the fuel (*chih^c*) being burnt, perhaps our life span; or things intended (*chih^b*) by the mind, what is concentrated on, attended to; or fingers (*chih^a*) handling and picking up the firewood, indicating and pointing to it. The sense of the passage becomes: All the activities involved in burning can not-know their own exhaustion because they simply do what they do—gathering firewood, thinking of nothing but gathering, oil quietly burning ...

Hsin: This may be the least likely reference of *ch'i*, but not an impossible one. The passage would then have a meaning somewhat as follows: When the firewood burns, it does not burn itself but only its fuel; it is as it is, burning. In fact, burning indicates its existence. There is no burning-in-general, on the one hand, with the firewood existing separately, on the other. To see a burning is to see the firewood, burning, and burning itself to extinction. And it does not-know it.

Huo: This is the most likely reference of *ch'i*, which indicates fire. We must watch against dualism here, to which most commentators have succumbed. Chuang Tzu has no business with the separation of our life into two—form versus substance, matter versus spirit, body skeleton versus life, firewood versus fire, and the like. For fire has to include firewood and fingers that feed the fire. Fire transmitting itself without knowing its finish is everything going on without finish. This is the closest the Chinese people go toward immortality. It is the Chinese im-mortality, which happens when we lose ourselves in the commonest sensation. Xavier Rubert de Ventós put it well:

> We do not *have* a sensation, but are possessed by and lost in it. The performer disappears and we become the vibrating string of an instrument. We do not know where the sensation begins or ends, or even if it does begin and end. Hegel observed astutely that this impersonal character is not a *trait* of sensual pleasure but is ... the sensual pleasure *itself*.... Sensual desire or satisfaction is not, then, something we possess but something that escapes from us—that 'bursts from us' ... as we all 'burst' into tears.[82]

In this situation we do not know where our sensation begins or ends; we are immortal.

After all this is said and analyzed, however, not much has been said that we did not know already. Chuang Tzu simply reminded us once more that as long as we follow the spinal artery of energy, we will be led to "living happily *ever* after," with fire, wants, suffering, and all. For that spinal artery we have, if we but follow it through, leads us to realize that it is also the cosmic spine, as the knife (whether in our hands or in our life) and the oxen of things dancingly showed us.

8.3. As for the *fire*. What does fire signify?

Our conscious handling (*chih*[a]) stops at the firewood. But what we cannot handle and manipulate is the fire, which goes on without our knowing it. And yet the fire also follows after the firewood. Fire has something to do with our fingers which manipulate the firewood, after all.

This may be another description of that with which the second chapter started. We the firewood, the withered wood and dead ashes, can overhear the sounds (effect) of the invisible wind (cause). We can overhear the effect; we have no idea about the cause. And the wind causes fire.[83]

In this connection the fire may echo the southern Darkness with which the first chapter began. Southern darkness means the bright-separate realm which we yet do not know. That realm is the destination of the P'ung Bird and that is what we do not know as to its "finish." It is the limitless Realm that we do not follow after (*sui*) but only stay on with (*yüan*) and settle in (*ch'u*); we will then not be burnt (as were mentioned in Chapter One, line 111, and Chapter Two, line 224).

Fire is of course in the Yang. To dwell in the Yang aspect of reality we must not-know (Yin) it, that is, we must be Yin to dwell in the Yang. That is how the endlessness of the Yang is ensured.

Fire is produced by "Wood" ("firewood") and produces "Earth", in the unending cycle of the Five Elementary Ways of the Universe; fire has a lot to do with transformation (*hua*; Chapter Two, 305). Yet fire destroys. Such co-incidence of opposites is described in the third chapter. Fire is an apt symbol for the coincidence of opposites.[84]

9. All in all, we can see four waves of life, as it were, in this chapter:

(*a*) Introduction
(*b*) Undoing the ox of a thing
(*c*) The commander and the pheasant
(*d*) Lao Tan and fire

Thus, (*a*) is the gist and introduction to what follows; (*b*) elaborates on (*a*) and sets the tone for the rest; (*c*) concerns living amidst the mortal dangers. Mutilation (*chieh*) echoes back to the undoing (*chieh*) in (*b*); "not good"

resonates forward to "not ... finish" in (*d*). Mutilation has a negative connotation that deepens the positive connotation of loosening; "not good" uses
something positive ("good") to warn ("not") of something negative ("fed in a
cage"). "Not ... finish" uses something negative ("not," "finish") to point to
the positive ("transmits"); (d) concerns death as a loosening (*chieh*) and a transmitting (*ch'uan*). Death is a going that is a going on—the fire with mortal
suffering, fire as life that does not know its finish.

Now, it is all too easy to see all this as Buddhist insight in Chinese dress,
describing our life that goes from birth (*a*) to nourishing by butchery (*b*) to
mortal dangers (*c*) to death (*d*). But we have here a simple clue telling us that
this is the Chinese way of *life* that *includes* such negatives. The clue is fire that
does not know its finish. For Buddhism the central goal is to blow off the fire
of our desires that causes unending cycles of painful rebirths (and redeaths).
Chinese sentiment affirms that the fire is good, or rather, *allows* such un-
endingness to be good; it is being trapped in it that is bad. And to believe that
it is bad is to be trapped in it. The Chinese Way of *life* allows fire to be fire,
and goes with it. This way of life *includes* all suffering, goes along with it, and
with Camus' Sisyphus "pronounces it as good." Life releases itself (*chieh*)
from suffering in suffering.

And this message is carried throughout the rest of the Inner Chapters:

> The marsh pheasant and the cage are transformed into the story of a tiger
> keeper that climaxes Chapter Four;
> The commander's singular-footedness as nourishing is borne out in the
> handicapped people to whom men and women flock as their fonts of
> virtues, in Chapter Five;
> Lao Tan's funeral becomes terminal patients looking forward to their illim-
> itable future transformations, in Chapter Six;
> The im-mortal notes of anticipation and fulfillment, a nourishing of life, in the
> midst of mortal suffering.

All strike the positive notes of anticipation and fulfillment, a nourishing of
life, in the midst of mortal suffering.

C. Our Understanding of the Message

Since this chapter is the summa of the Inner Chapters, many things can be
said about most of the themes mentioned in this chapter. This section of
Meditations, therefore, must confine itself to only a few of the themes, those
that are obviously significant today. And their reading will deliberately be less

speculative than spontaneously exegetical, at least less so than the last readings
of meditations for the previous two chapters.

1.1. Chuang Tzu starts Chapter Three with a big theme. One's life is
limited; one's task and desire of knowing things is limitless. To follow after the
unlimited with the limited endangers oneself. Knowing the danger there is in
the pursuit of knowledge, and yet trying to gain more knowledge in order to
save oneself from danger,[85] or not knowing the danger and blindly continuing
one's cognitive pursuit, taking it to be a worthwhile project[86] —these are
dangers indeed. This is because cognitive enterprise is an endeavor in which
one inherently overreaches oneself.[87]

Similarly, as one follows after external pomp and fame in doing "good"
(what one considers or knows to be good), one would surely be followed by
external punishment as if one were doing "evil" (what is publicly considered
evil). Since pomp is as dangerous as punishment, it should be avoided as much
as punishment.[88] In short, one cannot follow after limitless externals, such as
knowledge and fame, and survive. That "knowledge" is external and limitless,
and that "following" can be dangerous, deserve looking into.

1.1.1. To know is to know about life, that is, oneself living—knowledge
in the final analysis is self-knowledge. Furthermore, to know is to explain, that
is, to insert explanations between the knower and the known. Thus knowledge
means explanatory self-knowledge, which is an impossibility if not a self-
contradiction. This can be understood in two ways:

First, to explain oneself is both to objectify oneself and distance oneself,
and to approach oneself and become one with oneself. Secondly, we aspire to
know everything, including our knowing act itself. And this project cannot be
completed because as soon as we know what there is to know, we have an
additional item to know, namely, our very act of knowing our act of knowing
our act of knowing ... It is as frustrating as trying to learn Han-tan walk and
forgetting the old way of walking, or trying to flee from one's shadow of
ignorance.[89]

To distance *and* approach oneself tears oneself apart. In learning Han-tan
walk one ends up crawling home; continually fleeing from one's shadow,
one ends up falling down in decease. To pursue knowledge is to pursue an
infinite regress with our finite life, endangering life itself.[90]

1.1.2. Cognitive endeavor is to follow after knowledge. There are two
ways of following: following after someone and following on a path. To
follow after a person is to follow behind him, with a little distance between.
Knowing as explaining is such a following-after, for every explanation is a

distance between the explanation and the explained; yet in seeking to know, one strains oneself toward cognitively uniting oneself with the known. Such a project is self-defeating, for the same reason that knowing the act of knowing leads into a downward, narrowing spiral. This is as pathetic as mourning one's master; to mourn the master is to try to follow after him who is no longer among us. To follow on a path, in contrast, is like following the master's way of life when he is out of our way. We slip ourselves into his steps and become him. This is following on a path, the path of our master. And this can be effortless.

1.2. We must, then, not follow after (*sui*) knowledge, but instead follow (*yüan*) the path (*ching*) of our spinal arteries (*tu*). Instead of straining ourselves following after knowledge, we lose ourselves in the inner paths of life energies. Our paths become the constant warp of the fabric of life (*ching*), the spinal seam of a "garment" of life (*tu*). Action originating from here is like breathing following our inner control of the arteries of breaths of life. It is as self-centered as it is natural. In literally following ourselves, we lose ourselves in the vital center paths of life.[91]

Such activities from our inner depths, in constant naturalness unawares, are responsible (*chu*) for nourishing life (*yang sheng*), in as routine a fashion as the spinal arteries let the life energy go through and keep us alive, and as the warp and the spinal seam keep the fabric together as a garment. Now, all this is nothing special; just putting what is there where it belongs, putting ourselves back to our own inner vital center, letting us follow the spinal column in us. Such self-following nourishes life unawares. As the later *Chuang Tzu* says,

> To move without knowing where you are going, to sit at home without knowing what you are doing, traipsing and trailing about with other things, riding along with them on the same wave—this is the basic rule of life-preservation, this and nothing more.[92]

Such life nourishment is the thread (*tu*) that runs through the chapter till the last phrase, "not knowing its finish" (line 61).

1.3. These positive characterizations of life-nourishment are fulfilled by their negatives of suffering in the stories that follow. We can preserve our body by following our inner tube-and-thread, while (sometimes) we are cut-loose (*chieh*) as an ox is. We can keep our life intact and enjoy our years as a swamp pheasant does, while being mutilated as the singular-footed commander was. We can nourish our family while (at times) attending their funeral, as Ch'in Shih attended that of Lao Tan who was supposed to be undying. And we can live out our natural years while not knowing when they end with their suffering.

This negative description of desirables makes sense if we realize that in the inner thread of life, undoing an ox means the ox undoing itself, with which the butcher dances. Mutilation will also be an undoing "from heaven," an inevitable in our nature, a natural event. Although as risky as the pheasant in the marsh, our life of freedom is just as "good" (*shan*, 39). We may die as Lao Tan did, a release (*chieh*) from bondage (*hsüan*). And long live suffering, happily ever after; none knows its end.

In every life there is a co-crescendo of suffering and bliss; the more suffering, the more bliss. We nourish our life in suffering by the guiding secret (*chu*) of following on the inner vital arteries of life (*yüan tu*).

2.1. To follow, not after knowledge, but on the path of oneself seems to connote the life of a recluse. Not so, however. To follow the spinal column of the self is to become adept at dealing with things at *their* spinal core. A lowly agent of death, the cook, exemplifies and teaches the unity of butchery and nourishment to the highest agent of social bliss, Lord Wen Hui. Butchery is dressing the ox for dinner. Occasional obstacles in the process bring out the crucial relevance of staying on with the spine-meridian of the self and the thing. In concentrated caution (*tu*), the cook himself becomes as thickless as his knife to slowly enter the ox-interstices.

It is here that the knife passes through the ox as the spinal corridor passes through the body. Nothing special is in all this, just putting what there is where it is, that is, putting oneself at one's own center, thereby putting things at theirs. It is to follow the inherently-so, to stay on the natural veins, of things. William James said that all our speculations must come back home to their common corridor—their practical significance in life. Chuang Tzu would add that the corridor goes from one's own spine to the spines of things. How such following on the spines becomes a sailing in the situation is described as the cook's dance with the ox.

2.2. Speculatively we can assign three possible meanings of *tu* to the three segments of the story of ox-undoing.[93]

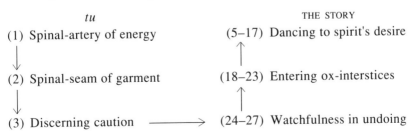

tu	THE STORY
(1) Spinal-artery of energy	(5–17) Dancing to spirit's desire
(2) Spinal-seam of garment	(18–23) Entering ox-interstices
(3) Discerning caution	(24–27) Watchfulness in undoing

The final segment perhaps needs looking into (lines 24–27). At first glance the segment seems a return to the rabble of cooks as the word *tsu* suggests (24, cf. 18); but three considerations prevent this interpretation: (*a*) the interpretation would be an anticlimax to the story; (*b*) it would leave the difficult places unexplained, making the whole operation irresponsibly smooth; (*c*) the interpretation also leaves the stoppage of vision (25) unexplained.

If *tsu* is taken instead to be "complex place" where tissues entwine, then line 25 emerges as the apex (not appendix) to the story. The line has three phrases; (*i*) tremblingly cautioning oneself, (*ii*) the gaze staying-stopping, (*iii*) the (knife's?) walk slowing down. Phrase (*i*) may be a summary of what follows, a cautious concentrated move, echoing the delicate move in line 26. Phrase (*ii*) is a re-emphasis of "the gaze staying-and-stopping" (15). Phrase (*iii*) is a re-emphasis of "the spirit walks as it desires" (15). In short, line 25 is now a redoubling of line 15, the very height of the cook's "way."

Wei is also significant, repeated three times. The word was not one of approbation in lines 2–3, "self-conscious contrivance." Here it is a continuation of *nan wei* (24), trouble-making. Here watchfulness is dissolved and unified into the total project of the spirit walking, the knife's spontaneous move; such unity is called "caution" (25). It is a beautiful integration of the totality of our resources, both mental and manual, both during (25) and after (27) the operation.

A popular Japanese interpretation takes *wei* (25) as an abbreviation of *wei chih* (in 27), "because of it." The line (25) would be "I tremblingly caution myself because of it; my gaze stops and stays on account of it; my move slows down because of it." The cook loses himself in all his concentration on the difficulties (*nan*) and complexities (*tsu*) of the ox (24). This is perhaps what a "concentration of the spirit" (Chapter One, line 96) means. The cook loses himself (in all his attentiveness) in the ox, dancing with it, says Chuang Tzu. Such integrated resonance is thus beautifully depicted as the dance, to which we turn.

2.3. Civilization came from religion and the arts. The arts came from play, which produced singing and dancing in nature. Singing and dancing were used both for molding our feelings, attitudes, and behavior, that is, for education, *and* for resonating with animals, men, nature, and gods, that is, for religion. All this is because singing and dancing balance and harmonize by tuning the resonance of things—that is, smooth our inner resonance, sublimate and unify our thinking, feeling, and willing, and harmonize them with nature. It is no accident that in China the phrase *li yüeh* ("ritual and music") appears routinely in literature of every genre.[94]

Singing and dancing meet in music, the music of instruments of men (words, tunes, rhythm, musical instruments), in which the inside and the outside, men and nature, sing and dance together. Music is the time-art, distinct from the space-art of painting and sculpture. Art re-presents nature, both in us and in things. The time-art vibrates and spreads the re-emergence of all *with* all, and in the process nourishes life.

All these activities, attitudes, and attainments are compressed and poignantly expressed in the dance of the butcher-knife, reminding the royal observer, Lord Wen Hui, of the ancient ritual tune of the dance for rain; it would have reminded us of ecological husbandry, including the lion capturing the lamb. The knife-dance was a beautiful sight, sending the Lord into ecstatic admiration. We notice here that the usual Mencian sentiment of a gentleman shying away from the kitchen is absent. The butcher knife in bloody dismemberment is sublimated in the unity of the knife dancing with the ox that quivers in tune. It is poetry and singing; it is quivering, slithering, rhyming, a time-art. It is nourishment with a knife.

Here there is no longer the cook or the ox, but only that thicklessness entering those interstices. Since no one can see the thickless or the spaces, only the entering becomes visible, or rather, noticeable. Or more accurately, it is the *rhythm* of entering that is noticed, and nothing else. And this is supreme unity, which nourishes in the ultimate sense. But since violence is cutting and hacking, chipping and breaking (18), such knife-entering and ox-undoing is not violent. It is the music that feeds.

2.4.   The butcher is depicted as a dancer to the force of life. The music is the ancient dance tunes of prayers for rain. That dance follows the Way (*tao*) of things, their natural veins and lines (*li*), their inherently-so (*ku-jan*). Such a dance goes with, stays on, the spinal artery of the energy of life.

And such a dance enables the butcher to slip into the right posture, the right route, the right rhythm. It is the Tao itself (not his muscle or skill) that unfolds his posture as it folds itself into his routing and his knife's going. The life energy (*ch'i*, if you wish) flows freely from the center of bodily gravity (*tan t'ien*) through the meridian-artery, and the flow is manifested in the butcher's knife as it stays on the route. The movement finds itself a rhythm which follows a music not of the butcher's own devising but of the ancient music of the collective prayer for rain.

To allow the movement to generate itself, the butcher must go through three stages of growth out of tension-imbalance (line 1), which kills *real* movement. As the tension goes, relaxation and centering come. As he wields his knife, he goes from preoccupation with the ox (nothing not-oxen), to meticulous dissection (the whole ox was never seen), to effortlessness (the spirit meets the ox, in which it walks as it desires) (13–15). This walk is a spontaneous tracing of the spinal artery, the veins and lines (*li*) of things.

The resemblance of this movement to that of *T'ai Chi Ch'üan*, a Chinese martial art, is uncanny. T'ai Chi Ch'üan is a lethal art *and* an art of life; so is butchery.

The kitchen fellow danced with the oxen, and in the dance they were undone or, rather, were themselves their own undoing. The dancing rhythm does not kill but undoes and nourishes, tuned with the ritual dance tunes of the spring. This dance is sacred, to which oxen are sacrificed—made sacred.

Matadors (those who sacrifice, make sacred) dance with the bulls, who are also knifed or, rather, knife themselves in the dance, to nourish the audience.

Both the Commander of the Right and the Marsh Pheasant are oxen, dancing the inevitabilities of life, freely undoing themselves in the risks of life.

The same principle applies to the martial arts, in which dancing rhythm quivers between the combatants. No killing is seen here, either, but undoing and nourishing—either you undo yourself to nourish me in our dancing, or I undo myself to nourish you in our dancing. The Chinese martial arts are the art of the dance of life in death.

And that is what happened in Lao Tan's death. Lao Tan danced with his disciples and undid himself; lines 6–10 of Chapter Three go with lines 56–59. These are dancing to and with the times of life. In this process Chuang Tzu managed to include the negative side of the dance in the dance itself—see line 18 (cf. lines 24–27, which corresponds with lines 50–55. Here again we have no killing, only undoing, a self-undoing in the rhythm of the dance of time and fulfilment (lines 20, 58; cf. 6/27 and 51–52, as well as 6/53–55, 57–58, 62–65, 74–75, and 95–97).

There is, however, a difference.[95] In T'ai Chi Ch'üan there is activity initiating itself to call for the life force, whereas the cook just follows along on the paths of lines and ligaments in the ox; he does not cut. The T'ai Chi act may be a balancing activity between two extremes to center oneself on oneself. The cook neither balances nor centers. He merely follows along and stays on.

Let us watch the butcher. He is now neither obsessed with the ox, seeing nothing but oxen everywhere, nor meticulously observant of minute details, never having seen the whole ox. His vision stops and stays. He lets the spinal spirit meet with the ox. The motion then begins.

The motion is the walk of the spirit as it desires. It is an operation based neither on a pre-established harmony (a downward deduction from an a priori principle) nor on a Hegelian synthesis (an ontological build-up). The motion is an ontological co-vibration.

Such resonance starts with staying on the throbbing rhythm of one's vital spinal arteries (which in their vacancy administer breathing and blood circulation). The resonance ends up vibrating with whatever it meets. We can say that the knife brings the ox to life, to dance with the knife, to the music co-resonated forth by the dance of the knife-with-ox. It is a symphonic dance that has its historic root in the ancient tunes of the sagely kings.

Such dancing resonance does not stay in one place but goes on smoothly, as smoothly as a thickless nothing goes through a spatial nothing. Every time, the knife goes in fresh and comes out fresh. The freshness is nineteen years old—as just from the grindstone, as just from the ecstasy of the first successful ox-loosening, or rather, the ox's self-loosening enabled by the butcher's knife.

2.5. Let us look closely at *tu*. Whether taken as the spinal artery of energy-that-breathes or as the spinal fold that sews two halves of a dress together, *tu* is a fullness of emptiness, vital un-self-conscious emptiness.

In the West, a sort of full emptiness is not unappreciated, as in the notion of universal. Verbs, for instance, are motions *plus* adverbial descriptions. To run is to move (universal) in the manner of running (description), without which there is no motion. That is, universal (core-motion) is a ghostly non-existence to be clothed with concrete description (manner of running). Conversely, the "manner" is non-existent when left to itself, without its universal. Description is always a description *of* something universal. A concrete description depends on the core-universal to be concrete. Thus universal is a fullness of emptiness, so full, in fact, that Plato calls it the Really Real, the Form of all actuals, albeit perhaps with mistaken connotations. Universal is full because it fills *all* sorts of descriptions. It is empty because it cannot exist by itself without those descriptions.

Chuang Tzu goes a step further, as it were, and takes the universal to be emptiness that is alive, a vital emptiness. The image of spinal artery can be helpful, says Chuang Tzu. Artery is an empty tube that carries, or rather, lets through, the flow of energy, whether in the form of blood, nerves, or *ch'i* the breathing-energy, in short, the energy of life. Such vital energy throbs and thrusts itself everywhere like a flood.[96] What regulates and makes it a particular living being (such as a man, or an ox) is that *tu*, that vital artery, that vital emptiness which lets through the energy of life in a particular manner.

It may be objected that the relation between the universal and the descriptive is reversed here. For it is now *tu* that makes *ch'i* concrete, not the other way round. One must admit that the Western analogy fails here. Both *tu* and *ch'i* are concretizing agents, and both are pervasive universals; both must come together to comprise concrete particulars. This is what the Neo-Confucians will later elaborate on, though in different formulations of *li*, *ch'i*, and the like. For our purpose, it suffices to point out that *tu* is the vital emptiness that lets through and lets be. *Ch'i* (or *shen*) is a becoming emptiness; *tu* is a letting emptiness. *Ch'i* starts *Ch'i Wu Lun*; *tu* starts *Yang Sheng Chu*.

To stay on in *tu* and flow with the concrete vicissitudes (dealing with an ox, the wild environment, politics, life-years) is the way to become as one is and to become free in whatever interchange one must undergo (*hua*); we see here an application of two key notions (*fen* and *hua*) that concluded the *Ch'i Wu Lun*.

So far "vital" in "vital emptiness" is explained—the true universal is what renders us alive, the principle of nourishing life. But how do we nourish life? By going *in* "emptiness." *Tu* is as empty as the spinal artery or the spinal fold. To become oneself is to become empty and loosened. And to go being-loosened is thereby to loosen others as well. The cook becomes thickless as the knife enters the inner spaces of the ox. He lets the spirit (*shen*) that pervades the universe go through him, that is, loosen him, and thereby loosens the ox.

Such empty going-through can be as free and risky as the marsh pheasant, as mutilating as the commander, and as death-ly as Lao Tan. The point is to go through one's own vital emptiness at one's spine.

Spine is an interesting notion. It is at the center of our *back*, invisible. It is yet the center, our backbone that supports us. Invisible, it symbolizes our lack of self-consciousness. At the center of our back, it symbolizes our vitality. We must be *on* it, to become as we are.

To live on is also invisible, that is, un-self-conscious, neither an activity nor a situation. The empty universal that is full is un-self-consciously alive, a vacancy that lets fill and lets through.

And so this chapter is about a "live" universal, saying that the true universal is alive (*yüan tu*), going through phases of life, tracing and staying on with the spinal meridian of the self and things, sustaining us throughout. Thus *yüan tu* (line 3) is an explication of *yang sheng chu*; the chapter throughout explains this. The living universal is the principle of life-nourishment.

Such a principle is like our *tu*, which un-self-consciously sustains us, letting the heart pump the blood constantly without our noticing it, much less helping it. We should stay on in this empty live universal, *tu*, and then we will be nourished. *Tu* is introduced in the beginning segment (1–4). How we stay on *tu* (*yüan tu*) is detailed in the second segment (5–29). The rest of the chapter is its application, until we become quite im-mortal.

2.6. *Sheng* is what proceeds forth from the ground upward,[97] that is, life giving birth to itself. *Shen* is what draws forth life throughout the universe.[98] When the spirit walks (roams?) as it desires, things begin to proceed from the ground, and grow. And the knife loosens life up (*chieh*; cf. *fen*) into the individual things. The knife is the force that nourishes[99] the individual growth.

Shuo Wen says that things (*wu*) begin with a leading of the oxen, the largest of the things we can lead.[100] K'ang Yin definitely identifies things (*wu*) with the cutting of oxen, complete with bloodstains.[101] There is no question but that the chapter proposes the origin of things (*wu*), in which their principle of sus-tenance is discerned.

For Chuang Tzu the so-called "cutting" can be a loosening out of things, if only we stay on the *tu* of things, including our own. Staying on the *tu* has been considered. We now see into how things come out of cutting-loosening.

If we but stay on *tu*, things come out by cutting. More accurately, we should say that painful cuttings and violence in the world shall become a loosening forth of things if we but live in *tu*. Such loosening appears both at the beginning, with the ox our nourishment, and at the end, with Lao Tan our "mother" (51) who nourishes.

What are those "things"? Chuang Tzu gave us five typical ones:

(*i*)   the ox of a thing, an ordinary thing: The story of butchery sets the stage for the rest, and echoes Chapters One and Two;

(*ii*)   the environment in which we move and feed, as implied in "heaven" (31–34) and "marsh" (35): The theme of how to survive in the hostile inevitables is treated in Chapter Four;

(*iii*)   our body and our identity (31, 33): This is elaborated into the "holy cripples" in Chapter Five;

(*iv*)   our livelihood typified in the marsh pheasant: It is expanded into Chapter Six;

(*v*)   our vicissitudes, even up to the funeral of our Lao Tan: Such ultimates are explained as a vivacious im-mortality in Chapter Seven.

We can see how in all the typical "things" of the world, the violence of cutting is really a loosening, an occasion for the nourishing of our identity. When we understand this, the danger of the boundlessness of knowledge (line 1) is turned into the ignorance of the endless transmission of the fire, the principle of life.[102] In Chuang Tzu's magic of the shift of perspectives, cutting is cultivation of life.

2.7. Jesus said, "Put back your sword in its place. For all who take the sword shall perish by the sword."[103] Unfortunately, Jesus himself did not touch the sword and perished nonetheless by the sword-like violence. Perhaps he did wield a sword of sort,[104] and so perished in the sword of a sort. His position in regard to the sword is ambiguous.

Chuang Tzu's position is straightforward, though just as paradoxical. There is a way, he says, of going along with the knife to loosen things and be nourished or even to let it loosen ourselves, and being at peace, at home, in life, even unto death. It is the simplest way—to follow along; yet it is the hardest way because it is pain and destruction from which we instinctively shrink. He who masters this Way of things is a free man dancing through the ups and downs of life (and death).

There are many I-It-ish responses to whatever I meet—I can dissect, analyze, and control It. When I respond to-the-Thou, that is, Thou-ishly, the presence of the Thou hovers and suspends itself like the spirit upon the waters. This vapor is not inactive but puts itself forth as a beneficent rain. This is the metaphor that gives us access to a dimension which is primordially dynamic, between the I and the Thou. This is the dimension of the eternal sources at which persons are nourished.

Such is what Gabriel Marcel sees in Martin Buber. See Marcel's essay that begins Paul Arthur Schilpp and Maurice Friedman (eds.), *The Philosophy of Martin Buber*, esp. pp. 47–48.

Chuang Tzu talked about sense-knowledge versus spirit, chipping-breaking versus entering, instead of the I-It versus the I-Thou. Except for such differences in terms and in connotations, Marcel's description has an uncanny affinity with Chuang Tzu, who predates both Marcel and Buber by almost twenty-four centuries. Chuang Tzu adds three more points: The beneficent rain is enshrined in the community ritual of the dance for rain, officiated by the emperor. The primordial dynamism of the I-Thou spirit is danced out. And the dance is often deadly in actual life, yet the dance remains the inner principle of nourishment.

2.8. Loosening or unravelling (*chieh*) seems to differ from dividing or separating (*fen*).

Chieh has many meanings. Originally it was a pictograph of (*a*) pulling horns out of an ox head, an act of (*b*) dismembering a butchered or sacrificed ox or animal. From this it came to symbolize any act of (*c*) undoing, loosening, dividing, dissolving, unraveling something into its component parts.[105]

Fen is a picture of knifing (*tao*) a thing into two (*pa*) parts, to separate and discriminate (*pien*) one from the other. Then it came to mean discerning and discriminating the right from the wrong, as in litigation.[106]

"Analysis," a household word in Western philosophy, lurks in all these meanings, but more prominently in *fen* than in *chieh.*

Related to these above two terms is *pien*, meaning striving to discern, discriminate, and distinguish (with a knife if needed) between right and wrong, good and bad, flavors, colors, and the like. The connotation of "analysis" seems to be less strong than *fen* and more so than *chieh.*[107]

Chuang Tzu seems to be averse to, though not denying the importance of, explicit analysis. He is eager to limit such analytical discrimination to a minimum (Chapter One, lines 56–57). He always couples analysis with its opposite, synthetic formation (Chapter Two, line 118), sometimes even coupling analysis with its denial (Two, line 177) or its transformation (Two, lines 304–5). In his description of the holy man in respect to the division of things, Chuang Tzu explicitly denies the activity of *pien* to the holy man (Two, line 176), with whom not even *fen* is mentioned.

Chieh in the vivid story of butchery in Chapter Three seems to describe well what Chuang Tzu means in Chapter Two, line 177: "In division there is no division." This is precisely what undoing an ox amounts to; here to divide is to nourish and to fulfill (both the Lord and the gods). Chuang Tzu seems to say that analysis should be for the sake of feeding and fulfilling our life. How does such undoing relate to nourishing?

Life-nourishment comes not in the result of undoing the ox (although undoing an ox does nourish us also in the form of beef), but in the very act, or rather, the very *knack*, of loosening itself. For Lord Wen Hui is not impressed with the delicious texture of the beef; he is impressed with the cook's dancing expertise and enjoyment of undoing (5–9). Nor is his concluding exclamation about having obtained nourishment of life aimed at the beef, but at the cook's words describing (not beef but) *how* he undoes the ox and how much he enjoys such undoing.

This point is quite important. For the act of butchery is anything but delicious and nourishing; the Mencian gentleman, we remember, distances himself from the kitchen (1A7). *Within* the bloody unseemliness of the knifing act Chuang Tzu sees nourishment.

Of course we must distinguish bloodiness from its expertise; it is the latter, not the former, that is celebrated. Having said so, however, Chuang Tzu is not blind to the fact that the two are practically inseparable, that we often find in actual life the expertise (and its enjoyment) only in bloodiness. We must know how to find the expertise in bloodiness without endorsing, much less enjoying, bloodiness. We remember Chuang Tzu distinguished the Cook Ting from ordinary cooks' chipping and breaking (18). The whole chapter concerns this important truth of life—to find nourishment in destruction. "Their division is their formation; their formation is their breakdown. Among all things, there exists no formation or breakdown; for they are again gone through into one" (Chapter Two, lines 118–119).

Let us look at the entire chapter along the single thread of *chieh*. The ox is the reasonable, the whole of things, the totality of reason. The knife is the unintelligible inevitables, the disasters in life. The ox is chipped, hacked, broken, and chopped into pieces. *We* should turn such intentional violence into a natural undoing of things.

The conversion of breaking and hacking into a loosening apart, especially when applied to ourselves, is illustrated in the story of the singular-footed commander. Political mutilation (*chieh*) is understood in terms of a natural loosening-apart (*chieh*), in which the commander became singular and unique (*tu*). We see that the commander has been hacked by a common cook. We see that the "reasoning" offered does not make sense, except in one way. The commander must have reflected on the event at the spinal core of his being; he must have accepted it as a part of his becoming of himself. Thus the staying on with his spinal artery made him understand. The event of political mutilation was a moment in the preservation of his personal integrity, a maintaining of his "body" (4). It is not a reasoning, but a meta-reasoning, a reflective or meta-reflective digestion. The event nourished him; he has grown into his unique self (*tu*). He is not knotted (*hsüan*) and hurt further, but has converted his *chieh* (singular-footedness) into a heavenly *chieh* (loosening, unrevelling, enlightenment).

Such a going along with one's inner spinal thread leads the marsh pheasant to keep his life whole (4), in all its risks and troubles of ten hops a peck, a hundred hops a drink (36–37). All the risks similar to the commander's are included in the peaceful strutting of the pheasant in the wild, which he would never exchange for the safety of the confines (*fan*) of culture (*chih*) and government.

After the two short stories (the commander, the pheasant), we come to the long one of Lao Tan's funeral. The supposedly immortal Lao Tan[108] has died. Long live Lao Tan! Thus the undoing is now carried to its ultimate, our death. In Lao Tan's death we are made to understand the im-mortality of the holy man. The spokesman for such truth is Mr. Ch'in whose given name is Shih, "losing," "loosing," "letting go," "loose," or "ease."[109]

This Mr. Easy-going, Mr. Loosing, or Mr. Losing-without-being-upset was a good friend of Lao Tan. But unlike Lao Tan, this man was quite obscure; not even Lao Tan's disciples knew him. This Mr. Loss came to the funeral of his good friend, uttered three ritual wailings, and went out. The mourning was over; Mr. Loss followed along with the loss. The cutting of the heavenly knife is completed by Mr. Loss's ritual mourning into a loosening of the Great Ox, on which Lao Tan rode away from the world of men. Mr. Loss who had been lost in the world (practically unknown) came to ease up and "nourish" our natural loss of Lao Tan our dear "mother" and "son." The loss is now part of the loosening of the entanglements (59). This is the "nourishment of our close relatives," the fulfillment of filial piety, not as young people weeping for their loss of parents, but as the filial son nourishing them. Lao Tzu the teacher is now our relative Lao Tan.[110]

In the end, whatever is pointed to (*chih*) in our understanding (*chih*) is exhausted in whatever firewood that we are, and when the fire of life travels in suffering by knives, we would be loosened away from the bother of knowing when it finishes (61). This is the way to "finish out our natural years" (4), the last characteristic of staying on with our spinal thread of vitality. This is also the loosening dance of the cook, the ordinary life of the lowly caste. In such ordinary living we live it up to the very limit, and we are happy. Our finish is our completion. This is anything but prudential stoicism; it is resiliently positive Taoism.

3.   The two stories which begin Chapters Two and Three (on things and on life) have something in common. In both stories there is music that gives birth to things. In one, pipings let hollows and cavities come alive as things in the heaven, in nature, and among men. In the other, the dance goes through hollows and cavities to loosen things apart and to nourish life. Ezekiel prophetically ordered the dry bones to come alive;[111] Chuang Tzu piped and danced out things. Ezekiel had the word of the Lord; Chuang Tzu had the wind and the spirit, and the Lord admired.

Such origination and nourishment of life and things are anything but conscious or contrived. Mr. Southern City Wall becomes as dead as withered log and dead ashes to overhear the pipings, the breath of the huge Clod belching, going, belching through. The invisible wind goes through the nothingness of hollows and cavities, and the pipings come out and the "dead" ears overhear.

Similarly, the Cook himself goes through a threefold decrease of the self, so as to go through thicklessly (in the spirit-ed knife) the interstices, and then the dancing music that loosens and nourishes happens. It is an un-self-conscious tracing of the invisible spinal fold, both of things and of oneself. It is the Way of things in which the Cook moves and has his being.

At the same time, there is a progress from the hearing to the loosening. The belching of the huge Clod's breath becomes the spontaneous walk of the spirit as it desires, *in* which the Cook and the ox dance together. The pipings that sound like things in three areas are now the concrete symphonic music that dances together the knife, the Cook, and the ox, and nourishes life. The noble Master Base of the South, who overhears absent-mindedly the as-if creation of things, is now the lowly Cook who actually creates the dance music that loosens and nourishes, the rain dance which echoes the belching of the Clod. The noble Master South Base as-if dies and overhears; the lowly Cook moves, creates, and comes alive. The noble Master keeps asking; the lowly Cook exultantly explains. In the Cook the music of creative piping becomes the dance of nourishing, and the passive overhearing of whatever activities out there, becomes the live demonstration of the act of nourishment. There is, then, progress.

"Progress" is at bottom a mutual enrichment of implications. The passive overhearing is really a powerful transforming. The active cutting is really an overhearing and a letting be, an entering of nothing into nothing, a nourishing dance, a music of nature.

4.   A little speculative imagination sees some surprising connections between the two stories of the cook and the commander.

The cook (*p'ao*) may be a cipher for a brotherly fellow (*pao*) who enfolds (*pao*) his fellow humans (even his Lord) by undoing an ox (a thing) to feed them.[112] In answer, the Lord gives the grace of admiration, who yet can mutilate his subjects (such as his commander) to fulfill their uniqueness.

The point is that brutality—both undoing (*chieh*) and mutilating (*chieh*) rhyme—can feed as the cook, and fulfill as the commander, if we but trace and stay on what we do not see (*shih*) or know (*chih*) at the spinal route (*tu, ching*), the Way things go (*tao*), the natural veins (*t'ien li*) of things. Then we see that to enfold is to loosen is to feed; to grace is to mutilate is to fulfill. A bewildering co-incidence of opposites that makes sense only in the marrow of our spine. And we would not "know" it.

5.1.   Our hearts roam with the pheasant strutting through the marshland, ten steps a peck, a hundred steps a drink, going along with the rhythm of the wild. It does not wish to hoard (*ch'u*) what is given or what it is born with (*yü*; 33). For to hoard something would hoard and cage you (*ch'u*) in that thing. Doing "good" we go near fame; and then we are caged in social externals. This is not "good" at all; we have now lost our strutting roaming freedom in the wild

(39). We must instead "good" the knife that cuts (27), the knife of nature.

For the marsh pheasant stays on with its spinal instincts when he struts through the swampland, ten steps a peck. He may become singular-footed as the commander, or die as Lao Tan. But he is happy, being himself, hoarding nothing, caged by none. And this is "good."

There is of course no guarantee that what "goods" my life also "goods" my death, as was said in Chapter Six (6/58). But as long as I am part of what "goods" things, I have a part in "good"-ing my life, and then I can affirm with my life and my death such conviction that life is good—what "goods" my life also "goods" my death, after all. And so, the cook "goods" his knife (and his knifing acts) as the pheasant "goods" his steps in the wild. This is a sort of Chinese existential ethics. We remember Camus' Sisyphus was good and well with his rock; *he* turned his rock into his bliss.

5.2. The story of the pheasant is pregnant with meaning precisely because of its peculiar uneventfulness, compared with other stories.

This story alone (*tu*; 33) has no loosening, no mutilation, no death. This alone has no dramatic activity, much less tragedy. This alone has no counterpart to cope with. It is as it is, as brief as it is uneventful.

And perhaps the point lies precisely here; one ought to live free as oneself, without any special description. The last line is a breeze compared with butchery, mutilation, and death. The line may even be an elaboration of the main point, not its contrast. For living *in* a cage is not condemned as much as being fed-in-a-cage, in short, being caged. To be in a cage is one thing; to be caged is quite another. *Fan*[a] ("cage") is said to be *fan*[b],[113] which has the additional connotation of national territory, cultural boundary. Perhaps we may do well to live in the territory of a tyrant, whether political or cultural. He who can live in it uncaged is the true wild pheasant. This pheasant lives a carefree life, though not risk-free.

And this is the zenith of the chapter—a free nonchalant Hsiao Yao Yu, eating and drinking as one hops and roams. We remember that the *P'ung* which started Chapter One was a big *fung*, phoenix, roiling the waters three thousand miles, flying nine thousand miles up for the Southern Darkness (lines 8–10). Here this regal Yin of Phoenix is as calm, small, and ordinary as a pheasant, trotting in the marshland, yet remaining a phoenix; what a contrast! Yet both birds *are* phoenixes by virtue of their common phoenix-like character: both are unbridled by the natural elements and human bondage, in which both are free and active.

Besides, as fish-*k'un* rhymes with phoenix-*p'ung* in their liquid *un*-sound, so marsh-*tseh* and pheasant-*chih* rhyme in the restful *h*-sound (or silence).

Perhaps the changing soaring epic journey was meant to end in an unhurried sauntering freedom among foods and drinks at the quiet ordinary marshland, which may well be the Southern Darkness dreamed by the *P'ung*.

5.3.   Connections, not contrasts, with other sections can be seen. *Pu* describes how we walk, now a step (*t'a*), now a stop (*chih*), one leg after another. When we have only one leg, the gait of walking becomes more pronounced, now a hop, now a stop. And thus *pu* echoes *chieh*, singular-footedness.[114] The pheasant's carefree steps (almost without destination) remind us of "not knowing its finish" (61) that finished this chapter. "King" (39) reminds us of Lord Wen Hui and Lao Tan. "Not good" (39) continues "good" in Lord Wen Hui's praise of the cook-butcher. He praised the cook yet could not *be* the cook; he is "not good," yet.

But of course the most important term here is *pu*, the strutting roaming walk of the pheasant, everywhere in the wild. Such *pu* reminds us of *ch'uo* that accompanies every character of the title, *hsiao yao yu*, "now walking, now halting."[115] Such strutting everywhere is another expression of "can ... can ... can ... " that began the third chapter (4).

Furthermore, the carefree pheasant is incarnated in the "cool" manner of Mr. Ch'in, the "losing-loosing," easy-going which cuts through all the "mushy" and thick atmosphere of mourning, the height of Confucianism.

The comparison can go on indefinitely. Enough has been said to show how the central story of the chapter, the hub of all things, is a brief description of the simple ordinary life of an unknown marsh pheasant.

6.1.   How about the two long elaborate stories in the chapter? We can say that they mirror each other.

The first story is thrilling at first, and later develops a problems of how *butchery* can be joyous dance and how the smoothness of loosening up an ox operates in complex places. The second story is puzzling at first as to how a friend of *Lao Tan* can be so casual in mourning his death (as well as how we can even mention our revered master teacher's death), and then explains how natural such an attitude is. The difficulty is hidden in the first story, in joy; it is on the surface in the second, in mourning.

Furthermore, in the first story the knife's spatial cruising is described in the time-language of music and dance. In the second story, the passing of our life-time is described in the space-language of being at "at home" and "settled."

Finally, the first story describes how a cook can be in command over an enormous ox, something less than us in value. The second story describes how our teacher is controlled by the inexorable passage of invisible time that finally robs him of his life, someone we look up to.

There may be more mirror-like contrasts between the two stories. But this does not mean that they are opposed. Quite the contrary, the first story should be read in the light of the second, and the second in the light of the first. To be in command over something lower is as shallow an impression as being overwhelmed by the onrush of our own death. The ox, the knife, and the cook are at one in the spontaneous symphonic dance of a nothing using a nothing to enter a nothing. The situation is similar to the master's being at home in the passage of time, settling himself in following along, in which sorrows and joys are irrelevant. Conversely, to be at home in change is to enter the rhythm of change, and the ecstasy of the spirit ensues in the dancing together with time. It is a loosening of the thing (in the first story) and of the self (in the second)—a loosening that is as nourishing in the knifing as it is natural in the dying.

6.2. But what is the undoing of the self? It is a fact beyond reason and understanding, because understanding is part of ourselves, whose very loosening is the fact. All reasoning and teaching, all human relations, all daily events, shall one day cease, unravelled and undone, at least for each of us, even for Lao Tan. To feel at home, loosening our knotted selves in the midst of such undoing of all we have and are, requires more than a neat packaging of logical points, for there is no such package. For, let us repeat to ourselves, everything goes, including our understanding. Without adequate understanding, however, we owe it to ourselves to become a Mr. Ch'in the loser-looser, the easy-goer, to be mournful without sorrow, to lose things and lives without looking glum over the loss.

The later *Chuang Tzu* offers many diverse explanations as to how this is possible.[116] Here it offers only a *how*—to come back to one's own un-unself-conscious spinal artery of life-energy, the spirit, and stay on it, And one will understand, without cognitively knowing about it. One will let go of things and be as much at ease in life as Mr. Ch'in the loser; one will *be* Mr. Ch'in.

7.1. Our life is limited, in which we can become im-mortal. This is the fascinating theme that concludes the chapter that is the summa of the Inner Chapters, which in turn are the gist of the entire *Chuang Tzu*. To look into the final sayings of the chapter, we must also look over the entire chapter, especially its beginning passages.

The concluding two lines (60–61) are so brief as to be almost unintelligible. This is perhaps because the conclusion needs to be forceful, and the briefer the sentence the more forceful it is. Now that everything is told (though again all too briefly), only the final punch is needed.

Chuang Tzu was, however, smart enough to add three new ciphers to spur us on—finger-pointer-manipulation (*chih*), firewood (*hsin*), and fire (*huo*). They are cryptically combined; those thirteen characters in two short sentences are unintelligible at the first reading. There must be a clue.

I have found the clue, I think, in the opening lines of the chapter (1–4):

"My life is limited but knowledge is unlimited; with the limited to follow the unlimited is already a danger" (1).

"… the spinal artery of energy …" (3).

"With it we can sustain our body, with it keep our life whole, with it nourish our family, with it live out our natural years" (4).

"Finger-pointing (*chih*) is exhausted in the making (*wei*) of firewood" (60).

"… not knowing …" (61).

"Fire transmits itself, not knowing its finish" (61).

"Knowing" appears in the first and the last sentence of the chapter; it is regarded as not good. Knowing is perhaps synonymous with various activities of following, fingering-pointing (*chih*) and making (*wei*).[117] My limited life echoes the exhaustion of fingering-pointing (*chih*). And perhaps line 3 is negatively summed up in the phrase, "not knowing," in the last line (61). And perhaps the *entire* line 61 summarizes line 4. And the reading of the whole chapter confirms this interpretation. The chapter concerns two themes, life in its loosening-suffering, and our dealing with it, either in our self-conscious knowing or in our un-self-conscious staying on at the spinal core of life.

With this as a clue, I take it that the main message of the concluding two sentences is twofold, expressed in two sets of connections: (*a*) knowing, with limitlessness, with suffering, and (*b*) not knowing, with finishing out our years, with the principle of nourishing life. Section 7.2 treats (*a*); 7.3 treats its transition to (*b*). 7.4 treats (b).

7.2.1. The concluding phrase of the chapter, "not knowing its finish," is all too vague. First, who or what is the subject? Fire? Life? The knower? "Fire does not know its exhaustion" means "The fire goes on without end." "Life does not know its finish" means "When we are, death is not, and when death is, we are not" (Epicurus). Or else it means "Life does not know the fire's finish," where fire could mean either "life" (and then the sentence affirms immortality) or "suffering," meaning, suffering is from heaven, of which we know nothing, or about which we can do nothing.

"Its" in "not knowing its finish" is also vague. Whose finish? Knowledge? Fire? And what is fire? If it means the ending of knowledge, then "not knowing its finish" says "Knowledge has no boundary" (1). If it means the finish of fire, then what does fire mean? Fire can mean life or suffering or both. If life is meant, then we have the problem raised by T'ang Chün-i, that is, life is taken to be limitless here, contradicting the beginning of the chapter asserting life to be limited.[118] But perhaps "does not know its finish" differs from "is endless." If "fire" means suffering, then the concluding phrase of the chapter borders on a Buddhistic pessimism that is foreign to Chuang Tzu. Or is it pessimism? Chuang Tzu wants us to live *through* the knifing suffering, converting suffering into a loosening which divides out (*fen*) things and changes (*hua*) things, as was concluded in the second chapter. Chuang Tzu calls the process "life nourishment" (*yang sheng*).

Perhaps Chuang Tzu's meaning is somewhat as follows: Life contains desirables (our nourishment) and detestables (suffering). To live is to have both which are inseparable through distinguishable. It is only when we give up (*pu*) trying to discern and discriminate (*chih*) that we can live out our years (*chin nien*), enjoy our subjective immortality (*pu chih ... chin*), and let the suffering be as it is (not knowing where it ends).

All this hinges on our giving up knowing (*pu chih*), that is, giving up using the limited life endeavor of cognition to follow up on the unlimited tangles of life and suffering, crisscrossing each other, defying our knowing.

7.2.2. Our knowing seems to be an ill-named dog which Chuang Tzu tried to hang. Since the chapter is about the principle of life, the object of knowledge should also be life and principle. The beginning sentence of the chapter should then mean "My life is limited, yet the knowledge of life and its principle is unlimited." We must leave "knowledge" undefined—it could be cognition, analysis, or even discernment. Whatever definition knowledge takes, even it takes all of them, the preceding interpretation holds. Taken in this way, this opening statement tallies with the usual saying, "life is larger than logic," although on the surface the latter statement contradicts the former.

Taken in this way, the opening statement also tallies with the chapter's next to last statement, "Finger-pointing exhausts itself in the making of firewood" (60). The "finger" here is the pointer, that *with* which we know, perhaps our limited life span, or even the grease or lard (*chih*) with which we burn and suffer, such as our talents. *Chih* can also mean our very knowing activity.

We use our fingers to forward the logs, one by one, and the manipulation of logs ends at each log.[119] Every log can be burnt up, yet the fire goes on, not knowing where it ends. Kuo Ch'ing-fan said that a log can mean one cycle of breathing in and out. "Such cycles of breathing go back and forth in the great void," he said. Man takes part in them, and lives on, as logs transmit fire. Fire comes and we can not refuse it, it goes and we cannot retain it. All that we can manipulate stops at logs. Yet our life goes on and we who are in its midst do not know it.

Knowledge—or more accurately, trying to follow knowledge—is impossible, both in the sense that life is too subtle and supple for our limited ability of cognition to handle, and in the sense that knowledge of all of its own events is too much for any individual life to bear. Knowledge, to be knowledge, would have to be limitless. We cannot possibly follow after knowledge and survive intact. Limitlessness or boundlessness here is not mathematical or philosophical infinite, something absolute, bloodless, in the domain of cognitive calculation. Limitlessness is simply something "without limit" from *my* perspective, something of which I do "not know the limit." Limitlessness is the freshness of that nineteen-years-old knife which is as if fresh from the grindstone.

From this perspective, we can now collate two sentences beginning and ending the Chapter:

"Fire transmits ... not ... finish" (61).
"... knowledge ... no limit" (1).

7.3. "Knowledge ... no limit" (1) is equivalent to "not knowing ... finish" (61). As we understand that our knowledge has no limit,[120] we will settle in not-knowing the finish of things, and thereby finish out our natural years. And then we say confidently that to know the exhaustion of life leads to dying an untimely death (danger and suffering [1–2]), and not to know the exhaustion of life leads to living out our years. It is this wise not-knowing (15, 61), of which the second chapter made so much, that turns the fire's finish into the natural finishing out of our years. Now, the loosening of an ox (things, life) is the loosening of entanglements, and the pheasant's risky life in the wild is the unique commander's living out of his singularity according to heaven.[121]

"O, my soul," said Pindar, "do not aspire to immortal life, but exhaust the limits of the possible."[122] Chuang Tzu quietly added, "and then you would not know your limits" (61).

7.4.1. Life goes on through one log *after* another. As logs fire them-selves, so fire transmits itself. As the cook manipulates the knife, the ox un-does itself. We may wish for fire by manipulating (*chih*) logs; we may not wish for the transmission of life by picking up the fire. Life goes on through one log after another of breathing cycles. We should not try to hang on to any particular "breath," or any particular "me"-consciousness. And the breathing-periods-as-a-whole are also *one* log, our natural life span. When this log is burnt, we can breathe out our breath, and we still do not know where it ends. The sub-jective evidence of the continuity of something called fire or life is that the subject does not-know, and this is the secret principle of life.[123] We are no longer endangered by trying to know life, that is, being conscious of and preoccupied with living longer.

But what is this nourishing principle of not-knowing? Not to know is not to try to know, but instead to stay along on one's spinal life artery. It is to live up to what one is at one's gut level, depending on, complying with, and obeying the natural grains of things and of oneself, that heavenly principle of nature (*t'ien li*). Having discarded cognitive pursuit, we now move and breathe with the spinal artery which enables our breathing. Our route of life will be the route of this spinal artery, the warp of the fabric of our life (*ching*); we live our life principle. And then we can loosen ourselves into the oxen of things, can be loosened out into the singularity of our uniqueness, loosened out into the wild of things, and loosened out of all life's entanglements. We live our principle.

7.4.2. And principle (*chu*) is etymologically connected with fire (*huo*). *Chu* is the picture of a lamp or (originally) lard candle above which the flame rises. In ancient days the fire (written as a dot) was also lit on a bundle of fire-wood carried by a boy at the religious ceremony for the ghosts and the spirits (*kuei shen*), who therefore came to be called *chu*. People paid homage to them, and so *chu* came to mean whatever or whomever the homage is paid to. In any case, *chu* is originally connected with lard-fat (*chih*) and fire.[124]

Perhaps Chuang Tzu meant to sum up the entire chapter in this way. As the fire burns to direct us in the dark, so this chapter describes the principle to direct us in our nourishment of life. As the fire burns from the grease and the wood, so the principle comes from our daily living. In fact, the daily ongoings *are* the way we burn. We must care for how we burn, and we may become death-less, without knowing our finish, in the same manner as our principle is valid without finish.

The connection of fire with life comes from an unexpected corner: Mary Caroline Richards, in *Centering*, talks about the making of pottery and the poetry of life, saying,

All the forces of the mineral world, in our skeleton as it were, ... want to grow rigid, want to congeal; all our habits ... weigh us down; the death-dance burns away the bone, burns away, and lets the living impulses rise, the vision rise. So it is difficult to ... invoke the sense of life ... unspeakable, what is left after the books are all ... burned, forgotten.[125]

This is the connection of life with fire, that fire releases life out of congealed life-materials. And *we* come to life, burning our fire. As our life is our fire, so the way we live teaches us our principle of nourishment. Nourish our fire well as we nourish ourselves; surrender ourselves to it as the potter surrenders his molded clay to the fire. The fire then takes over and "the fired pot is the child" (M. C. Richards).

And so, the three characters of the chapter title are completed. The second character, *Sheng*, appears on line 1 twice—the first time clearly, the second time implicitly, as the limitless. The first character of the title, *Yang*, appears in the final line (4) of the introductory section, four times—again, clearly once, and three other times implicitly (as *pao*, *ch'üan*, *chin*). Now we see how the last line of the chapter has *Chu* implied in the final line, in "fire" (*huo*).

If we look carefully, we can also see *yang*, *sheng*, *chu*, implicitly stamped throughout the chapter:[126]

Yang Sheng:
    Yang: In the story of the cook;
    Sheng: In the story of the Commander.
    Yang: In the story of the pheasant;
    Sheng: In the story of Lao Tan.
Chu: In the story of fire and firewood.

The chapter is a tapestry of life woven with the warp of the principle and the woof of the stories.

8.1. We remember how Mr. South Wall becomes as dead wood and ashes, losing his conscious, objective, and objectivating self, to participate in the never-ending chorus of the pipings of the universe. He becomes as dead and comes alive in things, as Chuang Chou becomes un-self-conscious in his dream and becomes a butterfly. Similarly here. We have to discard cognition and skill to enter the spirit. We have to exhaust our pointings at, and manipulation of, the firewood to not-know the finish of the transmission of fire.

All this is not death, but coming to be *as* dead. It is darkness that breeds.

We also remember that Chapter One starts with darkness and ends with a lying asleep. Chapter Two starts with a sitting, a position neither of standing nor of lying, and a trance, a situation neither of sleep nor of awakening. The second chapter ends with a dream, a situation neither of the total light of consciousness nor of the total darkness of dead sleep.[127] Chapter Three begins with a warning against knowledge and proposes staying on the spinal artery, which is again neither totally unconscious nor totally conscious. The third chapter ends with the fire that goes on without knowing the finish. If the dream of Chapter Two echoes the sleep of Chapter One, then the not-knowing of Chapter Three echoes the not-knowing of the dream of Chapter Two. Such not knowing is repeated in Chapter Four, both at the beginning and at the end. Roaming with the uncanny crippled begins Chapter Five, which ends with a sleepy gibberish of logical analysis. Both Chapter Six and Seven begin and end with an intertwining of knowing and not-knowing.

All this is about the pervasive obscurity and ambiguity, both within and outside the self, called *hun tun* (at the end of Chapter Seven); it pervades the Inner Chapters. If "living drunk and dying in a dream" is bad, living in a dream is proposed here, where things germinate and grow. The point is purposely to live there purposelessly.[128]

8.2. Let us arrange the third chapter according to the key terms and then see how the arrangement mirrors the Inner Chapters.

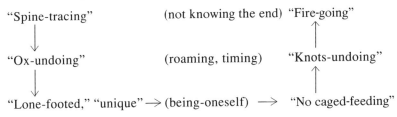

Cutting (and so suffering) becomes undoing, that is, unraveling problems, loosening ourselves from knots of time. Therefore there is no death but only finishing out our years without knowing it. This main theme is elaborated in other of the Inner Chapters:

Spine-tracing leads to the cosmic freedom which is dealt
    with in Chapter One;
Ox-undoing unravels tangles of things and thinking in
    Chapter Two;
Unique lone-footedness is treated as a sign of virtue to
    which people flock in Chapter Five;
No caged feeding in politics, where true men walk as the
    wild pheasant does, is treated in Chapter Four;
Knots-undoing concerns friends and deaths in Chapter Six;
    and

Fire-going-without-our-knowing concerns ultimate matters
    in Chapter Seven.
The mutual connections among these chapters, which come
    together in the inner principle of life-nourishment,
    are given in Chapter Three.

The connections are expressed in the key terms as set forth above, all indicating the Way to live our natural years. Chapter Three is the summary and
index of the Inner Chapters.

8.3.   At the center of all this is life (*sheng*), the be-all of all stories. Life
is what we *are*. Unfortunately life contains an inevitable ingredient, the
"knife," which cuts us this way and that, until we fall to the ground. It is up to
us to change our fall into the return of a clod of earth to the ground. This is to
convert the cutting into a loosening, and the loosening into a nourishing.

To go along with such inevitabilities, without trying to know the rational
connections between ourselves and the knife, is the way to survive. For this
to happen we must stay on the spinal artery of life-energy. We will then nourish
life.

To go along with suffering is to survive and nourish; thus the chapter about
nourishment has nothing but suffering. Suffering is what is obvious; nourishment is what is hidden. The chapter presents what is obvious to bring a
realization of what is hidden. If metaphor is a raft taking us from hither to
thither, then the chapter on life-nourishment is a metaphor. He who can take it
can take the journey from the hither of suffering to the thither of nourishment.
The journey is after all ourselves, life itself, in which suffering and nourishment are intertwined.

And now, after having hazarded some connections and implications
among the stories, we can go back to those stories again. We can forget all
speculations and simply read the stories. They shall come alive and nourish our
souls, or rather, our spines.

8.4.   Now we are in a position to settle back and understand what all this
means. Specifically two questions present themselves for consideration. (*a*)
Do all these pages so far on the first three chapters of the *Chuang Tzu* belong
to Chuang Tzu or to myself? (*b*) Do all these thoughts have any bearings on
life today? What do they *mean*? The second question (b) will be considered in
the Epilogue. Let us go briefly into the first question (*a*) here.

The *Chuang Tzu* is to myself as the firewood is to the fire. Fire differs from
the firewood. The fire transmits itself by drawing on the firewood. Without the
firewood there would be no fire, much less the firewood-fire; without fire, the
firewood is dead. Besides, in the fire we see the firewood—the fire is *that* sort

of fire. And in the firewood we see the fire—the firewood is there for the sake of making fire, or else it would not be firewood.

First, it is hoped that these pages make some contributions to the kind of Chuang Tzu scholarship that is not Chuang Tzu scholasticism. Although Chuang Tzu studies should no be embalmed in archaic irrelevance, they cannot afford to cut themselves off from historical scholarship and lose their authenticity to the picture of Chuang Tzu. These pages are hopefully not a false picture of Chuang Tzu. At the same time it cannot be doubted that these pages would not have been written in *this* manner were I not alive to write them.

Thus my *Companion* has the unmistakable peculiarity of my thinking, and at the same time it also belongs unmistakably to Chuang Tzu, not to Confucius or Plato. The unity is as inevitable as it is natural, and it is a peculiar one having two essential characteristics—it is a Chuang Tzu through myself.

The Butterfly as Companion

INCONCLUSIVE MEDITATIONS

The book of *Chuang Tzu* is a "scrapbook," a collection of bits of myths, legends, anecdotes, and their parodies. It makes fantastic reading. Colliding galloping nonsense is mingled with physics and myths, and logic is interspersed with alchemy and jokes. An Einstein talks with a Seneca and a Confucius changes his mind about Confucianism. Kings are taught by lowly artisans and butchers. In addition, there are the holy cripples and criminals, beauties and saints, sophists and despots. The book is a melange of delightful mess.[1]

Going through such a confusing collage the reader is yet somehow put at ease. He has been oppressed with suffering long enough. Now he can breathe again and smile. He is calmed and invigorated. Yet he stammers when asked *what* the book is about, what it is that he has gotten out of it. There is nothing specific at which he can point and say: This is the main point in the entire parade of seeming confusion. Such is the *Chuang Tzu*, a potpourri of meaninglessness that is profoundly wholesome.

The world has few works of literature that match the *Chuang Tzu* in such strange charm. The closest analogy in Chinese history is *ch'ing t'an*, Pure Conversation, during the dynasties of Wei and Chin (220–420 A.D.). But those conversationalists engaged in delightful and spicy talks for the sake of talking. They were brilliant recluses; the *Chuang Tzu* is not a book of recluses. The pure conversationalists were otherworldly; the *Chuang Tzu* is both otherworldly and this-worldly. They were at least coherent in their tenor; the *Chuang Tzu* is a montage of bits of seemingly contradictory stories. And in the very confusion and nonsense, the *Chuang Tzu* lifts us up as we go through it. This is a book of profound nonsense in which the sense of life emerges. It gives freedom to life, letting us "float around" *in* the world. Shen Fu wrote *Six Essays on Floating Life* in A.D. 1673 because Chuang Tzu wrote at least Seven Essays on Floating Life in the fourth century B.C. (cf. 1/42; 15/12). Both practiced their Roaming Essay on Floating Life (cf. 11/49; 20/6, 7).

In order to understand all this, we will look into what sense or "meaning" can be in such a book (Meditation A); how "saying" can be as surprisingly "ironic" as its meaning is startlingly wild and fresh (Meditation B); how all this amounts to "play" (Meditation C); and finally, what a "companion" to the *Chuang Tzu* can do to help us understand meaning, irony, and play in relation to our life (Meditation D).

A. Meaning

1. "Meaning" is so basic and pervasive that it cannot be clearly defined or described. To ask what meaning means begs the question, for every word describing meaning must itself be meaningful. We can only become aware of what meaning is by attending to the situation where meanings emerge—human experience. Philip Wheelwright said, "Every human experience has meaning."[2] We are "condemned to meaning," as Camus, Sartre, and Merleau-Ponty repeatedly said. All phenomenology is built on it; all philosophizing is to explain this fact of life.

Experiential meaning obviously transcends linguistic meaning, which is a special case of a meaningful situation in which we have our being as human. The Hebrew word for "word," *dābār,* has its Semitic root, *dbr,* hinterground. *Dābār* is a manifestation of the hinterground of meaning in the dynamic event. Every event has its "word"; to understand an event is to understand its meaning. Thus the plural *dᵉbārîm,* like its synonyms, *rēmata* (Greek) and *res gestae* (Latin), may mean "history." Christianity exploited this etymological connection and used the notion of "word" to describe the meaningful "mighty act of God" as the manifestation of His *word,* which "happened" (or "was born"; *egeneto*) in history.[3]

This connection among meaning, event, and word is not accidental. Our overwhelming *sense* of significance suggested by things seen or heard (the starry sky, conscience, music) is more than mere feeling or concept. To capture this "sense" is the purpose of art. It is the sense of the world for which beautiful things stand.

A Taoist poet, T'ao Ch'ien (372–427 A.D.). said (thirteen hundred years before Wordsworth was born):

> "Plucking chrysanthemums along the east fence;
> Gazing in silence at the Southern Hills;
> The birds flying home in pairs
> Through the soft mountain air of dusk—
> In these things there is a deep meaning [i].
> But when we are about to express it,
> We suddenly forget the words [*yen*].[4]

"In these things there is a deep meaning [literally, 'true intention']," T'ao Ch'ien said. All the situational elements—chrysanthemums, east fence, Southern Hills, flying birds, soft mountain air of dusk—all constitute a life configuration that *is* meaning, which is so pervasive that we "forget the words." It is only when we forget words *in* such a meaning-situation that we understand.

Similarly, an act can have a meaning that reaches further than verbal statement; the significance of an act may include an indefinite range of suggestions beyond intellectual exposition. Saying and thinking—however well done—are mere shadows. "Don't say; show me." To do is to say, and merely to say is not really to *say* at all.

If events and facts, charged as they are with significance, are yet ambiguous and elusive, this is what life is. Real meanings are ambiguous. To say that all this is "existential" talk does not go to the heart of the matter. The *word* "existential" is elusive to the point of being deceptive, even implying that thinking and its referent are separate. But the referred reality is charged with meaning; it *is* the meaning-matrix which renders the word "existential" significant.

There is something unique and decisive about the elusive factuality of experience. "Their behavior had no trail, their events had no records." Books are mere chaff and dregs when compared with wheel-chiselling, which we can only comprehend in our hand and feel in our mind.[5]

2.   What is a situational meaning? It is insight into a meaningful situation, an environment in which a coherent relation is *seen* among things. Then we say that the situation is meaningful. Such a pattern of togetherness which is meaning is made up of two interpenetrated elements: the symbol and the signified meaning. On the one hand, the life of a symbol is the meaning to which it points; the symbol exists only in its meaning. On the other hand, there is no meaning without the symbol; meaning manifests as meaning only in its symbol. Desymbolized meaning cannot be thought, and unthinkable meaning does not exist any more than a disembodied person does.

Thus meaning and symbol co-exist by a mutual indwelling. Symbol is not a dispensable instrument of meaning, but its essential ingredient and embodiment. And both meaning and its symbol are born of life and dwell in it. Such symbols as darkness and water were given to us with our experience, forcing themselves upon us. Yet the meaning of life is as ambiguous as its symbols are overwhelming, for those symbols are polythetic, evocative of many insights and applications.

The experience of a situation is meaningful when seen to be signified by a non-linguistic sign, such as "body language." Music pervades the air, and colors and smells charge the situation with polythetic coherence.

What is polythetic meaning? Its contrast, monothetic meaning, clarifies it. In a monothetic meaning-situation, "What is the point?" can be asked, but that question is out of place in a polythetic meaning-situation. The latter situation is merely charged with clouds of implications, still to break out into a thunderous clarity. It is polythetic[6] because it is non-thetic of articulate meanings. We cannot ask what it means because all we have is a peculiar con-figuration of situational factors, waiting to be "read off" by a perceptive observer.

Moreover, the very "situational pattern" is a product of the reading. Reading is a crucial shaping force, not a passive discovery of an already made meaning. In a polythetic situation the "reader" actively works out (constitutes) meanings from a significant situation. The constitution goes somewhat like this. Being non-thetic, the situational factors interest the observer who dwells in them, just as they are—or rather, he lets himself be immersed, as he is soaked in the sunshine while walking. Then the configuration can sooner or later suggest new meanings. Such a situation can be called "poetic," evoking enjoyment for its own sake before a definite meaning is perceived.

Thus the symbol is alive to the perceptive reader, on whose sensitivity the emergence of meaning depends. Conversely, the excellence of a polythetic symbol, whether situational[7] or semantic,[8] corresponds with the range, the variety, and the depths of meanings that the significant situation can call forth in the reader. When the reader is "bored" the situation loses its evocative power. The classical literature is a group of highly significant writings that bear repeated readings, capable of continual dehiscence of meaning. Similarly, we can call any situation that is highly charged with meaning "classical" or "historic."

Aristotle said in his *Rhetoric* (I. 3) that there are three elements in speech-making—the speaker, the subject, and the audience. Of these three, "it is the last one, the hearer, that determines the speech's end and object," for the whole purpose of the speech is to win the hearer over to the speaker's side.[9]

In order to show how revolutionary Aristotle was, yet how regretably short of the importance of the "hearer" Aristotle came, we must weigh the importance of each of the three elements in a general statement, "I tell you something." The statement has four words: "I" the speaker, the act (and manner) of "telling," "you" the hearer, and "something" told, the subject matter.

We usually say that the subject matter, "something" told, is the most important, for the conveyance of which the speech is made. Then, "I" the speaker is taken as the source of information, the guarantor of the conveyed message. Then comes the manner of conveyance, as to how accurately "it" is conveyed. The hearer is, then, left over as the least important. The information that is true universally (as in science) is for *anyone* interested. In short, in the modern world the order of importance in the sentence, "I tell you something," is: (1) "something" told, (2) "I" the speaker, (3) my manner of telling, and then (4) an anonymous "you" the hearer.

In contrast, Aristotle correctly perceived that the object of speech is to influence the hearer in some way with the how and the what of my telling. Otherwise there is no point in telling. This is the insight on which Aristotle founded his *Rhetoric*. However, Aristotle mistakenly judged the function of speech and the role of the hearer. For Aristotle the hearer is merely to be informed and won over to the *speaker*. Either as "member of the assembly," or as "a juryman," or "an observer," the hearer is to be persuaded and molded to the speaker's set objective. The rest of the *Rhetoric* is about the methods of persuasion. And so, for Aristotle the most important element in the sentence, "I tell you something," is (1) "I" the speaker. Then come in importance (2) "you" the hearer to be changed to my objective, then (3) the mode of my telling that changes you, and perhaps (4) whatever ("something") told for my purpose.

Chuang Tzu differs from both schemes described above. The contemporary mind regards "something" to be told as the most important, and "you" the hearer as the least important. Aristotle regards "I" the speaker as the most important, and "something" told as the least important. In contrast, Chuang Tzu regards "you" the listener as the main purpose of the speech, not in order to change you into my pre-set mold (Aristotle) but to arouse and release you into your own creativity. For this purpose the most effective means must be used; thus, the mode of "telling" comes next in importance. "I" the speaker is therefore of little significance. In fact, "I" should become so anonymous that you would not be influenced. Finally, "something" told is the least important. The hearer can be provoked into himself by anything—trivia, falsehood, irony, anything. The accuracy of what is conveyed is as irrelevant as it is necessary that I the speaker be anonymous. Thus the order of importance is (1) the hearer, (2) the persuasive telling, (3) the anonymous speaker, and (4) something told.

To sum up. The contemporary sentiment is a cognitive one, intent on the accurate conveyance of *information*. The Aristotelian mode is a rhetorical one, emphasizing molding the hearer to the *speaker's* objective. Chuang Tzu's style is an evocative one, stimulating the *hearer* to an ontological homecoming to the hearer himself.

Both the contemporary and the Aristotelian patterns of speech are directive—information to be conveyed as it is, a plan to be imposed on the hearer. In contrast, Chuang Tzu's pattern of speech is open-ended and indirective, intent on evoking in the hearer zest and thrust of the hearer's own life. Being indirective, descriptive sentences seem ill-suited here. But the *Chuang Tzu* has many sentences in descriptive *form*. This is because descriptive sentences can do many jobs:

(1) They can describe and inform.
(2) They can prescribe. "Little smile helps learning."
(3) They can recommend. "We usually want to help one another."
(4) They can perform, as John Austin said. "Now you are my pal."
(5) They can elicit the hearer's performance. "Zen is like learning the art of burglary."

When a description lets the hearer perform, it does not describe at all. "Zen is like learning burglary" says nothing about burglary or about Zen, but merely nudges the hearer to go on exploring Zen. "There is a fish or a bird" says even less; it does not even give us the "name" of what we should seek, but merely intrigues us into our own exploration.

"In the northern darkness there exists a very big fish, K'un, which is changed into a very big bird, P'ung. When the sea moves, the bird sets off for the southern darkness." Here description functions as a parable, a thrown-beside-the-inexpressible. The hearer is provoked into journeying and exploring on his own, and creatively discovers that "inexpressible."

Interestingly the preceding arrangement of sentential functions matches the order of a decrease in cognitive contents and an increase in hearer participation. When the sentence gives information, the hearer receives it. When it prescribes, the hearer follows. When it recommends, he can choose to accept it or refuse it. When it performs, he is influenced. When it elicits, he is on his own.

Where does the *Chuang Tzu* belong? It does not give us doctrines; it is not descriptive. It neither prescribes, nor recommends, nor performs. Instead, it performs some of these functions sometimes *so as to* lure us into living discernfully on our own.

That is why the *Chuang Tzu* has no view, no prescription, no achievements. This is why the *Chuang Tzu* seems vague yet is intriguing. Chuang Tzu is like a little child among us. He draws us into doing something for him, charms us into learning from him, but constantly reminds us that he is he and not us (for he has nothing we can take away), and we had better lead our life. He cleanses us by not cleansing us, that is, by being himself, thereby luring us into cleansing ourselves. This is an eliciting that is indirective, for which a poetic use of sentences (as described in the Prologue, in "The Poetic *Chuang Tzu*") is best.

3. Poetic self-division is a vibrant tension between antithetical meanings which are secretly related, and between those related meanings which are secretly antithetical. The poetic tension is most expressive when the explicit story and the suggested innuendoes vibrate across the distance, constituting an inherent dialectic with dramatic liveliness.

A symbol has a connotative fringe that has varying impacts on different ears. The evocation of self-creative novelty requires some slack between an expression and its overtone. It is not an irresponsible vagueness but a "soft focus," as Wheelwright calls, it, by which the hard outlines of a landscape are blurred; such blurred edges reveal the landscape most *truthfully*, in truth unmatched by conceptually exact plain speech.[10]

For such blurred ambivalence corresponds to a real ambivalence in the nature of things whose meanings are yet to be brought forth by and in the observer. Their precise expression is produced by a poetically controlled ambivalence which responds to the concrete vagueness. This is a significant obscurity required by the evocative expression of actuality. Paradoxically, the accuracy of communication (a sharing) requires literary ambivalence.

Creative novelty involves a hitherto-unheard-of regrouping of experience and events. We have no publicly accepted vocabulary for such new groupings. The task of an artist is precisely to formulate phrases not existing in any language, be it verbal, plastic, or musical.

Chuang Tzu goes as step further; his mission is a meta-artistic one. His task is to *induce* the hearer to formulate what does not exist in our existing vo-cabulary, be it verbal, plastic, musical, or behavioral. Chuang Tzu does not slave under logical universals but uses them toward universal plenitude. His meta-art enables the hearer to cut out a universe of experience that invigorates our ordinary discourse. That is, Chuang Tzu's meta-art stimulates the hearer into establishing the hearer's own concrete universality throughout the ups and downs of daily life. The hearer's own language then renovates the dictionary language.

All this is not as esoteric as it sounds. Ethical and esthetic statements were once regarded as "emotive" and "meaningless" because their meanings are *yet* to be evoked in the hearer. "Open the door" has a definite program of execution, but "Be kind to others" has none. "Roses are red" describes; "My love is a red, red rose" invites the hearer's active imagination to feel forth the intensive red-rose-like beauty of "my love," and through all this to envisage the inexpressible intensity of beauty. Artistic and ethical sentences are meaning-less, in the sense of being without a specific literal meaning, as of the moment of their utterance. Such lack of literal meaning makes for a pervasive evocative impact. The hearer's reaction to them produces sense and sensibility.

It is in this way that the *Chuang Tzu* intrigues the reader back to himself; it incites him into creating his own configurations of meaning, which render him *interested* in life. An "emotive" situation is a mother of meaning. An "emotive" sentence is meaning-less, non-thetically evocative of new meaning from the "emotive" situation.

4.   Language can, then, be divided into two kinds: exploratory language and explanatory language. Exploratory language opens our eyes to initiate feeling for new connection of things. By nature such language is metaphorical. Chuang Tzu calls it "lodged words (*yü yen*) and "goblet words" (*chih yen*).

Legge said that "'Yü Yen' are 'Lodged Words', that is, Ideas that receive their meaning or character from their environment, ... in which they are deposited." Wang Hsien-ch'ien said that "Lodged words are words that are entrusted and lodged" that is, "the intentive meaning that is here is entrusted, lodged, and expressed there."[11] Put differently, these words "lodge" us strategically here for us to see the new implications there.

Such lodging is often situational. Words must *tip* to the ever-changing trend of the situation, as if each one were a goblet tipping in and tipping forth its contents. And so the words are also called "goblet words." They are goblets tipping toward the situation so as to contain it as fully as they can. Lodged and gobletly, Chuang Tzu accords his language to the situation, and such is his invitation to the reader.

Chuang Tzu's goblet words lodge many meanings in a phrase or a story. As they come together and echo one another the reader comes to find one cross-connection after another, forgetting what Chuang Tzu originally had in mind. In "finding" meanings the reader makes them; as the reader progressively finds Chuang Tzu's words provocative and creative, Chuang Tzu makes the reader into a creative self. As the reader watches Chuang Tzu's words come alive in meaning, the reader discovers that these meanings have also been created by the reader's responses to the text. Thus, in reading, both the reader and the text come alive reciprocally; in the meantime, Chuang Tzu himself slips away.

5.   Such metaphorical use of language is risky. We will be confused if we are not aware of the connection between the temporary lodging and the proper residence of meaning, or if we are not aware of the situational meaning (yet unknown) *to* which the tipping of the linguistic goblet tends. We only see the

lodging and the inordinate tipping, and they both seem arbitrary and out of place. After all, it is painful to break our habitual perspective, in whose light such lodgings and tippings rightly seem odd. Chuang Tzu's words are indeed "useless," as even the professional word-juggler, Hui Shih the sophist, announced. It is so easy to be lost in the maze of exploration, where everything seems "odd, ... outlandish and bombastic."[12]

Thus it requires the reader's genius to turn the bewildering exploratory language into orderly explanatory language. Socrates complained that the soothsayers said something they themselves did not understand. But the job of understanding belongs to the *hearer*, not to the sayer. Socrates owed it to himself to explain what the Delphic oracle meant, "None is wiser than Socrates." In his struggle Socrates finally understood it by understanding the internal connection between knowledge and ignorance. But he failed to make the connection intelligible to *others*, his beloved Athenians. And that is perhaps the meaning of the charge of "impiety." Socrates' discovery amounts to being impious to *people's* capability to understand. He insulted the cultured Athenians. In his failure to make his discovery intelligible to them, he violated the sacred canon of communication, a mutual evocation; after all, the sacredness of the oracle lies in its being conveyed. That was the "impiety" of Socrates.

The difficulty of producing explanation out of exploration underscores the fact that the provocative language of exploration is always surprising to the point of senselessness. What shows such language to be inevitable, not senseless, is its evocation in the hearer of a coherent vision of new connections. The power of evocation is the proof that Chuang Tzu's language is a living nonsense, a profound frivolity.[13]

6. Gilbert Ryle compared the commodity-neutral paper and twine for packing commodity goods to the topic-neutral logical constants for packing natural language[14] What can be easily missed here is to let the convenience of "packing" blind us to the ever-present necessity of *improving* on the means of packing. Twine is now banned at the post office; packing tape is required. The paper box is being replaced by the foam and cellophane folder. Similarly logical constants are themselves to be "improved on" to accomodate, to pack adequately, the fascinatingly protean actuality of natural language that reflects our life world.

Interestingly enough, as the spilling of a package reveals its contents, so the failure of logic shows the contents packed therein. And there is no fixed logical way of exploring the ways of changing conventional logic. *Pace* Nowell Russell Hansen, there is no "logic of discovery." Although not arbitrary, exploration has no rule. Ryle's convenient coinage, "informal logic," is itself a contradiction in terms, for "form" is of the essence of logic. Besides, the coinage tends mistakenly to emphasize "logic" more than "informal."

Ryle said that the application of logic to the concrete situation is

> ... rather like what geometry is to the cartographer. He finds no Euclidean straight hedgerows or Euclidean plane meadows. Yet he could not map the sinuous hedgerows ... or the undulating meadows save against the ideally regular boundaries and levels in terms of which alone can he calculate out the relative positions and heights of the natural objects which he is to record from the visual observations. ... The possibility of his map being approximately correct or precise is the gift of Euclid.[15]

This is one side of the story, however. The truthful drawing *also* comes from noting how much the actual shape *deviates* from geometry. The crater's size gauges its creator (to change metaphor). Paradox is the logical crater from the impact of life, which is described best by paradox. Put it differently, the "signature" of the flow of experience is its novelty, to be expressed in elusive notions and phrases. These situational meanings must be constituted afresh, and cannot be stipulated a priori. The shifts of the situation demand conceptual dislocation.

Aristotle produced three kinds of hearers: judges, members of the assembly, and observers. His commentator, Edward Meredith Cope, says,

> Audiences are of two kinds; either mere 'spectators,' like the *theatai* in a theatre, [or] at the games, ... where there is no interest of a *practical* character ...; or else 'judges,' where some real interest is at stake, and they are called upon to pronounce a decision ... But these decisions, and those who pronounce them, again fall into two classes, according as they are referred to questions, (1) of political expedience and look to the *future*, or (2) of right or wrong in respect of *past* acts or facts.[16]

How tidy and barren such comment is! Aristotle was perhaps merely citing some examples from life, not trying out an exhaustive list of characteristics of various audiences. We remember Van Gogh, who exclaimed,

> I should despair if my figures were correct. ... If you take a photograph of a man digging ... he is sure to look as if he were not digging. ... I think Michaelangelo's figures magnificent, even though the legs are certainly too long and the hips and pelvis bones a little too broad. ...Well, yes, if you like, they are lies; but they are more valuable than the real values.[17]

Evocation of sensibility requires that our tendency to rely on ready-made method must be jolted to pieces. There is no "logic" of discovery, because logic is a system of interconnected highways, which are nowhere to be found during our trail-blazing. We have only many leads shooting in many directions. We must be sensitive to the confusing signals of the language of exploration.

The literal mind asks for a road map. But "where there is virgin forest, there can be no rails; where rails exist the jungle has long since been cleared."[18] Chuang Tzu simply says, "a path is made by people walking." The language of exploration whets our appetite for a walk into the uncharted land. The map comes later.

7.   In the meantime, the connections are many, and the language of exploration is polythetic in meaning and non-thetic in its evocative intent. It calls forth many potentials of associations.

First, there are novel connections among things and events. For example, a disciple eager to reform a despot was counselled by Chuang Tzu's "Confucius"[19] with the example of the tiger keeper, who tames the tiger by following along with it without meaning to tame it. Chuang Tzu connects the tiger keeper with the despot reformer.

Second, there are unexpected connections of the actual to the ideal. The reformation of despotism is connected to the reformation of the reformer's own ideal.

Third, there are hidden connections of the ideal to its ground. The tiger keeper, the political reformer, and the ideal are men's pipings to be connected to the earthly piping, both of which are symbolic of the heavenly piping.

Fourth, there are connections from the ground back to the actual situation. The heavenly embodied in the self lets go of the heavenly in the world. The heavenly is manifested in the world, in which we roam and play.

Chuang Tzu evokes all these connections. That is why his words seem confusing to the literal-minded. They seem "big and useless." That they are big and ironic but not useless can be seen by going into "irony."

B. Irony

1.   Meaning is connection seen among things. An idea is our reflection of meaning, and is our feat of association which enables us to understand one thing in terms of another. Such association can then be called metaphoric. Since association among things is our meaning and idea, our meaning and idea are metaphoric. Robert Frost even says that every philosopher has one big metaphor in him.[20] Johan Huizinga boldly declared that

Behind every abstract expression there lie the boldest of metaphors, and every metaphor is a play upon words. Thus in giving expression to life man creates a second, poetic world alongside the world of nature.[21]

Sadly, we are so used to our accustomed associations that we seldom see our thinking as metaphoric (much less poetic) until we explore something new. And then we become conscious of our language as metaphoric, understanding the strange in terms of the familiar.

Moreover, our language *after* our exploration is not only metaphoric but often ironic. For irony shakes us out of our fixed way of combining things. And we must be shaken off our familiar association before we can see the new world of exploration. Superficially an irony goes along with our usual conversation, only to make us realize that it points in a different direction. With the familiar meaning of words irony blasts the hearer's expectation.

For exploratory language appears to the unwary as relating unrelatables, as the language of incongruity. And incongruity breeds paradox and irony, in which the comic resides. Since life is larger than logic, we have many things in life to surprise us. Therefore "wherever there is life, there is contradiction, and wherever there is contradiction, the comical is present."[22]

Humor and irony induce self-recognition to liberate us from our prison of self-content. Yet this liberation is painful. Irony often appears as a sarcastic exposé.

Irony exhibits a collage of disrelations of things, and such a collage defies the *existing* order of things. But the ironist does not stand in another world beyond. His irreconcilables let in a new perception of reality to jar our old assumptions. The ironist lets memory, hope, and experience clash and challenge each other. The clash shocks the audience. Thus Socrates had to die, and Chuang Tzu had to be misread.[23] The illogical *Chuang Tzu* offends us.

Bigotry is fixation in a routine method of "packaging things," and is particularly vulnerable to ironic ridicule. Fortunately, in addition to our love of set routine we also have an urge to live a new life. After the initial shock we *can* reflect on what the ridicule of an ironist means.

Chunag Tzu goes a step farther, however. He counsels us that we must stop being obsessed with devising a new and better way of life in order to find it. The best method is "no method" (*wu fang*), which must *come* naturally. He says,

The ten thousand things live species by species, one group settled close to another. Birds and beasts form their flocks ..., grass and trees grow to fullest height. ... In this age of Perfect Virtue men live the same as birds and beasts, group themselves side by side with the ten thousand things.[24]

To devise the Confucian "logic" of humanness is to hurt this natural "method" or order (or ways) in which things simply settle side by side together. We must kick *our* methodical habit and become "il-logical," going along with the trend of things; we cannot and should not push the river. And then we can reflect the way (method) of natural grouping; we will have the natural knack of accomplishment. Our life will be a walking of heaven, and our death will be a change of things. We act according to what-cannot-be-helped.[25]

But first we must be "il-logical." The "brash and bombastic language" of the *Chuang Tzu* smashes our pride in logic and knowledge. We become without a logic of our own, "useless."[26] And then we become mobile as water, placid as a mirror, and can now respond to things as their echoes.[27]

The sentences above are words without words, unintelligible yet contain truths. These words stir us to self-scrutiny and world-discovery. For the stirrings initiate a new experience which reveals reality otherwise hidden.

Irony and laughter loosen (*chieh*) us for such stirrings to the new. To laugh is to see beyond the transitoriness of events; laughing at oneself liberates the self into self-scrutiny, thereby allows the situation to appear meaningfully albeit often startlingly.

2. Irony differs from sarcasm. Sarcasm laughs at the hearer; irony laughs with him. The ironist laughs at himself, and invites the hearer to do likewise. The ironist's laughter is spontaneous, and his attack is not contrived.

Irony is by nature self-referential, and includes its opposite. It goes out of itself and looks at itself with the other. This is an act of comprehensiveness, a peculiar quality of the philosopher. And so we cannot take a philosopher seriously who takes himself so seriously that he is unable to poke fun at his own theories. Light-heartedly to include one's own negation is to see beyond oneself. It is to play with any theory, any metaphor, and thus to be in any world; it is to roam happily everywhere.

An example of self-irony is the story which ends the second chapter—Chuang Chou dreaming of being a butterfly. Awakened, he realized that he was unmistakably Chuang Chou. And *then*, in this awakened state, he realized that he might be a butterfly currently dreaming of being Chuang Chou.

One of the ironies here is that he had to be *awakened* before realizing that he could be a butterfly, currently *dreaming*. Awakening to a dream, and becoming certain about one's uncertainty—this is clearly a self-involved incongruity. The incongruity is between (1) situation *a* and situation *b*, such as Chuang Chou and a butterfly, awakening and dreaming, knowing and being uncertain, and (2) that situation *a* internally supports situation *b*, and vice versa: awakening to a dream, being cocksure while dreaming, Chuang Chou dreaming being a butterfly, and a butterfly dreaming of being Chuang Chou. This may be a better way of expressing the Socratic paradox, "I know that I do not know, and herein lies my wisdom." For Chuang Tzu the irony consists of a twofold built-in mutuality: (*1*) mutual distinction (*yu fen*) and (2) mutual interchange (*wu hua*). The ironist "double walks" (*liang hsing*; Chapter Two, line 129), spanning his life on two roads: *a* and *b*, (1) and (2).

Likewise, we must be awakened to living two lives; we live one life to live the other, dreamed and awakened, onself and another self, in this world and not of it. Living the double life, we see how every utterance and event takes on a fascinating strangeness. The simple and the mundane is now a spectacular mirror of the deep darkness, the lake of heaven, the heavenly reservoir of existence.

Sadly, we are usually too much in the "dream" of the immediacy of literalism to appreciate the depths of reality mirrored in the mundane. We must be evoked and awakened to appreciate the dream. Metaphor evokes us by juxtaposing the incongruous to break our linguistic convention.

Metaphorical juxtaposition alludes to (lightly plays on) something unexpected. Allusive metaphor shakes loose from us our complacency. We are awakened to naturalness and become flexible, continually responding to life risibles. "Of the comical there is certainly enough everywhere, and at every time, if a man only has an eye for it; one could continue indefinitely, ..."[28]

Wheelwright said that logical precise steno-language is to imaginative expressive language what a black-and-white movie is to a technicolor movie, or what a regular snapshot is to the artist's depiction, with the softened focus that brings actuality close to us.[29] Similarly here. If the metaphorical expression is a soft-focus painting, then play language is a movie, soft-focused and on the move. Moreover, when a statement is made about a situation, the hearer becomes part of the situation itself and thereby contributes to the situational change. It is like a child observing other children play, who then joins them in the play. This is how alive the play language is to the situation. Play language invites us to participate in the play of life. The child is able to speak, just by being with those who speak (26/30).

The play language is more "literal" than the literal language, for play language subtly and truthfully changes *with* the ever-changing situation. This pliant shift of the play language is more accurate and more responsive to the situation than a rigid modification of the cognitive literal language. No matter how much the geometer modifies his lines, they cannot hope truly to represent the cartographer's "coastlines." The conceptual exactitude of literalism changes awkwardly, if it ever does modify itself, for cognitive exactitude canonizes rational truths held to be valid for all possible worlds, and our actual life takes place in a very definite world of constant change.

Play language in its evocative expressivity has nothing to do with Stoic *ataraxia*.[30] In their indifference to the pain and pleasures of life the Stoics do not play. Their indifference is the result of their practice of death. By removing themselves from life they render themselves unable to play. In contrast, Chuang Tzu's metaphorical language induces participation. Chuang Tzu's language is as much alive to life as children's play; it is a play language. This brings into play the topic of play in life.

C. Play

1. Subjectively to discover meaning and objectively to communicate it in irony is to roam and play in the world. What play is can be seen by examining (*1*) the four kinds of connection which end Meditation A on meaning and (*2*) awakening to a dream which characterizes Meditation B on irony.

First, as to the four connections of things with events, the actual with the ideal, the ideal with its ground, and that ground with the actual. These connections may remind us of Whitehead, who once typified Western philosophizing as follows:

> The true method of discovery is like the flight of an aeroplane. It starts from the ground of particular observation; it makes a flight in the thin air of imaginative generalization; and it again lands for renewed observation rendered acute by rational interpretation.[31]

One *could* say that the connection among things is a preparation for the flight. The connection between actuals and ideals is the takeoff. The connection of ideals and actuals to their ground is the flight itself—a strange flight underground. And the connection between the ground and actuals is the descent.

But Chuang Tzu's play only superficially resembles Whitehead's vision. Chuang Tzu has no dichotomy between the general and the particular, and he does not leave the particulars for abstract generalization. Chuang Tzu's movement is gradually to discern, *within* the particular experience, its constant reference to the ground and matrix. It is to see the pipings of earth *in* the pipings of men, and then to see the heavenly piping *in* the earthly. The heavenly piping is the heavenly reservoir, equalizer, the Tao. And then, once the Tao is thus seen, each particular actual entity is strangely seen to contain its own peculiar "seed power" (*chi, chung*), the incipient power to spring forth into itself. The heavenly reservoir is seen in the seed power; without seeing the one, the other cannot be seen. Yet they are distinct—the heavenly reservoir is the universal matrix, the seed power is the specific "virtue" of an individual entity. Chuang Tzu has no flight *from* particular observation to thin generalization, which is then applied to the concrete particulars.

This reminds us of that notorious traffic between an awakening and a dream. It takes the awakening to realize that we might well be in a dream; in a dream, we have no interrelation between the two. In such a situation awakening is only one mode of existence, not more valuable than dream. Awakening is no more real than dream is less trustworthy. And they are involved in each other; the one situation cannot exist without the other. We are awakened to such mutuality.

To go in this way from one mode of existence to the other, is to go to one *in* the other. When we realize that there is the universal reservoir of ontological plenitude behind all things, then we realize that each actuality is as it is, with its own seed-power to spring out as such. And to *realize* this point is to be awakened to the likelihood that we are something *other* than ourselves dreaming of being ourselves. This is the meaning of life, a self-referential irony of universal interdependence and interchange. Difference-and-interchange is at work, both horizontally among various things, and vertically between actuals-ideals and their ground. And this is what it means to *play*, for to be awakened to the meaning in life is to traverse all these modes in life.

Juxtaposition constitutes the comic and the ironic, says Kierkegaard.[32] Chuang Tzu adds that this is a playful roaming in life. Chuang Tzu looks at the tiger keeper, and admonishes the despot reformer to do likewise. This is a simulation of one mode of existence with another, patterning the despot reformer after the tiger keeper. And then we realize the story refers itself to something inexpressible. Chuang Tzu was talking about neither the circus ring nor politics, but their matrix. He lets both the casual world of circus and the serious world of politics play dissimulation, so that their mutual reference itself refers to their common matrix. What is this matrix?

We want language to become precise, having a specific one-to-one correspondence between words and their referents. In literalism the falsifiability principle is effective. Here analogy is the highest our language soars— reforming a despot is *like* keeping a tiger. But the meaning comes from and resides in its pervasive matrix. The meaning matrix is the universe itself where a living experience has polythetic meaning.

Furthermore, the human piping has the earthly piping, both of which come from and express the heavenly piping. In this final realm there is no longer analogy. It is not like anything. To this realm words and situations serve as *mute* metaphors. They are "mute" because they do not refer, either literally or analogically, but merely appeal and evoke. They are existential "metaphors" in that they ferry us over (*meta-pherein*) to the region yonder (*fang wai*). They are things of this world moving us with an intimation of charged vacancy. Among those metaphorical "things" we have philosophical theories.

Whitehead is correct that philosophical technicalities "remain metaphors mutely appealing to an imaginative leap." Unfortunately he attributed this to "weakness of insight and deficiencies of language."[33] To him the metaphorical nature of philosophical language is an obstacle to the final literal formulation of first principles.

Chuang Tzu would disagree. Chuang Tzu would think that the metaphorical nature of language (philosophical or otherwise) is as it should be. Metaphor is the humus out of which our fantasies and creations grow. Metaphor can be said to be the first principle of philosophy. The universe is itself metaphorical, alive with its power ceaselessly to move us from one realm of meaning to another. As soon as one realm is entered, it suggests another realm. Such suggestion may not be a smooth transition, but a jarring contradiction provoking our revolt. The result is an "imaginative leap," an innovation, a new vista, a new world.

This agrees with the characteristic of a metaphysical theory whose power consists in its range of vision. The more things can be encompassed in the vista of a theory the more powerful that theory is. When Newton's theory enables us to see some coherent connection between the ebbing of the tide, the falling of an apple, and the movement of the planets, that theory deserves the name of the "theory of *universal* gravity." Freud's theory of the unconscious also helps us recognize a connection between the slip of the tongue and jokes, between dreams and neuroses.

Similarly, the power of a person consists in the range of vision he commands, the range of territory in which he is at home. He who sees in the unjust steward or the corrupt judge the logic of the kingdom of God is powerful indeed. He whose name is Joy is acquainted with grief. He is at home on the wretched woodrack as he is in the bosom of the Father in heaven.

Such a wide range of meaning can be encompassed only with metaphor and irony. Irony says one thing and means another, or says several things at once by mentioning only one. This is how playful roaming takes place. We now understand Kant's predilection for expressions, "the play of imagination," "the play of ideas," "the whole dialectical play of cosmological ideas," in his Critiques. Such roaming freedom gives the poetic sensitivity of being able to laugh at taking the familiar connections we have among things for "reality." Set free from the rut of ordinariness, our life shall extend richly. If Kant is right in insisting that the power of imagination synthesizes the scattered manifold of sensations into a patterned intelligibility of our experience of perception, then the same power of imagination is also responsible for the dissolution of ordinariness into novelty.

Imaginative play carries many contextual connotations. They constitute a semantic tension within the play. The tension gives vitality to the expressive language of lived experience. The tension forms neither a complex unity nor a chaos of suggestions, neither a unity of monothetic meaning-components, nor a melange of cacophony. The uneasiness provoked by the unitive tension in Chuang Tzu's stories induces our own probes. This is what both Kierkegaard and Wheelwright called "indirection." Nothing that is suggested by expressive-metaphorical language is irrelevant, and the plenitude of experience is precisely echoed in the plenitude of meanings. And then many new worlds shall be born in new associations of fresh meanings. Such creative transition from one imaginative vision to another is called "play."

2. By definition play cannot be defined, as Wittgenstein correctly observed,[34] because play is free self-forgetful activity, whether in a game or in a leisurely roaming. Play defined is no longer play.

But play can be roughly characterized. With the suggestion of Chuang Tzu, play can be perceived in its two modes—a game played according to agreed-upon rules, and carefree roaming.

Game is play that requires an ingenious adherence to the rules; roaming is a self-immersing in the wind of whims, in response to the shift of atmosphere. But of course this is a caricature. Every play, whether a game or a roaming, involves both a conscious effort and a letting-go. The football game relies on a free flow with the situation; a stroll in the woods follows the laws of nature of psyche and ecology. Play has two elements—an intensity that sensitizes us for new awareness, and a self-forgetfulness that lets an object both be itself and reside in the subject. Play is exertion and enjoyment, an activity of the élan vital, protean and non-arbitrary.

Such esoteric description has practical significance. Free association heals our mental illness, because free association brings us back home to our self. The scientific breakthrough originates in our imaginative thought experiments in new perspectives and rules. Play is a "cross-indexing of things" which changes itself, freely reshuffling information from ever-new view-points, freely using computers to systematically follow up on whatever we playfully envisioned. Language has no rigid grammar or logic. Wittgenstein says,

> Doesn't the analogy between language and games throw light here? We can easily imagine people amusing themselves in a field by playing with a ball so as to start various existing games, but playing many without finishing them and in between throwing the ball aimlessly into the air, chasing one another with the ball and bombarding one another for a joke and so on. And now someone says: The whole time they are playing a ball-game and following definite rules at every throw.
>
> And is there not also the case where we play and—make up the rules as we go along? And there is even one where we alter them—as we go along.[35]

Isn't that the way we live, making and changing our rules as we go on playing within and with the world?

Roaming in life takes on a mutual transformation of many modes of existence. Chuang Tzu shows us that we are awakened to an ever-present possibility of changing back and forth between the butterfly-world and the human-world. Such play releases us (*chieh*) from the fear of poverty and death. On the death bed we praise the "creator"-force which prepares us for a new journey into new entities.[36]

We can say, then, that play is an activity with purposeless purpose, with non-serious seriousness. It is an activity of knowledge that is no knowledge, of great use that is useless, of no-self that nourishes the self. It is an other-worldly activity that is in this world. Let me explain.

(1) Play is purposeful without a purpose. Play is not random but coherent and meaningful, yet without purpose in a conventional sense, because it is not for anything but just for fun, for self-enjoyment.

Play is purposeful and purposeless because it is itself its own purpose.[37] Fulfilling itself, play is a *joyous* activity. It looks irresponsible because it is responsible for no observable objective. It is responsible to itself, and an outside observer is oblivious to such internal purpose. A bird sings, and an ornithologist says it is for the sake of courtship and species propagation. For the bird, however, to sing is to sing, for the bird is born to sing. Come spring it sings, and the rest takes care of itself. Flowers blossom with the spring sun, bees and birds come with flowers, and children play in response to them. All of them cannot help but be and do as they do and are. Their playful activities are part of self-purposeful living; they fulfill themselves in what they do.

The self-contained purposiveness of play is not limited to any territory, for play is playful everywhere, a self-contained wandering, going with any situation without being lost in it. When parents look for their children, it is the parents who are lost because *they* lost their children. Being "lost" is an adult concept, for adults do not play. Play is self-fulfilled everywhere, and the playful people ("children") are not lost.

(2) Play is activity that is useful and useless. It is useless because something is useful when it is for the sake of something *else*, and play is useful for nothing, that is, nothing other than itself—it is for itself. Therefore play is just as it is, a self-replenishment. When Hui Shih the sophist complained that Chuang Tzu's words are so playful that they are as useless as a big tree too gnarled for the carpenter to look at, Chuang Tzu replied,

> Now you have a huge tree, worrying about its no-use.
> Why not plant it in the village of not-any-existence,
>   the field of vast nothing,
> Go rambling away and doing nothing beside it,
> Roaming around and lying asleep beneath it?
> Not dying young by axes, there is nothing to harm.
> If there is nothing for which to be useful, how can there
>   be anything from which to distress and suffer?

This reply ends the first chapter, explaining the "use of the useless" (*wu yung chih yung*) that ends the fourth chapter. Without purpose, useful for nothing else, play is intrinsically valuable, self-cathartic, and self-invigorating.

(3) Curiously, playful self-enhancement is an activity of "no self" and "self-forgetting." It is an act of self-oblivion, as in play-acting *with* the despot; when he acts stupidly, we also act stupidly with him. We enmesh ourselves in play, in which we are transported beyond ourselves. Play is fun and enthusiasm, in which we have no self.

Yet precisely in such self-kenosis the true self is fulfilled, for it is I myself who have fun. In the fun of self-immersion the self grows into itself. The Cook Ting nourishes himself by disappearing into his thickless knife, dancing through the spaces in an ox. This is a selfless self-ing, a self-forgetting self-fulfillment. Similarly the tiger comes to fawn on its feeder who follows along with its nature. Such playful enthusiasm distinguishes Chuang Tzu from playless Stoicism and Buddhism.

(4) Play is non-rational though not irrational, non-cognitive though not ignorance, non-self-conscious though not unconscious.

Human beings and animals do "know" what they are doing while they play, for play has its own meaning, rule, sense, and coherence—which are beyond the physiological needs instinct, or reflexes (as Huizinga rightly reminds us). Therefore play is in some sense rational. This explains why

Huizinga vacillates between the rationality and irrationality of play.[38] The puzzlement can be solved by noting that both human beings and animals act according to their nature when they play. Is play rational? Well, is nature rational?

Seneca said that natural law is rational. But since "rationality" is meaningless outside the human sphere, rationality cannot be attributed to nature—so says the contemporary mind. Yet if this is correct, nature would be inexplicable. Besides, since we are a part of nature, our rationality must also be part of nature as well. Our rationality is powerless in nature of which it is a part.

And so "nature is not rational" is not quite correct, any more than "nature is rational" is. If we are rational, nature can neither be rational nor not rational.

It is still a mystery how "7+5=12" in our minds *applies* to the world. Kant proposed a famous "solution" in "judgments synthetic a priori,"[39] which unfortunately is a label for the enigma, not its solution. This is why Chuang Tzu harps on "How should I know...?" and "I don't know."[40] He has "knowledge of no-knowledge" (*wu-chih chih chih*).

Play is an embodiment of this strange knowledge. Play is activity neither of abstract cognition nor of a-rational instinct. Play is not computer intelligence, divisible, situation-free, impersonal, nor is it instinctive activity, physiologically reflexive. As a natural activity, play is reasonable and responsive without being either instinctive or cognitive.

(5) Play can be serious, as in a clown, and play can be non-serious, as in a trifle game. Few noted however that play can be either because it can be both.

A clown takes us by surprise, forcing us to see ourselves by saying something important in a special way. The saying catches the essential lunacy of our life, sobering us in our laughter. The clown's joke is no joke, then, starting us by nonsense into seeing our nonsensical lives. The holy conventions of civilization are fractured. William Zinsser said,

> ... there will never be a dearth of new lunacies—and dangers—for the humorist to detect and to fight. Lyndon Johnson ... of Vietnamization was brought down partly by Jules Feiffer and Art Buchwald. Joseph McCarthy and Spiro Agnew were brought down partly by Walt Kelly in the comic strip *Pogo*. H. L. Mencken brought down a whole galaxy of hypocrites in high places, and 'Boss' Tweed was partly toppled by the cartoons of Thomas Nast."[41]

With "throwaway non sequiturs," a "serious humor" operates "on a deeper current than most people suspect."[42] Our civilization owes its sanity to a long line of lampoonists from Socrates and Chuang Tzu till today.

Sadly, however, Zinsser denies that clowns and jokers are also just "fooling around," simply because they have the serious purpose of awakening the public. Johan Huizinga rules out laughter from his studies of play because laughter is too non-serious and without engagement.[43]   Harvey Cox agrees with all this, focusing himself on the indispensability of jarring juxtaposition of notions.[44]

All of them lose sight of the play's non-serious leisureliness which produces satirical seriousness. They forget that the indispensable satirical creativity is impossible without clownish "fooling around," which is, mind you, not for the sake of serious contrivance of jokes, much less of civilization.

Chuang Tzu goes a step further. For him, the "serious point" of irony is for the sake of non-serious playfulness in life. The mistake of "holy conventions" is in their holiness, trapping us in bigotry. Such mistaken seriousness is corrected by subtly serious points; these points naturally seep out of the non-seriousness of play, in which we live out our life as we like to see it lived.

(6) True life is lived in the world but not as its part, immersed in the world but not enmeshed in it, engaged but not totally committed. The true life is the life of play, serious yet not-serious.

Play can be serious, in which the rule is obeyed and the role is played truthfully. Yet play is also a play act which is enjoyed self-foregetfully; it is our imaginative overplay, a creative second-world, a world beyond yet within this world. For there is always the real self behind the mask. Although the real self must be forgotten into the masked self, the self can at any moment take off the mask. Otherwise play is not play. The enjoyment lies in its frivolity and dispensability. The realm beyond the ordinary world (*fang wai*) is the land of enchantment precisely because it is *casually* situated in the ordinary world (*fang nei*).

Play is enjoyed for its nimble freedom in *and* out of actuality, romping and roaming in varied realms of possibility. The enjoyment is in the combination of our serious immersion in the not-serious procedure of acting out a peculiar world, pretending to be someone else. The fun is in combining the serious *and* the not-serious engagements.

Such combination is an organic unity (*methexis*)[45] of mutual participation, not a mechanical conjunction of disjunctive entities. The seriousness of play resides in its casualness, and enjoyment lies in the inter-seeping of seriousness and not-seriousness.

Two "stooges" stood over the sunny bridge, jostling playfully over how one of them, Chuang Tzu, ever knew and enjoyed the minnows enjoying themselves playing around (*yu*) under the bridge. This is the story that ended the seventeenth chapter of the *Chuang Tzu*.

Such a jostling amounts to a double presentation of the unity of play. (*a*) We have here Chuang Tzu lost in the minnow's enjoyment. Chuang Tzu is one with them. (*b*) We also have Chuang Tzu's playful rebuke of Hui Shih (his jostling partner). Such rebuke plays Hui Shih's own game of sophistry, softly reminding Hui Shih that logical scrutiny only destroys the unity with minnows. (*c*) And *in* such play both stooges *presented* to us the joy of playing, even playing with logic and argumentation.

(7) In sum, play creates a magic circle out of the ordinary, a realm by itself, where no ordinary utility, knowledge, seriousness, order, and purpose fit. It has its own boundary and order, in which the self is enthused and transported, where no "serious point" need to be made, such as Cox, Kierkegaard, Socrates, and Zinsser insist should be made. It is a special reality distinct from the mundane world, as distinct as the butterfly dreamed by Chuang Tzu is from Chuang Tzu himself.

This magic circle is in this world (as the butterfly is in Chuang Tzu), transforming the ordinary into part of the magical. The transformation is as fascinating as Chuang Tzu wondering whether he has dreamed being a butterfly or *he* is the dream of the butterfly. To play with Nicholas of Cusa, the circle of play has its center everywhere and its circumference nowhere. The circle is everywhere in this world, yet we cannot find it in this world. It is the mystical circle of playful enchantment encompassing the world. "Confucius" was reported to have sighed that the great Realm (*ta fang*) of roaming lies beyond the ordinary realm (*fang wai*).[46] It is the realm of no realm (*wu fang*), spreading everywhere,[47] in which ten thousand things are embraced without partiality.[48]

3.   We have at least three kinds of play—spontaneity in roaming, obeying the rules in playing a game, and theatrical role-playing. The first kind seems to be basic, giving vigor and self-fulfillment to the other two. Self-forgetful moving with the situation makes possible the ingenious manipulation of rules in a game and self-transport in role-playing makes an enthusiastic play-act.

4.   Do the tragedies of life have a place in play? Despite the existence of tragedies in the Chinese theater, it is said that the Chinese people lack the tragic sense of life. This is perhaps due to a mistaken notion of play as only light-hearted merriment, which is chased away by the tragic occurrences of life.

Yet the Chinese people have tragedies in their theaters, and suffer at least as much as any other people. "Funeral odes" and "epitaphs" are accepted literary genres. Many prose poems on the "ruins of ancient palaces" and on the "onset of autumn" are full of pathos. In fact, whenever appropriate, the "sense of tragedy" intrudes into literary essay and so on, and so forth, so much so that (among many other writers) Ou-Yang Hsiu, in his "*Preface to Collected Poems of Mei Sheng-yu*," claimed that it is impoverishment that crafts writing into excellence.

That natural or political disasters are tragic is well known; that public fame is also disastrous, none but Chuang Tzu explicitly noted. To meet the latter sort of disasters well is an art.

The whole of a generation's praise added little to Mr. Sung Jung's diligence; Hsu Yu gently turned down Yao's throne-ceding (Chapter One, lines 54, 77–84). Tall Dryandra Tree told Jittery Magpie that holy men pursue no duties; to be ruler and herdsman is an obstinacy in a dream (Chapter Two, lines 232, 255). Fame punishes good deeds (Chapter Three, line 3). Chapter Four begins by warning that fame is an evil weapon; it ends by warning Confucius that virtue mutilates its pursuer (for politics). In Chapter Five an ugly popular man quietly leaves premiership (5/35–37); in Chapter Eight fames kills sages as profit kills robbers (8/23–26). This sentiment runs through the rest of the Chuang Tzu, as epitomized by Chuang Tzu, a fishing rod in hand, comparing being in office to being a turtle shell in the temple (17/ 82–84). In the notorious Chapter Twenty-Eight, all the sages committed suicide when offered high positions. Fame destroys us as much as natural or political disasters do; they equally make tragic heroes out of us.

The Chinese people are all too familiar with the tragic heroes morosely catalogued in Chapter Twenty-Eight of the *Chuang Tzu*. But the Chinese literary critical tradition rightly rejected that chapter, holding it to be spurious. The reason is simple: the sentiment is not Chuang Tzu's. Chuang Tzu offers a dancing *resolution (chieh)* of tragedies. In contrast, the Western tradition offers serious, if not tragic solutions to the so-called "problems of life," including the *problem* of pleasure.

Chuang Tzu's resolution was often described as hedonistic. Yet hedonism is a calculated quest for pleasure away from tragedies; in such quest the spontaneity of pleasure is calculated away. As the spontaneity goes, the pleasure disappears as well: thus the hedonistic paradox. Pleasure cannot be fled *to*.

In contrast, being neither tragic nor hedonistic, Chuang Tzu offers a playful resolution to life's pain. He wants us to play out life's tragedies. Despotism is one source of suffering, you say. Very well, then, despotism must be resolved by playing its senseless tyranny: refusing to play *its* game only increases our hazards, as the praying mantis waving its angry arms at the oncoming cart. We must be a tiger keeper to play with the tiger the game *it* sets for itself and for us. And then, without our meaning to make it so, the tiger comes to fawn on us. Similarly, the monkey keeper played along with the preference of the monkeys for four in the morning and three in the evening, instead of three in the morning and four in the evening. To insist that the two arrangements are identical is to refuse to play with them, courting disaster.[49]

In this manner we immerse ourselves in life negativities, playing along with the games set by a tiger or a tyrant. Sometimes we ponder about misfortunes such as deformities, whether political or genetic. We chant on misfortunes, as Chuang Tzu did at his friends' deathbeds or funerals, or as Men-sun Ts'ai did at his mother's funeral, or as Chuang Tzu did when poverty struck, or when his wife died. In the process of such self-immersion we are sad *with* the sad events, and in our sorrows we transcend them.[50] Undergoing the misfortunes in this manner is to undergo a transition to another stage of life, bearing different roles in the universe. Such transition is simply called "change" (*hua*).[51] It is an ontological transformation, a self-growth from this realm to the beyond. Those who play this game of life, no matter how unfortunate, strangely attract us. Describing such lives of playfulness, the *Chuang Tzu* attracts readers.

Play and pleasure are synonymous, as long as pleasure is not an everlasting giggle. Play can be play of sorrow, as long as play means a self-immersion in activities that prove to be self-enhancing, though not necessarily pleasurable in themselves.

In this connection, Aristotle's distinction of pleasure from happiness is helpful.[52] But Aristotle distinguished bodily pleasure from rational happiness. Such categorization of originally interfused elements brings us the problem of relating them back together. All this is foreign to Chuang Tzu.

For Chuang Tzu, to live is to "play it out," pain or pleasure—and then we will *find* bliss in the playing. Playing and bliss preclude no pain. We do not need to be pathological gigglers to be happy; we can be happy in sorrow, playing the world. The real misfortune which made Chuang Tzu sigh, "What a pity!" is not pain or suffering. What is truly pitiful is our failure to follow through on the ludic way, come what may.[53]

5.   What does play have to do with meaning and irony? The answer is twofold. First, the three notions can be regarded as labels to the stages on life's way. Secondly, such stages are stages of growth in more comprehensive inclusion. In short, play, meaning, and irony together characterize our growth in life.

To begin with, we grow in living more meaningfully, that is, in perceiving more and more connections among things previously thought to be unrelated or even contradictory. Growth in life is growth in the perception of unsuspected connections, which often shock common sense. Such shocks are expressed in ironies. He who can connect ironically is a mature man.

At the same time, to grow is to grow in spontaneity. To a mature person what is ordinarily seen as ironic is only part of his natural perception of things. He treads where none thought possible. He freely roams among the clashes of common meanings, savoring meaning in the very clash. He plays them as if playing one game after another. To go through the stages of meaning and irony is to reach and live in the stage of play.

Such growth is a process of inclusion. To go through meaning and irony to reach play, means to include meaning and irony in play. A ludic man roams in meaning to soar in irony.

Irony is growth into perceiving meaning in a seemingly meaningless connection among things. Play is growth into spontaneously handling ironies among the unusuals.

To see connections among things is to enter the world of meaning. To be jolted out of one's own perspective by this situational meaning, thereby to look at one's own world from the perspective of the sky out there, is to engage oneself in irony. To become spontaneous in going back and forth between meaning and irony, in and out of oneself in the situation, is to play, roaming and soaring playfully in tragedy even, playing things out.

One naively finds new connections in the meaning-matrix of the situation. One then becomes self-conscious, becoming reflexive and ironic about oneself and the situation. And then one become spontaneous in roaming in and out of oneself. One's spontaneity unifies non-self-aware naivete and self-reflective irony. One plays spontaneously in the world of things.

The *Chuang Tzu* describes how a mature person handles meaning and irony. An exhaustive elucidation is impossible because no one can exhaust the possibilities of play. But we can give a schematic intimation here.

Finding meaning-connection among things, we can play things according to *their* meaning, that is, play their game. We see fruits as sweet and stones as reliable. This is to connect fruits with sweetness and stones with reliability. Such connection enables us to eat fruits and build stone shelters. We then come to possess a map of the connections among things in which we roam. When obvious meanings clash, we hop, skip, and romp among them, enjoying a rough ride. And the game, the roaming, and the romping are played in an unlimited variety of ways. Such variety constitutes freedom and enjoyment of life, of which the *Chuang Tzu* is an exciting exploration.

Eugen Fink reported Schiller's saying, "Man is whole only when he plays," then added, "it is equally true that he is whole only when he works, when he struggles, when he confronts death, when he loves."[54] This is Fink's talk about Schiller's talk about man. Chuang Tzu goes further and says that man is whole only when he plays his work, his struggle, his death, his love. This would be Chuang Tzu's way of talking about Fink's talk about Schiller's talk about man. Here Chuang Tzu does not talk any more, but tells stories, plays humors, and lives. Here to tell is part of living, and living is one big talk without talking. This is the life of play, playing even with misfortunes as well as with talks.

D. "Companion"

1. The globe, the world, is our environment. An environment encloses the subject, enabling him to be himself. The globe is the environment in which, and in terms of which, the subject sees, knows, and moves. The global environment itself cannot be seen in its totality while the subject is living in it.

Yet the subject wants to see the globe as he sees everything else. This is life's élan of self-transcendence, its intentionality to brave the Gödelian impasse. This is life's metaphysical urge to contain the whole of environment within one of its parts, the human subject.[55]

The space sciences give us a way, actualizing Galileo's "standpoint of space." We used to see only an expanse of flat land. Now the astronauts help us see our global environment. The standpoint of space is the standpoint of nothingness, with which we roam in space while being on earth.

The astronauts' pictures of our globe (Chapter One, lines 11–13) symbolize our success in fulfilling our metaphysical dream of containing the whole in its part. For they are the pictures of our globe seen in space, yet we look at them on this globe. We have succeeded in living on the globe and looking at it, both at once, fusing the outer-space vision with the globe-living.

The ancient *Chuang Tzu* is just such a picture. To enjoy it is to lift ourselves from our environment while living in it. The feat gratifies our urge, cleanses us from petty perspectives and problems, and gives us serene joy. Chuang Tzu helps us soar into space as P'ung Bird while roaming on the earth, steeping in it like K'un Fish. This is what it means to live happily in human excellence, at which philosophy aims.

In order to enjoy the picture we must process it in the dark room and set it against an appropriate background. Similarly a commentator processes and presents the "picture" of a classic. The *Chuang Tzu* was produced in ancient China (the fourth century B.C.), and has been processed and re-processed by commentators in their historical, textual labors. Today the *Chuang Tzu* must be set against the contemporary Western background. For such coherent presentation to the contemporary reader the foregoing pages were devoted to exegeses, literary summaries, reconstruction of the total feel and sweep with phenomenological imagination, and even contrasts with the Western frame of mind.

Such an enterprise is long overdue. A commentary is a background work, processing and presenting the classic, yet the Chinese commentators on the *Chuang Tzu* have mainly toiled at processing. Kuo Hsiang and Wang Fu-chih are perhaps two notable exceptions, doing more presenting than processing. The preceding pages transpose their *sort* of labor to the contemporary West, where Chuang Tzu's picture (and its message) is urgently relevant.

Strangely, the unification of processing and presenting has been subject to controversies. The proverbial feuds among the philologists and the historians, or among the sinologists and the philosophers, help keep processing *separate* from presentation. This fact is less to be lamented than to warn us that the unification is not an automatic procedure but to be *achieved* by a toilsome dialectic, a sustained open-minded learning from one another. To be preoccupied with one at the cost of the other kills commentary.

Abstract generalization is an appropriate objective method of describing abstract concepts. To describe concrete notions (pity, piety, game, humanness), only the method of subjectivity (instantiation, re-enactment) is adequate. For concrete notions are concerned with life of subjectivity. There is no game-in-general; "game" is always a particular game with a particular set of rules to be actually played. There is no man-in-general; "man" is always this man in this life style and this series of daily undergoings. Socrates can criticize Euthyphro's examples as inadequate characterizations of "piety"; Socrates cannot criticize the *method* of instantiation as inappropriate for introducing us to "piety." There is no piety-in-general to be defined objectively and generally, as if to define another number.

The "definition" of a subjective notion must be its subjective description, that is, subjective concretization, a presentation of that notion at work. Objective researches on *tools* of presentation (words, texts) should not blind us to the subjective topic (life, play) of the *Chuang Tzu*. To engage in objective exegesis *alone* sadly bypasses the existential involvement of and with the *Chuang Tzu*.

Kant said that the structure of our experience is not in the objects experienced but supplied by the experiencing subject. Lakoff and Johnson said that the way we live, that is, the way we talk, think, and act, is structured by metaphor, an understanding of one experience in terms of another. For instance, the way we argue is structured by the way we fight; our argumentation operates under the metaphor, "Argument is war."[56]

Both Kant's transcendental shaping of experience and Lakoff and Johnson's discovery that our expression, however "literal," is metaphorical, shaping one experience in terms of *another*, testify how we live with a meta-élan, constantly going up to the meta-level and coming down to shape our life. To be human is to be self-reflexive and self-shaping. Our life is life of self-transcendence, talking *to* ourselves, being ashamed or proud *of* ourselves, going beyond and beside ourselves. Our sanity and insanity come from our looking *at* ourselves, laughing at ourselves, shaping ourselves metaphorically and transcendentally.

Chuang Tzu's job is to chart and capture our self-distancing, self-looking, self-shaping, self-transcending. This élan facilitates our enjoyment (even in miseries) of life, freely roaming in and out of ourselves, in and out of the world. We must capture Chuang Tzu's way by charting the way Chuang Tzu played with description and arguments. To describe and argue is one thing; to play with description and argument is quite another. To play is to operate on a metalevel. On way of playing with sentences is to state a thesis and then sweep it away clean in the next breath—and this is what Wang Fu-chih said Chuang Tzu was doing.[57] It is often remarked that childlikeness is not childishness, and what makes this distinction possible is precisely such playful self-transcendence. Like children, we forget ourselves in what we are doing, non-consciously and non-actively. We are free as the child without childish clumsiness.

2. How can we present the *Chuang Tzu*? One thing is certain. Preoccupation with words and phrases is obsession with tools and skills, making us forget the product. Preoccupation with analytical exegesis emaciates Chuang Tzu's evocative vigor in a list of platitudes or contradictions. Obsession with textual criticism leads astray from the forest of Chuang Tzu's central intention for the trees of words and phrases. All the master craftsmen in the *Chuang Tzu*—butcher, wheelwright, bellstand maker—warn us against the "machine mind."[58]

What Chuang Tzu needs is not interpretation but *transposition* of his evocative intention into our contemporary world. This transposition is accomplished by a re-presentation of the power of the original text which provokes us into looking afresh at the mysteries of ordinary things, the incredible depths of daily routines.

The *Westside Story* presents us with the *Romeo and Juliet* with all its raw impact as no amount of Shakespeare scholarship can hope to approximate. The contemporaneity of Chuang Tzu is an event, which the tradition of Chuang Tzu scholarship (however copious, venerable, and indispensable) cannot *alone* contrive. Chuang Tzu's impact can be felt today only by its re-presentation, a *companion* re-enacting his intention, like its shadow and its echo.[59]

If Chuang Tzu is a shadow of the reader, shadowing forth the reader's own self-creativity, then the *companion* is a shadow of the shadow, a penumbra that clarifies the contour of the shadow. The *companion* deepens and soft-focuses the shadow so that it appears as the shadow, neither an unintelligible shade nor the thing itself (Chapter Two, lines 290–94).

The danger is that often a *companion* is either too little or too much of a penumbra. It either merely "bites on the sentences and chews on the words," leaving the main intention of the text untouched, or explains too much "what it really means," intruding into the shadowhood of a shadow, again missing Chuang Tzu's original intention. And then the *companion* becomes a mere commentary, which either quibbles textually (textual scrutiny) or pontificates like a false Chuang Tzu (exegetical blunder). Chuang Tzu is a challenge; Chuang Tzu explained is Chuang Tzu emaciated.

Instead, the penumbra must clarify the shadow. The *companion* must present how Chuang Tzu's goblet words and bombastic sayings are structured, and how indispensable they are for Chuang Tzu's true intention. The *companion* must let Chuang Tzu come out and speak for himself.

A contemporary re-presentation of the *Chuang Tzu* co-reverberates with its original tonal rhythm. The ideal *companion* tunes in to resonate with the *Chuang Tzu*. Resonance originates meaning, rendering discourse meaningful. Such meaning-resonance is a primitive notion which cannot itself be analyzed further, though its adumbration is possible.

To tune into a resonance is to enter a *universe* of discourse in which significant dialogue resides. The universe here is the field of interaction of meaning; to live in it is to have one's thinking sympathetically criticized. Everyone learns from family disputes in which each recognizes the other as a member of the same family; the family habitat of significance is tacitly acknowledged in a family quarrel. Such an atmosphere is the humus that nourishes saplings. In such a family atmosphere the inevitability of self-growth crowds out arbitrariness.

The *Chuang Tzu* has goblet words and seeming nonsense to incite a tuning-in of mutual resonance. Chuang Tzu himself has no specific tune or universe of discourse. As Huang Chin-hung provocatively puts it, "Chuang Tzu has no view of his own."[60] Chuang Tzu allows us instead to produce our own universe of discourse in which many discourses sprout happily. Chuang Tzu's humus-discourse stoutly opposes a stunting of such elicitation. This is why in the "world of Chuang Tzu" things seem so arbitrary. The non-arbitrary character of such seeming arbitrariness is discernible precisely in the following criticism, saying that we (if not Chuang Tzu) espouse arbitrariness:

> ... your central philosophical claim is a kind of plea for play based on a profound critical awareness of our being cut off from what could be called definitive truth. But I cannot help wondering whether that suggestion is either arbitrary (why not rather mad debauchery) or betraying a sly reintroduction of esoteric 'knowledge'—*the* way to be human in a world in which there is no truth, as opposed to merely *a* way. ...There is no need to justify anything if nothing can be justified, and one simply does whatever one's heart desires without justification.
>
> Your work is very readable. It has a kind of sense of the freedom and zest, and joy that must have characterized Chuang Tzu. Maybe the content is irrelevant, for the style and feel of the *saying* of it makes it pointless to argue about *what* is said. It is a delight to read, though I think it will stick in the craw of most analytically sensitive philosophers.[61]

The first paragraph unwittingly reveals how we feel when we are faced with reality, of which the *Chuang Tzu* is a mere shadow. The second paragraph reveals how we ourselves should behave in such a situation. Wittgenstein would have approved of such combination.

Put differently, the first paragraph opposes any systematization of life; the second paragraph opposes any imprisonment of the self in necessity, both analytic and fatalistic. All of us thus live together, each in his own way, fully and happily, and this is the "system and significance of life," *the* way to live. Yet such a sense of life cannot be formulated objectively and analytically, as was complained in the first paragraph. Instead, the sense of life must be expressed and embodied, as we noticed in the second paragraph. The first paragraph frees the second; the second answers the first. In short, these two paragraphs express well the open non-arbitrariness of life as humanly lived.

"Life" can be described as something spontaneous and creative. Spontaneity is to the subject as creativity is to the observer. Neither spontaneity nor creativity can be commanded, nor can they be described definitively, much less defined or schematized exhaustively from outside. This partly because language fixates: to talk *about* spontaneity is to denature it.

What can be done with words here is to re-present spontaneity subjectively, that is, adumbrating it historically by telling stories (pointing to what has happened), or evoking the reader's participation in spontaneity by unusual juxtaposition of words and ideas (provoking novelty in the future). Chuang

Tzu combined both by montaging bits of stories and arguments, parodying history and argumentation, playing with them, satirizing them, thereby arousing the reader. To the question, "What is spontaneity?", the answer can only be, "Come and join in." To know spontaneity is to became spontaneous. An adumbration of spontaneity is then an aid to becoming spontaneous. If the *Chuang Tzu* is such an aid, then this *Companion* is an invitation and an appeal to that aid.

    3. Doubt may linger as to whether such a liberal, if not loose, notion of the author's intention deserves the reader's attention. To doubts like this a reminder can be given. Aristotle has been customarily regarded as "*the* Philosopher" who pronounced the last word on the truths of things; such a view has understandably alienated many a thinker. This view of Aristotle, however, is disputed by J. L. Ackrill, an Oxonian scholar on Aristotle and General Editor of the Clarendon Aristotle Series. He claims that Aristotle's remarkable achievements consist not in the final dogmas on things but in the capability of his ideas and arguments to continue provoking philosophers to controversy for more than two millennia. This evocative quality of Aristotle is what holds those Aristotelians spellbound.[62] A Plato scholar Gregory Vlastos told the same story about Socrates. For Vlastos, "Socrates' metaphysics" is Plato's later literary embellishments. The rugged authentic Socrates is that gadfly unsparingly inciting reason to its own elenchic paradoxes.[63]

    This is not to claim that the readings of Socrates and Aristotle cited above are beyond controversy. This is to say that, rightly or wrongly, people admire them for *that* reason, that is, for that arousal of people to thinking on their own. Far from being arbitrary and irresponsible, this is what is most treasured as the soul of a classic.

    This evocative character is also the soul of the *Chuang Tzu*. To be faithful to the text here is to be appropriate to its evocative thrust, with which the reader is confronted, thereby letting the reader become excited at recognizing himself. This is the task more faithful to the text, and more difficult, than its mere exegesis.

    Wing-tsit Chan said that Taoism imbues Chinese cooking.[64] Daily culinary chores are daily enactments of the Taoist principle of harmony. If this is the case, the *Chuang Tzu* can be taken as a recipe, with which the reader cooks his meal. The recipe is not itself edible but points to the dinner. The *Chuang Tzu* is as unfinished as the recipe is; as the recipe is not to be slavishly followed but to be creatively used in cooking to one's taste, so the *Chuang Tzu* is not the definitive blueprint of a zestful life but its incitement. For John Austin, performative utterance is itself performance; to say is to do. For Chuang Tzu, his book is a collection of evocatives; they *let*-do.

Accordingly, a *companion* to such a life-recipe book may include actual examples of what is "cooked" at the incitement of Chuang Tzu, as well as a modern version of Chuang Tzu's recipes.

One final note. An ideal *companion* to the *Chuang Tzu* as described here and throughout this book is extremely hard to come by. What has been written in the foregoing pages does not pretend to have achieved the ideal. What might save a failed *companion* is twofold. First, each reader is a unique individual who can immediately sense and recognize that a particular Chuang Tzu proposed in a *companion* is not *his* Chuang Tzu; the reader has an intuitive capacity to be dissatisfied. Secondly a bad *companion*, producing as it does a bad vignette of Chuang Tzu, can serve as an evocative penumbra, provoking the reader into a better understanding of Chuang Tzu on his own.

This *Companion* has been offered to the reader, whose dissatisfaction hopefully provokes his own original probe into the *Chuang Tzu*, and thereby into himself. To find his Chuang Tzu is to find himself in the world, and the world in himself—here at the end of this book, we are still (as we were at the beginning) urging you the reader to continue on, beyond the book, without the book, but still with the butterfly as companion.

NOTES

REFERENCES

Notes

R eferences to the *Chuang Tzu* beyond the first three chapters will be given in the
following form: chapter/line(s)—where chapter and line numbers are taken from *A
Concordance to the Chuang Tzu*, Harvard-Yenching Sinological Index Series. See note
1 of Notes to the Preface for extensive examples.

When English titles are given for books published in Chinese or Japanese, but not
yet published in English translation, such titles are put inside quote marks.

Full publication data for all citations will be given in References.

Notes to the Preface

1.   For *wu shih, wu shih wu chung,* and the like, see 17/15, 45, 46; 20/53; 21/29; 22/59,
60, 61, 63, 73; 25/17, 72; 27/9; 33/68. I omit references to *wei shih,* an expression which
is strewn all over the book. For the meaning of these numbers, see the preceding general
note.

2.   See the note preceding the Kuo Hsiang text in Chapter One, p. 35.

Notes to the Prologue

1.   See Chapter Two, lines 295–305. Chuang Tzu is "the Honorable Mr. Chuang," whose
given name is "Chou." What I call "Chuang Tzu" does signify *that* Chuang Tzu—of the
fourth century before Christ, a native of Meng, "an official in the lacquer garden" in
Meng, as he was described by the Grand Historian Ssu-ma Ch'ien. Often I also use the
name "Chuang Tzu" in a collective sense to mean Chuang Tzu's "friends" among whom
"there was no disagreement" (6/47, 62). They include the writers of the Outer and
Miscellaneous Chapters (from Chapter Eight to the last, Chapter Thirty-Three), and
perhaps anyone thinking and writing in his sentiment. "*The Chuang Tzu* " refers of course
to the book we have called by that name at least since Kuo Hsiang (fourth century A.D.).

The reason why I use "Chuang Tzu" in such a diffusive manner is a major fascinating
theme of this book. Chuang Tzu is an expert in friendship, as explicated in Aria II of my
previous book, *Chuang Tzu: World Philosopher at Play*; cf. note 3 on p. xiii. Chuang
Tzu's friendship immediately follows from his thinking, his philosophy of evocation and
freedom. His lived thinking defines and demands an atmosphere of friendship. The
Chuangtzu-esque freedom—soaring, sorting, nourishing—is responsible for this powerfully diffusive name of "Chuang Tzu." This *Companion* is an invitation to the reader to
join in and become "Chuang Tzu," the name signifying the reader himself. See also note
113 to Chapter Two.

2.   See, for instance, Peter A. French (ed.), *Philosophers in Wonderland,* pp. 23–56, for
such an approach, which is shared by Norman Malcolm's little classic, *Dreaming.*

3.   *Chuang Tzu,* 18/22–29. (See my comments toward the end of Meditation C in

Chapter Two and, in the Prologue, Meditation C, "Conversation With A Roadside Skull.")

4. Besides note 3, see 6/45–80.

5. See Friedrich Nietzsche's *Thus Spoke Zarathustra* and Albert Camus' *The Myth of Sisyphus*. For Chuang Tzu's *dissolution* of life's recurrence, see my comments in Chapter One, Meditation A.

6. For example, the whole of Section 6 in Meditation A of Chapter One.

7. 6/24.

8. Chapter Two, lines 118–19.

9. *Chih has two meanings: "partner," as A. C. Graham said in Chuang-tzû: The Seven Inner Chapters*, p. 124; and "material," as Burton Watson said in *The Complete Writings of Chuang Tzu*, p. 269. The story appears in 24/50.

10. The fifty-one references to Confucius in the *Chuang Tzu* exhibit the following pattern. When Confucius is called "Chung Ni," he is a teacher of true Tao, solemnly mouthing Lao Tzu's view. Exceptions are 5/24, 6/90, 17/14, 19/18, 26/18; they are perhaps parodies of Confucius as teacher. When Confucius is called "K'ung Tzu," he is always scolded by Lao Tzu, recluses, "sages" (cripples), social outcasts, or Robber Chih. Exceptions are 17/60, 18/29, 20/50, 25/36, and occurrences in Chapter Twenty-Seven. When Confucius is called "K'ung Ch'iu" he is depicted (without exception) as historical or personal friend.

Besides explicitly mentioning Confucius by name, Chuang Tzu has oblique allusions to Confucius's sayings. These allusions are "oblique" in that they are explicit enough to remind the reader of Confucius, yet they are somehow twisted into something different from, sometimes even opposed to, views in the *Analects*. I have found so many such allusions that they cannot be recorded here. The same situation holds for Mencius and Lao Tzu.

Chuang Tzu's ambiguous position in relation to Confucius has long been the subject of controversy among Chuang Tzu scholars. Some say that Chuang Tzu opposes Confuscius and so Chuang Tzu's book deserves burning. Others say that Chuang Tzu originates in Confucius. Yet others—Ssu Tung-po, Liu Tsung-yüan, Lu Shu-chih, Wang Fu-chih— say that Chuang Tzu promotes Confucius under the guise of opposing him. Yet others— Huang Chin-hung—say that Chuang Tzu used Confucius's words to express Chuang Tzu's own thoughts; Chuang Tzu after all does not oppose people, and the reason is that Chuang Tzu has no position. All these interpretations are one sided, with partial truths. They can be put in proper perspective by my interpretation that Chuang Tzu has a "position of no position."

Chuang Tzu was himself in his book, responding to thinkers contemporary with him, using their views as he liked. The reader is not sure whether Chuang Tzu really disagreed with them or was merely alluding to another side of their sayings, their alternative implications, which may well be quite different from their original intentions. Chuang Tzu's allusions are thus ironic, even gently humorous—neither helping nor opposing Confucius, but softly nudging the reader to *see*.

11. Confucius, *The Analects*, 1:15, 2:11, 5:9, 7:8.

12. Quoted in Lin Yutang, *The Wisdom of Confucius*, p. 157; cf. p. 39.

13. Watson, p. 302. I said, "Chuang Tzu said," but it is an abbreviation for "someone who embodies Chuang Tzu's sentiment said." I will do so continually in this book.

14.   Jean-Paul Sartre, *Nausea*, pp. 56–59. Cf. Gabriel Marcel, *The Mystery of Being*, I:192–94. Incidentally, both thinkers agree that story-telling is a sinister form of self-deception. I am ambivalent about that view. See Meditation A, Chapter Two.

15.   Søren Kierkegaard, *The Gospel of Suffering*, pp. 6–9.

16.   Confucius, *The Analects*, 7:1.

17.   H. J. Paton, *The Good Will*, pp. 16–17. Paton is a well-known Kant scholar.

18.   Akatzuka Tadashi, *Soshi*, 2 vols.

19.   A. C. Graham, *Chuang-tzŭ: The Seven Inner Chapters; Later Mohist Logic*; "Chuang-tzŭ's Essay on Seeing Things As Equal," *History of Religions*, Vol. 9.

20.   Han Shan, *Chuang Tzu Nei P'ien Chu*; Fukunaga Mitsuji, *Soshi*, 3 vols.

21.   Ch'en Ch'i-t'ien, *Chuang Tzu Ch'ien Shuo,* Introduction. Cf. Shen Hung, *Chuang Tzu*, pp. 10–11.

22.   There are some exceptions. For instance, Kuo Hsiang, Wang Fu-chih, and Chiao Hung, anthologized the insights of various historical writers. In our times we have Kuan Feng in his *Chuang Tzu Nei P'ien I-chieh ho P'i-p'an*; Ch'en Ku-ying in his *Chuang Tzu Chin-chu Chin-i,* 2 vols.; *Chuang Tzu Che-hsüeh T'an-chiu;* Fukunaga Mitsuji, *op cit.;* Akatzuka Tadashi, *op cit.*

They are a mere handful out of about one thousand titles on the *Chuang Tzu.* Yen Ling-fung's *Chuang Tzu Chih-chien Shu-mu* cites more than 690 titles of books and more than 240 titles of essays on the *Chuang Tzu* in Chinese and Japanese alone. I have consulted about fifty so far.

Sadly, even the above cited anthologies of insights are either predominantly literary in character, drawing on Chuang Tzu's phrases tempered with their occasional insights (as in historical writers) or appealing too much to Western philosophical categories to tarry and note Chuang Tzu's original subtleties (as in modern writers).

23.   Graham, *Chuang-tzŭ*, pp. 30–31.

24.   Burton Watson, *Chuang Tzu*, p. 373, modified; cf. *ibid.*, pp. 124, 293, 302–304.

25.   Hsüan Ying, Kuo Ch'ing-fan, and Ch'ien Mu, for instance, managed to produce wonderful anthologies of commentaries. Hu Shih in his introduction to Liu An's *Collected Commentaries on Huai Nan Hung Lieh* says that there are three kinds of collections possible: indexing of words and phrases, collection of the ancients' thought on the passages, and cultural historical narrative of ideas. See also Hu Shih's view on textual criticism in "Methodology of Textual criticism" in *Collected Works of Hu Shih*, IV: 1: 135-48.

On textual criticism on the *Chuang Tzu*, see Wang Shu-min, *Chuang Tzu Chiao-shih*, 2 vols.; *Chuang Hsüeh Kuan-k'uei*; Chang Ch'eng-ch'iu, *Chuang Tzu P'ien-mu K'ao*; Lang Ch'ing-hsiao, *Chuang Tzu Hsüeh-an*; Ma Hsü-lun, *Chuang Tzu I-cheng*; Chu Kuei-yao; *Chuang Tzu Nei-p'ien Cheng-pu*; Su Hsin-wu, *Kuo Hsiang Chuang Hsüeh P'ing-i*; etc.

26.   Huang Chin-hung's *"Chuang Tzu and His Literature"* is good in this respect.

27.   "Rongo yomi no Rongo shirazu."

28.   *Mencius* 7B3. Cf. Tsuda Saukichi, *Dōke no Shisō to sono Tenkai*, pp. 725–32. Sadly the book itself falls into the danger against which he warns the reader. On the general situation of textual criticism in China, see Ch'ien Mu, *Kuo-hsüeh Kai-lun*; *Hsüeh Yueh* (good on Chu Hsi); Yü Ying-shih, "I-li, K'ao-chu, Ts'u-chang," in Wei Cheng-t'ung (ed.), *Chung-kuo Cheh-hsüeh Ts'u-tien Ta-ch'uan*, pp. 629–52.

29.   On this question, see especially Søren Kierkegaard, *The Point of View of My Work as an Author*.

30.   Watson, p. 302.

31.   Cf. preceding note 1.

32.   Both these quotations are from Max Black, *A Companion To Wittgensteins's 'Tractatus'*, p. vii.

33.   Watson, pp. 193–94.

34.   Cf. Tsuda, *op. cit.* (in preceding note 28), pp. 408–10.

35.   Watson, pp. 84, 86.

36.   For a similar yet bloodier, more fatal, and less dialogal version of our father's-race-earth-*in*-us against whom we revolt, see Nikos Kazantzakis, *The Saviors of God*, pp. 63–84.

37.   "Poetic" is taken in the wide sense to be described here, not in the conventional sense of the literary style called poetry; poeticity differs from poetry. Chuang Tzu's poetic beauty is noted in, among others, Lin Yün-ming's *Chuang Tzu Yin*. Hsüan Ying's *Nan-Hwa-Ching Chieh*, Wang Fu-chih's *Chuang Tzu Chieh*, Ch'en Shou-ch'ang's *Nan-Hwa Chen-Ching Cheng-I*, Huang Chin-hung's "*Chuang Tzu and His Literature*," Lang Ch'ing-hsiao's "*Notes to Chuang Tzu Scholarship*," Liu Ta chieh's "*A History of the Development of Chinese Literature*," A. C. Graham's *Chuang-tzŭ: The Seven Inner Chapters*, Burton Watson's *The Complete Works of Chuang Tzu*, as well as Thomas Merton's *The Way of Chuang Tzu*.

   Wen I-to in his usual perceptiveness even gives us an exquisite appreciation of (1) Chuang Tzu's divine literary beauty, (2) the divinely beautiful principle of things, and (3) the divine unity of both, with various quotations appreciating Chuang Tzu from many angles and quarters. Wen thinks that imaginative novels in China (such as *The Monkey* and *The Scholars*) are the gifts of Chuang Tzu. He quotes Chuang Tzu's incomparable phrase, "skin like ice, snow" (Chapter One, line 92), saying, "*Are* not our sublimest healthiest views of beauty the standards already given, after all, by Chuang Tzu 2,000 years ago?" He adds, "In fact, what Chuang Tzu called 'healthy' seems to be at a higher level than where we fix our eyes on." (See Wen's essay, "Chuang Tzu" in "*The Collected Works of Wen I-to*," 2:275–90).

   Sadly, for all these universal praises of Chuang Tzu's poetic beauty, few commentators (not even Wen himself) elaborated on the mutual involvement between what Chuang Tzu said and how he said it, much less considering the philosophical implications of such involvement.

   Incidentally, I must resist the temptation to go into Martin Heidegger's poetizing and poetic indwelling. Suffice it here to note that Chuang Tzu in the fourth century B.C. executed, far more subtly and naturally than Heidegger, what Heidegger formidably talked *about* in the twentieth century. For a further comparison, see my *Chuang Tzu: World Philosopher at Play*, pp. 61 (note 1) and 82 (note 50).

38.   If not "begging the question," "going in a vicious circle," and the like.

39.   Martin Buber and Gabriel Marcel in the world of philosophy of the modern West perhaps come closest to Chuang Tzu in this regard. Plato is of course here, too.

40.   Francois Cheng, *Chinese Poetic Writing*, pp. xiii–xiv. Cf. James J. Y. Liu, *The Art of Chinese Poetry*, pp. 91–130; *Chinese Theories of Literature*, pp. 16–105.

41. Owen Barfield, *Poetic Diction*, p. 146. Cf. note 42.

42. On this point, as well as the points raised in the passage referred to in notes 41 and 43, see one of the leading literary critics of our time, Wang Meng-ou's *"General Introduction to Literature,"* pp. 95–107.

43. Barfield, pp. 145–46.

44. See Wang Meng-ou, *"Researches in Theories of Chinese Classical Literature,"* pp. 3–6, 156–59, 163–68, 280–85, 323–24, et passim (this book predominantly discusses Chinese poetry with sensitivity and erudition). His view agrees with Chow Tse-tsung (ed.), *Wen-lin*, pp. 155–66, and of course with Chuang Tzu's in 33/9.

45. See Wang Meng-ou, *"Researches,"* pp. 11–13, 22 (note 3). See also note 42 above.

46. This is the heroic romance of the Liang-shan outlaws. See Pearl S. Buck's translation, *All Men Are Brothers*, and Liu Ta-chieh, pp. 943–49.

47. This beautifully evocative imagery appears somewhere in Lin Yün-ming's *Chuang Tzu Yin.*

48. Cf. Chapter Twenty-One, and Chapter Twenty-Six, 26/48–49 (Watson, p. 302).

49. This statement is quoted on the book jacket of Normans Mailer's historical novel, *Ancient Evenings.*

50. Barfield, pp. 146–47.

51. Wen I-to, *"Myths and Poetry,"* pp. 181–92. His view was quoted approvingly by both Chow Tse-tsung, pp. 164–65, and Liu, *Literature,* pp. 67–68. Wang Li said in *"The Ancient Chinese"* (2:535f) that not only did poems in the *Shih Ching* (and the *Ch'u Tz'u*) rhyme but all pre-Ch'in literature is steeped in the rhyming convention of the *Shih Ching*. Most of the *I Ching* and *Tao Te Ching* is rhymed. So are quite often, other classics, and he cites from the *Tso Chuan*, the *Chan Kuo Ts'e*, the *Analects,* the *Mencius,* the *Chuang Tzu,* and the *Hsun Tzu*—all following the rhyming convention of the *Shih Ching.*

52. Barfield, pp. 41, 48.

53. Ch'en Shou-ch'ang, pp. 649–77, et passim. Graham, *Chuang-tzŭ,* passim. See also the delightful but incomplete and sometimes inaccurate translation by Thomas Merton, *The Way of Chuang Tzu.* It is sad also to note that the text is not as pictorial as the pictorial format of Gia-fu Feng and Jane English, *Chuang Tsu: Inner Chapters*—which, incidentally, seems to have been carefully consulted by Graham.

54. Lin Yutang (ed.), *The Wisdom of China and India,* p. 627.

55. Russel M. Geer (tr.), *On Nature by Lucretius.*

56. For remarks on the Chinese text used as a basis for the translations that follow, see my notes in Chapter One: (*a*) preceding the Kuo Hsiang Text and (*b*) at the beginning of the Translation. On the various editions and extant copies of the original *Chuang Tzu*, and their relations to Kuo Hsiang's compilation and its various copies, see Chang Ch'eng-ch'iu, *Chuang Tzu P'ien-mu K'ao,* pp. 1–18.

57. See note 52.

58. That is, the *original* text reproduced by Kuo Ch'ing-fan. Although the Kuo Hsiang text has only one *wu* throughout (the one we commonly use today), the Kuo Ch'ing-fan text has the distinction between the two *wu*'s,.

59. Recently (1986) a noted philosopher, P'ang P'u, said that *wang* means "what was but later becomes non-existent"; *wu*[a] means "there may be but we do not know"; another *wu*[b] indicates a pure nothing, non-existence. This is another way of interpreting the

Chinese notion of nothingness and its etymological foundations. See P'ang P'u, "On *Wu*", in T'ang Yijie, et al. (eds.), *"Chinese Culture and Chinese Philosophy."*

60. For a detailed description of Chuang Tzu's usage of *pu*, see Huang Chin-hung's *"Chuang Tzu and His Literature,"* pp. 111–46.

Notes to Chapter One

1. Jean-Paul Sartre, *Nausea*, pp. 56–59.

2. See, 3.2.b of Meditation C, and note 101. Cf. *The American Heritage Dictionary*, s. v. "yarn." Ludwig Wittgenstein says that a concept is an overlapping and crisscrossing, yarn-like, of characteristics, one taking over another, mutually reinforcing endlessly. See his *Philosophical Investigations*, I.66–71. Cf. note 201 to Chapter Two.

    Incidentally, although science is open to future revisions, such revisions are occasioned by the breakages of *uniform* applications of scientific theories. Uniformity of application indicates the closed nature of scientific theory. A revised theory in science is no longer the previous one, which must be discarded.

3. Lao Tzu, *Tao Te Ching*, Chapter 73.

4. See note 1.

5. See Chapter Two, line 182.

6. *Tao Te Ching*, Chapter 1.

7. In my "Invitation by a Butterfly," Prologue A.4.

8. On this issue of participatory provocation, or what I would rather call indirection and evocation, see my *Chuang Tzu: World Philosopher at Play*, pp. 29–60.

9. See the beginning of Chapter Twenty-Seven, as translated by Burton Watson in *The Complete Works of Chuang Tzu*, p. 303, and its note.

10. In my Translation I had "(In the) Northern Darkness (there) exists a fish; his name is K'un." *Yu* has two meanings, to have and to exist, and both meanings are present here. The fish belongs to the Northern Darkness, and the fish exists a such—the fish of Northern Darkness.

11. For connections among south, north, yin-yang, and five elementary ways, see Akatzuka Tadashi, *Soshi*, 1:26; Wen I-to, *"Myths and Poetry,"* pp. 140-41; and Murobashi Tetsuji, *Dai Kanwa Jiten*, s. v. "south" (2:562), "north" (2:442).

12. *A Concordance to the Chuang Tzu*, 11/35, 12/16, 22/30, cf. 22/56.

13. Norman J. Girardot said that *ming, hun tun,* and the gourd are mutually synonymous in his *Myth and Meaning in Early Taoism*. See my translation, Chapter One, lines 120–144.

14. We see as much irony in the later summary description, "In the *barren* north, ... there lived a fish" (lines 36-39) as in the name K'un, the smallest roe and the biggest Leviathan.

15. C. A. S. Williams, *Outlines of Chinese Symbolism and Art Motives*, s. v. "fish."

16. Such parsimony contrasts with other Taoist writings (except for *Tao Te Ching*) which love to embellish on fantastic details. See *Lieh Tzŭ* (tr. by A. C. Graham), p. 98; *Huai Nan Tzu*, S. P. C. K., 3/2a, 4/10b, 6/2b; Hiraoka Teikichi, *"A Study of Ch'i in the Huai Nan Tzu,"* pp. 269–72.

17. Watson, p. 138.

18.   Watson (p. 29, note 1) merely sums up the consensus of commentators on this point. See my gloss to Translation, line 1.

19.   To the Chinese mind, what sounds and/or looks alike means alike, that is, similarities in pronunciation and/or character formation are somehow connected with similarities in meaning. And so it is not out of line to explain a notion or develop an argument by way of such similarities. See 2/36–37 (in my translation, Chapter Two, line 122) and its explication by Fukunaga Mitzuji, *Soshi*, 1:57. Arthur Waley observes the same point regarding the notion of *shih*, "power-situation," in his *Three Ways of Thought in Ancient China*, p. 181. On the notion of *shih*, see also Roger T. Ames, *The Art of Rulership*, pp. 65–107, where a systematic treatment of its various implications appears. See note 50 to Chapter Two.

20.   4/33; 5/6; 6/23, 27–28, 54; 11/54; 12/6, 73; 13/22; 17/47; 18/13; etc.

21.   2/20, 6/55, 13/29, 15/19, 18/43, etc.

22.   6/50–82; 5/6; 13/14; 15/10; 18/22; etc.

23.   1/1; 6/54, 78; 18/43; etc.

24.   2/96; 4/17, 24, 33; 7/15; 11/54; 14/80–81; 16/9; etc.

25.   Chapters 2, 3, 6 (7, 13), 14, 15, 16, 18, 22.

26.   16/55ff., 18/22ff., 19/62, 22/77ff., 25/16, etc.

27.   The "Light and Lissome Bird" (Watson p. 93, 7/9) is "death," according to Wang Fu-chih, *Chuang Tzu Chieh*, p. 71.

28.   The Book of Poetry said, "The Hawk flies up to heaven; the fishes leap in the deep"—James Legge, *The Chinese Classics*, 4:445. Also cf. Akatzuka, 1:26–27).

29.   See my translation, Chapter Two, lines 105, 129, and my glosses to them. In addition, Chang Heng's "*Cosmology*" shows that the universe is shaped like a bird's egg; the heavens surround the earth as the egg white wraps its yolk. Their movement is like that of a wheel, turning without ceasing. And "refusing to rest in the ocean, P'ung cruises forth until it rests in the heavenly Pond," he continued, obviously referring to Chuang Tzu here. Cf. note 35.

30.   See Kuo Ch'ing-fan, *Chuang Tzu Chi-shih*, 3:730.

31.   Cf. 22/56–57.

32.   Cf. Watson, p. 302; 26/48–49.

33.   Cf. lines 163–64 and my gloss to line 47.

34.   The story of the Wheelwright concludes Chapter Thirteen; cf. notes 29, 111. The wheezing and belching of the huge Clod begins the first chapter (line 10) and the second chapter (line 15).

35.   Such perspective of the sky would have been called a "bird's eye view," were it not for the fact that the phrase is ambiguous; it can also mean the view in the eyes of a small bird, such a small doves (and cicadas), to be mentioned presently.

36.   Paul Tillich, *The Courage to Be*, pp. 143–51, 179–90.

37.   On becoming non-being, see my *Chuang Tzu: World Philosopher at Play*, Aria I.

38.   Although the phrase, "use of the useless," does not appear till later (4/90, 22/69, 26/31, 33), the phrase captures the gist of the dialogue here.

39.   *Hsüeh chiu* ("dove") may indicate such scholarship. *Hsüeh* is often taken to mean *yü* or *hsüeh*, though Kuo Ch'ing-fan said that they are alternative readings (1:9). Even

hsüeh is a "bird which *knows* the coming events" according to the *Shuo Wen Chieh Tzu* (4a/42).

In my opinion, (1) these proposals stem from the difficulties of interpreting *hsüeh* ("learning") in this context, (2) these alternative readings may well not be what Chuang Tzu had in mind (the *Chuang Tzu* does not support them), (3) *hsüeh* still has something to do with knowledge, and (4) two "authoritative quotations" (lines 6–7, 35) show that Chuang Tzu did have scholarship in mind when he told the story. In short, my interpretation is plausible.

40.   Akatzuka, 1:34.

41.   *Ibid.*, pp. 34–35.

42.   The cicada symbolizes longevity, if not "immortality and resurrection" (Williams, p. 71). Incidentally, the names of small animals are changed from those in the first description.

43.   Chuang Tzu later said that to peddle the ancient sagely ideals to our contemporary world is as tragically laughable as to push a boat over land (Watson, p. 160 or 14/37).

44.   A contemporary example of what Chuang Tzu has in mind may be the notion of "industrial waste" with which we do not know what to do, but which may contain something very useful.

45.   Cf. "nourishing the bird with what nourishes you [man]," thereby killing the bird (Watson, pp. 194, 208).

46.   All this is the "machine mentality" (12/56, Watson, p. 134; A. C. Graham (tr.), *Chuang-tzŭ: The Seven Inner Chapters*, p. 186).

47.   19/63. Cf. Watson, p. 206; Graham, p. 138.

48.   This is the concluding phrase of the First Chapter.

49.   See note 38.

50.   2/59, 61; 6/61; 24/66.

51.   And we may be surprised to find that we actually become what we have been imagining, as the reverie before death on what the future brings shows—we may become a "rat's liver" or a "bug's arm," a "rooster," a "crossbow pellet" or "cart-wheels" made out of the wood which has fed on our decays (Watson, pp. 84–85).

52.   Friedrich Nietzsche is well known for his courageous *amor fati* that conquers eternal recurrence by accepting it. Whether or not he regards eternal recurrence as *itself* meaningful remains a debatable topic.

Sophia Delza in her perceptive book, *T'ai Chi Ch'uan* (edited with an excellent foreword by Robert C. Neville) said, (pp. 176–78) that even when, and precisely because, we remember, repetitions can be meaningful due to the different contexts in which they happen. I wonder if she would have said so if the historical context were to remain the same.

53.   Even in the eighteenth chapter on Perfect Happiness, suffering is treated only as a foil for the main theme, "perfect happiness."

We can translate Chuang Tzu's sentiment into modern language as follows. Pain is a raw sensation as inherent in sensory organs and awareness as pleasure. But we can do something with pain as we can with pleasure. We can enhance it or reduce it with our consciousness; we can even go on living without noticing pain to a considerable extent. We can also accept it as part of life, in fact as a threshold of a new stage of existence. In these ways we can eliminate pain-as-enemy or as-problem. *How* we deal with pain is the problem, not pain itself.

54. Here Chuang Tzu and Nietzsche agree.

55. On this point of *non*-violent non-violence (as opposed to violent non-violence), see my *Chuang Tzu: World Philosopher*, Aria III.

56. Cf. Chapters Three, Four, Five, Six.

57. Christopher Nolan, *Dam-Burst of Dreams*, p. 123.

58. 11/13, 50; 14/2.

59. 6/15, 18.

60. 17/62, 18/39.

61. 8/31; 2/95; 6/14, 8/32.

62. This is the theme of the third chapter, which applies the theme of *hsiao yao yu* to human life full of suffering.

63. Many commentators from Hsiang Hsiu onward, through Kuo Hsiang, Liu I-ch'ing, Chih Tao-lin, to contemporary Kuan Feng and Mou Tsung-san, usually take this first chapter to be a description of stages of our spiritual progress from "dependence" on the world to "independence," reaching the realm of "self-possession" and life "in line with one's allotment."

In my opinion, all this is too disjunctive. In their seriousness they miss Chuang Tzu's playful dynamism. My critique can be divided into three points:

(1) The dependence-independence distinction deals with the outer world. Self-possession and living in line with one's allotment describe the inner self. Both sets of notions assume a *disjunction* between the outside and the inside.

Chuang Tzu has no such disjunction; in fact the whole point of the chapter is to abolish such disjunction. Cicadas and doves were chitchatting precisely on disjunction; they complained about the Bird being too big, engaging in a task entirely disproportionate to life, etc. Their smallness lies in obsession with the disjunction between the we (right) and the they (wrong). The small birds distinguished and excluded; the big Bird was silent. The chapter then builds up the theme of acceptance—even of the useless things.

(2) I agree with Mou (p. 182), saying that this chapter is about self-cultivation, not about knowing the material and practical world, within its net of limitations. But then Mou himself also has a disjunction between the inner self and the practical material world. He falls into Buddhistic absolute idealism which goes *beyond* this world. And that is not Chuang Tzu; *hsiao yao yu* is always a *yu* in this world.

(3) Furthermore, these people are without exception all too serious. They have lost that romping innocence of the cosmic frolic of Hsiao Yao Yu which *includes* both the big and the small, the foolish and the sagacious, the useful and the useless, of myriads of things. By tirelessly quoting other views, these commentators blur the peculiarities of Chuang Tzu, as if Chuang Tzu says what these "authorities" have already said, only less convincingly. Mou is worst in this regard. He commented on others' commentaries. And *his* comments are studded with quotations from Neo-Confucianism and Buddhism. Fortunately we are yet to explain Plato by *merely* quoting form Aristotle, Kant, and Wittgenstein. (Hsiang Hsiu, Kuo Hsiang, Liu I-Ch'ing, and Chi Tao-lin are conveniently anthologized in Kuo Ch'ing-fan's *Chuang Tzu Chi Shih*, 1:1–42. For Kuang Feng see his

Chuang Tzu Nei-P'ien I-Chieh ho P'i-P'an, pp. 11, 79, 84-88. For Mou Tsung-san, see his *Ch'ai-Hsing yü Hsüan-Li,* pp. 180–205.)

64.   Søren Kierkegaard, *Fear and Trembling;* it starts with the four readings of *Genesis* 22. And of course we remember how the New Testament recorded four seismic effects of Jesus' personality on his disciples. Did Kierkegaard have this in mind when he recorded his four readings, the four seismic effects, of Abraham on him?

65.   *Tao Te Ching,* Chapter 11. (The *Chuang Tzu* has thirty-three extant chapters.) The title of the first chapter captures the flexibility of the Pivot of Tao that, fitted to the center of the circle, responds endlessly (Chapter Two, line 105).

66.   See *Dai Kanwa Jiten,* 6:1184.

67.   See *Shuo Wen Chieh Tzu,* 7a/20, *Kuang Ya Shih Ku,* 3.

68.   Hsü Fu-kuan, *Chung-Kuo I-Shu Ching-Shen,* pp. 60–64.

69.   "Tao tao-able" is certainly a curious literary construction even in Chinese; it shows Lao Tzu's extreme parsimony. William McNaughton has "The Tao you can tao is not the Tao," in *The Taoist Vision,* p.10.

70.   The first Seven Chapters of the *Chuang Tzu* are usually called "the Inner Chapters," reputed to have been genuinely written by Chuang Tzu. These chapters are more ambiguous, balanced, profound, and vigorous than the others.

71.   Cf. Watson, p. 303.

72.   *Tao Te Ching,* Chapter 41.

73.   Xavier Rubert de Ventós, *Self-Defeated Man,* p. 61.

74.   Is it a mere accident that Socrates used birds and aviary to ponder on the problem of knowledge in the *Theaetetus* (196D-199C)?

75.   Chapter Two, line 261. Of this more later.

76.   Watson, p. 193.

77.   In *A Concordance to the Chuang Tzu,* Part A is from line 1 to line 13, Part C is from lines 35 to 47. That is, these two Parts have roughly equal number of characters. In Watson's translation, Part A takes up the first two pages, and Part C the last two pages, of the chapter. In my translation, lines are arranged not according to the number of characters but according to meaning clusters, and so Part A has less lines (34) than Part C (50).

78.   Cf. an interesting "inversion principle" in Kenneth G. Bailey, *Poet and Peasant,* pp. 48-50. My arrangement slightly modifies it.

79.   On lines 36 and 37 the Northern Darkness is explained as the "heavenly pond." But this belongs to Part B.

80.   The phrase, "still ... had not planted himself"— James Legge, *The Texts of Taoism,* 1:168; my translation, line 59—about Mr. Sung Jung Tzu may well have an implicit reference to the useless Shu *Tree planted* in the Village of Not-even-existence (line 161). "Tree" and "to plant" are translations of the identical character, *shu* (which rhymes with *Shu*). To be planted means to shy away from self-glorification (for Sung Jung Tzu literally means "Sung, glory, son") and to become roamingly nameless, meritless, self-less—in a word, useless.

81.   That is, "linkage" between the ordinary Mr. Self and the extraordinary Mr. Chieh Yü (Mr. Receiver of the Divine Man?). Interestingly, nobody claims to be the Divine Man. As the tao-able Tao is not the Tao, so the self-professed Divine Man is a fake.

82. I know that other commentators have other interpretations on the meaning of Hsü Yu. Kuo Ch'ing-fan, Ssu-ma Piao, Wang Fu-Chih, and Chien Wen Ti typically took it to be name of a historical personage. Akatzuka is more imaginative and, siding with Yang K'uan, dared to see in the name an allusion to a mountain god connected with a sun god.

I have chosen what is stated above, simply because my interpretation fits the literary context in the chapter much more directly and unequivocally. We can accept both those interpretation *and* my interpretation. The same situation holds for other names, such as Chien Wu, Lien Shu, and Chieh Yü. It is not implausible for Chuang Tzu to use those names in their original senses to allude to his ideas here, fully knowing that these names may have been those of historical persons and mythological gods.

Some commentators refuse to say what they "do not know." They quote only what is historically, textual-critically certain. Some others hazard what is appropriate in a literary context of the original text, confessing at the same time that they are only proposing a hypothesis.

I admire both the historical integrity of the former and the literary integrity of latter. Both may, of course, be wrong. What is historically correct may be contextually out of place: what is contextually plausible and illuminating may not be borne out historically and textual-critically. There is risk in any sort of literary interpretation of an ancient text.

Perhaps the *Chuang Tzu* requires both sorts of commentators. Both have conscientiousness, and that is what is needed for understanding the *Chuang Tzu* more than absolute accuracy, which is not only impossible but inappropriate in such an imaginative work of literature. What is required here is a *compelling* interpretation, not an accurate one. My ploy is, as mentioned in the Prologue, "The Poetic *Chuang Tzu*," not to follow but to *use* the historical commentaries to lean on the literary-contextual interpretation; imaginative literature must be treated imaginatively, and internal contextual evidence is weightier than external historical-textual evidence. In short, I think one must take the risk; one must confess its danger and plunge imaginatively but cautiously. Cf. Prologue, "Why Companion, Not Commentary."

Akatzuka said that Chien Wu, Lien Shu, Chieh Yü, and Mao Ku She are various pronounciations for various place-names connected with mountains.

Chien Wu: Pronounce *k'ü* (loan for *hsü*; see Bernhard Karlgren, *Gramatica Serica,* p. 146, 78a), meaning "hill."

Lien Shu: Pronounce *lu* ("plateau" and its god).

Chieh Yü: Pronounce *chü* (as in *chü ju*), meaning "marshland" (at the foot of a mountain).

Miao means "not visually certain."

Ku She: Pronounce *ke* ("spirits descending"). The spirits-descended Ku She mountain is where the Energy of Nature is gathered to raise wind, rain, and myriads of things (Akatzuka, p. 51–52).

Thus Chuang Tzu begins with the Darkness of Water, continues with the energies of various Mountains, and ends with the quietude of the Tree. Chuang Tzu begins the chapter with lives in water (*K'un*) and in the air (*P'ung,* cicadas, doves), continues with men and animals, and ends with trees.

83. Watson, p. 129.

84. Line 119 echoes the quietude of lines 30–38 (Part A) and lines 161—165 (Part C).

This division differs slightly from that of my Translation, where "use" is the main theme of the last section and "big" is the main theme of the first section. I agree with Kuan Feng (p. 87), Akatzuka (pp. 41–42), and others, that this threefold description of the sage is one of the central foci in Chuang Tzu. But I think it should be taken more as a literary device describing living actuality than as a definitive metaphysical system reflecting the structure of reality. Commentators tend to take Chuang Tzu's statements in the latter mold.

85. See note 80.

86. See, e.g., Martin Buber, *I and Thou*, tr. Ronald Gregor Smith, pp. 18–20. This is only one of his frequent intimations of pregnant silence in the I-Thou "encounter." Also see Max Picard, *The World of Silence*. For my thoughts on non-being, music, silence, etc., see my *Chuang Tzu: World Philosopher*, Aria I.

87. *On Nature*, I:215–614, 483–584.

88. See Henry G. Bugbee, Jr., *The Inward Morning*, pp. 125—126.

89. See 7/21, 23–26; 12/56; 18/45–46 (Watson, pp. 96, 134, 196).

90. Phyllis Trible, *God and the Rhetoric of Sexuality*, pp. 32—56.

91. *Ibid.*, pp. 35, 36.

92. Cf. *ibid.*, p. 32.

93. Even the other woman must have been brought back to her womb-sense, seeing that she did not contest Solomon's judgment.

94. The pre-Socratics are conveniently summed up in John Mansley Robinson, *An Introduction to Early Greek Philosophy*, pp. 5–6, 25–27, 93, et passim.

95. Watson, pp. 97, 124, 142, 372.

96. Cf. Watson, P. 137. "Ambi-guous" comes from "ambi" and "agere"; "ambiguus" in Latin means both "doubtful" and "driving hither and thither." *Oxford English Dictionary* adds, "The objective meanings, though second in Latin, seem earliest in English."

97. *Hua* can mean birth (Watson, p. 191)—cf. 4/33; 6/27; 12/6; 13/22, 29; 15/19; 18/13, 43; 20/59; 21/34. Also see *tsao hua*, 6/55, 59, 60; *feng hua*, 14/78, 79; *wu hua*, 2/96, 13/14, 15/10.

98. Murobashi Tetzuji in his *Soshi Heiwa* said that a European rendered *wu ho yu* as "Erewhon," the name (an anagram on "nowhere") of a Utopian novel by Samuel Butler (Chinese tr. by Li Chun-shih, p. 54).

99. On this ideogram see James Legge, 1:127. Cf. Mai-Mai Sze, *The Tao of Painting*, 1:108.

100. Watson, p. 87. Cf. Chapter Two, lines 112–114.

101. To say that the *Hsiao Yao Yu* chapter treats the theme of creation may raise some eyebrows among literary critics. There is no *clear* indication of creation in the chapter, and no commentator can be so irresponsible as to read his own fantasy into it.

There is such a thing as literal-prosaic explication of the text that kills its tenor, and also such a thing as creative interpretation with textual and contextual clues, so that the text is enlivened and equipped with an increased range of application. Especially in the imaginative text of the *Chuang Tzu* one must sin boldly, and beware of killing the spirit by adhering slavishly to the letter.

My contextual clues for "creation"-interpretation are two: (1) Many ancient essays and novels (including those of Chinese culture) *start* with cosmology and often cosmog-ony. Shrewd Chuang Tzu could not have failed to take advantage of this custom. (2) There are no other chapters in the *Chuang Tzu* which are totally devoted to this theme.

My textual clues for "creation"-interpretation are four: (1) Creation and creativity are intimately related throughout the *Chuang Tzu*. (2) The charismatic, potentially com-munal bird, P'ung, is traditionally related to (if not identified with) the Hun Tun, the primal Chaos before creation. This bird flies to the Southern Darkness, the bright-separatedness, perhaps the created world. Such flight strongly suggests the creation theme. (3) The living beings mentioned in this chapter roughly cover all possible kinds of beings in the world—flora, fauna, and humans of various sorts. (4) Wen I-to claims with plausibility that, having carefully examined forty-nine ancient myths and stories, he came to the following six conclusions:

(*a*) Gourd is used as an instrument against water (flood) and as a material for making humans;

(*b*) Gourd, bird egg, Fu Hsi, and Nü Wa are mutually related, both mythologically and etymologically;

(*c*) Gourd, Fu Hsi, and wood-virtue are mutually related in the same twofold manner;

(*d*) Gourd, Nü Wa, and Sheng (musical instrument) are also related in the same manner;

(*e*) Utensils in China started with the utilization of gourds;

(*f*) Gourd and "no-hand-feet," "no head-tail," "no ear-eye-mouth-nose" are re-lated—they all suggest primal Hun Tun, primal "meat ball."

Thus the following notions seem to be linked mythologically and etymologically in the notions of the gourd: creation of the universe and mankind, creativity and ingenuity, utility and survival, water, floating, fighting. K'un and P'ung at the beginning of the chapter seem to be related to gourd and hand salve toward the end of the chapter—and they all converge on the theme of creation. See Wen I-to, pp. 55–68. Norman J. Girardot further elaborates on the relations among egg, gourd, and deluge in his *Myth and Meaning*, pp. 169–256.

Furthermore, my "creation"-interpretation enables the reader to (1) link creation to creativity, laughter, levity, and imagination, and (2) see the hidden connection between the first and second chapters on the same theme of creation—the first chapter treats creation fantastically and cosmologically, complemented by the second chapter in an entertaining, logical, and ontological manner. In this way (3) the entire *Chuang Tzu* can be seen to be a parody of more formal and customary essays on things of the world. The *Chuang Tzu* can now be seen as a *Ch'i Hsieh*, a legendary book of jokes, where Chuang Tzu gigglingly quotes from his own font of imagination, thus inviting others to do the same—in other words, spreading the activity of creation.

In this context it is interesting to check on Epicurus' canon of scientific method, as reported in Lucretius' *On Nature*, tr. Russel M. Geer, p. 116 (note 6); cf. p. 48 (note 12) and p. xxviii. According to Epicurus (reported by Lucretius), a good and acceptable scientific hypothesis is what has fecundity of explanation and coherence with the observed data. On this principle, my "creation"-interpretation of the first chapter is a good scientific hypothesis—it fulfills (1) fecundity of explanation and 2) coherence with both the text of the *Chuang Tzu* and the context of life.

Our scholarly translator (Geer) complained that it leads to "fantastic conclusions." We must ask what is wrong with fantastic conclusions. They may militate against the rule of science—the principle of simplicity. Lucretius' explanation may have crowded the world with "unnecessary" "idols" and thin films of images emitted from objects that facilitate our senses.

Yet we have no inherent reason why a simple explanation should be true and a complex one false; simplicity may turn out to be *our* theoretical prejudice. At the very least, the Epicurean model may generate esthetically pleasing and evocative thoughts, which may evoke further scientific investigations.

A system (such as Lucretius' atomism) generated by the Epicurean canon of coherence (explanation and non-contradiction) could land us in factual irrelevance—the danger of the coherence theory of truth that plagues any metaphysical system. A "false statement" also means just this, that it is meaningful (logically coherent) and factually fatuous and irrelevant. But this bane, when recognized as such, is "interesting" (Whitehead) because its internal *contrast* between logical coherence and factual fatuity provokes imaginative investigation. Poetry is made up, among others, of these interestingly false statements. Bad science may be good poetry, the fertile humus for good science. Contemporary Western technology is built on the ruins of Athens and Rome. In this sense at least, the pre-Socratics (Thales, Heraclitus) and Roman scientists (Epicurus, Lucretius) are the precursors of modern science.

Now all this side glance at Lucretius and Epicurus has a point. *If* my creation-interpretation turned out to be a false over-interpretation, then it *can* at least be claimed that it is an interestingly false one, bound to stimulate further thinking. It is interesting because it makes for a coherent vision of the first and the second chapters. It is stimulating because—well, the reader is the judge here. See also the section on "story telling" (3.2.b) in this Meditation C.

102. Chapter Two, line 98. The *Chuang Tzu* is full of *k'o*; see 6/60, 90, 91; 11/11; 14/80; 21/27, 27/8; etc.

103. *Tao Te Ching*, Chapter 41.

104. Watson, p. 136.

105. W. K. C. Guthrie, *Sophists*, p. 187, note 3.

106. W. K. C. Guthrie, *Socrates*, p. 146.

107. Guthrie, *Sophists*, p. 188, note.

108. Watson, p. 269.

109. Chapter One, line 162.

110. Cf. note 9. Chuang Tzu's "goblet words" are "spillover words," according to Graham (*Chuang-tzŭ*, p. 26).

111. Cf. note 34; Watson, pp. 152–53.

112. Watson, p. 215.

113. Watson, p. 60.

114. *Shih erh wu ch'uan* (12/83). Thomas Merton has "They made no history" (*The Way of Chuang Tzu*, p. 76).

115. *Phaedrus* 275.

116. These are the statements that end Chapter Twenty-Five.

117. Kurt Gödel, *Foundations of Mathematics* (1969). Cf. *Gödel's Proof*, by Ernest

Nagel and James R. Newman. For its interesting application, see Douglas R. Hofstadter, *Gödel, Escher, Bach.*

118.   Cf. note 2. From Wittgenstein's remark that a notion such as "game" is a "yarn," it follows that any notion and any description is a "yarn," a story.

119.   Rudolf Bultmann, *Essays: Philosophical and Theological,* and *Existence and Faith.*

120.   Michael Polanyi and Harry Prosch, *Meaning,* p. 146.

121.   Paul Ricoeur, *The Conflict of Interpretations,* p. 5.

122.   In fact, being an ancient book, those stories may over the years have been thrown in together to make up a chapter.

123.   I have been using the word "principle" loosely and generally.

124.   See note 9.

125.   See an interesting book by George Lakoff and Mark Johnson, *Metaphors We Live By.*

126.   Lucretius, *On Nature,* II: 55–61.

127.   On computers and evocation, see my *Chuang Tzu: World Philosopher,* "Overture," especially, "C: Understanding."

128.   Professor Severin Swanson.

129.   6/81; 11/44, 45; 9/17 (8/22 is derogatory).

130.   Watson, pp. 152–53, 200, 205–6, 244–45.

131.   Watson, 284–85.

132.   For catching cicadas, see Watson, pp. 199–200, 219. For fishing, pp. 167, 187–88, 228–29, 296, 302. For archery, pp. 201, 267. For hunting, p. 270. For horse racing, p. 206, cf. pp. 244–45. For music, pp. 267–68. For watching fish play, pp. 188–89. For bird watching, pp. 218–19.

Notes to Chapter Two

1.   Cf. note 13. As the phrases, *wan wu i ch'i* (17/44) and *pien hua ch'i i* (14/20) show. This radical democracy, where each thing is unique-and-equal, is neither esoteric nor ancient. See Meditation B.1.1. According to Henry Alonzo Myers, this is the very tissue and foundation of human equality and of American democracy. Myers said, "Each man is to himself equal to the great world of his own experience. In what matters most to men this world has the same import to all; it teaches the lesson of his own infinite worth. And so men, who are equal to the same thing, are equal to each other..." (*Are Men Equal?— An Inquiry into the Meaning of American Democracy,* p. 32). Myers claims that he was merely summing up the common sentiment of Emerson, Whitman, Melville, and Lincoln. Chuang Tzu anticipated them by nearly 2,400 years, summing up no one's view.

For all the etymological information in the text of my Meditation here see *Shuo Wen Chieh Tzu* and *Dai Kan Wa Ji-ten* under *ch'i, wu,* and *lun.* For peculiar interpretations of *ch'i* and *wu,* see K'ang Yin, *Wen-Tzu Yuan-Liu Ch'ien-Shuo,* pp. 495, 226 (it has no entry on *lun*). For *lun* and *wu,* see A. C. Graham, *Later Mohist Logic,* pp. 194, 210.

2.   *Cheng chih, ch'i chih* (9/3).

3.   These are two important phrases that conclude Chapter Two; they will be referred to again and again in the following pages.

4.   Cf. Samuel Todes and Charles Daniels, "Beyond the Doubt of a Shadow, with an Addendum by Samuel Todes, 'Shadow in Knowledge: Plato's Misunderstanding of Shadows, and of Knowledge as Shadow-Free,'" in Don Ihde and Richard M. Zaner (eds.), *Dialogues in Phenomenology*, pp. 86–113. This interesting article criticizes the Platonic notion of shadow-free knowledge. Unfortunately, Todes still thinks that shadow is subordinate and dependent on the thing of which it is a shadow. The complete interdependence between knowledge and ignorance is advocated in David L. Hall, *Eros and Irony*, pp. 124–27.

5.   A. C. Graham should be given credit for discovering Chuang Tzu's practice of quoting from the Mohist Canons of logic. See his "Chuang-tzǔ's Essay on Seeing Things as Equal," *History of Religions*, 9:139. Cf. also his *Chuang-tzǔ*, pp. 52–56.

6.   See Watson, *Chuang Tzu*, p. 375, and *Mencius* 7A4, "All things are complete in me."

7.   Although commentators usually take the name to refer to a real historical personage, a legendary beauty that effected a profound political change in Chin, the name is not without its symbolic meaning of "lady beautiful", implying, perhaps, that the truly beautiful life is life that changes its (her?) mind. In addition, this story may well contain a political and moral satire on loyalty, as well as on our longing for immortality. The life that relents from sorrow to joy is the life of Beginnings Without End, to borrow the title of Sam Keen's book celebrating the changing of marital mind.

8.   It is significant that "attitude" is the only thing we can discuss here, now that all argumentation is stripped of its unqualified validity. Usually we say that to "argue" for the relativity of all judgings and arguings is itself an argument and so is self-contradictory. But this standard argument assumes the universal validity of argumentation, which Chuang Tzu's three points come to discredit. These points are neither argumentation nor irresponsible fantasy; they are an observation of our actual situation. In the end, relativism as an ism is also a judgment, having little to do with Chuang Tzu's rational observation.

9.   I had some thoughts on the monkey-keeper in my *Chuang Tzu*, pp. 73–74.

10.   The personal name, "Chuang Chou," may well be an expression of the *recognized* personal identity, equivalent to the *wo*-self. See Meditation B and   note 28.

Another understandable reason why the personal name was used here even when told by the dreamer himself, may be that the point of the story is puzzlement over personal identity—"Chuang Chou? Or the butterfly?" In this context, it is awkward if not dogmatic to assert "*I* dreamed *I* was a butterfly," etc.; to say "he" or "it" is false, for it was after all "myself" dreaming; to say "he/it/I" is cumbersome, awkward, and perhaps false as well, because "I" am neither a three-in-one personality nor either one of them. It is precisely this sort of puzzlement that is the point of the story. Therefore, the best way out is to use the personal name, "Chuang Chou," and a common name, "butterfly."

11.   Watson, pp. 209–10, modified.

12.   We are reminded here of Chiao Hung's *Chuang Tzu I*, a collection of personal discoveries in the *Chuang Tzu* by notable Chinese thinkers. Although some thoughts in it are more valuable than others, it has a significant title, *Chuang Tzu I* "wings ('aids') to the *Chuang Tzu*." The present *Companion* has roughly the same intention, without the pretentious connotations of "wings" (cf. line 293).

13.   See note 1. Incidentally, *lun* has an uncanny resemblance to Plato's "dialectics,"

the art to *dialegesthai*, which is the verb *dialegein* in the middle voice. The middle voice means "that the agent is the person affected or benefited by the action." Thus to *dialegesthai* is to converse and discriminate things into their kinds, that is, "sorting things into their kinds by taking counsel with each other." It is to sort for oneself by learning from each other in conversation that is serious, open, critical, and cordial. See I. M. Crombie, *An Examination of Plato's Doctrines*, II: 562–63. Specifically, *logos* or *legein* is to take account of things, a selective critical gleaning or collecting, counting, reckoning, explaining. See Gerhard Kittel (ed.), *Theological Dictionary of the New Testament*, 4:69–84.

Similarly, *lun*ᵃ means *lun*ᶜ or more widely *lun*ᵇ, which means *lei, teng ch'a* ("classes," "ranks"), putting order into things, classifying them into kinds and species, etc. Thus Graham's interpretation, "sorting things out, thereby evening them" is correct (*Mohist Logic*, p. 194). See Shih Yung-mao, *Chuang Tzu Cheng*, as quoted in Chang Mo-sheng, *Chuang Tzu Hsin-Shih*, pp. 32–33. The similarity between *lun* and *logos* is thus apparent.

*Lun*ᵃ can, furthermore, have another meaning, *lun*ᵈ (or *kuan*) meaning fishing line or string of musical instrument, people's blue belt, the "line" of occupation, whatever is begun, woven by people about things, and so, knowledge, clarity on things (*Huai Nan Tzu*, 16/7a, 2/3b). In this sense, *lun*ᵃ means also knowledge, sayings, teachings, what is heard, order and arrangement of things, and the like. (Cf. *Dai Kan Wa Ji-ten*, 8:1104). James Legge has "to arrange," in the *She King* [*Shih Ching*], p. 412); Arthur Waley has "to reel" in *The Book of Songs*, No. 59.

14.   Cf. the Buddhistic merry-go-round of all things which is anything but merry—the endless cycles of rebirths and redeaths.

15.   Watson, 152–53. Cf. notes 29, 34, 111 to our Chapter One.

16.   Chapter Two, lines 155–60.

17.   Al Chuang-liang Huang, *Embrace Tiger, Return to Mountain—The Essence of T'ai Chi*, p. 35.

18.   Graham, *Chuang Tzu̇*, p. 48. In that cosmic satire, *The Hitchhiker's Guide to the Galaxy* (p. 7), Douglas Adams says, "It would sort itself out."

19.   Akatzuka, pp. 65–66.

20.   *Dai Kan Wa Ji-ten*, s. v. "ch'i."

21.   Note 19.

22.   *Ibid.*, note 19.

23.   Fukunaga Mitsuji, *Soshi*, 1:32

24.   T'ao Ch'ien's poem is quoted by Fung Yu-lan in *A Short History of Chinese Philosophy* (p. 23) and referred to as describing "Taoism at its best." I have much modified Arthur Waley's translation, quoted there.

25.   Confucius, *The Analects*, 2:7, 16:12. See Fang Chi-ling *Lun-Yu Hsin-Ch'uan*, p. 28; and Uno Tetsujin, *Rongo*, 1:194.

26.   I translated *yü* as "counterpart." Watson has "companion," which he correctly reported "is interpreted variously to mean his associates, his wife, or his own body." I doubt if any of these possible (dictionary) meanings of *yü* fits this context. In the light of the context of both here and line 104, I would take *yü* (or *ou*) to mean: (1) *wo* the identifiable and objectifiable self which forms a pair of opposites with its "objects" of

attention, whatever they are; and/or (2) those objects, the so-called "things." Both belong together in the subject-object dichotomy. For simplicity, I would refer to *wo*-self only.

"Sitting" has a special meaning for Chuang Tzu. Neither lying, standing, or running, sitting is the pose in which all life activities are concentrated. See 2/1 (here), (2/93, 27/22); 4/32; 6/92, 93; 23/16; 24/61.

27. Can it be described as "serpentine"? Cf. 19/43–44, 20/27, 30. Fukunaga (2:538) described this characteristic as sinuous and slithery, trailing and moving along with the counterpart. Cf. also 20/58 and Fukunaga 2:543, 562. One now can go into groups of animals and birds without disturbing them (20/36). See also various examples given in Chapter Nineteen. All this describes a radical democracy (togetherness) of things and beings, a *ch'i wu*.

28. Except for line 268. Chuang Tzu is quite consistent in Chapter Two in his distinction of *wu* and *wo*. To my knowledge commentators have three interpretations of what the distinction means.

(a) Yang Fu-chi and Chao Te said that *wu* is said from the point of view of the self; *wo* from that of others.

(b) Chu Kuei-yao said that *wu* is in the subject-nominative case; *wo*, in the objective-receptive case.

(c) Huang Chin-hung said that *wu* is spirit and *wo* is body. (See Huang, "Reader in the Chuang Tzu," pp. 67)

These interpretations differ in the following ways. Interpretation (a) is the distinction of perspective. *Wo* is an identifiable self, which others can identify as a subject as well as an object. *Wu* is an identifying agent, but itself not identifiable as such. Interpretation (b) is a subject-object distinction; while (c) is another simple Cartesian dualism. Mind or spirit is something that cannot be objectified, nor can it be recognized by the senses, but can be identified as such; body can be objectified *and* identified.

My view is that (a) is correct, to which (b) is a corollary. Interpretation (c) is inadmissible; even mind-spirit as dead ashes is recognizable as such by someone else (Mr. Yen-Ch'eng).

Combing all occurrences of *wu* and *wo* in the chapter, I came across three problem cases, of which only one is really problematic.

(i)   "I (*wu*) heard this from the Master" (line 231; 2/73).
(ii)   "What do you, my (*wu*) dear sir, take it to be like?" (line 236; 2/75).
(iii) ". . . you do not win over me (*wu*) . . ." (line 268; 2/85).

Case (i) is connected with a hearing (*wen*) of an important message, to which *wu* is an appropriate subject; (ii) uses *wu* in a possessive case, which is a usual usage of *wu*. Only case (iii) is a problem. Debate is between two identifiable selves (*wo*); and the context bears out our interpretation, for *wo* is used throughout here (lines 265–79) except for this line.

Kuo Hsiang's text is the reputed old text, if not the oldest available, and it has *wu*, as does many other texts. My bold assumption is that Kuo Hsiang miscopied the original text and others followed his text without question. I have found, however, five texts which have *wo*: Lin Yün-ming, Lu Shu-chih, Kuan Feng, Nishida Nagazaemon, and Sakai Kanzō. Sakai said that his text is from *Ssu-Pu Ch'ung-K'an*.

The above interpretation of the distinction between *wu* and *wo* is in line with W. A. C. H. Dobson who said, "*wu*: PERSONAL PRONOUN, first person determinative, *non-status*, ... *wo*: First person, *exalted form*, occurs in both self-standing and determinative usage, 'I' 'we' 'my' 'our' 'me' ..." (*A Dictionary of the Chinese Particles*, pp. 789, 786; emphasis mine). See also Huang Chin-hung and Ch'en Ku-ying for the preceding three interpretations of the distinction between *wu* and *wo*.

From a purely literary and grammatical point of view, Wang Li said,

> ... *wu* can be used as a subject-term ... but usually not used as an object-term. Chuang Tzu's '*wu* loses *wo* '(Chapter Two) is a model case in point. The sentence cannot be switched to '*wo* loses *wu*' or '*wu* loses *wu*.' But this is only a matter of word-position; in a negation, when an object-term is placed before a verb, we can again use *wu*.

Then he cited Confucius' *Analects* 11/24 and this notorious line 268. (See Wang Li, *Ancient Chinese*, 1:352; cf. pp. 260–61 for further explanation of this convention.) Thus Wang Li's explanation both supports the transcendental character of *wu*, and weakens its exceptional character on line 268, where *wu* is as it is, merely because of literary convention.

Ma Shih Wen T'ung (pp. 43–44) said that *wu* is used as subject-term (in both the nominative and the possessive cases), and only rarely (only after negatives) is it used as object-term. *Wo* in contrast is freely used in all cases.

Etymology seems also to support the distinction between *wu* as the transcendental self and *wo* as the objectifiable-identifiable self. According to the *Shuo Wen Chieh Tzu*, the character for *wo* contains a "mouth" pictogram, signifying a self-calling. *Wo* contains a picture of a hand put to a "saw," meaning a reflexive doing-to-oneself, and objectifying of the identifiable self. Wang Li disagrees, saying that the word *wo* for "self" is a meaningless borrowing from this character meaning "saw"—in *"The Ancient Chinese,"* 2:541–42.

29. Can we call it the basic self (*pen wu*) or the true self (*chen wo*)?

30. The *wo*-self is not analogous to Kant's "empirical ego," which is one item in the network of experience *constituted* by those imposing categories of the transcendental Ego. This transcendental Ego is not the *wo*-self either, since the former is not objectifiable, while the latter is.

31. *Tao Te Ching*, Chapter 3.

32. "To lose" is *sang*, "to loosen" is *chieh*. If the first word is explained in Chapter Two, then the second word is explained in Chapter Three.

33. *Shih tzu-chi* (line 33) has three possible meanings:

(1) Kuo Hsiang and Wang Hsien-ch'ien have *tzu ssu,* meaning "arise" (*ch'i),* that is, "lets (things) arise of themselves." Few commentators have adopted this interpretation.

(2) Huang Chin-hung has *tzu i,* meaning "stop," "end," "finish" (*chih*). Many commentators adopted this interpretation (Kuan Feng, Ssu-ma Piao), taking the phrase to mean "lets (things) stop themselves."

(3) Ch'ien Mu, Wu Ju-lun have *tzu chi,* meaning "become oneself" (*ch'eng chi*). Watson adopted this, saying, "so that each can be itself" (p. 37).

34. Watson. p. 124.

35. Chapter Two, lines 5, 10, 13, 17, 27, 31, 34.

36. Chapter Two, lines 197–215, 245–49; cf. 272.

37. Genesis 1:4, 15:12; Deuteronomy 4:11, 5:23; Psalms 18:11, 112:4, 139:12; Isaiah 45:7.

38. Matthew 5:43–48. Also see note 37.

39. Perhaps this is why Kuo Hsiang, Akatzuka, and Fukunaga say the heavenly piping is just the as-is (*ku jan*) of things themselves and nothing else. On this point see my *Chuang Tzu*, pp. 76–86.

40. See *Dai Kan-Wa Ji-ten*, 8:875. This is Fukunaga's point in his explication of "piping."

41. See note 33.

42. David L. Hall, *Eros and Irony*; Robert C. Neville, *Reconstruction of Thinking*.

43. Objectively *k'o* is "can," as in Translation (lines 98, 111). Subjectively, *k'o* is "right" and "approval," as taken here. For simplicity, I follow the second meaning here.

44. This is Kuo Ch'ing-fan's view in his commentary on the *Chuang Tzu*.

45. Cf. Jean-Paul Sartre's "nihilation" in his massive *Being and Nothingness*.

46. See this chapter, Meditation A.1.

47. Cf. Suzuki Shuji, *Sōshi*, p. 61; my *Chuang Tzu: World Philosopher*, pp. 63–64.

It is interesting to compare Hofstadter in this context. In his celebrated *Gödel, Escher, Bach* (pp. 477–79), Douglas R. Hofstadter spoke of "jumping out of the system." What Chuang Tzu has here is a jump out of the circle, but in such a way that it is at the same time jumping into it deeply, for he proposes a jump into the center, the very soul of the circle. Hofstadter said that we cannot jump out of the overriding system of physics (the universe), but can jump out of a subsystem into another subsystem. Chuang Tzu said that we can and should jump out of the circle (of the universe of things) so we can be at its very center and amidst things.

Unless we understand things in Chuang Tzu's way, we will have problems here. How does, for instance, Hofstadter know that there is an overriding system that we cannot jump out of (a ghost of Gödel here)? How does he know that we cannot jump out? How does he know that that system is physics? To these questions Chuang Tzu has two answers: (1) the circle is that of interdependence, and (2) we participate in it, flipflopping our identities with those of others—our subjectivity is caught in it. We know all this in the form of uncertainty.

Some interesting stylistic implications follow from these observations. The center is where we can comfortably "respond infinitely" to the circle of things, for the center is the essence of the circle. The circle (the system, our reason) cannot explain the center's operation, and the circle is all we have (we being one of those things that comprise the circle) with which to express the center. Therefore the center cannot be coherently and systematically described, but can only be evoked in metaphors. Hence the style of the entire *Chuang Tzu*.

The style of such expression-evocation at the center is that of freedom. Such freedom cannot be copied or explained by rules. This is what distinguishes the truly *human* from mere things in the physical universe. Hofstadter missed this point when he confused meta-level freedom with absolute brute (as it were) transcendence. We cannot and need not transcend this world. But we are free in regard to it because of our freedom in the metaphorical sense.

48.   The monkey story (cf. note 52) reminds us of a Zen master who was reputed to have sauntered into a heated argument, and told one of the arguers, "You are right." Then, turning to the opponent, the master said, "You are right." Upon hearing this, a bystander inquired, "But Master, they are opposed to each other; how could they be both right?" The master thought for a while, then said to the bystander, "You are right, too." Similarly, T'ai Chi Ch'uan is an art of death (martial art) and an art for health (practiced at the YMCA). It is both.

Incidentally, the monkey story has another implication in the complementarity of things. "Benefit" is at the same time a "drawback" of a sort. Achilles has his heels, and his heels may well be the cause for his being what he is. Samson's hair is the secret of his strength and the occasion for his fall, what made him strong and what made his fall. What made him strong *is* what made him fall; formation is breakdown (118). For another implication, see my *Chuang Tzu*, pp. 73–74.

49.   *Chih* is literally *finger,* and can mean (1) a pointer, signifier, intention (*chih*[b]), intended meaning; or (2) *what* is meant, meaning or things referred to (*so chih*).

Similarly, *ma* is literally *horse,* and can mean (1) things as represented by cattle (due to noticeable size); or (2) sign (*ma*). Thus according to meaning (1), *chih* is the pointer and *ma* is the pointed reality. According to meaning (2), *chih* is the intended meaning, and *ma* is the sign referring to the meaning. Cf. my *Chuang Tzu*, p. 72.

See Akatzuka, 1:89, Hsiao Ch'un-po, p. 30; and Hsü Fu-kuan, *Chuang Tzu Chih Iao, Kung Sun Lung Tzu Chiang Shu*, pp. 13–18, 45–53.

50.   Fukunaga, 1:57. Liu Hsieh's *Wen Hsin Tiao Lung* is full of such examples. This is the familiar principle of "sound covers meaning," "sound must be united to intention," and "every form and sound of a word must be united to implied intention." I suspect that this is derived from Six Graphic Principles for the written Chinese. See note 20 to Chapter One. Cf. James J. Y. Liu, *The Art of Chinese Poetry*; James Legge, *The She King*, pp. 1–171 (especially 96–126); and Wang Li, *Han Yü Shih Kao*. Cf. Plato's view on letters and syllables as endowed with ontological significance in Crombie, *Plato's Doctrines*, II:115–17, 202ff., 241–60, and 411–16.

51.   *Chih*, usually "of," can be taken as a verb, "to reach."

52.   On the logical implications of *hsing* (and its opposite, *chih*), see Graham, *Mohist Logic*, pp. 177–78. Graham translated *liang hsing* as "letting both alternatives proceed," in his *Chuang-tzǔ*, p. 54. Watson has "walking two roads" (p. 41). Fung Yu-lan has "following two courses at once" (*Chuang Tzǔ*, p. 53), which Thomas Merton followed in *The Way of Chuang Tzu*, p. 44. Gia-fu Feng and Jane English have "taking both sides at once" in *Chuang Tsu: The Inner Chapters*, p. 30. James R. Ware has "travelling by two" in *The Sayings of Chuang Chou*, p. 23, adding, "or the identity of contraries." James Legge has "both sides of the question are admissible" in *The Texts of Taoism*, I:185. All in all, the monkey keeper (B.7.1) is the man of resourcefulness, of profound common sense, of *liang hsing*, letting two courses proceed.

53.   Cf. Graham, *Mohist Logic*, p. 177.

54.   This is Watson's rendering (p. 42).

55.   This is an alternative interpretation to my rendering of lines 148–49. Cf. my comments in glosses there.

56.   Cf. 18/22, which Watson renders as "You and I came to watch the process of change, and now change has caught up with me" (p. 193).

57.   Graham, *Chuang-tzŭ*, p. 48.

58.   Watson, pp. 128–29.

59.   This is the theme of Chapter Five. For meditations on non-being, see my *Chuang Tzu*, Aria I, especially pp. 85–86.

60.   Akatzuka (2:769) said that this may have been out of Hui Shih's thoughts.

61.   The saying reminds us of *Mencius* 7A4.

62.   See A. C. Graham, *Mohist Logic*, pp. 225–26. Unfortunately Graham lumped together *fang* with *kui* or *fa*. To my understanding, at least, in Chuang Tzu *fang* is sharply distinguished from *fa* and *kui*; the former is natural, the latter are conventional. But Graham was not exclusively treating Chuang Tzu in the book.

63.   As is usually interpreted; see my glosses on lines 183–84.

64.   Akatzuka mistakenly cited a reference to the *Huai Nan Tzu* as from T'ien Wen Hsun (in 1:111). Kuo Ching-fan (1:91) quoted the *Huai Nan Tzu* without specifying the source. The correct reference is: *Huai Nan Tzu*, "Pun Ching Hsun," 8.5a.

65.   If *Pao Kuang* is taken to mean *Yao Kuang*, Benetnash Star that shines at the base of the Big Dipper and directs all things (as Chu Kuei-yao, Wang Shu-min, and Graham did), then Pao Kuang tells Yao that he should not be a sun but an undisturbing directive star. This will be an elaboration (if not correction) of Confucius' words in his *Analects* 2:1. See Chu Kuei-yao, *Chuang Tzu Nei-P'ien Cheng-pu*, p. 69; Wang Shu-min, *Chuang Tzu Chiao-Shih*, 1:22; Graham, *Chuang-tzŭ*, p. 57.

66.   Although Akatzuka also noted the significance of junior Shun gently persuading his senior Yao, he claimed this section to be a later addition because (1) it does not reject various traditional "virtues" as the heavenly piping story does; (2) it has some stock phrases of Taoism—such as "big debates do not speak," "the debates of no speaking"— lacking in originality; and (3) it strains itself on rhetorical exercise, even mixing metaphors ("pouring ... light"), and is not as coherent as the heavenly piping story (1:111–12).

In my opinion, his view is plausible, unconvincing, and inconclusive. (1) Chuang Tzu can be regarded here as radically changing, if not rejecting, traditional virtues; "Five Things" is a parody on the traditional "Five Virtues." This section seems to be an elaboration on the heavenly piping story. (2) Using traditional Taoist phrases has as little to do with lack of originality as not using them is a sign of originality. What is important is to see how the phrases (Taoist or not) are *used*. This section displays an original manner of using Taoist phrases. (3) It is curious to accuse an essay of being spurious because of its rhetorical beauty, which should not be taken as sign of weakness. Besides, the so-called mixing of metaphors is really one of rapid successions of images toward the end of the section to clinch the argument. Perhaps Pao Kuang is also used as a transition to the final mini-story about Yao and Shun; such usage in turn explains what Pao Kuang means. Furthermore, the water-image of the inexhaustible Heavenly Reservoir or Treasury and the light-image of Shaded Light are not so far apart; a "pouring of light" is not a mixing of metaphors. Finally, the Treasury and the Light share in common such, qualities as hiddenness, preservation, storing rich resources, preciousness, and the like.

67.   Lines 197, 199, 201; 203, 204; 208, 211 215; 219.

68.   Lines 202, 205, 241.

69.   Cf. 4/28–29, "yet to begin to be 'Hui'," where "Hui" as mentioned by Hui himself signifies the identifiable phenomenal self, *wo*.

70. Akatzuka (1:115) even surmised that these names may be patterned after divine names in ancient mythology, Ch'i and Erh (or Ni) of pre-Yin dynasty—see Index.

71. This is Graham's (p. 58) rendering.

72. See *Huai Nan Tzu*, 19:12a, for the famous story.

73. See 12/20–21.

74. Akatzuka 1:115.

75. The connection with *t'ien ni* is proposed by Kuo Hsiang, and that with *t'ien yen*, by Pan Ku.

76. "Ultimate" (*chih*) means "going to the ground (of things)" (*Shuo Wen Chieh Tzu Ku Lin*, 9:952–56); "divine" (*shen*) means "stretching to draw forth things" (*ibid.*, 2:86–88). Chuang Tzu may have meant that when a man goes down to the root of things, he can stretch himself to draw forth things. Incidentally, is there here a frivolous and sarcastic reference to Mencius's reverent use of *tuan* to refer to the budding of morality (2A6)?

77. As in the butterfly dream that ends this chapter and in the latter half of Chapter Six. Since, in Chuang Tzu's mind, death is the beginning of life (22/10–11, Watson p. 235), he uses the phrase, "death and life" (28 times), and only rarely (three times) uses the ordinary phrase, "life and death," as in *Han Fei Tzu*, 100:7+—see Wallace Johnson, *A Concordance to Han-fei Tzu*.

78. One is reminded here of the rugged pragmatism of Art Linkletter in his *Yes, You Can*, which reads like a Taoist handbook to success—"put wrong to work for you," "strength in your inner life," "when things go wrong, turn them into a plus," "set goals, but not concrete goals," and so on. It is almost daemonic or divine, or holy (*sheng*) in Chinese sense, that is, stretching oneself to listen as you live on. (Cf. *Ku Lin*, 2:86–88 for *shen*, 9:1086–88 for *sheng*).

79. For *chu* see *Dai Kanwa Jiten*, 8:260; for *ch'üeh*, see *ibid.*, 12:842-43.

80. Do we have here a pun on "you" (*nü* or *ju*) and "abandon" (*wang*, a combination of *wang* and *ju*)? Could the sentence imply "I will say something to you without (having) you (in mind), and you must also self-lessly listen''? In any case, this manner of saying is the true human piping that echoes heavenly piping, self-lessly (as if dry wood and dead ashes) and naturally.

81. Does *ai* have a remote reference to "underbrush of mugwort"(*p'ung a*i; line 193)?

82. If Graham is correct (in his *Mohist Logic*, p. 191) in noting that *Li* is *li* , a linkage or connection, in meaning and in reality, then *Li Chi* may have an added meaning of someone learning to see new connections among things, even the linkage of grief and joy, death and life. Such linkage is not disimilar to "mutuality of death and life," mutual "dependence of yes and no," "going double," and "heavenly treasury."

83. Lieh Tzu's story of Mr. Yin of Chou and his underling exchanging their roles in their dreams belongs to Lieh Tzu's ingenious concretization of this point by Chuang Tzu (line 258). See the "King of Chou" chapter in A. C. Graham (tr.), *The Book of Lieh-tzû*, pp. 68-69. The entire chapter (pp. 58-73) is worth pondering in this context.

84. If a logician seeks freedom by spinning his logical web that firmly fetters him, as Nietzsche said (see below), then a way of releasing him is to spin with him his own logical web, but in a reverse manner. Chuang Tzu has Mr. Tree turn such logical spinning back on Mr. Magpie, telling him gently, "I say you are dreaming, and I am, too." Such freedom! One can even put it as follows: If logic is a sort of mythology concocted out of our imaging, then it is only appropriate to use logic to produce myth, and metaphor to

envisage reality freely. (On Nietzsche's saying, see Friedrich Nietzsche, *The Wanderer and His Shadow*, as it appeared in R. J. Hollingdale [ed. and tr.], *A Nietzsche Reader*, p. 57.)

85.   *T'ien ni is t'ien yen,* which is *t'ien chün;* they are synonymous.

86.   I have another rendering in my Translation (lines 280–89). Akatzuka (1:121-29) is unnecessarily complex and confusing here. Kanaya Osamu (1:82–87) is good. Chu Kuei-yao (80–82) is very good.

87.   The story appeared also in note 48, in connection with the monkey-story (lines 126–29). The story of a Zen master is the same in both contexts, because the same point is made in both contexts. *T'ien chün* was there; *t'ien ni* is here. This is Chuang Tzu's amazing consistency.

88.   Is *wang liang* synonymous with *liang wang,* a parody of *liang hsing* ("double walk"; line 129)? For if there is a going-both-ways, then there will be a going-neither-way. Furthermore, if *ching* is not just taken as *ying* but as the scene-appearing power, that is, the power of the sun and moon to let appear as they are, then *wang liang* would be darkness (*ming*) of neither light nor appearance. Unfortunately, no commentator I know of went into such etymological speculation. Although Chu Kuei-yao has many interesting observations about *wang liang,* they are mostly irrelevant.

89.   Ch'u Po-hsiu in his *Kuan Chien,* as quoted in Chiao Hung's *Chuang Tzu I,* 5:57 (or p. 37 in the 1970 edition).

90.   Butterfly is a "sign of conjugal felicity" (Williams, *Outlines of Chinese Symbolism,* pp. 51–52). The first three stories also have the process of change. Snakes shed their skin as they grow; cicadas change from chrysalises into winged creatures. See Hiraoka Teikichi, *Enanji no Arawareta Ki no Kenkyo,* pp. 52–55. But this sort of change is one-directional, unless we include parents begetting eggs and chrysalises. For various views of various peoples on "butterfly," see James Hastings (ed.), *Encyclopedia of Religion and Ethics,* I:506a.

   Hua is generally taken to mean birth from seed or *chi* and then going back (death) to its original seed or *chi.* Cf. "wind-change" means fertilization (14/79; Watson, p. 166: Legge, I:361). According to *Huai Nan Tzu* there is an infinity of *huas* (2:6a). *Hua* has an implication of interchange, then, as also according to Tsai I's *Yueh Ling Chang Chu* (as quoted in Hiraoka, pp. 52–53).

91.   Graham, *Chuang-tzŭ,* p. 48; *Mohist Logics,* p. 194.

92.   This is Graham's translation in his *Chuang-tzŭ,* p. 60.

93.   As a wheel in the potter's hand, as in the story toward the end of Chapter Thirteen, Watson, pp. 152–53.

94.   Chuang Tzu has subtle but definite distinctions in implications among the following words, all having to do with difference and area:

   Ni means "grass just born", hence *natural* distinction (*Ku Lin,* 7:202). Chuang Tzu sticks to this meaning throughout; see 2/90, 92; 17/20; 27-29, especially 19–35; 27/1, 5, 9, 10. Such a distinction is as natural and subtle as the rainbow, or rather, the outer rainbow (*ni*), the faint lines of distinctions in nature, hence, natural horizon. Cf. *Dai Kanwa Jiten,* 1:844; *Shuo Wen T'ung Hsün Ting Sheng,* quoted in *Dai Kanwa Jiten,* 12:60.

   Fen in contrast is a contrived artificial distinction. It came from an image of a knife (*tao*) separating (*pa?*) things apart. See *Ku Lin,* 2:983-84. Akatzuka probably defined it too narrowly when he said that *fen* is a hierarchical distinction instituted by "ritual propreity" (1:108). Again, Chuang Tzu is consistent in using *fen* in this sense; 2/35, 56, 96; 5/2; 9/12, 15; 10/12; 17/15; 19/21; etc.

There are three words which lie between the preceding contrastive terms: *chen, feng,* and *yü.*

Chen is "raised paths between fields", the limits of borders of the Fields (*Ku Lin,* 10:1302–3; Akatzuka 1:108), and hence, boundaries instituted by men according to the natural contour of the earth. See 2/55, 17/44.

Feng means originally raised mound, hence, border that follows such a mound, then it came to mean land fiefed; and, eventually, any distinction instituted by men. See 1/40, 41; 2/41, 55; 23/61; 29/30; 30/23, 24; at 7/31 it has an entirely different meaning (*Ku Lin,* 10:1158; *Dai Kanwa Jiten,* 4:6).

Yü is similar to *feng* except that it is widely used to mean a state, an area, and the like (*Ku Lin* 10:316), and is not used in Chapter Two. See 5/34; 17/19, 20; 24/46, 92.

In general, we can see two groups of words, one natural, the other contrived, all carefully used by Chuang Tzu:

Natural (HEAVENLY)	*Contrived* (HUMAN)
ni	*fen*
feng	*chen*
t'ien	*wang*
wu (original, authentic)	*wo* (empirical, identifiable)
fang	*fa*

The list is of course only illustrative, neither definitive nor exhaustive. Happiness and wholeness come when we (i) maintain or rather discern the distinction between the natural and the contrived, and (ii) induce the latter to merge into the former.

95.   This is one of the fresh phrases of Maurice Merleau-Ponty in his *The Visible and the Invisible*, p. 155, a beautiful page.

96.   On the whale songs as singing the world, see Don Ihde, *Sense and Significance*, pp. 162–63. Sadly he did not dwell on it.

97.   Watson, p. 152–53. Cf. note 93.

98.   The world-singing differs from the world singing itself out. The former is earthly piping; the latter is heavenly piping, which originates the former.

99.   Cf. Violet S. De Laszlo (ed.), *The Basic Writings of C. G. Jung*, pp. 78, 304–5, 314, 460, 462. The quotation is taken from Aniela Jaffé (ed.), *Memories, Dreams, Reflections by C. G. Jung*, pp. 87–88 (my emphasis).

100.   *Memories*, p. 88. I am grateful to that indomitable motherly Mrs. Dorothy Lovett for calling my attention to this dream of Jung's in *Memories*.

101.   See preceding note.

102.   John A. Sanford, *The Man Who Lost His Shadow.*

103.   See note 83.

104.   Kuan Feng, quoting Liu's opinion, in his *Chuang Tzu Nei P'ien I-Chieh ho P'i-P'an*, p. 117.

105.   I took this interpretation of *wu* from K'ang Yin, *Wen Tzu Yüan Liu Ch'ien Shuo*, pp. 226–28. Jean-Paul Sartre has an uncanny resemblance to this view in his *Being and*

Nothingness and *Nausea*, stating how our consciousness, the for-itself (nothingness) carves things out of the in-itself (being). Unfortunately, *Shuo Wen Chieh Tzu Ku Lin* merely says that the number of things of heaven and earth begin with leading oxen, which are big and noticeable and so taken as representative of things in general. All star constellation and counting of time begin with the leading of an ox (2:1082–85).

106.   *Chieh*, "to mutilate," a homonym of *chieh*, "to undo," perhaps.

107.   Graham, *Chuang-tzŭ*, pp.23–24.

108.   *Chieh, hsüan chieh, an shih,* and *ch'u shun* in Chapter Three further explicate *fen* and *hua*.

109.   During a later description of such identity-in-change (6/45-66, 75-82), the word *hua* appears often at key places.

110.   Marie C. Swabey, *Comic Laughter*, pp. v–vi.

111.   Søren Kierkegaard, *The Concept of Irony*.

112.   A. C. Graham, "Chuang-tzu's Essay on Seeing Things as Equal," *History of Religions*, 9:137–38. This view remains unchanged up to his recent *Chuang-tzu*, p. 48.

113.   Watson, p. 373. I attribute this paragraph to "Chuang Tzu." There are many essays and metaphors and stories in the *Chuang Tzu*. As can be seen from the many stylistic differences, they are undoubtedly the work of different authors. But the men who speak in them are so symphonic one with another that we may see a single figure variously multiplied in them, namely the Chuang Tzu. They resonate among themselves to form that series of natural, moving, and transforming experiences that can only be termed a personal way from a mere conscious being to true existence as the indwelling in the Tao of beings. I would not hesitate to take any passage from the *Chuang Tzu* to be from Chuang Chou's insights. This does not mean that every passage in the *Chuang Tzu* explicates and represents Chuang Tzu's sentiment as perfectly as every other passage; no book does that for any author. This does mean that amid all the human imperfections and slippages of those writers, the collection of writings we call the *Chuang Tzu* today exhibits an amazing coherence and consistent atmosphere that is unmistakably Chuang Tzu's. Cf. note 1 to the Prologue.

114.   See preceding note 113.

115.   A. C. Graham, "Chuang-tzu's Essay ...," p. 139.

116.   *Mencius* 7A4, *Chuang Tzu* 2, line 163.

117.   *Mencius* 3A5, *Chuang Tzu* 2, line 117.

118.   *Mencius* 3A4. I purposely dwelt on Mencius because of the proverbial textual puzzlement over Chuang Tzu's apparent reticence on Mencius, despite their proximity and contemporaneity.

119.   Graham, "Chuang-tzu's Essay ...," p. 137.

120.   I omit another possible meaning, *lun*, "wheeling," of which I took advantage in A (the beginning, and 1.3) and in B (13.3, 13.4).

121.   I omit the origin of things, a loosening of the oxen of things, which I described in B (13.9). Cf. note 105.

122.   Cf. *Dai Kanwa Jiten*, 7: 635. For *wu wu* see 20/7 and 22/50, 75. Heidegger also used the phrases, "thinging things," "the world worlds," "nothing nothings," and the like.

123.   James Legge said of *ch'i* that it means "'corn earing evenly'; hence, what is level, equal, adjusted, and here [*Analects* 2:3] with the corresponding verbal force." Legge took

ch'i to mean fasting or religious adjustment on *Analects* 7:12. See James Legge, *The Chinese Classics*, 1:146, 198. See also *Shuo Wen Chieh Tzu Ku Li*, 6:310-13. K'ang Yin has a rather bloody interpretation of "arranging the cut pieces of meat in order" (pp. 495–96). See also my Meditations, the beginning of A, and B (1.1–4).

124. Watson, p. 105, modified.

125. Watson, p. 214.

126. I take *pien* to mean a sustained and systematic discrimination, disputation, namely, systematization. Graham's phrase occurs in his "Chuang-tzŭ's Essay ..., " p. 137.

127. Wang Fu-chih, Wang Hsien-ch'ien, Chang Ch'eng-ch'iu, Hsüan Ying, Lin Hsi-i, Li Chung-i, Lu Shu-chih, Juan Yü-sung, Chang Wen-ch'ien, Wang Hou-chai, and James Legge, among others, held the first interpretation.

Huang Chin-hung, Kuan Feng, Ch'ien Mu, Liu Wen-tien, Kuo Ch'ing-fan, Kuo Hsiang, Ch'en Ku-ying, Wu I, F. H. Balfour, and Burton Watson, among others, held the second interpretation. Besides the standard commentaries of those writers, see the following: Chang Ch'eng-ch'iu, *Chuang Tzu P'ien-Mu K'au*, pp. 56-58; Wu I, *Hsiao Yao te Chuang Tzu*, pp. 76-78.

128. On the "goblet" manner of saying see 3.2; also Overture, A, in my *Chuang Tzu*.

129. The phrase, "ambiguities of life," is a favorite of both Maurice Merleau-Ponty and Paul Tillich. Every chapter of Merleau-Ponty's *Phenomenology of Perception* leads up to and ends with "ambiguities of life." The third volume of Tillich's *Systematic Theology* is built around ambiguities of life as the correlate of the Holy Spirit.

130. Watson, p. 90.

131. *Ibid.*, pp. 199–200, 205–206.

132. *Ibid.*, p. 271.

133. *Ibid.*, pp. 244–45.

134. *Ibid.*, pp. 237, 254.

135. T'ang Chün-i, *Chung-kuo Che-hsüeh Yüan-lun, Yüan Tao P'ien*, 1:353–55; Wu I, *Hsiao Yao te Chuang Tzu*, pp. 84–85.

136. The ancient Greeks also noted cosmic musicality, as in *The Republic*, III:400c–403c. (Cf. Francis M. Cornford, *The Republic of Plato*, pp. 88–92, especially p. 89), and *The Nicomachean Ethics*, II:1105a20 (cf. Martin Ostwald translation, No. 75, p. 39, note 14). Unfortunately they did not pursue the matter further. To my knowledge, only Chuang Tzu took cosmic musicality seriously enough to make it a ruling metaphor for the universe. On the modern development of Greek intimations of music and mathematics (with a side glance at India), see Ernest G. McClain, *The Pythagorean Plato; and The Myth of Invariance*.

137. Cf. mutual shadowings-forth and dreaming-about toward the end of the chapter. Cf. also Watson, pp. 166, 195–96.

138. If human piping is music, then earthly piping is musical (yet to be music), and heavenly piping is what evolves both forth. This relation finds its unexpected manifestations in, for instance, the book of *Joshua*, Chapter 2, which exhibits the spies as human piping, Rahab's intuitive responses as earthly piping, and God as heavenly piping.

139. 14/79. Cf. Watson, p. 166. Graham did not translate "wind change" (*Chuang-tzŭ*, p. 134).

140.   When the first chapter mentioned "the rectitudes of the heaven and earth, ... the changes of six breaths" (63–64), the phrase describes heavenly piping, the primal wind, on which Lieh Tzu did not rely but only on the earthly wind, earthly piping. Lieh Tzu was justifiably ranked a second-rate magician (Chapter One, lines 60–69).

What is the primal wind? Chinese linguistic common sense say that wind, breath (*ch'i*), heaven (*t'ien*), and life (*sheng*) are inherently related. The character *feng* ("wind") has in it the characters *pa* ("eight") and *ch'ung* ("insect"); the wind is the living breath (*sheng ch'i*) that wind-changes (*fung hua*)—that is, fertilizes insects in eight directions in eight days, as was explained in the *Ku Lin* 10:1015–1021. K'ang Yin says, however, that *fung* as wind is related to *fung* as phoenix, the big Bird that began the *Chuang Tzu* (in his *Wen Tzu Yüan Liu Ch'ien Shuo*, pp. 180–81). Phoenix of course symbolizes peace, prosperity, and the sun for summer and harvest (Williams, *Outlines of Chinese Symbolism*, pp. 323–26). Both *Ku Lin* and K'ang Yin agree that the wind is symbolic of life power, then.

Let us compare all this naturalism with the Greek view. Chuang Tzu's "piping" (related to "wind") *seems* to parallel the Greek notion of "wind" or inspiration (*pneuma*). Under Stoic influence, *pneuma* is a sort of material force whose breath sets the Pythia in an ecstatic prophetic infilling with deity. It evokes physical effects as the wind may also do: streaming hair, panting breath, violent filling, seizing, or snatching away in a Bacchantic frenzy of *ekstasis* or *mania*, as Chrysostom said in his First Epistle to the Corinthians.

The longest list of traditional effects of the spirit (*pneuma*) includes fiery phenomena (Lucan, *De Bello Civili*, V:169–74, 190–93, 211–18), the giving of oracles linked with the sound of a wind-instrument (Vergil, *Aeneid*, 6.82ff), and the ecstatic speech of the sibyl and Delphic prophecy. The Pythia, sitting on a tripod, receives the mantic *pneuma* as it rises up from a cleft in the earth below her; the reception is an act of holy marriage, at which the Pythia receives the generative *pneuma* of Apollo in her womb (*Auct. Sublim.*, 13,2).

In other words, as something "other" coming from without, pneuma fills the interior of the house either with the thunderous sound or a costly divine aroma. The bridegroom-spirit is a male overcoming female resistance. It powerfully possesses the whole man (the chosen) and carries him off like a stormy wind, chasing the understanding out, taking its place.

Plato and Stoicism later conceived breath materially as mist arising by warmth, carried up by air or water out of a cleft or a well; the Delphic *pneuma* is one of the many natural forces of the earth, manifesting themselves in various places and have extraordinary effects, mostly beneficial but sometimes harmful. *Pneuma* is "wine," inflaming-opening the soul for ideas of the future to enter. The soul is joined to *pneuma* as the eye to light, giving rise to prophetic enthusiasm. The soul is the material instrument with which the god sound forth. Later, breath became light, illuminating from above our vision. (For more details, see an essay on *pneuma* by Hermann Kleinknecht in Gerhard Kittel [ed.], *Theological Dictionary of the New Testament*, 6:334–57.)

What is striking in all these is that the Greek piping is violently ecstatic, divinely possessed, and even sexual in connotation. None of these characteristics exists in Chuang Tzu's piping, thoroughly natural and ordinary, *in* which he saw something extraordinary. Considering how ancient Chuang Tzu was (fourth century B.C.), such sane naturalism is simply unusual. In short, Chuang Tzu's "piping" (*lai*) and "wind" (*fung*) do not parallel the Greek wind or inspiration (*pneuma*), much less are there mutual borrowings among them.

141. I have probed into this matter in my *Chuang Tzu*, pp. 79–87.

142. This is Maurice Merleau-Ponty's favorite phrase in *The Structure of Behavior* and *Phenomenology of Perception*.

143. Aristotle, *Metaphysics*, III:1005a19–1009a14.

144. Plato, *The Republic*, VI:508, just before the allegory of the Cave (VII: 514–21).

145. Watson, pp. 134–35.

146. David L. Hall worried about "principle" as our cognitive "principality," a totalistic external cognitive imposition. In my opinion, this danger obtains when the principle is *detached* from that of which it is principle, either by thinking or by rulership. The internal principle of a being is its vigor, root, and coherence. David Hall has, in the same book in which he worried about "principle," an interesting Polanyi-esque interplay of principle with metaphor. See his *Eros and Irony*, pp. xii, 12, 224–25.

147. These are Mr. Menuhin's words in Yehudi Menuhin and Curtis W. Davis, *The Music of Man*, pp. 24–25.

148. On mutual resonance, see Watson, pp. 267–68.

149. *Ibid.*, p. 157.

150. Ch'en Ku-ying reports that many commentators agree that all distinctions (this and that, right and wrong) are subjective illusion for Chuang Tzu. All things are equal and there is no difference whatever. Chuang Tzu is thus said to have flattened things into indiscriminate identity (*Chuang Tzu Chin Chu Chin I*, 1:65, 73).

I disagree. Chuang Tzu insisted that we should not be fixated (*chih erh pu hua*, 4/17) in one position, for differences among things and theories are partially due to differences of perspectives and the positions we take. We must become free in the dynamics of actual differences we see in the universe, and walk two roads (*liang hsing*).

But all this argues neither for nor against the *real* differences among things and theories. If anything, Chuang Tzu strongly hinted at real differences in actuality since mutual involvement and interchange of contraries and opposites assumes that there *be* differences. Yet we cannot assert it categorically, because (*a*) we do not know, because (*b*) we the judging subjects are ourselves caught in interchanges among things.

From such a "view," which is no view, arises a peculiar series of "heaven"-words— "heavenly equality," "heavenly horizon," "heavenly piping," and the like, all of which point to the unity of all. But this unity like the "one" of "one finger" and "one horse," is a pluralistic unity. It is the *ch'i* where each entity equally has its unique place in the economy of nature, not a mathematical identity (*teng*, which never occurs in the Seven Inner Chapters in the *Chuang Tzu*). Chuang Tzu used instead *chün*, a dynamic creative equality, like the "potter's wheel" freely turning out various earthenware things (cf. Watson, pp. 85–86).

All this is proposed from an objective point of view. Subjectively speaking, what this amounts to is a mutual transformation of things (*wu hua*), which is equivalent to going to sleep peacefully, and with a start waking up (cf. line 300; and Watson, p. 85.)

All in all, Chuang Tzu wanted not a flattening of things into uniformity but a dynamic interchange among things and our participation therein.

151. "We can see this if we go on far enough in such manner as our finger/no-finger argument," Chuang Tzu seems to say. See note 49 for many meanings of "finger."

152. For Mencius, see 7A1, 4; for Hui Shih, see Watson, p. 375.

153. This is the consensus of the majority of commentators; Ch'ien Mu is clearist on this interpretation in his *Chuang Tzu Ch'üan Chien*, p. 17.

Two commentators took exception to this interpretation. Wing-tsit Chan has "Speech and the one then make two. These two (separately) and the one (the two together) make three" (see his *Sourcebook in Chinese Philosophy*, p. 186). Wang Fu-Chih goes further and takes neither-arising-nor-stopping of the vital-spring-power (ch'i *chi*), its rising, and its stopping, to be three (see his *Chuang Tzu Chieh*, p. 22).

154. *Shuo Wen* says "wind" is the breath (*ch'i hsi*) of life. See note 140.

155. See note 45.

156. See Sartre, *Being and Nothingness*, p. 113.

157. This is James Legge's sentence in *The Texts of Taoism*, 1:197, where he identified this dream story with Buddhist maya.

158. Jean-Paul Sartre began his *Being and Nothingness* with these stories.

159. This can be seen by a careful reading of *The Apology* in which Socrates "inferred" from his knowledge of ignorance the divine mission to examine the Athenians.

160. "Intimate presence" is made up of *intimus* (inmost), *int-us* (within), and pre-sence, a being-before. And so intimate presence is literally "(someone) being before (me) inside." See *Oxford English Dictionary*, s. v., "intimate," "presence."

161. Lucretius, *On Nature* , IV:1037–1286. Cf. note 88 to my Meditations on Chapter One, and note 19 to the Prologue, D. "The Poetic *Chuang Tzu*."

162. This is one of the early and hence clear versions of the now familiar scenario in biomedical ethics, the basic adversarial pattern of which has not changed since. Patrick Romanell, "Ethics, Moral Conflicts, and Choice," in *American Journal of Nursing*, 77:850–55, esp. pp. 854–55.

163. *Yu* ("friend") in China etymologically means intersection-interchange of both hands (*erh yu hsiang chiao*), both legs (*chiao ching*), with the same intentions (*t'ung chih*), as hands helping mouths (*shou k'ou hsiang chu*), and becoming one body as brothers (*hsiung ti i t'i*) (*Ku Lin*, 3:1053–57). "Friend" in the West is etymologically related to caressing and touching (*Oxford English Dictionary*, s. v., "friend").

164. In Chapter One, 3.2.c.i, life is said to be a union of self-referential consistency and self-referential inconsistency.

165. Such as Han Shan, Chang Ping-lin, among others.

166. George Lakoff and Mark Johnson, *Metaphors We Live By*, p. 3.

167. *Ibid.*, p. 5; cf. pp. 56, 77, 117.

168. *Ibid.*, p. 48; cf. p. 103.

169. *On Nature*, I:43–40, II:430–50, IV:220–70. For a lucid short presentation of atomism and its mode of thinking, see Lancelot Law Whyte, *Essay on Atomism,* esp. Chapters 1, 2, and 6.

170. For a clear and illuminating description of Zeno, see John Mansley Robinson, *An Introduction to Early Greek Philosophy* , pp. 127–40.

171. W. V. Quine, *The Ways of Paradox*, p. 11. "Veridical" paradoxes are "truth-telling" paradoxes, and "falsidical" ones express falsehoods, as defined in p. 5. "Antino-

mies" are paradoxes that produce self-contradictions "by accepted ways of reasoning," and demands that "some tacit and trusted pattern of reasoning must be made explicit and henceforward be avoided or revised" (p. 7).

172. See Quine, *Ibid.*, p. 5.

173. For Aristotle, motion is essentially incomplete, an interim stage of a thing on its way from potentiality to actuality (*Nicomachean Ethics*, 1174a18–b7). And in his *Physics*, VI–VIII, he used this idea of motion to refute Zeno.

174. Plato likewise praised sight, saying, "sight is by far the most costly and complex piece of workmanship" *(The Republic*, VI:507). And "... sight is the most piercing of our bodily senses" (*Phaedrus*, 250). Plato's imagery was, not surprisingly, predominantly visual and geometric. These quotations are from Benjamin Jowett's translation, the first slightly revised. For more citations on "sight" in ancient Greece, see Wilhelm Michaelis's essay on it in G. Kittel (ed.), *Theological Dictionary of the New Testament*, V:316–24, where it is said that "the Greek were 'a people of the eye'."

175. A. C. Ewing, among others, argued vigorously for such a "jump." One can of course go too far in this direction, as can one in everything else. I brought this point to our attention not to defend it at length but simply to caution against fastidious analyticity. Cf. H.D. Lewis (ed.), *Clarity Is Not Enough.*

176. The notion of "self-evidence" must depend on the judging subject and the climate of thinking at the time. Quine, of all persons, said that "the falsidical paradoxes of Zeno must have been, in his day, genuine antinomies. We in our latter-day smugness point to a fallacy: the notion that an infinite succession of intervals must add up to an infinite interval. But surely this was part and parcel of the conceptual scheme of Zeno's day. ... One man's antinomy is another man's falsidical paradox, give or take a couple of thousand years" (*The Ways of Paradox*, p. 11).

177. This does not of course imply that all aphoristic sayings are profound simply because of their illogicality. This only makes a negative point, that is, lack of sufficient logical steps (whatever "sufficient" may mean) may not necessarily mean lack of truth. On the contrary, It may mean too much and too deep a truth for logical steps to express adequately, and convince us of its depth and its truth, in a limited amount of time and space.

178. R. J. Hollingdale (tr.), *Nietzsche: Thus Spoke Zarathustra*, p. 67.

179. This metaphor end Chapter Twenty-Six of the *Chuang Tzu.*

180. This saying ends Chapter Twenty-Two.

181. In fact, Chuang Tzu scolded Hui Shih of having been in love with his own talk; see the end of Chapter Five.

182. This question ends Chapter Twenty-Five.

183. They start Chapter Twenty-Seven. They will be the theme of 3.2.

184. These three sayings or words begin Chapter Twenty-Seven. I realize that my interpretation is not shared by anyone so far, though it bears some resemblances to many standard interpretations. I offer it tentatively, but without apologies. For other interpretations see Watson, pp. 303–304; Graham, *Chuang-tzu*, pp. 25–26; Legge, *Taoism*, 1:155–56, 2:142–44.

185. The change from the old script (*chou wen*) to the new (*li wen*) during the Ch'in-Han period (221 B.C. to 220 A.D.) was more in script form than in syntax. Cf. Ch'ien Mu, *Kou Hsueh Kai-lun*, pp. 80–124; and Wang Ch'ung, *Lun Hung*, Chapter 28.

186. The vast majority of commentaries (such as the 208 commentaries cited by Kuan Feng, pp. 370–403) labored on textual emendation of *this* sort, that is, manipulation of the text on the basis of their common sense. They disliked paradoxes which challenged their common sense.

187. As a conscientious commentator of Taoism laments recently, "A very real obstacle in attempting to give a coherent account of Taoist philosophy is its ambiguous use of language ... [Taoist writers] use the same locution to connote very different concepts ... used on different levels with diametrically opposite meanings ..." (Roger T. Ames, *The Art of Rulership*, p. 33). Graham also said, "Chuang-tzŭ's refutation ... is highly elliptical, and it is possible that he intends his effect of making the mind fly off in a new direction at every re-reading" (*Chuang-tzŭ*, p. 55). The problem for us is what to make of this peculiar writing style.

188. See Chapter One, lines 10, 16–19, 60–64; Chapter Two, lines 15–34.

189. I. M. Crombie, *An Examination of Plato's Doctrines*, 2 vols. Only the second volume will be quoted.

190. This does not mean that Chuang Tzu is not a philosopher. This means that Chuang Tzu so criticized the conventional *mode* of philosophizing that the very assumption behind the question—"Why do we call Chuang Tzu a philosopher?"—must be itself questioned, the assumption, namely, that Chuang Tzu is indeed a conventional philosopher. For if we take philosophy to be basic rational criticism, then since Chuang Tzu criticized the overall mode of philosophizing, he can be called a philosopher in a special sense, in fact a truer sense than any philosopher commonly so called.

191. *Ibid.*, pp. 517–19.

192. *Ibid.*, p. 568.

193. Max Black, *The Prevalence of Humbug*, pp. 33–36.

194. *Ibid.*, p. 31.

195. Watson, pp. 112–13.

196. Chapter Two, lines 195–305, the final segments of the chapter.

197. David L. Hall develops this theme in a different context in *The Uncertain Phoenix* and *Eros and Irony*.

198. See Immanuel Kant, *Critique of Pure Reason*, A vii—xii (pp. 7–9 in Norman Kemp Smith's translation), and Michael Polanyi, *They Study of Man*, pp. 11-13.

199. Chapter Two, lines 100, 169. Cf. Aristotle, *Metaphysics*, 1012*b*, 15-18.

200. Chapter Two, lines 195–219.

201. Ludwig Wittgenstein, *Philosophical Investigations*, Sections 66–71. Cf. note 2 to Chapter One.

202. One of the magnificent modern system-builders in the best sense is Robert C. Neville. See especially his *Reconstruction of Thinking*.

203. *Ibid.*, p. 312.

204. Although "universal" and "consistent" are not completely equivalent in meaning, they are sufficiently intertwined in meaning to warrant their being used interchangeably. I did not bother to be fastidious about their distinction.

205. The distinction and debates are conveniently summed up in Kuan Feng, p. 93, fn.

206.   The distinction and debates are described in Kuan Feng, pp. 117–18; Chang Ch'eng-ch'iu, pp. 57–58; and Huang Chin-hung, pp. 67.

207.   *Wu-lun* commonly means "public opinion."

208.   This accounts for the fame of the phenomenology of Marcel and that of Merleau-Ponty, designed to overthrow this assumption, though not with non-egology.

209.   Lieh Tzu later expanded such identity-interchange into a fantastic scale. See A. C. Graham, *The Book of Lieh-tzŭ*, pp. 66-73 (and 58-74).

210.   Robert Neville mentioned thinking as "an aspect of a much larger process, most of which is not only described scientifically as physical but is experienced as that" *(Reconstruction*, p. 106).

211.   This point render Graham's point moot when he said that "Chuang-tzŭ never does say that everything is one ... [He] always speaks subjectively of the sage [as] treating [all things] as one" *(Chuang-tzŭ*, p. 56). Graham took for granted the dichotomy of subject versus object.

212.   See note 187.

213.   Cf. Chapter Two, line 55; more correctly *wu chi*, Chapter One, line 67. Cf. 4/14.

214.   Chapter Two, lines 34, 55–59.

215.   Franz Kafka, *The Complete Stories and Parables,* ed. by Nahum N. Glatzer, p. 459.

216.   This saying begins Lao Tzu's *Tao Te Ching*. Cf. *Chuang Tzu*, Chapter Two, lines 182–89.

Notes to Chapter Three

1.   T'ang Chün-i says (in his *Chung-kuo Che-hsüeh Yüan-lun, Yüan-Tao P'ien I* (1973, p. 356) that *Hsiao Yao Yu* proposes the ideals of "the Perfect Man, Divine Man, and Holy Man," and that *Ch'i Wu Lun* speaks of losing oneself, abolishing the dichotomies of the other-self and the thing-self, thereby attaining the knowledge of the True Master, the True Self that is "one with everything, being born with the Heaven and earth." Thus T'ang takes the previous two chapters to be exclusively concerned with the human self, and seems to have missed the fantastic cosmological (first chapter) and ontological (second chapter) dramas.

2.   Wang Fu-chih's phrase, *li ming,* which describes Southern Darkness may be a duplication of *ming* ("clarity"; see *Shuo Wen Chieh Tzu Ku Lin*, 4:248–53, esp. p. 253). But it also makes sense to take *li* as different from *ming*. See Wang Fu-chih's *Chuang Tzu Chieh*, p. 1.

3.   Chapter One, lines 97, 108–11, 138–39, 155, 164–65.

4.   Chapter Two, lines 35–52, 69-77, 224–29, 245–51.

5.   Ch'en Ku-ying, Ch'ien Mu, Huang Chin-hung, Legge, Kuan Feng, and Wang Fu-chih, among others, defended the first interpretation. Kuo Hsiang, Liu Wen-tien, Wang Hsien-ch'ien, and Watson, among others, defended the second interpretation.

6.   Chapter Two, lines 57–59, cf. 66–68, 76–77.

7.   Chapter Three, lines 4, 29, 58.

8.   A somewhat similar view is expressed by T'ang Chün-i, who in his typically careful

manner said that this chapter treats the way of harmonizing our knowledge with our life, so that they would not clash and damage each other. This way of harmony is what nourishes the principal body of life, which is after all what originates our cognition. See his *Yüan Lun*, I:356.

9.   Watson, *Chuang Tzu*, p. 55, note 1.

10.   Graham, *Chuang-tzŭ*, p. 62. He also said, "The most obviously mutilated of the *Inner Chapters* is the shortest, *What matters in nurturing life* (chapter 3). It opens with what looks like the start of an introductory essay similar to that of chapter 6, but breaks off at 3.2. The rest consists of three stories, with a little fragment about the pheasant of the marshes between the second and the third (3.14). We must assume considerable losses, involving in particular most of an introductory essay." ("How Much of the *Chuang-tzŭ* did Chuang-tzŭ write?" in *Journal of the American Academy of Religion*, 47:459–502; the passage quoted comes on p. 472). This article describes *how* Graham pulled sections from later chapters of the *Chuang Tzu*. In his *Chuang-tzŭ*, pp. 62–63, 25/ 51–54 is dropped (without explanation). I am more impressed with the dexterity of his textual-criticism than with its plausibility. Why the chapter is thought to be mutilated is still beyond me.

11.   Akatzuka, *Sōshi*, II:367, 420–31, 700. Fukunaga, *Sōshi*, III:73–74, 156–59, 475.

12.   Chang Ch'eng-ch'iu casually footnoted that "because of the shortness of the chapter some claimed that part of the chapter has been lost-scattered; but such a claim is incorrect" (*Chuang Tzu P'ien-Mu K'ao*, p. 63). He discloses neither who said so nor why they are wrong.

13.   T'ang Chün-i mentioned a contradiction between the first and the last sentences of the chapter: the chapter begins by saying that life is limited and knowledge is unlimited. The chapter ends with life (fire) being limitless and knowledge (fuel-logs) being limited (p. 356). T'ang then devoted three pages (pp. 357–59) to solving this problem. But the problem arises only when we interpret "fire" as life and "fuel logs" as knowledge; nothing compels us to do so.

14.   I have noted what I found in glosses to the translation. There is undoubtedly more for those who have eyes to see.

15.   Austin Farrer, a scholastic Oxonian with poetic perceptiveness, sees the unity of the ancient text of the New Testament with poetic and philosophic depth, and claims that the "short ending" of Mark's Gospel is as it should be (no mutilation), and "decoded" the Book of Revelation. He claims that there is a literary inevitability both to the "short ending" of Mark's Gospel and to the coherence of Revelation. See his *Glass of Vision*, especially the last chapter, and his *Rebirth of Images*.

16.   Hu Shih, "On the Methodology of Textual Criticism" available in *Collected Works of Hu Shih*, 4:135–52. The illustration appears in pp. 136–37.

17.   "Fire" can mean either "life" (to agree with the funeral that precedes it) or "suffering," as Kao Heng noted in his *Chuang Tzu Chin-chien*, p. 12.

18.   *Sui* is usually translated as "pursue." But *sui* implies less of the pursuer in active charge than of a following after, even a trailing.

19.   By the supreme Ruler, perhaps, if we follow the traditional interpretation of *ti*. But perhaps not against the Ruler's entanglements, as Wang Fu-chih, Lin Hsi-i, and even Kuo Ching-fan said. Cf. also my gloss to line 59.

20. This may well be the sixth way of looking at the third chapter. I put it here simply to facilitate its relation with the Inner Chapters.

21. Chi'ien Mu's intuition that this chapter may have been written *prior* to Chapters One and Two may be justified, then, although his reason for saying so is curious. He said that it is because Wen Hui Chün is Liang Hui Wang. See his *Chuang Tzu Tsuan-Chien*, p. 24.

Incidentally, a comparison with *Lieh Tzu* is instructive. We all know that Lieh Tzu quoted extensively from Chuang Tzu, and elaborated on many of Chuang Tzu's stories with eerie details. Yet, interestingly, Lieh Tzu did not touch Chapters Three and Five in the *Chuang Tzu*. These chapters specifically deal with Chuang Tzu's strong theme of how to "live happily ever after" *amidst* suffering, and that without esoteric mystification. Lieh Tzu leaned heavily on Chuang Tzu's Chapters One and Nineteen and (to a less extent) on Chapters Six and Thirty-Two. (See Ch'en Shou-ch'ang, *Nan-Hua Chen-Ching Cheng-I*, pp. 711–38; Kobayashi Nobuaki, *Lessi*, p. 437.) These are chapters of fantastic imagination, bordering on mystical roaming. This shows how Lieh Tzu developed only one side of the *Chuang Tzu*, the mystical side. And this set the path of later developments of Taoism, such as Huai Nan Tzu, Wei Chin Pure Conversationists, and Huang Lao Taoist religion. Even when these later Taoists adopted Chuang Tzu's "nourishment" they heavily leaned on the magical-medicinal side. They missed the pristine unity of the mystical-empirical vitalism in the original Chuang Tzu.

22. Kuo Hsiang, Wang Fu-chih, Lin Hsi-i, Wang Hsien-ch'ien, T'ang Chün-i, are typical examples.

23. Chapter Two, 3.2, and its note 28.

24. Bertrand Russell's famous distinction between knowledge by acquaintance and knowledge by description (in *The Problems of Philosophy*, ch. 5) merely describes the *problem* of knowing. For in either knowledge the cognitive dilemma applies. In fact, he described not two kinds of knowledge but two aspects of knowledge in all its ramifications.

25. Michael Polanyi devoted his entire life to explicating this point; see especially *The Study of Man*, and *The Tacit Dimension*.

26. For *tu*, cf. *Ku Lin*, 4:82–83; for *yüan*, cf. *Ku Lin*, 10:659.

27. See Lin Hsi-i, *Chuang Tzu K'ou-i*, 4:1b; cf. 20/30, which is supposed to be the way of deathlessness. See Watson, p. 213.

28. Typically by *Hsüan Ying* and Kuan Feng. But even they merely noted this alternative meaning; they did not go into its possible implication.

29. See my gloss to line 5.

30. "Name" and "fame" are synonymous both in Chinese and in English. I omit a sideline stab at Mencius mentioned in my gloss to line 5.

31. "Thing" (*wu*) in Chinese has a lot to do with "ox," as will be explained when we get to Meditation C.

32. Cf. Williams, *Outlines*, pp. 282–83.

33. Chu Kuei-yao, *Chuang Tzu Nei-P'ien Cheng-Pu*, pp. 89–91; Wang Shu-min, *Chuang Tzu Chiao-Shih*, I:29; Akatzuka, I:580.

34. Cf. Ou Yang-hsiu, "A Versed-Essay on the Autumn Sounds," anthologized, e.g., in *Ku-Wen Kuan-Chih*, ed. by Hsieh Ping-ying, et al., pp. 583–85. Although describing the

murderous chills of autumn, the essay seems to have been patterned after the beginning sentences of Chuang Tzu's second chapter (lines 1–27).

35. This beautiful phrase comes later in the *Chuang Tzu*, 20/7, cf. 11/62. Cf. Aria I in my *Chuang Tzu*.

36. The later endless outputs of Taoist esoteric writers are elaborations of these all-too-brief phrases.

37. When I mentioned Chuang Tzu, Professor John E. Smith of Yale University greatly chuckled and said, "Do you remember that cook and his knife?"

38. Cf. *Ku Lin*, 2:205–209; and Williams, *Outlines*, p. 295; and Wang Li, pp. 123, 152, 180, 433.

39. As in Ch. Two, lines 131–33, 195–201; 4/26–28; 6/90–92; 19/18–19, 46–49, 56–57; 21/15-17, 23/58-60, 24/62-65. For twice "three," see Ch. Two, lines 154-57, 6/39-40. For three times "three," see 6/43–45, 27/17–18. Chuang Tzu also has five stages of growth, such as 7/15–27, 14/9–11, 19/62–64, perhaps patterning after the Five Elementary Ways of things.

40. Cf. *Ku Lin*, 3:448–52; Williams, *Outlines*, p. 294.

41. Cf. *Ku Lin*, 10:1070–73. See Akatzuka, I:426.

42. Cf. *Ku Lin*, 11:574–76; *Dai Kanwa Jiten*, 1:356–57.

43. Cf. *Ku Lin*, 7:140–41; *Dai Kanwa Jiten*, 1:758.

44. On *shen* ("spirit"), see *Ku Lin*, 2:86–88 (cf. *shen* ["the divine"]in *Ku Lin*, 11:779–87); Fukunaga Mitsuji, *Sōshi*, II:346-50. On the medical significance of *shen* see Ted J. Kaptchuk, *The Web That Has No Weaver: Understanding Chinese Medicine*, pp. 45–46; Shanghai Chinese Medical Association (ed.), *Tsang Hsiang Hsüeh Shuo Teh Li-Lun Yü Yün-Yung*, pp. 19–20.

45. Diels, Frag. 45; Burnet, Frag. 71; Philip Wheelwright, *Heraclitus*, pp. 58–59 (Frag. 42). Graham haltingly captured this in his *Chuang-tzu*, p. 35, n.72.

46. The story of conversing with a roadside skull is in Watson, pp. 193–94. See Prologue, C.

47. "Desire" (*yü*) in the Inner Chapters is *always* combined with its negative (*pu*), never used as it is to describe the ideal self, much less the ideal Tao.

48. *Ku Lin*, 5:163–65.

49. K'ang Yin, *Wen-Tzu Yüan-Liu Ch'ien-Shuo* (1979), p. 325.

50. *Ku Lin*, 10:375–84; *Dai Kanwa Jiten*, 5:711.

51. I have lost the reference in Heidegger. Incidentally, Chuang Tzu's later pages say "to thing things" (11/62, 20/7; see note 35). Chuang Tzu does have "to nothing a nothing" (22/67, cf. 17/32, 23/71).

52. *Ku Lin*, 6:184–87; K'ang Yin, p. 466.

53. *Ku Lin,* 10:117–20; K'ang Yin, p. 250; *Dai Kanwa Jiten*, 3: 669–70.

54. See preceding note.

55. *Ku Lin*, 4:950–51; K'ang Yin, p. 224; *Dai Kanwa Jiten*, 10: 361–62.

56. Cf. Ch. Two, lines 69, 136. All the verbs there can be understood by what I say here.

57. *Ku Lin*, 2:1083–85; K'ang Yin, pp. 226–28; Wang Li, pp. 93, 94, 141.

58. *Ku Lin*, 2:983–84.

59. See Ch. Two, lines, 95, 112–15, 119, 131–32, 147, 195–201.

60. Strangely the third chapter does not mention or use the word "things" (*wu*), but "ox" (*niu*) is an obvious cipher for things. See note 57.

61. Ch. Two, line 170, cf. 130–31.

62. Ch. Two, lines 304–5.

63. When commenting on "to nothing nothings" (22/67), Fukunaga refers us to Chapter Two, lines 156–57. See his *Soshi*, 3:691.

64. See Ch. Two, lines 118, 177, 304.

65. The phrase "to thing things" appears in 20/7, 22/50, 75. The phrase, "to nothing nothings," appears in 22/67 (cf. 17/32).

66. Watson, *Chuang Tzu*, p. 51, note 4.

67. See preceding note.

68. Comparing with 5/59, we can see that the phrase in line 58 is the opposite of injury, and nourishing is implied.

69. Kuan Feng, Ch'en Ku-ying (and probably Lin Hsi-i, Ch'ien Mu, and Kanaya Osamu) are those who think these stories separate.

70. Thomas Merton, *The Way of Chuang Tzu*, p. 48.

71. I owe an initial inspiration of this point to my former student, Mr. Pinkney J. Garrison, III.

72. This is Fung Yu-lan's translation of Kuo Hsiang in Fung's *Chuang Tzu*, p. 69.

73. "Why Companion, Not Commentary" also recognizes the virtue of this quotation. In fact, this *Companion* may be compared to an elaboration and re-enactment of this story of Lao Tan's death.

74. Ma Hsü-lun takes *shih* to mean *i*, "enjoying," or "a loss." Akatzuka takes *shih* to mean *chi*, "fast" (passing).

75. On various meanings of nourishing, see *Ku Lin*, 5:82–83; *Dai Kanwa Jiten*, 12:394–95. The inferior can indeed nourish the superior, but not in the way the superior nourishes the inferior, that is, coupled with instruction.

76. Akatzuka said *fan^a* means "palace garden"; Huang Chin-hung said *fan^a* is *fan^b*, "hedges." See the similar stories of a confined bird in 18/33–39 and 19/72–76, which may have been inspired by the story here.

77. 14/9–11 in Watson, *Chuang Tzu*, p. 155. I tried my ethical probes into this passage in my "Deconcentration of Morality: Taoist Esthetics of Person-Making," *Chinese Studies*, December 1983, pp. 625–55, especially pp. 643–44.

78. 24/61–65 in Watson, *ibid.*, p. 271. Cf. Graham's slightly infelicitous rendering in his *Chuang-tzu*, p. 105; I fail to share his interesting comments there.

79. This is a slightly clumsy but accurate rendering by Arthur Waley in *The Analects of Confucius*, p. 141 (a translation of 9:12).

80. See notes 31, 51, 63, 65,

81. Kao Heng took this view in his *Chuang Tzu Chin Chien*, pp. 11–12. So also did Han Shan serenely. For further comments on such views see Chiao Hung's *Chuang Tzu Yü*, pp. 39–40; Akatzuka, 1:153–54. Kuo Ch'ing-fan is refreshingly different.

82. Xavier Rubert de Ventós, *Self-Defeated Man*, pp. 5–6.

83. *Ku Lin*, 8:708–12, Williams, *Outlines*, pp. 179–83.

84. See note 83, referring to writings that also say fire is full outside and hollow inside,

that one year is "one fire," that fire starts in the south, the god of fire is the god of the south, that fire is not independent but must go along with firewood, and so on.

85. This is Kuo Ch'ing-fan's view.

86. This is Yeh Yü-lin's view.

87. In Watson, *Chuang Tzu* (p. 76), Chuang Tzu accuses the logician Hui Shih precisely of such straining, externalizing, and exhausting his limitations in an endless cognitive pursuit.

88. Pomp and punishment rhyme not only in sound (*ming, hsing*) but in life. As Chuang Tzu later says in Chapter Four, "Virtue is corrupted by fame-pomp-name (*ming*); knowledge comes out of contention (*cheng*). Fame is a people-beater; knowledge is a device for contention. Both are ominous weapons, not those with which to fulfill activities" (4/6–7; cf. Watson, p. 55).

89. For these two stories see Watson, *Chuang Tzu*, pp. 187 and 348. The first story concerns the futility of cognitive pursuit; the second concerns the futility of moral endeavor. This is also the order in Ch. Three, lines 1–4.

90. Cf. Ch. Two, lines 69–84.

91. A somewhat similar sentiment is expressed by the holy men's "breathing from the soles" (Watson, p. 78), that is, breathing from the root of oneself, and breathing in intimate contact with the ground.

92. Watson, *Chuang Tzu*, p. 253; cf. p. 247.

93. On the three meanings of *tu*, see this chapter, Meditation B.2.1 (and note 26). On the three sections in the story of ox-loosening, see also B.4.3.

94. Since the *Shih Ching* ("The Book of Poetry"), life, writing, and music have been entwined in China, as eloquently expressed in *Wen Hsin Tiao Lung* ("Dragon Carvings of a Literary Mind") by Liu Hsieh (Chapters 6–10, 33, 48–49); Han Yü's (A.D. 768–824) "To Meng Tung Yeh"; Ou-yang Hsiu's (1007–72) "Autumn," "To Yang Chih"; and so on. (Those three essays are collected in *Ku Wen Kuan Chih*. Only Ou-yang's "Autumn" has to my knowledged been translated into English. See Herbert A. Giles, *Gems of Chinese Literature*, pp. 164–65, "An Autumn Dirge"; and Arthur Waley, *Translations from the Chinese*, pp. 317–19, "Autumn.") For contemporary thinkers, see Wen I-to, *Myths and Poetry*, pp. 181–200; Hsü Fu-Kuan, "*The Esthetic Spirit in China*," pp. 1–143.

95. I here follow William L. Prensky's interpretation of T'ai Chi Ch'üan in his "Tai Chi—Spiritual Martial Art," *Parabola*, IV:68–73. Prensky may have confused *Chi* ("ultimate") with *ch'i* ("breath"). Cf. also Al Chung-liang Huang, *Embrace Tiger, Return to Mountain—The Essence of T'ai Chi*. I have a strong suspicion that one strain in the T'ai Chi Ch'üan art must have come from the story of the cook here, though I have no proof.

96. Mencius' phrase, "the vast *ch'i*" (2A2) complements Chuang Tzu here. It is true that Chuang Tzu did not mention *ch'i* in this chapter, though he did in the next chapter in a similar context (4/27–28). Chuang Tzu used *shen* (15) which moves as it desires, now dancingly (6–9), now playfully (22), now cautiously (25–27). And *shen* is an inclusive notion for *ch'i*; *ch'i* is vital, *shen* is universal. And so for brevity and clarity's sake *ch'i* was used here.

97. *Ku Lin*, 5:1036–38 explains *sheng*.

98. See Meditation B.4.5.1 in this chapter, for *shen*.

99. See *Ku Lin*, 5:82–83 for *yang*.

100. See *Ku Lin*, 2:1082-85 for *wu*.

101. See K'ang Yin, *Wen-Tzu Yuan-Liu*, pp. 226-28, for *wu*.

102. On the etymological connection between the principle (*chu*) and the fire (*huo*), see 7.4.2.

103. Matthews, 26:52.

104. Matthews, 10:34.

105. *Ku Lin*, 4:950–51, and K'ang Yin, *Wen-Tzu*, p. 224, explain *chieh* well.

106. *Ku Lin*, 2:983, and K'ang Yin, p. 240, explain *fen*.

107. *Ku Lin*, 10: 1377–78, explains *pien*.

108. In the report about the tradition concerning Lao Tan, Ssu-ma Ch'ien said that "none knew where he went to in the end" (trans. by D. C. Lau in *Lao Tzu: Tao Te Ching*, p. 8).

    Tsuda Saukichi said that since Lao Tzu the man did not exist, it is natural to say that "none knew where he went in the end"—in *Ju-Tao Liang-chia Koan-hsi Lun (Ju-ka to Do-ka no Kosho ni Tsuite)*, p. 5. I hesitate to accept this sanguine view which is based on the inconclusive hypothesis of Lao Tzu's non-existence. In any case, what the *Chuang Tzu* text said here concerns not Lao Tzu's actual existence (or non-existence) but only the common impression about Lao Tzu, and how Chuang Tzu struck a deadly blow to the assumed reverence behind that impression.

109. All these explanations of *shih* are from *Ku Lin*, 9:1289–90. Cf. Akatzuka, 1:151. *Ch'in* can mean, besides being a proper name for a country or a man, "ground grain" (*Ku Lin*, 6:475–49). But I did not exploit this etymological possibility.

110. The immortal teacher "Lao Tzu" now acquires the historical im-mortality of our close relative "Lao Tan." Cf. Chuang Tzu's careful usage of two names in my gloss to line 40.

111. *Ezekiel* 37.

112. *P'ao* ("kitchen") may mean *pao* ("brother"; Ma Hsü-lun and Chu Kuei-yao). *Pao* ("unfolding") is my own speculation.

113. E.g., by Huang Chin-hung.

114. For *pu* see *Ku Lin*, 2:1426-28.

115. As James Legge said, quoting *Shuo Wen*, in *The Texts of Taoism*, I:127. See *Ku Lin*, 3:13–17 for *ch'uo*, and my Meditations C.2 to Chapter One, where I used *ko* (after Legge). (*Ko* must be Cantonese for *ch'uo*.)

116. For example, Chapters 13, 16, 21, 22, 23, 24, 25, 26, end with such explanations on how to end our lives well, to end our lives without ending them.

117. In line 2, a repeat of line 1, the phrase *wei chih* ("making-after knowledge") seems to confirm the synonymity of knowing with making and following.

118. See T'ang Chün-i, "*The Fundamental Treatise of Chinese Philosophy, Inquiry into Tao*," I:356. He was quoting from Hsü T'ing-huai's quotation from others. He took it seriously and tried to solve it by some logical manuvers which I consider invalid. He opted for an Epicurian subjective immortality in pp. 363–64.

119. This is Kuo Ch'ing-fan's view.

120. To "understand" is to stand under and to undergo. Such experiential realization has nothing to do with that explanatory cognition which splits the knower from the known. Chuang Tzu's rejection of the latter does not extend to the former.

121. And T'ang Chün-i's problem (see note 118) is dissolved.

122. Quoted by Robert E. Meagher in *Albert Camus*, p. 25.

123. Besides Epicurus' "When death is, we are not, when we are, death is not," as recent as 1947 C. J. Ducasse said something as follows:

> ...we do not experience unconsciousness in ourselves, for to experience it would mean being conscious of being unconscious, and this is a contradiction. ... Nor do we ever experience unconsciousness in another person, but only the fact that, sometimes, some or all of the activities of his body cease to occur. That consciousness itself is extinguished at such times is thus only a hypothesis which we construct to account for certain changes in the behavior of another person's body ... (from *Is Life After Death Possible?*).

But while Ducasse argued about such subjective immortality and Epicurus stoically lived it, Chuang Tzu presented it in the full bloodiness of the knife and the fire. And since the theme hinges on the subject who lives it, Chuang Tzu's im-mortality differs from the others' subjective immortality.

124. On *chu* and its connections with fire (*huo*), lard or animal fat (*chih*), and religious ceremony to the spirits, see *Ku Lin*, 4:1441–44.

125. *Centering: In Pottery, Poetry and the Person*, p.22.

126. Line 3 can be taken to be a presentation of the principle (*chu*) of nourishment of life; *yüan tu* is the content, and *ching* is the equivalent, of *chu*. Taken this way, the introductory passage of lines 1 through 4 can be seen to present the entire three characters of the chapter title.

127. *Ku Lin*, 6: 256–67 says that dream is the twilight zone of the dusk where things are not clearly visible.

128. The first and third chapters give us all the famous Five Elements. The first chapter starts with water. The third chapter ends with wood and fire, and gives earth (26) and metal (8). In the Theory of Five Elementary Ways, water produces wood (Ch. One, Lines 1, 21), wood produces fire, Ch. Three lines (60, 61), fire produces earth (not in Chuang Tzu), earth produces metal (reversed in Ch. Three, line 26), and metal produces water (not in Chuang Tzu). Water is supposed to put out fire; Chuang Tzu merely goes from water (the first chapter) to fire (third chapter). Thus Chuang Tzu seems to follow the Theory of Five Elementary Ways only partially. This means that I failed to see any meaningful relation between the two.

129. See further, note 101, Chapter One.

Notes to the Epilogue

1. Its author was supposed to be an obscure official called Chuang Chou who lived around the fourth century B.C. (born between 390 and 359, died between 300 and 270) in an obscure place called Meng (wherever that was), and served at Lacquer Garden (whatever that meant). It was reputed that he wrote only seven of the thirty-three extant chapters of the book which bears his name. The rest of the book is thought to have been from the brushes of his friends, men of kindred spirit. Thus the author and the book are already a testimony to mutual evocation, to be elaborated in this chapter. On the author

and the book of *Chuang Tzu*, see a convenient summary of various views in *Huang Chin-hung, Hsin-I Chuang Tzu Tu-Pen*, pp. 1–32. See also note 1 to the Prologue.

2.   Philip Wheelwright, *The Burning Fountain*, p. 7.

3.   T. F. Torrance, *Royal Priesthood*, p. 1.

4.   The poem is translated by, among others, R. H. Blyth in his *Zen in English Literature and Oriental Classics*, p. 61.

5.   Watson, *Chuang Tzu*, pp. 138, 153, modified.

6.   The term "polythetic" is used by Alfred Schütz in his *Collected Papers II: Studies in Social Theory*, p. 172. Recently Jacques Derrida used "polysemic," "polysemy," or "non-semantic"—see his *Marges de la Philosophie*, pp. 365–93. I prefer "polythetic" to "polysemic" because semantics smacks verbalism, although I agree that "polythetic meaning" is "polysemy."

7.   As in the "limiting situations" of, say, vocational choice or deciding on a spouse.

8.   As in poetry, aphorisms, and the like, where words *strike* the hearer more than they express something.

9.   Aristotle, *Rhetoric*, I:3, especially 1358b. I followed W. Rhys Roberts' translation.

10.   Wheelwright, *Burning Fountain*, p. 87.

11.   Legge, *The Texts of Taoism*, 1:156; Wang Hsien-ch'ien, *Chuang Tzu Chi-Chieh*, p. 181 (at Chapter 27).

12.   Watson, *Chuang Tzu*, p. 373.

13.   Similarly, Socrates was impious to the cultured Athenians, not because he failed to make his discovery intelligible to them, but because he failed to inspire them by his discovery. Socrates was novel without being evocative, and so he confused and irritated them. His was a tragic case of the risked and failed evocation.

14.   Gilbert Ryle, *Dilemmas*, pp. 115–29.

15.   *Ibid.*, p. 123.

16.   Edward Meredith Cope, *The Rhetoric of Aristotle*, I:52.

17.   From *The Letters of a Post Impressionist*, p. 23; quoted by Wilbur Marshall Urban, *Language and Reality*, p. 473.

18.   Ryle, *Dilemmas*, p. 126.

19.   Watson, *Chuang Tzu*, p. 63.

20.   Robert Frost, "Between Prose and Verse," *The Atlantic Monthly*, January 1962, p. 51. He says, "every philosopher has one big metaphor in him. That's all he has."

21.   Johan Huizinga, *Homo Ludens*, p. 4.

22.   Søren Kierkegaard, *Concluding Unscientific Postscript*, p. 459. Cf. pp. 378, 413.

23.   For a catalogue of misreadings of the *Chuang Tzu* see "Prelude" in my *Chuang Tzu—World Philosopher at Play*, pp. 1–28.

24.   Watson, *Chuang Tzu*, p. 105. Cf. pp. 166, 195–96.

25.   15/10-14. Although reputedly inauthentic, this passage is a pithy summary of at least one aspect of Chuang Tzu.

26.   Watson, *Chuang Tzu*, pp. 35, 63–66, 75, 299.

27.   *Ibid.*, p. 372.

28.   Kierkegaard, *Postscript*, p. 462, note.

29.   Wheelwright, *The Burning Fountain*, pp. 74, 87.

30. Joseph Needham made this mistake in his *Science and Civilization in China*, II:63–68.

31. Alfred North Whitehead, *Process and Reality*, p. 7. The passage appears unchanged in "Corrected Edition," ed. by David Ray Griffin and Donald W. Sherburne, p. 5.

32. Kierkegaard, *Postscript*, pp. 448–51, 489.

33. Whitehead, *Process and Reality*, p. 6 (p. 4 in Corrected Edition).

34. Ludwig Wittgenstein, *Philosophical Investigations*, 3rd ed., Sections 21–27, 66–71, 75, 83, 100, 200, 562–68, et passim.

35. *Ibid.*, Section 83, p. 39e.

36. Watson, *Chuang Tzu*, pp. 52–53, 85, 91.

37. C. J. Ducasse is correct in calling play "autotelic" activity, performed for its own sake as opposed to art as "endotelic" and work as "ectotelic." See his "Creative Work, Art, and Play" in Vincent Tomas (ed.), *Creativity in Art*, pp. 71–83 (reprinted from C. J. Ducasse, *The Philosophy of Art*). Sadly Ducasse was mainly interested in art, regarding play as having only a "trampery" end, and to be studied for the sake of clarifying art.

38. Johan Huizinga vacillated between the rationality and the non-rationality of play in his *Homo Ludens*, pp. 5–27. My thoughts on play may put some sense into his confusion.

39. Immanuel Kant, *Critique of Pure Reason*, B15; see especially Norman Kemp Smith's translation.

40. See, for example, in Chapters Two, Six, and Twenty-Two of the *Chuang Tzu*.

41. William Zinsser, *On Writing Well*, p. 163.

42. *Ibid.*, p. 163. Liu Hsieh stressed this corrective function (with many examples) of humor and metaphor used by the Chinese people toward their rulers, in his *"Dragon Carvings of a Literary Mind,"* Chapter 15.

43. Huizinga, *Homo Ludens*, p. 6.

44. Harvey Cox, *The Feast of Fools*.

45. Wheelwright, *The Burning Fountain*, p. 77.

46. Watson, p. 86.

47. On *fang wai* see 6/66. On *ta fang* see 17/5, 20/16, 24/107–108, 25/80. On *wu fang* see 11/65, 14/25, 22/32. Unfortunately, Watson translated *fang* variously as "method," "direction," "realm." Incidentally, *to fang* ("diverse methods") is not popular with Chuang Tzu: 8/1, 3-4, 33/69. Cf. *to* ("many") in 17/16, 42.

48. Watson, p. 182.

49. *Ibid.*, pp. 62–63; p. 41 (or Chapter Two, lines 125–29 in my translation).

50. *Ibid.*, pp. 52, 68–76, 84–88, 91, 191–92, 223–24, 269, 271.

51. *Ibid.*, pp. 88, 192–93.

52. Aristotle, *Nicomachean Ethics*, VII and X.

53. "What a pity!" appears in three situations: (1) Watson, *Chuang Tzu*, pp. 38, 247, 267, 361; (2) *ibid.*, pp. 152, 338, 377; (3) *ibid.*, pp. 140, 247, cf. 224, 271.

54. In Jacques Ehrmann (ed.), *Game, Play, Literature*, p. 20. This book reprints Eugen Fink's essay from *Yale French Studies*, No. 41 (1968).

55. Besides Ernest Nagel and James R. Newman, *Gödel's Proof*, Douglas R. Hofstadter's *Gödel, Escher, Bach: An Eternal Golden Braid*, should be cited as a highly interesting presentation of Gödel. It must not have occurred to Hofstadter that he has shown us that

Gödel perhaps explained our *metaphysical urge* to see (Escher) and hear (Bach) *more* than we usually see and hear. He manifested his metaphysical insensitivity in his cavalierly mechanistic treatment of the meta-level jumping (pp. 473–79).

56. For Kant, see his *Critique of Pure Reason*; for Lakoff and Johnson, see George Lakoff and Mark Johnson, *Metaphors We Live By*.

57. Wang Fu-chih, *Chuang Tzu Chieh*, p. 76 (toward the beginning of the Outer Chapters).

58. The master craftsmen appear in Watson, *Chuang Tzu*, pp. 41, 50–51, 63, 152–53, 199–201, 204–7, 228–31, 244–45, 265–67. The phrase, "machine hearts (or minds)," appears in *ibid.*, p. 134.

59. Cf. "The Great Man in his teaching is like the shadow that follows a form, the echo that follows a sound" (*ibid.*, p. 124).

60. Huang Chin-hung, *Chuang Tzu Chi Ch'i Wen-Hsüeh*, pp. 67–68, 110, 147–49 189, 261, 282; his "Chin San-Shih Nien-Lai Chih Chuang-Tzu-Hsüeh," in *Han-Hsüeh Yen-Chiu T'ung-Hsün*, Vol. I, No. 4 (October, 1982), p. 147; *Hsin-I Chuang Tzu Tu-Pun*, p. 8.

61. I am greatly indebted to Professor William Springer of the University of Texas at El Paso for furnishing me with the criticism.

62. J. L. Ackrill, *Aristotle the Philosopher*, pp. 1–4.

63. Gregory Vlastos (ed.), *The Philosophy of Socrates*, pp. 1–21, 90–93, etc.

64. See Wing-tsit Chan's introduction to *The Way of Lao Tzu*, p. 3; and his introduction to Lao Tzu in Wing-tsit Chan (ed.), *A Source Book of Chinese Philosophy*, p. 136. For the Chinese "art" of cooking, its "spirit" and its "essence," see "the largest, most comprehensive Chinese cookbook ever published for the Western world," *The Thousand Recipe Chinese Cookbook* by Gloria Bley Miller. Part One in it sounds like a veritable introduction to Taoism.

For a less spontaneous and more academic rendition of the same point, see *Food in Chinese Culture: Anthropological and Historical Perspective*, edited by K. C. Chang.

Sadly, the book has only one citation from the *Chuang Tzu* about food—the story about ox-undoing. Actually Chuang Tzu mentioned food at almost every critical turn. The Big Bird's epic journey needed six months' (preparation of) foodstuffs; Lady Li changed her heart at sumptuous feasts; the holy man's meals differ from those of commoners; the holy man rains for food; the tailorbird is content with a bellyful of drinks from the river; the goose that cannot cackle faces being butchered for human consumption; the quantity and the quality of their foods manifest the poverty of Lao Tzu and Chuang Tzu, and the baseness or nobility of various birds; and so on.

References

Works in Chinese and Japanese

Note: Some of the following citations represent Chuang-Tzu scholarship, but not comprehensively, seeing that Chuang Tzu's work is now about twenty-four centuries old. The following are just a handful of works found to be instructive (not just concerning Chuang-Tzu scholarship). They are arranged in alphabetical order by the romanized surnames of authors and editors.

赤塚忠　莊子　東京集英社
Akatzuka, Tadashi, *Sōshi*, 2 vols. Tokyo: Shu-ei-sha, 1974, 1977.

張默生　莊子新釋　臺北時代書局
Chang Mo-sheng. *Chuang Tzu Hsin-shih*. Taipei: Shih-tai Shu-chü, 1974.

張成秋　莊子篇目考　臺灣中華書局
Ch'ang Ch'eng-ch'iu. *Chuang Tzu P'ien-mu K'ao*. Taiwan: Chung-hua Shu-chü, 1971.

陳啟天　莊子淺說　臺北中華書局
Ch'en Ch'i-t'ien. *Chuang Tzu Ch'ien-shuo*. Taipei: Chung-hua Shu-chü, 1978.

陳鼓應　莊子哲學探究　臺北日盛印製廠
Ch'en Ku-ying. *Chuang Tzu Che-hsüeh T'an-chiu*. Taipei: Jih-sheng Yin-chih Ch'ang, 1975.

陳鼓應　莊子今註今釋　臺北商務印書館
Ch'en Ku-ying. *Chuang Tzu Chin-chu Chin-i*, 2 vols. Taipei: Shang-wu Yin-shu-kuan, 1975.

陳壽昌　南華真經正義　臺北新天地書局
Ch'en Shou-ch'ang. *Nan-hua Chen-ching Cheng-i*. Taipei: Hsin T'ien-ti Shu-chü, 1972 (reprint of the original).

焦竑　莊子翼　臺北廣文書局
Chiao Hung. *Chuang Tzu I*. Taipei: Kuang-wen Shu-chü, 1970, 1979 (reprint of the original).

錢穆　莊子纂箋　香港東南印務出版社
Ch'ien Mu. *Chuang Tzu Tsuan-ch'ien*. Hong Kong: Tung-nan Yin-wu Ch'u-pan-she, 1951, 1963.

錢穆 學籥 香港南天事業公司
Ch'ien Mu. *Hsüeh Yüeh*. Hong Kong: Nan T'ien Shih-yeh Kung-ssu, 1958.

錢穆 國學概論 臺灣商務印書館
Ch'ien Mu. *Kuo-hsüeh Kai-lun*. Taiwan: Shang-wu Yin-shu-kuan, 1931, 1966.

朱桂曜 莊子內篇證補 臺灣商務印書館
Chu Kuei-yao. *Chuang Tzu Nei-p'ien Cheng-pu*. Taiwan: Shang-wu Yin-shu-kuan, 1935

方驥齡 論語新詮 臺北中華書局
Fang Chi-ling. *Lun-yü Hsin-ch'üan*. Taipei: Chung-hua Shu-chü, 1978.

福永光司 莊子 東京朝日新聞社
Fukunaga, Mitsuji. *Sōshi*, 3 vols. Tokyo: Asahi Shin-bun-sha, 1966, 1967.

馮友蘭 中國哲學史 上海商務印書館
Fung Yu-lan. *Chung-kuo Che-hsüeh Shih*. Shanghai: Shang-wu Yin-shu-kuan, 1934.

憨山大師 莊子內篇憨山註 臺北新文豐出版股份有限公司
Han Shan. *Chuang Tzu Nei-p'ien Han Shan Chu*. Taipei: Hsin Wen-feng Ch'u-pan Ku-fen Yu-hsien Kung-ssu, 1974 (reprint of the original).

平岡禎吉 准南子に現れた氣の研究 東京理想社
Hiraoka, Teikichi. *Enanji ni Arawareta Ki no Kenkyu*. Tokyo: Li-so-sha, 1968.

何敬群 莊子義繹 香港人生出版社
Ho Ching-ch'un. *Chuang Tzu II*. Kong Hong: Jen-sheng Ch'u-pan-she, 1966.

蕭純伯 莊子治要 臺北商務印書館
Hsiao Ch'un-po. *Chuang Tzu Chih-yao*. Taipei: Shang-wu Yin-shu-kuan, 1972.

謝冰瑩等註釋 古文觀止 臺北三民書局
Hsieh Ping-ying, et al. (eds.) *Ku-wen Kuan-chih*. Taipei: San-min Shu-chü, 1971.

徐復觀 中國藝術精神 臺灣學生書局
Hsü Fu-kuan. *Chung-kuo I-shu Ching-shen*. Taiwan: Hsüeh-sheng Shu-chü, 1966.

徐復觀 公孫龍講疏 臺灣學生書局
Hsü Fu-kuan. *Kung-sun Lung Chiang-shu*. Taiwan: Hsüeh-sheng Shu-chü, 1966.

許慎　說文解字註（段玉裁註）　九龍實用書局
Hsü Shen. *Shuo-wen Chieh-tzu Chu* (commented on by Tuan Yü-ch'ai).
Kowlung: Shih-yung Shu-chü, 1963 (reprint).

許慎　引用於劉安撰劉文典集解　淮南鴻烈集解
臺灣商務印書館
Hsü Shen. (Commentator in Liu An and Liu Wen-tien version of) *Huai
Nan Hung-lieh Chi-chieh*. Taiwan: Shang-wu Yin-shu-kuan, 1969 (reprint
of the original).

宣穎　莊子南華經解　臺北宏業書局
Hsüan Ying. *Chuang Tzu Nan-hua Ching Chieh*. Taipei: Hung-yeh Shu-chü,
1977 (reprint of the original).

胡適　中國古代哲學史　臺灣商務印書館
Hu Shih. *Chung-kuo Ku-tai Che-hsüeh Shih*. Taiwan: Shang-wu
Yin-shu-kuan, 1919, 1958.

胡適　胡適文存　臺北遠東圖書公司
Hu Shih. *Hu Shih Wen-ts'un*, 4 vols. Taipei: Yüan-tung T'u-shu Kung-ssu,
1934.

胡適　序文劉安劉文典註　淮南鴻烈集解　臺灣商務印書館
Hu Shih. Introduction to Liu An and Liu Wen-tien version of *Huai Nan
Hung-lieh Chi-chieh*. Taiwan: Shang-wu Yin-shu-kuan, 1978 (reprint).

黃錦鋐　莊子及其文學　臺北東大圖書有限公司
Huang Chin-hung. *Chuang Tzu chi Ch'i Wen-hsüeh*. Taipei: Tung-ta
T'u-shu Yu-hsien Kung-ssu, 1977

黃錦鋐　新譯莊子讀本　臺北三民書局
Huang Chin-hung. *Hsin-i Chuang Tzu Tu-pen*. Taipei: San-min Shu-chü,
1974.

黃錦鋐　"近三十年來之莊子學"　臺灣漢學研究通訊
Huang Chin-hung. "Chin San-shih Nien Lai Chih Chuang Tzu Hsüeh,"
in *Han-Hüeh Yen* ("*Newsletter for Research in Chinese Studies*"), Vol. I,
No. 1 (January 1982), pp. 3–5.

金谷治　莊子　東京岩波文庫
Kanaya, Osamu. *Sōshi*, 4 vols. Tokyo: Iwanami Bunko, 1981.

康殷　文字源流淺說　北京榮寶齋
K'ang Yin. *Wen-tzu Yüan-liu Ch'ien-shuo*. Peking: Jung Pao Chai, 1979.

高亨　莊子今箋　臺灣中華書局
Kao Heng. *Chuang Tzu Chin Ch'ien*. Taiwan: Chung-hua Shu-chü, 1973.

小林信明　列子　東京明治書院
Kobayashi, Nobuaki. *Lesshi*. Tokyo: Meiji Sho-in, 1967.

關鋒　莊子內篇譯解和批判　北京中華書局
Kuan Feng. *Chuang Tzu Nei-p'ien I-chieh ho P'i-p'an*. Peking: Chung-hua Shu-chü, 1961.

郭慶藩　莊子集釋　北京中華書局
Kuo Ch'ing-fan. *Chuang Tzu Chi-shih*. Peking: Chung-hua Shu-chü, 1960 (re-typeset, punctuated).

郭慶藩　莊子集釋　臺灣中華書局
Kuo Ch'ing-fan. *Chuang Tzu Chi-shih*. Taiwan: Chung-hua Shu-chü, 1973 (reprint of the original).

郭象　莊子南華真經　臺北藝文印書館
Kuo Hsiang. *Chuang Tzu Nan-hua Chen-ching*. Taipei: I-wen Yin-shu-kuan, 1968 (reprint of the original).

郭紹虞　語言通論　臺灣華聯出版社
Kuo Shao-yü. *Yü-wen T'ung-lun*. Taiwan: Hua-lien Ch'u-pan-she, 1976.

郎擎霄　莊子學案　臺北河洛圖書出版社
Lang Ch'ing-hsiao. *Chuang Tzu Hsüeh-an*. Taipei: Ho-lo T'u-shu Ch'u-pan-she, 1974.

林希逸　莊子口義　臺灣弘道文化事業有限公司
Lin Hsi-i. *Chuang Tzu K'ou-i*. Taiwan: Hung-tao Wen-hua Shih-yeh Yu-hsien Kung-ssu, 1971 (reprint of the original).

林紓　莊子淺說　上海商務印書館
Lin Shü. *Chuang Tzu Ch'ien-shuo*. Shanghai: Shang-wu Yin-shu-kuan, 1923.

林雲銘　標注補義莊子因　臺北蘭臺書局
Lin Yün-ming. *Piao-chu Pu-i Chuang Tzu Yin*. Taipei: Lan-t'ai Shu-chü, 1969 (reprint of the original).

林雲銘　增註莊子因　廣文書局
Lin Yün-ming. *Tseng-chu Chuang Tzu Yin*. Taipei: Kuang-wen Shu-chü, 1968 (reprint of the original).

劉勰　文心雕龍輯註　（黃叔琳註）　香港中華書局
Liu Hsieh. (Commented on by Huang Shu-lin), *Wen Hsin Tiao Lung Chi-chu*. Hong Kong: Chung-hua Shu-chü, 1973 (reprint of the original).

劉勰　文心雕龍　香港商務印書館
Liu Hsieh. *Wen Hsin Tiao Lung Chu*, 2 vols. Hong Kong: Shang-wu Yin-shu-kuan, 1960, 1964.

劉大杰　中國民學發展史　臺灣中華書局
Liu Ta-chieh. *Chung-kuo Wen-hsüeh Fa-chan Shih*. Taiwan: Chung-hua
Shu-chü, 1968.

劉文典　莊子補正　昆明：雲南人民出版社
Liu Wen-tien. *Chuang Tzu Pu-cheng*, 2 vols. K'un-ming: Yün-nan Jenmin
Ch'u-pan-she, 1947, 1980.

陸侃如年世金註釋　文心雕龍　濟南齊魯書社
Lu K'ang-Ju, and Mou Shih-chin (commentators). *Wen Hsin Tiao Lung
I-chu*, 2 vols. Chi-nan: Ch'i Lu Shu-she, 1981.

陸樹芝　莊子雪　儒雅堂藏板嘉慶四年
Lu Shu-chih. *Chuang Tzu Hsüeh*. Ju-ya T'ang collection, 1799 (oringinal in
the library of the University of Tornoto).

呂祖謙　東萊博議　宋晶如章榮註釋　香港廣智書局
Lü Tsu-ch'ien. *Tung-lai Po-i* (commented on by Sung Ching-ju, and Chang
Jung). Hong Kong: Kuang-chih Shu-chü, no publication date.

馬建忠　馬氏文通　北京商務印書館
Ma Chien-chung. *Ma-shih Wen-t'ung*. Peking: Shang-wu Yin-shu-kuan,
1983 (reprint)

馬叙倫　莊子義證　臺北弘道文化事業有限公司
Ma Hsü-lun. *Chuang Tzu I-cheng*. Taipei: Hong-tao Wen-hua Shih-yeh
Yu-hsien Kung-ssu, 1970.

牟宗三　才性與玄理　臺灣學生書局
Mou Tsung-san. *Ts'ai-hsing yü Hsüan-li*. Taiwan: Hsüeh-sheng Shu-chü,
1983.

諸橋轍次　大漢和辭典　東京大衆館
Murobashi, Tetsuji. *Dai Kan-wa Jiten*, 13 vols. Tokyo: Tai-shu-kan, 1960.

諸橋轍次　莊子平話　李君奭譯　臺灣專心企業有限公司
Murobashi, Tetsuji. *Sō-shi Hei-wa*, tr. Li Chün-shih. Taiwan: Chuan-hsin
Ch'i-yeh Yu-hsien Kung-ssu, 1972.

西田左衞門　老子莊子(上)　東京至誠堂
Nishida, Saemon. *Loshi, Sōshi (jō)*. Tokyo: Si-sei-do, 1931.

歐陽修　"秋賦"　謝冰瑩等編譯註　古文觀止
Ou-yang Hsiu. "Ch'iu-sheng Fu," in Hsieh Ping-ying, et al., commentators.
Ku-wen Kuan-chih, pp. 583–85.

龐朴　公孫龍子譯註　上海人民出版社
P'ang P'u. *Kung-sun Lung Tzu I-chu.* Shanghai: Jen-min Ch'u-pan-she, 1974.

龐朴　說"無"　深圳大學國學研究所
P'ang P'u. "Shuo 'Wu'," see Shen-chen Ta-hsüeh, pp. 62–74.

斐學海　古書虛字集釋　北京新華書店
P'ei Hsüeh-hai. *Ku-shu Hsü-tzu Chi-shih.* Peking: Hsin-hua Shu-tien, 1939, 1954, 1982.

坂井煥三　莊子新釋　東京弘道館
Sakai, Kanzō. *Sōshi Hsin-shaku.* Tokyo: Kō-dō-kan, 1930.

上海市中醫學會　臟象學說的理論與運用
　香港醫學衛生出版社
Shanghai-shih Chung-i Hsüeh-hui. *Tsang-hsiang Hsüeh-shuo te Li-lun yü Yün-yung.* Hong Kong: I-hsueh Wei-sheng Ch'u-pan-she, 1974.

沈洪　莊子　臺北商務印書館
Shen Hung. *Chuang Tzu.* Taipei: Shang-wu Yin-shu-kuan, 1969.

深圳大學國學研究所主編　中國文化與中國哲學　東方出版社
Shen-chen Ta-hsüeh Kuo-hsueh Yen-chiu So (ed.) *Zhongguo Wenhua yü Zhongguo Zhexüe.* Peking: Tung-fang Ch'u-pan She, 1986.

蘇新鋈　郭象莊學平議　臺灣學生書局
Su Hsin-wu. *Kuo Hsiang Chuang Hsüeh P'ing-i.* Taiwan: Hsüeh-sheng Shu-chü, 1980.

鈴木修次　莊子　東京清水書院
Suzuki, Shūji. *Sōshi.* Tokyo: Shimizu Sho-in, 1974.

唐君毅　中國哲學原論原道篇　香港新亞研究所
T'ang Chün-i. *Chung-kuo Che-hsüeh Yüan-lun, Yüan-tao P'ien*, Vol. 1. Hong Kong: Hsin Ya Yen-chiu So, 1973.

丁福保編　說文解字詁林　臺北鼎文書局
Ting Fu-pao (ed.) *Shuo-wen Chieh-tzu Ku-lin*, 12 vols. Taipei: Ting-wen Shu-chü, 1983 (reprint of the original).

曹礎基　莊子淺註　北京中華書局
Ts'ao Ch'u-chi. *Chuang Tzu Ch'ien-chu*, Peking: Chung-hua Shu-chü, 1980.

津田左右吉　道家の思想て其展開　東京岩波文庫
Tsuda, Saukichi. *Dōke no Shisō to sono Tenkai.* Tokyo: Iwanami Bunko, 1939.

宇野哲人　論語　東京新教出版社
Uno, Tetsujin. *Rongo*, 2 vols. Tokyo: Shin-kyo Shup-pan-sha, 1953.

王充　論衡校釋　臺灣商務印書館
Wang Ch'ung. *Lun Heng Chiao-shih*. Taiwan: Shang-wu Yin-shu-kuan, 1964.

王夫之　莊子解　香港中華書局
Wang Fu-chih. *Chuang Tzu Chieh*. Hong Kong: Chung-hua Shu-chü, 1976 (reprint).

王夫之　莊子通　北京中華書局
Wang Fu-chih. *Chuang Tzu T'ung*. Peking: Chung-hua Shu-chü, 1962 (reprint).

王先謙　莊子集解　臺北世界書局
Wang Hsien-ch'ien. *Chuang Tzu Chi-chieh*. Taipei: Shi-chieh Shu-chü, 1964 (reprint).

王力　漢語史稿　北京中華書局
Wang Li. *Han-yü Shih-kao*, 3 vols. Peking: Chung-hua Shu-chü, 1980.

王夢鷗　古典文學論探索　臺北正中書局
Wang Meng-ou. *Ku-tien Wen-hsüeh Lun T'an-so*. Taipei: Cheng-chung Shu-chü, 1984.

王夢鷗　文學概論　臺北藝文書局
Wang Meng-ou. *Wen-hsüeh Kai-lun*. Taipei: I-wen Yin-shu-kuan, 1976.

王叔岷　莊學管闚　臺灣藝文印書館
Wang Shu-min. *Chuang Hsüeh Kuan-k'ui*. Taiwan: I-wen Yin-shu-kuan, 1978.

王叔岷　莊子校釋　臺灣臺聯國風出版社
Wang Shu-min. *Chuang Tzu Chiao-shih*, 2 vols. Taiwan: T'ai-lien Kuo-feng Ch'u-pan-she, 1972.

王引之　經傳繫詞　香港太平書局
Wang Yin-chih. *Ching-ch'uan Hsi-ts'u*. Hong Kong: T'ai-p'ing Shu-chü, 1974 (reprint).

韋政通編　中國哲學辭典大全　臺北水牛出版社
Wei Cheng-t'ung (ed.) *Chung-kuo Che-hsüeh Ts'u-tien Ta-ch'üan*. Taipei: Shui-niu Ch'u-pan-she, 1983.

聞一多　神話與詩　臺中籃燈文化事業有限公司
Wen I-to. *Shen-hua wü Shih*. Taichung: Lan-teng Wen-hua Shih-yeh Yu-hsien Kung-ssu, 1975.

聞一多　聞一多全集　北京新華書店
Wen I-to. *Wen I-to Ch'üan-chi*. Peking: Hsin-hua Shu-tien, 1982.

吳怡　逍遙的莊子　臺北新天地書局
Wu I. *Hsiao Yao te Chuang Tzu*. Taipei: Hsin T'ien-ti Shu-chü, 1971.

葉玉麟　莊子白話註解　臺北華聯出版社
Yeh Yü-lin. *Chuang Tzu Pai-hua Chu-chieh*. Taipei: Hua-lien Ch'u-pan-she, 1961.

嚴靈峯　莊子知見書目　臺北成文出版社
Yen Ling-feng. *Chuang Tzu Chih-chien Shu-mu*. Taipei: Ch'eng-wen Ch'u-pan-she.

余英時　"義理、考據詞章"　韋政通　中國哲學辭典大全
Yü Ying-shih. "I-li, K'ao-chü, Ts'u-chang," in Wei Cheng-t'ung (ed.) *Chung-kuo Che-hsüeh Ts'u-tien Ta-ch'üan*, pp. 639–52.

Works in English

Note: Translations of, and writings about the *Chuang Tzu* will be found under the
following names: Chan, Feng, Fung, Girardot, Graham, Legge, Lin, Merton, Waley,
Ware, Watson, and Wu. Also see *Concordance.*

Ackrill, J. L. *Aristotle the Philosopher.* New York: Oxford University Press,
1981.

Adams, Douglas. *The Hitchhiker's Guide to the Galaxy.* New York: Harmony
Books, 1979.

American Heritage Dictionary, The. Boston: Little, Brown, 1982.

Ames, Roger T. *The Art of Rulership* Honolulu: University of Hawaii Press,
1983.

Aristotle, *Nichomachean Ethics*, trans. by Martin Ostwald. New York:
Macmillan, 1962.

—. *Rhetoric*, trans. by W. Rhys Roberts. In *The Complete Works of Aristotle*,
2 vols., ed. by Jonathan Barnes. Princeton, N.J.: Princeton University Press,
1984.

Bailey, Kenneth G. *Poet and Peasant.* Grand Rapids, Mich.: Eerdmans, 1976.

Barfield, Owen. *Poetic Diction.* Middletown, Conn.: Wesleyan University
Press, 1978.

Black, Max. *A Companion to Wittgenstein's 'Tractatus'.* Ithaca, N.Y.: Cornell
University Press, 1964.

—. *The Prevalence of Humbug and Other Essays.* Ithaca, N.Y.: Cornell
University Press, 1983.

Blyth, R. H. *Zen in English Literature and Oriental Classics.* New York:
Dutton, 1960.

Buber, Martin. *I and Thou*, trans. by Ronald Gregor Smith. Edinburgh:
Clark, 1937.

Buck, Pearl S. (trans.) *All Men Are Brothers.* New York: John Day, 1933;
repr. 1968.

Bugbee, Henry G., Jr. *The Inward Morning.* New York: Collier, 1961.

Bultmann, Rudolf. *Essays: Philosophical and Theological*, trans. by James
C. G. Grieg. New York: Macmillan, 1955.

—. *Existence and Faith*, trans. by Schubert M. Ogden. London: Hodder and
Stoughton, 1961.

Camus, Albert. *The Myth of Sisyphus*, trans. by Justin O'Brien. New York:
Alfred A. Knopf, 1955.

Chan, Wing-tsit (ed. and trans.) *A Sourcebook in Chinese Philosophy.*
Princeton, N.J.: Princeton University Press, 1963.

—. (ed. and trans.) *The Way of Lao Tzu*. Indianapolis: Bobbs-Merrill, 1963.

Chang, K. C. (ed.) *Food in Chinese Culture: Anthropological and Historical Perspectives*. New Haven: Yale University Press, 1977.

Cheng, Francois. *Chinese Poetic Writing*. Bloomington, Ind.: Indiana University Press, 1982.

Chow Tse-tsung (ed.) *Wen-lin*. Madison, Wis.: University of Wisconsin Press, 1968.

A Concordance to the Chuang Tzu, Harvard-Yenching Sinological Index Series. Cambridge, Mass.: Harvard University Press, 1956.

Cope, Edward Meredith (ed.) *The Rhetoric of Aristotle*, [the Greek text] with a Commentary. Cambridge: At the University Press, 1877; reprint ed., New York: Arno Press, 1973.

Cornford, Francis M. (ed. and trans.) *The Republic of Plato*. London and New York: Oxford University Press, 1941.

Cox, Harvey. *The Feast of Fools*. New York: Harper and Row, 1969.

Crombie, I. M. *An Examination of Plato's Doctrines*. London: Routledge & Kegan Paul, 1963.

Davis, Curtis W. See Menuhin, Yehudi,

De Laszlo, Violet S. (ed.) *The Basic Writings of C. G. Jung*. New York: Modern Library, 1959.

Delza, Sophia. *T'ai Chi Ch'üan*. Albany: State University of New York Press, 1985.

Derrida, Jacques, *Margins of Philosophy*. Chicago: University of Chicago Press, 1982.

Dobson, W. A. C. H. *A Dictionary of the Chinese Particles*. Taipei: Shuang-Yeh Shu-Tien, 1976.

Ducasse, C. J. *Is Life After Death Possible?* The Agnes E. and Constantine E. Forester Lecture, 1947.

—. *The Philosophy of Art*. New York: Dial Press, 1929.

Ehrmann, Jacques (ed.) *Game, Play, Literature*. Boston: Beacon Press, 1971.

Farrar, Austin. *Glass of Vision*. Glasgow: Dacre Press, 1948.

—. *Rebirth of Images*. Glasgow: Dacre Press, 1949.

Feng, Gia-fu, and Jane English (trans.) *Chuang Tsu: Inner Chapters*. New York: Vintage Books, 1974.

French, Peter A. (ed.) *Philosophers in Wonderland*. St. Paul, Minn.: Llewellyn, 1975.

Frost, Robert. "Between Prose and Verse," *The Atlantic Monthly*, Vol. 209, No. 1 (January 1962).

Fung Yu-lan. *A History of Chinese Philosophy*, 2 vols., trans. by Derk Bodde. Princeton, N.J.: Princeton University Press, 1952, 1953.

—. *A Short History of Chinese Philosophy*, ed. by Derk Bodde. New York: Macmillan, 1948.

—. (trans.) *Chuang Tzu: A New Selected Translation with an Exposition of the Philosophy of Kuo Hsiang*, reprint ed. New York: Gordon Press, 1975.

Geer, Russel M. (trans.) *On Nature by Lucretius.* Indianapolis, Ind.: Bobbs-Merrill, 1965.

Giles, Herbert A. (ed. and trans.) *Gems of Chinese Literature.* New York: Paragon/Dover, 1965.

Girardot, Norman J. *Myth and Meaning in Early Taoism.* Berkeley, Calif.: University of California Press, 1983.

Graham, A. C. *Chuang-tzŭ: The Seven Inner Chapters and Other Writings from the Book* Chuang-tzŭ. London: George Allen & Unwin, 1981.

—. "Chuang-tzŭ's Essay on Seeing Things as Equal," *History of Religions,* Vol. 9, Nos. 2 and 3 combined (November 1969-February 1970), pp. 137-159.

—. "How Much of *Chuang-tzŭ* Did Chuang-tzŭ Write?" *Journal of American Academy of Religion*, Vol. XLVII, No. 3-S, Thematic Issue (Sept. 1975).

—. *Later Mohist Logic, Ethics and Science.* Hong Kong: Chinese University Press/London: University of London Press, 1978.

—. *Chuang-tzŭ*: Textual Notes to a Partial Translation. University of London Press, 1982.

—. (trans.) *The Book of* Lieh-tzŭ. London: John Murray, 1960.

Guthrie, W. K. C. *Socrates.* Cambridge: Cambridge University Press, 1971.

—. *Sophists.* Cambridge: Cambridge University Press, 1971.

Hall, David L. *Eros and Irony.* Albany: State University of New York Press, 1982.

—. *The Uncertain Phoenix.* Albany: State University of New York Press, 1982.

Hastings, James (ed.) *Encyclopedia of Religion and Ethics.* New York: Scribner's, 1920.

Hofstadter, Douglas R. *Gödel, Escher, Bach.* New York: Random House, 1980.

Hollingdale, R. J. (ed. and trans.) *A Nietzsche Reader.* New York: Penguin Books, 1977.

Huang, Al Chung-liang. *Embrace Tiger, Return to Mountain— The Essence of T'ai Chi.* Moab, Utah: Real People's Press, 1973.

Huizinga, Johan. *Homo Ludens*, trans. by the author. Boston: Beacon Press, 1955.

Ihde, Don. *Sense and Significance.* Pittsburgh: Duquesne University Press, 1973.

— and Richard M. Zaner (eds.) *Dialogues in Phenomenology.* The Hague: Martinus Nijhoff, 1975.

Johnson, Wallace. *A Concordance to Han-fei Tzu.* San Francisco: Chinese Materials Center, 1975.

Jung, C. G. *Memories, Dreams, Reflections*, ed. by Aniela Jaffé. New York: Pantheon, 1961.

Kafka, Franz. *The Complete Stories and Parables*, ed. by Nahum N. Glatzer. New York: Quality Paperback Book Club, 1985.

Kant, Immanuel. *Critique of Pure Reason*, trans. by Norman Kemp Smith. London: Macmillan, 1963.

Kaptchuk, Ted J. *The Web That Has No Weaver: Understanding Chinese Medicine.* New York: Congdon and Weed, 1983.

Karlgren, Bernard. *Grammata Serica.* Taiwan: Ch'eng-wen, 1965.

Kazantzakis, Nikos. *The Saviors of God*, trans. by Kimon Friar. New York: Simon and Schuster, 1960.

Keen, Sam. *Beginnings Without End.* New York: Harper and Row, 1977.

Kierkegaard, Søren. *The Concept of Irony*, trans. by Lee M. Capel. Bloomington: Indiana University Press, 1965.

—. *Concluding Unscientific Postscript*, trans. by David F. Swenson and Walter Lowrie. Princeton, N.J.: Princeton University Press, 1941.

—. *Fear and Trembling*, trans. by Walter Lowrie. Princeton, N.J.: Princeton University Press, 1941.

—. *The Gospel of Suffering*, trans. by David F. and Lilian M. Swenson. Minneapolis: Augsburg, 1946.

—. *The Point of View of My Work as an Author*, trans. by Walter Lowrie; ed. by Benjamin Nelson. New York: Harper, 1962.

Kittel, Gerhard (ed.) *Theological Dictionary of the New Testament.* Grand Rapids, Mich.: Eerdmans, 1967.

Lakoff, George, and Mark Johnson. *Metaphors We Live By.* Chicago: University of Chicago Press, 1980.

Lau, D. C. (trans.) *Lao Tzu: Tao Te Ching.* Baltimore: Penguin Books, 1963.

Legge, James (ed. and trans.) *The Chinese Classics*, 5 vols., reprint ed. Hong Kong: Hong Kong University Press, 1960.

—. (ed. and trans.) *The Texts of Taoism*, 2 vols., reprint ed. New York: Dover, 1962.

Lewis, H. D. (ed.) *Clarity Is Not Enough.* London: George Allen & Unwin, 1963.

Lin Yutang (ed.) *The Wisdom of China and India.* New York: Modern Library, 1942.

—. (ed. and trans.) *The Wisdom of Confucius.* New York: Modern Library, 1938.

Linkletter, Art. *Yes You Can.* New York: Simon and Schuster, 1979.

Liu, James, J. Y. *The Art of Chinese Poetry.* Chicago: University of Chicago Press, 1962.

—. *Chinese Theories of Literature.* Chicago: University of Chicago Press, 1975.

Lucretius, *On Nature;* see Geer, Russel M.

Mailer, Norman. *Ancient Evenings.* Boston: Little, Brown, 1983.

Malcolm, Norman. *Dreaming.* London: George Allen & Unwin, 1956.

Marcel, Gabriel. *The Mystery of Being,* 2 vols., trans. by G. S. Fraser. Chicago: Regnery/Gateway, 1960.

Matthews, Robert Henry. *A Chinese-English Dictionary.* Cambridge: Harvard University Press, 1943.

McClain, Ernest G. *The Myth of Invariance: The Origin of the Gods, Mathematics and Music from the* Rg Veda *to Plato.* Stony Brook, N.Y.: Nicholas Hays, 1976.

—. *The Pythagorean Plato.* Stony Brook, N.Y.: Nicholas Hays, 1978.

McNaughton, William. *The Taoist Vision.* Ann Arbor: University of Michigan Press, 1971.

Meagher, Robert E. *Albert Camus.* New York: Harper/Colophon, 1979.

Menuhin, Yehudi, and Curtis W. Davis. *The Music of Man.* New York: Methuen, 1979.

Merleau-Ponty, Maurice. *Phenomenology of Perception*, trans. by Colin Smith. London: Routledge & Kegan Paul, 1962.

—. *The Structure of Behavior*, trans. by Alden L. Fisher. Boston: Beacon Press, 1963.

—. *The Visible and the Invisible*, ed. by Claude Lefort; trans. by Alphonso Lingis. Evanston, Ill.: Northwestern University Press, 1968.

Merton, Thomas (ed. and trans.) *The Way of Chuang Tzu.* New York: New Directions, 1965.

Miller, Gloria Bley. *The Thousand Recipe Chinese Cookbook.* New York: Simon and Schuster, 1966, 1984.

Myers, Henry Alonzo, *Are Men Equal? — An Inquiry into the Meaning of American Democracy.* Ithaca, N.Y.: Cornell University Press, 1963.

Nagel, Ernest, and James R. Newman. *Gödel's Proof.* New York: New York University Press, 1958.

Needham, Joseph. *Science and Civilization in China:* Vol. II, *History of Scientific Thought.* Cambridge: At the University Press, 1956.

Neville, Robert C. *Reconstruction of Thinking.* Albany: State University of New York, 1981.

Nietzsche, Friedrich. *Thus Spake Zarathustra*, trans. by R. J. Hollingdale. Baltimore, Md.: Penguin Books, 1961.

Nolan, Christopher. *Dam-Burst of Dreams.* Athens, Ohio: Ohio University Press, 1981.

Oxford English Dictionary, The, 12 vols. Oxford: At the Clarendon Press, 1933. ("A corrected re-issue" of *A New English Dictionary on Historical Principles*, 1884-1927.)

Paton, H. J. *The Good Will.* London: George Allen & Unwin, 1927.

Picard, Max. *The World of Silence*, trans. by Stanley Godman. South Bend, Ind.: Regnery/Gateway, 1952.

Polanyi, Michael. *The Study of Man.* Chicago: University of Chicago Press, 1959.

—. *The Tacit Dimension.* Garden City, N.Y.: Doubleday, 1966.

— and Harry Posch. *Meaning.* Chicago: University of Chicago Press, 1975.

Quine, W. V. *The Ways of Paradox and Other Essays.* New York: Random House, 1966.

Richards, Mary Caroline. *Centering.* Middletown, Conn.: Wesleyan University Press, 1964.

Ricoeur, Paul. *The Conflict of Interpretations*, trans. by Don Ihde. Evanston, Ill.: Northwestern University Press, 1974.

Robinson, John Mansley. *An Introduction to Early Greek Philosophy.* Boston: Houghton Mifflin, 1968.

Romanell, Patrick. "Ethics, Moral Conflicts, and Choice," *American Journal of Nursing*, Vol. 77, No. 5 (May 1977). Unwin, 1927.

Rubert de Ventós, Xavier. *Self-Defeated Man.* New York: Harper/Colophon, 1971.

Russell, Bertrand. *The Problems of Philosophy.* London: Oxford University Press, 1921.

Ryle, Gilbert. *Dilemmas.* Cambridge: Cambridge University Press, 1964.

Sanford, John A. *The Man Who Lost His Shadow.* Ramsey, N.J.: Paulist Press, 1983.

Sartre, Jean-Paul. *Being and Nothingness*, trans. by Hazel E. Barnes. New York: Philosophical Library, 1956.

—. *Nausea*, trans. by Lloyd Alexander, New York: New Directions, 1964.

Schilpp, Paul Arthur, and Maurice Friedman (eds.) *The Philosophy of Martin Buber.* LaSalle, Ill.: Open Court, 1967.

Schütz, Alfred. *Collected Papers*: Vol. II, *Studies in Social Theory*, ed. and trans. by Arvid Brondersen. The Hague: Martinus Nijhoff, 1964.

Seneca, Lucius Annaeus. *Moral Essays*, 3 vols., trans. by John W. Basore. Cambridge, Mass.: Harvard University Press, 1920-1935.

Swabey, Marie C. *Comic Laughter.* New Haven, Conn.: Yale University Press, 1961.

Sze, Mai-Mai. *The Tao of Painting.* New York: Pantheon, 1956.

Tillich, Paul. *The Courage To Be.* New Haven: Yale University Press, 1952.

—. *Systematic Theology*, 3 vols. Chicago: Chicago University Press, 1951-1963.

Tomas, Vincent (ed.) *Creativity in Art.* Englewood Cliffs, N.J.: Prentice-Hall, 1964.

Torrance, T.F. *Royal Priesthood. Scottish Journal of Theology*. Occasional Papers, No. 3. Edinburgh: Oliver and Boyd, 1955.

Trible, Phyllis. *God and the Rhetoric of Sexuality*. Philadelphia: Fortress Press, 1978.

Urban, Wilbur Marshall. *Language and Reality*. London: George Allen & Unwin, 1939.

Vlastos, Gregory (ed.) *The Philosophy of Socrates*. Garden City, N.Y.: Doubleday, 1971.

Waley, Arthur. *Three Ways of Thought in Ancient China*. Garden City, N.Y.: Doubleday, 1956.

—. (trans.) *The Analects of Confucius*. New York: George Allen & Unwin, 1938.

—. (ed. and trans.) *The Book of Songs*, reprint ed. New York: Grove Press, 1960.

—. (ed. and trans.) *Translations from the Chinese*. New York: Knopf, 1919.

Ware, James R. (trans.) *The Sayings of Chuang Chou*. New York: Mentor, 1963.

Watson, Burton (trans.) *The Complete Writings of Chuang Tzu*. New York: Columbia University Press, 1968.

Watson, Lyall. *Heaven's Breath: A Natural History of the Wind*. New York: Morrow, 1985.

Wheelwright, Philip. *The Burning Fountain*. Bloomington: Indiana University Press, 1968.

—. *Heraclitus*. New York: Atheneum, 1971.

Whitehead, Alfred North. *Process and Reality*. New York: Macmillan, 1929.

—. *Process and Reality*, Corrected Edition, ed. by David Ray Griffin and Donald W. Sherburne. New York: Free Press, 1978.

Whitman, Walt. *The Complete Poetry and Prose*, 2 vols. NY: Pellegrini & Cudahy, 1948.

Whyte, Lancelot Law. *Essay on Atomism from Democritus to 1960*. Middletown, Conn.: Wesleyan University Press, 1961.

Wieger, Leo. *Chinese Characters*, reprint of 2nd ed. New York: Paragon/ Dover, 1965.

Williams, C.A.S. *Outlines of Chinese Symbolism and Art Motives*. New York: Dover, 1941.

Wittgenstein, Ludwig. *Philosophical Investigations*, [the German text of *Philosophische Untersuchungen*] with trans. by G.E.M. Anscombe. New York: Macmillan, 1953; 3rd ed., 1968.

Wu, Kuang-ming. *Chuang Tzu: World Philosopher at Play*. New York: Crossroad/Chico, Calif.: Scholars Press, 1982.

—. "Deconcentration of Morality: Taoist Esthetics of Person Making," *Chinese Studies*, Vol. I, No. 2 (Dec. 1983).

Zinsser, William. *On Writing Well.* New York: Harper and Row, 1980.

INDEXES

Compiled by James D. Parsons

GUIDE TO THE INDEXES

There are four Indexes here—

Index of Names: Chinese and Japanese
Index of Names: Mostly Western
Index of Themes: In Chinese
Index of Themes: In English

The Chinese entries in these Indexes are accompanied by full Wade-Giles transcription, with superscript numerals representing tone numbers. Chinese words appear in alphabetical order according to their romanized forms; words with the same romanization are ordered by tone numbers. (Please note that tone changes, occurring in speech but not represented in written Chinese, are not indicated in transliteration here. Note also that each of the "aspirated" consonants is treated here as a distinct consonant —that is, words beginning with *ch'*, *k'*, etc., follow all words beginning with *ch*, *k*, etc.)

Other numerals, described in the order in which they appear in each entry, are used here as follows:

(*a*) The Roman numerals **I, II,** and **III** in boldface type refer to chapter numbers, and the boldface Arabic numerals immediately following them refer to line numbers of the Kuo Hsiang Text (and the Translation) of the first three chapters of the *Chuang Tzu* as reproduced in this book. Examples: **I.1; II.15,296; III.60–61;** ... (no space between line numbers).

(*b*) Page numbers are in the style in which they appear on the pages: ix, xi, 27, 404, ... (space between page numbers).

(*c*) Numerals inside parentheses following page numbers—for instance, 158–59(77), 431(210)—refer to line numbers in the Glosses, or to note numbers in the Notes.

(*d*) Numerals separated by a slash—4/15, 6/4, etc.—refer to chapter and line numbers (beyond the first three chapters) as they appear in *A Concordance to the Chuang Tzu*: see note, p. 399.

(*e*) The numeral "0" indicates the appearance of a word or phrase in a chapter title.

Some of the significant variant usages that occur in different editions of the Chinese text of the *Chuang Tzu* are enclosed in brackets.

Several Chinese phrases and one Japanese name, with too many characters to fit into the general format, have been put into an Appendix, following the Index of Themes in English.

The English section of the Index of Themes contains many references to words in the Chinese section. Separate references from Chinese to English are unnecessary, since references to the English section are naturally provided in the Chinese section by the immediate gloss of every Chinese word.

The names of all authors mentioned in Meditations have been drawn into the Index of Names; but, from the Glosses and Notes, only those authors whose views are quoted or discussed are cited here. The letter "q" following a page number indicates the presence there of a significant quotation.

Shu-Huey Y. Jenner reviewed the Chinese sections of these Indexes in galleys and made a number of significant improvements.

—J. D. P.

INDEX OF NAMES

Chinese and Japanese

Mostly Western

INDEX OF THEMES

In Chinese

經	ching¹	(the) path, passage; constancy, standard, **III.3,17**; 290(3), 308, 336

經　ching¹　warp (of the fabric of our life), 355

經脈　ching¹ mo⁴　main veins, 293(17)

經首　ching¹ shou³　(name of a piece of music), **III.9**

逕庭　ching¹ t'ing²　extravagance, **I.89**; 64(89)

景　ching³　shadow, scene-manifesting power, **II.290**; 422(88); *see* 425(126)

徑　ching⁴　route or passage, 290(3)

鳩　chiu¹　pigeon, 319

久　chiu³　a long time, 319

九　chiu³　(number) nine, 319

就　chiu⁴　follow, **II.233**; 161(96)

周　chou¹　comprehensive, 165–66(180)

籀文　chou⁴ wen²　"old" script (form of writing), 429(185); *see* li⁴ wen¹

朱學　Chu¹ hsueh²　Chu Hsi scholarhship, 13; *see* Names: **Chu¹ Hsi¹**

族　chu²　gathering, **III.18,24**; 319

主　chu³　principle; lord, **III.0**; 301–03, 306–07, 336–37, 355–56, 438(124); *see* chün¹

莊學　Chuang¹ hsueh²　Chuang Tzu scholarship, 13

狀事　chuang⁴ shih⁴　description, 158(77)

憰　chueh²　swindle, **II.262**; 212

決起　chueh² ch'ih³　leap, rise, **I.21**

終　chung¹　end, 169(288)

中　chung¹　middle, **II.105**; 28

種　chung³　seed, seed power, 187, 378

中　chung⁴　fall in with, **I.147,148,156**; **III.8,9**; 28

重言　chung⁴ yen²　weighty words, heavy words, 86, 263; *see* chih¹ yen², ch'ung² yen², yü⁴ yen²

啄　chuo² (*or* cho²)　peck, 296(35–37)

居　chü¹　(marker for emphasis), **II.5**; 155(5); *see* ho² chu¹

狙　chü¹　monkeys, **II.127,207**; *see* Names: chü¹ Kung¹

俱　chü¹　two, more than two, **II.271,278**

矩(矩)　chü³　square, 65(149)

沮洳　chü³ ju²　disillusioned, 409(82)

瞿　chü⁴　jittery (magpie), 209, 421(79); *see* Names: **Chü⁴ Ch'üeh⁴ Tzu³**

覺　chüeh²　awakening, **II.254,300**; 205, 211; *see* ta⁴ chüeh²

勻(均)　chün¹　balance, equality, 156(27), 162(129), 280–82

鈞　chün¹　balance wheel, 221, 427(150); *see* huan², lun¹

君　chün¹　ruler, lord, **II.65,66**; 291(5); *see* chü³

長　ch'ang²　long, tall, **II.230**

常　ch'ang²　normal, normalcy, **II.170**

塵埃　ch'en² ai¹　dust storm, 58(11)

成　ch'eng²　form, **II.81,112,135–38,145–47**

成己　　ch'eng² chi³　form oneself, 417(33)

成心　　ch'eng² hsin¹　formed mind; make up one's mind, **II.78**

成形　　ch'eng² hsing²　formed figure (or body), **II.69**

乘　ch'eng²　ride, **I.63**

齊　ch'i²　**1** all (without exception), 86; **2** arrange, equalize; equality, parity, **II.0**; 171–72, 178, 189, 192, 197, 203, 216, 220–22, 230, 234–38, 255, 265–66, 277, 302, 413(1), 424–25(123), 427(150); *see* **lun⁴, wu⁴** ("things")

齊諧　ch'i² hsieh²　all harmony, **I.6**; 58(6), 59(6), 73, 86–87

齊物　ch'i² wu⁴　unity among things; things arranging and sorting themselves, **II.0**; 248; *see* **wu⁴ lun⁴**

齊物論　*Ch'i² Wu⁴ Lun⁴*　(title of Chapter Two), 78, 104, 172, 178–81, 227, 230, 233–39, 245–46, 254–57, 259, 263–66, 272, 274–76, 302, 342, 413(1), 431(1)

綦　ch'i²　base, basis, **II.1**; 182

其　ch'i²　he, his; that, they, **I.12**...; **II.62**...; **III.31**...; 157(62–68), 158–59(77), 160(93,94), 168(271), 331–32

其…亦　　ch'i² ... i⁴　that ... also, **II.77**; 158(77)

其人　　ch'i² jen²　that man; those people, **III.48**; 297(48), 330

其子　　ch'i² tzu³　his sons, **II.144**; 163(144)

祈　ch'i²　pray, request, 296(38)

蘄　ch'i²　pray, request, **III.38,52**; 296(38)

豈　ch'i³　how could? 158(77)

起　ch'i³　(let things) arise (of themselves), 417(33); *see* **tzu⁴ ssu⁴**

氣　ch'i⁴　vapor, atmosphere, breath energy, **I.42,64,94**; **II.15,228**; 17, 56(1), 63(64), 64(94), 69, 321, 339, 341–42, 426–27(140), 436(96); *see* **sung¹ fung¹, yün² ch'i⁴**

氣息　ch'i⁴ hsi²　(vital) breath, 428(154)

棄己　ch'i⁴ chi³　abandon oneself, 242

竅　ch'iao⁴　hollow, **II.26**; 189

且　ch'ieh　besides, indeed, **I.14**...; **II.255**; 60(14), 62(45), 159(78), 168(255), 292(9)

且夫　　ch'ieh³ fu¹　"besides, mind you," 60(14)

竊竊然　ch'ieh⁴ ch'ieh⁴ jan²　so saucy, saucy, **II.257**; 168(257)

持　ch'ih²　keep, hold, 169(291)

親　ch'in¹　family (members), parents, **III.4**; 290(4), 296(60)

欽光　ch'in¹ kuang¹　august brillance, 186(190–93)

秦失　ch'in² shih¹　great loss, **III.41**; 296–97(41)

秦　ch'in²　*see* Names: **Ch'in²**

清談　ch'ing¹ t'an²　pure conversation, 363

160–61(96), 168(252), 173, 175, 194–97, 221, 292(15), 420(62), 422–23(94), 440(47)

方 **fang¹** square, **II.184;** 166(184)

fang¹ k'o³ fang¹ pu⁴ k'o³ *see* Appendix

方內 **fang¹ nei⁴** (situated in) the ordinary world, 384

方生 **fang¹ sheng¹** co-thriving, 277

方生之說 **fang¹ sheng¹ chih¹ shuo¹** (the) theory of co-birthings, **II.96;** *see* sheng¹, wu⁴ hua⁴

方生方死 **fang¹ sheng¹ fang¹ ssu³** now living[,] now dead, **II.97;** 184, 193

方外 **fang¹ wai⁴** realm beyond the ordinary world, region yonder, 379, 384, 385, 440(47)

放勳 **fang⁴ hsün¹** (honorary title, *lit.* "shining forth of merit"), 166(190–93); *see* Names: Yao²

非 **fei¹** not-that, 30, 159(82), 203, 295(31–34)

非指 **fei¹ chih³** no-pointer, 30

分 **fen¹** division, distinction (human, contrived), **II.304;** 169(280–82), 170(304), 178, 185, 191, 204, 216, 221, 228–30, 275, 322–23, 342–45, 353, 422–23(94), 424(108), 437(106)

封 **feng¹** fief, border, mound, **I.137,139;** 28, 165(170), 191, 201, 204, 216, 221, 275, 323, 422–23(94)

風, 鳳, 封 **feng¹·⁴** *see* **fung¹**

夫 **fu¹** in fact (marker of sentence beginning), **I.14,103,144; II.78;** 60(14), 64(103), 65(144), 159(78)

扶搖 **fu¹ yao²** whirlwind, **I.9;** 60(9), 64(92)

伏 **fu²** hide, 66(156)

風 **fung¹** wind, 59(2), 426–27(140)

風化 **fung¹ hua⁴** wind change; copulation, 410(97), 426–27(140)

鳳 **fung⁴** phoenix (bird), 71, 349, 426–27(140); *see* **p'ung²**, **wu²** ("phoenix tree")

好 **hao⁴** be given to; find good, **III.12;** 292(12), 319

合 **ho²** match, correlate; harmony, **I.50; II.174; III.9;** 63(50), 165(174), 292(8–9)

何 **ho²** why?, what? 61(22)

何居 **ho² chu¹** why? **II.5**

何居乎 **ho² chu¹ hu¹** why is this? **II.5;** 155(5)

何以 ⋯ 為 **ho² i³ ... wei²** what does he need ... for? **I.22;** 61(22)

和氣 **ho² ch'i⁴** harmonious vitality, 166(188)

奚以 ⋯ 為 **hsi¹ i³ ... wei²** what [is] all this ... about? **I.22;** 61(22)

息 **hsi²** breathing, rest, **I.10;** 57–58(4,8,10), 58(10)

昔 **hsi²** of old, earlier, yesterday, **II.295;** 169(295)

郤 **hsi²** seam, **III.16;** 292–93(16)

徙 **hsi³** set-off, departure, self-translation, **I.8;** 98

戲　　hsi⁴　play, frolic; roam, play games, 110

系　　hsi⁴　ties, bonds, 297–98(59)

相待　hsiang¹ tai⁴　waiting on one another, mutual dependence, 173

　　　hsiang¹ tai⁴ jo⁴ ch'i² ...　see Appendix

相與　hsiang¹ yu³　having to do with, interaction, 19

　　　hsiang¹ yu³ yu² qu² ...　see Appendix

嚮然　hsiang⁴ jan²　so swing, I.8; 291(8); see hua⁴ jan², huo⁴ jan²

消　　hsiao¹　dissolve, 84

逍　　hsiao¹　roam, I.0; 84

逍遙　　hsiao¹ yao²　roam, play, I.0; 62(47), 83, 221

逍遙遊　*Hsiao¹ Yao² Yu²*　(title of Chapter One), 69, 83–84, 96, 169(288), 228, 230, 274–75, 349–50, 407–08(63), 410–12(101), 431(1)

小　　hsiao³　small:

小成　　hsiao³ ch'eng²　small accomplishment; formation, II.92; 160(92)

小知　　hsiao³ chih¹　small understanding, I.27; II.35

笑　　hsiao⁴　laugh; laughter, 87, 97

諧　　hsieh²　harmony, joke, I.6; 58(6), 59(6), 86

薪　　hsin¹　firewood, III.60; 298(60), 331–32, 352

心　　hsin¹　mind-heart, thought, 183, 189, 259; see ch'eng² hsin¹, chi¹ hsin¹

心齋　hsin¹ chai¹　mind-fasting, 183, 189

心室　hsin¹ shin⁴　mind-chamber, 259

心思　hsin¹ ssu¹　thought and anxiety, 298–99(60–61) see ssu¹

新　　hsin¹　new; renewal, 20, 23, 290(4)

信已　hsin⁴ i³　certain enough, II.58; 157(58)

形　　hsing²　bodily figure, II.69; 158(72)

刑　　hsing²　cane, punish; punishment, III.53; 289(3), 297(53–55), 308, 436(88); see ming²

硎　　hsing²　grindstone, whetstone, III.20; 294(20), 308; see yen², yen⁴

行　　hsing²　walk, II.58,71,112,290; III.15; see liang³ hsing², liang³ wang³

兄弟一體　hsiung¹ ti⁴ i¹ t'i³　brothers united as one, 428(163)

虛　　hsü¹　empty, I.70; II.26; 63(70), 154(2), 156(26), 189

虛室　hsü¹ shih⁴　empty chamber, 4/32

墟　　hsü¹　hill, I.70; 63(70), 409(82)

噓　　hsü¹　sigh deeply, II.2; 154–55(2), 156(26)

　　　hsü²-hsing² hsiang²-pan⁴ ...　see Appendix

緒業　hsü⁴ yeh⁴　business, 163(144)

懸　　hsüan¹　bond, bondage, III.59; 298(59)

懸解　hsüan¹ chieh³　knot-loosening, 229, 297–98(59), 309, 337, 346, 424(108)

玄冥　hsüan² ming²　mysterious darkness, 56(1), 59(1); 6/45, 17/78

麗　　li⁴　beauty, **II.247**; 168(247)

麗姬　　li⁴ chi¹　see Names: **Li⁴ Chi¹**

利害之端　li⁴ hai⁴ chih¹ tuan¹　buddings of benefit (and) harm, **II.229**; see
　　　　　tuan¹

隸文　　li⁴ wen²　"new" script (form of writing), 429(185); see **chou⁴ wen²**

兩　　liang³　double, 169(290)

兩行　　**liang³ hsing²**　double walk, **II.129**; 162(129), 169(290), 175, 199,
　　　　245, 376, 419(52), 422(88), 427(150); see 419(48)

兩罔　　**liang³ wang³**　(going) neither (way); penumbra, 169(290), 215,
　　　　422(88); see **wang³ liang³**

旒　　liu²　pennant, 182

六　　liu⁴　(number) six, 63(64), 165(174)

六氣　　**liu⁴ ch'i⁴**　the force of the universe (lit. "six [cosmic] breath
　　　　[energies]"), 63(64), 93

六合　　**liu⁴ ho²**　"Six Correlates," 165(174)

六月息　**liu⁴ yueh⁴ hsi²**　six-month's blowing, sixth month blowing, **I.10**;
　　　　58(10), 60(10)

攄, 抒空　(lu²), shu¹; shu¹ k'ung¹　hollow out, 65(142)

轆轤　　lu⁴ lu²　potter's wheel, pulley, 171, 180; see **t'ao² chün¹**

亂　　luan⁴　confuse; confusion, 164(148), 172

倫　　lun²⁽ᵈ⁾　human relations, 414–15(13); see **II.172,173**

侖　　lun²⁽ᵈ⁾　sheaf of pages, 171, 413(1), 414–15(13)

綸　　lun²⁽ᵉ⁾　strings, **II.144**; 414–15(13)

輪　　lun²⁽ᶜ⁾　wheel, 171, 179, 221–22, 414–15(13), 424(120); see **chün¹**,
　　　　huan²

論　　lun⁴⁽ᵃ⁾　(to) sort, (to) reason, **II.0,174**; 171, 179, 204, 221, 230,
　　　　234–38, 245, 248–49, 255, 263, 265–66, 382, 413(1), 414–
　　　　415(13)

履　　lü³　see **li³⁽ᵇ⁾**

馬　　ma³　horse, **II.109,110**; 196–98, 419(49)

碼　　ma³　(sentence marker), see **II.109,110**; 196–98

滿志　　man³ chih⁴　heart fully satisfied, **III.27**; 295(27), 325

曼衍　　man⁴ yen²　flow far; vicissitudes, **II.281**; 179, 229, 245

芒　　mang²　dark, futile, muddled; futility, **II.76–77**; 167(235), 239, 242;
　　　　see **ming²** ("deep and dark")

茫昧　　mang² mei⁴　vague, 169(290)

莽眇之鳥　mang³ miao³ chih¹ niao³　light and lissome bird, 7/9

茫漠　　mang² mo⁴　wide, 167(235)

茫洋　　mang² yang⁴　wide, 167(235)

昧　　mei⁴　darkness, foolishness, 200

孟浪　　meng⁴ lang⁴　vague romanticism, **II.235**; 167(235)

夢蝶主人　meng⁴ tieh² chu³ jen²　(the) Butterfly Dreamer, 246; see **hu² tieh²**

怒　　nu⁴　rage up; angry uprising, **I.3; II.16;** 57(3,4), 155–56(16), 189

怒 而 飛　　**nu⁴ erh² fei¹**　rage up and fly off, **I.3;** 57(3,4), 61(21)

女　　(nü³) ju³　you, 421(80)

偶　　ou³　pair, counterpart, **II.3,104;** 154(3), 156(24), 415–16(26)

八　　pa¹　(number) eight, **II.173;** 165(173)

八 德　　**pa¹ te²**　"Eight Virtues," **II.173;** 165(173), 165(173–76)

胞　　pao¹　brother, 291(5), 348, 437(112); *see* **p'ao²**

包　　pao¹　enfold, 348

保　　pao³　maintain, 356

保 身　　**pao³ shen¹**　maintaining one's body (= total self), 229

葆 光　　pao³ kuang¹　shaded light, **II.189;** 166(189), 242, 245, 267; *see*
　　　　　　Names: **Pao³ Kuang¹**

碑 文　　pei¹ wen²　epitaph, 385

北　　pei³　north; northern, **I.1,36;** *see* **nan²**

北 冥　　**pei³ ming²**　northern darkness, **I.1;** 56(1)

本 我　　pen³ wu²　basic self, 417(29)

比　　pi³　benefit, **I.50;** 63(50)

鄙　　pi³　despise, 169(148)

彼　　pi³　that, those, they, **III.52;** 61(26), 159(82), 160(95), 193, 202, 203,
　　　　297(52)

彼 是　　**pi³ shih⁴**　that and this-yes, **II.96...;** 194–95

庇　　pi⁴　protect, 63(50)

辟　　pi⁴　trap, avoid, hesitate, **I.156;** 66(156)

飆　　piao¹　hurricane, 60(9), 64(92)

辯, 變　　pien⁴　change, 63(64)

變 化 齊 一　　**pien⁴ hua⁴ ch'i² i¹**　(all) changes arranged into one, 413(1); 14/20

辨, 辯　　pien⁴　discrimination; distinguish, 63(64), 246, 344–45

辯　　pien⁴　distinction, change, debate, **I.64; II.89,176,219;** 63(64),
　　　　160(89), 165(173–76), 165(176), 167(219), 221, 229, 437(107)

搏　　po²　beat, 59(9)

搏　　po²　capture, hit, 59(9)

礴　　po²　widespread; extend, 64–65(106)

不　　pu⁴　no, not, **I.1...; II.181...;** 28, 30, 159(82), 166(186), 353

不 知　　**pu⁴ chih¹**　not knowing, not understanding, **I.29; II.124,185,198,-
　　　　252; III.61;** 184, 289(2), 353

不 知 盡　　**pu⁴ chih¹ chin⁴**　not knowing the end, 353

不 盡　　**pu⁴ chin⁴**　not finished, not exhausted, 298(60–61)

不 齊　　**pu⁴ ch'i²**　unequal, 234

不 亦　　**pu⁴ i⁴**　not ... rather, **II.9;** 155(9)

不 亦 悲 乎　　**pu⁴ i⁴ pei¹ hu¹**　Is it not sad! **I.34;** 62(35)

不 若　　**pu⁴ jo⁴**　not like, **II.108;** 161(108)

不 能 入　　**pu⁴ neng² ju²**　cannot enter, **III.58;** 309

繩 絡 之   **sheng² lo⁴ chih¹**   wrap with cords, 65(142)

省 嗇   **sheng³ se⁴**   dispense with, 164(148)

聖 人   **sheng⁴ jen²**   holy man, **I.69; II.100,129,148...;** 161(100)

盛 旺   **sheng⁴ wang⁴**   beautiful, brilliant, prosperous, 296(39)

失   **shih¹**   lose; loss, III.41; 296(40–41), 296–97(41)

詩   **shih¹**   poetry, 24

十   **shih²**   (number) ten, **II.194; III.36;** 319

十 九   **shih² chiu³**   (number) nineteen, **III.19;** 318–19

始   **shih³**   beginning, **II.131...,154...,247; III.13,48;** 168(247)

使   **shih³**   let, 197

使 如   **shih³ ju²**   allowed (to become) as, 183

使 獨   **shih³ tu²**   let (oneself be rendered) unique (and one-footed), 229;
         see Names: Commander of the Right

使 自 己   **shih³ tzu⁴ chi³**   let (oneself) be oneself, 186, 189, 417(33)

是   **shih⁴**   be (as copula), 159(82)

是   **shih⁴⁽ᵇ⁾**   yes, this, **I.112; II.100,129,262; III.23,31...;** 12, 65(112),
         159–60(82), 160(95), 162(129), 193, 195, 198–99, 202, 203, 211,
         221, 295(31–34), 323

     shih⁴ chih¹ wei⁴ ...   *see* Appendix

是 非   **shih⁴ fei¹**   yes (and) no; yes-no, **II.82; III.31...;** 159(82), 192, 194,
         203, 295(31–34)

是 已   **shih⁴ i³**   this only, 157(58), 162(123); *see* **III.29,30,123**

是 以   **shih⁴ i³**   this with ... **II.129; III.23;** 294(23)

室   **shih⁴**   chamber; *see* **hsin¹ shih⁴**

釋   **shih⁴**   let go of, throw away, **III.11;** 292(11)

勢   **shih⁴**   power, situation, 405(19)

視   **shih⁴**   see, 292(13–15), 348

飾, 拭   **shih⁴**   wipe, 295(27)

事 而 無 傳   **shih⁴ erh² wu² ch'uan²**   things (happen) yet no (thing is) passed on,
         412(114); 12/83

手 口 相 助   **shou³ k'ou³ hsiang¹ chu⁴**   hand (and) mouth mutually help,
         428(163)

受   **shou⁴**   receive, **III.54;** 297(53–55)

淑(俶)   **shu²**   beginning, 168(262)

倏   **shu²**   formed, speedy, 86; *see* Names: **Shu²**

鼠   **shu³**   rat(s), **I.159;** 66(190,160,161)

數   **shu⁴**   number; several, **III.20;** 294(20)

樹   **shu⁴**   plant; tree, **I.59,146;** 63(59), 65(146)

述   **shu⁴**   report of affairs or events, 24

順   **shun⁴**   compliance, 230

所 指   **so³ chih³**   meaning, thing(s) referred to, 419(49)

斯   **ssu¹**   and then, **I.17;** 61(17)

則　tse² then, **II.272**; 160(93,96), 168(262), 168(272)

則 已 矣　tse² i³ i³ this ... only, **I.13**; 60(13), 62(35), 63(57)

則 ⋯ 斯　tse² ... ssu¹ then, **I.17**; 61(17)

奏　tsou⁴ perform, **III.8**; 291(8)

族　tsu² complexity, band, gathering; common; rabble, **III.24**; 294(24–27), 321, 324, 338

族 庖　tsu² p'ao² common cooks, **III.18**

醉 生 夢 死　tsui⁴ sheng¹ meng⁴ ssu³ living drunk and dying in a dream, 357

縱　tsung⁴ let go, let loose, 346

作　tsuo⁴ start up, 156(26)

獨　tu² alone, unique, **III.33**; 296(33); *see* **shih³ tu²**

獨 且　tu² ch'ieh³ leave alone; alone indeed, **II.78,84**; 159(78), 160(84)

獨 立 志 操　tu² li² chih⁴ ts'ao¹ (of) independent mind and behavior, 169(291)

督　tu² (the) spinal route; investigate, **III.3**; 290(3), 292(9), 313–14, 336–37, 341–42, 348, 433(26)

督 ⋯ 經　tu² ... ching¹ the *tu* meridian through the spine, 292(9)

端　tuan¹ bud, beginning, **II.217**; 167(217), 421(76); *see* **jen² i⁴ chih¹ tuan¹, li⁴ hai⁴ chih¹ tuan¹**

遯　tun⁴ escape, 297(53–55)

遁　tun⁴ escape, **III.53,55**; 297(53–55)

冬　tung¹ (ancient pronunciation of **chung¹**), 162(122)

子　tzu³ mister, master; person, **I.60...**; 182

自　tzu⁴ from, by; (the) self, **II.95**; 160(95)

自 己　tzu⁴ chi³ become oneself, **II.33**; 417(33); *see* **ch'eng² chi³**

自 取　tzu⁴ ch'ü³ adopt oneself (as oneself), 189

自 已　tzu⁴ i³ stop, end, finish (itself), 417(33)

自 然　tzu⁴ jan² what is as it is, 184

自 已　tzu⁴ ssu⁴ arise (of) itself, 417(33); *see* **ch'i³**

自 為　tzu⁴ wei² what does as it does, 184

少　t'a¹ step, 350

太 極 拳　T'ai⁴ Chi² Ch'uan² a Chinese martial art, 340, 419(48), 436(95)

湯　t'ang¹ (symbol of **ta⁴**), huge, **I.35**; 62(35)

韜　t'ao¹ contained, hidden, 164(148)

陶 鈞　t'ao² chün¹ potter's wheel, 162(129); *see* **lu⁴ lu²**

特 操　t'e⁴ ts'ao¹ behave especially (as oneself), **II.291**; 169(291)

提 刀 而 立　t'i² tao¹ erh² lih⁴ hold the knife and stand up, 295(27)

體　t'i³ substance (of all conduct), 198

蜩　t'iao² cicada, **I.20**; 61(20)

調 調　t'iao² t'iao² wavering, **II.27**; 156(27)

天　t'ien¹ heaven; heavenly, natural, **I.3,12,18...**; **II.2,100,110,163**; **III.31–34,53,55**; 58(12–19), 66(158), 305, 309, 325, 423(94), 426(140)

天 機　t'ien¹ chi¹　originating power, 241, 253

天 池　t'ien¹ ch'ih²　heavenly pond, **I.5,36**

天 鈞　t'ien¹ chün¹　heavenly wheel, heavenly balance, **II.129;** 162(129), 422(85)

天 府　t'ien¹ fu³　heavenly treasury, 199, 245, 267

天 下　t'ien¹ hsia⁴　under heaven, **I.70...; II.161;** see Appendix: **tz'ang²** **t'ien¹ hsia⁴ yu²** ...

天 籟　t'ien¹ lai⁴　heavenly piping(s), **II.12,31;** 184; see **lai⁴, jen² lai⁴, ti⁴ lai⁴**

天 理　t'ien¹ li³　heaven-given lines, **III.16,31–34,53,55;** 348; 355

天 倪　t'ien¹ ni²　heavenly horizon, heavenly equality, **II.281;** 162(129), 169(280–82), 191, 206–07, 229, 245, 421(75), 422(85)

天 研　t'ien¹ yen⁴　heavenly natural whetstone, 207, 421(75), 422(85); see **yen⁴**

聽　t'ing¹　listen, **II.241;** 186, 295(28–29); see **wen²**

莛　t'ing²　stalk(s), **II.116;** 161(116)

藏　ts'ang²　store, **III.27;** 295(27), 296(38)

操　ts'ao¹　behavior, **II.291;** 169(291)

存　ts'un²　(being) present; (in time) presence, **II.60,91,174,192;** 157(60), 204

塗　t'u²　road, 65(149)

圖　t'u²　set one's eyes on, **II.148;** 164(148)

圖 南　t'u² nan²　be set on heading south, **I.19,42;** 61(19), 164(148)

土　t'u³　earth, soil:

土 委 地　t'u² wei³ ti⁴　soil thrown to the ground, **III.26;** 295(26)

摶　t'uan²　circling up as a whirlwind, **I.9;** 59(9)

屯　t'un²　lump, collection, gathering, 168(244)

通　t'ung¹　go through, bleed, **II.117,120;** 198–99, 203

通 暢　t'ung¹ ch'ang⁴　go through without obstruction, 169(288)

通 達　t'ung¹ ta²　worldly wise, 199

通 為 一　t'ung¹ wei² i¹　go through to make into one, 18, 162(117)

同 志　t'ung² chih⁴　same intention; comrade, 428(163)

　　tz'ang² t'ien¹ hsia⁴ yu² ...　see Appendix

此　tz'u³　this, these, here, 61(26), 162(124), 163(137,138,140), 202, 203, 289(2)

萬 物　wan⁴ wu⁴　myriads of things, **I.106; II.110,163,194,244**

萬 物 一 齊　wan⁴ wu⁴ i¹ ch'i²　myriads to things arranged into one, 413(1); 17/44

汪 洋　wang¹ ya²　vast horizon of deep waters, 207

王　wang²　king; royal, **I.121,134–35; II.176,248; III.39**

王 倪　wang² ni²　see Names: **Wang² Ni², (Mr.) Royal Horizon**

亡　wang²　lose, die, **II.69;** 158(69),421(80)

亡，毋　wang², wu⁴　denial (in general), 30

罔　wang³　nothing, **II.290**; 169(290), 403–04(59)

罔罟　**wang³ ku³**　net, **I.156**; 7, 66(156)

罔兩　**wang³ liang³**　nothing doubled, double neither; penumbra, **II.290**; 169(290), 422(88); *see* Names: **(Mr.) Double Nothing, (Mr.) Penumbra**

妄　wang⁴　abandon, **II.241**; 167(241), 187, 421(80)

妄言　**wang⁴ yen²**　abandoned words, **II.241**

忘　wang⁴　forget, **II.69**; 158(69)

威　wei¹　awesome, 165–66(183)

為　wei²　do, make, mean, call, **I.1,2,15,79,125,162; II.117,120,125,161,-162; III.2,3,24;** 18, 19, 59(2), 65(125), 164(161,162), 289(2), 294(24–27), 298(60–61), 313, 322, 338, 352

為戒　**wei² chieh⁴**　become cautious, 295(25)

為知　**wei² chih¹**　seek knowledge, **III.2;** 289(2), 437(117)

為一　**wei² i¹**　make one, unify, **II.117;** 161(117)

為無為　**wei² wu² wei²**　"doing by not doing" (Lao Tzu), 184

微礙　wei² ai⁴　slight obstruction, 293(17)

萎　wei³　crooked withered grass, 322

委　wei⁴　entrust to, submit; *see* t'u² wei³ ti⁴

謂　wei⁴　be called, **II.112,129,160,173,203–04,303; III.55,59;** 59(2), 164(161,162), 191, 202

未　wei⁴　(not) yet, 30

未嘗　**wei⁴ ch'ang²**　(not) yet tried, **III.17;** 293(17)

未始　**wei⁴ shih³**　yet to begin, **II.131,155,157;** 30, 164(155), 197

未始有　**wei⁴ shih³ yu³**　yet to begin to be, 200–04, 206, 323

未有　**wei⁴ yu³**　yet to exist, 30

為　wei⁴:

為之　**wei⁴ chih¹**　because of (it), **III.27;** 294(24–27), 338

為是　**wei⁴ shih⁴**　for this reason, 12

　wei⁴ shih⁴ erh² yu³ ...　*see* Appendix

為是以故　**wei⁴ shih⁴ i³ ku⁴**　for this reason, 161(116)

為是故　**wei⁴ shih⁴ ku⁴**　*see* ku⁴ wei⁴ shih⁴

聞　wen²　hear, **II.11–12,17; III.28;** 181, 186, 295(28–29) 416–17(28)

文　wen²　non-metered writing, 24

文理　**wen² li³**　the natural grain of the jade of things, 171

問　wen⁴　ask, 186

我　wo³　self, I; objectifiable self, **II.10,235;** 16, 155(10), 167(235), 183, 185–87, 193, 206, 216, 228, 240–42, 276, 415–16(26), 416–17(28), 417(29,30), 422–23(94)

我齋　**wo³ chai¹**　self fasting, 183

巫　wu¹　shaman, 30

用　　　yung⁴⁽ᵃ⁾　use, usefulness, **I.83,125,140; II.128;** 198–99; *see* **wu² yung⁴**

用, 庸, 通　yung⁴-yung¹-t'ung¹　used, used to; adapted, adept at, 198

魚　　　yü²　fish, **I.1,36; II.214;** 57(1); *see* Names: **K'un¹**

余　　　yü²　I for one, 167(230), 228

　　　　yü² wu² so³ yung⁴ ...　see Appendix

余　　　yü²　I for one, **I.83; II.241,245,246,261**

於　　　yü²　of, in, to, 28

愉　　　yü²　happy, 170(298)

愚者　　yü² cheh³　fool(s), **II.256**

鴛　　　yü³　(species of) small bird, 405–06(39)

與　　　yü³　(together) with, **III.31;** 18, 28, 296(31), 296(33), 348

語助　　yü³ chu⁴　(marker for emphasis), 294(24–27)

耦　　　yü⁴　counterpart, **II.3,104;** 155(3), 183; see ou³

寓　　　yü⁴　dwell, lodge, 155(3), 169(289), 214–15

　　　　yü⁴ chu¹ wu² ching⁴　*see* Appendix

寓諸庸　yü⁴ chu¹ yung¹　dwell in the ordinary, 199

寓言　　yü⁴ yen²　lodging words, 263, 370; *see* **chih¹ yen², chung⁴ yen²,**
　　　　　　ch'ung² yen²

欲　　　yü⁴　desire, **III.15;** 319, 321, 434(47)

遇　　　yü⁴　meet, **III.15;** 292(13–15)

育　　　yü⁴　raise, nourish, 296(38)

喻　　　yü⁴　show, **II.298;** 170(298)

域　　　yü⁴　territory, 422–23(94)

元　　　yüan²　origin(s), 321, 323

圓　　　yüan²　round; circle, **II.184;** 166(184)

緣　　　yüan²　staying on with, 289(1), 298(60–61), 306, 308, 314, 332–33,
　　　　　　336, 433(26)

緣督　　yüan² tu²　spine tracing, 313–15, 337, 342, 438(126)

雲氣　　yün² ch'i⁴　cloud breath (energy), **I.42,94; II.228;** 64(94)

運　　　yün⁴　(of ocean tides) move, 57(3,4)

In English

abandon, abandoned, 187, 191; *see* **wang⁴**

abrogation by fulfillment, 198

absolute realism, 325

abstract: ... generalization, 390; ...
painting and absolute music, 208; *see*
concrete

absurdity: "the ... of life" (Camus), 15

accumulation of significant notions, an,
264–65

accuracy, accurate, 367, 369, 376

activity, act, action, active, 201, 213, 257,
298(60,61), 323, 336, 345, 365, 380–
83, 387, 436(88); the ... of creation,
410–11(101)

actual, actuality, **II.128;** 25, 27, 72–73,
101, 181, 184, 203–04, 206–07, 216,

joy that trails the facts of ..., limitless knowledge, limited ..., logic of ..., making ... coherent, making sense of ..., meaning of ..., tragic sense of ..., true ..., unity of ..., way of ..., what it means to be alive, what ... is, *sheng*¹

light, 86, 112, 188, 223–24; ... of deep darkness, 112; *see kuang*¹

limit(s), limited, **I.12,88**; 311, 313, 320, 335, 354; "... of the possible" (Pindar), 354; *see ya*²

limitless, 311, 313, 335, 354; ... knowledge, limited life, 306, 311

listen, listener, 68, 186–87, 193, 210, 226, 240, 259, 321, 421(80); *see* hear, reader, *t'ing*¹

literal, literalism, 376–79; ... meaning, ... mind, 369, 373

literary criticism, 15

live, 7–8, 15–16, 18, 381, 387; ... happily in human excellence, 389; (to) ... humanly, 7; ... rightly, 81; ... out our (natural) years, 336, 358; *see* (the) way to ..., (the) way we ..., *sheng*¹

living, 15, 22, 93, 198, 233, 274, 335, 381; ... among things 201; "living drunk and dying in a dream" (proverbial Chinese saying), 357; ... in the original world of yet-to-begin-to-be, 204; ... the coherence we create, 8; ... two lives, 376; *see* Chuang Tzu's ... in death, our very mode of ..., *sheng*¹, *tsui*⁴ *sheng*¹ *meng*⁴ *ssu*³

lodge, lodging, **II.149,289**; 212–214; *see chi*⁴, *yu*⁴

lodged words, lodging words, 12, 21–22, 263, 370; *see* doublet words, goblet words, *yu*⁴ *yen*²

logic, logical, 6, 99, 101–02, 104, 107, 179, 194, 220, 230, 237, 256–59, 277, 373, 375, 421–22(84); the ... of life, 107, 256–57; the ... of lucid con-

sciousness, 220; the ... of mathematics, 272; the ... of poetry, 272, 274; the ... of the comical, 264; the ... of the kingdom of God, 379; logical: ... necessity, 261–62; ... rules, 179, ... scrutiny, 269; *see* Confucian ... of humanness, consistency, life ..., no ... logical, two logical roads, ways of changing ...

loop (word and chart), 23, 90, 106, 238, 304, 306–09, 337, 357

loosening, loosen, **III.20,59**; 315, 318, 322–25, 328–30, 334, 342, 344, 351, 358; ... of the Great Ox, 347; *see* undo, *chieh*³

loss of the self, 211, 218, 239, 243, 246, 250; *see* self, *sang*¹ *wo*³

love, **II.135**; 169, 200, 224–25, 251–52, 302; ...'s formation, 200; *see* forming of ...

ludic: ... man, 388; the ... way, 387

machine mind, 241–42, 391; *see chi*¹ *hsin*¹

magic: ... circle, 385; the ... of darkness, 73; *see* realm beyond the ordinary

making: ...-doing *wei*, 18; ... life coherent, 7–8, 67–69; ... sense of life, 7, 67–69; ... the reader into a creative self, 370; ... spring and autumn of heaven and earth, 17; *see* life, reader, self, *wei*²

man, men, people, **I.100,105,108**; **II.74–76,130,180,206–07,209,213,- 243,272; III.31–34,48**; 202, 223, 272, 318, 330, 374, 388–90; *see* divine ..., every reasonable ..., great ..., holy ..., people, true ..., *jen*²

many new worlds, 380; *see* world

mask, 384

meaning, xiv, 10–11, 31, 67, 87, 197, 231, 267, 318, 364–66, 369, 373–74, 377, 382, 387–88, 392; ... and connection, 373; ... and symbol, 365; the ... matrix, 378, 388; the ... of life, 7, 365, 378; *see*

APPENDIX

見 之 調 調 之 勺 勺
chien⁴ chih¹ t'iao²-t'iao² chih¹ tiao¹-tiao¹   see their silence; see them waver, wavering—quiver, quavering, **II.27;** 181

凡 形 聲 字 必 兼 會 意
fan² hsing² sheng¹ tzu⁴ pi⁴ chien¹ hui⁴ i⁴   Every form and sound of a word must be united to implied intention, 419

方 可 方 不 可
fang¹ k'o³ fang¹ pu⁴ k'o³   Now yes, now no, **II.98;** 184, 193

相 待 若 其 不 相 待
hsiang¹ tai⁴ jo⁴ ch'i² pu² hsiang¹ tai⁴   mutual dependence that is no mutual dependence, 246

相 與 於 無 相 與, 相 為 於 無 相 為
hsiang¹ yü³ yü² wu² hsiang¹ yü³, hsiang¹ wei² yü² wu² hsiang¹ wei²   having to do with something (without) having to do with (it), 19, 78

徐 行 翔 伴 而 歸
hsu³-hsing² hsiang²-pan⁴ erh² kuei¹   slowly walking home, 62

以 天 地 為 春 秋
i³ t'ien¹ ti⁴ wei² ch'un¹ ch'iu¹   with the skies and the earth to make spring and autumn, 17, 18

意 在 此, 言 寄 於 彼
i⁴ tzai⁴ tz'u³, yen² chi⁴ yü² pi³   the intentive meaning that is entrusted and lodged here and expressed there, 370

槁 木 … 死 灰
kau¹-mu⁴ ... ssu³-hui¹   dry wood ... dead ashes, **II.6;** 184

不 用 而 寓 諸 庸
pu⁴ yung⁴ erh² yü⁴ chu¹ yung¹   discard obsession with "use" and dwell in the ordinary, 199

是 之 謂 兩 行
shih⁴ chih¹ wei⁴ liang³ hsing²   this is (what is) called "double walk," **II.129;** 162(129); *see* liang³ hsing²

津 田 左 右 吉
Tsuda, Saukichi   15, 437(108)

藏 天 下 於 天 下
tz'ang² t'ien¹ hsia⁴ yü² t'ien¹ hsia⁴   The underheaven is safely tucked away in the underheaven, 18

為 是 而 有 畛 也
wei⁴ shih⁴ erh² yu³ chen³ yeh³　　for this (reason) boundaries exist, **II.170**

无 責 於 人, 人 亦 无 責
wu² tse² yü² jen², jen² i⁴ wu² tse²　　No one bothers it, as it bothers on one, 18

无 為 而 无 不 為
wu² wei² erh² wu² pu⁴ wei²　　Doing nothing, and nothing is left undone, 19

因 是 因 非, 因 非 因 是
yin¹ shih⁴ yin¹ fei¹, yin¹ fei¹ yin¹ shih⁴　　As following on yes so following on no, as
following on no so following on yes, **II.99**

余 无 所 用 天 下 為
yü² wu² so³ yung⁴ t'ien¹-hsia⁴ wei²　　For me there exists no use for things under
heaven, **I.83**

寓 諸 無 [无] 竟
yü⁴ chu¹ wu² ching⁴　　dwell where there is no boundary, **II.289;** 169(289); *see*
wu²⁽ᵃ⁾, wu²⁽ᵇ⁾

Conversion Table: Wade-Giles To Pinyin

This Conversion Table is designed for use with the version of the Wade-Giles system of transcription used in this book—see Prologue, D.10 (d). On this chart, letters and groups of letters not accompanied by hyphens (e.g., **i**) represent complete syllables; letters with hyphens represent the beginning (*y-*), middle (*-i-*), or end (*-i*) of syllables. Those items which do not change in going from Wade-Giles to Pinyin are in *italic* type; items that change are in **boldface** type.

WADE-GILES → PINYIN

a / -a =	*a / -a*
ai / -ai =	*ai / -ai*
an / -an =	*an / -an*
ang / -ang =	ang / -ang
ao / -ao =	**ao / -ao**
ch- (generally) =	**zh-**
ch- (before -i, -i-, except -ih) =	**j-**
ch'- (generally) =	**ch-**
ch' (before -i, -i-, except -ih) =	**q-**
e / -e =	*e / -e*
-eh =	**-e**
-ei =	*-ei*
en / -en =	*en / -en*
-en (after y-) =	**-an**
-eng / -eng =	eng / -eng
-erh =	**-er**
f- =	*f-*
h- =	*h-*
hs- =	**x-**
i =	**yi**
-i =	*-i*
-ia =	*-ia*
-iang =	*-iang*
-iao =	*-iao*

WADE-GILES → PINYIN

-ieh =	**-ie**
-ien =	**-ian**
-ih =	**-i**
-in =	*-in*
-ing =	*-ing*
-iu (generally) =	*-iu*
-iu (after t-) =	**-iou**
-iung =	**-iong**
j- =	**r-**
k- =	**g-**
k'/ =	**k-**
l- =	*l-*
m- =	*m-*
n- =	*n-*
-o (generally) =	**-uo**
-o (after f-, m-, p-, w-) =	*-o*
-ou =	*-ou*
p- =	**b-**
p'- =	**p-**
s- =	*s-*
sh- =	*sh-*
sz-[ss-] =	**s-**
t- =	**d-**
t' =	**t-**

WADE-GILES → PINYIN

ts- =	**z-**
ts'- =	**c-**
tz- =	**z-**
tz'- =	**c-**
-u (generally) =	*-u*
-u (after sz- [ss-], tz-) =	**-i**
-u (after y-) =	**-ou**
-ua =	*-ua*
-uai =	*-uai*
-uan =	*-uan*
-uang =	*-uang*
-uei =	**-ui**
-ui =	*-ui*
-un =	*-un*
-ung =	**-ong**
-uo =	*-uo*
-ü (generally) =	**-u**
-ü (after n-) =	*-ü*
-üan (generally) =	**-uan**
-üan (after i-) =	*-üan*
-üeh =	**-ue**
-ün =	**-un**
w- =	*w-*
y- =	*y-*

—Compiled by James D. Parsons